Britain 1979 An official handbook

Britain 1979

An official handbook

London: Her Majesty's Stationery Office

Her Majesty's Stationery Office

Government Bookshops
49 High Holborn, London WC1V 6HB
13a Castle Street, Edinburgh EH2 3AR
41 The Hayes, Cardiff CF1 1JW
Brazennose Street, Manchester M60 8AS
Southey House, Wine Street, Bristol BS1 2BQ
258 Broad Street, Birmingham B1 2HE
80 Chichester Street, Belfast BT1 4JY

*Government publications are also available
through booksellers*

Obtainable in the United States of America
from Pendragon House Inc.
2595 East Bayshore Road
Palo Alto
California 94303

£7 net

ISBN 0 11 700971 7

Contents

Diagrams

Maps

Photographs

Acknowledgement is made for photographs to:

British Railways Board for Advanced
passenger train (facing p 38); *British
Hovercraft Corporation Ltd* for 'Super 4'
hovercraft (facing p 38); Eric Hosking,
F.R.P.S., F.I.I.P., for Gentian, Bee Orchid,
Primrose and Cowslip (facing p 39);
Superform Metals Ltd for superplastic alloy
(facing p 134); *International Computers
Ltd* for miniature circuit (between pp 134
and 135); *Tate & Lyle Ltd* for sugar-based gum
(between pp 134 and 135); *Mears Bros Holdings
Ltd* for tower (facing p 135); *United Kingdom
Atomic Energy Authority* for nuclear fuel
reprocessing (facing p 135); *Metropolitan
Police Publicity Branch* for traffic control
room and information room (facing p 390);
Davy-Loewy Ltd for support structure
(between pp 390 and 391).

Introduction

Britain 1979 is the thirtieth official handbook in the series prepared and revised each year by Reference Division of the Central Office of Information. The contents are based on information available up to September 1978. The handbook is widely known as an established work of reference and is the mainstay of the reference facilities provided by the British Information Services in many countries. It is distributed overseas in a limited free edition and is on sale by Her Majesty's Stationery Office throughout the world.

Britain 1979 is primarily concerned to describe the machinery of government and other institutions, together with the necessary physical and social background, and to show the part played by government in the life of the country. It does not attempt an analytical approach to current events.

The factual and statistical information it contains is compiled with the co-operation of other government departments and agencies, and of many other organisations. Sources of more detailed and more topical information (including statistics) are mentioned in the text and in the Bibliography towards the end of the book.

Reference Division
Central Office of Information, London
September 1978

1 The Land and the People

THE PHYSICAL BACKGROUND

Britain, formally known as the United Kingdom of Great Britain and Northern Ireland, constitutes the greater part of the British Isles, a group of islands lying off the north-west coast of mainland Europe. The largest islands are Great Britain (comprising the mainlands of England, Wales and Scotland) and Ireland (comprising Northern Ireland and the Irish Republic). Off the southern coast of England is the Isle of Wight and off the extreme south-west are the Isles of Scilly; off north Wales is Anglesey. Western Scotland is fringed by numerous islands and to the north-east are the Orkneys and Shetlands. All these have administrative ties with the mainland, but the Isle of Man in the Irish Sea and the Channel Islands between Great Britain and France have a large measure of administrative autonomy and are not part of England, Wales, Scotland or Northern Ireland.

TABLE 1: Area of the United Kingdom

	Total		Land		Inland water	
	square km	square miles	square km	square miles	square km	square miles
United Kingdom	244,103	94,249	241,019	93,058	3,084	1,191
Great Britain	229,983	88,797	227,536	87,852	2,447	945
England	130,441	50,363	129,725	50,087	716	276
Wales	20,768	8,019	20,640	7,969	128	49
Scotland	78,775	30,415	77,171	29,796	1,604	619
Northern Ireland	14,120	5,452	13,483	5,206	637	246

Care should be taken when studying British statistics to note whether they refer to England, to England and Wales (considered together for many administrative and other purposes), to Great Britain, which comprises England, Wales and Scotland, or to the United Kingdom (Great Britain and Northern Ireland) as a whole. United Kingdom statistics and other data occasionally include the Isle of Man, 588 square km (227 sq miles), and the Channel Islands, 194 square km (75 sq miles).

The latitude of 50° North cuts across the southernmost part of the British mainland (the Lizard Peninsula) and latitude 60° North passes through the Shetland Islands. The northernmost point of the Scottish mainland, Dunnet Head, near John o' Groats, is in latitude 58° 40'. The prime meridian of 0° passes through the old observatory at Greenwich (London), while the easternmost point of England is nearly 1° 45' East and the westernmost point of Northern Ireland is 8° 10' West. It is just under 1,000 km (some 600 miles) from the south coast to the extreme north of mainland Britain and just under 500 km (some 300 miles) across in the widest part. There are numerous bays and inlets and no place is as much as 120 km (75 miles) from tidal water.

The seas surrounding the British Isles are shallow—usually less than 90 metres (50 fathoms or 300 feet)—because the islands lie on the continental shelf. To the north-west along the edge of the shelf the sea floor plunges abruptly from 180 metres (some 600 feet) to 900 metres (about 3,000 feet). These shallow waters are important because they provide excellent fishing grounds as well as breeding grounds for fish. The North Atlantic current, the drift of warm water which reaches the islands from across the Atlantic, spreads out over the shelf and its ameliorating effect on the air is thus magnified. The effect of tidal movement is also increased by the shallowness of the water.

Geology and Topography

Despite its small area, Britain contains rocks of all the main geological periods. In general, the oldest rocks appear in the highland regions in the north and west, and the youngest in the lowland areas in the south and east. This is mainly the result of persistent slow sinking over many millions of years in the south and east accompanying the formation of the deep North Sea and English Channel sedimentary basins.

Beneath the lowland areas in the south and east of England lie the younger rocks. The harder chalk and limestone formations stand out as ranges of low, grass-covered hills (rarely reaching 300 metres, 1,000 feet, above sea level) separated by clay vales of rich farm land. These younger formations rest on an old volcanic foundation present at a depth of a few hundred metres under much of central England. This volcanic foundation, containing the oldest British fossils, comes to the surface as craggy hillocks in north-west Leicestershire. At greater depths beneath southern England lies the continuation of the older rock formations of Belgium and the Rhineland.

The south-western peninsula of England, mainly the counties of Devon and Cornwall, is composed of very old slate and sandstone formations into which has been forced a large mass of metal-bearing granite whose outcrops now form most of the high ground such as Dartmoor.

Still older rocks form most of the mountainous and hilly terrain in Wales, the English Lake District, the southern uplands of Scotland and the southern border counties of Northern Ireland.[1] These rocks were subjected to compressions 400 million years ago which folded the strata and turned muddy sediment into slate. In Wales and the Lake District thick volcanic formations, eroded by rivers and Ice-Age glaciers, form spectacular mountain scenery.

Carboniferous limestone formations form the Mendip Hills, south of Bristol, and the Pennines range in northern England. In Scotland similar strata of a partly volcanic character underlie the midland valley. These and other carboniferous strata contain the coal measures which were the foundation of British industrial expansion. The outcrops and shallow seams of coal which have now largely been exhausted were found on the edge of the plains and up the valleys leading to the high land. Most of the present deep coal workings lie underneath the fertile lowlands. The continental shelf under the North Sea contains large, exploitable quantities of oil and natural gas.

The Scottish Highlands are built from very thick formations of crystalline rock, now deeply eroded, which was deposited between 1,000 million and 500 million years ago. Far older rocks, including the oldest in Britain, emerge from beneath the Highlands on the north-western seaboard of Scotland and in the Outer Hebrides, forming barren and rocky land. On the mainland of Scotland a cover of red sandstone between 800 million and 1,000 million years old has been partly eroded, leaving imposing isolated peaks.

Extensive areas in Antrim in Northern Ireland and in the islands of the Inner

---

[1] The highest peaks are: in Scotland, Ben Nevis, 1,342 metres (4,406 feet); in Wales, Snowdon, 1,085 metres (3,560 feet); and in England, Scafell Pike (in the Lake District, Cumbria), 978 metres (3,210 feet). The highest peak in Northern Ireland is Slieve Donard, 852 metres (2,796 feet).

Hebrides are composed of volcanic lava flows which erupted 50 million to 60 million years ago when the North Atlantic Ocean was in the process of opening out. The lavas and the roots of the volcanoes which fed them are deeply eroded into wild mountain scenery.

The landscape of Britain is mainly the result of cycles of uplift and erosion in the past 25 million years, culminating in the last Ice Age. Around 750,000 years ago great glaciers built up in the mountainous areas of Britain and Scandinavia and spread out as ice-sheets into the lowland areas. The mountains and the valleys were formed by the glaciers while the ice sheets deposited a thick blanket of boulder clay, gravel and sand over the lowlands north of a line from Bristol to London. Large lakes of meltwater held back by the ice gradually dried up, leaving deposits of sand and silt. Throughout much of the country the blanket of glacial debris affords soils of great fertility.

Britain's complex geology is one of the main reasons for its rich variety of scenery and the stimulating contrasts found within short distances, particularly on the coasts. The ancient rocks of the highland area often reach the coast in towering cliffs; elsewhere the sea may penetrate in deep lochs, as along much of the west coast of Scotland. Bold outstanding headlands are notable features in other parts of the varied coastline: the granite cliffs of Land's End; the limestone masses and slates of the coast of south-west Wales; the red sandstone of St. Bees Head on the coast of Cumbria; and the vertically jointed lavas of Skye and the island of Staffa in the Inner Hebrides. Even around the lowlands there are striking contrasts. In some parts the soft, white limestone—the chalk—forms white cliffs as at Dover and in the Needles off the Isle of Wight; while other parts of the south and south-east coastline have beaches of sand or shingle. The eastern coast of England between the Humber and the Thames estuary is mostly low-lying, and for centuries some stretches of it have been protected against the sea by embankments.

The marked tidal movement around the shores of Britain sweeps away much of the sand and mud brought down by the rivers and makes the estuaries of the short British rivers[1] valuable as natural harbours.

Climate Britain has a generally mild and temperate climate. The prevailing winds are south-westerly and the weather from day to day is controlled mainly by a succession of depressions from the Atlantic. The weather is subject to frequent changes but to few extremes of temperature. Although the winds are largely determined by those of the eastern Atlantic, occasionally during the winter months easterly winds may bring cold, dry, weather which, once established, may persist for many days or even weeks. During the summer months the Azores high pressure system usually extends its influence north-eastwards towards north-west Europe, and the depressions take a more northerly course, often passing entirely to the north of the country.

Winds South-westerly winds are the most frequent, and those from an easterly direction the least; such winds occur about one-third as often as south-westerlies although easterly winds are appreciably more frequent in the spring than at any other time of the year. In hilly country, wind direction may differ markedly from the general direction owing to local topography. Winds are generally stronger in the north than in the south, stronger on the coasts than inland, and stronger in the west than in the east. The strongest winds

---

[1] The longest rivers in England—the Severn and the Thames—are only about 354 and 338 km (220 and 210 miles) long respectively; those in Scotland (the Tay and the Clyde) about 188 km and 170 km (117 and 106 miles) long.

usually occur in the winter; the average speed at Lerwick, Shetland Islands, varies from about 29 km/h (18 mph) in January to about 19 km/h (12 mph) in August, while at Kew Observatory, on the western outskirts of London, the average speed varies from about 15 km/h (9 mph) in January to about 12 km/h (7 mph) in August. The stormiest region is along the north-west coast with over 40 gales a year; south-east England and the east Midlands are the least stormy, with gales occurring on about 2 days a year inland and on some 10 to 15 days on the Channel coast.

Temperature

Near sea level in the west the mean annual temperature ranges from 8°C (46°F) in the Hebrides to 11°C (52°F) in the extreme south-west of England; latitude for latitude it is slightly lower in the east. The mean monthly temperature in the extreme north, at Lerwick (Shetland), ranges from 3°C (°37F) during the winter (December, January and February) to 12°C (54°F) during the summer (June, July and August): the corresponding figures for the Isle of Wight, in the extreme south, are 5°C (41°F) and 16°C (61°F). During a normal summer, the temperature occasionally rises above 30°C (86°F) in the south, but temperatures of 32°C (90°F) and above are infrequent. Minimum temperatures depend largely on local conditions, but − 10°C (14°F) may occur on a still, clear winter's night in inland areas. Lower temperatures are rare.

Rainfall

Britain has an annual rainfall of about 1,100 mm (over 40 inches), while England alone has some 830 mm (about 33 inches). The geographical distribution of annual rainfall is largely governed by topography and exposure to the Atlantic, the mountainous areas of the west and north having far more rain than the lowlands of the south and east. Between 3,800 and 5,000 mm (roughly 150–200 inches) of rain fall on the summits of Snowdon, the Lake District and north-west Scotland during the average year, whereas some places in the south-east of England record less than 500 mm (about 20 inches). Rain is fairly well distributed throughout the year, but, on the average, March to June are the driest months and October to January the wettest. A period of as long as three weeks without rain is exceptional, and is usually confined to limited areas.

Sunshine

The distribution of sunshine shows a general decrease from south to north, a decrease from the coast inland, and a decrease with altitude. During May, June and July (the months of longest daylight) the mean daily duration of sunshine varies from five hours in northern Scotland to eight hours in the Isle of Wight; during the months of shortest daylight—November, December and January—sunshine is at a minimum, with an average of half an hour a day in some parts of the Highlands of Scotland and two hours a day on the south coast of England.

Visibility

In fine, still weather there is occasionally haze in summer and mist and fog in winter. Fogs have become less frequent and less severe as a result of changes in fuel usage and the operation of clean air legislation. In London, for example, the frequency of dense fogs in winter is about half what it was 20 years ago.

Soil and Vegetation

Many parts of the surface of highland Britain have only thin, poor soils, with the result that large stretches of moorland are found over the Highlands of Scotland, the Pennines, the Lake District, the mountains of Wales and in parts of north-east and south-west England. In most areas the farmer has cultivated only the valleys and the plains where soils are deeper and richer;

villages and towns are often separated by uplands with few if any habitations.

With the exception of a few patches of heath and forest, almost the whole of lowland Britain has been cultivated, and farmland covers the area except where there are urban and industrial settlements. Elaborate land drainage has been developed through the centuries to bring under cultivation the fertile soil of the low-lying fenland of Lincolnshire and part of East Anglia.

With its mild climate and varied soils, Britain has a diverse pattern of vegetation. When the islands were first settled, oak forest probably covered the greater part of the lowland, giving place to extensive marshlands, forests of Scots pine on higher or sandy ground and perhaps some open moorland. In the course of the centuries the forest area was progressively diminished and, in spite of planting by estate owners in the eighteenth and nineteenth centuries and the establishment of large forests by the Forestry Commission in the past 50 years, woodlands now occupy only about 8 per cent of the land area. The greatest density of woodland occurs in northern Britain, in some parts of south-east England and on the Welsh border. Yet much of Britain appears to be wooded because of the numerous hedgerows and isolated trees. The most common trees are oak, beech, ash and elm and, in Scotland, pine and birch. The number of elms, especially in southern England, has been severely reduced since the late 1960s by 'Dutch' elm disease.

There are various types of wild vegetation, including the natural flora of woods, fens and marshes, foreshores and cliffs, chalk downs and the higher slopes of mountains; the most widespread is that of the hilly moorland country, which consists mainly of heather, grasses, gorse and bracken, with cotton grass in the wetter parts. About 82 per cent of Great Britain however is used for agriculture (including rough grazing land) with most of the prime farming land in England. The amount of land in urban use is less than a tenth of the amount of agricultural land.

Farming land is divided into fields by hedges, stone walls or fences and, especially in the mixed farms which cover most of the country, presents a pattern of contrasting colour. The removal of hedges to facilitate mechanical farming has resulted in a more open landscape in certain parts of the country. The cool temperate climate and the even distribution of rainfall ensure a long growing season; streams rarely dry up, grassland is green throughout the year with many wild flowers from spring to autumn; in most years there is scarcely a month without some flowers in hedgerows and woodlands.

Fauna

The fauna of the British Isles is, in general, similar to that of the rest of north-western Europe, though there are fewer species. Some of the larger mammals, including the wolf, the bear, the boar and the reindeer, have become extinct; but red deer, protected for sporting reasons, flourish in the Scottish Highlands and on Exmoor in the counties of Devon and Somerset, roe deer are found in Scotland and in the wooded areas of southern England, and fallow deer (which are probably not indigenous) have been introduced into parks and are wild in some districts. The badger, a nocturnal animal, is rarely seen; there are foxes in most rural (and many semi-urban) areas, and otters are found along many rivers and streams. Common and grey seals may be seen on parts of the coast, though not usually in the same localities. Smaller mammals include mice, rats, voles, shrews, hedgehogs, moles, squirrels (the imported grey much more numerous than the native red), hares, rabbits, weasels and stoats.

About 460 species of birds have been recorded in the British Isles. Some 200 species breed; the rest are regular migrants to, or pass through, the country, or are casual stragglers. Visitors to Britain are often struck by the abundance, variety and tameness of song birds in towns and villages. The pigeon, blackbird and chaffinch are widely distributed but sparrows usually predominate near houses. London and some other large towns have huge flocks of starlings which congregate to roost on buildings, especially in winter. Most species of birds have maintained their numbers over the last few decades, owing to their success in adapting themselves to man-made surroundings, and in London there has been an increase in the number of species breeding as a result of the improvement in the environment brought about by anti-pollution measures. Some large birds, on the other hand, have tended to decrease, but several species, such as the osprey and the ruff, have re-established themselves after disappearing from Britain in the nineteenth century.

Many species of gulls and other sea birds nest around the coast, and gulls may regularly be seen feeding far inland; some nest in inland sites such as gravel pits and sewage farms. The drainage and reclamation of marshlands have diminished the natural habitat of ducks, geese and other aquatic birds, but the survival of such species is largely assured on the nature reserves and bird sanctuaries which have recently been established on an increasing scale. Nearly all British wild birds are protected; the principal exceptions are those considered injurious to agriculture and birds shot for sport in the open season.

About 30 kinds of freshwater fish are found, salmon, trout, pike, roach, dace and perch being widely distributed. Stocks of trout, rainbow trout (an introduced species), carp, tench and roach are frequently supplemented by introductions for angling purposes. In a number of rivers measures to control pollution have resulted in fish becoming more numerous. In the Thames in London, for example, where pollution levels have been reduced to a quarter of those in the 1950s, over 90 kinds of fish have been found, compared with only one in 1958.

Reptiles and amphibians are few. The former are represented by three species of snakes, of which only the adder is venomous, and three species of lizards, including the snake-like slow-worm. The amphibians are represented by three species of newts and five species of frogs and toads. Most British reptiles and amphibians are indigenous but at least one, the marsh frog, has been recently introduced from continental Europe. Ireland has no snakes.

There are more than 21,000 different kinds of insects. Among the largest are the rare swallowtail butterfly (8–10 cm, 3–4 inches) and the stag beetle (6 cm, $2\frac{1}{2}$ inches). The insect fauna is less varied than that of continental Europe and lacks a number of common European species. With modern methods of pest control, extensive insect damage to crops or timber and serious outbreaks of diseases spread by insects are not common but there is some anxiety that chemical protection against insects may be reducing the population of creatures which feed on them, and of their predators in turn. These and other effects of agricultural chemicals on wildlife are the subject of special safeguards.

THE DEMOGRAPHIC BACKGROUND

The people who now inhabit Britain are descended mainly from the people who inhabited the area nine centuries ago. The last of a long succession of invaders and colonisers from Scandinavia and the continent of Europe were the Normans, a branch of the Norsemen or Scandinavian Vikings who, after settling in northern France, intermarrying with the French, and assimilating their language and customs, crossed to England and conquered it in 1066.

Obviously it is not possible to estimate the relative importance of various early peoples—pre-Celts, Celts, Romans, Anglo-Saxons and the Norsemen, including the Danes—in the ancestry of the present English, Scots, Welsh and Irish. Over most of England and the lowlands of Scotland the language which soon came to predominate was English, mainly a marriage of Anglo-Saxon and Norman-French, while the use of Celtic languages persisted in Wales, Cornwall, the Isle of Man, the highlands of Scotland and in Ireland.

The available records do not enable any precise estimates to be made of the size of population or of the extent or direction of population movement until the beginning of the nineteenth century. It is believed, however, that at the end of the eleventh century the population of Great Britain was about 2 million, while at the end of the seventeenth century reasonable contemporary estimates put the population at about 6½ million. The main factor in this gradual growth of population was a slow natural increase, with high death rates and, in particular, very high infant and maternal mortality. Immigration from the continent of Europe has been an influence at certain times and immigration from Commonwealth countries more recently.

Statistics and Censuses

From the beginning of the nineteenth century there is relatively plentiful and reliable information about the British people—their number, sex, age, geographical distribution, births, marriages, deaths, occupations, language, and family structure. Most of it comes from two main sources: the regular flow of statistical information based on compulsory registration of births, marriages and deaths, and the periodic censuses taken regularly every ten years since 1801 (because of war there was no census in 1941). The last census was in 1971; the next will be held in 1981.

Numbers

Britain's estimated mid-1977 home population was 55,852,000 (see Table 2, below). The populations of the Isle of Man, Jersey, and Guernsey and associated islands are about 56,000, 72,000 and 53,000 respectively. In 1975, 1976 and

TABLE 2: Populations 1901–77[a]   *thousands*

		1901 census	1931 census	1961 census	1971 census	1977 mid-year estimate
England	Males	14,714	17,839	21,012	22,355	22,581
	Females	15,795	19,520	22,448	23,663	23,770
	Persons	30,509	37,359	43,461	46,018	46,351
Wales	Males	1,014	1,294	1,292	1,328	1,341
	Females	1,004	1,300	1,352	1,404	1,427
	Persons	2,019	2,593	2,644	2,731	2,768
Scotland	Males	2,174	2,326	2,483	2,515	2,501
	Females	2,298	2,517	2,697	2,714	2,695
	Persons	4,472	4,843	5,179	5,229	5,196
Northern Ireland	Males	590	601[b]	694	755	761
	Females	647	642[b]	731	781	776
	Persons	1,237	1,243[b]	1,425	1,536	1,537
United Kingdom	Males	18,492	22,060	25,481	26,952	27,184
	Females	19,745	23,978	27,228	28,562	28,668
	Persons	38,237	46,038	52,709	55,515	55,852

[a] Figures may not add up to the totals shown because of rounding.
[b] Estimates.

1977 for the first years since records began (other than in war) the population fell slightly. This trend, common to much of western Europe, is mainly the result of a sharp fall in the birth rate (see below). Births in 1977 just outnumbered deaths but the direction of net migration, as in other recent years, was outward.

The total population of New Commonwealth and Pakistani ethnic origin (including children born in Britain and children with only one parent of such ethnic origin) was 1·8 million in 1977, about 3·4 per cent of the total population of Great Britain.

Now that population growth has, for the time being at least, stopped, many official policies, such as those on housing, the planning of the new towns and the supply of school teachers, have been re-examined in the light of the implications, for the short term, of a static or declining population.

Projections for the future suggest that the traditional increase in population will continue, though at a much slower rate than was expected a few years ago. Britain's total population is expected, on 1977 estimates, to be about 56 million in 1986, 57·5 million in 2001 and 58·3 million in 2017.

The country as a whole has a population density of about 229 people to the square kilometre (593 per square mile), but in England the figures are 355 people to the square kilometre (920 per square mile), and in London 4,411 people per square kilometre (11,432 per square mile).

Birth Rates

Annual births have fallen by some 33 per cent since the mid-1960s. The birth rate has declined from 18 live births per 1,000 people in 1966 to 11·8 in 1977, an unprecedentedly low figure. The most recent information suggests that the fall in the birth rate may be coming to an end. The number of births in 1977 was 656,000 (compared with 980,000 in 1966), of which about 10 per cent were illegitimate.

Several factors may have contributed to this change. Family planning, particularly the use by women of the contraceptive pill, has become more widespread, and sterilisation of men and women has also become more common. An appreciable proportion of pregnancies outside marriage and of pregnancies to older women are ended by legal abortion.

There are indications that the proportion of childless marriages may be increasing a little, and for marriages which do produce children there is a continuing tendency for the interval between marriage and the first birth to be longer. The numbers of third and later children born have fallen substantially. The biggest falls have been in the births of third and later children to manual workers, but the pattern is similar for all social classes. A rise in first and second births to professional families appears to be an exception, but may be due to an increase in the number of families in those groups.

The fertility of women born overseas, particularly those from the Irish Republic, the West Indies and the Indian sub-continent, was higher on average in 1971 than that of the indigenous population, but has since been falling. The population of New Commonwealth and Pakistani ethnic origin contains a larger proportion of young people than the indigenous population and so contributes disproportionately to the number of births.

Mortality

At birth the expectation of life for a man is just over 69 years and for a woman it is nearly 76 years. The corresponding expectations in 1901 were 48 years for men and 52 years for women. The improving health of the population has mainly had the effect of increasing young people's chances of reaching the older age groups. Life expectancy in the older age groups has increased relatively little.

The general death rate has remained about the same for the past 50 years, at about 12 per 1,000 population, but this figure takes no account of the ageing population, and at every age there has been a considerable decline in mortality—particularly among children and young adults.

The causes of the decline in mortality include better nutrition, rising standards of living, the advance of medical science, the growth of medical facilities, improved health measures, better working conditions, education in personal hygiene, and the smaller size of the family, which has reduced the strain on mothers and enabled them to take greater care of their children.

Mortality from tuberculosis is a tiny fraction of what it was in the mid-nineteenth century, and mortality from acute infectious diseases in infancy has virtually been eliminated. The infant mortality rate (deaths of infants under one year old per 1,000 live births) was 14·5 in 1976; neonatal mortality (deaths of infants under four weeks old per 1,000 live births) was 9·9; and maternal mortality was 0·13 per 1,000 live births.

United Kingdom population changes and projections

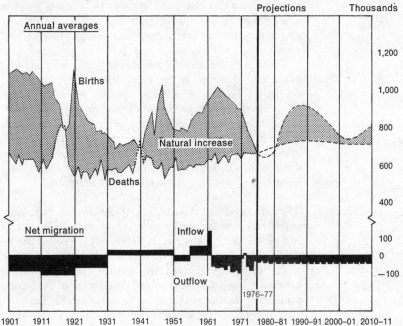

The mortality from each major cause often reflects factors directly linked to occupation and the wide variations between the life patterns and living standards of the different social classes.

Migration

Traditionally Britain has a net outflow of people to the rest of the world (net loss by migration between 1871 and 1931 for instance was about 4 million) though there have been exceptional periods—in the 1930s when there was a considerable flow of refugees from continental Europe, and in the late 1950s and early 1960s, mainly the result of a large influx of people from the West Indies and the Indian sub-continent.

The traditional pattern of migration in Britain has been maintained in the past few years.

Between 1967 and 1976 Britain lost about half a million people by migration:

2·6 million emigrants and 2·1 million immigrants; in both totals about a third of the people were returning to their country of origin.

Sex Ratio

There are about 6 per cent more male than female births every year. Because of the higher mortality of men at all ages, however, there is a turning point, at about 45 years of age, at which the number of women exceeds the number of men. This imbalance increases with age so that there is a preponderance of women among the elderly. In the population as a whole there are more than 105 females to every 100 men.

Marriage and Divorce

Marriage trends since the 1930s have been towards a higher proportion of people marrying and an earlier age pattern. The proportion of the population of Great Britain who are or have been married has risen from about 52 per cent in 1939 to 59·4 per cent in 1976, while the proportion of single persons in the population aged 15 years or over has fallen from 33·3 per cent to 23·1 per cent. This change has been due mainly to an increase in marriage rates among men and women in their late teens and early twenties although recent years suggest that the trend towards early marriage may not be continuing. The average ages of people marrying for the first time in 1976 were roughly 25 for men and 23 for women, compared with ages half a year younger in 1970.

Changes in the law and social attitudes have made divorce easier, and the number of divorces in the 1970s has increased sharply. In 1976 about 10 decrees of divorce were made absolute for every 1,000 married people in England and Wales. If current divorce rates were to continue, the proportion of future marriages which would ultimately end in divorce would come to at least a fifth. The average age of people at the time of divorce in England and Wales is about 38 for men and 36 for women. Remarriage rates among younger divorced people are high, and births in remarriage are likely to become a more important component of total births in the future.

Age Structure

The estimated age distribution of the British population in mid-1977 was roughly as follows: under 15 years, about 22 per cent; 15–64, 63 per cent; and 65 and over, 14 per cent. Some 17 per cent of the population were over the normal retirement ages (65 for men and 60 for women).

The changing age structure has for the time being produced a balance between those who are primarily producers of resources and those who are primarily consumers that is more unfavourable than at any time since the early 1930s. This 'dependency ratio' of children and older people to the size of the population of working age is, however, projected to fall from 67 per cent in 1976 to 58 per cent in 2001. This will be the result principally of the decreasing proportion of children in the population.

Perhaps the main feature of the changing age structure is the increasing number of elderly people, reflecting birth patterns in the early years of the century and the final decades of the nineteenth. Between mid-1970 and mid-1977 the number of people over the normal retirement ages rose by 8 per cent. Proportionately there was a particularly large increase in the number of people aged 85 and over, 20·5 per cent over the same period.

Distribution of Population

The population of England is, and has been for centuries, greater than that of all other parts of Britain. The distribution of the British population by country, is shown in Table 2 on p 7.

The standard regions of England, sub-divisions of the country used for

most statistical and economic planning purposes, have the following populations (provisional mid-1977 estimates): East Anglia 1,827,400; East Midlands
3,746,900; Northern 3,116,000; North-West 6,518,600; South-East
16,833,500; South-West 4,278,700; West Midlands 5,154,300; and Yorkshire
and Humberside 4,875,900.

Table 3 gives figures of some of Britain's largest urban areas. About half
the population lives in a belt across England with south Lancashire and
West Yorkshire at one end, and the London area at the other, having the
industrialised Midlands at its centre. Other areas with large populations are:
the central lowlands of Scotland; north-east England from north of the
river Tyne down to the river Tees; south-east Wales; the Bristol area; and the

TABLE 3: Size and Population of Some of the Main Urban Areas, Mid-1977

	Area		Population estimate (provisional)
	square km	square miles	
			(thousands)
Greater London	1,580	609·7	6,970·1
Birmingham	264	102·0	1,050·1
Glasgow	157	60·5	832·1
Leeds	562	217·0	735·0
Sheffield	368	141·9	547·4
Liverpool	113	43·6	536·9
Manchester	116	44·9	491·6
Bradford	370	142·9	462·2
Edinburgh	135	52·0	463·9
Bristol	110	42·3	409·9
Belfast	140	54·0	357·6
Coventry	97	37·3	340·5
Cardiff	120	46·3	278·9

English Channel coast from Poole, in Dorset, eastwards. Less densely populated
areas are the eastern fringes of England between the Wash and the Thames
estuary, and the far south-west. The seven major metropolitan areas which
have been denoted as 'conurbations' in successive population censuses accommodate a third of Great Britain's people while comprising less than three per
cent of the total land area. They are: Greater London, Central Clydeside, Merseyside, South East Lancashire, Tyneside, the West Midlands and West Yorkshire. Most of the mountainous parts including much of Scotland, Wales and
Northern Ireland and the central Pennines in northern England, are very
sparsely populated.

These differences in average density between different regions have been
widening. There has been a geographical redistribution of the population from
Scotland and the northern regions of England to East Anglia, the South-West
and the East Midlands. The proportion resident in Greater London and most
of the metropolitan counties of England has recently been falling. People,
particularly the young and skilled, have tended to leave city centres and
conurbations, although such migration may not necessarily mean a change of
job but rather an increase in the distance of travel to and from work.

Language   In England, Wales, Scotland and Northern Ireland, English is the language
predominantly spoken. In Wales, however, Welsh, a form of British Celtic,
was spoken by 21 per cent of the population (some 542,000 people) aged three
years and over at the time of the 1971 census. The Welsh Language Council, an

official body, promotes the use of the language. The Welsh Language Act 1967 affirms the equal validity of Welsh with English in the administration of justice and conduct of government business throughout Wales. The number of bilingual schools is increasing. In Scotland some 88,000 persons in 1971, mainly in the Highlands and western coastal regions, were able to speak the Scottish form of Gaelic. A few families in Northern Ireland still speak the Irish form of Gaelic. The Cornish variety of Celtic is no longer effectively a living language, although there is a revival of cultural interest.

Some of the country's ethnic minorities have their own languages, normally as well as English. Among the Asian community, for example, the most usual languages are Punjabi, Gujarati, Bengali or Urdu.

Immigration Control and Nationality

Immigration into Britain is controlled by the Immigration Act 1971. The Act confers a right of abode—and exemption from control—on citizens of the United Kingdom and Colonies who are connected with Britain by birth, adoption, naturalisation or registration or are children or grandchildren of such persons, on citizens of the United Kingdom and Colonies from overseas who have been resident in Britain for a continuous period of five years, and on Commonwealth citizens with a parent born in the United Kingdom. Those having this right of abode are known as 'patrials'. In general, others wishing to enter Britain for employment must hold work permits. Exceptions are. Commonwealth citizens with a grandparent born in Britain, certain permit-free categories, and nationals of European Community countries. The dependants of work permit holders and of those who may enter without work permits may also be admitted.

Under the British Nationality Act 1948, people born in the United Kingdom, the Channel Islands, the Isle of Man, a ship or aircraft registered in the United Kingdom, or a territory which is still a colony, are, with insignificant exceptions, citizens of the United Kingdom and Colonies by birth. Citizenship may also be acquired: by descent from a father who is himself a citizen otherwise than by descent and, in certain specified circumstances, from a father who is a citizen by descent only; by registration, for citizens of Commonwealth member countries or of the Irish Republic, for minor children and for women married to citizens of the United Kingdom and Colonies; in consequence of a United Kingdom adoption order; and, for aliens, by naturalisation. The requirements for naturalisation include five years' residence in the United Kingdom or Colonies, good character, a sufficient knowledge of English and the intention to reside in the United Kingdom or a colony. The requirements for registration are similar except that most Commonwealth and Irish citizens settled in Britain by 1973 have the right to be registered after completing five years' ordinary residence without satisfying any other requirement. Over 27,500 people acquired citizenship by naturalisation and registration in 1977.

A citizen of the United Kingdom and Colonies does not forfeit his citizenship by acquiring or possessing the nationality or citizenship of another country (although he can lose it automatically if the territory from which he derives it becomes independent); nor does a woman who is a citizen of the United Kingdom and Colonies lose her citizenship by marriage to a foreign national. Indeed, a citizen cannot be deprived of his citizenship against his will except in very exceptional circumstances (for example, if he has obtained naturalisation or registration as a citizen by fraud). Any man or woman who is a citizen is, however, at liberty to renounce citizenship if he or she possesses or acquires the nationality or citizenship of another country.

Citizens of the other independent Commonwealth countries are, in United Kingdom law, British subjects or Commonwealth citizens and, as such, enjoy full political and civic rights if resident in Britain.

The Government has suggested for public discussion various ways in which the law on nationality might be changed.

THE SOCIAL FRAMEWORK

This section gives some points of general interest about household structure and social characteristics in Britain as a background to the information given in later chapters. It deals with topics in very broad and informal terms and many exceptions apply to the generalisations.

The way of life of the people of Britain has been changing rapidly throughout the twentieth century. As in many other countries underlying causes include two major wars, a lower birth rate, longer expectation of life, a higher divorce rate, widening educational opportunities and technical progress, particularly in communications and transport and a better standard of living. One of the features of the change in social attitudes has been the development of a more informed tolerance of others' behaviour and an unwillingness to penalise individuals with particular problems. Relationships between the generations, too, are changing, and young people are more ready to criticise traditional values and institutions and to seek greater influence in shaping society.

The following account applies primarily to Great Britain. Many of the same factors are at work in Northern Ireland but their effect is modified by both the Province's history and the emergency of recent years.

Homes and the Environment

The majority of people (some 97 per cent) live in private households (in families or on their own). The remainder include residents in hotels, and people in the armed services and in educational or other institutions. Of approximately 27·5 million married people at the time of the 1971 population census about 25 million were estimated to be married couples living together in some 12·5 million separate families containing some 46 million people, the remainder living either on their own or with other persons or families, except for a small number living in institutions. Nearly 8 million of the families, comprising 32 million people, contained a married couple and their children or grandchildren. There were, in addition, 1·2 million families consisting of a parent living with children or grandchildren. About half, mostly women, were bringing up between them about 1 million dependent children; the rest were living with adult children or grandchildren.

The average size of households has continued to fall progressively, from over four persons in 1911 to 3·1 in 1961 and 2·8 in 1976. It is estimated that in 1976 21 per cent of households consisted of one person only, 32 per cent of two, 17 per cent of three, 17 per cent of four and 13 per cent of five or more. However, about half of the small households (one or two persons) contained a person over 60 years old while of the remaining 40 per cent about half were older people and couples whose children had left home, and the other half consisted of young couples.

Four British households out of five live in houses rather than flats. Terraced housing, most of it built in the early years of the present century, still provides accommodation for over a quarter of all households. In inner urban areas, which have increasing priority in the Government's housing and planning policies, slum clearance and redevelopment have been major features of post-1945 public housing programmes, but, with help from public funds, the modernisation and conversion of sub-standard housing has increasingly been encouraged as an alternative to clearing and rebuilding. Emphasis in new building is on low-rise, high density layouts, often incorporating gardens or patios. Nearly half of Britain's housing stock has been built since 1945.

The main housing development of the past 50 to 60 years, however, has been suburban. Many British families now live in houses grouped in small terraces, or semi-detached or detached, usually of two storeys with gardens, and providing two main ground-floor living rooms, a kitchen, from two to four bedrooms, a bathroom, and one or two lavatories. Many such houses, built in the 1920s and 1930s, are located in 'ribbon development' along main roads, but recent patterns have involved housing estates set back from the main thoroughfares with amenities such as health and community centres.

Housing standards are continually improving; some 93 per cent of households in Great Britain have exclusive use of a bath or shower, and 97 per cent sole use of a lavatory—high percentages by international standards. Most housing built nowadays is centrally heated. About 54 per cent of British households have a telephone, 56 per cent have the use of one or more cars, 49 per cent some form of central heating, 88 per cent a refrigerator, 71 per cent a washing machine, 22 per cent a deep freeze and 3 per cent a dish washer.

Over half of all families now own their own homes, though half of these home owners still have further repayments of mortgages to make. Most of the other households rent an unfurnished house or flat either from a local authority (an increasing trend) or from a private landlord (a falling trend). People in unskilled manual jobs are more likely to live in rented accommodation, particularly local authority housing, than people in non-manual occupations. One-third of all families move house every five years.

An important influence on the planning of housing and services has been the growth of car ownership. Greater access to motorised transport and the construction of a network of modern trunk roads and motorways have resulted in a considerable increase in personal mobility and changed leisure patterns, as well as changes in the design of housing and shopping areas. Most detached or semi-detached houses in new suburban estates have garages, and out-of-town shopping centres, frequently including large supermarkets, are often specially planned for the motorist and offer an alternative to shopping in the centres of older towns. The 32 new towns and the 'expanding towns' (generally seen as one of the most successful achievements of British planning since 1945) have set high standards in accommodating people and traffic.

The growth in car ownership has brought very great benefits but also a number of problems, notably, in many towns and cities, increased congestion, noise and air pollution. Public transport, too, has been affected, and many services have been reduced or eliminated, especially in rural areas. The people without access to a car include those among the poorer sections of the community, or the elderly or infirm; mobility allowances help the disabled. Priority to ensure the maintenance of the remaining essential public transport services is a feature of the Government's transport policy, and special fare concessions are made for groups such as old age pensioners and invalids.

In a densely populated modern industrial society there is much scope for conflict between the need for communal facilities and the desire to preserve existing beauty or places of historic interest, and between potential users of a new service and people whose way of life is threatened by the need to accommodate it. As a result the activities of the established amenity societies, such as the National Trust and the Council for the Protection of Rural England, are supplemented to a growing extent by those of groups formed expressly to safeguard the amenities of a particular area and to publicise the views of the people they represent.

Growing public concern about the dangers both to health and to the natural environment which can be caused by the disposal of industrial and human waste, by exhaust fumes and by the rising volume of noise is reflected in the appointment by the Government of a standing Royal Commission on Environmental Pollution, a Clean Air Council and an Advisory Council on Noise. Voluntary societies include the National Society for Clean Air, the Noise Abatement Society, the Keep Britain Tidy Group, Friends of the Earth, and the Council for Nature.

The Economic and Social Pattern

Marked improvements in the standard of living have taken place during the twentieth century. Nonetheless considerable inequalities of income and wealth, among them regional disparities, remain. The gap between social classes in such matters as infant mortality rates, educational progress, working conditions and ill-health remains wide. There has been a long-term tendency to a reduction in the proportion of semi-skilled and unskilled workers, and an increasing number of people in professional or managerial occupations are children of manual workers.

The working population comprises nearly half the total population. For a long period an increase in real earnings was a principal factor in British working and social life. Between 1950 and 1975 real personal disposable income[1] more than doubled to £41,625 million, an average annual rise of 4·4 per cent. It fell by about 0·2 per cent in 1976, and by about 1 per cent in 1977.

The combined effect of the tax system and the receipt of transfer payments and direct and indirect benefits in kind is to redistribute incomes on a more equal basis. Changes in the distribution of income between the late 1950s and 1974–75 were not very pronounced, but there had been an almost continuous decline in the share of the top 5 per cent of income recipients from about 20 per cent of income before tax in 1959 to just under 17 per cent in 1974–75, accounted for largely by the drop in the share of the top 1 per cent from about 8 per cent to 6 per cent over the same period. (The fall in the share of the top 1 per cent since 1938–39 had been about two-thirds.) The share of the bottom 20 per cent had increased between 1959 and 1975 from 5·3 to 6·2 per cent. However, more recently during a period of inflation and wages restraint when the standards of living of all income groups have been falling, those of higher income groups have tended to fall more, and customary differentials between higher and lower employment incomes have been reduced.

There is very little knowledge about long-term trends in the distribution of wealth, but such estimates as there are show a substantial fall in the share owned by the richest people in the community. In 1975 about 24 per cent of personal wealth was owned by the top 1 per cent of the adult population, and over 76 per cent by the top 20 per cent. The value of state pension rights has an especially marked effect on these figures; it lowers the share of the top 1 per cent by a third while the share of the bottom 80 per cent of the adult population is increased by two-thirds. The proportion of personal wealth held in the form of physical assets rose from less than a third in 1960 to almost 50 per cent in 1975, reflecting especially the increasing importance of dwellings. There has been a marked decline in the relative importance of company securities in the composition of personal wealth.

---

[1] Total personal income less taxes on income, national insurance contributions, transfers abroad (net) and taxes paid abroad, adjusted to take account of inflation.

The volume of consumer spending in Britain has increased little in the past two or three years, after allowing for inflation, although there were signs of growth in early 1978. Over the period 1970–76 there were significant changes in the pattern of expenditure. Consumers' expenditure on food remained fairly level, but that on alcoholic drink, particularly wines and spirits, increased substantially. By contrast, expenditure on tobacco in 1976 was below the 1970 level. A large increase in spending on radio and electrical goods was mainly due to people buying colour televisions, and well over half the television broadcast licences are issued for colour sets. Expenditure on television rental, too, more than doubled, while that on admission to cinemas, theatres, spectator sports and the like increased by about 15 per cent.

Some 11·5 million visitors to Britain in 1977, a record number, spent a total of £2,179 million. This expenditure has increased dramatically, and, although little is known about visitors' spending patterns, it is likely that most of the increase was on meals and accommodation and on items such as clothing and footwear. It therefore presumably helped to keep up real expenditure levels when spending by British residents was, at most, rising slowly.

The general level of nutrition is high. The movement towards a greater use of convenience (including frozen) foods, and imported foods in the 1960s, has been partly offset by a reversion to a slightly less expensive diet. The last 20 years or so have seen a gradual decline in total food supplies per person, which is regarded as consistent with reductions in physical activity and the greater proportion of less active people in the population. The trend is common to most developed countries. A greater willingness to try unfamiliar foods has given rise to a wider availability of imported products, as well as to restaurants serving the national dishes of other countries.

Over the period 1966–76 total consumption of beer (Britain's most popular alcoholic drink) rose by 32 per cent; that of spirits by 100 per cent; and that of wine 114 per cent.

The Role of
Women

The greatest social changes have probably been in the economic and domestic lives of women. Almost all theoretical sex discrimination in political and legal rights has been removed.

The changes have been significant but, because tradition and prejudice can still handicap women in their working careers and personal lives, major legislation to help to promote equality of opportunity and pay has been passed during the 1970s.

At the heart of women's changed role in society has been the rise in the number of women at work, particularly married women. As technology and society permit highly effective and generally acceptable methods of family planning there has been a decline in family size. Women as a result are involved in child-bearing for a much shorter time and, related to this, there has been a rapid increase, which is still continuing, in the number of women with young children who return to work when their children are old enough not to need constant care and attention.

Since 1951 the proportion of married women who work has grown from just over a fifth to a half. Compared with their counterparts elsewhere in the European Community, British women comprise a relatively high proportion of the workforce, about two-fifths, but on average they work fewer hours, about 31 a week. There is still a significant difference between women's average earnings and men's, but the equal pay legislation which came into force at the end of 1975 appears to have helped to narrow the gap between women's and men's basic rates. During the 1970s women's wages have risen proportionately more than men's but remain relatively low because women tend to work in lowly-paid sectors of the economy, they often work in predominantly female workforces, and they work less overtime than men.

As more and more women joined the workforce in the 1960s and early 1970s there was an increase in the collective incomes of women as a whole and a major change in the economic role of large numbers of housewives. Families have come to rely on married women's earnings as an essential part of their income rather than as 'pocket money' or a means of buying 'extras'. At the same time social roles within the family are more likely to be shared, exchanged and altered.

Ethnic and National Minorities

Britain has a long history of accommodating minority groups and in the last hundred years or so a variety of people have settled in the country, some to avoid political or religious persecution, others seeking a better way of life and an escape from poverty.

Many Irishmen have made homes in Britain, and comprise the largest single minority group. Many Jewish refugees started a new life in the country towards the end of the nineteenth century and in the 1930s, and after 1945 large numbers of other European refugees, Poles in particular, also came to settle. The large communities from the West Indies and the Indian subcontinent date from the 1950s and the early 1960s. There are also sizeable groups of Americans, Australians, Chinese and various European communities such as Greek and Turkish Cypriots, Italians and Spaniards. In the last generation British society has therefore become more multi-racial as ethnic minority groups from almost all parts of the world have made a permanent home in the country. Although a small proportion of the total population, they represent a significant element in certain areas.

The minority communities tend to live mainly in the urban centres, especially the largest towns, and in particular areas within these centres. The most recent immigrants, such as the West Indians and the Asians, are usually concentrated in the poorer inner city areas, whereas earlier arrivals have tended to move out to the suburbs.

Most minorities share a way of life that is broadly similar to that of the British community as a whole, though some of the newer arrivals, mainly from Commonwealth countries and sometimes with a poor command of the English language, may face problems of limited employment opportunities and inadequate housing. In areas with large and fairly recently-arrived immigrant populations arrangements are made in schools and elsewhere to enable host and minority communities to understand each other's traditions better and to help immigrants who need special language training.

Leisure Trends

Most people have considerably more free time, more ways in which to spend it and higher real incomes than had previous generations. Agreed hours of full-time work are usually from 35 to 40 hours a week, although many people actually work somewhat longer (about 45 on average for manual workers) because of voluntary overtime work, while the hours worked by women and girls average somewhat less. Most employees work a five-day week.

Almost all full-time employees are entitled to a paid holiday each year in addition to public holidays and in practically every case the minimum period is three weeks.

The number of holidays taken in Great Britain by British residents was 36 million in 1977 compared with 31 million in 1966. More than two holidays in five in Great Britain are spent at the home of a friend or relative, and over a quarter involve camping or caravanning. Holidays abroad in 1977 numbered 7·75 million, compared with 5·5 million in 1966, and well over half involved 'package' arrangements. Spain is by far the most popular destination, and receives well over a quarter of all British holiday-makers abroad. A third of the population each year, however, takes no holiday away from home.

Leisure patterns generally are determined by age, sex, social class, income, access to a car and education. The most common activities are home based, with television-watching the most popular; about 96 per cent of households have a television set and in winter the population aged five and over spend on average 20 hours a week watching programmes.

Other popular pursuits include: listening to the radio or records; needlework and other hobbies; going out for a drink to a public house (the 'pub' or 'local' is a traditional social centre for many people); gardening (a majority of British families have some garden or allotment despite the high proportion living in urban areas); eating out; open-air outings; games and sports (as both spectator and participants); going to social clubs[1]; film going (especially among young people); visits to buildings and museums; social and voluntary work; and attending leisure centres.

---

[1] These include clubs run by political groups; trade unions; church groups; social, cultural and academic groups; youth clubs and organisations; and groups of local business and professional people. The longer-established clubs organised on a national basis include the Working Men's Clubs and Institutes, the Townswomen's Guilds and the Women's Institutes.

2 Government

GENERAL SURVEY

The origins and traditions of the United Kingdom are to be found in each of its four component parts: England, Wales, Scotland and Northern Ireland. England was united as a kingdom a thousand years ago, and Wales became part of the kingdom during the Middle Ages. The thrones of England and Scotland were dynastically united in 1603, and in 1707 legislation passed in the two countries provided for the establishment of a single Parliament of Great Britain with supreme authority both in England and Wales and in Scotland. Ireland had had links with the kingdom of England since the thirteenth century, and in 1800 the creation of the United Kingdom was completed by a union joining the Irish Parliament to that of Great Britain. In 1922 Southern Ireland (now the Irish Republic) became a self-governing country. The six counties of Northern Ireland had in 1920 been given their own subordinate Parliament, and voted to remain within the United Kingdom. Arrangements in Northern Ireland are described on p 53.

The United Kingdom Parliament at Westminster in London—with an elected chamber comprising members from English, Scottish, Welsh and Northern Ireland constituencies—therefore represents people whose backgrounds and traditions vary considerably from one part of the country to another. It has ultimate authority for government and law-making, but administrative arrangements have developed in such a way as to take account of the particular needs of different areas.

The United Kingdom is a member of the Commonwealth and of the European Community.

Devolution Two Acts of Parliament became law in July 1978, providing for the establishment in Scotland and in Wales of assemblies (elected by simple majority) with responsibility for a wide range of their domestic affairs. The Scottish Assembly would have powers of primary legislation, with an executive body to administer devolved matters. The Welsh Assembly would have executive responsibility in devolved matters, but no law-making powers.

The Acts also provide that before assemblies can be elected referendums must be held in both Scotland and Wales, in which at least 40 per cent of those entitled to vote must approve the establishment of the assembly. If in either country such a vote is not obtained, the Secretary of State must lay an order for the repeal of the Act. If a general election is called before orders for the referendums have been laid, the referendums cannot then be held until at least three months after the date of the election.

Channel Islands and Isle of Man The Channel Islands and the Isle of Man (which are Crown dependencies, not part of the United Kingdom) have their own legislative assemblies and systems of local administration and of law, and their own courts. At the same time, they have a special relationship with the United Kingdom because of the antiquity of their connection with the Crown. The United Kingdom Government is responsible for their defence, their international relations and, ultimately, their good government. They have separate arrangements with the European Community which take into account their special relationship with the United Kingdom.

The Constitution The United Kingdom constitution is formed partly by statute, partly by common law and partly by conventions, which have never been codified and are not directly enforceable in a court of law, but which, nevertheless, are regarded as rules of the constitution. Because the constitution is not contained in any single document, and because it can be altered by the passing of an Act of Parliament or by general agreement to vary, abolish or create a convention, it can the more readily be adapted to changing political conditions and ideas.

The organs of government are readily distinguishable although their functions often intermingle and overlap. They are:

1. the legislature, the supreme authority in the realm (see p 23);
2. the executive, which consists of: (a) the Government—that is the Cabinet and other ministers of the Crown, who are responsible for initiating and directing national policy (see p 36); (b) government departments, most of them under the control of ministers and all staffed by civil servants, which are responsible for administration at the national level (see p 39); (c) local authorities, which administer and manage many services at the local level (see p 61); and (d) public corporations which may be responsible for the operation of particular nationalised industries or, for example, of a social or cultural service, and which are subject to ministerial control in varying degrees; and
3. the judiciary, which determines common law and interprets statutes, and is independent of both the legislature and the executive.

THE MONARCHY

The monarchy is the most ancient secular institution in the United Kingdom. Its continuity has been broken only once in over a thousand years; and, in spite of interruptions in the direct line of succession, the hereditary principle upon which it was founded has never been abandoned. The royal title in the United Kingdom is: 'Elizabeth the Second, by the Grace of God of the United Kingdom of Great Britain and Northern Ireland and of Her other Realms and Territories Queen, Head of the Commonwealth, Defender of the Faith. The form of the royal title is varied for those other member nations of the Commonwealth[1] of which the Queen is head of State, to suit the particular circumstances of each.

The seat of the monarchy is in the United Kingdom. In the Channel Islands and the Isle of Man the Queen is represented by a Lieutenant-Governor. In the other member nations of the Commonwealth of which the Queen is Sovereign, her representative is the Governor-General, who is appointed by her on the advice of the ministers of the country concerned and is wholly independent of the United Kingdom Government. In the United Kingdom dependencies the Queen is usually represented by governors who

[1] The other members are (those of which the Queen is head of State are marked with an asterisk): Australia*, Bahamas*, Bangladesh, Barbados*, Botswana, Canada*, Cyprus, Fiji*, The Gambia, Ghana, Grenada*, Guyana, India, Jamaica*, Kenya, Lesotho, Malawi, Malaysia, Malta, Mauritius*, Nauru, New Zealand*, Nigeria, Papua New Guinea*, Seychelles, Sierra Leone, Singapore, Solomon Islands*, Sri Lanka, Swaziland, Tanzania, Tonga, Trinidad and Tobago, Uganda, Western Samoa and Zambia. (Nauru is a special member, participating in functional activities but not in meetings of Heads of Government.)

are appointed by the Crown, having various executive and legislative powers, and are responsible to the United Kingdom Government for the good government of the countries concerned.

Succession, Accession and Coronation

The title to the Crown derives partly from statute and partly from common law rules of descent. Lineal Protestant descendants of Princess Sophia (the Electress of Hanover, grand-daughter of James I of England and VI of Scotland) are alone eligible to succeed, and although succession is not bound to continue in its present line, it cannot now be altered other than by common consent of the member nations of the Commonwealth of which the Queen is head of State. Rules of descent provide that the sons of the Sovereign are in order of succession to the throne according to their seniority; if there are no sons, the daughters succeed in order of their seniority. When a daughter succeeds, she becomes Queen-Regnant and the powers of the Crown are vested in her as fully and effectively as though she were a king. By convention, the consort of a king takes the rank and style of her husband; the converse, however, does not apply and the constitution has never attached any special rank or privileges to the husband of the Queen-Regnant although in practice he fills an important role in the life of the nation.

There is no interregnum between the death of one Sovereign and the accession of another. Immediately on the death of his or her predecessor the new Sovereign is proclaimed at an Accession Council to which all members of the Privy Council are summoned. The Lords Spiritual and Temporal, the Lord Mayor, aldermen and other leading citizens of the City of London, and the High Commissioners in London of the member nations of the Commonwealth are also invited to attend.

The coronation of the Sovereign follows the accession after an interval of possibly a year or more. The ceremony has remained much the same in substance for over a thousand years although the details have frequently been modified to bring it into conformity with the customs of the time. The coronation service is held at Westminster Abbey in the presence of representatives of the Lords, the Commons and all the great public interests in the United Kingdom, of the Prime Ministers and leading citizens of the other Commonwealth countries and of representatives of foreign States.

Acts of Government

The Queen is the personification of the State. In law, she is the head of the executive, an integral part of the legislature, the head of the judiciary, the commander-in-chief of all the armed forces of the Crown and the temporal 'governor' of the established Church of England. In practice, as a result of a long evolutionary process during which the absolute power of the monarchy has been progressively reduced, the Queen acts on the advice of her ministers which she cannot constitutionally ignore. She reigns, but she does not rule. The United Kingdom is governed by Her Majesty's Government in the name of the Queen.

Within this framework, and in spite of a trend during the past hundred years towards assigning powers directly to ministers without any necessity for royal intervention, there are still important acts of government which require the participation of the Queen. These include the summoning, prorogation and dissolution of Parliament; giving Royal Assent to Bills passed by both Houses of Parliament; making appointments to all important State offices, including those of government ministers, judges, officers in the armed forces, governors, diplomats and all the leading positions in the established Church of England; conferring peerages, knighthoods and other

honours[1]; and remitting all or part of the penalty imposed on a person convicted of a crime. An important function is the appointment of the Prime
Minister. This is normally automatic, and the Queen must invite the leader of
the political party commanding a majority in the House of Commons to form
a government. If, however, no party has a majority, or if the majority party
has no recognised leader, the Queen must select a Prime Minister, and can
consult anyone she wishes. In international affairs, the Queen as head of
State has the power to declare war and make peace, to recognise foreign
States and governments, to conclude treaties and to annexe or cede territory.

With rare exceptions (such as in the appointment of the Prime Minister)
these and other acts involving the use of 'royal prerogative' powers are nowadays exercised by government ministers who are responsible to Parliament
and can be questioned about a particular policy. The law does not require
Parliament's prior authority before such powers can be exercised, but Parliament has the power to pass legislation to restrict or abolish a prerogative right.

Ministerial responsibility for the exercise of powers by the Crown does not,
however, detract from the importance of the Queen's participation in the
smooth working of government. She holds meetings of the Privy Council,
gives audiences to her ministers and other holders of office at home and
overseas, receives accounts of Cabinet decisions, reads dispatches and signs
innumerable State papers; she must be informed and consulted on every
aspect of the national life; and she must show complete impartiality.

Such is the significance attached to these royal functions that provision has
been made for a regent to be appointed to fulfil them if the Sovereign is totally
incapacitated (or is under the age of 18 years on accession to the throne). The
regent would be the Prince of Wales, and thereafter those in succession to the
throne who are of age. In the event of the Sovereign's partial incapacity or
absence abroad, provision is made for the appointment of Counsellors of State
(the Duke of Edinburgh, the four adult persons next in succession to the
Crown, and the Queen Mother) to whom the Sovereign may delegate certain
royal functions. Counsellors of State may not, however, dissolve Parliament
(except on the express instructions of the Sovereign), or create peers.

**Ceremonial and
Royal Visits**

Ceremonial has always been associated with British kings and queens, and,
in spite of the changes that have taken place in the outlook of both the Sovereign
and the people, many traditional customs and usages remain. Royal marriages
and royal funerals are marked by public ceremony. The birthday of the
Sovereign is officially celebrated early in June by Trooping the Colour on
the Horse Guards Parade and is also celebrated as Commonwealth Day.
State banquets take place when a foreign monarch or head of State visits the
United Kingdom; investitures are held at Buckingham Palace; and royal
processions add significance to such occasions as the opening of Parliament,
when the Queen drives in state from Buckingham Palace. The Queen and
other members of the royal family visit many parts of the United Kingdom
every year, and their presence at the inauguration of scientific, artistic,
industrial and charitable works of national importance encourages nation-
wide interest and publicity. The Queen pays State visits to foreign governments, accompanied by the Duke of Edinburgh, and undertakes lengthy
tours in other countries of the Commonwealth. Other members of the royal
family pay official and private visits overseas.

---

[1] Although most honours are conferred by the Queen on the advice of the Prime
Minister, a few are conferred on her personal selection—the Order of the Garter, the
Order of the Thistle, the Order of Merit and the Royal Victorian Order.

Royal Income and Expenditure

More than three-quarters of all expenditure arising from the official duties of the royal family is borne on the accounts of public departments—including, for example, the costs of the royal yacht, the Queen's Flight, travel by train and the upkeep of the royal palaces. Apart from this the Queen's public expenditure on staff and expenses incurred in carrying out official duties as head of State is financed from the Civil List, approved by Parliament. Her private expenditure as Sovereign is met from the Privy Purse, which is supplied mainly from the revenues of the Duchy of Lancaster[1]; and her personal expenditure as a private individual from her own personal resources. Annual allowances approved by Parliament are specifically made to certain other members of the royal family. No allowances are made to the Queen's eldest son, the Prince of Wales, who as Duke of Cornwall is entitled to the net revenue of the estate of the Duchy of Cornwall (he has voluntarily agreed to surrender half the revenue to the nation). The Queen meets from her Privy Purse the official expenses of members of the royal family for whom Parliament has not specifically provided.

PARLIAMENT

The supreme legislative authority in the United Kingdom is the Queen in Parliament, that is to say, the Queen and the two Houses of Parliament—the House of Lords and the elected House of Commons.

The three elements of Parliament are outwardly separate; they are constituted on different principles; they work in different places; and they meet together only on occasions of symbolic significance such as the State opening of Parliament when the Commons are summoned by the Queen to the House of Lords. As a law-making organ of State, however, Parliament is a corporate body and cannot as a rule legislate without the concurrence of all its parts.

The Parliament at Westminster can legislate for the United Kingdom as a whole, or any of the constituent countries separately, or for any combination of them. Parliament can also legislate for the Channel Islands and the Isle of Man, which are Crown dependencies and not part of the United Kingdom, and have subordinate legislatures[2] which legislate on island affairs.

Because it is not subject to the type of legal restraints imposed on the legislatures of countries with formal written constitutions, Parliament is free to legislate as it pleases: generally to make, unmake, or alter any law; to legalise past illegalities and make void and punishable what was lawful when done and thus reverse the decisions of the ordinary courts; and to destroy established conventions or turn a convention into binding law. It can prolong its own life beyond the normal period without consulting the electorate.

In practice, however, Parliament is slow to exercise its supremacy in this way. Its members bear in mind the common law which has grown up in Britain throughout the centuries and have tended to act in accordance with precedent and tradition. Moreover, although the validity of an Act of Parliament that has been duly passed, legally promulgated and published by the proper authority cannot be disputed in the law courts, no Parliament would be likely to pass an Act which it knew would receive no public support. The system of

---

[1] The Duchy of Lancaster is an inheritance which, since 1399, has always been enjoyed by the reigning Sovereign; it is kept quite apart from his or her other possessions and is separately administered by the Chancellor.

[2] The legislatures of the Channel Islands (the States of Jersey and the States of Guernsey) and the Isle of Man (the Tynwald Court) consist of the Queen, the Privy Council and the local assemblies. It is the duty of the Home Secretary, as the member of the Privy Council primarily concerned with island affairs, to scrutinise each legislative measure before it is submitted to the Queen in Council.

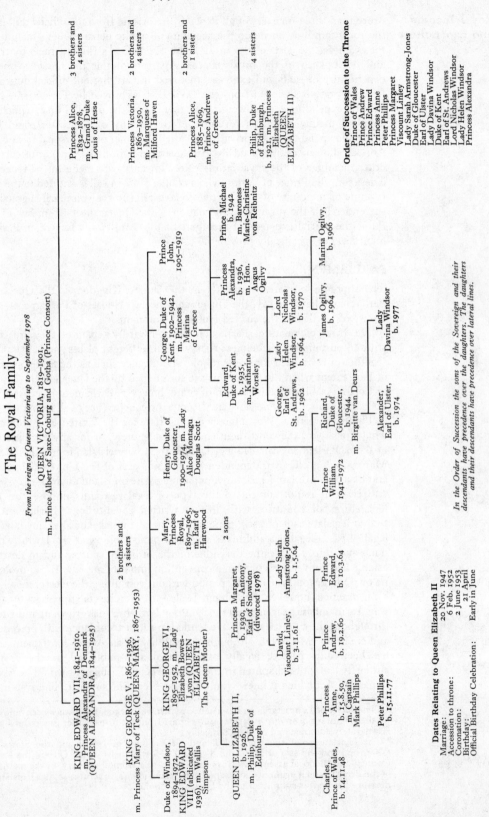

The Royal Family

From the reign of Queen Victoria up to September 1978

QUEEN VICTORIA, 1819–1901,
m. Prince Albert of Saxe-Coburg and Gotha (Prince Consort)

Order of Succession to the Throne

Prince of Wales
Prince Andrew
Prince Edward
Princess Anne
Peter Phillips
Princess Margaret
Viscount Linley
Lady Sarah Armstrong-Jones
Duke of Gloucester
Earl of Ulster
Lady Davina Windsor
Duke of Kent
Earl of St. Andrews
Lord Nicholas Windsor
Lady Helen Windsor
Princess Alexandra

In the Order of Succession the sons of the Sovereign and their descendants have precedence over the daughters. The daughters and their descendants have precedence over lateral lines.

Dates Relating to Queen Elizabeth II

Marriage:	20 Nov. 1947
Accession to throne:	6 Feb. 1952
Coronation:	2 June 1953
Birthday:	21 April
Official Birthday Celebration:	Early in June

party government in Britain ensures that Parliament legislates with its responsibility to the electorate in mind.

As a member of the European Community, the United Kingdom recognises various types of Community legislation, including regulations, which take direct effect in member countries, and directives, which are binding as to the result achieved upon each member State to which they are addressed, but allow the national authorities to choose the form and method of implementation. Britain has made arrangements for holding direct elections to the European Assembly in June 1979. A more detailed account of Britain's membership of the European Community is given in Chapter 3.

The Functions of Parliament

The main functions of Parliament are (1) to pass laws regulating the life of the community, (2) to scrutinise government policy and administration, particularly proposals for expenditure. In discharging these two functions Parliament helps to bring the relevant facts and issues before the electorate. By custom, Parliament is also consulted before the ratification of all important international treaties and agreements, the making of treaties being, in theory at least, a royal prerogative exercised on the advice of the Government and not subject to parliamentary approval.

The Meeting of Parliament

A Parliament (in the sense of a parliamentary period) has a maximum duration of five years, but may be, and nearly always is, dissolved, and a general election held, before the end of this term. The maximum life has been prolonged by legislation passed in the usual way in such rare circumstances as during the two world wars. Dissolution is ordered by the Queen on the advice of the Prime Minister, by means of a royal proclamation which, besides dissolving the existing Parliament, orders the issue of writs for an election, and announces the date on which the new Parliament is to meet (not less than 20 days after the dissolution). The proclamation is very soon followed by the issue of writs in each constituency to cause an election to be held on the day named.

The life of a Parliament is divided into sessions. Each usually lasts for one year—beginning and ending most often in October or November and interspersed with 'adjournments' at night, at weekends, at Christmas, Easter and the spring holiday and during a long summer recess starting late in July or early in August. The average number of 'sitting' days in a session is about 175 in the House of Commons and about 140 in the House of Lords. At the start of each session the Queen's speech in the House of Lords outlines to the members of both Houses the Government's broad policies and proposed legislative programme. Each session is terminated by prorogation, a prerogative act which appoints the day of meeting in a new session (on rare occasions Parliament has been dissolved without prorogation), and a short speech is made on behalf of the Queen summarising Parliament's work during the past session. Parliament then 'stands prorogued' until the new session opens. Whereas an adjournment does not affect uncompleted business, the effect of a prorogation is at once to terminate nearly all parliamentary business, so that all public Bills not completed in the session lapse, and must be reintroduced in the next unless they are to be abandoned.

The House of Lords

The House of Lords consists of the Lords Spiritual and the Lords Temporal. The Lords Spiritual are the Archbishops of Canterbury and York, the Bishops of London, Durham and Winchester, and 21 other bishops of the Church of England, according to their seniority as diocesan bishops. The Lords Temporal consist of (1) all hereditary peers and peeresses of England, Scotland,

Great Britain and the United Kingdom who have not disclaimed their peerages under the Peerage Act 1963, (2) all life peers and peeresses created by the Crown under the Life Peerages Act 1958, and (3) those Lords of Appeal in Ordinary who are appointed to assist the House in the performance of its judicial duties. Hereditary peerages carry with them a right to sit in the House of Lords (subject to certain statutory disqualifications), provided the holder is 21 years of age or over, but anyone succeeding to a peerage may, within 12 months of succession, disclaim that peerage for his or her lifetime. Disclaimants lose their right to sit in the House of Lords but they gain the right to vote at parliamentary elections and to offer themselves for election to the House of Commons. No hereditary peerage has been conferred since 1965.

Not all peers with a right to sit in the House of Lords attend the sittings of that House. Those who do not wish to attend may apply for leave of absence for the duration of a Parliament.

Peers who frequently attend the House of Lords (the average daily attendance is about 280) include elder statesmen and others who have spent their lives in public service. They receive no salary for their parliamentary work, but they are entitled to recover expenses incurred in attending the House (except for judicial sittings) and certain travelling expenses.

The House of Lords is presided over by the Lord Chancellor, who takes his place on the woolsack as *ex officio* Speaker of the House. In the absence of the Lord Chancellor his place may be taken by a deputy speaker appointed by the Crown or a deputy chairman appointed by the House or, if neither a deputy speaker nor a deputy chairman is present, by a speaker chosen by the Lords present. The first of the deputy speakers is the Lord Chairman of Committees, who is appointed each session and takes the chair in all committees, unless the House otherwise directs. The Lord Chairman and the Principal Deputy Chairman of Committees are salaried officers of the House. The permanent officers include the Clerk of the Parliaments, who is responsible for the records of proceedings including judgments and for the promulgation of Acts of Parliament; the other Clerks at the Table; the Gentleman Usher of the Black Rod, who is also Serjeant-at-Arms in attendance upon the Lord Chancellor; and the Yeoman Usher who is Deputy Serjeant-at-Arms.

The House of Commons

The House of Commons is a representative assembly elected by universal adult suffrage and consists of men and women from all sections of the community. There are 635 seats in the House of Commons (516 for England, 36 for Wales, 71 for Scotland, 12 for Northern Ireland[1]).

General elections are held after a Parliament has been dissolved and a new one summoned by the Sovereign. If a vacancy occurs in the House as a result of the death or resignation[2] of a member, or as a result of his elevation to the House of Lords, a by-election takes place. Members are paid an annual salary and an allowance for secretarial and research expenses. They also have a number of other allowances, including travel allowances, a supplement for London members and, for provincial members, subsistence allowances. The

---

[1] A Speaker's Conference recommended in February 1978 that Northern Ireland's representation should be increased to 17.
[2] If a member wishes to resign from the House, he may apply for what is technically an office of profit under the Crown (Bailiff of the Chiltern Hundreds or Steward of the Manor of Northstead) which automatically disqualifies him from membership of the House but to which, in fact, no remuneration attaches.

basic salary for members is £6,897 a year. Some members receive less than this, with a minimum of £6,554; a £312 a year increase permitted under the Government's pay policy for 1975–76 was not paid to members, or was reduced, if it would have carried their earnings from parliamentary and other sources over the £8,500 limit for pay rises. (For ministers' salaries, see p 38.)

The chief officer of the House of Commons is the Speaker, who is elected by the members to preside over the House. Other parliamentary officers of the House are the Chairman of Ways and Means, and two deputy chairmen who act as Deputy Speakers; these officers are elected by the House on the nomination of the Government and, like the Speaker, neither speak nor vote other than in their official capacity.

Permanent officers of the House (that is, those who are not members of Parliament) include the Clerk of the House of Commons, who conducts the business of the House in the official departments under his control and is the accounting officer for the House of Commons Estimates, and the Serjeant-at-Arms, who attends upon the Speaker, executes the orders of the House, is the official housekeeper of the Commons part of the building, and is responsible for its security.

Parliamentary Electoral System

For electoral purposes the United Kingdom is divided into constituencies, each of which returns one member to the House of Commons. To ensure equitable representation, four permanent Boundary Commissions (for England, Wales, Scotland and Northern Ireland) make periodic reviews of constituencies and recommend any redistribution of seats that may seem necessary in the light of population movements or for some other reason.

Election to the House of Commons is decided by secret ballot. British subjects (except Members of the House of Lords) and citizens of the Irish Republic resident in the United Kingdom are entitled to vote provided they are 18 years of age or over, are registered in the annual register of electors, and not subject to any legal incapacity to vote (that is, are not convicted offenders in penal institutions or persons found guilty of illegal election practices within the past five years). Service voters (that is, members of the armed forces, Crown servants and staff of the British Council employed overseas, together with their wives and husbands if accompanying them) may also be registered for an address in a constituency, if they normally reside there. Each elector may cast one vote at a polling station in person, but service voters, voters who are abroad on polling day because of the nature of their occupation (and their wives or husbands who accompany them) may vote by proxy. Absent voting facilities also exist for merchant seamen. Voters entitled to vote by post include those who have a service vote but happen to be in the United Kingdom at the time of an election, persons employed on polling day as constables or by the returning officer, candidates in another constituency and their wives and husbands, and electors who are blind or physically incapacitated.

Voting is not compulsory but, of about 40 million people entitled to vote in the most recent elections in February and October 1974, some 78·1 per cent and 72·8 per cent respectively cast their votes. The candidate who polls the most votes in any constituency is elected; an absolute majority (a greater number of votes than those cast for all other candidates combined) is not required.

Anyone, man or woman, who is entitled to vote and who has reached the age of 21 can stand for election. Undischarged bankrupts, clergymen of the Church of England, Church of Scotland, Church of Ireland and Roman

Catholic Church, peers, and certain people holding offices of profit under the Crown are, however, not eligible. The House of Commons Disqualification Act 1975 defines those who may not become a member of Parliament. They include holders of judicial office, civil servants and some local government officers, members of the regular armed forces, members of the police forces and members of public corporations and government commissions. A candidate usually belongs to one of the main national political parties, although smaller parties or groupings also nominate candidates, and individuals may be nominated without party support.

The maximum sum of money that a candidate may spend on his election campaign is £1,750, plus 1½ pence for each elector in a borough constituency or 2 pence for each elector in a county constituency. A candidate may send by post (free of postal charge) an election address to each elector in his constituency. All other expenses, apart from the candidate's personal expenses, must not exceed the statutory limit.

The Party System

The party system, existing in one form or another since the seventeenth century, is an essential element in the working of the constitution.

The present system is based upon the existence of organised political parties, each laying its own policies before the electorate. Whenever there is a general election or a by-election, the parties may put up candidates for election; any other citizen who wishes may also stand. The electorate then indicates, by its choice of candidate at the poll on election day, which of the opposing policies it would like to see put into effect. The percentages of votes cast for the main political parties in the October 1974 general election and the resulting distribution of seats in the House of Commons are given in Table 4.

TABLE 4: Percentages of Votes Cast, and Members Elected,[a] in the October 1974 General Election

Party	% of Votes Cast	Party	Members Elected
Labour	39·3	Labour	319
Conservative	35·8	Conservative	276
Liberal	18·3	Liberal	13
Others	6·6	Scottish National	11
		United Ulster Unionist	10
	100·0	Plaid Cymru (Welsh Nationalist)	3
		Social Democratic and Labour (Northern Ireland)	1
		Independent (Northern Ireland)	1
		The Speaker	1
			635

[a] In September 1978, the party strengths (excluding the Speaker and his three deputies) were as follows: Labour 306; Conservative 282; Liberal 13; Scottish Nationalist 11; Unionists (Northern Ireland) 10; Plaid Cymru 3; Scottish Labour 2; Social Democratic and Labour 1; Independent 1; Vacant 2.

The party which wins the majority of seats (although not necessarily the majority of votes) at a general election, or which is able to command a majority of supporters in the House of Commons, usually forms the Government. By tradition, the leader of the majority party is appointed as Prime Minister by the Sovereign; and about 100 of its members in the House of Commons and the House of Lords receive ministerial appointments on the advice of the Prime Minister. The largest minority party becomes the official Opposition with its own leader[1] and its own council of discussion or 'shadow Cabinet'; while the members of any other parties or any independents who have been elected may support or oppose the Government according to their party's or their own view of the policy being debated at any given time.

The effectiveness of the party system in Parliament largely rests on the relationship between the Government and the Opposition. Depending on the relative voting strengths of the parties in the House of Commons, the Opposition might seek to overthrow the Government by securing a sufficiently large adverse vote on a major policy issue. In general, however, its aims are to contribute to the formulation of policy and its expression in legislation by constructive criticism of the Government's approach; to oppose specific government proposals that it considers objectionable; to secure concessions on government Bills; and to increase support outside Parliament and enhance its chances of success in by-elections or at the next general election.

The detailed arrangements of government business are settled, under the direction of the Prime Minister and the Leaders of the two Houses by the Chief Government Whips, in consultation with the Chief Opposition Whips. The Chief Whips together constitute the 'usual channels' often referred to in the House of Commons when the question of the possibility of finding time for debating some particular issue is discussed. The direction of the business of the Houses is primarily the responsibility of the Leaders of the Houses and it is their duty to provide all reasonable facilities for the House to debate matters about which they are concerned.

Outside Parliament, party control is exercised by the national and local organisations. Inside Parliament, it is exercised by the Chief Whips and their assistants (chosen within the party) whose duties include keeping members informed of forthcoming parliamentary business, maintaining the voting strength of their parties by ensuring the attendance of members at important debates, and conveying upwards to the party leadership the opinions of their back-bench members. The Chief Government Whip in the House of Commons is Parliamentary Secretary to the Treasury; of the other Government Whips, three (one of whom is deputy Chief Whip) are officers of the Royal Household, five hold titular posts as Lords Commissioners of the Treasury and seven are paid Assistant Whips. Salaries are likewise paid to the Chief Opposition Whip and his counterpart in the House of Lords, and to two of the Assistant Whips for the Opposition in the House of Commons. The Government Whips in the House of Lords hold offices in the Royal Household and sometimes act as spokesmen for the Government in debates.

Annual financial assistance from public funds helps opposition parties in Parliament to carry out their business. It is limited to parties which had at least two members elected at the last general election or one member elected and a minimum of 150,000 votes cast. The formula is: £550 for every seat and £1.10 for every 200 votes, up to a maximum of £165,000. The Government is considering whether public funds should be made available to political parties for their work outside Parliament, and to candidates for election expenses.

---

[1] The Leader of the Opposition in the House of Commons receives an annual salary for that post, as well as a parliamentary salary; in the House of Lords the Leader of the Opposition receives an annual salary.

Parliamentary Procedure

Parliamentary procedure is based on custom and precedent, mainly formulated in standing orders governing details of practice in each House. The system of debate is much the same in the two Houses: for instance, every matter is determined upon questions put from the chair or woolsack and resolved in the affirmative or negative, as the case may be; and members speak from wherever they have been sitting and not from a rostrum. The main difference is that in the House of Lords the office of Speaker carries with it no authority to check or curtail debate, such matters being decided by the general sense of the House, whereas in the Commons the Speaker has full authority to give effect, promptly and decisively, to the rules and orders of the House. He must guard against abuse of procedure or any infringement of minority rights, and he has a discretion whether to allow or disallow any closure motion (that is, a motion to end discussion so that the matter may be put to the vote). He has certain powers to check irrelevance and repetition in debate, and to save the time of the House in various other respects. In case of grave disorder he can adjourn the House or suspend the sitting on his own initiative.

Voting in the House of Commons is carried out under the direction of the Speaker, and it is his duty to pronounce the final result. If an equal number of votes is cast for and against the motion under debate, the Speaker must give the casting vote, but he does so only in accordance with rules which preclude an expression of opinion on the merits of the question.

The procedure on voting in the House of Lords is similar to that in the House of Commons, except that the Speaker or chairman has an original, but no casting, vote—the House of Lords being generally governed by the principle that unless there is a majority in favour the question is decided in the negative. When the House is sitting judicially (see pp 84 and 95) the question is put in such a way that, if the votes are equal, there is no interference with the judgment under appeal.

The House of Commons has a public register of members' pecuniary interests. Members with a direct pecuniary interest in a matter before the House must abstain from voting in connection with it, though in order to operate as a disqualification the interest must be immediate and personal, and not merely of a general or remote character. In any proceedings of the House or in transactions with other members or with ministers or civil servants, members must disclose any relevant pecuniary interest or benefit.

All proceedings of either House are public, except on extremely rare occasions; the minutes (in the House of Commons called Votes and Proceedings and in the House of Lords, Minutes of Proceedings) and the speeches (The Official Report of Parliamentary Debates, *Hansard*) are published daily. The records of the Lords from 1497 and of the Commons from 1547, together with the parliamentary and political papers of certain past members of the Houses, are available to the public in the House of Lords Record Office. Radio broadcasting of the proceedings of both Houses of Parliament began in April 1978, but parliamentary proceedings are not transmitted on television. A Parliamentary Sound Archive has been established.

Legislative Proceedings

The law undergoes constant reform in the courts as established principles are interpreted, clarified or refashioned to meet new circumstances, but substantial changes are the responsibility of Parliament and the Government through the normal legislative process.

Draft legislation takes the form of a parliamentary Bill. Most Bills are public Bills involving measures relating to public policy, but there are also private Bills which deal solely with matters of individual, corporate or local interest.

Public Bills can be introduced either by a Government minister or by a 'private member' of either House of Parliament who does not hold office in the Government. Most public legislation is in practice drafted on behalf of ministers, and has the support of the Cabinet before being presented to Parliament by the appropriate minister.

In the modern legislative process, before a Government Bill is finally drafted, there is normally considerable consultation with, for instance, professional bodies, voluntary organisations and other agencies interested in the subject matter of the proposals, such as major interest groups and 'pressure' groups which aim to promote a specific cause. Proposals for legislative changes are sometimes set out by the Government in 'White Papers' which may be debated in Parliament before the introduction of a Bill. From time to time consultative documents, sometimes called 'Green Papers', are published setting out for public discussion major ministerial proposals which are still at the formative stage.

Public Bills can be introduced in either House. As a rule, however, Government Bills likely to raise political controversy go through the Commons before the Lords, while those of an intricate but uncontroversial nature often pass through the Lords first. A Bill with a mainly financial purpose must be introduced in the Commons, and a Bill involving taxation or the spending of public money must be based on resolutions agreed to by that House, often after debate, before it can be introduced. If the main object of a Bill is to create a public charge, it can only be introduced by a minister, which gives the Government considerable control over legislation.

At the beginning of each session private members of the Commons ballot for the chance to introduce a Bill during time specially allocated for private members' Bills; the first 20 are successful. A private member may also present a Bill after question time on notice given, or seek leave to introduce a Bill under the 'ten minute rule' which allows two speeches, one in favour of and one against the measure, after which the House decides whether to allow the Bill to be brought in. Private members' Bills do not often proceed very far, but a few become law. If one secures a second reading, the Government usually introduces any necessary money resolution. Private members' Bills may be introduced in the House of Lords at any time, without notice, but the time that can be given to them in the Commons is strictly limited.

The process of passing a public Bill is similar in both Houses of Parliament. The Bill receives a formal first reading on introduction, it is printed, and after a while (between one day and several weeks depending on the nature of the Bill) it is given a second reading after a debate on its general principles and merits. In the Commons a non-controversial Bill may be referred to a second reading committee to recommend whether it should be taken as read a second time. After a second reading in the Commons, a Bill is usually referred for detailed examination to a standing committee (see p 33). If the House so decides, the Bill may be referred to the whole House sitting in committee. The House may vote to limit the time devoted to examining a Bill by passing a timetable motion, commonly referred to as a 'guillotine'. In the Lords a Bill is considered by a committee of the whole House as a matter of course, unless the House decides to refer it to a Public Bill Committee. The committee stage is followed by the report stage, during which previous amendments may be altered and new amendments incorporated. At the third reading a Bill is reviewed in its final form. In the Commons this stage is taken without a debate unless there is a motion in the name of six members that the question 'be not put forthwith'—a procedure of which substantial use is made.

After the third reading a Commons Bill is sent to the Lords where it goes through broadly the same stages. Similarly a Bill which starts in the Lords and is passed by that House is then sent to the Commons for all the stages there. Amendments made by the second House generally must be agreed by the first, or a compromise reached, before a Bill can become law.

Most Government Bills introduced and passed in the Lords pass through the Commons without difficulty because of their non-controversial nature. However, should any non-governmental Lords Bill be unacceptable to the Commons it would not generally become law because no debating time would be allotted to it. The Lords, on the other hand, cannot in general prevent a Bill insisted upon by the Commons from finally becoming law. In the normal course of events they either accept a Commons Bill without changes, or they amend and return it for consideration by the Commons, who frequently agree to the amendments made. In practice, the Lords pass without amendment such financial Bills as the Finance Bill, which authorises taxation, or the Consolidated Fund or Appropriation Bill, which authorises national expenditure. A Bill that deals only with taxation or expenditure must become law within one month of being sent to the Lords, whether or not they have agreed to it, unless the Commons directs to the contrary. If no agreement is reached between the two houses on a non-financial Commons Bill (or an amendment to it) the Lords can in practice delay the Bill (with certain exceptions) for about 13 months. At the end of this time it becomes law in the form originally passed by the Commons. The limitations on the power of the Lords are based on the belief that the principal legislative function of the non-elected House nowadays is to act as a chamber of revision, complementing, not rivalling, the elected House.

When a Bill has passed through all its parliamentary stages, it is sent to the Queen for royal assent, after which it is part of the law of the land and known as an Act of Parliament. The royal assent has not been refused since 1707.

Private Bills, which can be promoted by people or organisations outside Parliament, go through substantially the same procedure as public Bills, but most of the work is done in committee, where proceedings follow a semi-judicial pattern: the promoter must prove the need for the powers or privileges he seeks, and objections on the part of the opposing interests are heard. Both parties may be legally represented.

Delegated
Legislation

The system of delegated legislation, which is used to relieve pressure on parliamentary time, empowers ministers and other authorities to regulate administrative details after a Bill has become an Act. In order to minimise the risk that powers thus conferred on the executive might supersede or weaken parliamentary government, they are normally delegated to the Queen in Council or to authorities directly responsible to Parliament, that is, to government ministers, government departments for which ministers are responsible, or to organisations whose regulations are subject to confirmation or approval by ministers who thereby become responsible to Parliament for them. Moreover, the Acts of Parliament by which particular powers are delegated normally provide for some measure of parliamentary control over legislation made in the exercise of these powers, for instance, by reserving to Parliament the right to affirm or annul the orders themselves. Certain Acts also require direct consultation with organisations which will be affected thereby before rules and orders (in the form of statutory instruments) are made.

A joint committee of both Houses reports on the technical propriety of statutory instruments. In the Commons, in order to save time, they are often referred to standing committees with any decisions reserved to the House.

Parliamentary Committees

Committees of the Whole House

Either House may resolve itself into a committee, known as a committee of the whole house, to consider Bills in detail, clause by clause, after their second reading. A committee of the whole house is presided over by the Chairman of Ways and Means (the Chairman of Committees in the House of Lords) or a deputy chairman.

Standing Committees

House of Commons standing committees include those which examine public Bills at the committee stage and, in certain cases, at the second reading and report stages; two Scottish standing committees; the Scottish Grand Committee; the Welsh Grand Committee; and the Northern Ireland standing committee. Ordinary standing committees have no distinctive names, being referred to simply as Standing Committee A, B, C, and so on. Each has between 16 and 50 members with the balance of the parties reflecting as far as possible that in the House as a whole. The Scottish Grand Committee, which comprises all 71 Scottish members and ten to 15 others, considers the principles of Scottish Bills referred to it at second reading stage, the Scottish estimates and other matters relating exclusively to Scotland. The Welsh Grand Committee, with all 36 Welsh members and up to five others, considers Bills referred to it at second reading stage, and matters relating exclusively to Wales. The Northern Ireland committee considers matters relating specifically to the province. A standing committee on regional affairs comprising the 516 members from English constituencies considers matters relating to the English regions. The Lords equivalent to a standing committee, a Public Bill Committee, is rarely used.

Select Committees

Select committees are generally set up, by either House, to help Parliament with the control of the executive by examining some aspect of administration and reporting to the House. They may be appointed as occasion demands, or for a session, or for the rest of the life of a Parliament. On rare occasions a parliamentary Bill is examined by a select committee (a procedure additional to the usual legislative process). Select committees are constituted on a party basis, in approximate proportion to party strength in the House.

Select committees in the Commons include committees on public accounts, expenditure, privileges, House of Commons' services, nationalised industries, the Parliamentary Commissioner for Administration, science and technology, race relations and immigration, overseas development, and European Community secondary legislation. The Committee of Selection and the Standing Orders Committee have duties relating to private Bills, and the Committee of Selection also chooses members to serve on standing committees.

In their scrutiny of administrative activity and government policies, the committees question ministers, senior civil servants and interested bodies and individuals. They bring before Parliament and the public generally, through their hearings and published reports, a body of fact and informed opinion on many important issues and they build up considerable expertise in their subjects of inquiry.

In the House of Lords there are sessional committees on the European Community, standing orders (Private Bills), personal Bills, procedure, offices, privileges, leave of absence, Lords' expenses and selection, and the Appeal and Appellate Committees.

Joint Committees

The two Houses may agree to set up joint select committees, and joint committees are also appointed in each session to deal with Consolidation Bills and delegated legislation.

Party Committees

In addition to the official committees of the two Houses there are several important party organisations or committees. The Conservative and Unionist Members Committee, popularly known as the 1922 Committee, consists of the back-bench membership of the party. The Parliamentary Labour Party is a corporate body comprising all members of the party in both Houses; when the Labour Party is in office a liaison committee acts as a channel of communication between the Government and its back-benchers in both Houses; when the party is in opposition the Parliamentary Labour Party is organised under the direction of a Parliamentary Committee.

Parliamentary Control

Control of the Government in power is exercised in the final analysis by the ability of the House of Commons to force the Government to resign either by passing a resolution of 'no confidence' or by rejecting a proposal which the Government considers so vital to its policy that it has made it a 'matter of confidence' or, ultimately, by refusing to vote the money required for the public service. A number of opportunities for a searching examination of government policy by both the Opposition and the Government's own back-benchers are provided in parliamentary procedure. These include:

1. Question time, which is an hour of parliamentary time on Monday, Tuesday, Wednesday and Thursday during which ministers, in rotation, answer questions put to them on matters for which they are responsible. Parliamentary questions are one means of eliciting information about the Government's intentions, as well as a way of airing, and possibly securing redress of, grievances brought to members' notice by constituents.
2. The right of members to use motions for the adjournment of the House to initiate discussions on constituency cases or matters of public concern. There is a half-hour adjournment period at the end of public business; and immediately before the adjournment for each recess (Christmas, Easter, spring and the summer) a day is spent discussing matters raised by private members. Moreover, if a member wishes to discuss a 'specific and important matter that should have urgent consideration' he may, at the end of question time, ask leave to move the adjournment of the House. If the Speaker accepts the terms of the motion, he asks the House for leave for it to be put forward. Leave can be given unanimously, or if 40 or more members support the motion, or if fewer than 40 but more than ten support it and the House (on a vote) is in favour. Once leave has been given, the matter is debated for three hours, usually on the following day.
3. The 29 'supply' days each session, which were formerly used to discuss details of proposed government expenditure, and which are nowadays time for the Opposition to choose subjects for debate. (Scrutiny by small committees has been found more apt for detailed expenditure proposals.)

Procedural opportunities for criticism of the Government also arise during the debate on the address in reply to the Queen's speech at the beginning of a session, during debates or motions of censure for which the Government gives up part of its own time, and during debates on the Government's legislative proposals.

Opportunities for criticism of the Government are also provided in the House of Lords at question time and during debates on specific motions.

The involvement of Parliament, and more particularly the House of Commons, in the management of the revenues of the State and payments for the public service is described in Chapter 17, Finance.

Arrangements have been made in Parliament to keep members informed about European Community developments, and to enable them to scrutinise and debate matters which are to be decided in Community institutions.

Parliamentary Commissioner for Administration

The Parliamentary Commissioner for Administration is an independent statutory officer whose function is to investigate complaints of maladministration when so requested by members of the House of Commons on behalf of members of the public. His powers of investigation extend to actions taken by central government departments in the exercise of their administrative functions, but not to policy decisions (which are the concern of the Government and can be questioned in Parliament). Certain administrative actions also outside his jurisdiction include matters affecting relations with other countries and the activities of British officials outside the United Kingdom.

In the performance of his duties, the Parliamentary Commissioner has access to all departmental papers, and reports his findings to the member of Parliament who presented the case. The Parliamentary Commissioner reports annually to Parliament and may submit such other reports as he thinks fit.

Parliamentary Privilege

Each House of Parliament enjoys certain rights and immunities designed to protect it from unnecessary obstruction in carrying out its duties. These rights apply collectively to each House and individually to each member.

For the Commons the Speaker formally claims from the Crown 'their ancient and undoubted rights and privileges' at the beginning of each Parliament. These include freedom of speech in debate; freedom from arrest in civil process; and the right of access to the Crown, which is a collective privilege of the House. Further privileges include the right of the House to control its own proceedings (so that it is able, for instance, to exclude strangers if it so wishes); the right to pronounce upon legal disqualifications for membership and to declare a seat vacant on such grounds; and the right to penalise those who commit a breach of its privileges.

The privileges of the House of Lords include: freedom of speech in debate; freedom of access to the Sovereign for each peer individually; and the right to commit for contempt. These privileges are not formally claimed by the Speaker as in the House of Commons; they exist independently.

THE PRIVY COUNCIL

Until the eighteenth century, the Sovereign in Council, or Privy Council, was the chief source of executive power in the State. As the system of Cabinet government developed, however, the Privy Council became less prominent. Many of its powers were transferred to the Cabinet as an inner Committee of the Privy Council, and much of its work was handed over to newly created government departments, some of which were originally committees of the Privy Council. Nowadays the Privy Council is responsible for advising the Sovereign to approve Orders in Council, of which there are two kinds, differing fundamentally in constitutional principle: those made by virtue of the royal prerogative, such as Orders approving the grant of royal charters of incorporation; and those made under statutory powers, which are the highest form of delegated legislation. It is an accepted principle that members of the Privy Council attending meetings at which Orders in Council are made do not thereby become personally responsible for the policy upon which the orders are based; this rests with the minister responsible for the subject matter of the order in question, whether or not he was present at the meeting.

The Privy Council also advises the Crown on the issue of royal proclamations, some of the most important of which relate to prerogative acts (such as summoning or dissolving Parliament) of the same validity as Acts of Parliament. The Privy Council's own statutory responsibilities, which are independent of the powers of the Sovereign in Council, include powers of supervision over the registering bodies for the medical and allied professions.

Apart from Cabinet Ministers, who must be Privy Counsellors and are sworn of the Council on first assuming office, membership of the Privy Council (which is retained for life) is accorded by the Sovereign on the recommendation of the Prime Minister to certain eminent persons in independent monarchical countries of the Commonwealth. There are usually about 340 Privy Counsellors. The whole Privy Council is called together only on the death of the Sovereign or when the Sovereign announces his or her intention to marry.

Committees of the Privy Council

There are a number of Privy Council committees whose meetings differ from those of the Privy Council itself in that the Sovereign cannot constitutionally be present. These advisory committees may be prerogative committees, such as those which deal with legislative matters submitted by the legislatures of the Channel Islands and Isle of Man and with applications for charters of incorporation; or they may be provided for by statute as are those for the universities of Oxford and Cambridge and the Scottish universities.

The Judicial Committee of the Privy Council is the final court of appeal from the courts of the United Kingdom dependencies, courts of independent members of the Commonwealth which have not elected to discontinue the appeal, courts of the Channel Islands and the Isle of Man, and certain other courts, some professional and disciplinary committees and church sources.

The administrative work of the Privy Council committees is carried out in the Privy Council Office under the Lord President of the Council, a senior Cabinet minister. He is assisted by a Minister of State and a Parliamentary Secretary, and has special responsibility for devolution policy (see p 19) and other work relating to the development of political institutions.

HER MAJESTY'S GOVERNMENT

Her Majesty's Government is the body of ministers responsible for the administration of national affairs.

The Prime Minister is appointed by the Crown, and all other ministers are appointed by the Crown on the recommendation of the Prime Minister.

The majority of ministers are members of the House of Commons. However, the Government must be fully represented by ministers in the House of Lords as it requires spokesmen of standing to expound its policy and justify its actions to that House. The Lord Chancellor is always a member of the House of Lords.

Composition

The composition of the Government is subject to variation from time to time, both in the number of ministers and in the titles of some offices. The creation of a paid ministerial office with entirely new functions requires legislation, but the abolition of an office, the transfer of functions from one minister to another, or a change in the designation of a minister may be effected by Order in Council. Ministers may be classified as follows:

Prime Minister

The Prime Minister is also First Lord of the Treasury and Minister for the Civil Service. The head of the Government became known as the Prime Minister during the eighteenth century. The unique position of authority enjoyed by the holder of this office derives from his ability to command a majority in Parliament and from his power to submit his own choice of ministers to the Queen and to obtain their resignation or dismissal individually. By convention, the Prime Minister always sits in the House of Commons.

It is the duty of the Prime Minister to inform the Sovereign of the general business of the Government; to preside over the Cabinet; and to exercise a general supervision over departments, settling departmental differences and approving important departmental decisions where reference to the Cabinet is not required.

The Prime Minister's other responsibilities include making recommendations to the Sovereign for the appointment of Church of England archbishops, bishops and deans and the incumbents of some 200 Crown livings, as well as for appointments to high judicial offices, such as the Lord Chief Justice, Lords of Appeal in Ordinary, and Lord Justices of Appeal. He also advises the Crown on appointments of Privy Counsellors, Lord-Lieutenants and certain civil appointments, such as Lord High Commissioner of the General Assembly of the Church of Scotland, Poet Laureate, Constable of the Tower, and some university appointments which are in the gift of the Crown. The Prime Minister makes similar recommendations for appointments to various public boards and institutions, such as the British Broadcasting Corporation, as well as to various royal and statutory commissions. He likewise makes recommendations to the Sovereign for the award of many civil honours and distinctions and of Civil List pensions (awarded to people who have achieved eminence in science and the arts and who are in some financial need) and selects the trustees of certain national museums and institutions.

Departmental
Ministers

Departmental ministers are in charge of government departments. The holders of these offices, who are usually in the Cabinet, are known as 'Secretary of State' or 'Minister', or they may have a special title, as in the case of the Chancellor of the Exchequer (who is responsible for the Treasury and a number of sub-departments).

Non-Departmental
Ministers

Non-departmental ministers include the holders of various traditional offices—the Lord President of the Council, the Chancellor of the Duchy of Lancaster, the Lord Privy Seal, the Paymaster General—and from time to time Ministers without Portfolio. Usually these ministers have few or no departmental duties and are thus available to perform any special duties which the Prime Minister may wish to entrust to them.

Lord Chancellor
and Law Officers

The Lord Chancellor holds a special position, being a Minister of the Crown with departmental functions and also head of the judiciary in England and Wales. The four Law Officers of the Crown are: for England and Wales, the Attorney General and the Solicitor General; for Scotland, the Lord Advocate and the Solicitor General for Scotland.

Ministers of State

Ministers of State are usually appointed to assist ministers in charge of government departments in which the work is particularly heavy or complex or where it involves frequent travelling abroad. It is possible for a Minister of State to be given a place in the Cabinet and to be paid accordingly.

Junior Ministers

Junior ministers generally have the title of Parliamentary Secretary or, where the senior minister is a Secretary of State, Parliamentary Under Secretary of

State. They share in parliamentary debates, answering parliamentary questions, and assisting in departmental duties. In certain cases, however, they may be given responsibility, directly under the departmental minister, for specific aspects of the department's work. The Parliamentary Secretary to the Treasury and the other Lords Commissioners of the Treasury are in a different category as Government Whips (see p 29).

Ministerial Salaries

The salaries of ministers in the House of Commons range from £6,050 a year for junior ministers and £8,250 to £10,450 for more senior ministers to £14,300 for Cabinet ministers. The Prime Minister receives £22,000 a year. Ministers in the House of Lords receive an additional sum of £520 a year if junior and £208 a year if senior. The Lord Chancellor receives £22,228 a year, including £2,500 for his speakership of the House of Lords.

Ministers in the House of Commons, including the Prime Minister, also have parliamentary salaries of £3,529 (£4,299 for non-Cabinet ministers) and are entitled to claim the allowances paid to all members of the House.

The Cabinet

The Cabinet is composed of about 20 ministers personally selected by the Prime Minister and may include the holders of departmental and non-departmental offices. Its origins can be traced back to the informal conferences that the Sovereign held with his leading ministers, independently of the Privy Council, during the seventeenth century. After the Sovereign's withdrawal from an active role in politics in the eighteenth century, and the development of organised political parties stimulated by successive extensions of the franchise from 1832 onwards, the Cabinet assumed its modern form.

The functions of the Cabinet are: the final determination of the policy to be submitted to Parliament; the supreme control of the national executive in accordance with the policy agreed by Parliament; and the continuous co-ordination and delimitation of the authority of government departments. The exercise of these functions is vitally affected by the fact that the Cabinet is a group of party representatives, depending for its existence upon the support of a majority in the House of Commons.

Cabinet Meetings

The Cabinet meets in private and its proceedings are strictly confidential. Its members are bound by their oath as Privy Counsellors not to disclose information about its proceedings. The Official Secrets Acts forbid the publication of Cabinet as well as of other State papers (although after they have been in existence for 30 years they may be made available for inspection in the Public Record Office) and a resigning minister wishing to make a statement involving disclosure of Cabinet discussions should first obtain the permission of the Sovereign through the Prime Minister.

In normal times the Cabinet meets for a few hours once or twice a week during parliamentary sittings, and rather less frequently when Parliament is not sitting. Additional meetings may be called by the Prime Minister at any time if a matter urgently requiring discussion should arise. To keep the amount of work coming before the Cabinet within manageable limits, a great deal of the work of the Cabinet is carried on through the committee system, which involves the reference of any issue either to a standing Cabinet committee or to an *ad hoc* committee composed of the ministers primarily concerned. The committee then considers the matter in detail and either disposes of it or reports upon it to the Cabinet with recommendations for action. Ministers not in the Cabinet may attend its meetings for discussion of matters affecting their departments; they may also be members of Cabinet committees.

Modern Transport

Britain's advanced passenger train has a unique suspension system and is capable of speeds up to 250 kph (155 mph).

'Super 4', the world's largest hovercraft, has a capacity for carrying 416 passengers and 60 vehicles at a speed in excess of 65 knots.

The Countryside

Nant Mills Waterfalls, Gwynedd, North Wales.

Right: John o' Groats, Scotland, the north-east point of mainland Britain and (*far right*) Land's End, England, the south-west point.

Tollymore Forest
Park, County Down,
Northern Ireland.

Flowers

Above: Gentian (*Gentiana*). There are numerous species of Gentian with several of them found only in Scotland.

Above right: Bee Orchid (*Ophrys apifera*). A native perennial of field edges, pastures and grassy slopes on calcareous ground.

Wood Anemone (*Anemone nemorosa*). Common in woods throughout Britain.

Cowslip (*Primula veris*). Found in meadows in England and Wales.

Far right: Primrose (*Primula vulgaris*). Grows in woods, hedgerows and grassy places.

The Secretary of the Cabinet and senior officials of the Cabinet Office attend meetings of the Cabinet and its committees as appropriate.

Ministerial Responsibility

The term 'ministerial responsibility' refers both to the collective responsibility which ministers share for government policy and actions and to ministers' individual responsibility to Parliament for their departments' work.

The doctrine of collective responsibility, which was fully accepted by the middle of the nineteenth century, means that the Cabinet is bound to offer unanimous advice to the Sovereign, even when its members do not hold identical views on a given subject. Consequently it means that the policy of departmental ministers must be consistent with the policy of the Government as a whole. In principle, once the Government's policy on a particular matter has been decided, each minister is expected to support it, unless he chooses to resign, as he is free to do if he cannot agree with his colleagues on a matter of general policy or on a single major issue. On rare occasions, ministers have been allowed free votes in the House of Commons on government policies involving important issues of principle. In the exceptional circumstances preceding the referendum in June 1975 on British membership of the European Community, ministers were free to campaign in the country against the Government's recommendation. This freedom did not, however, extend to parliamentary proceedings and Government business.

The individual responsibility of a minister for the work of his department means that, as political head of that department, he is answerable for all its acts and omissions and must bear the consequences of any defect of administration, any injustice to an individual or any aspect of policy which may be criticised in Parliament, whether he is personally responsible or not. Since the majority of ministers are members of the House of Commons, they are available to answer questions and to defend themselves against criticism in person. Departmental ministers who are in the House of Lords must be represented in the Commons by someone qualified to speak on their behalf, usually a Minister of State or a Parliamentary Secretary.

Departmental ministers normally decide all matters within their responsibility, although on important political matters they will usually wish to consult their colleagues collectively, through the Cabinet or a Cabinet committee. Any decision by a departmental minister binds the Government as a whole.

The responsibility of ministers for their departments is an effective way of bringing government under public control, for the knowledge that any departmental action may be reported to and examined in Parliament discourages the taking of arbitrary and ill-considered decisions.

On assuming office ministers must resign directorships in private and public companies. In all other respects they must order their affairs in such a way that there is no conflict between their public duties and their private interests.

GOVERNMENT DEPARTMENTS

Government departments are the main instruments for giving effect to government policy when Parliament has passed the necessary legislation. They may, and frequently do, work with and through local authorities, statutory boards, and government-sponsored organisations operating under various degrees of government control.

A few departments have existed for over 200 years. Many more have come into existence during the past half-century to match the widening scope of government activity. The election of a party of a different political complexion does not necessarily affect the number or general functions of government departments, although a radical change in policy may be accompanied by some organisational change.

The work of some departments (for instance, the Ministry of Defence) covers the United Kingdom as a whole. Other departments (for example, the Department of Employment) cover England, Wales, and Scotland, but not Northern Ireland. Others, such as the Department of Education and Science and the Department of the Environment, are mainly concerned with affairs in England. There are separate departments for Scotland, Northern Ireland and Wales.

A department is usually headed by a minister. Certain departments in which questions of policy do not normally arise are headed by a permanent official, and a minister with other duties is responsible for them to Parliament. For instance, the minister in charge of the Civil Service Department is responsible for the Central Office of Information, Her Majesty's Stationery Office, and the Department of the Government Actuary; and Treasury ministers are responsible for the Board of Customs and Excise, the Inland Revenue, the Department for National Savings and a number of small departments including the Treasury Solicitor's Department, the Royal Mint, and the National Debt Office. Generally, departments receive their funds directly out of money provided by Parliament and are staffed by the Civil Service.

Internal Organisation

Departments differ in size and in the volume, type and complexity of their work. Since each department makes its own arrangements for discharging its duties, there are variations in internal organisation. Most departments, however, have certain features in common: for instance, the minister of a major department is likely to have at the head of his officials a permanent secretary, sometimes assisted by one or more second permanent secretaries, and also one or more deputy secretaries, and a varying number of under secretaries and assistant secretaries. Usually major departments also have a principal finance officer and a principal personnel and organisation officer. Many departments also have their own legal advisers or solicitors, economists and statisticians and their own information divisions. The Government Statistical Service, which includes the Central Statistical Office (CSO), the Business Statistics Office (BSO), the Office of Population Censuses and Surveys and the statistics divisions of the major departments, provides a service of statistical information and advice. Each department compiles statistics relating to its own policy area and publishes them, usually through its own publications. Information about individual industries is published by the BSO in *Business Monitors*.

Some departments maintain a regional organisation, and some that have direct contact with the public throughout the country also have local offices.

Advisory Bodies

Many government departments are assisted by advisory councils or committees (several hundred in all) which undertake research and collect information, mainly to enable ministers to ascertain informed opinion before coming to a decision involving a legislative or executive act. In some cases there is a statutory obligation on a minister to consult a standing committee, but usually advisory bodies are appointed at the discretion of the minister concerned because he feels the need for their advice.

The membership of the advisory councils and committees varies according to the nature of the work involved, and may include civil servants and representatives of varying interests and professions—for instance, industrialists, trade unionists, university and industrial scientists, educationists, lawyers and local government councillors and officers.

In addition to these standing advisory bodies, there are *ad hoc* committees which the Government frequently sets up to examine and make recommendations on specific matters. For certain important inquiries Royal Commissions, whose members are selected on the grounds of their wide experience and diverse knowledge, may be appointed (by royal warrant). Royal Commissions examine written and oral evidence from government departments and interested organisations and individuals, and on this evidence submit recommendations. The Government may accept the recommendations in whole or in part, or it may decide to take no further action or to delay action. Inquiries may also be undertaken by departmental committees, appointed by the head of the appropriate department.

Distribution of Functions

The following pages provide an outline of the principal functions of the main government departments. They are arranged in alphabetical order, except for the Cabinet Office, the Civil Service Department, and the Treasury (which, in view of their central positions, are placed first) and the Scottish and Northern Ireland departments (which are grouped at the end of the section). Further information on the work of departments is given in later chapters under the relevant subject headings.

The Cabinet Office

The Cabinet Office, headed by the Secretary of the Cabinet, under the direction of the Prime Minister, comprises the Cabinet Secretariat, the Central Policy Review Staff, the Central Statistical Office and the Historical Section.

The Cabinet Secretariat serves ministers collectively in the conduct of Cabinet business. It operates as an instrument in the co-ordination of policy at the highest level. Functions of the office include circulating the memoranda and other documents required for Cabinet or Cabinet committee business, preparing agenda for meetings of the Cabinet and its committees, recording their discussions and circulating the minutes, keeping in touch with the progress of action on decisions, and safeguarding the security of documents.

The Central Policy Review Staff advises ministers collectively on major issues of policy.

The Central Statistical Office is concerned with the preparation and interpretation of the statistics necessary to support economic and social policies and management. It is directly responsible for the central economic aggregates such as the national accounts, balance of payments, financial statistics and measures of output; it co-ordinates the statistical work of other departments and agencies; and it prepares a number of statistical publications.

The Historical Section of the Cabinet Office is in the process of completing the official histories of the second world war, and is responsible for the preparation of official histories of certain peacetime events.

The Civil Service Department

The Civil Service Department is under the control of the Prime Minister as Minister for the Civil Service. Responsibility for day-to-day work is delegated to a senior minister. The Department's Permanent Secretary is also the official head of the Home Civil Service.

The Department is responsible for personnel management in the Civil Service, which includes policy and central arrangements for recruitment, training (including the Civil Service College), promotion, general career management, catering, welfare and retirement. It is also responsible for expenditure on civil service manpower for pay, pensions, and conditions of service in the Civil Service, and for the co-ordination of pay and pension policies in the public sector as a whole. Further responsibilities include advising on the development and application of new systems and techniques in management and administration; the provision of central management services covering subjects and techniques such as organisation and methods, operational research and management accounting; and central planning, procurement and co-ordination of data processing in government.

The Civil Service Commission

The Civil Service Commission, which is responsible for the recruitment of all permanent civil servants, forms part of the Civil Service Department. In matters concerned with recruitment policy, the commissioners are responsible to ministers in the normal way, but in the selection of individuals for appointment, they act under Order in Council and are completely independent of ministers.

Parliamentary Counsel Office

The Office of the Parliamentary Counsel is responsible for the drafting of all Government Bills, except Bills or provisions of Bills extending exclusively to Scotland, which are handled by the Lord Advocate's Department. The Office drafts all financial and other parliamentary motions and amendments moved by the Government during the passage of Bills; advises departments on questions of parliamentary procedure; and attends sittings (and committees) of both Houses as required. In addition the Parliamentary Counsel draft subordinate legislation when specially instructed, and advise the Government on legal, parliamentary and constitutional questions falling within their special experience.

The Treasury

Nominally the heads of the Treasury are the Lords Commissioners: the First Lord of the Treasury (always the Prime Minister), the Chancellor of the Exchequer and five junior Lords. In practice, the Lords Commissioners never meet as a board and their responsibilities are carried by the Chancellor of the Exchequer assisted by the Chief Secretary to the Treasury, the Financial Secretary and a Minister of State. The Parliamentary Secretary to the Treasury is the Chief Government Whip in the House of Commons.

The Treasury is the government department primarily responsible for the development of Britain's overall economic strategy. Its Public Services Sector is responsible for controlling aggregate public expenditure and for most of the individual public expenditure programmes; the Domestic Economy Sector is concerned with fiscal, monetary and counter-inflation policies, and with the Treasury's contribution to industrial policies, including control of public expenditure on industry and agriculture; the Overseas Finance Sector is responsible for balance of payments policies, the management of Britain's foreign currency reserves, international monetary questions, financial relations with other countries and the aid programme; and the Chief Economic Adviser's Sector is responsible for the preparation of short-term and medium-term economic forecasts and for specialist advice on broad economic policies.

The Ministry of Agriculture, Fisheries and Food

The Ministry of Agriculture, Fisheries and Food is responsible for administering government policy for the agriculture, horticulture and fishing industries in England, and for matters relating to the food and drink industries in Britain generally. Directed by the Minister of Agriculture, Fisheries and Food (who is assisted by a Minister of State and a Parliamentary Secretary) its functions include the administration, in co-operation with the Intervention

Board for Agricultural Produce, of agricultural support, and in particular the Common Agricultural Policy of the European Community. The Ministry also administers schemes such as those designed for the control and eradication of animal and plant diseases and for the improvement and drainage of agricultural land; and it exercises responsibilities relating to applied research and development. In addition it is concerned with the safety and quality of food including standards of composition, labelling and advertising, food additives and contaminants; and it has certain responsibilities for ensuring public health standards in the production and handling of basic foods in cargoes, stores and slaughterhouses. Where appropriate these measures and those of the Community are being harmonised.

The Ministry's responsibilities extend to Scotland and Wales regarding the operational control of certain diseases of animals. It also acts on behalf of the Secretary of State for Wales in certain matters relating to, for instance, fisheries and the provision of agricultural advice.

The Ministry maintains relations with other Commonwealth and foreign countries and participates in certain of the activities of a number of international organisations concerned with agriculture, fisheries and food, and trade in food products, such as the Food and Agriculture Organisation of the United Nations, and the Organisation for Economic Co-operation and Development and the General Agreement on Tariffs and Trade.

The Intervention Board for Agricultural Produce

An executive department subject to the direction and control of ministers responsible for agriculture, the Intervention Board for Agricultural Produce is responsible for the implementation in the United Kingdom of the market support arrangements and certain other aspects of the European Community's Common Agricultural Policy provided for under the guarantee section of the European Agricultural Guidance and Guarantee Fund. In consultation with the Ministry of Overseas Development, the Board is responsible for sending cereals to developing countries under the Food Aid Convention 1971, and for administering occasional Community donations of other commodities to developing countries and areas of national disasters.

The Board of Customs and Excise

The primary work of the Board of Customs and Excise is to collect and administer the customs and excise duties, including value added tax, imposed from time to time in the annual Finance Acts or by other legislation, and to advise the Chancellor of the Exchequer on any matters connected with them. The Board is also responsible for preventing and detecting evasion of the revenue laws.

The Board undertakes, for other departments, a wide range of non-revenue agency work, for instance, the enforcement of prohibitions and restrictions on the import and export of certain classes of goods, exchange currency control, and the compilation of United Kingdom overseas trade statistics from customs import and export documents. Parliamentary responsibility for the Board's work is exercised by Treasury ministers.

The Ministry of Defence

The Ministry of Defence is the government department responsible for defence policy and for the control and administration of the three armed services—Navy, Army and Air Force (including the procurement of defence equipment). The Secretary of State for Defence is in charge of the department, assisted by a Minister of State. Three Parliamentary Under Secretaries of State are severally responsible for each of the three armed services.

The Department of Education and Science

The Department of Education and Science is responsible for the general promotion of education in England; for the Government's relations with universities in Great Britain; and for fostering the progress of civil science both in Britain and internationally. The Department also has responsibilities relating to the library service, support for the British Library and the administration of the Victoria and Albert and Science Museums in London.

The Secretary of State for Education and Science is assisted by a Minister of State and a Parliamentary Under Secretary of State. A second Minister of State in the department is responsible for the arts, and deals with policy on the promotion of the arts and on libraries and museums.

Among the matters relating to the development of school and post-school education for which the Department has responsibility are the broad allocation of resources for education, the capital programmes for the building of new schools and other institutions, the supply, training and superannuation of teachers, and the basic standards of education. The Department works in co-operation with local education authorities whose duty it is to provide and run the schools and colleges in their areas. Its relations with the universities are conducted through the University Grants Committee. Activities concerning civil science are discharged through five research councils: the Medical Research Council, the Agricultural Research Council, the Natural Environment Research Council, the Social Science Research Council and the Science Research Council. On questions of scientific policy an advisory board for the research councils advises the Secretary of State.

The Department of Employment

The Department of Employment has overall responsibility for manpower policies in Britain, either directly or through statutory agencies, and for the formulation of labour legislation. It is also responsible for monitoring labour market trends, including pay, and for producing statistics on them and on retail prices (from which the rate of inflation is calculated). The Department is responsible for the payment of unemployment benefit through its local offices; for the issue of work permits to workers from overseas; and for the Race Relations Employment Advisory Service.

The Secretary of State for Employment is assisted by a Minister of State and two Parliamentary Under Secretaries of State.

The Department of Energy

The Department of Energy is concerned with the development of government policies for the supply and use of all forms of energy. It discharges functions connected with the nationalised coal and gas industries in Great Britain and the electricity industry in England and Wales; is responsible for the United Kingdom Atomic Energy Authority; and is the sponsoring department for the nuclear power and oil industries including the British National Oil Corporation. It is also responsible for the policy for the development of offshore oil and gas resources in the British sector of the continental shelf; and it sponsors, through the Offshore Supplies Office in Glasgow, the suppliers of equipment to the offshore operators. The Department also represents Britain in international discussions on energy policy, including relations and co-operation with oil-producing countries. It is the co-ordinating and sponsoring body for energy conservation policy, in addition to implementing measures not falling directly to any other department. The Department also encourages the development of new sources of energy, being assisted by the Energy Technology Support Unit at Harwell, Oxfordshire. The Secretary of State for Energy is supported by a Minister of State, who is especially concerned with the development of North Sea oil and gas resources, and by two Parliamentary Under Secretaries of State.

The Department of the Environment

The Department of the Environment, under a Secretary of State, is responsible in England for a wide range of functions relating to the physical environment in which people live and work.

The Secretary of State is concerned primarily with the strategic issues of policy and priorities, including public expenditure, which determine the operations of the department as a whole. He is also responsible for urban affairs and inner city renewal; new towns; local government; and regional affairs. He is assisted by a Minister for Housing Construction, who is responsible for the finance and policy of the housing programme; the construction industries; and planning, development control and land. A Minister of State has special responsibilities for sport and recreation; the control of pollution; water and sewerage; minerals; countryside affairs; and the Property Services Agency (which provides nearly all government common services relating to land, property, buildings and furnishings). There are four Parliamentary Under Secretaries of State.

The Department is also concerned with the conservation of historic towns and buildings and ancient monuments, and research into planning matters, building and construction, environmental pollution and resources.

Export Credits Guarantee Department

The Export Credits Guarantee Department, which is a separate government department within the responsibility of the Secretary of State for Trade, offers two main facilities to British exporters; insurance against the risk of not being paid for goods and services; and access to special fixed interest rates for export finance. The Department also provides support for 'buyer credits' (loans made direct to overseas buyers for capital goods contracts enabling the supplier to be paid on cash terms); insurance against the political risks of new overseas investment for up to 15 years; partial protection for large capital goods contracts against an unexpectedly high rise in costs; and support for the issue of performance bonds.

The Foreign and Commonwealth Office

The Foreign and Commonwealth Office provides, mainly through diplomatic missions, the means of communication between the British Government and other governments and international governmental organisations for the discussion and negotiation of all matters, including economic issues, falling within the field of international relations. In particular the Department is responsible for alerting the British Government to the implications of developments overseas; for protecting British interests overseas, including commercial interests; for protecting British citizens abroad; and for explaining British policies to, and wherever possible cultivating friendly relations with, governments and peoples overseas. The Department is also responsible for the discharge of British responsibilities in the associated States (mainly for defence and external affairs) and dependent territories. In the dependent territories, each of which has its own internal administration, the British Government is finally responsible for good government and for the relations between these territories and other countries.

The Secretary of State for Foreign and Commonwealth Affairs is assisted by three Ministers of State and two Parliamentary Under Secretaries of State.

The Department of Health and Social Security

The Department of Health and Social Security is responsible in England for the administration of the National Health Service; the social services provided by local authorities for the elderly and handicapped, socially deprived families, and children in care; and for certain aspects of public health, including hygiene. Throughout Great Britain it is responsible for the collection of social security contributions and the payment of benefits. The Department is concerned in making reciprocal health and social security arrangements with other countries and in the administration of European Community social security regulations for immigrant workers. It also represents the United Kingdom in the World Health Organisation.

Through its Supplementary Benefits Commission the Department is responsible for determining awards of non-contributory benefits and Family Income Supplement, for reception centres, and for assessing the means of people applying for legal aid. The Department also has responsibilities in connection with pensions and welfare services (including in some cases the provision of medical and surgical treatment) for war pensioners in the United Kingdom, the Channel Islands and the Isle of Man, and, through its various agencies, for United Kingdom war pensioners living in other countries.

The Department is headed by the Secretary of State for Social Services who is assisted by a Minister for Social Security (of Cabinet rank), a Minister of State (Health) and two Parliamentary Under Secretaries of State (one of whom has special responsibilities for disabled people).

The Home Office

The Home Office deals with those internal affairs in England and Wales not assigned to other government departments. The Home Secretary is the channel of communication between the Crown and the public, and between the United Kingdom Government and the Governments of the Channel Islands and the Isle of Man. He exercises certain prerogative powers of the Crown, of which the most important are the prerogative of mercy and the maintenance of the Queen's Peace. He is also concerned with: the administration of justice; criminal law; the treatment of offenders; probation; the prison service; public morals and certain public safety matters; the police, fire and emergency services; immigration and nationality; community relations; administration of the community development project; co-ordination of government action in relation to voluntary social services; and legislation on sex discrimination and race discrimination policy. He also deals with the broad questions of national broadcasting policy.

Other Home Office responsibilities include: addresses and petitions to the Queen and preparation of presentations to Parliament; preparation of patents of nobility for peers, and formal proceedings for the granting of honours; requests for the extradition of criminals; scrutiny of local authority by-laws; grant of licences for scientific experiments on animals; exhumation and removal of bodies; firearms; dangerous drugs; general policy on liquor licensing laws; gaming and lotteries; charitable collections; and theatre and cinema licensing.

The Home Secretary is assisted by two Ministers of State and a Parliamentary Under Secretary of State.

The Department of Industry

The Department of Industry, under a Secretary of State, is responsible for general industrial policy and for industrial aspects of regional policy including financial assistance to industry under the Industry Act. Some regional industrial policy functions in Scotland and Wales are exercised by the Scottish and Welsh Offices. The department sponsors individual manufacturing industries, and is responsible for the nationalised industries: the British Steel Corporation; the Post Office, British Aerospace and British Shipbuilders. It is also responsible for industrial research and development, including civil aerospace research and the supervision of industrial research establishments and for the provision of technical services to industry. The Design Council and the National Research Development Corporation come within its sphere.

The Department's regional offices also serve the Departments of Trade, Energy, and Prices and Consumer Protection.

The Secretary of State for Industry is assisted by two Ministers of State and two Parliamentary Under Secretaries of State.

The Central Office of Information

The Central Office of Information (COI), a common service department, produces information and publicity material, and supplies publicity services required by other government departments; these departments are responsible for the policies expressed. In the United Kingdom, it conducts press, television, radio and poster advertising; produces booklets, leaflets, films, radio and television material, exhibitions, photographs and other visual material; and distributes departmental press notices. For the Foreign and Commonwealth Office it supplies British information posts overseas with press, radio and television material, publications (including magazines), reference services, films, exhibitions, photographs, and display and reading-room material. The COI provides exhibition services (except for trade and cultural exhibitions); and organises tours (other than those sponsored by the British Council and the British Overseas Trade Board) for visitors officially invited to Britain. There are nine regional information offices in England providing services for the home departments and assisting the overseas services by supplying material and by arranging tours for overseas visitors; similar services are provided on a mutually agreed basis by the information staffs of the Scottish, Welsh and Northern Ireland Offices.

The Board of Inland Revenue

The Board of Inland Revenue administers the laws relating to income tax, corporation tax, capital gains tax, stamp duty, capital transfer tax, petroleum revenue tax, development land tax and certain other direct taxes, and advises the Chancellor of the Exchequer on any matters connected with them. It is also responsible for the valuation of land and buildings for such purposes as compensation for compulsory purchase and, in England and Wales, local rates (a form of local taxation).

The Law Officers' Department

The Law Officers of the Crown for England and Wales (the Attorney General and the Solicitor General) appear on behalf of the Crown in important civil and criminal proceedings and in proceedings before international tribunals such as the international court at The Hague and the European Commission and Court of Human Rights at Strasbourg. The Attorney General is the senior legal adviser to the Government. He has the ultimate responsibility for the enforcement of the criminal law and his consent is necessary before proceedings for a number of criminal offences can be commenced; the Director of Public Prosecutions is subject to his superintendence. Legal proceedings for the enforcement of public rights and on behalf of the interests of charity are conducted in his name and the functions of the Queen's Proctor, who has certain duties connected with the operation of the divorce laws, are exercised under his direction. The Attorney General is also spokesman for the Lord Chancellor in the House of Commons on matters affecting the administration of justice. The Solicitor General is subject to the authority of the Attorney General, with the same rights and duties. The Law Officers, who are leading barristers and are always members of the House of Commons, are assisted, particularly in parliamentary work, by a Parliamentary Secretary.

The Lord Chancellor's Office

The Chancellorship is a legislative, judicial and executive office held by an eminent ex-member of the judiciary or of the Bar and carrying Cabinet rank.

In addition to his functions as Speaker of the House of Lords and Custodian of the Great Seal, the Lord Chancellor may sit judicially as a member of the Appellate Committee of the House of Lords or of the Judicial Committee of the Privy Council.

He is also the minister primarily responsible for the administration of the courts and of the law. The Home Secretary has important responsibilities in respect of the criminal law but the Lord Chancellor appoints magistrates and recommends to the Crown most other appointments to the judiciary in England, Wales and Northern Ireland. His responsibility for the courts and for their administrative staff is exercised through six regional (or circuit) offices and their sub-offices.

The Lord Chancellor is responsible for court procedure and for law reform, including appointing the members of the Law Commission, and for presenting the commission's reports to Parliament.

In addition he appoints the chairmen of certain administrative tribunals in England and Wales, and (with the Secretary of State for Scotland) the members of the Council on Tribunals; and he is responsible for the administration of the Judge Advocate General's Department,[1] the Department of the Official Solicitor[2] and the Public Record Office (which preserves, and provides access to, the national archives).

Ordnance Survey

The Ordnance Survey is responsible for the surveying and mapping of Great Britain. This includes geodetic surveys and associated scientific work, topographic surveys and the production of maps at appropriate scales from these surveys. The Department also undertakes a considerable amount of agency work for other departments, particularly the Ministry of Defence, and for the Institute of Geological Sciences and the Land Registry. Parliamentary responsibility for the Ordnance Survey is exercised by ministers of the Department of the Environment.

The Ministry of Overseas Development

Subject to the overall responsibility of the Secretary of State for Foreign and Commonwealth Affairs, overseas development functions are the responsibility of a Minister of State, known as the Minister for Overseas Development, who is assisted by a Parliamentary Secretary.

The separate Ministry of Overseas Development is responsible for Britain's policy of financial and technical co-operation in developing countries. It is concerned with the aid programme as a whole and its detailed composition. The provision of financial assistance includes both grants and loans (the latter mostly interest-free) and support for multilateral aid agencies, such as the IBRD (World Bank); technical co-operation comprises the supply of British experts and equipment, the training of overseas personnel, and the support of research and advisory services.

---

[1] The Judge Advocate General's Department advises the Secretary of State for Defence and the Defence Council on legal matters arising out of the administration of military law, and reviews the proceedings of army and air force courts martial.
[2] The Official Solicitor is concerned with the interests of minors and people with a mental disability involved in proceedings in the High Court, who would otherwise not be represented. In addition he protects the interests of people committed to prison for contempt of court, acts as Receiver for people with a mental disability, and can be appointed as Judicial Trustee in complex and disputed trusts.

The Paymaster General's Office

The Paymaster General's Office acts generally as a banker for government departments other than the Boards of Inland Revenue and Customs and Excise, for which separate arrangements exist. Money granted by Parliament is transferred (in such sums as may be required from day to day) from the Exchequer account to the account of the Paymaster General at the Bank of England. Most departmental payments are made by means of payable orders drawn on the Paymaster General's Office; their recipients obtain payments through the commercial banks, whose accounts at the Bank of England are in turn reimbursed by the Paymaster General's Office. The Department is also responsible for the regular payment of many public service pensions.

The Office of Population Censuses and Surveys

The Office of Population Censuses and Surveys, whose director is the Registrar General for England and Wales, is concerned with the administration of the law relating to non-Anglican marriages and to the registration of births, deaths and marriages in England and Wales; and with the control of the local registration service. Its work also includes the preparation and publication of reports on vital, medical and demographic statistics, taking the periodical census of the population, and, through the Social Survey Division, supplying the Government with a wide range of statistical findings resulting from sample surveys.

The Department of Prices and Consumer Protection

The Department of Prices and Consumer Protection is responsible for general policy and legislation on prices. It also deals with consumer affairs, and sets policy for consumer credit, fair trading, monopolies, mergers and restrictive practices, consumer and home safety, and weights and measures, including metrication, quality assurance and standards. It is responsible for the Price Commission, the Monopolies and Mergers Commission, the Consumer Protection Advisory Committee, the Metrication Board, the British Hallmarking Council, the Hearing Aid Council and the Nationalised Industry Consumer Councils. It is the sponsoring department for the British Standards Institution and for the National Consumer Council. The Secretary of State for Prices and Consumer Protection also appoints the Director General of Fair Trading. The Secretary of State is assisted by a Minister of State and a Parliamentary Under Secretary of State.

The Department of the Procurator General and Treasury Solicitor

The Treasury Solicitor provides a common legal service for a large number of government departments in England and Wales. The duties of his department include instructing Parliamentary Counsel on Bills and drafting subordinate legislation, representing other departments in court, and giving general advice on the interpretation and application of the law. The Department undertakes a considerable amount of conveyancing connected with the transfer of property, administers the estates of persons dying without known relatives and intestate, and deals with the outstanding property and rights of dissolved companies. The Statutory Publications Office is staffed and controlled by the Treasury Solicitor, who reports annually on its work to the Statute Law Committee (a body appointed by the Lord Chancellor from among the judiciary and legal profession in Great Britain).

Some government departments are wholly dependent on the Treasury Solicitor for their legal work; some have their own legal staffs for a proportion of the work and draw on the Treasury Solicitor for special advice and, often, for litigation and conveyancing; others, whose administrative work is based on or deals with a code of specialised law or involves a great deal of legal work, have their own independent legal sections.

The Treasury Solicitor is also the Queen's Proctor (an officer who has certain duties in connection with the divorce laws).

Her Majesty's Stationery Office

Her Majesty's Stationery Office (HMSO) is the publisher for Parliament and Government. The Controller is the Queen's Printer of Acts of Parliament and the copyright of all British government documents is vested in him. Official publications are sold by government bookshops in London, Edinburgh, Cardiff, Belfast, Manchester, Bristol and Birmingham, and through agents and booksellers overseas. HMSO is the United Kingdom agent for publications of the European Community and of other principal international organisations.

HMSO provides a wide range of printing, duplicating, photocopying, and micro-copying facilities for Parliament and Government in its eight printing works and other establishments, and through commercial contractors. It operates five binderies, two of which are involved in the repair of manuscripts from national archives. HMSO is the central purchasing organisation providing the home and overseas public service with paper, printing, binding, books, office supplies and office machinery, and supporting services, such as addressing, and distribution and maintenance of office machinery.

The Department of Trade

The Department of Trade is responsible, under a Secretary of State, for commercial policy and relations with overseas countries. It promotes British commercial interests overseas, negotiates trade and commercial matters, and administers British protective tariffs. It sponsors the work of the British Overseas Trade Board in export services and government support for overseas trade fairs and provides an information service to industry largely through the eight regional offices. It is responsible for companies legislation, supervision of the insurance industry, the insolvency service and for patent, trade mark and copyright matters. Other responsibilities include civil aviation, marine and shipping policy, tourism, the hotel and travel industries, the newspaper, printing, publishing and film industries, and the distributive and service trades. The Secretary of State is assisted by two Parliamentary Under Secretaries of State.

The Department of Transport

The Department of Transport, headed by a Secretary of State, is responsible in England for the main inland transport industries, including railways, buses, freight and ports. It is also responsible for the planning and construction of motorways and trunk roads, although responsibility for the appointment of inspectors at public inquiries and decisions on their reports is shared with the Department of the Environment. The Department of Transport is further responsible for local transport, road and vehicle safety, and vehicle and driver licensing. The Secretary of State is assisted by a Parliamentary Under Secretary.

The Welsh Office

The Secretary of State for Wales, a Cabinet minister, has full responsibility in Wales for ministerial functions relating to child care, health, housing, local government, education (except universities), town and country planning, new towns, water and sewerage, roads, agriculture (with some exceptions), forestry, tourism, national parks, ancient monuments and historic buildings, and shared responsibility for the administration of urban grants to areas of acute social deprivation. He has direct ministerial responsibility in Wales for selective financial assistance to industry, as well as a general responsibility for economic development. This aspect of the Secretary of State's work has been strengthened by the establishment of a Welsh Development Agency, responsible to him, with important industrial and environmental functions. The Secretary of State has certain responsibilities relating to the national library and the national museum. He is assisted by two Parliamentary Under Secretaries of State.

The Welsh Office maintains close and continuous working relationships with the government departments mainly concerned with economic and industrial affairs. Advice on the implications for Wales of national policies, particularly in the economic field, is also available to the Secretary of State through the Welsh Council. The main Welsh Office is in Cardiff, with branches throughout Wales and a small ministerial office in London.

SCOTLAND

Scotland has its own system of law and a wide measure of administrative autonomy. The Secretary of State for Scotland, a United Kingdom Cabinet minister, has responsibility in Scotland (with some exceptions) both for the formulation of policy and for its execution in such matters as agriculture and fisheries, education, local government and environmental services, social work, health, housing, roads and certain aspects of shipping and road transport services. He is also responsible for a range of other functions from police and fire services to sport and tourism. At ministerial level he is assisted by two Ministers of State and three Parliamentary Under Secretaries of State.

The United Kingdom Government's administrative functions arising from these responsibilities are carried out principally by five Scottish departments based in Edinburgh and known as the Scottish Office. A management group including five heads of departments under the chairmanship of the Permanent Under Secretary of State advises the Secretary of State, particularly on questions, such as the allocation of resources and forward planning, with which more than one of the departments are concerned.

The Secretary of State also has a major and expanding role in the planning and development of the Scottish economy. He has important additional functions related to industrial development, with his assumption of responsibility for selective financial assistance to industry in Scotland and the establishment of the Scottish Development Agency which is responsible to him. He also has responsibilities for the activities in Scotland of the Manpower Services Commission, the Training Services Agency and the Employment Services Agency.

He plays a full part in the Government's determination of energy policy and exercises a co-ordinating function over activities in Scotland—such as the location of industry, the creation of employment and the land-based facilities needed for North Sea oil and gas—which are not his direct responsibility but have an important effect on the country's economy. United Kingdom government departments with significant Scottish responsibilities have offices in Scotland with delegated powers, and work closely with the Scottish Office.

The Secretary of State is responsible for legal services in Scotland, and other important functions are exercised by the two Scottish Law Officers: the Lord Advocate and the Solicitor General for Scotland. On many domestic matters, in order to reflect distinctive Scottish features and the different conditions and needs of the country and its people, there is separate legislation relating wholly to Scotland, or else clauses of special application to Scotland only are inserted in Acts which otherwise apply to the United Kingdom generally.

The Department of Agriculture and Fisheries for Scotland

The Department of Agriculture and Fisheries for Scotland has a general responsibility for, and in most cases administers, government measures for the promotion and development of farming in Scotland. It also has responsibilities for the oversight and protection of the Scottish inshore, deep sea and freshwater fisheries, and functions relating to certain harbours.

The Scottish Development Department

The Scottish Development Department is concerned with a number of services affecting the physical development of Scotland, such as town and country planning, housing, roads, water supplies and sewerage, coast protection, flood prevention, building standards and the prevention of river and air pollution (most of which are administered by local authorities). The Department is also responsible for general policy in regard to local government organisation and for ancient monuments and historic buildings; certain transport functions including oversight of the Scottish Transport Group; and assistance for shipping services, ferry services, pier work, and air services in the Highlands and Islands.

The Scottish Economic Planning Department

The Scottish Economic Planning Department is responsible for industrial and economic development including the Scottish aspects of regional and industrial policies and the economic aspects of North Sea oil and gas development; selective assistance to industry; oversight of the Scottish Development Agency; rural development, including supervision of the Highlands and Islands Development Board; electricity; and new towns. The Department also acts as agent in Scotland for certain of the services of the departments of Trade, Industry, and Prices and Consumer Protection.

The Scottish Education Department

The Scottish Education Department is responsible for the development of public education in Scotland in all its forms (except universities). Through its Social Work Services Group the Department has a responsibility for the guidance of local authorities in their provision and development of social work services. It is also concerned with sport, including the financing of the Scottish Sports Council, and with the development of the arts, and has responsibility for the administration of the National Galleries of Scotland, the Royal Scottish Museum (including the Scottish United Services Museum), the National Museum of Antiquities of Scotland, and the National Library of Scotland.

The Scottish Home and Health Department

The Scottish Home and Health Department is responsible for the central administration of functions relating to law and order, including the police service, criminal justice (other than the conduct of prosecutions) and legal aid and the administration of penal institutions. It also has responsibility for the administration of the National Health Service in Scotland, legislation relating to public service superannuation schemes in Scotland and the administration of the teachers' and National Health Service superannuation schemes. The Home and Health Department is the central authority in Scotland for the fire service, for certain home defence and emergency services, and for legislation concerning shops, theatres, cinemas, licensed premises and land tenure matters.

Other Administrative Departments

In addition to the main departments, there are a number of other Scottish departments, all of which work in varying degrees under the direction of the Secretary of State. Such departments include the Department of the Registrar-General for Scotland (the General Register Office); the Scottish Record Office; and the Department of the Registers of Scotland. There are also Scottish branches of the Great Britain and United Kingdom departments under the direction of controllers, who are responsible for ensuring that the execution in Scotland of the policy and procedure of their departments is in accordance with Scottish conditions and needs.

**The Scottish
Law Officers**

The Law Officers of the Crown for Scotland (the Lord Advocate and the Solicitor General for Scotland) are the chief legal advisers to the Government on Scottish questions and the principal representatives of the Crown for the purposes of litigation in Scotland. The Lord Advocate is also closely concerned with questions of legal policy and administration and is himself responsible for the institution and direction of all prosecutions on indictment in Scotland, and the control of summary prosecutions in the Sheriff and District Courts, which are conducted by officials of the Procurator Fiscal Service. In some of this work the Lord Advocate is assisted by the Lord Advocate's Department and the Scottish Courts Administration. The members of the Lord Advocate's Department also act as legal advisers on Scottish questions to certain government departments who have no Scottish legal adviser of their own. The work relevant to prosecutions is centred in the Crown Office in Edinburgh.

The Parliamentary Draftsmen for Scotland, incorporated in the Lord Advocate's Department, are responsible to the minister concerned and to the Law Officers for the drafting of government Bills affecting the law of Scotland.

*The Scottish
Courts
Administration*

The Scottish Courts Administration has a general responsibility to the Secretary of State for the organisation, administration and staffing of the courts and court offices, and is responsible to the Lord Advocate for certain functions in the field of law, including the programme of the Scottish Law Commission, proposals for law reform and questions involving private international law, international conventions and associated problems, the jurisdiction and procedure of the Scottish courts, and enforcement of judgments.

**NORTHERN
IRELAND**

Northern Ireland formerly had its own subordinate legislature responsible for a broad range of domestic matters; the Government of Ireland Act 1920 enacted a constitution which, while preserving the supreme authority of the United Kingdom Parliament and reserving certain matters to that Parliament, provided Northern Ireland with its own legislature and executive to deal with domestic 'transferred' matters. This structure remained in force until 1972 when, following several years of sectarian violence and terrorism in Northern Ireland, a period of direct rule was introduced, with executive powers exercised by a Secretary of State for Northern Ireland and laws made by Order in Council. In 1973 a new type of constitution for the Province provided, among other things, for the devolution of powers to a legislative assembly and a 'power-sharing' executive. These arrangements came into force in January 1974, but following widespread opposition in Northern Ireland the Assembly was prorogued in May 1974. In July 1974 the Northern Ireland Act was passed, providing for the election of a Constitutional Convention to consider what arrangements for the government of Northern Ireland would be likely to command most widespread acceptance throughout the community. The Act provided that, in the interim period (defined as one year from the passing of the Act), the United Kingdom Government and Parliament should continue to be responsible for law and order, electoral matters and business of national importance, such as foreign policy, defence and certain aspects of taxation, while the Secretary of State for Northern Ireland should be responsible to the United Kingdom Parliament for the devolved services (such as agriculture, commerce, education, health, finance and the environment). It further provided that, during this period, laws for Northern Ireland on matters formerly within the competence of the Assembly should be made by Order in Council. The Northern Ireland

Assembly was dissolved at the end of March 1975, and elections to the Constitutional Convention and its first meeting took place in May of that year. In March 1976, the Convention was dissolved, having failed to reach agreement on the central issue of a system of government which would provide for a form of partnership and participation. Direct rule as provided for in the Northern Ireland Act has since been extended for further periods of a year and Northern Ireland departments continue to be under the direction and control of the Secretary of State for Northern Ireland. The Government's principal aim, however, is for a system of devolved government to be established, in which both Protestant and Roman Catholic communities participate.

The Northern Ireland Office
The Northern Ireland Office is the department of the Secretary of State for Northern Ireland who, assisted by two Ministers of State and two Parliamentary Under Secretaries of State, has overall responsibility, and is fully answerable to Parliament, for the government of Northern Ireland. In addition to exercising personal responsibility for constitutional developments, law and order and security in Northern Ireland, the Secretary of State is closely concerned with financial and economic matters in the Province. The four other ministers are in charge of the various Northern Ireland departments, the activities of which are co-ordinated as necessary.

Northern Ireland Departments
The Northern Ireland departments' functions are listed below.

Department of Agriculture
The Department of Agriculture is responsible for the development of Northern Ireland's agricultural, forestry and fishing industries. Its functions also include the collection of agricultural census data, the compilation of statistics, the provision of extensive advisory services to farmers, and the promotion of agricultural research, education and training. The Department acts as agent of the Ministry of Agriculture, Fisheries and Food in agricultural support and the implementation of the European Community's common agricultural policy.

Department of the Civil Service
The Department of the Civil Service is responsible for the general management and control of the Northern Ireland Civil Service.

Department of Commerce
The Department of Commerce is concerned with the development of Northern Ireland's industry and commerce, and with the administration of schemes of assistance to industry. The Department also has responsibilities in connection with electricity and other fuel undertakings; harbours (other than fishery harbours); the tourist trade; the regulation and inspection of mines and quarries; mineral development; consumer protection; the registration of companies, societies, credit unions and insurance and unit trusts; and the administration of an industrial science department.

Department of Education
The Department of Education is responsible for central policy, co-ordination and financial control of the education (apart from universities), youth and library services and for the oversight of the five education and library boards which are responsible for the local administration of these services; for teacher training; and museums. It also makes awards for teacher training and postgraduate studies; formulates and sponsors policies for the improvement of community relations and community services; and distributes grants for the arts and various recreational and community facilities.

*Department of
the Environment*

The Department of the Environment is responsible for housing, planning, comprehensive development, the construction and maintenance of roads and bridges, water supply and sewerage services, local government, the Development Officer service, transport and traffic matters (including road safety), pollution control, amenity lands (country parks, nature reserves and areas of natural beauty), environmental public health, historic buildings and ancient monuments, street lighting and the fire service.

*Department of
Finance*

The Department of Finance's responsibilities include the control of the expenditure of the Northern Ireland departments, liaison with the United Kingdom Treasury and the Northern Ireland Office on financial matters, and economic and social planning and research.

The Department has also responsibility for: rating policy and the collection of rates; borrowing; loan advances; charities and charitable funds; the provision and maintenance of public buildings; building regulations and liaison with the construction industry; property valuation; Ordnance Survey; public records; the registration of births, marriages and deaths; the registration of title of land; miscellaneous licensing; the registration of clubs; and Ulster Savings.

*Department of
Health and
Social Services*

The Department of Health and Social Services is responsible for all aspects of health and personal social services and the administration of the social security schemes.

*Department of
Manpower Services*

The Department of Manpower Services has responsibility for the administration of government policy in relation to the employment and training of labour. It operates employment service and careers offices; administers a comprehensive training programme; compiles statistics on employment and unemployment; and undertakes research into employment matters. It provides a factory inspectorate and deals with industrial relations and the rehabilitation and employment of the disabled.

It is also responsible for sponsorship of the direct labour organisation of Enterprise Ulster and has functions in relation to the Industry Training Boards, Northern Ireland Training Executive, Fair Employment Agency, the Equal Opportunities Commission and the Labour Relations Agency.

THE CIVIL SERVICE

A civil servant in Britain is a servant of the Crown (not being the holder of a political or judicial office), who usually is paid wholly and directly out of money voted by Parliament and works in a civil capacity in a department of government. Some civil servants work for Crown bodies, which are not government departments (the Manpower Services Commission and its agencies are examples), and are paid out of government grants to these bodies. Including part-time staff (two part-time officers being reckoned as equivalent to one full-time), there are about 738,000 civil servants (just over one-third of them women), roughly 343,000 of whom are engaged in the provision of public services, such as, paying sickness benefits and pensions, collecting taxes and contributions, running employment services; staffing prisons, and providing services to industry and agriculture. About 253,000 are employed in the Ministry of Defence, including the Royal Ordnance factories and Royal Dockyards. The rest are about equally divided between: central administrative and policy duties; service-wide support services, such as accommodation, printing and information; and largely financially self-supporting services, for instance those provided by the Department for National Savings and the Royal Mint.

Over 75 per cent of civil servants work outside the London area, and further dispersal from the capital is taking place.

The total of civil servants includes about 171,000 industrial staff, mainly manual workers in government industrial establishments, whose pay and conditions of service are largely separately administered, and differ quite substantially from those for non-industrial grades.

Stability of administration is ensured by the political neutrality of the service. Although a civil servant works under the authority and direction of the minister of the department to which he is appointed, legally he is a servant of the Crown. A change of minister, whether due to ministerial changes within a government or the advent of a government of a different political complexion, does not involve a change of staff.

Ministers sometimes personally appoint special advisers, who are nonetheless civil servants and are paid from public funds, to give them advice on policy matters. Such appointments lapse when the Government's term of office ends.

Structure

Following the report of the Fulton committee which in 1968 assessed the structure, recruitment and management, including management training, of the service, the Civil Service has been undergoing a programme of reshaping and modernisation to make it more effective in carrying out its changing tasks.

The structure of the Home Civil Service is being redesigned to provide for a more flexible deployment of staff so that talent can be used to the best advantage and the highest levels of the Civil Service seen to be open to people of outstanding ability, whatever their specialist background or original method of entry to the service. These structural changes involve the abolition of classes, and are being allied with personnel management policies designed to ensure that, although work requiring specialist skill is always done by appropriately qualified individuals, people with the necessary aptitudes are given opportunities to gain suitably wide experience to fit them for higher posts.

At the top levels of the Civil Service, where staff are predominantly concerned with higher management and policy, there is an open and unified structure, with three grades—permanent secretary, deputy secretary and under secretary—available for all types of posts. Posts at these levels are filled by the people most suitable for them without regard to their academic background or to whether they were previously in a specialist or administrative stream.

At other levels the structure is being based on a system of occupational groups, which are the basic groupings of staff for the purposes of pay, recruitment and personnel management, and categories which consist of one or more occupational groups having a common pay and grading pattern. Ten categories have so far been created, and the groups of staff that are so far members of them are shown below.

Categories

There are five groups within the General Category. The Administration Group contains some 250,000 staff. Their functions range from the formulation of policy advice to ministers and the implementation of government policies to the performance of clerical duties. The Economist Group contains about 390 staff. They provide economic advice and undertake economic analysis. The Statistician Group (some 530 staff) undertakes the collection and analysis of statistics required for government purposes. The Information Officer Group (some 1,400 staff) carries out a variety of specialised press, publicity, public relations and information work. The Librarian Group (some 380 staff) carries out the professional librarian duties in departmental libraries.

The Science Category contains the Science Group (16,700 staff), which is responsible for conducting scientific research and testing in numerous government laboratories and testing establishments, and for providing advice on scientific policy. Its members also participate in the planning and management of advanced technology procurement projects.

There are three groups in the Professional and Technology Category. The Professional and Technology Group contains some 40,000 staff and includes a range of professionals—architects, surveyors, quantity surveyors, and electrical and mechanical engineers—and appropriate supporting staff, whose main function is to plan and oversee a wide range of government construction and procurement activities, and to carry out certain inspection and regulatory activities. The Graphics Officer Group contains about 490 staff responsible for the preparation of all forms of artwork applied to the wide range of requirements within the government service. The Marine Services Group contains about 600 staff who operate the civilian-manned vessels of the Royal Maritime Auxiliary Service.

Within the Training Category the Instructional Officer Group comprises some 5,750 staff employed on instruction in a trade, craft or subject, or on ancillary or supervisory duties connected with instruction.

The Legal Category contains the Legal Group (England and Wales) and the Legal Group (Scotland), a total of some 980 staff who carry out a wide range of legal work for government departments.

The Police Category consists of a single Police Group of some 4,450 staff who form an internal constabulary to carry out normal police functions in Ministry of Defence establishments.

The Secretarial Group within the Secretarial Category comprises 22,000 typists, who work mainly in small groups, some 4,600 personal secretaries who work mainly for senior civil servants, and 1,800 superintendents and controllers.

The Data Processing Category contains a single group of 8,600 staff who operate processing equipment in computer and other machine installations.

The Research Officer Category contains the Social Science Research Group, and the Resource and Planning Research Group, a total of some 460 staff who carry out a wide range of research work.

The 44,500 staff employed in the single group within the Social Security Category work in local offices of the Department of Health and Social Security.

The ten categories already established account for over 70 per cent of the non-industrial staff. The intention is that the remainder (including support staff such as paperkeepers, messengers and office-keepers) will be absorbed into existing categories or, where this is impossible, into additional categories set up for the purpose.

The Diplomatic Service

The Diplomatic Service was established in 1965 as a separate service of the Crown and provides the staff for service in the Foreign and Commonwealth Office and at United Kingdom diplomatic missions and consular posts in foreign and in independent Commonwealth countries. Its functions include advising on policy, negotiating with overseas governments and conducting business in international organisations; promoting British exports and the advancement of British trade; administering British aid, presenting British ideas, policies and objectives to the people of overseas countries; and protecting British interests abroad.

The Service has its own grade structure, linked for salary purposes with that of the Home Civil Service. It also has secretarial, communications and security officer branches. Specialists and advisers from home departments or the armed forces may serve at overseas posts on loan or attachment and it is intended to build a closer working relationship between the Diplomatic Service and the Home Civil Service.

The Northern Ireland Civil Service

Northern Ireland has its own Civil Service which, subject to regional differences, is modelled on its counterpart in Great Britain, recruitment being effected through its own Civil Service Commission. Interchange of staff between the two Civil Services occurs to a minor extent only, and is a matter for departmental agreement in individual cases.

Public Services of Overseas Dependent Territories

Britain's dependent territories fill vacancies in their public services by the appointment of suitably qualified local candidates wherever possible; but when vacancies cannot be filled by this means generally the Foreign and Commonwealth Office, the Ministry of Overseas Development and the Crown Agents for Oversea Governments and Administrations are asked to recruit other candidates, principally from the United Kingdom. Hong Kong has its own Government office in London with responsibility for recruiting to the Hong Kong public service.

Recruitment

Recruitment to the Civil Service is the responsibility of the Civil Service Commission which, working in conjunction with departments, ensures that staff are selected on the basis of fair and open competition. The selection of junior staff such as those engaged in clerical and manual work, is undertaken almost entirely by departments. The commission, however, always issues the 'certificate of qualification' necessary for permanent appointment. The appointment of a successful candidate is made by the department concerned.

For the Administration Group, which forms the central part of the Home Civil Service, entry is at three levels relating broadly to the academic achievements of university honours graduates; 18-year-old school-leavers; and 16-year-old school-leavers. The selection procedure for the highest of these levels (the Administration Trainee entry) comprises qualifying tests, followed by a series of tests and interviews at the Civil Service Selection Board and an interview by the Final Selection Board. The next level (the Executive Officer entry) selection from among those possessing the necessary academic qualifications is in two stages, a set of qualifying tests followed by an interview. For the clerical entrants selection is normally by interview of those holding the prescribed educational qualifications.

Entry to the professional and technical grades usually requires appropriate qualifications, and selection is on the basis of past record and by interview.

Training

In all except the smallest government departments, there are full-time training officers and instructors whose task it is to help identify the training needs of the staff and to organise courses, both general and technical, to provide for their varying requirements. A substantial number of management courses is run within the Civil Service both by departments and by the Civil Service College. Use is also made of external management courses in business schools, the Administrative Staff College, Henley, and other centres.

Methods of training within the Civil Service combine lectures, discussion groups, instructional visits and case-studies with the use of many audio-visual aids such as closed-circuit television and video-tape recordings, instructional films and self-instructional programmes. There is also a considerable amount of 'on-the-job' training. Civil servants are regularly moved between the different branches of their department and sometimes between departments so that they can gain as wide an experience as possible of Civil Service work.

In order that they may continue their education, arrangements are made for the release of civil servants under the age of 18 to attend appropriate courses usually on one day a week ('day release' schemes). Adult staff are assisted financially to undertake, mainly in their own time, private studies leading to recognised educational or professional qualifications in approved subjects. There are also opportunities for civil servants in mid-career to obtain fellowships or otherwise to go on sabbatical leave to undertake research in areas of interest to themselves or their departments.

Training is co-ordinated by the Training Division of the Civil Service Department which is responsible, in conjunction with the Civil Service College, for the analysis and determination of training needs to be met centrally, and which exercises advisory functions in regard to departmental training. Central training is provided by the Civil Service College which offers a wide range of courses and seminars (some of a broad developmental nature and others more job-related) for civil servants, including those in specialist groups, at various levels up to and including that of under secretary. Subjects include structure and machinery of government, management studies, social administration and social policy, economics, accountancy and financial management, statistics and operational research, computers, information systems and management services; many of the courses are multi-disciplinary. The College also provides courses on European institutions and has reciprocal training arrangements with other European countries.

Promotion

A period of probation (varying according to grade, with extensions in certain instances) is the rule for all new entrants to the Civil Service.

Promotions are made partly through centrally conducted examinations and partly by the departments themselves. Promotions or appointments to deputy secretary-level posts and above and all transfers between departments at these levels are approved by the Prime Minister, who is advised by the official head of the Home Civil Service.

Normally promotion is from grade to grade, but arrangements exist for accelerated promotion for staff who have shown exceptional promise.

Conditions of Service

Machinery for negotiation on conditions of service affecting the Civil Service as a whole is provided by the National Whitley Council, which is composed jointly of official and staff representatives. Negotiating machinery for separate sections of the service is provided through the various staff associations which civil servants are encouraged to join (for instance, the Civil and Public Services Association, the Society of Civil and Public Servants and the Institution of Professional Civil Servants), and through departmental Whitley Councils.

In general, the civil servant receives a salary which is based on a fair comparison with that paid for broadly comparable work outside the service and usually he receives annual increments up to the maximum of the scale of the grade to which he belongs. There is a pension scheme. The aim of the Civil Service is to ensure that every civil servant who is capable and efficient realises his or her full potential.

It is possible for staff to interrupt their careers, or to have special leave granted, to look after domestic responsibilities, and staff who resign may apply later to rejoin the service in the grade they held at the time of resignation.

Civil servants are required to work a specified number of hours each week. Certain grades are eligible for overtime pay for any hours worked in excess of the standard hours, but this does not apply to the higher grades whose salaries are determined on the assumption that they will work as long as necessary without additional pay. The standard working week for office staff is 42 hours (41 in London). Annual leave varies according to grade and length of service up to a maximum of 30 working days a year.

Sick leave on full pay, less any national insurance benefit received, may be granted to civil servants for up to six months in a 12-month period, and thereafter on reduced pay up to a maximum of one year's sick leave in any four years; any officer whose health is permanently impaired may be retired.

Political and Private Activities

The position and functions of a civil servant remain the same whichever political party is in power; and it is his duty to serve the Government of the day irrespective of his own political opinion. The extent to which he is free, as a private individual, to participate in political activities varies according to grade. For this purpose civil servants are divided into three groups: those who are completely free to engage in all kinds of national and local political activities (although if they intend standing for Parliament, they must resign their appointment before nomination day on the understanding that if not elected they will be reinstated in their previous capacity within a week of the declaration of the election result); those who are free, subject to the acceptance of the need for discretion and with the permission of the department, to take part in most activities except parliamentary candidature; and those who are debarred from national political activities though they may seek permission to take part in local government political activities. In the non-industrial Civil Service the completely free groups are mostly ancillary staff such as cleaners and messengers. The intermediate group includes mainly members of the clerical and typing grades and the granting of permission by the department depends, broadly, on the nature of the work done. The remainder are not allowed to take part in national political activities. Permission is usually granted to members of all groups to engage in local political activities to the maximum extent consistent with the reputation of the Civil Service for political impartiality and the avoidance of any conflict with official duties. Where permission is granted, it is subject to a code of discretion and to the obligation to notify the department of election or co-option to a local council. A committee of inquiry, set up by the Government to review the rules governing political participation by civil servants, has said that it considers these arrangements to be unnecessarily restrictive and has recommended that the group allowed to take part in national political activities with departmental permission should be substantially enlarged.

All civil servants enjoy the right to register their private political opinions on appropriate occasions, for instance, at general or local authority elections. They may also engage in such private activities as they wish, provided that these do not in any way conflict with their official duties, nor with the provisions of the Official Secrets Acts 1911 and 1920, and the Prevention of Corruption Act 1926. However, since a civil servant must not use his official position to further his private interests, he is subject to certain restrictions in commerce and business: for instance, he may not hold private interests in public contracts and he may not use official information in writing, broadcasting or lecturing without the approval of his department.

Security

As a general rule the political views of civil servants are not a matter of official concern, but there are some civil duties in which secrecy is so vitally important to State security that the Government does not feel itself justified in employing anyone to carry them out whose reliability is in doubt. For this reason no one who is known to be a member of, or actively associated or in sympathy with, the Communist Party or with Fascist organisations, or is liable to be a security risk in any other respect, is employed on secret work.

Each government department is responsible for its own internal security, and the Security Service, which operates independently under a Director-General who is responsible for its efficiency to the Home Secretary, deals with national security. In addition, there is a Security Commission which, if requested by the Prime Minister in consultation with the Leader of the Opposition, may investigate and report on breaches of security in the public service and, in certain circumstances, advise whether any change in security arrangements is necessary or desirable.

LOCAL GOVERNMENT

The local government system comprises a pattern of elected councils for defined areas. The councils represent their own localities, provide a local level of democracy and make available a wide range of services.

The specific powers and duties of local authorities are conferred on them by Act of Parliament (or by measures made under the authority of an Act). The actual administration and the exercise of discretion within statutory limits are the responsibility of the local authority, but, in respect of certain services, Acts of Parliament dealing with local government give government ministers defined powers, some of which are designed to secure a measure of national uniformity in the standard of service provided or to safeguard public health, while others are for the protection of the rights of individual citizens. For some services the minister concerned has wide powers of supervision; for others there are strictly limited powers. Government policy is to ensure that central government controls over local authorities are kept to the minimum necessary.

In addition to their statutory powers, ministers concerned with local government give assistance to local authorities by the general issue of advisory circulars and by giving advice in individual cases.

The main links between local authorities and the central Government are: in England, the Department of the Environment; in Scotland, the Scottish Development Department; in Wales, the Welsh Office; and in Northern Ireland, the Department of the Environment for Northern Ireland.

Principal Types of Local Authority

The main pattern of local government organisation in England and Wales (outside Greater London) is a division of the country into 53 large county authorities, within which there are 369 smaller district authorities. Both types of authority have independent, locally elected councils, and have separate functions to perform. County authorities normally provide the large-scale local government services, while the districts are responsible for the more local ones (see pp 63–4). However, in six of the English counties, which are in heavily populated areas and known as 'metropolitan' counties, responsibility for certain large-scale services rests with the district authorities. In England populations in the non-metropolitan counties range from 288,000 to about 1·4 million (the Isle of Wight with a population of about 112,000 is an exception), and in the metropolitan counties from 1·2 to 2·7 million. District authorities within metropolitan counties have populations of between 167,000 and 1·1 million; other districts' populations average between 75,000 and 100,000, although many fall outside this range. The local government system in Wales closely resembles that in non-metropolitan areas of England. Populations in the counties range from 102,000 to 540,000, and the districts have populations of between 19,600 and 282,000. English parish councils or meetings in villages and small towns serve as focuses for local opinion as bodies with limited powers of local interest. In Wales community councils have similar functions.

Greater London—an administrative area of about 610 square miles (1,580 sq km) and a population of some 7 million—is administered by the Greater London Council, the councils of 32 London boroughs (with populations ranging from 136,000 to 331,000) and the Corporation of the City of London (the historic centre which has a resident population of about 6,800).

On the mainland of Scotland local government is on a two-tier basis: nine regions are divided into 53 districts, each area having its own elected council. There are three virtually all-purpose authorities for Orkney, Shetland and the Western Isles. Provision is made for local community councils to be formed. These councils have no statutory functions and are not local authorities.

The pattern of local authorities, and of their electoral arrangements, is kept up to date by Boundary Commissions for England, Wales and Scotland.

In Northern Ireland there are 26 district councils which are responsible for local environmental and other services. Statutory bodies and local offices, responsible to central departments, administer major services such as roads, education, health, and housing. Populations of the districts range from 13,000 to over 350,000.

Constitution and Election of Councils

Local authority councils consist of a number of elected unpaid councillors presided over by a chairman. They can claim flat-rate attendance allowance as of right (without proof of loss of earnings) on the performance of council business; they are also entitled to travelling and subsistence allowances. Parish and community councillors cannot claim for duties within their own areas.

In England, Wales and Northern Ireland each council annually elects a chairman and vice-chairman. Some districts have the ceremonial title of borough, or city, both granted by royal authority (except in Northern Ireland where they are granted by the Secretary of State). In boroughs and cities the chairman is normally known as the Mayor (in the City of London and certain other large cities, he is known as the Lord Mayor). In Scottish regions and islands areas the chairman is called the convener and the chairman of the district councils of each of the four cities is called the Lord Provost. No general title is laid down for the chairmen of the other district councils, but some are known as conveners, while others continue to use the old burghal title of 'provost'.

The term of office of a councillor elected to any form of local government is usually four years. In England and Wales county council elections took place in 1977 and will be held every fourth year thereafter. Metropolitan district elections are held for a third of the seats in each year when there is no county council election. Non-metropolitan district councils may adopt the same procedure or opt for whole council elections; the latter took place in 1976 and are being held again in 1979 and every following fourth year. In London elections to the Greater London Council were held in 1977 and elections to the London borough councils in 1978. In Scotland elections for the regions and islands areas took place in 1978. Elections for the districts were held in 1977. Elections for the district councils in Northern Ireland took place in 1977 and will be held every fourth year thereafter.

Any person (including a member of the House of Lords) is entitled to vote at a local government election in Great Britain provided that he or she is 18 years of age or over, is a British subject or a citizen of the Irish Republic, is not subject to any legal incapacity and is registered as a local government elector for the area for which the election is held. A person qualifies for registration as a local government elector if, on the qualifying date for the register (compiled annually), he or she is resident in the council area. In Northern Ireland the qualification for voting is a little different.

A candidate for election as councillor—man or woman—normally stands as a representative of one of the national political parties, as a member of an association representing some local interest, or as an independent. He must be a British subject or a citizen of the Irish Republic and aged 21 or over. In addition, he must be registered as a local government elector in the area of the local authority to which he seeks election; or have resided or occupied (as owner or tenant) land or other premises in that area during the whole of the 12 months preceding the day on which he is nominated as a candidate; or, in that 12 months, have had his principal or only place of work there. A candidate is also subject to a number of statutory disqualifications designed to ensure that unsuitable people do not offer themselves for election.

Local authority areas are generally divided into electoral areas for local council elections. Administrative counties in England and Wales are divided into electoral divisions returning one or more councillors. Districts in England, Wales and Northern Ireland are divided into electoral 'wards'. In Scotland in the regions and islands areas the electoral areas are called electoral divisions, each returning a single member; the districts are divided into wards, similarly returning a single member. For parish or community council elections in England and Wales, each parish or ward of a parish (or, in some cases, a combination of parishes) forms an electoral area which returns one or more members. For elections to the Greater London Council, Greater London is divided into electoral divisions, each returning one councillor.

Voting takes place at polling stations arranged by the returning officer concerned, and under the supervision of a presiding officer appointed for the purpose. The procedure for local government voting in Great Britain is similar to that for parliamentary elections, although facilities for postal voting are more restricted. In Great Britain each elector has one vote for each seat contested in his electoral area: he need not record all his votes, but must not give more than one vote for each candidate. In Northern Ireland local government elections are held on the basis of proportional representation and for this purpose electoral wards are grouped into district electoral areas. Facilities for postal voting are available.

Functions and Services

The functions of local authorities are far reaching. Some are framed primarily as duties mandatory on an authority, others are purely permissive.

Broadly speaking, functions in England and Wales are divided between county and district councils on the basis that county councils are responsible for matters requiring planning and administration over wide areas or requiring the support of substantial resources. Within the metropolitan areas district councils are responsible for functions needing substantial resources because they have populations large enough to give such support. District councils as a whole administer functions of more local significance. In London the division of functions is slightly different.

In England all county councils are responsible for such matters as strategic planning, transportation planning, highways, traffic regulation, consumer protection, refuse disposal, police and the fire service. Education, libraries and the personal social services are functions of county councils in non-metropolitan areas and of district councils in metropolitan areas. All district councils are responsible, for instance, for environmental health, housing, decisions on most planning applications and refuse collection. They may also provide off-street car parks subject to the consent of the county council. Powers to operate some functions—such as the provision of museums, art galleries and parks—are available at both levels; arrangements depend on local agreement.

In Greater London the London boroughs and the Corporation of the City of London are responsible for the same range of functions as district councils in metropolitan areas (with the addition of consumer protection). The Greater London Council (GLC) deals only with those services which by their nature require unified administration and control over the whole area. In the inner London area education is administered by the Inner London Education Authority, an independent committee of the GLC. Responsibility for highways in London is divided according to the type of road: the main strategic road network is a matter for the GLC, while the London boroughs look after the other roads. The boroughs are primarily responsible for the provision of housing, although the GLC also maintains a stock of housing. It is additionally involved in such matters as the provision of housing outside London for people from the London area, assisting the inner London boroughs in relation to slum clearance, the provision of accommodation for people on the London boroughs' housing waiting lists, and the rehousing of its own tenants and those of the London boroughs whose accommodation needs have changed. The police force in the London area (see p 78) is directly responsible to the Home Secretary.

In Wales the division of functions between county and district councils is much the same as that between county and district councils in non-metropolitan areas of England. The main differences are that Welsh district councils are responsible for refuse disposal; they may, subject to the consent of the county council, provide on-street as well as off-street car parking facilities; and they may, exceptionally, exercise library and consumer protection functions.

Local authorities in England and Wales may arrange for most of their functions to be carried out on their behalf by another local authority. The exceptions to this general rule are functions relating to education, police, the personal social services and national parks.

In Scotland the regional and district authorities discharge local government functions in a way broadly similar to that of authorities in England and Wales, including some at both levels. Orkney, Shetland and the Western Isles, because of their isolation, have single, virtually all-purpose authorities.

In Northern Ireland, local environmental and certain other services are administered by the district councils, but responsibility for planning, roads, water supply and sewerage services is exercised in each district by a local office of the Department of the Environment for Northern Ireland working closely with the district council and its staff. Area boards, responsible to appropriate central departments, administer locally education, public libraries and the health and personal social services. The Northern Ireland Housing Executive, responsible to the Department of the Environment, administers housing.

Internal Organisation of Local Authorities

Local authorities are free to a very considerable extent to make their own internal arrangements and to choose the means and methods by which they discharge their responsibilities. Most councils use the committee system, whereby questions of policy and principle are decided in full council, and committees are appointed to administer the various services. Parish and community councils in England and Wales are often able to do their work efficiently in full session although they appoint committees from time to time as necessary. Some councils have established policy advisory or co-ordinating committees with powers to originate policy, subject to the approval of the full council. The powers and duties of local authority committees (which may be advisory or executive) are usually laid down in the appointing council's standing orders.

A council is free to delegate all its powers to committees, except its powers in connection with raising loans, levying rates (see p 66), or making financial demands on other authorities liable to contribute, which are legally reserved to the council as a whole.

Local authorities can make arrangements among themselves for the discharge of their functions. These include co-operation through joint committees, joint teams and the loan of staff. One authority may discharge functions for another, and may also supply others with a range of goods and services.

The public and the press are admitted to all meetings of a council (and of committees) but may be excluded while a particular item is considered if the council (or committee) resolves that publicity for that matter would be prejudicial to the public interest.

Officers and Employees

The execution of council policy rests with salaried officers and employees, of whom there may be tens of thousands in the larger authorities. Some 2·8 million people are employed by local authorities in Great Britain. These include administrative, professional and technical staff, manual workers and teachers. Although a few appointments, such as chief education and fire officers and the director of social services, must by law be made by all the authorities responsible for the functions concerned, councils are individually responsible within national policy requirements for determining the size and composition of their work forces and the way they should be used. An authority must not, however, employ one of its own councillors. In Northern Ireland, each council must by law appoint a clerk of the council as its chief officer.

As a general rule, employees are of three kinds: heads of departments or chief officers, whose duties are mainly of an administrative and managerial kind; subordinate officers employed in an administrative, a professional, clerical or technical capacity; and manual workers who are employed to do the physical work for which the council is responsible. Senior staff appointments are usually made at the instance of the committee or committees particularly concerned; most junior appointments are made by heads of departments, who are also responsible for engaging manual workers. Appointments and engagements always conform to the council's set establishment, and committees are informed of any appointments which they have not made themselves.

Rates of pay and conditions of service for local authority staff are within the jurisdiction of the employing council, although there are recommended scales.

Local Government Finance

Local authority expenditure in the United Kingdom (on both current and capital accounts) was about £20,000 million in 1977. A clear distinction is made between capital and current expenditure. Capital expenditure (just under a quarter of the total) is financed partly from the current account surplus (about half), from borrowing (two-fifths) and the remainder from grants and other incomes. Housing, the major element, accounted for over half in 1977. Current expenditure by local authorities accounts for just over a quarter of total current account spending by central and local government. The education service represents over a third of this expenditure, followed by the police, personal social services, roads (including lighting), public health and debt interest. Current expenditure is financed mainly from central government grants (about three-fifths) and from local rates paid by occupiers of land and building (about one-third). Each local authority is responsible for its own finance, although in a few cases several authorities combine to organise a specialist service which it would be uneconomic for each authority to provide on its own.

Government Grants

Government 'rate support grants' to local authorities are paid in aid of revenues generally. Grants are also paid towards the cost of specific services—either towards current expenditure, such as on the police, or towards capital expenditure, such as on the acquisition and clearance of derelict land. (In Wales, approved schemes for the acquisition and clearance of derelict land are financed by the Welsh Development Agency.) Annual subsidies are paid for local authority housing.

Rate support grants are distributed among authorities in three parts: the 'needs' element which is designed to give most help to authorities whose spending needs are greatest; the 'resources' element, which is used to supplement the rate income of authorities whose rateable value per head of population falls below a standard figure, prescribed for each year; and the 'domestic' element, which compensates authorities for loss of rate income from reductions in rate poundage which they are required to give to householders. The formula for distributing the 'needs' element is subject to annual variations. Grants are also made towards the cost of rate rebates for people with low incomes.

In Northern Ireland the district councils receive specific grants plus a general grant used to supplement the resources of those councils whose rateable value resources are below the standard level.

Rates

Rates are local taxes paid by the occupiers of land and property (with certain exceptions, see below) to meet part of the cost of local services. Each occupier's payment is calculated annually by the rating authority by multiplying the rateable value of his property (broadly equivalent to its annual rental value) by the rate poundage—an amount per £ of rateable value fixed by the authority according to its projected financial needs. In England and Wales rateable values are assessed periodically by the Board of Inland Revenue (see p 47). The last general revaluation of all property was in 1973. Disputes about rating assessments are heard by local valuation courts, and on appeal by the Lands Tribunal. Public undertakings have their rates separately determined. Crown property is not rateable but payments are made, based on values assessed by the Treasury Valuer, in lieu of rates.

In Scotland valuation is carried out by assessors appointed by the regional and islands councils. The last general revaluation was in 1978. Appeals are heard by the valuation appeal committees of each valuation area and thereafter by the Lands Valuation Appeal Court of the Court of Session.

In Northern Ireland valuations are carried out by the Valuation Officer of the Department of Finance. There is a right of appeal. The present valuations came into force in 1976.

Responsibility for levying and collecting rates in England and Wales lies with the district councils and London borough councils. Each county council (and the Greater London Council) determines what rate will be required to meet its estimated expenditure and district councils (and London borough councils) include this element in the rate they levy. Householders benefit from domestic rate relief and those with lower incomes may also qualify for rate rebates; both reliefs are financed by government grants. Rates may be paid by instalments, normally in ten one-monthly payments. Rating relief is available in certain circumstances on premises adapted for the use of the disabled. Agricultural land and buildings (apart from living accommodation) and places of religious worship are exempted from rate payments. Charities pay half the full rate on premises they occupy for charitable purposes and may be given further relief by rating authorities, who can also reduce or remit the rates for a wide range of non-profit-making bodies. Rates may be levied on empty properties at any percentage up to the full amount and in the case of empty commercial property a rating surcharge may be payable.

In Scotland every authority determines a rate for its own services, but the collection of rates and the administration of rating is the responsibility of regional and island councils. Industrial (including freight transport) premises in Scotland are rated at a half of net annual value and the right to pay rates in instalments extends to all ratepayers. There is empty property rating in Scotland but no empty property surcharge.

In Northern Ireland there are two rates: one set by the district councils and one set by the Department of Finance. Both are collected by the Department and the appropriate part paid over to the respective councils. Industrial (including freight transport) premises are rated at a quarter of net annual value and the degree of charitable exemption is decided by the Valuation Office. Empty properties are not rated.

Loans

Loans may be raised by local authorities to finance capital expenditure under general powers conferred by national legislation. For items of expenditure in key sectors (such as education, housing and roads) local authorities in England and Wales must seek approval from the government department concerned before raising loans. For other capital expenditure, each authority receives an annual loan authorisation within which it determines what sums to borrow and what projects to undertake. The GLC applies annually for parliamentary sanction to raise the money it needs for capital expenditure while the City of London has ancient charter powers to cover its borrowings. In Northern Ireland long-term borrowing by district councils is subject to approval by the Department of the Environment for Northern Ireland. In Scotland departmental approval is given to capital expenditure, not to loans.

Local authorities may raise long-term loans by means of private mortgages, issuing stock upon the Stock Exchange and bonds which may or may not be quoted on the Stock Exchange. Local authorities also have right of access to the Public Works Loan Board, financed by the Exchequer, or, in Northern Ireland, to the Government Loans Fund, for long-term borrowing to finance a proportion of their reckonable capital payments, and may borrow temporarily for a limited proportion of their current outstanding loan debt.

Control of Finance

Internal control of finance is normally exercised on behalf of the council concerned by a finance committee, whose function it is to keep the financial policy of the council under constant review. (There is no statutory requirement for local authorities to appoint a finance committee, but they have to make proper arrangements for the administration of their financial affairs.) Local authorities must have their accounts audited. Those in England and Wales can choose between the district auditor (appointed by the Secretary of State for the Environment) and an approved private auditor (or partly both). In Scotland the auditing of accounts is the responsibility of an independent Commission for Local Authority Accounts in Scotland appointed by the Secretary of State for Scotland, and in Northern Ireland it is carried out by independent local government auditors appointed by the Department of the Environment.

**Local
Government
Complaints
System**

A complaints system for local government in England and Wales involves independent statutory Commissions for Local Administration (one each for England and Wales) comprising a number of local commissioners, each responsible in a particular area of the country for investigating citizens' complaints of maladministration by local authorities. In Scotland there is a single Commissioner for Local Administration. The commissioners help local authority councillors to protect the interests of constituents.

In Northern Ireland a Commissioner for Complaints deals with complaints alleging injustices suffered as a result of maladministration by district councils, and certain other public bodies.

THE FIRE SERVICES

The fire services in Great Britain are organised on a local basis, subject to a measure of central control. The cost is borne by local authorities, aided by central government through the rate support grant (see p 66). Every part of the country is covered by a public fire brigade. Northern Ireland has its own service responsible to the Northern Ireland Department of the Environment.

Fire Authorities

Each of 68 fire authorities in the United Kingdom must by law make provision for fire-fighting purposes, and in particular maintain a brigade of sufficient strength to meet efficiently all normal requirements (in some parts of Scotland, authorities are combined to provide fire cover). Other fire-fighting organisations are maintained, for instance, by the Army and Air Force Departments of the Ministry of Defence; by the Department of Industry at certain establishments; and by some large industrial and commercial concerns.

Central Control

The Home Secretary and the Secretary of State for Scotland have central responsibility for the fire service in England and Wales and in Scotland respectively. Central control is directed mainly towards ensuring the operational efficiency of brigades. Ministers have statutory powers to make regulations on such matters as appointments and promotions, standards of training and equipment, pensions, and disciplinary matters. Their approval is also required for reductions in the operational establishments of fire brigades. Each minister is advised by a Central Fire Brigades Advisory Council, consisting of officers of the respective home departments, representatives of the local authority associations, and of the associations representing members of fire brigades, and other persons with special qualifications, appointed by the minister concerned. Inspectorates of fire services advise the ministers on operational and technical matters.

Personnel

Most fire brigade establishments include part-time retained personnel to augment and support the full-time strength in return for a retaining fee and call-out and attendance fee. Volunteer members (who receive no remuneration) undertake to attend a fire if called upon. Fire authorities also employ people for duties in controls communications and mobilising and staff duties. Some brigades have schemes for the employment of juniors of 16–18 years, prior to their enrolment as regular members at the age of 18.

Each fire authority must draw up a scheme showing the establishment of personnel, the number and location of fire stations and the number and type of appliances considered necessary for the provision of fire cover for its area. Establishment schemes vary according to the fire risks in the area concerned. In the United Kingdom there are about 31,240 full-time and 16,130 part-time operational members of fire brigades.

Recruits and junior ranks in the fire service in England and Wales receive practical training in basic firemanship at collective training schools run by the larger fire authorities. In Scotland similar training is carried out at a central training school. Management and command training is provided for the higher and middle ranks at the Fire Service Staff College, where high-level operational studies are also conducted. Fire prevention, practical firemanship, advancement and instructor training for junior and middle ranks is provided at the Fire Service Technical College. Both colleges are maintained by the Home Office and the Scottish Home and Health Department. Facilities for officers from overseas fire services to study the organisation, current training methods, appliances and equipment of British fire brigades are arranged by the Home Office Fire Department.

Equipment

Every fire authority must buy such appliances and equipment as may be necessary to meet efficiently all normal fire-fighting requirements in its area. Certain items of equipment are standardised so that there is complete interchangeability when a fire is attended by personnel and appliances from more than one area. The principal types of fire-fighting appliances are bought by fire authorities to requirement specifications approved by the Home Office and the Scottish Home and Health Department on the advice of the respective Central Fire Brigades Advisory Councils. These specifications ensure that minimum standards are maintained, and allow sufficient freedom of design to meet special circumstances and encourage further developments.

In the United Kingdom some 5,000 fire-fighting appliances are used (including pumps, turntable ladders, hydraulic platforms, water tenders, emergency tenders, foam tenders and hose-laying lorries), and are housed in just over 2,000 fire stations.

Operational Methods

Each fire authority must appoint a Chief Fire Officer (Firemaster in Scotland) for its fire brigade. The appointment must be approved by the Home Secretary or by the Secretary of State for Scotland.

Central control is exercised by the Chief Fire Officer from brigade headquarters. Divisional officers in charge of the geographical divisions into which most brigade areas are divided are responsible for mobilising forces to deal with outbreaks of fire in their divisions. Constant communication is maintained between divisional and brigade headquarters and, if at any time an outbreak of fire should grow beyond the capabilities of a division, help is sent from one or more neighbouring divisions, or even from the area of another fire authority. Under arrangements for mutual help made by all fire authorities, the nearest available force is sent to a fire, regardless of area boundaries.

Special Services

Fire authorities have discretion to employ their brigades and equipment for purposes other than fire-fighting, and they are used in a variety of emergencies (such as rail, road and aircraft accidents, collapse of buildings, flooding of premises, leakage of noxious gas or liquids and the rescue of people or animals from dangerous situations) for which no charges are made. Brigades are also used, by prior arrangement, for such purposes as emptying swimming pools and filling water tanks.

Fire Prevention

Fire authorities are concerned with fire prevention measures relating to most buildings to which the public have resort or in which they are employed. The authorities are also under a statutory duty to give advice on fire prevention, restricting the spread of fires, and means of escape in case of fire. Courses in fire prevention are held at the Fire Service Technical College for fire brigade officers.

Fire precautions are not normally required by law in private dwellings, so that, in addition to enforcement duties, brigades are also involved in educational and publicity activities to promote fire safety in the home.

Central government is advised on all these fire prevention matters by the Joint Fire Prevention Committee of the Central Fire Brigades Advisory Councils, representing the service and central and local authorities.

Research   Research into the different aspects of fire is undertaken by a number of government departments and other organisations. A comprehensive programme of research into fire brigade operations, organisation, fire-fighting appliances and equipment is conducted by the Home Office with the help of the fire service under the auspices of the Joint Committee on Fire Research of the Central Fire Brigades Advisory Councils. Individual research projects are undertaken by the Home Office Scientific Advisory Branch or, under contract to the Home Office, by other government agencies, notably the Fire Research Station, which is part of the Building Research Establishment of the Department of the Environment, or by private consultants.

The Fire Research Station is the main organisation undertaking the study and investigation of the technical aspects of fire. Its work is supervised by a steering committee, the membership of which is drawn from the Department of the Environment, the Home Office and independent sources.

3 Membership of the European Community

Britain, together with the Irish Republic and Denmark, joined the original six countries—Belgium, France, the Federal Republic of Germany, Italy, Luxembourg and the Netherlands—in the European Community on 1 January 1973.

British membership of the Community was endorsed, after renegotiation of the terms of membership, in June 1975 by a more than two-to-one majority in the first national referendum to be held in Britain. The period of transition following accession ended on 31 December 1977. Britain plays a full and positive part in all Community activities. Details of Britain's participation in specific policies of the Community are contained in the appropriate chapters.

Formation of the European Communities

The European Community consists of three communities set up by separate treaties—the European Coal and Steel Community, the European Economic Community and the European Atomic Energy Community.

The European Coal and Steel Community

The European Coal and Steel Community (ECSC), set up in 1952, established a common market for coal and steel and formed the model for the 'community' approach to economic integration. The ECSC is designed to ensure an orderly supply of coal and steel to member countries, to promote the rational expansion and modernisation of production and to provide better conditions of employment and living for the employees in the industries. The Treaty of Paris, signed in 1951, which established the ECSC, provided for the abolition of duties and quantitative restrictions (or charges having the same effect) on trade in coal and steel between member states; of discrimination by producers in prices, delivery terms or transport rates; of any measures which hampered free choice of supplier; and of restrictive practices resulting in the collusive sharing or exploitation of markets. The treaty also provided for action by the Community over a wide field of activity in the coal and steel industries, the work of the Community being financed mainly by a levy on production. The Community provides funds for capital investment, research and other programmes, as well as loans to help create new jobs where coal seams are being exhausted or where restructuring of the steel industry is taking place. Grants to assist redundant coal and steel workers until they find new employment, or while they are undergoing retraining, are also made.

The European Economic Community

The European Economic Community (EEC) was created by the Treaty of Rome signed by the six countries in 1957. It aimed to promote a continuous and balanced economic expansion by establishing a common market and progressively approximating the member states' economic policies. The preamble to the Treaty included among the basic objectives of the EEC the laying of the foundations for a growing unity among European peoples, the improvement of their living and working conditions, the progressive abolition of restrictions on trade, and the development of the prosperity of overseas countries. The initial steps towards the attainment of these objectives were the creation of a customs union, abolition of internal tariffs and other barriers to trade and establishment of a common external tariff, the development of a common policy for agriculture, and the introduction of measures to establish the free movement of labour, capital and services. At the same time, provision was made for the overseas countries which had special links with the member countries to have preferential treatment in aid and the development of trade. This principle has since been embodied in the Lomé Convention of 1975, which covers 53 countries in Africa, the Caribbean and the Pacific, and in the arrangements made in 1976 with the British dependent territories and the other Community countries' overseas countries and territories (see p 358).

The European Atomic Energy Community

The European Atomic Energy Community (Euratom) was set up by a second treaty signed in Rome in 1957, which provided for the co-ordinated development of members' atomic energy industries and of their other peaceful nuclear activities. Euratom has worked to develop a co-ordinated research programme (for power production, industrial and medical purposes), to ensure the dissemination of technical information, to facilitate the co-ordination of investment in the nuclear field, to ensure an adequate supply of nuclear ores and fuels, and to develop wider commercial outlets. Since 1959, there has been a common market for all nuclear materials and equipment, with a common external tariff on imports of nuclear materials, while the Community has established common nuclear legislation and a common control system for nuclear materials to prevent their diversion to purposes other than those declared.

The Treaty of Accession

The Treaty of Accession was signed by the applicant countries and the original member states in January 1972. Britain thereby became a party to the two treaties of Rome establishing the EEC and Euratom, adjusted as necessary to take account of enlargement. Accession to the ECSC was effected by a decision of the Council of Ministers.

In 1977, following a transitional period during which tariffs on trade in industrial products between Britain and the original six members were progressively reduced, the internal tariffs were abolished and the phased introduction of the common external tariff on British imports from countries neither members of the Community, nor having any special arrangements with it, was completed. Britain had also adopted, progressively, the Community system of agricultural support under the Common Agricultural Policy (CAP). The treaty provided for a slightly longer period of adjustment with regard to payments to the Community budget (see p. 75). Other provisions included those relating to participation in the Community's institutions and to its relations with Commonwealth and other countries.

European Communities Act

The European Communities Act became law in October 1972 and made the legislative changes necessary for Britain to comply with the obligations entailed by membership of the Community and to exercise the rights of membership. The Act gave the force of law in Britain to that part of Community law which is directly applicable in member states. It also contained detailed legislation (in part repealing or amending existing statutes) to implement Community obligations.

Community Law

Community policies are implemented by means of regulations, which are legally binding and directly applicable in all member countries; directives, which are binding, as to the result to be achieved, on those member states to which they are addressed but allow national authorities to decide on the means of implementation; decisions, which are binding on those to whom they are addressed (for example, member states, firms, or individuals); and recommendations and opinions, which have no binding force.

Institutions

The separate institutions established by the treaties for each of the three Communities were merged in 1967. The institutions (the Council of Ministers, the Commission, the European Assembly, the Court of Justice, the Court of Auditors, and the Economic and Social Committee), together with other bodies and organs dealing with specific subjects, provide a framework within which the interests of the member states are represented and reconciled, and common policies formulated and administered. Each state has one representative on the Council; in the other institutions Britain's representation is in line with that of the other large member states (France, Federal Republic of Germany, and Italy). English is one of the six official languages of the Community.

The Council of Ministers is the final decision-making body for all major Community questions and is the only institution established by the treaties whose members, usually the foreign minister or other ministers appropriate to the subject of discussion, directly represent each member country. Most council decisions are taken on the basis of a proposal by the Commission. Where member states' vital interests are involved, the Council's practice is to proceed only on the basis of unanimity. Some issues may be decided by majority, or qualified majority, with votes weighted according to provisions in the Treaty of Accession. A Committee of Permanent Representatives (COREPER) has been established to assist the Council by preparing its meetings and co-ordinating the work of the Council's other subordinate bodies and working groups.

The Presidency of the Council (the chairmanship of meetings of the Council and its subordinate bodies) changes at six-monthly intervals. Britain held the Presidency for the first time from January to June 1977.

The Commission is responsible for formulating detailed policy proposals for submission to the Council of Ministers, for promoting the Community interest and attempting to reconcile national viewpoints and for implementing the provisions of the treaties and Community measures. It has some limited powers of decision relating mainly to the detailed administration of the CAP. It is composed of 13 commissioners nominated by the member governments; two are from Britain. In January 1977, a former British Cabinet Minister took office as President of the Commission. The President, who is appointed for a two-year renewable term, acts as the Commission's representative and is responsible for its general administration. Each of the other commissioners is responsible for one or more of the main Community activities. The Commission is pledged to act independently of national or sectional interests and to formulate its proposals and administer policy in the interests of the Community as a whole. Its proposals are made only after extensive consultation with officials of the national governments and with producers, trade unions, employers' associations and many others.

The Court of Justice interprets and adjudicates on the meaning of the treaties and of any measures taken by the Council of Ministers and Commission under them, hears complaints and appeals brought by or against Community institutions, member states or individuals and gives preliminary rulings on questions referred to it by courts in the member states. As a court of final appeal, its procedure in such cases is broadly similar to that of the highest courts in member states; its rulings are binding on member countries, Community institutions and individuals. The Court consists of nine judges, assisted by four advocates-general.

The European Assembly is composed of 198 nominated members of the parliaments of member states, sitting according to party affiliation and not nationality. Britain is entitled to nominate 36 members. The Assembly is consulted on and debates all the major policy issues of the Community. Members of the Assembly may question the Council of Ministers and Commission and have the power to dismiss the Commission by a two-thirds majority. The Assembly may reject in its entirety the Community's draft annual budget as presented by the Commission and approved by the Council; a formal conciliation procedure has been adopted for use in the event of disagreement between the Assembly and the Council of Ministers on matters with major budgetary or financial implications. In future the Assembly is to be directly elected and its size is to be increased to 410 members, with 81 from Britain. The first direct elections in Britain are to be held on 7 June 1979.

Policy-making in the European Community

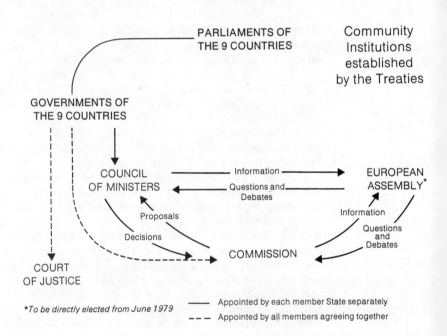

PARLIAMENTS OF THE 9 COUNTRIES

Community Institutions established by the Treaties

GOVERNMENTS OF THE 9 COUNTRIES

COUNCIL OF MINISTERS

Information

Questions and Debates

EUROPEAN ASSEMBLY*

Proposals

Decisions

Information

Questions and Debates

COMMISSION

COURT OF JUSTICE

*To be directly elected from June 1979

——— Appointed by each member State separately

– – – Appointed by all members agreeing together

A new Community institution, the European Court of Auditors, was set up in October 1977, under a treaty of 22 July 1975; it has replaced two previous bodies and carries out a continuous audit of the handling of Community funds by all member states and institutions.

The Economic and Social Committee is a consultative body representing a cross-section of economic interests. Its members—representing employers' organisations, trade unions and other interests—are consulted by the Council of Ministers and Commission during the formulation of policy. Britain is entitled to send 24 members out of a total of 144.

In addition to, and separately from, the institutions operating within the Community framework established by treaty, the member states have set up the European political co-operation machinery for the consideration of important problems of foreign policy. The British Government attaches considerable importance to Community co-operation in this area. The Community foreign ministers meet in this framework four times a year. Under the foreign ministers there is a structure of specialised committees. The country having the Presidency of the Council of Ministers provides the Secretariat. Close contact is maintained with Community institutions when this is appropriate, and decisions are made on the basis of consensus. Ministers meeting within the framework of political co-operation have adopted a code of conduct on employment practices for member states' companies operating in South Africa. Among other problems considered have been the prospects for negotiated settlements in the Middle East and in Rhodesia, and the co-ordination of the member states' policy at the Belgrade meeting on security and co-operation in Europe (see p 104).

The Community's heads of State or of Government meet at least three times a year as the European Council. This Council operates outside the Treaty framework and may consider both Community matters and those arising in the context of political co-operation. It discusses issues unresolved in the Council of Ministers as well as the general problems facing the Community, and lays down guidelines and an overall political direction for future work.

The Community Budget

All member countries contribute to a common budget for certain specific purposes, such as agricultural support (administered by the European Agricultural Guidance and Guarantee Fund, often known by its French initials FEOGA), the European Social Fund (used to finance occupational retraining and re-adaptation programmes, and to encourage manpower mobility), the Regional Development Fund, and administrative costs. The budget is financed by an 'own resources' system; that is, all levies on agricultural imports and all customs duties collected in member states are earmarked for the Community budget, with the exception of a 10 per cent rebate to cover collection costs. Hitherto these funds have been supplemented by direct contributions from the six original member states on the basis of their gross national product (GNP). It is intended that, from 1 January 1979, these contributions be replaced by a proportion (equivalent to a flat rate of up to 1 per cent) of the proceeds of the value added tax (VAT) collected on a harmonised base.

The Treaty of Accession provided that the new member states would participate in the full 'own resources' system as from 1 January 1980. In the intervening years their contributions would be allowed to rise by carefully graduated percentages.

A 'correcting mechanism' has been established providing for repayments to a member state whose contribution to the Community budget is seriously out of line with its share of total Community GNP and its economic situation.

4 Justice and the Law

THE LAW

Although the United Kingdom is a unitary State, it does not have a single body of law. England and Wales, Scotland and Northern Ireland each have their own legal systems and law courts. Common opinions on broader issues, and a common final court of appeal in civil matters have resulted in substantial identity on many points, but considerable differences remain in law and in procedure and practice. In Northern Ireland legal procedure and practice have for centuries closely resembled those of England and Wales but there are often differences in enacted law. However, a large volume of modern legislation applies throughout the United Kingdom.

Sources of Law

The main sources of law in the United Kingdom are legislation, common law and European Community law. Legislation consists of Acts of Parliament, orders, rules and regulations made by ministers under the authority of an Act of Parliament, or by-laws made by local government or other authorities exercising powers conferred upon them by Parliament. Common law is the ancient law of the land as deduced from custom and interpreted by the judges. Generally speaking it has never been precisely defined or codified but forms the basis of the law except when it has been superseded by legislation.

Community law (see p 72) arises out of the United Kingdom's membership of the European Community and is largely confined in impact to economic and certain social matters. In certain circumstances it prevails over domestic law. Community law is normally applied by the domestic courts, but the most authoritative rulings are given by the European Court of Justice (see p 73).

Branches of the Law

A feature common to the domestic legal systems of the United Kingdom is the distinction made between the criminal law and the civil law. The criminal law is concerned with wrongs against the community as a whole while civil law is concerned with the rights, duties and obligations of individual members of society between themselves.

CRIMINAL JUSTICE

Four distinct stages are involved in the British system of criminal justice: the enactment of criminal legislation which, for instance, defines prohibited acts, establishes criminal courts and provides for the treatment of offenders; the prevention of crime and the enforcement of the law—largely matters for the police service; the determination by the courts of the guilt or innocence of people accused of crimes, followed by the selection of appropriate sentences for the guilty; and the treatment of convicted offenders.

A Royal Commission has been set up to examine the powers and duties of the police in England and Wales, the rights and duties of suspects and accused people, and the process of and responsibility for the prosecution of criminal offences.

The Criminal Law

The criminal law, like the law generally, undergoes constant reform in the courts as established principles are interpreted, clarified or refashioned to meet new circumstances. Substantial changes in the law are the responsibility of Parliament. In practice most legislation affecting the criminal law is government-sponsored, but there is often consultation between government departments and bodies representing the legal profession, the police and the probation and prison services. The views of voluntary bodies are also considered.

Crime Statistics Chief constables in England and Wales have a duty to supply statistics relating to offences, offenders, criminal proceedings and the state of crime in their areas. Crime statistics are published annually by the Home Office and further information about crime trends (as well as about police matters) is contained in the annual reports of Her Majesty's Chief Inspector of Constabulary and (for London) the Commissioner of Police of the Metropolis. Similar arrangements operate in Scotland and Northern Ireland.

The differences in the legal systems of the constituent countries make it impractical to analyse in detail trends in criminality for the United Kingdom as a whole. In considering trends for a single country, it has to be remembered that the number of offences recorded as known to the police does not cover all offences committed since some offences go undiscovered and others are not reported to the police. Nevertheless it is clear that, as in western Europe generally, there has been an upsurge in crime since the early 1950s.

As Table 5 shows, there has been a rise in the rate of indictable offences recorded as known to the police in the past few years in most of the main offence groups; in 1977 in England and Wales there were some 5,014 indictable offences per 100,000 population.

In 1977, 428,740 people were convicted by courts in England and Wales of indictable offences. Of these about 16 per cent were women and about 47 per cent were under 21 years of age. Not all apprehended offenders are proceeded against in court. For indictable offences 114,984 people were given formal oral cautions by the police; of these 90 per cent were under 21. For non-indictable offences (excluding motoring offences) oral cautions were given to 34,328 people of whom 49 per cent were aged under 21.

TABLE 5: Known Indictable Offences per 100,000 Population
(England and Wales) 1973–77

Offence Group	1973	1975	1977
Homicide	1	1	1
Violence against the person (excluding homicide)	124	143	166
Sexual offences	52	48	43
Burglary	800	1,061	1,230
Robbery	15	23	28
Theft and handling stolen goods	2,031	2,577	3,028
Fraud and forgery	225	250	246
Criminal damage (excluding damage value £20 and under)	107	160	252
Other offences	16	17	20
TOTAL	3,371	4,280	5,014

Source: *Home Office*

Criminological Research A wide range of criminological and other social research is carried out by the Home Office Research Unit and by the research branch of the Scottish Home and Health Department. The results of the research are published in learned journals, the Home Office Research Studies series and the Scottish Office

Social Research Studies series. Research is also carried out in university departments, much of it financed by the Government. The principal university research establishment is the Institute of Criminology at Cambridge.

Criminal Injuries Compensation Scheme

The Criminal Injuries Compensation Scheme provides *ex gratia* compensation to victims of crimes of violence and people hurt as a result of attempts to arrest offenders and prevent offences. It is administered by a board consisting of legally qualified members appointed by the Home Secretary and the Secretary of State for Scotland after consultation with the Lord Chancellor. Compensation, which is assessed on the basis of common law damages and usually takes the form of a lump sum payment, has totalled over £50 million since the scheme began. The results of a review of the scheme were published in 1978 (see p 438).

The scheme does not apply in Northern Ireland where there is statutory provision in certain circumstances for compensation from public funds for criminal injuries caused to people and also for malicious damage to property (see below). Compensation for property damage includes losses of profits arising from the damage.

Measures to Combat Terrorism

Various temporary measures to deal with terrorism in connection with Northern Ireland have affected some aspects of the British criminal justice system. Under the Prevention of Terrorism (Temporary Provisions) Act 1976, organisations concerned in terrorism connected with Northern Ireland affairs and occurring in the United Kingdom can be proscribed. The appropriate Secretary of State can exclude people concerned in terrorism from Great Britain or Northern Ireland. If the person is not a British citizen he can be excluded from the United Kingdom as a whole. The Act provides powers for the arrest and detention of suspected terrorists. There is also a system of controls at ports on passengers travelling between Great Britain and Ireland.

The Criminal Jurisdiction Act 1975 creates extra-territorial offences under Northern Ireland law so that it is possible to try in the province a person accused of certain offences committed in the Irish Republic. It also enables evidence to be obtained in Northern Ireland for the trial of offences in the Irish Republic. Reciprocal legislation has been passed by the Irish Parliament.

Trials in Northern Ireland criminal courts of offences involving terrorism are heard by a judge sitting without a jury to obviate the possibility of intimidation of jurors.

As a result of the civil disturbances in the province since 1968, over £38·4 million has been paid from public funds in compensation for personal injuries and about £248 million for damage to property.

THE POLICE SERVICE

Crime prevention and crime investigation, the preservation of the peace and the bringing to trial of offenders are primarily the concern of the police service. The action of the British police in enforcing the law rests mainly upon common consent, for there are only a small number of officers in relation to the population (roughly one officer to 450 people). Officers do not normally carry firearms (their only weapon is a wooden truncheon) and there are strict limitations on police powers.

Forces

There are 43 police forces in England and Wales, eight in Scotland and one in Northern Ireland. Each force is responsible for law enforcement in its own area, but there is constant co-operation among them.

Outside London most counties (regions or islands in Scotland) have their own police forces, though in the interests of efficiency several have combined their forces. In London, the Metropolitan Police Force, with headquarters at

New Scotland Yard, is responsible for an area within a radius of about 24 kilometres (15 miles) from the centre but excluding the City of London, where there is a separate force. The strength of the regular police force in Great Britain is about 120,000 (including about 8,890 policewomen), the size of individual police forces depending on the area and population which they serve. The strength of the Metropolitan Police Force is 22,240.

In addition to the regular police forces, constabularies are maintained by the British Railways Board, the United Kingdom Atomic Energy Authority, the Ministry of Defence and a few other public bodies. Considerable numbers of people are employed by commercial security organisations which are subject to the ordinary law of the land.

Police Authorities and Chief Constables

Each of the regular police forces is maintained by a police authority, a committee consisting of local councillors and, in England and Wales, magistrates. The police authority for the Metropolitan Police Force is the Home Secretary. In Northern Ireland the police authority is appointed by the Secretary of State.

The primary duty of the police authority is to provide an adequate and efficient police force in the area for which it is responsible. Its functions, some of which are subject to ministerial approval, include appointing the chief constable, deputy chief constable and assistant chief constables and, if necessary, calling upon them to retire; fixing the authorised establishment (maximum permitted strength of the force); and providing buildings and equipment. In the Metropolitan Police area the chief officer of police and his immediate subordinates are appointed on the recommendation of the Home Secretary.

Chief constables are responsible for the direction and control of police forces and for the appointment, promotion and discipline of all ranks below deputy or assistant chief constable. They are generally answerable to the police authorities on matters of efficiency, and must submit a written report every year.

Central Authorities

The Home Secretary, the Secretary of State for Scotland and the Secretary of State for Northern Ireland are concerned with the organisation, administration and operation of the police service. They approve the appointment of chief constables, and may require a police authority to retire a chief constable in the interests of efficiency, call for a report from a chief constable on any matters relating to the policing of his area, or cause a local inquiry to be held. They are also empowered to make regulations covering such matters as police ranks; qualifications for appointment, promotion and retirement; discipline; hours of duty, leave, pay and allowances; and uniform and equipment. Some of these regulations are first negotiable on the Police Council (a negotiating body on which are represented the police authorities, police staff associations and ministers); others are discussed on representative advisory bodies, together with any general questions affecting the police service.

All police forces in Great Britain (except the Metropolitan Police for which the Home Secretary is directly responsible) are subject to inspection on behalf of the Secretaries of State. Inspectors of constabulary carry out, under Her Majesty's Chief Inspector of Constabulary and Her Majesty's Chief Inspector of Constabulary for Scotland, a formal annual inspection of the forces in their regions, inquiring into efficiency and reporting to the Home Secretary or the Secretary of State for Scotland. Annual reports are published, covering the whole range of police matters. The inspectors also maintain close touch with forces for which they are responsible, and have various advisory functions.

In Northern Ireland periodic inspections of the Royal Ulster Constabulary are made by Her Majesty's Chief Inspector of Constabulary.

Finance

The income of police authorities comes from central and local government. The Government's contribution, a half of approved expenditure (a third in the City of London), is conditional on the Home Secretary or the Secretary of State for Scotland being satisfied that the force is being efficiently administered and maintained.

Officers and Ancillary Staff

In general, entry to the regular police force is open to men and women between the ages of 18½ and 30. A chief constable may approve the appointment of especially suitable older men and women.

The standard police ranks in England, Scotland and Wales, except in the Metropolitan Police and City of London Police areas, are: chief constable, assistant chief constable, chief superintendent, superintendent, chief inspector, inspector, sergeant and constable. The chief officer in the Metropolitan Police area, the Commissioner of Police of the Metropolis, is assisted by a deputy commissioner and four assistant commissioners. Next in rank are deputy assistant commissioners, and then commanders; from chief superintendent the ranks are the same as in the regions. In the City of London the ranks are the same as in the regions except that the chief officer is the Commissioner of Police and the second in command is an assistant commissioner. Police ranks in Northern Ireland are very similar to those in the rest of the United Kingdom.

Cadet training is designed to prepare boys and girls between 16 and 18½ years of age for a police service career. They have no police powers but, in addition to their educational studies and physical and adventure training, are instructed in elementary police work.

In order to release as many uniformed police officers as possible for operational duties, police authorities employ some 40,000 civilians on administrative duties (pay, records, finance and other general subjects), technical duties (fingerprint, scenes of crime and control room work) and other duties, including catering and domestic work.

Traffic wardens (of whom there are nearly 5,460) discharge specified duties normally undertaken by the police. They may be authorised to serve fixed penalty notices[1] for some minor traffic offences; to man police car pounds (except in Scotland and Northern Ireland); to enforce some aspects of the vehicle excise laws; and to obtain the names and addresses of people thought to have committed certain types of traffic offence. They may also be authorised to direct traffic, to act as parking attendants at street parking places, and as school-crossing patrols. Wardens are under the control of the chief constable.

Each police force has an attachment of special constables, who volunteer to perform police duties without pay in their spare time. In England and Wales, they act as auxiliaries to the regular force when required. In Scotland they are employed only in emergencies although they may be assigned for duty for training. In Northern Ireland there is a largely part-time (and paid) reserve.

Status and Duties

A police officer in Great Britain is an independent holder of a public office; he is an agent of the law of the land, not of the police authority nor of the central Government, and he may be sued or prosecuted in respect of any wrongful act he may commit in the performance of his duties. Strict procedures govern the way complaints against police officers are handled and an independent element has been introduced into the way complaints are investigated.

---

[1] A fixed penalty notice gives the recipient the option of paying a specified sum to the clerk of the appropriate court instead of having his case tried in the ordinary way.

Members of the police service may not belong to a trade union nor may they withdraw their labour in furtherance of a trade dispute. All ranks, however, have their own associations which can make representations to ministers or to police authorities on matters of interest or concern to their members.

Police work ranges from the protection of people and property, road or street patrolling and traffic control to crime prevention, criminal investigation and the arrest of offenders. In urban areas, particularly, police officers often have to deal with social problems and, where necessary, they bring in other social agencies and expert help. In England and Wales they also prosecute accused people (see p 82).

The main departments in all forces are the uniform department, the criminal investigation department, the traffic department and specialised departments, including river or marine police, mounted police, and dog handlers.

Common Services

A number of common services are provided by the central government departments and by arrangements made between forces. The most important of these are: training services; a forensic science service in England and Wales with seven regional laboratories (in addition to the Metropolitan Police Laboratory); telecommunications services which supply and maintain police radio equipment; and central and provincial criminal records which are available to all forces. In addition, regional crime squads, consisting of teams of experienced detectives from several forces, and operating under a committee of chief constables, investigate major crimes involving inquiries in more than one police area. The Scottish Crime Squad assists forces in the investigation and prevention of crime.

Certain special services such as liaison with the International Criminal Police Organisation (Interpol) are provided for other British forces by the Metropolitan Police Force. The services of the Force are available, on request, to assist any other police force in England and Wales in criminal investigation, as are the services of the Fraud Squad, which is run jointly by the Metropolitan Police and the City of London Police for the investigation of company frauds.

Research into technical services is organised in separate units within the Home Office Police Department: the Forensic Science Service Unit and its regional laboratories; a Central Research Establishment staffed by scientists; and a Directorate of Telecommunications with one section of engineers engaged solely on research and development. The Police Scientific Development Branch is staffed by scientists and technicians assisted by police officers seconded from the Police Research Services Unit; the Branch and the Unit are concerned with operational research into police methods and the development of equipment for police forces. The Economic Planning Unit, composed mainly of economists and accountants, is responsible for the development of a planning–programming–budgeting system for the police; this includes the production of programme accounts and studies of the use of resources.

Powers of Arrest

In England and Wales arrest may be made on a warrant issued by a judicial authority on sworn information laid before it or without warrant. An arrested person is entitled to ask the police to notify a named person, such as a relative or a solicitor, about his or her arrest. The police may delay notification if they think it necessary in the interests of the investigation, the prevention of crime or the apprehension of offenders.

Anyone arrested without a warrant may be released by the police on bail and must be so released if he or she cannot be brought before a magistrates' court within 24 hours, unless the alleged offence is serious. If remanded in custody, the defendant must be brought before a magistrates' court as soon as practicable. People granted bail have to surrender to custody at an appointed time and place. On appearance before a magistrates' court, a defendant may be refused bail only if there are substantial grounds for believing that he or she might abscond, commit further offences or otherwise interfere with the course of justice; if bail is refused by the magistrates, the defendant can apply to a judge of the High Court and, if committed to the Crown Court, may apply for bail to that court. In 1976 some 83 per cent of people committed for trial by magistrates were given bail.

Once anyone has been charged with an offence, the police may not put any further questions to him, save, in exceptional circumstances, to prevent or minimise harm or loss to any person or to the public, or to clear up an ambiguity in a previous answer or statement. This is laid down by the Judges' Rules which do not have the force of law but carry very great weight.

A person detained in custody who thinks that the grounds for his detention are not lawful[1] may apply for a writ of habeas corpus against the person who detained him, this person being required to appear before the court on the day named to justify the detention. An application for such a writ is normally made to a divisional court of the High Court either by the person detained or by someone acting on his behalf.

In Scotland the police have similar powers of arrest as have the police in England and Wales. Although the Judges' Rules do not apply, an arrested person must be cautioned and have the charge read over to him. Thereafter, only his voluntary statements are used in evidence at his trial, and the court will reject any statements made by him unless it is satisfied that they have been fairly obtained. When anyone is apprehended he must be brought before a court with the least possible delay. Where a prosecution on indictment is contemplated, the accused is brought before a judge for judicial examination and the judge may then commit him for trial or for further examination. Eight days may elapse between commitment for further examination and commitment for trial.

People in custody in Scotland, other than those charged with murder or treason, may be liberated on bail by the sheriff or, if the offence is within the jurisdiction of a summary court other than the sheriff court, by that court or by the police. Even in the case of murder or treason, bail may be granted at the discretion of the Lord Advocate or the High Court of Justiciary. There is a right of appeal to the High Court by the accused person against the refusal of bail, by the prosecutor against the granting of bail, or by either party against the amount fixed. The writ of habeas corpus does not apply in Scotland, but the High Court of Justiciary has power to release anyone unlawfully detained and trials must be brought to a conclusion within 110 days of committal to custody.

CRIMINAL COURTS

Prosecution

The decision to prosecute normally rests, in England and Wales, with the police and in Scotland with public prosecutors. In Northern Ireland there is a Director of Public Prosecutions (see p 83). In England and Wales (and very exceptionally in Scotland) a private person may institute criminal proceedings. Police have powers to issue cautions (warnings in Scotland) instead of prosecuting, especially in the case of young people.

---

[1] Detention is lawful in pursuance of criminal justice, for contempt of court or of either House of Parliament and when expressly authorised by Parliament. It is also lawful in the case of persons found to be mentally disordered.

England and Wales In England and Wales some offences can only be prosecuted by, or with the consent of, the Attorney General or the Director of Public Prosecutions, the latter acting under the superintendence of the Attorney General and being responsible to him. Where the consent of the Attorney General is required, the Director is in practice responsible for prosecution; offences in the category include crimes such as bribery and corruption of officials, and the use and possession of explosives.

The Director has to prosecute cases such as treason and murder. The police must report to him a further list of offences, including serious offences against the person, sedition, criminal offences by police officers, and offences relating to obscene or indecent publications. The Director does not necessarily prosecute all such cases referred to him but may do so in any that appear to be important or where he thinks intervention is necessary; otherwise proceedings are conducted by solicitors employed by the police. The Director also considers whether proceedings should be taken in cases reported to him by government departments. In addition he advises the police and others concerned with the administration of the criminal law.

When cases go for trial, barristers in private practice are instructed to appear on the Director's behalf; at the Central Criminal Court in London, these are drawn from a panel of 'Treasury Counsel' appointed by the Attorney General.

Scotland The prosecution process in Scotland is different from that in the rest of the United Kingdom. The Lord Advocate (see p 99) is responsible for the prosecution of all crimes but delegates most of the work to the Solicitor General (see p 99), to ten Advocates Depute and to procurators fiscal. The permanent adviser to the Lord Advocate on prosecution matters is the Crown Agent who is head of the procurator fiscal service and is assisted by a staff of civil servants known as the Crown Office. Prosecutions in the High Court of Justiciary are prepared by the Crown Office while crimes tried before the sheriff and district courts are prosecuted by the procurators fiscal who are lawyers and full-time civil servants. The police investigate offences known to them and report to the procurator fiscal who decides whether or not to prosecute, subject to the discretion and control of the Crown Office.

Northern Ireland The Director of Public Prosecutions for Northern Ireland, who is responsible to the Attorney General, prosecutes all offences tried on indictment. He can also prosecute such summary offences or classes of summary offence as he considers should be dealt with by him, for example, those which he regards as serious or offences of a political or sectarian kind. Other summary offences are prosecuted by the police.

Courts in England and Wales Magistrates' courts deal with about 98 per cent of criminal cases in England and Wales, and conduct preliminary investigations into the more serious offences. The Crown Court, situated in a number of towns and cities, takes all criminal work above the level of magistrates' courts.

Magistrates' Courts Magistrates' courts hear and determine charges against people accused of 'summary offences', that is those that can be legally disposed of by magistrates sitting without a jury. There are some 700 courts and some 23,500 magistrates. Each court normally consists of a bench of three lay unpaid magistrates whose function is to ascertain the facts of a case and apply the law to them. The magistrates are advised on points of law and procedure by a clerk to the justices (or one of his assistants) who is normally legally qualified and is also in charge of the court's administrative arrangements. Magistrates are appointed by the Lord Chancellor.

In inner London and some other large urban areas where the pressure of work is heavy and continuous there are also professional 'stipendiary' magistrates who are full-time, salaried and legally qualified. They usually preside alone.

Magistrates must as a rule sit in open court, but when they make preliminary inquiries into a more serious case to see whether there is sufficient evidence to justify committal for trial in the Crown Court the evidence must not be reported in the press at the time except at the defendant's request, unless the magistrates discharge him.

Magistrates cannot usually impose a sentence of more than six months' imprisonment or a fine exceeding £1,000. If an offence carries a higher maximum penalty, they may commit the offender for sentence to the Crown Court if they consider their own power inadequate.

To hear cases involving people under the age of 17 brought before the court in 'care' (see p 92) or criminal proceedings, and to deal with applications for the adoption of children, magistrates' courts sit as juvenile courts, either in a different room or building from other courts, or at a different time; only limited publicity is allowed. If a young person under the age of 17 is charged jointly with someone of 17 or over, the case is heard in the ordinary magistrates' court. If the young person is found guilty, that court remits the case to a juvenile court, unless it wishes to dispose of the case by discharge or fine.

The Crown Court

The Crown Court is responsible for trials of the more serious cases, the sentencing of offenders committed for sentence by magistrates' courts, and appeals from magistrates' courts. It has about 90 centres and is served by High Court judges, full-time 'circuit judges' and part-time recorders. All contested trials in the court take place before a jury. A High Court judge sits alone for the most serious cases. A circuit judge or recorder sits with between two and four magistrates for appeals and committals for sentence from magistrates' courts and may sit with magistrates to try the less important cases.

The Crown Court may impose a fine of any amount on a convicted offender and, within the maximum penalty determined for the offence by Parliament, any other custodial or non-custodial penalty.

In 1977 the Crown Court tried 68,547 people; 46,957 pleaded guilty to at least one charge and 21,590 not guilty to all charges. About a half of defendants charged with one offence and pleading not guilty were acquitted.

Appeals

A person convicted by a magistrates' court may appeal to the Crown Court against the sentence imposed and, if he contested his guilt, the conviction. Where the appeal is on a point of law, either the prosecutor or the defendant may appeal from the magistrates' court to the High Court, which sits in London and some regional centres (see p 94). Appeals from the Crown Court, either against conviction or against sentence, are usually made to the Court of Appeal (Criminal Division). A further appeal from the Court of Appeal to the House of Lords can be brought if the court certifies that a point of law of general public importance is involved and it appears to the court or the House of Lords that the point is one that ought to be considered by the House. A prosecutor or defendant may appeal to the House of Lords from a decision of the High Court in a criminal case.

The Attorney General may seek the opinion of the Court of Appeal on a point of law which has arisen in a case where a person tried on indictment is acquitted; the court has power to refer the point to the House of Lords if necessary. The acquittal in the original case is not affected, nor is the identity of the acquitted person revealed without his consent.

Scotland

There are three criminal courts: the High Court of Justiciary, the sheriff court and the district court. The High Court tries serious crimes such as murder, treason and rape while the sheriff court is concerned with less serious offences and the district court with minor offences.

Criminal cases are heard either under solemn procedure, when proceedings are taken on indictment and the judge sits with a jury of 15 members, or under summary procedure, when the judge sits without a jury. All cases in the High Court of Justiciary and the more serious ones in the sheriff courts are tried by a judge and jury. Proceedings are taken under summary procedure in the less serious cases in the sheriff courts, and in the district courts.

A government committee is considering the effect on the criminal courts and the prosecution system of the volume of minor offences dealt with by summary prosecution and whether some other process could be devised to deal with such offences while maintaining safeguards for accused persons.

District Courts

District courts are the administrative responsibility of the district and islands local authorities (see p 62). The judges are lay justices of the peace including up to one-quarter of the membership of district and islands authorities who may be nominated as *ex officio* justices. In Glasgow there are three stipendiary magistrates who are full-time salaried lawyers.

Sheriff Courts

Scotland is divided into six sheriffdoms which are further divided into sheriff court districts, each of which has a sheriff who is the judge of the court.

The High Court of Justiciary

The High Court of Justiciary is Scotland's supreme criminal court. It is both a trial court and an appeal court. Any one of the following judges is entitled to try cases in the High Court: the Lord Justice General (the head of the court), the Lord Justice Clerk (the next judge in seniority) or one of the Lord Commissioners of Justiciary who preside at sessions of the court in other towns. The main seat of the court is in Edinburgh where all appeals are heard.

Appeals

All appeals are dealt with by the High Court of Justiciary. In both solemn and summary procedure, an appeal may be brought against conviction, or sentence, or both. The High Court cannot order a retrial if it sets aside a conviction. Appeals are heard by three or more judges; there is no further appeal to the House of Lords.

Children's Hearings

Children under 16 years (and in some cases people between 16 and 18) who have committed an offence or are considered to need compulsory care may be brought before an informal children's hearing comprising three members of the local community (see p 93).

Northern Ireland

The day-to-day work of dealing summarily with minor local criminal cases in Northern Ireland is carried out by magistrates' courts presided over by a professional, paid resident magistrate. Young offenders under 17 years and young people under 17 who need care, protection and control are dealt with by juvenile courts consisting of the resident magistrate and two lay members (at least one of whom must be a woman) with special qualifications for dealing with juveniles. Appeals may be made to a county court.

The county courts and the High Court of Justice share a similar jurisdiction in criminal matters, except that the most serious cases, such as murder, are tried in the High Court only. Other cases are heard at the court where the trial can be heard soonest. For people convicted of serious crimes there may be an appeal to the Court of Criminal Appeal and from there to the House of

Lords. Government proposals to reform the system have been passed by Parliament. The main changes proposed are the establishment of a Crown Court for the trial of all criminal cases on indictment and the abolition of the Court of Criminal Appeal and the transfer of its jurisdiction to the Court of Appeal.

Trial

All criminal trials in the United Kingdom take the form of a contest between the prosecution and the defence.

Since criminal law in Britain presumes the innocence of the accused until his guilt has been proved, the prosecution is not granted any advantage, apparent or real, over the defence. A defendant has the right to employ a legal adviser for his defence and if he cannot afford to pay he may be granted legal aid wholly or partly from public funds. If remanded in custody he may be visited in prison by his legal adviser to ensure that his defence is properly prepared. In England and Wales during the preparation of the case, the prosecution usually informs the defence of any relevant documents which it is not proposed to put in evidence and discloses them if asked to do so. The prosecution should also inform the defence of any witnesses whose evidence may assist the accused and whom the prosecution does not propose to call. The defence or prosecution may suggest that the mental state of the defendant is such that he is unfit to be tried. A jury must decide whether or not this is so. If they find that it is, the defendant is admitted to a hospital specified by the Home Secretary in England and Wales, and in Northern Ireland to one specified by a health and social services board (see p 114).

Criminal trials in England and Wales are normally held in open court and the rules of evidence (which are concerned with the way facts may be proved and what facts may not be proved) are rigorously applied. If evidence is admitted in contravention of the law, a conviction can be quashed on appeal.

During the trial the defendant has the right to hear and subsequently to cross-examine (normally through his lawyer) all the witnesses for the prosecution; to call his own witnesses who, if they will not attend the trial of their own free will, may be legally compelled to attend; and to address the court either in person or through his lawyer—the defence having the right to the last speech at the trial. Moreover, the defendant cannot be questioned unless he consents to be sworn as a witness in his own defence. When he does testify, he may only be cross-examined about his character or other conduct in exceptional circumstances and generally, the prosecution may not introduce evidence of such matters. Although confessions made in the course of previous judicial proceedings are admissible as evidence if they have been made upon oath, no confessions made in any other circumstances are admitted unless it can be proved that they were made voluntarily.

The Jury

In jury trials the judge determines questions of law, sums up the evidence for the benefit of the jury, and discharges the accused or passes sentence. Only the jury decides whether the defendant is guilty or not guilty. If the jury cannot reach a unanimous verdict, the judge may direct it to bring in a majority verdict provided that, in the normal jury of 12 people, there are not more than two dissentients. If the jury returns a verdict of 'not guilty', the prosecution has no right of appeal against the verdict and the defendant cannot be tried again for the same offence. From a verdict of 'guilty' there is a right of appeal by the defendant to the appropriate court.

A jury is completely independent of the judiciary. Once members are sworn in, they are protected from interference of any kind. Both the prosecution and the defence can object to particular jurors. In England and Wales people whose names appear on the electoral register are liable for jury service; in Scotland, where the minimum age for jurors is 21, not all those on the register are eligible to serve as the minimum voting age is 18.

Scotland

At summary trials in Scotland the accused is asked to plead to the charge at the first calling of the case and, if he pleads guilty, the court may dispose of the case. Where the plea is 'not guilty', the court may proceed to trial at once or, more usually, may appoint a later date.

In Scottish trials on indictment, the first 'pleading' proceedings take place in the sheriff court, when the accused person is called upon to plead guilty or not guilty. If he pleads not guilty, the case is continued to the second 'trial' proceedings in the appropriate court. If he pleads guilty, and the case is to be dealt with in the sheriff court, the sheriff may dispose of it at once. If it is a High Court case, it is continued to the second proceedings for disposal.

The trial proceedings are held at least nine days after the pleading proceedings, either before the sheriff or the High Court, with a jury of 15. Evidence is presented without opening speeches, and there are closing speeches for the prosecution and for the defence, followed by the judge's charge to the jury. The jury may return a verdict of 'not guilty' or 'not proven', both of which result in acquittal, or they may find the accused 'guilty', in which case the court proceeds to deliver sentence. The verdict may be by a simple majority. With a few minor exceptions, no person may be convicted without the evidence of at least two witnesses, or corroboration of one witness by facts and circumstances which clearly implicate the accused in the crime.

SPECIAL COURTS
Coroners' Courts

Most of the work of coroners' courts involves the investigation of violent and unnatural deaths or of sudden deaths where the cause is unknown. Cases may be brought to the notice of the local coroner (a senior lawyer or doctor appointed by local government) by doctors, the police, various public authorities or members of the public, and it is his duty to hold an inquiry into how, when and where the deceased died. If the death is a sudden one of which the cause is unknown, the coroner need not hold an inquest in court, but may order a post-mortem examination to determine cause of death. If, however, he has reason to believe that the deceased died a violent or unnatural death or died in prison or other circumstances provided for by statute, he must hold an inquest.

In Scotland the office of coroner does not exist. The procurator fiscal inquires privately into all sudden and suspicious deaths in his district and may report the result of his inquiries to the Crown Agent.

Coroners in Northern Ireland are mostly senior lawyers; the work of their courts is similar to that of coroners' courts in England and Wales.

Courts Martial

Courts martial have jurisdiction over serving members of the armed forces and in certain circumstances their dependants and other civilians who accompany them outside the United Kingdom. The courts do not deal with certain serious offences if committed in the United Kingdom, such as treason, murder, manslaughter, treason-felony and rape. Other non-military criminal offences committed by servicemen in the United Kingdom are also normally dealt with in the ordinary courts.

TREATMENT OF OFFENDERS

Although custodial treatment is an important part of British penal practice, it is increasingly seen as the last resort in dealing with people who break the law.

Sentencing

The criminal courts' discretion to select the sentence most appropriate for an offender is modified by statutory provisions designed to ensure that prison sentences are kept to a minimum. In England, Wales and Northern Ireland a person who has not previously served a custodial sentence of a particular kind may not be sentenced to custodial treatment of that kind unless he is legally represented or has chosen not to be, and in the case of imprisonment unless the court is satisfied that no other sentence will suffice. In England and Wales, extended sentences longer than the normal maximum term may be imposed on persistent offenders. In the case of murder there is a mandatory penalty of imprisonment for life. This is the maximum penalty for a number of serious offences such as robbery, rape, arson and manslaughter. A few very rare serious offences, such as treason, carry the death penalty but it is not mandatory.

In Scotland, unless the sentence is limited by statute, the maximum penalty is determined by the status of the court trying the accused. In trials on indictment, the High Court may impose a sentence of imprisonment for any term up to life and the Sheriff Court up to two years. In summary cases, the sheriff may impose up to six months' imprisonment.

Non-Custodial Treatment

Non-custodial treatment includes fines; probation; absolute or (in England, Wales and Northern Ireland) conditional discharge for up to three years (one year in Northern Ireland)—a discharge being made when the court feels that there is no need to impose punishment on a convicted person; and 'binding over' where the offender is required to pledge money, with or without sureties, to keep the peace and be of good behaviour.

A recent innovation is the community service order for offenders convicted of imprisonable offences in England and Wales. Similar schemes are to be introduced in Scotland and Northern Ireland. Examples of work done include decorating houses and flats for old people and building adventure playgrounds for children. Between 40 and 240 hours' service may be ordered within a period of 12 months.

An offender in England, Wales and Northern Ireland may also with his consent have his sentence deferred for up to six months to enable a court to arrive at the most appropriate sentence, taking into account his conduct after, for instance, some expected change in his circumstances.

The courts may order an offender to pay compensation for any personal injury, loss or damage resulting from his offence and, in the case of major crimes against property, bankruptcy proceedings may be brought against him in England and Wales. In Scotland a committee has reported to the Secretary of State and the Lord Advocate on the question of the potential role of the criminal court in ordering reparation by the offender to the victim.

In England, Wales and Northern Ireland a judge is free to pass a suspended sentence of not more than two years. The sentence is not served by the offender unless he is convicted of a further offence punishable with imprisonment; in that event the suspended sentence normally takes effect and another sentence may be imposed for the new offence. An offender receiving a suspended sentence of more than six months may be made subject to supervision by a probation officer for all or part of the period. Under the Criminal Law Act 1977 courts in England and Wales will have power, when passing a sentence of between six months' and two years' imprisonment, to order that part should be served and the rest held in suspense; the suspended part will be not less than one quarter nor more than three quarters of the whole.

In certain circumstances the courts may order the forfeiture of property involved in the commission of a crime. An offender convicted of a serious crime may be disqualified from driving if a motor vehicle was used in its commission.

In most circumstances, a person convicted of a criminal offence need not reveal or admit it after a rehabilitation period of from six months to ten years depending on the nature of the sentence imposed. This does not apply to those who have received a prison sentence of more than $2\frac{1}{2}$ years.

Probation

Probation is designed to secure the rehabilitation of an offender while he continues his ordinary life under the supervision of a probation officer, whose duty it is to advise, assist and befriend him. Before making a probation order (which lasts for between one and three years), the court must explain its effects and make sure that the probationer understands that if he fails to comply with the requirements of the order he will be liable to be dealt with again for the original offence. A probation order can be made only if the offender is 17 years of age or over (14 in Northern Ireland) and must have his consent; it usually requires the probationer to keep in regular touch with the probation officer, to be of good behaviour and to lead an industrious life. It may also require him to live in a specified place, or in appropriate circumstances, to submit to treatment for a mental condition.

In England and Wales the probation service is administered locally by probation and after-care committees consisting of local magistrates and co-opted members with legal and specialist interests. In Northern Ireland it is administered by the Northern Ireland Office. Probation officers are usually members of small teams, although each has a large measure of independence in his or her casework with an offender.

Probation and after-care committees may, with the approval of the Home Secretary, provide and maintain day training centres (which offenders may be required to attend for up to 60 days), bail hostels, probation hostels and other establishments for use in connection with the rehabilitation of offenders. The service is also responsible for administering the community service scheme.

In England, Wales and Northern Ireland, the services of probation and after-care officers are available to every criminal court.

In Scotland, offenders subject to probation orders or to after-care supervision following release from a penal institution are supervised by specially approved local authority social workers.

Prisons

Although the courts have made proportionately less and less use of prison as a penalty for criminal activity, there has been an increase in the prison population as a result of the rise in crime. In 1977 the average number of people in prisons, borstals, and detention centres was about 41,570 in England and Wales and 4,870 in Scotland; there are 135 prison service establishments and the size of the prison service in 1977 was 24,500.

Prisons to which offenders may be committed directly by a court are known as 'local prisons'; all are closed establishments. Other prisons, which may be open or closed, receive prisoners on transfer from local prisons (open prisons do not have physical barriers to prevent escape). Sentenced prisoners in England and Wales are classified into four groups for the purposes of security. Separate prisons cater for women prisoners.

People awaiting trial are entitled to privileges not granted to convicted prisoners and, as far as practicable, are separated from convicted prisoners. Prisoners under 21 are separated from older prisoners.

Many British prisons were built during the nineteenth century and are unsatisfactory by modern standards. Overcrowding is also a problem. However, a number of new prisons have been built in the past few years, and existing establishments are being redeveloped and modernised, as far as limited resources allow.

Remission of Sentence and Parole

All prisoners in Great Britain serving a determinate sentence of more than one month, except those sentenced to imprisonment for life, are allowed remission of one-third of their sentence provided that this does not reduce their sentence to less than 31 days (in Scotland, 30 days). Remission may be forfeited for serious misconduct in prison. In addition, prisoners serving fixed sentences of more than 18 months become eligible for consideration for release on parole after serving one-third of their sentence or 12 months, whichever expires later.

The parole licence remains in force until the date on which the prisoner would have been released had not parole been granted. The licence prescribes the conditions with which the offender must comply when on parole. About 10 per cent of prisoners granted parole in England and Wales in 1977 were recalled to prison.

Prisoners serving life sentences are also eligible for release on licence, after consultation with the judiciary and on the recommendation of the Parole Board. Those released in this way remain on licence for the rest of their lives and are subject to recall at any time should the circumstances warrant it.

In Northern Ireland, where there is no parole scheme, prisoners receive one-half remission on determinate sentences, provided that remission does not reduce the sentence to below 31 days. For those serving over a year, a court can order all or part of the outstanding balance of the remitted period to be served in the event of reconviction for an imprisonable offence in the remitted period, in addition to any penalty imposed for a further offence.

Prison Industries

The main aim of the prison industries is to give inmates training and experience to assist them to get and keep jobs when released. Prison industries generally consist of clothing and textile manufacture, weaving and knitting, engineering, woodwork, laundering, light engineering work, and electrical and mechanical production. A wide range of semi-skilled work is available and there is one industrial prison. Some products such as clothing are for use by the prison service, while others are supplied for government departments or sold on the open market. The farming and horticultural industries contribute to the prison food provision. A few prisoners are employed outside prison. Small payments are made to inmates for the work they do; in some prisons, incentive schemes provide an opportunity for higher earnings on the basis of output and skill.

Education

Education for those in custody is financed by the prison service and provided by the local education authorities. Each prison in England and Wales has an education officer assisted mainly by part-time teachers and a small number of full-time ones. Education is compulsory for young offenders below school leaving age. Education resources for other inmates are devoted to teaching and improving literacy and the provision of vocational training. Some prisoners study for public examinations (including those of the Open University). When resources permit there is teaching in recreational and leisure pursuits.

Physical Education

The purposes of physical education and remedial gymnastics are to promote health and fitness and to ensure that inmates are physically competent to sustain the demands of outside employment. Physical education is voluntary for adults but those under 21 have to attend a certain number of classes. Many establishments, however, do not have the proper facilities.

Medical Services

The prison medical service has a general responsibility for the physical and mental health of all those in custody. Each establishment has accommodation for sick people and there are some larger prison hospitals (some with up to 100 beds) to which patients can be transferred if necessary. Four prisons have surgical units and patients can also be transferred to hospitals within the National Health Service. There is one specialist psychiatric prison and some other centres in the prison service where patients can receive psychiatric care. In some establishments there is special treatment for alcoholics.

Psychological
Services

Prison psychologists are involved in the evaluation of treatment programmes and regimes, contribute to the management and treatment of individuals and groups, take part in advisory and training work with prison staff, and clinically examine selected inmates.

Privileges and
Discipline

All prisoners, from the beginning of their sentence, have a general right to write and receive letters and to be visited by their relatives at regular intervals. They also have such privileges as additional letters and visits, the use of books, periodicals and newspapers, and the right to make purchases from the canteen with money they have earned in prison. Depending on the facilities available, they may be granted the further privileges of dining and recreation in association and watching television in the evening.

Breaches of discipline are dealt with by the prison governor, or by the board of visitors (visiting committee in Scotland), who have power to order, among other penalties, forfeiture of remission and forfeiture of privileges. Boards of visitors consist of lay people, two of whom must be magistrates.

Welfare

The welfare of prisoners is the general concern of all the prison staff. Much of this work is the responsibility of probation officers (in Scotland social workers) stationed in prisons who help prisoners in their relations with individuals and agencies outside and make plans for after-care on release.

Prisoners may also receive visits from specially appointed prison visitors whose work is voluntary and, in England and Wales, is co-ordinated and guided by the National Association of Prison Visitors.

Chaplains give spiritual help and advice to inmates and are increasingly involved in management decisions affecting their needs and quality of life. A chaplain of the Church of England (in Scotland of the Church of Scotland, and in Northern Ireland of the Church of Ireland and of the Presbyterian Church), a Roman Catholic priest and a Methodist minister are appointed to every prison. Ministers of other denominations are appointed or specially called in as needed.

Discharge

All prisons in England and Wales arrange pre-release preparations for prisoners. Any person serving a sentence of four years or more is considered for outside employment for a period before release. If selected, work is found outside the prison for about the last six months of sentence; during the period the prisoner may live in a separate part of the prison or in a hostel outside. Normal wages are paid so that he can resume support for his family.

Periods of home leave may be granted in the last nine months of sentence to those serving two years or more to enable them to contact people, such as potential employers, able to assist them on release.

After-care

The aim of after-care, run by the probation and after-care service, is to assist the offender on his return to society by offering him the help of a skilled case worker. Compulsory supervision by a probation officer is given to offenders under 21 when released, adult offenders released on parole, and those released on licence from a sentence of life imprisonment. A voluntary system is offered to the remainder. After-care is also provided by a number of voluntary societies, most of which are members of the National Association for the Care and Resettlement of Offenders. Hostels and other forms of accommodation are provided, often with some financial help from the Home Office.

In Northern Ireland after-care duties are carried out by probation and after-care officers and in Scotland by local authority social workers.

Children in Trouble

England and Wales

In England and Wales no child under ten years can be held guilty of any offence. A child aged ten to 16 years who is alleged to have committed an offence may be the subject of criminal proceedings or of 'care' proceedings, both of which are normally held before juvenile courts (see p 84).

In care proceedings the fact that a child is found guilty of an offence is not in itself sufficient justification for the making of a care order; the court must also be of the opinion that the child is in need of care or control which he is unlikely to receive unless an order is made. In criminal proceedings a court may make a care order without the need to consider whether the child is in need of care or control; this applies to a child found guilty of an offence punishable in the case of an adult by imprisonment.

A number of orders are available to courts in both care and criminal proceedings. A care order commits the child to the care of the local authority, so that the authority becomes responsible for deciding where the child should be accommodated, for example, with foster parents or in a community home (see p 125). The care order must be reviewed every six months by the authority, and can be ended at any time by the court; normally it expires at the age of 18 or 19. For children who are too severely disturbed or disruptive to be treated in other child care homes, 'youth treatment centres' are being provided by the Department of Health and Social Security.

Under a supervision order (usually valid for three years or less) a child normally remains at home under the supervision of a local authority social worker or a probation officer. He or she may be required to undergo 'intermediate treatment' which is a compromise between measures involving complete removal from home and those which do not. It consists of participation under a supervisor in a variety of constructive and remedial activities through a short residential course or, more usually, attendance at a day or evening centre. An intermediate treatment fund, administered by the Rainer Foundation with the help of government finance, has been created to give grants to individuals, groups or organisations willing to provide intermediate treatment facilities.

A court may also order a parent or guardian to enter into recognisances to take proper care of the child and to exercise proper control over him; such an order may only be made in criminal proceedings with the consent of the parent or guardian. In care proceedings, the court may order a stay in hospital in accordance with the mental health legislation.

In criminal proceedings the courts may also order payments of compensation, or impose fines or grant a conditional or absolute discharge. If the offender is a boy, he may be ordered to spend a total of (normally) 12 to 24 hours of his spare time on Saturdays at an attendance centre (up to three hours on any one occasion). The centres are for boys found guilty of offences for which older people could be sentenced to imprisonment, and provide physical training and instruction in handicrafts or some other practical subject. For boys aged 14 or over courts may make a detention centre order (see p 93), and young people of 15 and over may be committed to the Crown Court with a view to passing a sentence of borstal training (see p 93). In the case of a very serious crime, detention in a place approved by the Home Secretary may be ordered.

Scotland

In Scotland the age of criminal responsibility is eight years but prosecution of children in the criminal courts is rare and can take place only on the instructions of the Lord Advocate; court proceedings usually apply only to very serious offences such as murder or assault. Instead children under 16 years who have committed an offence or need care and protection may be brought before an informal children's hearing which decides the most appropriate measures of care and treatment (see p 125). An official 'reporter' decides whether a child should come before a hearing. If the grounds for referral are not accepted by the child and his parents, the case goes to the sheriff court (sitting in its civil capacity) for proof. It can then come back to the hearing. The sheriff also decides appeals against a decision of a children's hearing.

Northern Ireland

The age of criminal responsibility in Northern Ireland is ten. Children aged 16 and under charged with committing a criminal offence may be brought before a juvenile court. If found guilty of an offence punishable by imprisonment in the case of an adult, the child may be sent to a training school or be placed under supervision. Children brought before the courts in need of care and protection may be placed in care locally. The law relating to young offenders is under review.

Young Adult Offenders

Offenders aged 17 to 20 years are recognised as a category distinct from child and adult offenders. The main non-custodial measures are generally the same as those used in dealing with adults, although in the London and Manchester areas an attendance centre order (usually made for younger boys, see p 92) may be given. The custodial sentences available are: detention in a detention centre, borstal training and imprisonment.

Some 12 senior detention centres provide a means of treating young male offenders (age 17–21) in Great Britain for whom a long period of residential training away from home does not seem necessary or justified by the offence, but who need to be taught respect for the law through some form of custody. There are also six junior centres for boys aged 14 to 16 years. The normal period of detention is three months but in England and Wales there is power to award up to six months and, exceptionally, nine months. Life in a centre is brisk and formal, demanding the highest possible standards of discipline and achievement. Training comprises a normal working week of 40 hours, including an hour each day devoted to physical training, with considerable attention paid to education. All offenders discharged from a detention centre are supervised for a year.

Borstal training is remedial and educational, based on personal training by carefully selected staff. Emphasis is placed on vocational training in skilled trades. There is much freedom of movement and many borstals are open establishments. Offenders are placed as near their homes as possible in order to maintain their ties with the local community. The training system is available to offenders aged 15 to 20 years (16 to 20 years in Scotland and Northern Ireland). Courts rarely order borstal training unless they have already tried fines, probation or detention centre training, perhaps all three. The training period usually ranges from six months to two years and is followed by supervision in the community.

A person under 17 years cannot be sentenced to imprisonment in England and Wales, and no court may pass a sentence of imprisonment on an offender aged 17 to 20 years unless satisfied that no other method of dealing with him is appropriate. Sentences of up to two years may be ordered by a court to be suspended. Prisoners under the age of 21 at the time of their sentence are classified as 'young prisoners', and serve their sentences separately from older prisoners unless they are reclassified as adults and treated as such in an adult prison. In Scotland no offender under 21 years may be sent to prison; where neither borstal nor detention training is suitable for an offender aged 16 to 20 years, detention in a special 'young offenders' institution may be ordered.

CIVIL JUSTICE

The Civil Law

The main sub-divisions of the civil law of England, Wales and Northern Ireland are: family law, the law of property, the law of contract and the law of torts (covering injuries suffered by one person at the hands of another irrespective of any contract between them and including such concepts as negligence, defamation and trespass). Other branches of the civil law include constitutional and administrative law (particularly concerned with the use of executive power), industrial law, maritime law and ecclesiastical law. Scottish civil law has its own, often analogous, branches.

**CIVIL COURTS
England and
Wales**
*Magistrates'
Courts*

The limited civil jurisdiction of magistrates' courts extends to matrimonial proceedings for custody and maintenance orders, adoption orders and affiliation and guardianship orders. The courts also have jurisdiction concerning nuisances under the Public Health Acts and the recovery of rates. Committees of magistrates license public houses, betting shops and clubs.

County Courts

The jurisdiction of the 300 or so county courts covers, for instance, actions founded upon contract and tort (with minor exceptions) where the amount claimed is not more than £2,000; trust and mortgage cases, where the amount does not exceed £15,000; and actions for the recovery of land where the net annual value for rating does not exceed £2,000. Cases outside these limits may be tried in the county court by consent of the parties, or may in certain circumstances be transferred from the High Court to the county court.

Other matters dealt with by the county courts include hire purchase, the Rent Acts, landlord and tenant and adoption cases. In addition, undefended divorce cases are heard and determined in county courts designated as divorce county courts (defended cases are transferred to the High Court) and outside London bankruptcies are dealt with in certain county courts. The courts also deal with complaints of racial and sex discrimination in education and the provision of goods, facilities, services and premises (see p 135). Where small claims are concerned (especially those for less than £200 involving consumers), there are special facilities for arbitration and simplified procedures.

All judges of the Supreme Court (comprising the Court of Appeal, the Crown Court and the High Court) and all circuit judges and recorders have power to sit in the county courts, but each court has one or more circuit judges assigned to it by the Lord Chancellor, and the regular sittings of the court are mostly taken by them. The judge normally sits alone, although on the request of a party the court may, in exceptional cases, order a trial with a jury.

*The High Court
of Justice*

The High Court of Justice is divided into the Chancery Division, the Queen's Bench Division and the Family Division. Its jurisdiction, which is both original and appellate and covers all civil and some criminal cases, is vested in all its divisions. In general, however, particular types of work are assigned to a particular division—distribution of work being governed by statute, the rules of court and the practice of the court. The Family Division, for instance, is concerned with all jurisdiction affecting the family, including that relating to adoption and guardianship of children. The Chancery Division deals with the interpretation of wills and the administration of estates. Maritime and commercial law is the responsibility of admiralty and commercial courts of the Queen's Bench Division.

There are 74 High Court judges, each of whom is attached to one division on appointment but may be transferred to any other division during his term of office. The Lord Chancellor is president of the Court of Appeal and of the Chancery Division—the administration of the Chancery Division being the responsibility of the senior judge known as the Vice-Chancellor. The Queen's Bench Division is presided over by the Lord Chief Justice of England, who ranks next to the Lord Chancellor in the legal hierarchy, and the Family Division is headed by the President. Outside London (where the High Court sits at the Royal Courts of Justice) sittings of the court are held at 23 Crown Court centres.

For the hearing of cases at first instance, High Court judges sit singly. Appellate jurisdiction in civil matters from inferior courts is exercised by courts of two (or sometimes three) judges, or by single judges of the appropriate division, nominated by the Lord Chancellor.

Appeals

Appeals in matrimonial proceedings heard by magistrates' courts go to a divisional court of the Family Division of the High Court. Affiliation appeals are heard by the Crown Court, as are appeals from decisions of the licensing committees of magistrates. Appeals from the High Court and the county courts are heard in the Court of Appeal (Civil Division) and may (with leave of the court or of the House of Lords) go on to the House of Lords, which is the ultimate court of appeal in civil cases.

The *ex officio* members of the Court of Appeal are the Lord Chancellor, the Lord Chief Justice, the President of the Family Division and the Master of the Rolls; the ordinary members are 16 Lords Justices of Appeal.

The judges in the House of Lords are the nine Lords of Appeal in Ordinary, who must have a quorum of three, but usually sit as a group of five, and sometimes even of seven. Lay peers do not attend the hearing of appeals (which normally take place in a committee room and not in the legislative chamber), but peers who hold or have held high judicial office may also sit. The president of the House in its judicial capacity is the Lord Chancellor, and proceedings take the form of the normal proceedings of the House: judgments are given as speeches to a motion, and the decision is in the form of a vote.

Scotland

The main civil courts are the sheriff courts and the Court of Session.

Sheriff Courts

The civil jurisdiction of the sheriff court extends to most kinds of action and is normally unlimited by the value of the case. Much of the work is done by the sheriff, against whose decisions an appeal may be made to the sheriff-principal or directly to the Court of Session.

The Court of Session

The Court of Session sits only in Edinburgh, and has jurisdiction to deal with all kinds of action, subject to a few exceptions. The main exception is an action exclusive to the sheriff court, namely one where the value claimed is less than £500. The Court of Session has sole jurisdiction in divorce and certain other actions. The court is divided into two parts: the Outer House, a court of first instance, and the Inner House, which is mainly an appeal court. The Inner House is divided into two divisions of equal status, each consisting of four judges—the first division being presided over by the Lord President and the second division by the Lord Justice Clerk. Appeals to the Inner House may be made from the Outer House and from the sheriff court. From the Inner House an appeal may go to the House of Lords. The judges of the Court of Session are the same as those of the High Court of Justiciary. The Lord President of the Court holds the office of Lord Justice General in the High Court (see p 85).

The Scottish Land Court   The Scottish Land Court is a special court whose jurisdiction relates to agricultural tenancies and similar matters. It consists of a judge (ranking equally with the judges of the Court of Session) and four laymen who are specialists in agriculture.

Northern Ireland   Minor civil cases in Northern Ireland are dealt with in magistrates' courts, but as in England and Wales most civil actions are heard in the county courts. The superior civil law court is the High Court of Justice and appeal may lie to the Court of Appeal. Together, these two courts comprise the Supreme Court of Judicature and their practice and procedure are similar to those in the corresponding English courts. The House of Lords is the final civil appeal court. Under legislation passed in 1978, the administration of both criminal and civil courts will be unified.

Civil Proceedings   In England and Wales civil proceedings are instituted by the aggrieved person; no preliminary inquiry as to the authenticity of the grievance is required. Actions in the High Court are usually begun by a writ of summons served on the defendant by the plaintiff, which notifies the defendant that the plaintiff has a claim against him and states the nature of the claim. If the defendant intends to contest the claim, he informs the court. Documents setting out the precise question in dispute (the pleadings) are then delivered to the court. County court proceedings are initiated by a 'request' served on the defendant by the court; subsequent procedure is simpler than in the High Court.

A decree of divorce must be pronounced in open court, but the special procedure introduced for a limited class of case in 1973 and extended to most undefended cases in 1977 dispenses with the need to give evidence in court and provides for written evidence to be considered by the registrar.

Civil proceedings, because they are a private matter, can usually be abandoned or compromised at any time without leave of the court—the parties to a dispute being able to settle their differences through their solicitors before the stage of actual trial is reached. Actions that are brought to court are usually tried by a judge without a jury, except in cases involving claims for defamation, false imprisonment, or malicious prosecution, when either party may insist on trial by jury, or in a case of fraud, when the person against whom fraud is alleged may claim this right. The jury decides questions of fact and damages awarded to the injured party; majority verdicts may be accepted.

Judgments in civil cases are enforceable through the authority of the court. Most are for sums of money and may be enforced, in cases of default, by seizure of the debtor's goods or by attachment of earnings (a court order requiring an employer to make periodic payments to the court by deduction from the debtor's wages). Other judgments can take the form of an injunction restraining someone from performing an illegal act. Refusal to obey a judgment directing the defendant to do something or to refrain from doing something may result in imprisonment for contempt of court. Arrest under an order of committal may be effected only on a warrant of the court.

The general rule is that the costs of the action (the barristers' fees, solicitors' charges, court fees and other payments) are in the discretion of the court. Normally, the court orders them to be paid by the party losing the action.

In Scotland proceedings in the Court of Session or ordinary actions (of a value exceeding £500) in the sheriff court are initiated by serving on the defender a summons (an initial writ in the sheriff court). In Court of Session actions the next step is the publication of the action in the court lists. If the defender intends to contest the action, he must inform the court; if he does not appear, the court grants a decree in absence in favour of the pursuer. In ordinary actions in the sheriff court the defender is simply required to enter appearance within a certain number of days after service of the initial writ, and if he does so this is followed by a formal appearance in court by the parties to the dispute or their solicitors.

In summary causes (actions normally of a value less than £500) in the sheriff court the procedure is less formal. The statement of claim is incorporated in the summons, which is a printed form obtained from the sheriff clerk. The procedure is designed to enable most actions to be carried through without the parties involved having to appear in court. They (or their representatives) need appear only when an action is defended or there is some doubt about the method of paying the debt.

Proceedings in Northern Ireland are similar to those in England and Wales.

Restrictive Practices Court

The Restrictive Practices Court is a specialised United Kingdom court which deals with monopolies, and restrictive trade practices. It comprises five judges and up to ten other people with experience and expertise in industry, commerce or public life.

Administrative Tribunals

Administrative tribunals consist of persons or bodies exercising judicial or quasi-judicial functions outside the ordinary hierarchy of the courts. As a rule, they are set up by Act of Parliament or under powers conferred by statute, which also govern their constitution, functions and procedure.

The continuing expansion of governmental activity and involvement in the social and economic affairs of the nation has greatly multiplied the occasions on which the individual may find himself at issue with the administration, with a group of people or with another individual. Consequently there has been a substantial growth of administrative tribunals adjudicating in disputes arising under regulatory or welfare legislation. Such tribunals include those concerned with: land and property; national insurance; supplementary benefits; employment rights; mental health; transport; taxation; and many which do not fall into any specified group. Usually they consist of an uneven number of people so that a majority decision can be reached. Members are normally appointed by the minister concerned with the subject but other authorities (for instance, the Lord Chancellor) have the power of appointment in appropriate cases. The Lord Chancellor (or the Lord President of the Court of Session in Scotland) makes appointments in most cases where a lawyer chairman or member is required. Members usually hold office for a specified period.

There are also tribunals which enforce professional discipline (for example of doctors and solicitors) but these are entirely different in constitution from the statutory tribunals and have no jurisdiction over the general public.

Appeals on a point of law from all the more important tribunals may be made in England and Wales to the High Court, in Scotland to the Court of Session and in Northern Ireland to the Court of Appeal. An appeal may also be made to a specially constituted appeal tribunal, to a minister of the Crown or to an independent referee. The Employment Appeal Tribunal which hears appeals on questions of law from decisions of industrial tribunals (see p 324) has High Court and Court of Session status. The Council on Tribunals (appointed jointly by the Lord Chancellor and the Lord Advocate) exercises general supervision over tribunals and reports on particular matters, those peculiar to Scotland being dealt with by the Scottish Committee of the Council.

ADMINISTRATION OF THE LAW

GOVERNMENT RESPONSIBILI- TIES

The United Kingdom judiciary is entirely independent of the Government and is not subject to ministerial direction or control. There is no minister of justice. Responsibility for the administration of justice rests with the Lord Chancellor, the Home Secretary and the Secretaries of State for Scotland and Northern Ireland. Also concerned is the Prime Minister who recommends the highest judicial appointments to the Crown.

England and Wales

The Lord Chancellor is the head of the judiciary (and sometimes sits as a judge in the House of Lords). He is concerned with court procedure and is responsible for the administration of all courts other than magistrates' courts. He also appoints magistrates. On the civil law side, law reform and supervision of the legal aid and advice scheme are matters for him.

The Home Secretary is concerned with the criminal law (including law reform), the police service, prisons and the probation and after-care service. He also exercises a general supervision over magistrates' courts, with some specific responsibilities (such as approving the appointment of justices' clerks). On matters relating to crime prevention and the treatment of offenders, he is advised by the Advisory Council on the Penal System. Prison policy and the administration of custodial centres are functions of the Home Office Prison Department and the Home Secretary appoints to each centre a board of visitors representing the local community to investigate and advise him on the state of the buildings, administration and the treatment of inmates. The boards have certain disciplinary powers in relation to serious breaches of discipline and they hear applications or complaints from inmates. The Home Secretary is advised by a special Parole Board on the release of prisoners on licence.

Responsibility for the treatment of offenders under the age of 17 is shared by the Home Office and the Department of Health and Social Security.

The Home Secretary is also responsible for advising the Queen on the exercise of the royal prerogative of mercy to grant a free pardon in connection with a person's conviction, or to remit all or part of a penalty which may have been imposed on an offender by a court.

The Secretary of State for the Environment is responsible for providing accommodation for all the superior courts in England and Wales, except for the Central Criminal Court, which is the responsibility of the City of London.

The Attorney General and the Solicitor General, the Law Officers of the Crown for England and Wales, are the Government's principal advisers on English law, and represent the Crown in appropriate domestic and international cases. They are senior barristers, elected members of the House of Commons and hold ministerial posts. The Attorney General is also Attorney General for Northern Ireland.

As well as exercising various civil law functions, the Attorney General has ultimate control over the institution and withdrawal of criminal proceedings; the Director of Public Prosecutions (see p 83) is subject to his superintendence. The Attorney General is concerned with the institution and prosecution of certain types of criminal proceedings, but he must exercise an independent discretion, and must not be influenced by his Government colleagues. The Solicitor General is, in effect, the deputy of the Attorney General.

Scotland

The Secretary of State for Scotland recommends the appointment of all judges other than the most senior ones. He also appoints the staff of the High Court of Justiciary and the Court of Session and is responsible for the composition, staffing and organisation of the sheriff courts. District courts are staffed and administered by the district and islands local authorities.

The Secretary of State is also responsible for crime prevention, the police and the penal system. He is advised on parole matters by the Parole Board for Scotland.

The Lord Advocate and the Solicitor General for Scotland are the chief legal advisers to the Government on Scottish questions and the principal representatives of the Crown for the purposes of litigation in Scotland. The Lord Advocate is closely concerned with questions of legal policy and administration; he is also responsible for the Scottish parliamentary draftsmen, and for the public prosecution of all major crimes (see p 83).

Northern Ireland In Northern Ireland the judiciary are appointed by the Queen on the advice of the Lord Chancellor. The Northern Ireland Office, under the Secretary of State, deals with the staffing and general organisation of the county and petty sessions courts and is responsible for the police and the penal system.

THE PERSONNEL OF THE LAW The courts of the United Kingdom are the Queen's Courts since the Crown is the historic source of all judicial power. The Queen, acting on the advice of ministers, is responsible for all appointments to the judiciary.

Judges Full-time judges do not engage in politics, except for the Lord Chancellor, who is head of the judiciary, speaker of the House of Lords and a Cabinet minister. With the exception of lay magistrates, judges are normally appointed from practising barristers (advocates in Scotland) or solicitors. Lay magistrates in England and Wales need no legal qualifications but on appointment they undertake to complete a period of basic training, so that they may obtain a sufficient knowledge of the law, including the rules of evidence, and may understand the nature and purpose of sentencing. A special committee advises the Lord Chancellor on training policies. The Scottish district court justices of the peace likewise need no legal qualifications, and the Secretary of State for Scotland is responsible for training. In Northern Ireland lay magistrates serving on juvenile courts undertake training courses; resident magistrates are drawn from practising solicitors or barristers. In certain circumstances (for instance, in cases of misconduct or proven incapacity) judges of the inferior courts in England and Wales and Northern Ireland may be removed from their position by the Lord Chancellor, and in Scotland, by the Secretary of State on a report by the Lord President of the Court of Session and the Lord Justice Clerk.

In order to safeguard and perpetuate the independence of the judiciary from the executive, however, superior judges in England and Wales and Northern Ireland (other than the Lord Chancellor who, as a Cabinet minister, changes with the Government) are subject to a power of removal only by the Sovereign on an address presented by both Houses of Parliament; in Scotland there is no statutory provision for removal of judges of the Court of Session or High Court of Justiciary from office and it is probable that special legislation would be required to effect such a dismissal.

The Legal Profession The legal profession is divided into two branches: barristers (advocates in Scotland) and solicitors. Barristers are known collectively as the 'Bar', and collectively and individually as 'counsel'. Solicitors undertake legal business for lay clients, while barristers advise on legal problems submitted through solicitors and present cases in the higher courts although certain functions are common to both. Although an individual is free to conduct his own case most people prefer to be legally represented in the more serious court cases.

Royal commissions are inquiring into the provision of legal services and considering the structure, organisation, entry, training and remuneration of the legal profession.

In England and Wales every barrister and every student wishing to become a barrister must be a member of one of the four Inns of Court (Lincoln's Inn, Inner Temple, Middle Temple and Gray's Inn). To become a student member of an Inn, an entrant must normally have a law degree from a United Kingdom university or polytechnic. People with other degrees and 'mature' students may also be accepted, but they must pass a diploma in law. All students must pass the professional examinations run by the Council of Legal Education. After training, a student can be called to the Bar, but may not practise independently until he has completed a year's pupillage with an established barrister. The governing body of the profession is the Senate of the Inns of Court and the Bar. The Bar Council (composed of those members of the Senate who are elected by the Bar) maintains the standards and independence of the profession and improves its services.

A prospective solicitor in England and Wales must be considered suitable by the appropriate committee of The Law Society (the professional organisation of solicitors) and he must enter into 'articles of clerkship' with a practising solicitor of not less than five years' standing before he can begin his professional career. The term of articles lasts for two to four years, depending upon the educational qualifications of the student. An articled clerk must pass the necessary examinations prescribed by The Law Society and, unless he has been a barrister or is a law graduate of a university, he is generally required to attend a course of studies at a recognised law school. Once a solicitor is qualified, he may become a member of The Law Society.

In Scotland prospective advocates and solicitors undergo much the same training. While the respective professional organisations—the Faculty of Advocates and The Law Society of Scotland—have their own professional examinations, candidates usually obtain exemption from them by including the necessary subjects in a law degree of a Scottish university. The prospective advocate must, thereafter, undergo a period of training (either of 21 months or of 12 months depending on whether or not he has been granted exemption from nine months' training) in a solicitor's office, followed by about nine months' pupillage with a practising advocate. The prospective solicitor must serve an apprenticeship of two years in a solicitor's office before he can begin his professional career.

In Northern Ireland barristers are members of the Inn of Court of Northern Ireland; there is also a General Council of the Bar of Northern Ireland. The professional organisation for solicitors is The Incorporated Law Society of Northern Ireland.

LEGAL AID, ADVICE AND ASSISTANCE

Legal aid is provided for people of limited means to pay for the cost of advice and assistance and for legal representation in court proceedings. Lawyers' costs and the expenses of litigation are paid out of a fund provided by the State. The fund is entitled to be reimbursed from contributions which assisted people may have to pay according to their means and costs, damages recovered from legally aided people's opponents in litigation, and a government grant.

Advice and Assistance

Where court proceedings are not involved, people with limited means can obtain help from a solicitor on any legal matter either free or subject to a contribution. This includes giving advice, writing letters, drafting wills and obtaining opinions from a barrister. A solicitor may act for a client until his costs and expenses reach a total of £25 (£45 for undefended divorce cases), but authority must be obtained for this limit to be exceeded. A person seeking help has to give the solicitor brief details about his income and savings. The income limit laid down by the scheme is reviewed at least annually.

In some urban areas law centres exist to provide free legal advice; all have at least one full-time salaried lawyer and most employ community workers. There are also voluntary legal advice centres in many parts of the country and many Citizens Advice Bureaux provide legal advice.

Aid in Civil Proceedings

Legal aid for civil court proceedings is available to people whose disposable incomes and disposable capital do not exceed certain prescribed amounts,[1] but a contribution is payable according to the level of the applicant's income; if that is below a prescribed amount, legal aid is given free of any contribution. As in the case of legal advice and assistance, the qualifying income limits for aid are reviewed at least once a year.

An applicant for legal aid must also show that he has reasonable grounds for taking or defending the proceedings. Provided his application is successful the case is then conducted in the ordinary way, except that no money passes between the assisted person and his solicitor—payments being made in and out of the legal aid fund. The costs of an action which an assisted litigant loses against an unassisted opponent may also, subject to certain conditions and if the court so orders, be met out of the fund. Solicitors and counsel have a duty to review the case at each stage to see that it is not being pursued unreasonably at public expense. Legal aid is not generally available in cases where redress is sought for alleged defamation or for representation in most proceedings in administrative tribunals.

The civil legal aid schemes are run by The Law Society, The Law Society of Scotland and The Incorporated Law Society of Northern Ireland, under the general guidance respectively of the Lord Chancellor, the Secretary of State for Scotland and the Secretary of State for Northern Ireland.

Aid in Criminal Proceedings

In criminal proceedings in England and Wales a legal aid order may be made by the court concerned if it appears to be in the interests of justice and that a defendant's means are such that he requires financial help in meeting the costs of the proceedings in which he is involved. An order must be made when a person is committed for trial on a charge of murder or applies for leave to appeal from the Court of Appeal (Criminal Division) or the Courts Martial Appeal Court to the House of Lords. No person can be given a custodial sentence for the first time unless he is legally represented.

Voluntary duty solicitor schemes at many magistrates' courts provide 'stand-by' help for unrepresented defendants.

The criminal legal aid scheme in England and Wales is administered by the courts, under the overall responsibility of the Home Secretary.

The arrangements for aid in criminal proceedings in Scotland and Northern Ireland are broadly similar, but in Scotland there is a statutory duty solicitor scheme for accused people in custody in sheriff, and district, court cases and the 'interests of justice' test applies only in summary cases.

---

[1] Assessments of disposable income and capital are made by the Supplementary Benefits Commission and are governed by regulations which allow for deductions from gross income for maintenance of dependants, interest on loans, income tax, rent and other matters for which a person may reasonably provide out of income, and deductions for furniture and other household effects from his capital.

LAW REFORM   The duty of keeping the law under review in order to ensure that it meets the needs of modern society lies in England and Wales with the Law Reform Committee, the Criminal Law Revision Committee and the Law Commission, and in Scotland with the Scottish Law Commission. The Law Reform Committee and the Criminal Law Revision Committee are standing committees of judges and distinguished practising and academic lawyers, appointed respectively by the Lord Chancellor and the Home Secretary, to examine such aspects of the civil and criminal law as may be referred to them by the appropriate minister.

The Law Commission is a permanent body consisting of five lawyers of high standing, charged with the duty of scrutinising the law with a view to its systematic development and reform, including the possibility of codification, the elimination of anomalies, the repeal of obsolete and unnecessary enactments, and the reduction of the number of separate enactments. It reports to the Lord Chancellor. The Scottish Law Commission, which has a constitution similar to that of the English body and similar functions, reports to the Lord Advocate. The work of the two commissions has led to changes in many areas of the law, the repeal of some 950 obsolete Acts and the pruning of the contents of nearly 1,400 others.

5 Defence

Britain's defence policy is based firmly on the North Atlantic Alliance, and this commitment was emphasised by the decision, taken in January 1978 following a period of retrenchment, to increase defence expenditure in line with an Alliance agreement (see below). In other respects, defence policy continues to be centred around the conclusions of the 1974 Defence Review, which aimed at reducing defence costs as a proportion of national resources while maintaining a modern and effective defence system. As a result of the review, completed in early 1975 following consultations with Britain's allies, defence forces are being concentrated on those areas in which a British contribution to collective defence will be most effective in ensuring the nation's own security and that of its allies. Thus the North Atlantic Treaty Organisation (NATO) remains the primary charge on Britain's defence resources, and Britain has withdrawn from its non-NATO commitments wherever this has been consistent with its fundamental military and political obligations. At the same time, general purpose forces are being maintained as insurance against the unforeseen.

At the end of 1976, reductions in planned defence expenditure for 1978–79 were announced as part of the overall reductions in public expenditure programmes (see p 186). About half of the savings are coming from the equipment programme, about one-fifth from works and accommodation stores, and the balance from miscellaneous changes. The Government's overriding objective is to keep to the minimum the effect of the reductions on Britain's front-line contribution to NATO.

Following the NATO agreement in May 1977 that all member countries should aim at an annual increase of defence expenditure of about 3 per cent in real terms for the period 1979–84, Britain has announced a 3 per cent increase in real terms in the defence budget for 1979–80 and a further 3 per cent increase for 1980–81. The latter figure is subject to review in the light of economic circumstances, and no decisions have been taken beyond 1981 since it will be necessary before reaching conclusions to take account of developments in arms control and defence as well as in the economy.

POLICY

Europe

Britain's basic security depends on the strength of the North Atlantic Alliance, and it is to NATO that by far the greater part of Britain's military forces is committed. Britain makes a major contribution to the full range of deterrent capabilities, both conventional and nuclear, required to maintain NATO's defensive posture. Within NATO, Britain plays an important part in the efforts of the European members to assume, through closer co-operation, an increasing responsibility for Western defence. In the 'Eurogroup' Britain and ten other European members are working to improve their contribution to the Alliance and to achieve a more effective collective result from the available resources. The sub-groups of the Eurogroup, each of which concentrates on a specific area such as training or logistics, make an important contribution towards the strength of the Alliance by increasing co-operation among its members. Britain also participates in the independent European Programme Group of all European members of the Alliance; the group has been set up to extend co-operation among European countries in defence equipment and to contribute to greater equipment co-operation throughout the Alliance.

Britain is playing a major part in the efforts to reduce tension and achieve more lasting peace in Europe. It is working to ensure that the agreements signed in Helsinki with the Soviet Union and Eastern European countries on security and co-operation in Europe, which were reviewed at a meeting in Belgrade from October 1977 to March 1978, will contribute to increased stability and improved relations. It is also seeking to achieve progress in the negotiations for mutual and balanced force reductions in Central Europe.

Beyond Europe Britain retains responsibility for the protection of its remaining dependencies; is a member of the Central Treaty Organisation (CENTO); and retains a consultative commitment to the Five Power Defence arrangement with Australia, New Zealand, Malaysia and Singapore. In addition, the armed forces continue to give assistance to communities overseas, particularly in such activities as disaster relief and development work.

United Nations and other International Organisations Britain also plays an active part in the United Nations (UN) and other international bodies working to eliminate the sources of tension and conflict between nations and to promote arms control and disarmament. It supports the peace-keeping efforts of the UN—supplying the largest national contingent to the UN Peace-Keeping Force in Cyprus. Britain played an active role in the UN special session on disarmament which took place from May to July 1978. In addition, it is a frequent contributor to debates in the Conference of the Committee on Disarmament and has played a leading part in strengthening the regime of non-proliferation of nuclear weapons through the International Atomic Energy Agency and other bodies.

PLANNING AND CONTROL

Supreme responsibility for national defence rests with the Government as a whole, which is responsible to Parliament. The formulation of defence policy is the responsibility of the Secretary of State for Defence. In recent years the emphasis in defence organisation has been on increased central policy control and the co-ordinated planning of the defence effort. The Ministry of Defence (see p 43) ensures effective co-ordination of policy and administration concerning the Services. The Secretary of State is assisted by a Minister of State, and by three Under-Secretaries of State—for the Navy, Army and Air Force respectively. They, together with the Chief of the Defence Staff, the three Service Chiefs of Staff, the Permanent Under-Secretary of State for Defence, the Vice-Chief of Defence Staff (Personnel and Logistics), the Chief Scientific Adviser and the Chief of Defence Procurement, form the Defence Council, which deals with major aspects of defence policy. The Chiefs of Staff Committee is responsible for giving professional advice on strategy and operations, and on the military implications of defence policy. The day-to-day management of the three Services is the responsibility of the Admiralty, Army and Air Force Boards of the Defence Council.

Expenditure Information about defence policy and the armed forces is provided in an annual *Statement on the Defence Estimates* (Cmnd. 7099 in 1978, published in February). The defence estimates for 1978–79 totalled £6,919 million, which represents about 4·75 per cent of gross domestic product at market prices. Of the total expenditure £2,996 million (43 per cent) is on personnel (pay, allowances, pensions), £2,770 million (40 per cent) on equipment, and the remaining £1,153 million (17 per cent) on buildings and miscellaneous stores and services. (See also diagram below.)

Functional analysis of defence expenditure 1978–79

Production, repair and associated
facilities in Britain £449m

War and contingency stocks £178m

Training £604m

Research and development £872m

Reserve and auxiliary formations £122m

Other support functions £1,255m

Air force general purpose forces £1,107m

Navy general purpose combat forces £1,017m

Nuclear strategic force £93m

European theatre ground forces, £1,251m

Other Army combat forces £74m

Miscellaneous expenditure and receipts —£103m

Total £6,919 million

DEPLOYMENT

NATO Strategy   The basis of the NATO strategy of flexibility in response, which retains the principle of forward defence, is that credible deterrence of military aggression of all kinds is essential. While NATO must be ready to use nuclear weapons if necessary, its conventional forces must be maintained to enable it to respond to aggression at a variety of levels, the level of response being that which enables NATO to maintain the territorial and maritime integrity of the Alliance and thereby to gain time for negotiations to end a conflict. The strategy requires a comprehensive range of mobile and well-equipped conventional forces, and of tactical and strategic nuclear weapons.

Britain's NATO Contribution   Britain makes a major contribution to the forces required by NATO's present strategy. Together with its tactical nuclear forces, the British Polaris strategic force provides a unique European contribution to NATO's nuclear deterrent. Virtually all ships of frigate size and above are earmarked for assignment in an emergency to NATO. The Royal Navy also contributes to NATO's Standing Naval Force Atlantic, Standing Naval Force Channel, and the Naval On Call Force Mediterranean. The British Army of the Rhine (BAOR) and Royal Air Force (RAF) Germany are deployed in the Federal Republic of Germany and there is a Field Force in Berlin. The main combat element of BAOR is First (British) Corps which is being reorganised, and by 1979 will comprise four new-style armoured divisions, an artillery division, and a new infantry formation. Its peacetime strength of around 55,000 would be more than doubled on mobilisation by reinforcements and reserves from Britain (see p 110). Virtually all the RAF's combat and combat support aircraft are assigned to NATO. RAF Germany is a tactical air force including strike/attack, reconnaissance, close support and air-defence aircraft. In addition, combat units based in Britain provide an important part of NATO's mobile reinforcement capability. These include the ground elements of the United Kingdom Mobile Force, the British contribution to the Allied Command Europe Mobile Force (Land) and three squadrons of 22 Special Air Service Regiment. RAF Strike Command provides forces for strike/attack, reconnaissance, close support, air defence and maritime patrol and anti-submarine warfare, together with transport forces and air elements for the United Kingdom Mobile Force and Allied Command Europe Mobile Force (Air).

Northern Ireland

At home a major task of the armed forces since 1969 has been to assist the civil authorities in Northern Ireland in the maintenance of law and order, and they have operated to counter the terrorist activities of extremist organisations.

Outside NATO

In the Mediterranean, British forces are deployed in Gibraltar, in Malta until March 1979, and in Cyprus to meet Britain's commitment to the United Nations Force and to provide for the security of the Sovereign Base Areas. In Hong Kong, units of all three Services provide a garrison for external defence, and a Gurkha battalion is stationed in Brunei. A Royal Marines detachment is maintained in the Falkland Islands; and in the Caribbean, units of the Army and the RAF provide a garrison for the external defence of Belize.

THE ARMED FORCES

Service Organisation

Britain's armed forces consist of the Royal Navy, the Army and the Royal Air Force.

The Royal Navy has four main arms: the Naval General Service, which mans and maintains the surface fleet; the Fleet Air Arm; the Submarine Service; and the Royal Marines, who primarily provide an amphibious striking force. The Royal Navy has a unified sea command, Commander-in-Chief, Fleet; and the Naval Home Command, Portsmouth, under a Commander-in-Chief, with subordinate area commands based at Plymouth, Chatham and Rosyth.

The Army is organised into some 30 arms and services which include the Household Cavalry, the Royal Horse Artillery, the Royal Armoured Corps, the Royal Regiment of Artillery, the Corps of Royal Engineers, the Royal Corps of Signals, the Regiments of Foot Guards and Regiments of Infantry, the Special Air Service Regiment, the Army Air Corps, the Royal Corps of Transport, the Royal Army Medical Corps, the Royal Army Ordnance Corps and the Corps of Royal Electrical and Mechanical Engineers. At home the Army is under a single command, United Kingdom Land Forces, with subordinate district commands; Northern Ireland remains a separate command while the emergency continues.

The Royal Air Force general purpose forces are organised in two operational commands, Strike Command and Royal Air Force Germany. Support and training organisations are grouped within one United Kingdom command.

Women's Services

The three women's Services, the Women's Royal Naval Service, the Women's Royal Army Corps, and the Women's Royal Air Force are integral parts of the armed forces, and servicewomen serve alongside servicemen in Britain and overseas. Nursing services are provided by Queen Alexandra's Royal Naval Nursing Service, Queen Alexandra's Royal Army Nursing Corps and Princess Mary's Royal Air Force Nursing Service.

Manpower Britain's armed forces excluding non-United Kingdom personnel totalled about 323,500 on 1 January 1978, 75,500 in the Royal Navy and Royal Marines, 163,100 in the Army and 85,000 in the Royal Air Force. The forecast total for 1 April 1979 is 322,500. The average number of civilian staff expected to be employed by the Ministry of Defence during 1978–79 is 266,800.

Functional analysis of defence personnel 1978–79

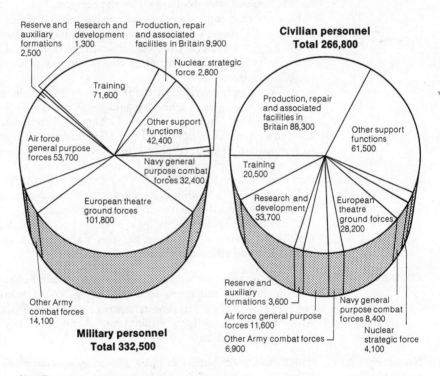

Note: These are average strengths and include locally enlisted personnel.

Engagements Britain's armed forces consist entirely of personnel serving on a voluntary basis. Engagements available to non-commissioned ranks range from three to 22 years, with a wide freedom of choice on the length and terms of service. Recruits to non-commissioned ranks of all three Services are committed for only a minimum period of service (about three years, excluding training) and, subject to that minimum, may leave at any time at 18 months' notice. Discharge may also be granted on compassionate grounds, by purchase, or on grounds of conscience (applications being assessed by an independent tribunal). Commissions may be granted for short, medium and long terms. In all three Services there are opportunities for promotion from the ranks. Entry to commissioned ranks is on the basis of educational and other qualifications. All three Services have schemes for university cadetships.

Training

Entrants to non-commissioned ranks are given basic training, and further and specialist training is given during the course of their careers. Young service-men and women are encouraged to study for educational qualifications, all three Services providing extensive facilities for the consolidation and develop-ment of their personnel's education. Trade and technical training, though primarily designed for Service purposes, leads for about half the total number of service personnel to nationally recognised qualifications.

Service technical training is highly valued in industry, which is a significant advantage on return to civilian life. To assist such resettlement the Services provide an advisory service, familiarisation attachments to civilian organisa-tions, and opportunity and assistance to study for suitable civilian qualifica-tions. There are also opportunities for short- and longer-term retraining both before and after discharge from the Services.

Entrants to commissioned ranks receive initial training at the Britannia Royal Naval College, Dartmouth, the Royal Military Academy, Sandhurst, the Royal Air Force College, Cranwell, or similar institutions. This is followed by specialist training, often including degree courses at university or Service establishments.

Staff training is provided by the Royal Naval Staff College, Greenwich, the Army Staff College at Camberley, and the Royal Air Force Staff College at Bracknell. The National Defence College at Latimer is designed to fit selected mid-career officers of all three Services for key posts that contribute to formulation of defence policy in the Ministry of Defence and on inter-national staffs. Specially selected senior officers and officials from Britain, the Commonwealth, NATO, CENTO and other countries attend the Royal College of Defence Studies in London, which provides the wider background necessary for those destined to fill higher appointments.

Considerable operational training is carried out through joint-Service and inter-allied exercises. All three Services provide training facilities for the armed forces of allied and Commonwealth countries.

COMBAT FORCES

Combat forces are functionally divided into the nuclear strategic force (costing an estimated £93 million in 1978–79), Royal Navy general purpose combat forces (£1,017 million), European theatre ground forces (£1,251 million), other Army combat forces (£74 million) and Royal Air Force general purpose forces (£1,107 million).

Nuclear Strategic Force

The British contribution to NATO's strategic deterrent is provided by the Royal Navy's force of four Polaris nuclear submarines—*Resolution, Repulse, Renown* and *Revenge*. Each can remain on underwater patrol for long periods and is equipped with 16 Polaris missiles, armed with nuclear warheads, with a range of about 4,500 km (2,800 miles).

Royal Navy General Purpose Combat Forces

Britain's maritime forces are concentrated in the Eastern Atlantic and English Channel, where they provide the majority of forces readily available to NATO. However, they retain an ability to be deployed world-wide in defence of allied or national interests. Nearer home there is an increasing commitment arising from the need to protect Britain's offshore resources, in particular the North Sea oil and gas installations, and to continue the traditional task of fishery protection.

Equipment

HMS *Invincible*, the first of a new class of anti-submarine warfare cruiser, was launched in 1977. Its prime role will be to deploy the Sea King anti-submarine helicopter. The cruiser will also provide a command and control function for maritime task forces and will contribute to area air defence with its Sea Dart missile system and Sea Harrier maritime vertical short take-off and landing (V/STOL) aircraft. The aircraft carrier HMS *Ark Royal* also deploys the Sea King helicopter and operates Buccaneer strike aircraft (equipped with the Anglo-French Martel air-to-surface missile), Phantom air-defence and Gannet airborne early warning aircraft. Sea Kings are also embarked on the anti-submarine warfare cruiser HMS *Hermes* and the command helicopter cruisers HMS *Blake* and *Tiger*, which are responsible for directing and controlling naval forces. There are the County class guided-missile destroyers, all armed with Seaslug and Seacat surface-to-air missiles and four with the Exocet surface-to-surface guided-missile system, the Type 82 guided-missile destroyer HMS *Bristol* (equipped with the Sea Dart area air defence missile system and the Ikara anti-submarine guided weapon system), and three of the new class of Type 42 Sea Dart guided-missile destroyers. Other surface vessels include 49 general purpose frigates (comprising 26 Leander class, seven Tribal class, eight Rothesay class and eight of the new Type 21 Amazon class), two anti-aircraft frigates, two aircraft direction frigates, two anti-submarine frigates, 38 mine counter-measure vessels and five new Island class offshore patrol vessels. The frigate classes are variously armed with automatic guns, surface-to-air missile systems, underwater detection and anti-submarine weapons. Most have the Wasp helicopter embarked, which is being replaced, where appropriate, by the Anglo-French Lynx.

Exocet missile systems are being installed in some Leander class and Type 21 frigates, giving these vessels a better surface-to-surface capability. Some Leander class frigates are also equipped with the Ikara anti-submarine weapon. Ten nuclear-fleet submarines are in service, including the first four of the Swiftsure class, as are 17 conventional patrol submarines. There is also an amphibious capability comprising the two assault ships HMS *Fearless* and HMS *Intrepid* and the Royal Marines Commando Forces, supported by HMS *Hermes* which retains a secondary role as a commando ship. Support will also be available from HMS *Bulwark* which is to return to full operational service as an anti-submarine warfare cruiser, but will, like HMS *Hermes*, retain an amphibious lift capability.

Ships under construction include HMS *Illustrious*, the second of the new anti-submarine warfare cruisers, and three of the new Type 22 class frigates which will be armed with the Sea Wolf surface-to-air and Exocet anti-ship missile systems. In addition, work is in hand on three nuclear-fleet submarines, including the first of a new class, seven Type 42 Sea Dart destroyers, and two of a new class of glass-reinforced plastic mine counter-measure vessels.

European Theatre Ground Forces   The European theatre ground forces consist of BAOR, and the forces stationed in Britain, the main elements of which have primary roles in support of NATO (see p 105).

Other Army Combat Forces   Other Army combat forces comprise land forces stationed overseas to meet treaty commitments to Commonwealth and other countries (see p 106).

Equipment   Armoured regiments are equipped with the Chieftain main battle tank. A new series of tracked combat reconnaissance vehicles is in service, including Scorpion and Scimitar, mounting respectively a 76mm and a 30mm gun, Striker, carrying the Swingfire anti-tank missile, and Sultan, a command vehicle. The primary tracked armoured personnel carriers used by mechanised infantry battalions are the FV432, and entering service with the infantry is the crew-portable Milan anti-tank weapon system. Artillery units are equipped with the Abbot 105mm self-propelled gun, 155mm and 175mm self-propelled guns, and Field Artillery Computer Equipment (FACE). A new 105mm light gun is entering service and will be joined by the FH70 155mm field howitzer. Tactical nuclear support is provided by the Lance missile system. Air defence is provided by the Rapier low-level surface-to-air missile system and the Blowpipe man-portable very-low-level missile.

Royal Air Force General Purpose Forces

The Royal Air Force general purpose forces consist of aircraft for air defence, strike/attack, reconnaissance, offensive support, airborne early warning, maritime patrol and anti-submarine warfare, transport and in-flight refuelling, together with RAF Regiment field squadrons.

Equipment

Phantom and Lightning aircraft, together with Rapier and Bloodhound surface-to-air missiles, are employed in air defence. Radar warning is provided by Shackleton airborne early warning aircraft and by the ground radars and control and reporting centres of the United Kingdom Air Defence Ground Environment system. Jaguars, Buccaneers and Vulcans operate in the strike/ attack role; Jaguars, Canberras and Vulcans are employed for reconnaissance; Jaguars and the Harrier V/STOL aircraft for offensive support (with the Harrier also having a tactical reconnaissance capability); Nimrods for long-range maritime patrol and anti-submarine warfare and for offshore surveillance and fishery protection duty.

The VC10 provides strategic transport and the Hercules (which also has a strategic capability) is used for tactical transport over medium ranges. For short-range tasks, the Wessex and Puma helicopters are used, while for search and rescue operations Wessex, Whirlwind and Sea King helicopters are used in Britain. Victor tankers are used for in-flight refuelling, which gives added range and flexibility to combat aircraft.

RESERVE FORCES

Reserve and auxiliary forces are an integral part of the armed forces. Apart from their essential military role—to supplement the regular forces in time of war or emergency with trained personnel able immediately to take their places in the Services either as formed units or as individual reinforcements—they form an important link between the Services and the civil community. Some of their members have a reserve liability following a period of regular service (regular reserve); others are volunteer men and women who devote their spare time to training for the roles they would undertake in war or an emergency. On 1 January 1978 regular reserves totalled 176,200, and volunteer reserves and auxiliary forces 75,300. Cadet forces, which make a significant contribution to recruitment to the regular forces, totalled 141,000.

Royal Navy

The Royal Navy regular reserve consists of various categories of former full-time officers and ratings liable to recall in emergency, including the Royal Fleet Reserve, which consists of men with recent experience of regular service. The volunteer reserves comprise the Royal Naval Reserve, with its associated women's reserve, and the Royal Marines Reserve. Both carry out regular part-time training, the former to man a number of operational minesweepers and support maritime and other headquarters, the latter to reinforce the regular corps and in particular the Royal Marine Commandos.

Army

The Army reserves comprise the Territorial and Army Volunteer Reserve (TAVR) and regular reserves consisting of ex-regular servicemen.

The TAVR's primary role is to reinforce the ground forces committed to NATO and to assist in maintaining a secure United Kingdom base in support of the forces deployed in Europe. It consists of independent units, organised on a local basis with regular Army and permanent civilian staff, and sponsored units of specialists recruited on a country-wide basis. They undergo regular part-time training. The task of regular reservists would be to bring regular and TAVR formations to war strength.

Ulster Defence Regiment

The Ulster Defence Regiment is a locally-recruited, largely part-time force designed to support the regular forces in Northern Ireland.

Royal Air Force

The Royal Air Force Reserve consists of former regular officers and personnel with a reserve liability, and the Royal Air Force Volunteer Reserve, which includes the university air squadrons. The Royal Auxiliary Air Force consists of units which would support regular formations in an emergency.

CIVIL DEFENCE

CIVIL DEFENCE

Civil defence arrangements are principally based on the extended and adapted use of existing public services operated by nationalised industries, local authorities, police authorities and government departments. Supplementary effort from individual volunteers and voluntary organisations would be brought in, either at the discretion of local authorities or in response to a national appeal, in time of crisis. A central point of recent policy has been to improve the preparedness of local government to meet a war emergency. Since there is common ground between such planning and the preparations and organisation for a major peace-time emergency or national disaster, activities have also been directed towards creating a closer relationship in local planning for the different emergencies of peace and war.

Within an annual budget of £26·3 million, emphasis is placed on a high quality of central and local government planning. Studies and seminars are arranged by the Home Office on staff college lines.

Arrangements also include an emergency system for decentralised governmental control and communications. The United Kingdom Warning and Monitoring Organisation, which includes the civilian Royal Observer Corps, is organised to provide public warning of an attack, of the location and strength of nuclear explosions, and of the distribution and level of radioactive fall-out.

DEFENCE PROCUREMENT

Responsibility for the procurement (that is, research, development and production) of defence equipment, including aircraft, ships, ordnance, guided weapons and electronics, lies with the Procurement Executive within the Ministry of Defence. The Executive is responsible for maintaining liaison between the Service users and the machinery for procurement, and co-ordination with industry in the formulation of programmes; this ensures a co-ordinated and cost-effective approach.

Research and Development

The major part of research is undertaken by the Ministry of Defence's research and development establishments, but the Ministry also sponsors a substantial amount of research by industry and the universities. The research and development establishments have a very wide technological capability, which has civil as well as military applications: for example, support is given to civil aerospace projects and advanced aero-engines. On the development side, the establishments collaborate closely with the Ministry's contractors by monitoring their progress, and by assisting in testing programmes and in solving particular technical problems.

Modern defence equipment is becoming ever more complex, and its development requires a high initial investment; in 1978-79 the total cost of British equipment research and development is estimated at £876 million. The search for a more efficient use of these resources has caused attention to be concentrated on collaborative projects, which enable the cost of development and production to be shared with other countries. In some cases the outright purchase of foreign equipment is the most economical solution. Nevertheless, the importance of maintaining a sound national industrial base for defence procurement is recognised, and there is close consultation between government and industry both in the National Defence Industries Council and through other specialised machinery.

Collaboration between Britain and other European countries is already extensive, and may be expected to increase, particularly through the work of the European Programme Group. Successful joint projects so far include the Anglo-French Jaguar aircraft, the Martel air-to-surface missile, the Lynx, Puma and Gazelle helicopters and the Anglo-Belgian family of armoured combat reconnaissance vehicles. Production and development of the Tornado multi-role combat aircraft (MRCA) with the Federal Republic of Germany and Italy is continuing and good progress is being made in the development, with these two countries, of the medium artillery pieces FH70 and SP70. Equipment collaboration also facilitates joint logistic support and training arrangements, like those taking place among the five European countries which have agreed to purchase the Lance surface-to-surface missile system from the United States.

National Projects   A considerable number of projects, covering all the main equipment areas, are under development. They include a complete range of new avionic and sonic equipment which will greatly improve the effectiveness of the Nimrods; an air defence variant of the Tornado, which is planned to replace the Phantom; a search and rescue version of the Sea King helicopter with a greater range and capability; a new range of logistic vehicles for battlefield support; a new type of tank armour, Chobham Armour, which weight for weight provides greatly improved protection for armoured vehicles; and the Wisp and Wideye remotely-piloted helicopters. An airborne early warning (AEW) version of the Nimrod is being developed, equipped with an advanced AEW radar, which will be interoperable with any other AEW system other NATO countries may decide to procure.

Production   Following the development of defence equipment, either nationally or in co-operation with allies, production is usually undertaken by private industry on a contract basis or by the Royal Ordnance Factories and Royal Dockyards. Production may also be undertaken on a collaborative basis. The Defence Sales organisation provides support, assistance and advice to British industry and the Royal Ordnance Factories in promoting the sales of defence equipment overseas. In 1978-79 the value of exports of British defence equipment is expected to reach £900 million.

6 Social Welfare

The British social welfare system comprises the National Health Service, the personal social services and social security. Education is described in Chapter 7, and housing in Chapter 9. The National Health Service supplies, largely free, the best medical service available to all, irrespective of means. The local authority personal social services and voluntary organisations provide advice and help to elderly people, disabled people and children in need of care. The social security system is designed to secure a basic standard of living for people in financial need by providing income support during periods of inability to earn, helping families and compensating for disablement.

Although public spending on health and personal social services has increased in real terms, the rate of growth has had to be cut because of restrictions on central and local government expenditure. Protection of the elderly, the sick and the poor is a central part of the Government's social programme, and pensions and other social security benefits have been unaffected by cuts in public expenditure and are raised annually.

In the health service, priority is being given to services for the mentally ill, the mentally handicapped, the elderly, families with children and primary health care. Efforts are being made to distribute resources more fairly between different parts of the country. The Government is also placing even greater emphasis than hitherto on the need to obtain value for money. Among additional money-saving measures being studied are cuts in administrative costs, more preventive medicine, a more efficient utilisation of hospital beds, more day hospital treatment and improved systems of purchasing supplies.

The Government in collaboration with local authorities has continued to build up the personal social services. Joint finance and planning between health and local authorities aims to prevent overlapping of services and to encourage the development of community services such as hostels for patients discharged from mental hospitals. In deciding their priorities, some local authorities attach greater importance than others to the personal social services and to the various categories of people in need of help, with the result that provision can vary from area to area.

Central government is responsible directly for the National Health Service, administered by health authorities and boards acting as its agents, and for the social security system. It has an indirect responsibility for the personal social services administered by local government authorities.

Spending on social welfare in 1977 was: health £6,730 million, personal social services £1,266 and social security £13,213 million.

NATIONAL HEALTH SERVICE

The National Health Service is based upon the principle that medical care and advice should be readily available to everyone, at little or no cost. Health services are available largely free of charge to everyone ordinarily resident in Britain. Visitors can also use the Service if they require immediate treatment for an unforeseen emergency; they are expected to pay if the purpose of their visit is to seek treatment. There are reciprocal health arrangements with some countries (see p 121). The Service is administered by appointed statutory authorities and is financed largely from general taxation, but other sources of revenue include charges for some items and a small part of the national insurance contribution (see p 126).

Since the beginning of the Service in 1948 (a period in which there have been considerable advances in standards of living, nutrition and scientific medicine), the infant mortality rate has been halved. The health of children has steadily improved with the decline of the major infectious diseases, and deaths from tuberculosis, poliomyelitis and diptheria have fallen steeply. As part of the general growth of facilities under the National Health Service, staffing has improved markedly. Since 1965, for example, the hospital medical staff in England, Wales and Scotland has increased by nearly 53 per cent and the nursing staff by over 32 per cent.

Although major advances have been made in the provision of health facilities, certain problems remain, notably regional disparities in health provision and a shortage of resources resulting from the need to restrain the growth in public expenditure. An additional problem is the high cost of technologically advanced equipment required for diagnosis and treatment. To help alleviate some of these difficulties the Government is allocating more funds to the less-favoured regions. Greater emphasis is being placed on preventive services (such as screening and health surveillance of children, immunisation, family planning and measures to discourage cigarette smoking) and on developing the services provided by family doctors, dentists and ophthalmic practitioners, district nurses, midwives and health visitors. A continued rise in standards in general practice is expected as a result of compulsory vocational training schemes for family doctors.

A Royal Commission is considering the best use and management of the financial and manpower resources of the National Health Service.

ADMINISTRATION The health ministers—the Secretary of State for Social Services in England and the Secretaries of State for Scotland, Wales and Northern Ireland—are responsible for all aspects of the health services in their respective countries. Within each of the four countries the health departments (the Department of Health and Social Security in England, the Scottish Home and Health Department, the Welsh Office and the Department of Health and Social Services in Northern Ireland) are responsible for strategic planning. Area health authorities in England and Wales, health boards in Scotland and health and social services boards in Northern Ireland are responsible for planning and operational control of all health services in their area. In England, because of its greater size and population, there is an additional tier of regional authorities responsible for regional planning and certain services best administered on a regional basis (for example, research and major capital building work).

There are 14 regional health authorities and 90 area health authorities in England, 8 area health authorities in Wales and 15 health boards in Scotland. They are statutory agencies of central government and co-operate closely with local authorities responsible for social work, environmental health, education and other services. In general the areas covered by area health authorities and health boards correspond with those of the major local authorities.   Health and local authorities in England, Wales and Scotland co-operate by means of joint planning arrangements and joint consultative committees.

In Northern Ireland the four health and social services boards act as agents for the Department of Health and Social Services.

Area authorities and health boards in Great Britain have discretion to determine the pattern of services best suited to their areas but they have to take account of national priorities. In most areas the day-to-day running of services is carried out by management teams in districts which usually contain a district general hospital and have a population of between 200,000 and 500,000, though some are considerably larger (in Scotland and Wales they may be much smaller in the remoter areas). In Scotland a Common Services Agency organises certain central services; there are similar agencies in Wales and Northern Ireland.

The health authorities and boards consist of unpaid part-time members. All chairmen and members of the English regional authorities and the Scottish health boards, and the chairmen of the English and Welsh area health authorities are appointed by the Secretary of State concerned after consultation with professional, local authority, university and other interests. Two-thirds of the members of the area health authorities are appointed by the regional health authorities in England and the Secretary of State in Wales; these include at least one university nominee and some professional members who work within the Service. The remainder are appointed by the corresponding local authorities, Area authorities in areas containing a university medical school are known as area authorities (teaching) and in addition to two university nominees contain at least two members with teaching hospital experience. University medical and dental schools are responsible for teaching medical students and the National Health Service provides hospital clinical facilities for their training.

There is statutory provision for professional advisory committees at national, regional and area level; the authorities have a duty to consult with these committees. The main national advisory bodies are the Central Health Services Council in England and Wales, the Scottish Health Service Planning Council in Scotland and the Health and Social Services Council in Northern Ireland. The Health Advisory Service for England and Wales reports to the Secretaries of State on conditions in hospitals and the community health service.

The Scottish Hospital Advisory Service reports to health boards and the Secretary of State.

Public representation in the Service for England and Wales is provided by community health councils. These consist of about 20 to 30 members, half of them appointed by local government councils and the rest mainly on the nomination of voluntary bodies interested in local health services. They have access to the area health authority, the right to secure information and the right to visit hospitals.

In Scotland local health councils have been set up by the health boards to represent the interests of the public. District committees exercise this function in Northern Ireland.

Health Service Commissioners

Legislation provides for the appointment of three Health Service Commissioners (for England, Scotland and Wales) to investigate complaints from members of the public about the health service. All three posts are held by the Parliamentary Commissioner for Administration (see p 35). His health service jurisdiction covers the failure of a health authority to carry out its statutory duties, maladministration, and injustice or hardship caused by a failure in a service. A complaint can only be considered if the complainant has sent it first to the health authority and given it sufficient time to investigate and reply. Matters outside his jurisdiction include action taken solely in the exercise of clinical judgment and the action of family practitioners (see p 116).

The commissioner reports annually to ministers who lay the reports before Parliament; he also publishes at regular intervals full texts of his reports of investigations without, however, naming individuals or institutions.

In Northern Ireland the Commissioner for Complaints (see p 68) investigates complaints concerning the health service, but not the actions of medical practitioners or the professions supplementary to medicine.

Finance

About 88 per cent of the cost of the health services falls on the Treasury while the rest is met from the national health service contribution paid with the national insurance contribution and from some charges.

There are charges for medical prescriptions but these do not apply to children under 16 years, expectant and nursing mothers, women aged 60 and over and men aged 65 and over, patients suffering from certain medical conditions, war and Service disablement pensioners (for treatment of their disability), and families with very low incomes, including those receiving supplementary benefits and family income supplement. In addition there are charges for treatment in the general dental service (but not for examination only or for treatment given to people under 21 years or women who are pregnant or have borne a child in the past year); for dentures (except for children under 16 or still at school, and women who are pregnant or have borne a child in the past year); for spectacles (except children's standard spectacles); and for some other articles. Certain low income groups are exempt from dental and optical charges (those receiving supplementary benefit or family income supplement and those receiving free prescriptions or welfare foods).

A limited amount of accommodation may be made available at a small charge for hospital patients wanting privacy as long as it is not needed on medical grounds for non-paying patients.

Provision is also made at certain hospitals for patients to be treated as private patients on payment of the whole cost of their accommodation and treatment. The Government is phasing out private pay beds in National Health Service hospitals (for private health provision, see p 121).

Hospital medical staffs are salaried and can be employed full-time or part-time. Part-time hospital doctors are free to accept private patients. General medical practitioners are self-employed and paid by a system of fees and allowances designed to reflect responsibilities, work load and practice expenses.

Dentists providing treatment in their own surgeries are paid on a prescribed scale of fees according to the treatment they have carried out. Pharmacists dispensing on their own premises are paid on the basis of the prescriptions they dispense. Ophthalmic medical practitioners and ophthalmic opticians taking part in the general ophthalmic service are paid approved fees for each sight test made; opticians who dispense spectacles are paid according to the number and type of pairs supplied.

PRIMARY HEALTH CARE

Primary health care is in the hands of doctors, dentists, opticians and pharmacists working within the Service as independent practitioners, and district nurses, midwives and health visitors employed by the health authorities.

Family Practitioner Services

The family practitioner services cover the services given to patients by doctors, dentists, opticians and pharmacists of their own choice. They are administered in England and Wales by family practitioner committees established by the health authorities, in Scotland by the health boards and in Northern Ireland by the Central Services Agency.

There are nearly 26,000 family doctors under contract to the National Health Service. A doctor may not normally have more than 3,500 patients; the average number in Great Britain is about 2,300 and in Northern Ireland 2,150. Access to most other parts of the health service is obtained through the family doctor.

Some 960 ophthalmic medical practitioners and about 7,080 ophthalmic and dispensing opticians are engaged in the general ophthalmic services which provide for the testing of sight and provision of spectacles. Patients requiring treatment are dealt with through the hospital eye service.

There are over 13,800 dentists taking part in the health service.

There are about 10,700 retail pharmacies under contract to the National Health Service with responsibility for the dispensing of prescriptions except for the small number dispensed by hospital pharmacies and some family doctors.

District Nurses, Midwives and Health Visitors

District nurses attend to people needing nursing at home or elsewhere outside hospital. Although almost all babies are born in hospital, there is a domiciliary service for mothers having their babies at home, midwives and family doctors caring for mothers and babies after birth. Midwives also assist births in hospital. Health visitors are concerned with the health of the household as a whole and provide services for families with young children and care for elderly people; they take part in health education, assist in preventing ill-health, and work closely with family doctors, district nurses and social workers.

Group Practices and Health Centres

Family doctors often work as members of health care teams with health visitors, district nurses, and sometimes midwives or social workers. About four-fifths are in partnership or group practices. About a fifth of the doctors in Great Britain and almost a half in Northern Ireland work in nearly 1,000 modern and well-equipped health centres built and maintained by the health authorities. Additional services at health centres may include child health clinics, family planning, ante-natal care, dentistry, ophthalmic and pharmaceutical services, chiropody and health education.

HOSPITALS AND SPECIALIST SERVICES

The hospital and specialist services include district general hospitals with treatment and diagnostic facilities for in-patients, day-patients and out-patients, hospital maternity departments, infectious disease units, psychiatric and geriatric facilities, rehabilitation facilities, convalescent homes and all forms of specialised treatment. A number of specialist hospitals for mentally ill, mentally handicapped and elderly people are also provided. In the long term the Government plans to replace the majority of mental illness hospitals by facilities based on psychiatric units in district general hospitals. Mentally handicapped people are cared for in hospital and in the community; it is long-term government policy to shift the emphasis from hospital to community care but, where hospital treatment is required, it will be provided in small units near to the patient's own home. It is also government policy to provide more geriatric beds in general hospitals, while elderly people needing longer term care will increasingly be admitted to smaller community hospitals.

Hospitals

A large proportion of the hospitals in the National Health Service were built in the nineteenth century; some trace their origins to much earlier charitable foundations, such as the famous St. Thomas' and St. Bartholomew's hospitals in London. Much has been done to improve and extend existing hospitals, some of which are housed in inconvenient buildings, and many new hospitals have been or are being opened. The most recent development in hospital design is the 'nucleus' hospital of some 300 beds which will make a more intensive use of space and facilities; it can be used either as the first stage of a new hospital or as an extension of an existing hospital. Building work on the first nucleus hospital began in 1978.

There are 2,700 NHS hospitals with nearly half a million beds and a nursing and midwifery staff of about 425,000 (whole time equivalent). There are 38,620 medical staff including over 14,260 consultants.

Rehabilitation

Rehabilitation is an important part of medical care beginning at the onset of illness or injury and aimed at helping people to live as normally as possible. Rehabilitation is especially important for elderly, disabled and mentally-ill people who need such help in order to become self-sufficient. Facilities are provided in the majority of hospitals and at special centres. The work is carried out by teams of doctors, nurses, physiotherapists, remedial gymnasts, occupational therapists, speech therapists and social workers. The hospital departments work closely with the Disablement Resettlement Service of the Manpower Services Commission (the Department of Manpower Services in Northern Ireland).

Medical services may include the provision, free of charge, of artificial limbs and eyes, hearing aids, surgical supports, wheel chairs, and other appliances. Very severely physically handicapped patients may be issued with electrical control equipment which enables them to operate devices such as alarm bells, radio and television, a telephone, and heating. The controls are operated by continuous depression of a microswitch or by sustained suction through a pneumatic tube with a pipe-stem mouthpiece. Nursing aids for the handicapped at home can be borrowed.

Local authority social workers, home helps and occupational therapists are available to hospital patients who, because of their illness, have difficulties on their return home.

Hospices

Some 40 hospices provide care for the dying either directly in residential homes or through the provision of nursing and other assistance in the patient's own home. About ten are financed entirely by the NHS; the remainder, most of which receive support from public funds, are run by independent charitable organisations. Control of symptoms and psychological support for the patient and his family form the central features of hospice care. The hospice movement, which is world-wide, originated in Britain.

Drug Dependence

Treatment for narcotic addiction is available at drug treatment clinics. Some doctors are licensed by the Home Secretary to prescribe heroin and cocaine to addicts (in Northern Ireland licensing is the responsibility of the Department of Health and Social Services). Doctors do not require a licence to prescribe methadone and other controlled drugs to addicts, but all doctors must notify the Home Office of any patient they consider to be addicted to certain controlled drugs.

Hospital services have treatment for drug misusers including accident and emergency services for people who take overdoses. Several voluntary bodies organise rehabilitation facilities including accommodation, day centres and counselling. The Advisory Council on the Misuse of Drugs advises ministers on measures to prevent the misuse of dangerous drugs or to deal with the social problems connected with their misuse.

Alcoholism

Treatment is provided for alcoholics as part of the general psychiatric service. In the National Health Service there are some 23 specialised treatment units as well as a day hospital. Three experimental detoxification centres are being sponsored by the Department of Health and Social Security. Closely linked with treatment are community services (including those provided by voluntary organisations) covering prevention, advice and rehabilitation.

Parents and Children

Special preventive health services, including free dental care, are available for expectant and nursing mothers and young children. A feature of the service is the education of parents before and after the birth by means of talks, discussion groups, demonstrations and classes. Very young children are tested for vision, hearing, speech and language deficiencies so that any handicap can be identified. Family planning advice and help is provided at many clinics and welfare foods (dried milk and vitamins) are distributed from them.

Sick children are treated at home or in hospital as out- or day-patients. If admission to hospital is necessary, the Government encourages health authorities to accommodate them in children's departments staffed by paediatricians and specially trained nurses.

The school health service, which is part of the National Health Service, organises health surveillance of school children including medical inspection and dental inspection and treatment where appropriate. The staff of the school health service work closely with local education authorities in the medical assessment of handicapped children thought to need special attention.

Child guidance facilities provide help and advice concerning children with psychological or emotional problems. These are run by local social services and education authorities and by the health authorities. In Scotland child guidance clinics are run by education authorities.

Family Planning

Free family planning facilities are available to everyone through family planning clinics, hospitals and a domiciliary service. Most family doctors provide a similar service for women only.

Abortion

Under the Abortion Act 1967 termination of a pregnancy may take place if two registered doctors think that its continuance would involve a greater risk to the life of the pregnant woman (or of injury to her physical or mental health or that of any existing children in the family) than if the pregnancy were ended. Termination may also be allowed if the two doctors think that there is a substantial risk of the child being born with severe physical or mental abnormalities. Abortions may be carried out in National Health Service hospitals or in premises officially approved for the purpose. The Department of Health and Social Security has issued guidance on counselling women with unwanted pregnancies. The Abortion Act does not apply in Northern Ireland.

Blood Transfusion

The blood transfusion service has more than 2 million voluntary blood donors. There are 19 regional transfusion centres in Britain recruiting donors and organising donor sessions in towns and villages, factories and offices, and in establishments maintained by the armed forces. Donors must be between the ages of 18 and 65. The regional centres are also responsible for blood grouping and testing, maintaining blood banks, providing a consultant service to hospitals, teaching in medical schools, and instructing doctors, nurses and technicians. There are four central laboratories which prepare blood products and undertake research.

Ambulance Services

Where necessary on medical grounds, free transport by ambulance is provided by the health authorities. The work of the ambulance service falls into two categories: emergency work dealing with sudden illness, urgent maternity cases, and accidents of all kinds; and non-urgent work providing transport for people needing out-patient treatment at hospitals, clinics and day hospitals.

The London Ambulance Service is probably the largest of its kind in the world, catering for eight million residents and non-residents in an area of

1,580 sq km (610 sq m). It uses over 1,000 vehicles at 85 ambulance stations and has a staff of 2,700. On an average day it receives 1,500 emergency calls (one call every minute) and carries out 7,000 non-urgent patient journeys.

In some areas the ambulance service is augmented by volunteers using their own cars.

HEALTH EDUCATION

Health education in England, Wales and Northern Ireland is promoted by the Health Education Council which assists in the development of programmes of health education with the health authorities, professional organisations, voluntary bodies and industry. Central health education services in Scotland are organised by the Scottish Health Education Unit, which is part of the Common Services Agency. Major themes of publicity campaigns are the encouragement of family planning, correct diet and exercise, and warnings against cigarette smoking and excessive consumption of alcoholic drink. Although expenditure for health education is met largely from central government funds, the Health Education Council is free to determine its own priorities and programme.

Within the National Health Service, medical officers advise health authorities on health education, and specialist officers have executive responsibility.

SAFETY OF MEDICINES

Under the Medicines Act 1968, which came into force in 1971 and applies to the whole of the United Kingdom, the health and agriculture ministers are responsible for licensing the manufacture, marketing and importation of medicines for human and veterinary use. The Medicines Commission advises the ministers on policy regarding medicines and a Committee on Safety of Medicines advises the health ministers on the safety, efficacy and quality of new medicines and monitors adverse drug reactions. A review of medicines on the market began in 1975, the health ministers being advised by the Committee on the Review of Medicines. The Act also controls the advertising, labelling, packaging, distribution, sale and supply of medicines.

THE HEALTH PROFESSIONS

Only people whose names are on the medical and dental registers may practise as doctors and dentists in the National Health Service. Registration as a doctor requires five or six years' training in medical school and hospital, with an additional year's experience in a hospital; for a dentist, four or more years at a dental school are required. The governing body of the medical profession is the General Medical Council and that of the dentists is the General Dental Council. The British Medical Association is the doctors' main professional association; that of the dentists is the British Dental Association.

The minimum period of hospital training required to qualify for registration as a nurse is normally three years. Training may be in general, sick children's, mental or mental subnormality nursing. An enrolled nurse takes a two-year course. The examining bodies of the nursing profession in England and Wales and in Scotland are the general nursing councils. Midwives in England and Wales and in Scotland must have the certificate of the appropriate Midwives Board. The examining body for nurses and midwives in Northern Ireland is the Northern Ireland Council of Nurses and Midwives. Most pupil midwives are already registered general nurses or sick children's nurses; for them the two-year midwifery training period is reduced to one year and for other registered and enrolled nurses to 18 months. The Royal College of Nursing and the Royal College of Midwives are the professional bodies for nurses and midwives. Health visitors are registered general nurses who have undergone at least the first part of the midwifery course or obstetric nursing before taking a year's course in health visiting, promoted by the Council for the Education and Training of Health Visitors. District nurses are state registered or state enrolled nurses, the majority of whom have undertaken additional training.

A retail or hospital pharmacist must have his or her name entered in the register maintained by the Pharmaceutical Society of Great Britain, the governing body of the profession, or, in Northern Ireland, in the register of the Department of Health and Social Services. Four years' academic study and practical training are necessary for registration. The dispensing of all medicines on doctors' prescriptions and sale of certain specified medicines can be carried out only by, or under the supervision of, a registered pharmacist. Under the Opticians Act 1958 the General Optical Council regulates the professions of ophthalmic optician and dispensing optician; only registered ophthalmic opticians (or registered medical practitioners) may test sight. Training of ophthalmic opticians takes four years including a year of practical experience under supervision. Dispensing opticians may take a two-year full-time course with a year's practical experience or a part-time day-release course while employed with an optician.

State registration may be obtained by chiropodists, dietitians, medical laboratory technicians, occupational therapists, orthoptists, physiotherapists, radiographers and remedial gymnasts. The governing bodies are eight boards, corresponding to the eight professions, under the general supervision of the Council for Professions Supplementary to Medicine. A professional training lasting two to four years is needed to qualify for registration. Only members of those professions who are state registered may be employed in the National Health Service and some other public services.

Dental auxiliaries (who have undergone a two-year training course) and dental hygienists (who have undergone a training course of about a year) may carry out some simple dental work under the direction of a registered dentist.

HEALTH ARRANGEMENTS WITH OTHER COUNTRIES

Britain has special health arrangements with other member states of the European Community under which most United Kingdom nationals are entitled to receive urgent medical treatment in another Community country on the same basis as insured nationals of that country. There are also reciprocal arrangements with some other countries.

PRIVATE MEDICAL TREATMENT

Though practically all residents in Britain use the National Health Service, a number of people sometimes prefer to pay for private consultations and treatment. Among the major users are the families of subscribers to the provident schemes which make provision for private health care in return for annual subscriptions. It is the Government's policy to phase out private facilities from National Health Service hospitals, but patients will remain free to seek medical treatment, and doctors to practise, in private hospitals or nursing homes. Some of these are run by charitable institutions.

ENVIRONMENTAL HEALTH

Environmental health officers employed by local authorities are responsible for the control of air pollution and noise, the inspection of offices, the investigation of unfit housing, and refuse collection and disposal. Doctors who specialise in community medicine and are employed by the health authorities advise local authorities on the medical aspects of environmental health. They may also assist the water authorities responsible for water supply and sewerage.

Environmental health officers are also stationed at ports and airports where they carry out a range of duties concerned with shipping, inspection of imported foods and disease control.

In Northern Ireland district councils are responsible for noise control, collection and disposal of refuse, clean air, and food composition, labelling and hygiene.

Safety of Food

It is illegal to sell food which is injurious to health, unfit for human consumption, or not of the nature, substance or quality demanded. In England and Wales the composition, labelling and description of food are the concern of food and drugs authorities (county councils, London borough councils and the City of London Corporation) while food hygiene and the safety and fitness of food are the concern of district councils, London borough councils and port health authorities. Premises where food or drink is prepared, handled, stored or sold must conform to certain hygiene standards. Environmental health officers may take for analysis or for bacteriological or other examination samples of any food on sale for human consumption. There are special regulations controlling the safety of particular foods such as milk, meat and ice-cream. The Department of Health and Social Security, the Ministry of Agriculture, Fisheries and Food and the Welsh Office are the central departments responsible for giving advice and making regulations. Expert committees of these departments periodically review regulations dealing with food.

In Scotland regional and islands councils are responsible for food standards and labelling, and district and islands councils for food hygiene. District councils in Northern Ireland are responsible for food hygiene, food standards and labelling.

CONTROL OF INFECTIOUS DISEASES

The health authorities have general responsibility for the prevention of disease and co-operate with the local authority environmental health services. The area health authorities and health boards carry out programmes of vaccination and immunisation against diphtheria, measles, rubella (females only), poliomyelitis, tetanus, tuberculosis and whooping cough. Although vaccination is voluntary, the Government encourages parents to obtain protection for their children from these diseases.

The Public Health Laboratory Service provides a network of bacteriological and virological laboratories throughout England and Wales which conduct research and assist in the diagnosis, prevention and control of epidemic diseases. Its largest establishment is the Central Public Health Laboratory at Colindale, in north-west London, which includes the National Collection of Type Cultures, the Food Hygiene Laboratory, and reference laboratories specialising in the identification of infective micro-organisms. In addition it has a surveillance centre, opened in 1977, which investigates and monitors human communicable diseases. In Scotland bacteriological work is done mainly in hospital laboratories. In Northern Ireland a central public health laboratory shares the bacteriological work with hospital laboratories.

PERSONAL SOCIAL SERVICES

Responsibility for personal social services rests with the social services authorities (local authority social services departments in England and Wales, social work departments in Scotland and health and social services boards in Northern Ireland). Many of their services are directed towards the same groups of people needing health services, for example, many elderly or disabled people. Other groups helped are young families with social problems, children deprived of a normal home life, the mentally disordered and young offenders. Close co-operation is maintained between local authority social services departments and health authorities. In Scotland local authorities also undertake duties similar to those of the separate probation and after-care service in England and Wales (see p 89).

The Personal Social Services Council advises ministers on policy issues and provides information and advice to all concerned with the personal social services in England and Wales, based on research projects or inquiries sponsored by the council. Its members are from local government, voluntary, educational and research bodies, and professional organisations. There is cross-representation with the Central Health Services Council and the Central Council for Education and Training in Social Work. Finance comes from central and local government. In Scotland there is an Advisory Council on Social Work and in Northern Ireland a Central Personal Social Services Advisory Committee. Advice on health and personal social services for children in England and Wales is given by the Children's Joint Committee; its members are nominated by the Central Health Services Council, the Personal Social Services Council, and the Secretaries of State for Social Services and Wales.

The Handicapped

Social services authorities have a duty to provide social services for handicapped people. In Great Britain they are required to ascertain the number of handicapped people in their area and to publicise services. A wide range of facilities may be available including advice on personal and social problems arising from disability, assistance in overcoming the effects of disability, adaptations to people's homes (such as fitting ramps, ground floor toilets and grab rails) and various aids to living. In certain circumstances a telephone or a television set may be installed. Other facilities include social and occupational clubs, residential homes and the organisation of outings and holidays. In addition some authorities make arrangements for the teaching of handicrafts and other occupations. Voluntary organisations also provide services for disabled people.

Help available from other sources includes social security, medical treatment, special education, employment and training services and specially designed housing and means of access to public buildings.

The Elderly

Services for elderly people are provided by statutory and voluntary bodies to help them to live at home for as long as possible. These may include the advice and help of social workers, domestic help, delivery of cooked meals, sitters-in, night attendants and laundry services as well as day centres, clubs and recreational workshops. In many areas 'good neighbour' and friendly visiting services are arranged by the local authority or a voluntary organisation. Social services authorities also provide residential accommodation for the elderly and infirm and have powers to register homes run by voluntary organisations or privately. The newer homes usually have accommodation for 30 to 50 residents. About 2,500 homes for elderly people are provided by local authorities in England which house about 1·5 per cent of the population over the age of 65. There are similar homes in Scotland, Wales and Northern Ireland.

Local authorities, as part of their responsibility for public housing, build flats specially designed for elderly people; some of these blocks have resident wardens. Housing associations also build this type of accommodation.

The Mentally Ill and the Mentally Handicapped

Social services authorities have a duty to make arrangements for helping the mentally ill or mentally handicapped in the community, and for prevention and after-care services. Recent developments in the treatment of mental illness, which enable patients either to be treated at home or to be discharged from hospital more quickly provided support is available in the community, are adding to demands for these services and particularly for social work support. Arrangements include training centres for the mentally handicapped, day centres for the mentally ill, as well as social centres and a variety of residential care for the mentally ill and mentally handicapped of all ages. Social workers help patients and their families to deal with social problems arising from mental illness or handicap and can arrange compulsory admission (on a medical recommendation) of mentally disordered people to hospital in certain circumstances.

Help to Families Social services authorities, through their own social workers or a voluntary organisation, make available help and advice to families facing special problems. The home help service provides practical assistance at home for sick and disabled people, elderly people and expectant mothers.

Some authorities make direct provision for the special needs of unmarried mothers and their babies, but most contribute to the cost of work done by voluntary organisations and other bodies.

Child Care Social services authorities are responsible for child care. This includes the provision of day care for children under five, often with special social or health needs, in day nurseries and part-time nursery groups, voluntary and private day nurseries (registered with the local authority), and play groups.

The authorities have a duty to offer advice, guidance and assistance to families in difficulties in order to promote the welfare of children. The aim is to intervene at an early stage to diminish the need to receive children into care or bring them before a juvenile court.

Cases of child abuse are the concern of health and local authorities which have established joint area review committees to represent the views of the professions and agencies and to agree on local policies and practices for handling these cases.

Authorities have a duty to receive into their care any child under the age of 17 who has no parent or guardian or who has been abandoned or whose parents are unable to provide for him if they are satisfied that such intervention is in the interests of the child. The child remains in care until he is 18 years old unless discharged to the care of parents, other relatives or friends before that time. When taking a decision on a child in care, the authorities have to give first consideration to the need to safeguard and promote the welfare of the child. Where children are in care, efforts are made to work with their families in order, where appropriate, to enable the child to return home.

Children in England and Wales may be brought before a juvenile court if they are neglected or ill-treated, exposed to moral danger, beyond the control of parents, not attending school or (if ten years or over) have committed an offence. At the same time it must be shown that the child is in need of care or control which he is unlikely to receive unless a care or other relevant order is made by the court. Local authorities are responsible for undertaking, through social workers, inquiries and consultations with parents, schools and the police. A child may be committed to the care of a local authority under a care order if the juvenile court is satisfied that he is in need of care or control. As an alternative the court may issue a supervision order for a period of up to three years. Supervision is carried out by a social worker or a probation officer.

In Northern Ireland the court may send the child to a training school (see p 93), commit him to the care of a fit person (which may include a health and social services board) or make a supervision order.

In Scotland children in trouble (see p 93) or in need may be brought before a children's hearing which can impose a supervision requirement on a child if it thinks that compulsory measures of care are appropriate. Under these requirements most children are allowed to remain at home under the supervision of a social worker but some may be sent to a residential establishment while under supervision. Supervision requirements are reviewed at intervals of not more than one year until terminated by a children's hearing.

When practicable, children in care are boarded out with foster parents, who receive an allowance to cover the cost of maintenance. If a foster home is not the most suitable place for a child or if one cannot be found for him, he may be placed in a children's home, a voluntary home or other suitable residential accommodation. Community homes for children in care in England and Wales comprise local authority and voluntary children's homes and community homes with education on the premises which provide long-term care usually for the more difficult children. In Scotland local authorities are responsible for placing children in their care either in foster homes, in local authority or voluntary homes, or in residential schools. In Northern Ireland there are residential homes for children in the care of the health and social services boards, although training schools and remand homes are administered separately.

Regulations regarding conduct of community homes and registered voluntary homes and the boarding out of children in care are made by central government.

Voluntary Organisations

Voluntary organisations, many of which were pioneers in child care, continue to play a valuable part in this work. Children's homes run by voluntary organisations are subject to inspection by social work service officers of the central government.

Voluntary bodies concerned with the welfare of children in their own homes include local family casework agencies and the Family Service Units. The National Society for the Prevention of Cruelty to Children and its Scottish counterpart maintain inspectors and visitors to investigate reported cruelty or neglect.

Adoption

Adoption of children is strictly regulated by legislation and some 12,000 adoption orders were made in England and Wales in 1977 and 1,600 in Scotland; the Registrars General keep confidential registers of adopted children. Local authorities have the power to act as adoption agencies and eventually will be obliged to offer such a service. Adoption societies (over 55 societies arrange adoptions) must be registered with their local authority.

Adoptions of minors under the laws of most European and Commonwealth countries are recognised but this does not confer British citizenship on the adopted person.

Social Workers

The effective operation of the social services is largely dependent upon the availability of professionally qualified social workers trained in the methods of social work. Training courses in social work are provided by universities, polytechnics and colleges of further education; their length depends upon previous educational qualifications and can last from one to four years. The Central Council for Education and Training in Social Work recognises social work courses and offers advice to people considering entry to the profession.

Professional social workers (including those working in the National Health Service) are employed by social services authorities. Others work in voluntary organisations or in the probation service (see p 89). Not all social workers employed by social services authorities are professionally qualified, but efforts are being made to increase the number of trained personnel.

SOCIAL SECURITY

National insurance, industrial injuries insurance, child benefit, family income supplement, supplementary benefits, and war pensions constitute a comprehensive system of social security. The payment of many benefits depends on prior payments to the national insurance scheme, while others are available without contribution conditions. The former are paid from the national insurance fund consisting of contributions from employed people and their employers, self-employed people and the Government. Non-contributory benefits are financed from general taxation revenue. Two or more benefits cannot normally be paid for the same set of circumstances.

The Department of Health and Social Security administers these services in Great Britain; within the department, the Supplementary Benefits Commission is responsible for the system of supplementary benefits. In Northern Ireland the Department of Health and Social Services administers social security with the exception of supplementary benefits which are provided through the Supplementary Benefits Commission for Northern Ireland. Pensions and welfare services for war pensioners and their dependants are the responsibility of the Department of Health and Social Security throughout the United Kingdom. Appeals relating to claims for the various benefits are decided by independent tribunals.

A series of Acts in the 1940s established a comprehensive social security system which became operative in July 1948. Benefits were flat-rate but as the level of earnings rose in the 1950s and the 1960s the gap between earnings and benefits tended to widen. In the 1960s, therefore, a modest earnings-related addition to retirement pension was started based on graduated contributions; this principle was extended to unemployment and sickness benefit and, later in 1975, to maternity allowance. In the 1970s new benefits have included better pension arrangements for widows, pensions for people aged 80 and over who have not qualified for a national insurance retirement pension, and more benefits for disabled people (see p 130). The most important advance since the 1940s is the new earnings-related state pension scheme providing improved retirement, widows', widowers' and invalidity pensions.

CONTRIBUTIONS

Employees and Employers

Class 1 contributions are earnings-related and cover the employee for retirement pension, sickness and invalidity benefits, unemployment benefit, maternity benefits, widows' benefits, and death grant. Earnings-related supplements to sickness and unemployment benefit and maternity allowance are also covered. Industrial injuries benefits, although non-contributory, are payable from the national insurance fund. Additional payments are made for dependants.

The contribution paid by the employee varies; if he is not a member of a 'contracted-out' occupational pension scheme run by his employers (see p 128), his contribution is 6·5 per cent of earnings up to £120 a week (the upper earnings limit) provided that these earnings are at least £17·50 (the lower earnings limit). The employer pays 10 per cent of the same earnings range. If the employee is a member of a 'contracted-out' occupational pension scheme, a lower Class 1 contribution is payable, namely 6·5 per cent of earnings up to the lower earnings limit and 4 per cent of earnings between the two limits; the employer's contribution is 10 per cent and 5·5 per cent respectively Contributions are collected through the 'Pay As You Earn' income tax system. The employer also pays to the Exchequer a national insurance surcharge of 3·5 per cent of the earnings range for each of his employees (see p 342).

Self-employed People

Self-employed people pay a flat-rate Class 2 contribution of £1·90 a week and a Class 4 contribution amounting to 5 per cent of net profits or gains between £2,000 and £6,250 a year. Self-employed contributors receive basic retirement pension (see below) and the same benefits as employees with the exception of unemployment benefit, earnings-related supplements, and industrial injuries benefits.

Married Women and Widows

Certain married women and widows retain the right to pay Class 1 contributions at the reduced rate of 2 per cent when employed and to pay no Class 2 contributions when self-employed. This right is being phased out and is retained only by those entitled to it at 5 April 1978. Reduced contributions do not count for the purposes of benefit. The employer's contribution is not affected.

Voluntary Contributions

Voluntary Class 3 contributions of £1·80 are payable by people wanting to safeguard rights to some benefits. Class 3 (and Class 2) contributions are paid by stamping a national insurance card or by direct debit of a bank or National Girobank account.

Exemptions

Some people do not have to pay contributions. Employees who continue working after pensionable age (60 for women and 65 for men) do not pay contributions though the employer remains liable. People earning less than the lower earnings limit are not liable for contributions, neither are their employers. Self-employed people with earnings below £950 a year and those over pensionable age may be excused payment of contributions.

BENEFITS

For most of the benefits there are two contribution conditions. First, before benefit can be paid at all, certain contributions have to be paid; secondly, the full rate of benefit cannot be paid unless contributions have been paid or credited up to a specific level over a specified period. There are special rules to help a widow who does not become entitled to a widow's pension at widowhood or when her children have grown up, to qualify for sickness, unemployment or maternity benefit in the period before she can have established or re-established herself in insurance through her own contributions; there are also provisions to help a divorced woman who was not paying contributions during her marriage. The main benefits (payable weekly) are summarised below. The rates quoted are those effective from November 1978; allowances for children include child benefit.

Social security benefits are reviewed every year and increased if their value has fallen through inflation. Long-term benefits, such as basic retirement pension, are linked with percentage increases in average earnings or retail prices, whichever is the higher. Short-term benefits like sickness or unemployment benefit are tied to percentage increases in retail prices.

Retirement Pension

A state retirement pension is payable to women at the age of 60 and to men at the age of 65. The weekly rate of basic pension is £19·50 for men and women qualifying on their own contributions and £11·70 for a woman qualifying on her husband's contributions. In 1978 the new state pension scheme came into operation and will mature fully after 20 years of contributions; the retirement pension will consist of the basic pension plus an additional pension of 25 per cent of earnings between the lower earnings limit and the upper earnings limit (see p 126). If there are fewer than 20 years' contributions, a proportionate rate of additional pension will be payable, that is 1·25 per cent of earnings between the earnings limits for each year of contributions paid under the scheme.

Employers are free to 'contract-out' their employees from the state scheme for additional pension and provide their own occupational pension in its place provided that the latter is at least as good as the state additional pension. The State remains responsible for the basic pension. Lower national insurance contributions are payable if contracting-out takes place.

Rights to basic pension are safeguarded for mothers who are away from work looking after children or for people giving up work to care for severely disabled relatives. Women contributors receive the same pension as men with the same earnings.

A small pension is also payable to those people who contributed to the state graduated pension scheme which operated between 1961 and 1975.

Basic pension is protected against inflation by annual increases. It is raised in line with average percentage increases in earnings or prices, whichever is the higher. Additional pension will be calculated by revaluing earnings in line with the general movement of earnings, and any pension awarded will keep up with the average percentage increase in retail prices. Since 1978 the small graduated pension has been protected against inflation.

In real terms the value of the retirement pension for a married couple has more than doubled since 1948.

A non-contributory retirement pension of £11·95 for a man, single woman or widow and £7·30 for a married woman (including an age addition of 25p) is payable to people over the age of 80 who have not qualified for a contributory pension or who qualified for one at a lower rate than the non-contributory pension. The age addition is also paid to all other pensioners aged over 80.

Mothers and Children
Maternity Benefits

A maternity grant of £25 is payable for each living child born and for a still-born child if the pregnancy lasts for at least 28 weeks. Maternity allowance is £15·75 a week and is payable normally from 11 weeks before the expected week of confinement until the sixth week following the birth. The allowance is payable only to working women who have paid full Class 1 or Class 2 contributions. An earnings-related supplement may also be payable.

Child Benefit

The non-contributory child benefit is the main social security benefit for children. The April 1979 rate is £4 for each child (£6 for the first child of single-parent families). Income tax allowances for children are being phased out gradually and their value transferred to child benefit which is tax free and payable to the mother. Benefit is payable for children up to the age of 16 and for those up to the age of 19 if they continue in full-time education: benefit is not payable if the young person is taking a degree, teacher training or any other advanced course or if the education is sponsored by an employer.

Child's Special Allowance

A contributory child's special allowance of £9·35 for each child, inclusive of child benefit, is payable to a mother on the death of a former husband if the marriage was dissolved or annulled and if the husband was contributing to the support of the children.

Guardian's
Allowance

A non-contributory guardian's allowance of £9·35, inclusive of child benefit, is payable to someone who takes an orphaned child into his or her family, provided that one of the dead parents satisfied a residence condition and that the claimant is entitled to child benefit for the child.

Other Benefits

Additions for children are payable with widows', sickness, unemployment and other benefits.

Widows

A contributory widow's allowance is payable for the first 26 weeks of widowhood at the rate of £27·30 plus £9·35 for each child, inclusive of child benefit. An earnings-related supplement may also be payable. After this a widowed mother receives a widowed mother's allowance of £19·50 plus £9·35 for each child, inclusive of child benefit. Widow's pension is payable to a widow who is 40 years or over when her husband dies or when her entitlement to widowed mother's allowance ends; the rates payable range from £5·85 for widows of 40 to £19·50 for widows of 50 or over. Payment continues irrespective of earnings until the widow remarries or begins drawing retirement pension.

Under the new state pension scheme widow's pension and widowed mother's allowance will consist of a basic pension and an additional pension earned by the deceased husband's contribution. If the widow is aged between 40 and 50 when widowed (or when her children have grown up), she gets part of the additional pension.

A man whose wife dies when they are both over pension age will be able to inherit his wife's pension rights just as a widow inherits her husband's rights.

Industrial Injuries

There are also benefits for widows under the industrial injuries scheme (see p 130). A pension of £27·30 is payable for the first 26 weeks of widowhood. A widow may also receive an earnings-related addition if sufficient Class 1 contributions have been paid by the deceased husband on earnings in excess of the lower earnings limit in the relevant tax year. Thereafter, she can receive a pension of £20·05 a week if she was aged 50 at the date of her husband's death, or has dependent children or fulfils certain other conditions; otherwise, she receives £5·85 a week. If she had been living apart from her husband, a pension is payable only if she was receiving or entitled to receive at least £0·25 a week for her maintenance from him.

In addition allowances are paid for children under the child benefit age limits. For widows they are £9·35 for each child inclusive of child benefit. Other beneficiaries receive £4·85.

Certain other dependants, such as parents and other relatives, may be entitled to pensions, allowances or gratuities.

Sick and Disabled People

There is a large variety of benefits for people unable to work because of sickness or disablement.

Sickness Benefit

Contributory sickness benefit of £15·75 a week is payable for 28 weeks. There are allowances of £9·75 for a wife or other adult dependant and £4·85 for each child inclusive of child benefit. An earnings-related supplement may be payable for up to six months but total benefit (including the flat-rate benefit) cannot exceed 85 per cent of the reckonable weekly earnings on which the supplement is based.

Invalidity Pension

Invalidity pension is £19·50 plus £11·70 for a wife and £9·35 for a child, inclusive of child benefit, and is payable when sickness benefit ends if the beneficiary is still incapable of work. An invalidity allowance (ranging from £1·30 to £4·15 according to age) is paid with the pension to those people who become sick more than five years before retirement age.

Under the new pension scheme, invalidity pension will be replaced by a basic pension and an additional earnings-related pension calculated in the same way as the new retirement pension.

Industrial Injuries Benefits

Various benefits are payable for injury or disablement caused by an accident at work or a prescribed disease.

Injury benefit for an adult is £18·50 a week plus £9·75 for an adult dependant and £4·85 for each child, inclusive of child benefit. It is paid when the employed earner is incapable of work and payment can continue for a maximum of 26 weeks beginning on the date of the accident or development of the disease. A person entitled to sickness benefit who draws injury benefit instead, also receives an earnings-related supplement (see p 129).

When injury benefit ceases disablement benefit may be paid if, as the result of the industrial accident or prescribed disease, there is a loss of physical or mental faculty. The amount depends on the extent of the disablement as assessed by a medical board; it varies from £31·90 a week for 100 per cent disablement to £6·38 for 20 per cent disablement, but for disablement of less than 20 per cent a gratuity is normally paid.

In certain circumstances disablement benefit may be supplemented as follows: unemployability supplement at the weekly rate of £19·50; invalidity allowance according to age (see above); constant attendance allowance of up to £12·70 a week normally, or up to £25·40 in exceptionally severe cases; an allowance of £12·70 a week payable in addition to constant attendance allowance in certain cases of exceptionally severe disablement; a special hardship allowance of up to £12·76 for a person who is unfit to return to his regular job or to do work of an equivalent standard; and hospital treatment allowance which raises the disablement benefit to that for a 100 per cent assessment during hospital treatment for the industrial injury. Increases of disablement benefit for dependants may be payable with unemployability supplement. There are benefits for widows and their children (see p 129).

Other Benefits

An attendance allowance of £15·60 is paid to severely disabled people requiring a great deal of attention by day and at night. A lower rate of £10·40 may be paid to those who need help either by day or at night. A non-contributory invalidity pension of £11·70 is payable to people of working age unable to work and not qualifying for the national insurance invalidity pension; it is also payable to disabled housewives incapable of work and unable to perform their normal household tasks.

A weekly invalid care allowance of £11·70 is payable to people (aged between 16 and pension age) who cannot go out to work because they are caring for a severely disabled relative receiving an attendance allowance.

Physically disabled people unable to walk may be entitled to a mobility allowance of £10 a week to help pay their transport costs. The allowance is intended for people aged between 5 and 65 (males) or 5 and 60 (females). At present the age group 5–58 is covered. An independent organisation called Motability assists those disabled drivers and disabled passengers wanting to use their mobility allowance to rent a vehicle.

Unemployment Benefit

Unemployment benefit at the same rate as sickness benefit (see p 129) is payable for up to 312 days (not counting Sundays) in any one spell of unemployment; periods which are 13 weeks or less apart count as one spell

Earnings-related supplement may be payable on the same basis as that for sickness benefit. Anyone claiming unemployment benefit has to be registered for employment at a local office of the Manpower Services Commission (in Northern Ireland the Department of Manpower Services) which helps people to find jobs.

Death Grant A death grant is payable on the death of a contributor or a contributor's near relative. It is normally £30 for an adult and a smaller sum for a child.

SUPPLEMENTARY BENEFITS Every person aged 16 or over who is not in full-time work and who does not have enough money to live on may be entitled to supplementary benefit. It is not awarded to people attending school or for the requirements of people involved in a trade dispute (dependants of strikers, however, are covered). In Northern Ireland a residence condition must also be satisfied. The benefit takes the form of a supplementary allowance for people under the minimum retirement age, and a supplementary pension for those over. The benefit is the amount by which a person's needs exceed his available resources, both being defined by rules approved by Parliament. The calculation of needs is based on different amounts for single people and family groups (for blind people there are special higher amounts) with, in each case an addition for rent. A higher long-term scale is used for retirement pensioners and for people under pension age who have received supplementary benefit for more than two years without having to sign on for work. Additions can be made for special dietary or heating requirements. A single payment of benefit may be made to meet an exceptional need. When resources are calculated, most social security benefits are taken into account in full. Part of most other income including part-time earnings, disablement benefit and war widow's pension is ignored, as is the capital value of an owner occupied house or capital resources of less than £1,250.

The payment of a supplementary allowance to an able-bodied person of working age may be conditional on registering for employment at an unemployment benefit office of the Department of Employment or, in Northern Ireland, the Department of Manpower Services. The supplementary benefits scheme is administered by a Supplementary Benefits Commission within the Department of Health and Social Security and there is a similar commission in Northern Ireland.

The Supplementary Benefits Commission also has a duty to influence people without a settled way of living to lead a more normal life. It provides temporary accommodation for them in 21 reception centres, one of which is administered by a local authority on its behalf. For men who have been unemployed for long periods and who are receiving supplementary allowances, it runs 17 re-establishment centres, three of which have residential accommodation, where they are given help to fit them again for work. These provisions do not apply in Northern Ireland.

FAMILY INCOME SUPPLEMENT Family income supplement is a cash benefit for families (including single parents) with small incomes where the head of the family is in full-time work and there is at least one dependent child. It is payable when the gross weekly income of a family falls below a prescribed amount, fixed at £46 a week where there is one child plus £4 for each additional child. The weekly rate of the supplement is half the difference between the family's income and the prescribed amount up to a maximum of £10·50 for a one-child family and this is increased by £1 for each additional child.

WAR PENSIONS AND RELATED SERVICES

The war pensions scheme is administered throughout the United Kingdom by the Department of Health and Social Security. Pensions are payable to people disabled as a result of service in the armed forces or from injuries received in the merchant navy or civil defence during war-time.

The current basic pension for 100 per cent disablement for a private soldier is £31·90 a week, but the amount varies according to rank and the degree of disablement. Allowances for a wife and children are paid in addition to the basic pension. There is a wide range of supplementary allowances, the main ones being for unemployability (£20·75 a week), constant attendance (up to £12·70 and, exceptionally, £25·40 a week), comforts (£2·70 or £5·40 a week), and lowered standard of occupation (up to £12·76 a week). An age allowance (between £2·20 and £6·80 a week) is payable to disabled pensioners who are aged over 65 or over and whose assessment is 40 per cent or more.

Pensions are also paid to war widows and war orphans. The standard rate of pension for widows of private soldiers is £25·30 a week, with additional allowances for their children and, in certain cases, a rent allowance (up to £9·60 a week). There is an additional allowance of £2·40 for widows aged 65 which is increased to £4·80 at the age of 70. Parents or other relatives who were dependent on a person whose death resulted from service in the Forces may receive pensions if they are in financial need.

The Department of Health and Social Security maintains a welfare service for war pensioners, war widows and war orphans. It works in close co-operation with many voluntary and ex-Service organisations who give financial aid and personal help to disabled ex-Service men and women and their families.

TAXATION

Social security benefits (other than child, maternity, unemployment, sickness, invalidity, injury or disablement benefit) are included in the taxable income on which income tax is assessed. On the other hand various income tax reliefs and exemptions are allowed on account of age or liability for the support of dependants. Supplementary benefit, family income supplement, attendance allowances and war disablement pensions are not taxable.

PREVENTING ABUSE

Measures are taken to ensure that social security payments go only to those for whom they are intended. Increased efforts are being made to cut down on fraudulent claims, the number of prosecutions rising from 15,400 in 1975 to 26,000 in 1977; the conviction rate is about 98 per cent. The size of the problem, however, remains small; as far as can be established, only £3·2 million was identified in 1976–77 as lost through fraud—about £0·03 for every £100 paid in benefits. The value of benefits unclaimed by people entitled to them is believed to be very many times greater than that of the money lost by fraud.

OTHER WELFARE BENEFITS

In addition to payments provided under the social security legislation, there are a number of other benefits for which people with low incomes may be eligible. These include legal aid and assistance (see p 100), rent rebates and allowances (see p 176), rate rebates (see p 66), exemption from health service charges (see p 116) and free school meals (see p 143).

VOLUNTARY SERVICES

The State services are complemented by those provided by voluntary organisations and by individual volunteers. Voluntary organisations, especially the churches, pioneered the development of many social services by providing schools, hospitals, clinics, dispensaries and social and recreational clubs. However, these facilities were not uniformly spread throughout the country and did not cover everyone in need. Gradually the State accepted responsibility for the major services by developing a comprehensive structure to ensure a minimum standard of living and well-being for the population.

State and voluntary social services work in co-operation. Central and local government make grants to the voluntary agencies. Public authorities plan and carry out their duties taking account of the work of voluntary organisations. Local authorities and voluntary agencies provide residential care for elderly, disabled, mentally ill and mentally handicapped people and for children. It has been estimated that about 5 million people take part in some voluntary work during the course of a year.

Co-ordination of government interests in voluntary social service throughout Britain is the responsibility of the Home Office Voluntary Services Unit. The Volunteer Centre, a national centre for information and research on voluntary work, was established in 1973 with the aid of a government grant. There are many full-time and part-time local volunteer bureaux.

In England and Wales the Charity Commission, a Government agency, gives free advice to trustees of charities, making schemes to modify their purposes or facilitate their administration when necessary. It maintains central and local registers of charities which are open to public inspection, and it investigates and checks abuses, though it has no power to act in the administration of a charity.

Voluntary Organisations

There are thousands of voluntary organisations ranging from national bodies to small individual local groups. Most are members of larger associations or are represented on local or national co-ordinating councils or committees. Some are chiefly concerned with giving personal service, others in the formation of public opinion and exchange of information. Some carry out both functions.

The main voluntary body in England which aims to provide central links between voluntary organisations and official bodies is the National Council of Social Service, which brings together most of the principal voluntary agencies for consultation and joint action, either as a whole or in groups of those concerned with particular aspects, such as youth work. There are also the Scottish Council of Social Service, the Council for Social Service for Wales and the Northern Ireland Council of Social Service, which perform similar functions.

Organisations concerned with personal and family problems include the voluntary family casework agencies like the Family Welfare Association, Family Service Units, and the National Society for the Prevention of Cruelty to Children; marriage guidance centres affiliated to the National Marriage Guidance Council; the National Council of Voluntary Child Care Organisations; the National Council for One Parent Families; and the Samaritans, who help people who are near to committing suicide.

Community service of many kinds is given by young people, particularly those belonging to a number of national and local organisations, for example, Community Service Volunteers, Task Force, Scouts, Girl Guides and school groups.

Voluntary service to the sick and disabled is given by—among others—the British Red Cross Society, St. John Ambulance, the Women's Royal Voluntary Service and the Leagues of Hospital Friends. A number of societies exist to help people with particular disabilities and difficulties. These societies include the Royal National Institute for the Blind, the Royal National Institute for the Deaf, MIND (National Association for Mental Health), the National Society for Mentally Handicapped Children, the Spastics Society, Alcoholics Anonymous, Age Concern, Help the Aged and their equivalents in Scotland and Northern Ireland.

National organisations whose social work is specifically religious in inspiration include the Salvation Army, the Church Army, Toc H, the Committee on Social Service of the Church of Scotland, the Church of England Children's Society, the Church of England Council for Social Work, the Young Men's Christian Association, the Young Women's Christian Association, the Society of Friends, the Catholic Marriage Advisory Council and the Jewish Welfare Board.

A wide range of voluntary personal service is given by the Women's Royal Voluntary Service, which brings 'meals on wheels' to housebound invalids and old people, provides flatlets and residential clubs for the elderly, helps with family problems and assists in hospitals and clinics, as well as doing relief work in emergencies.

Some 710 Citizens' Advice Bureaux give explanation and advice to the citizen who is in doubt about his rights or who does not know about the State or voluntary services which could help him. There are law centres and housing advisory centres in some areas.

EQUAL OPPORTUNITIES FOR WOMEN

The Sex Discrimination Act 1975, one of the most comprehensive on this subject in the world, makes discrimination between men and women unlawful in employment, education, training and the provision of housing, goods, facilities and services. Discriminatory advertisements which breach the Act are also unlawful. Sex discrimination is defined as treating a person less favourably than another on the grounds of his or her sex. Northern Ireland has similar legislation.

Under the Equal Pay Act 1970 (and corresponding legislation in Northern Ireland), women are entitled to equal pay with men when doing work that is the same or broadly similar or work which has been given an equal value under a job evaluation scheme.

The Equal Opportunities Commission assists in the enforcement of both Acts and promotes equal opportunities between the sexes. There is a separate commission in Northern Ireland.

Preventing Sex Discrimination

Employers must not discriminate against a man or woman because of his or her sex. This applies to recruitment, promotion, the provision of benefits, dismissals and training. It is also unlawful for employers to discriminate against a person on grounds of marriage. There are a limited number of exceptions including employment in private households and employment in jobs where a person's sex is a 'genuine occupational qualification', such as acting. Employers of not more than five people are exempt from the Act.

Co-educational schools, colleges and universities may not discriminate in the provision of facilities or in their admissions. Single sex establishments are permissible, however, and there are arrangements for such institutions to move gradually towards co-education if they wish.

It is unlawful to discriminate against a man or a woman in the sale or letting of land, houses, flats and business premises. The law applies equally to public and private housing, furnished and unfurnished. The Act does not apply to lettings in a small dwelling occupied by the landlord or a near relative.

Discrimination is also unlawful in the provision of goods, facilities and services. For example, banks, building societies or finance companies must not refuse to give credit, mortgages or loans to women on the same terms as would be applied to men. Exceptions include services provided in certain special care establishments such as hospitals; places used for religious purposes where religious susceptibilities would be offended; places where it is necessary to preserve decency or privacy; competitive sports in which for reasons of physique women would be at a disadvantage; and life insurance and similar matters where risk is assessed on reliable actuarial or other data.

It is unlawful to publish or place advertisements which contravene the Sex Discrimination Act whether for jobs, goods, facilities or services.

Complaints Complaints of discrimination may be brought before the county courts in England and Wales or the sheriff courts in Scotland, except for complaints concerning employment which are dealt with by industrial tribunals (see p 324). Complaints concerning State educational establishments must first be made to the relevant Secretary of State before they can be brought before a court. Only the Equal Opportunities Commission is responsible for handling complaints about discriminatory advertisements and can bring proceedings in matters concerning advertising. Where necessary, legal advice or assistance, or legal aid if the case is taken to court, are available for complainants with low incomes (see p 100). Legal aid is not available for industrial tribunal cases but applicants can receive advice and assistance.

Equal Opportunities The Equal Opportunities Commission helps to enforce the Sex Discrimination
Commission Act and the Equal Pay Act. Its roles are to eliminate sex discrimination and to promote equal opportunities. The Commission advises people of their rights under both Acts, and in certain circumstances, may give financial help or assist individuals to prepare and conduct a case before a court or tribunal. It may also attempt to secure a settlement. The Commission has power to conduct formal investigations and, if satisfied that practices are unlawful, it can issue non-discrimination notices requiring that discriminatory practices cease. For certain formal investigations, the Commission has the power to require a person to give information and to attend hearings to give evidence. In addition it reviews the workings of both Acts and may submit proposals for amending them to the Home Secretary.

RACE RELATIONS

After the 1950s considerable numbers of people entered Britain from Commonwealth countries in the West Indies, Asia and Africa to take up employment, many with the intention of settling permanently, and they make an important contribution to the economy and the public services. In 1977 the population of New Commonwealth[1] and Pakistani ethnic origin was estimated at some 1·8 million (about 3·4 per cent of the total population) of whom 40 per cent were born in Britain. Nearly three-quarters live in the south-east and the west Midlands. Although, as Commonwealth citizens, they enjoy full political and civic rights, many suffer from social and economic disadvantages. This can partly be attributed to the fact that many initially lack the skills needed in an industrial society and occupy low-status jobs in poor environments of the older towns. Another factor, the extent of which is difficult to determine, is that of racial discrimination.

The difficulties experienced by residents of the older inner city areas are being alleviated by continuous social programmes which benefit the whole community and others which are directed at areas of special social need. Additional teachers have been appointed to schools with ethnic minorities and

---

[1] All Commonwealth countries except Canada, Australia and New Zealand and including, therefore, people from Cyprus, Malta and Gibraltar.

government grants are available to local authorities with substantial ethnic minority groups towards the salaries of extra staff, such as interpreters, health visitors and helpers in schools and community homes. Language teaching is recognised to be of prime importance in schools and schemes arranged for adults include classes at their place of work and language groups run by voluntary organisations. The welfare of ethnic minorities and good relations between minorities and the local community are promoted by community relations councils and other voluntary bodies.

A major report published in 1976, while showing that many members of minority groups were at a disadvantage in terms of the level of their jobs or the quality of their housing, found that minorities did not regard racial discrimination as their main difficulty in making a life in Britain but saw themselves as relative newcomers in a country where prices were rising and jobs hard to get. Only a small proportion of Asians and West Indians believed that they had personally encountered discrimination. Policies for promoting equality of opportunity among ethnic minorities are pursued against a background of legislation designed to protect them from discrimination.

Race Relations Act

The Race Relations Act 1976 makes discrimination unlawful on grounds of colour, race or ethnic or national origin in the provision of goods, facilities and services, in employment, training and related matters, in education, in housing and in advertising. It strengthens the previous legislation passed in 1968 which, in turn, widened the scope of the first race relations legislation enacted in 1965. The 1976 Act brings the law against racial discrimination into line with that against sex discrimination (see above), and gives complainants direct access to civil courts and, in the case of employment complaints, to industrial tribunals. Complaints concerning educational establishments are made first to the appropriate education minister. The remedies available from the courts are damages, a declaration of rights or an injunction. Industrial tribunals are also able to declare the rights of parties, make recommendations or award compensation. Legal aid (see p 101) is available to complainants with low incomes.

The 1976 Act also strengthens the criminal law on incitement to racial hatred. A prosecution made under the Act may only be brought in England and Wales by, or with the consent of, the Attorney General.

Commission for Racial Equality

The Commission for Racial Equality was established under the Act to work towards the elimination of discrimination and to promote equality of opportunity and good relations between different racial groups. It has powers to investigate unlawful discriminatory practices and to issue non-discrimination notices, enforceable in the courts, requiring that such practices should cease. The Commission has sole responsibility for those contraventions of the Act which do not result in a particular person being discriminated against, for example, discriminatory advertisements and instructions; it may also assist individuals with their complaints. It has an important educational role and has power to issue codes of practice in employment.

The Commission supports and co-ordinates the work of nearly 100 local community relations councils operating in areas with significant minority groups; their purpose is to promote harmonious community relations. It makes grants towards the salaries of community relations officers and towards special projects which help to improve community relations or to assist members of the ethnic minorities. Particular encouragement is given to self-help schemes run by members of the minority communities.

7 Education

British education aims to develop individual abilities to the full and to shape those abilities for the benefit of society as a whole. Compulsory schooling takes place between the ages of five and 16, although some provision is made for children under five and many pupils remain at school beyond the minimum leaving age. Post-school education (mainly at universities, polytechnics and further education colleges) is organised flexibly to provide opportunities for academic work, vocational training and continuing study throughout life.

Considerable educational change has taken place in the last 15 years or so. New methods of teaching and learning have increasingly been used, particularly in modern languages, mathematics and science. Informal techniques designed to awaken children's curiosity and interest have been introduced, especially in primary schools. Secondary education has been extensively re-organised into comprehensive schools which dispense with selection procedures for entry at 11-plus and provide a wide range of studies for children of all abilities. Post-school facilities have also been expanded, particularly for advanced studies in the higher education sector.

Most expenditure on education comes from public funds; some £7,853 million in 1977 which represented 6·3 per cent of the gross national product.

Priorities

Following the period of substantial innovation and change the Government initiated a national debate on school educational issues, involving teachers, administrators, parents, employers, trade unionists and others. Two of the broad themes raised concerned the content of curricula and the links between schools and industry.

There is a general concern that schools' curricula should meet the needs of modern Britain, and that there should be a coherent and soundly-based means of assessment for individual pupils, for schools and for the educational system as a whole. The Assessment of Performance Unit of the Department of Education and Science which promotes the development of methods of assessing and monitoring the performance of children at school is concentrating on the development of tests suitable for national monitoring in English language, mathematics and science. Some of the costs are being met by the Welsh Office which is also sponsoring assessment of the use and development of the Welsh language in schools in Wales.

The Government is encouraging further links, especially locally, between schools and industry, to try to ensure that every pupil grows up with a basic understanding of the economy and the activities which are necessary for the creation of the country's wealth (particularly manufacturing industries), and to encourage more of the able pupils to consider and prepare for careers in productive industry. Many organisations already work to improve liaison between school and industry; national initiatives include the Schools Council Industry Project, being mounted with the Confederation of British Industry and the Trades Union Congress, and the Confederation's own project 'Understanding British Industry'.

Within the necessary strict financial limitations the Government remains committed to improving educational provision for all. Nursery education for children of pre-school age is being expanded, and priority in the allocation of resources is being given to those with social and educational disadvantages and to handicapped children. In many 'priority areas' within large cities, for instance, special annual payments are made to teachers working in schools of exceptional difficulty, and extra funds are allocated for school building.

The recent fall in birthrate (see p 8) has already caused the number of primary school children to decrease sharply, and over the next few years the secondary schools will face a similar decline. The trend is having its effect on teacher training programmes (see p 147) and the development of the higher education system in the 1990s is being discussed in this context.

The Government is anxious that more young people in the 16 to 18 age group should stay in full-time education in schools and colleges, and is discussing with local authorities the possibility of a statutory system of awards which could ensure this.

Administration

Educational responsibilities are devolved in varying degrees to ministers of the four countries of Britain. The Secretary of State for Education and Science is responsible for all aspects of education in England, and for universities, civil science and the arts throughout Great Britain. The Secretaries of State for Wales, Scotland and Northern Ireland have full educational responsibilities in their countries except that the Secretaries of State for Wales and Scotland are consulted about university-level education but are not responsible for it.

Administration of publicly provided schools and further education is divided between the central government departments (the Department of Education and Science, the Welsh Office, the Scottish Education Department, and the Department of Education for Northern Ireland), local education authorities (education and library boards in Northern Ireland), and various voluntary organisations. Their relationship is based on consultation and co-operation.

Local education authorities are responsible for the provision of school education and most post-school education outside the universities, and provide grants to students proceeding to higher education (including universities). In Scotland the central institutions (for higher education) and colleges of education (for teacher training), which are administered by independent governing bodies, are financed directly by the Scottish Education Department and grants to students are also paid by the Department. In Northern Ireland the Ulster College (an institution of higher education) is likewise administered by an independent board of governors and is financed directly by the Northern Ireland Department of Education. Colleges of education are controlled by the Department or voluntary agencies.

Universities are administratively independent and their governing bodies are appointed according to the terms of their individual charters or statutory provisions. The Government exercises its responsibilities in relation to the universities through the University Grants Committee (see p 145).

SCHOOLS

Parents are required by law to see that their children receive efficient full-time education, at school or elsewhere, between the ages of 5 and 16.

Over 11 million children attend Britain's 38,000 schools. Most receive free education financed from public funds, but a small proportion (very roughly four per cent) attend schools wholly independent of public financial support.

Boys and girls are taught together in most primary schools and in an increasing number of secondary schools. Over 80 per cent of pupils in maintained secondary schools in England and Wales and over 50 per cent in Northern Ireland attend mixed schools. In Scotland nearly all secondary schools are mixed. Most of the independent schools for younger children are co-educational, but of those providing secondary education the majority are single-sex.

Management

Schools supported from public funds are of two main kinds in England and Wales: county schools and voluntary schools. County schools are provided and maintained by local education authorities wholly out of public funds. Voluntary schools have mostly been established by religious denominations and receive varying amounts of public finance according to type ('aided', 'controlled' and 'special agreement'). Nearly a third of the 28,350 schools maintained by local education authorities in England and Wales are voluntary schools: some 5,860 are Church of England, 2,660 are Roman Catholic, and 340 belong to other groups and religious denominations. Each publicly maintained school has a body of managers or governors, some or all of whom are appointed by the local education authority. In Scotland most of the schools supported from public funds are provided by education authorities and are known as public schools (in England this term is used for a type of independent school, see p 140).

In Northern Ireland there are two main categories of school: voluntary schools which are mainly, though not exclusively, under Roman Catholic management receiving grants of up to 85 per cent of capital costs and up to 100 per cent of running costs, and controlled schools owned and managed by the Area Education and Library Boards and having all their expenditure met from public funds. Government policy is to encourage integration between Protestant and Roman Catholic school education where there is a local desire for it, but there is no question of enforcing integrated education against the wishes of local communities.

Fees

In England and Wales no fees are charged to parents of children attending maintained schools, and books and equipment are free. In Scotland, education authorities may charge fees where this can be done without prejudice to the adequate provision of free school education (although no authorities make use of this power). In Northern Ireland no fees are charged to parents of children attending grant-aided schools, with the exception of grammar schools, where a small proportion of pupils are admitted on a fee-paying basis.

Nursery and Primary Schools

Facilities for informal education and play for children aged two to five are provided free in public sector nursery schools and nursery classes in public sector primary schools, and are also available for a fee in a few independent schools and a large number of 'pre-school playgroups' organised by voluntary organisations or by groups of parents. Apart from children only just under five, the proportion of children aged two to four who attend public sector schools remains low (the supply of places being inadequate to meet the demand for them) though attendance, particularly part-time attendance, has been increasing very rapidly in recent years.

Compulsory education begins at five when children in England and Wales go to infant schools or departments; at seven they go on to junior schools or departments. The usual age of transfer from primary to secondary schools is 11 in England, Wales and Northern Ireland but an increasing number of local authorities in England are establishing 'first' schools for pupils aged 5 to 8 or 10 and 'middle' schools covering various age ranges between 9 and 14. In Scotland, the primary schools take children from 5 to 12, normally having infant classes for children under 7, although in some areas there are separate infant schools.

Secondary Schools

The public or State system of education aims to give all children an education suited to their particular abilities. About 80 per cent of the maintained

England and
Wales

secondary school population in England and Wales attend some 3,600 comprehensive schools which take pupils without reference to ability or aptitude and provide a wide range of secondary education for all or most of the children of a district. They can be organised in a number of ways including schools that take the full secondary school age-range from 11 to 18; middle schools whose pupils move on to senior comprehensive schools at 12 or 13, leaving at 16 or 18; and schools with an age-range of 11 or 12 to 16 combined with a sixth-form or 'tertiary' college for pupils over 16. Most of the remaining children receive their secondary education in 'grammar' and 'secondary modern' schools to which they are allocated after selection procedures at the age of 11. In order to hasten progress towards the re-organisation of secondary school provision along comprehensive lines, the Education Act 1976 gives the Secretary of State powers to require local authorities, if they have not already done so, to submit plans for such re-organisation.

A small number of selective grammar schools have in the past received direct grant payments from central government funds. The system is, however, being phased out. Of the 170 such schools 51 chose to enter the maintained sector as voluntary aided comprehensive schools, and most of these have done so, or will do so in the next few years. Those which did not choose to enter the maintained sector will become wholly independent (see below).

Scotland

Secondary education in Scotland is almost completely organised according to the comprehensive principle and virtually all pupils in education authority secondary schools are in schools with a non-selective intake. The majority of schools are six-year comprehensive schools. Because of local circumstances there are some comprehensive schools whose courses may extend to four years or less and from which pupils may transfer at the end of their second or fourth years to a six-year comprehensive school.

Northern Ireland

In Northern Ireland selective secondary education is being eliminated in favour of a comprehensive system.

Independent
Schools

Independent schools in England and Wales receive no grants from public funds but all are open to inspection and must register with the appropriate government education department which has power to require them to remedy any objectionable features in their premises, accommodation or instruction and to exclude any person regarded as unsuitable to teach in or to be the proprietor of a school. In default, the appropriate Secretary of State can, in effect, close a school, but schools have a right of appeal to an independent tribunal against any of the requirements. There are about 2,300 registered independent schools.

Independent schools cater for pupils of all ages. The largest and most important of them are the public schools,[1] which accept pupils at about 12 or 13 years of age usually on the basis of a fairly demanding examination. There are about 470 public schools in England and Wales, most of them single-sex (about half of them for girls) and at least partly boarding; but there are some coeducational schools and certain boys' schools have recently begun to admit girls direct to their top forms. Combined tuition and boarding fees in the public schools are about £2,000 a year, but some of this may be remitted for children winning competitive scholarships. A number of preparatory schools, day and boarding, coeducational and single-sex, prepare children for entry to the public schools.

---

[1] 'Public schools' are usually taken to mean those schools in membership of the Headmasters' Conference, the Governing Bodies Association or the Governing Bodies of Girls' Schools Association. They should not be confused with the State-supported public schools in Scotland.

Special Education

Special education is provided for children who require it because of physical or mental disability either in ordinary schools or special schools (including hospital schools). It has long been governmental policy to send as few handicapped children as possible to special schools, and by a law yet to be brought into effect such children will have to be educated in ordinary schools whenever practicable and compatible with efficient teaching. There are, however, some 1,800 separate special schools (both day and boarding) for a number of categories of disability. These are the blind, partially sighted, deaf, partially hearing, delicate, educationally subnormal (mentally handicapped in Scotland), epileptic, maladjusted, physically handicapped, autistic and those suffering from speech defects. There is no separate category for the delicate in Scotland. As many children have multiple handicaps, there is a growing tendency to relate educational provision to an assessment of overall needs.

A new framework of special education, based on the concept of special educational need, was recommended by the Warnock Committee in 1978 (see Bibliography p 441). It would cover not only children with disabilities of mind or body but also those who have significant difficulties in learning, many of whom are at present the concern of remedial services, as well as those with emotional behavioural disorders.

Teachers

Teachers in publicly maintained schools are appointed by local education authorities or schools, governing bodies or managers. There are more than 535,000 teachers (including the full-time equivalent of part-time teachers) in publicly maintained schools in Britain and the pupil/teacher ratio was about 20 to 1. Teachers must hold qualifications approved by the appropriate education department. Their salaries are determined by nationally negotiated scales taking account of qualifications, responsibilities and experience.

Curricular Control

In England and Wales the secular curriculum in maintained schools is the responsibility of the local education authority, or, in the case of secondary schools, of the schools' governors. In practice there is a very high degree of devolution to headteachers, particularly in nursery and primary schools. In Wales, the Welsh language is taught and is used as either the main or secondary medium of teaching in some schools. Her Majesty's Inspectors of Schools are responsible to the Department of Education and Science and the Welsh Office for the inspection of all schools including independent schools. They review and report on the content and value of the education provided and are available as advisers. Local education authorities also employ inspectors to guide them on maintained schools. Teachers' organisations and institutions concerned with the education and training of teachers are additional sources of advice. Further guidance and encouragement for school-based research and development is available to teachers through the Schools Council for Curriculum and Examinations. The Council, an independent body representative of all educational interests, acts as an advisory body and sponsors and carries out research and development work on curricula, teaching methods and examinations in primary and secondary schools. The Schools Council Committee for Wales carries out similar activities in Wales.

Local education authorities have been asked to review their curricular arrangements. In the light of the review the Government is to seek to establish a broad consensus on a framework for the curriculum and on whether part of it should be protected because there are aims (such as the achievement of basic literacy and numeracy at the primary stage) common to all schools and pupils at certain stages.

In Scotland the function of Her Majesty's Inspectors is in general the same;

the content and balance of the curriculum is kept under continuous review by the Consultative Committee on the Curriculum. Provision is made, where appropriate, for the teaching of Gaelic. Northern Ireland has a Schools Curriculum Committee which works in close liaison with the Schools Council; the Inspectorate of the Department of Education helps and advises teachers and inspects and evaluates the work of all schools.

Religion in Schools

In England and Wales by law all children in county or voluntary schools receive religious instruction and take part in a daily corporate act of worship unless their parents choose otherwise. In county schools, and sometimes in voluntary schools, religious instruction of a non-denominational character is given which may include the study of comparative religions. (In areas with large immigrant populations this can take the form of lessons on comparative cultures.) In all kinds of voluntary school there is opportunity for denominational instruction. In Scotland, subject to safeguards for the individual conscience, religious instruction must be given, but the content is determined by education authorities or, more commonly, by the schools themselves. Roman Catholic children generally have their own schools. In controlled schools in Northern Ireland clergy have a right of access which may be used for denominational instruction; in voluntary schools corporate worship and religious education are controlled by the management authorities.

Curricular Innovation

The freedom of schools to frame their own curricula has facilitated quite rapid change and experiment, partly stimulated by the Schools Council and other organisations. The general purpose has been to adapt curricula to reflect technological advance and social change; and to enable to respond to the needs of individual children. Greater emphasis has also been placed on appreciation of music and the arts.

Among the most clearly observable general trends in new teaching methods have been the increased emphasis, particularly for younger children, on 'learning by doing'; the efforts to reduce or modify 'streaming' (grouping according to ability) in such a way as to minimise its ill effects on children placed in a lower stream; and the increased importance attached to pupils' motivation. At the same time greater use is being made of new educational aids. The broad direction of changes in the school curriculum was among the subjects discussed in the national debate on education (see p 137).

Broadcasting is a major resource for school teachers—most schools can receive television, and almost all have radios. Relaxation of copyright for educational purposes enables many schools to make recordings for more flexible use within the school timetable. Films and slides are also used, often in conjunction with tape recordings for audio-visual presentations. These may be prepared by the schools themselves, but commercial products, including the BBC's 'Radiovision' programmes, are available.

The Council for Educational Technology for the United Kingdom and the Educational Foundation for Visual Aids advise those connected with education on the use of audio-visual aids. In Scotland this function is undertaken by the Scottish Council for Educational Technology.

Computers are increasingly used to assist learning by means of calculation, information retrieval and the simulation of situations. They are also used in planning timetables and helping in the management of courses.

Secondary School Examinations

There is no national school-leaving examination in England and Wales, but secondary school pupils may attempt examinations, in various subjects, leading to the Certificate of Secondary Education (CSE) or the General Certificate of

Education (GCE). The CSE is designed for pupils completing five years' secondary education and is normally taken at the age of 16. It is controlled by 14 Regional Examining Boards, consisting mainly of teachers serving in the schools which provide the candidates. The highest grade in the CSE (grade 1) is widely accepted as being of the same standard as at least grade C at GCE 'Ordinary' level. The GCE examinations are conducted by eight independent examining bodies and are set at two levels: Ordinary ('O') and Advanced ('A'). Normally candidates taking 'O' level are about 16 years of age, although some take it earlier, at the discretion of their head teacher. 'A' levels are usually taken after a further two years' study. Control over the scope and standards of the examinations is exercised by the Schools Council (see p 141) to ensure national comparability. Entries for both levels of the GCE are accepted from candidates at further education establishments and from candidates entering privately.

Grade C or above in various subjects at GCE 'O' level and the equivalent CSE grade 1 are usually considered to be qualifications for entry to courses of further education and training. Since the inception of the CSE the number achieving the highest grade has increased steadily as the popularity of the examination has grown while GCE 'O' level subject performances have also improved. The 'A' level examination is at the standard for entrance to university and for entry to many forms of professional training.

In Scotland examinations are conducted by the Scottish Certificate of Education Examination Board. School pupils in the fourth year of secondary courses sit an examination at 16 years for the Ordinary grade of the Scottish Certificate of Education, and pupils in the fifth or sixth year are presented for the Higher grade. Passes at the Higher grade are the basis for entry to university or professional training. For those who have completed their main studies at the Higher grade but wish to continue their studies in particular subjects there is a Certificate of Sixth Year Studies.

In Northern Ireland candidates may take the Northern Ireland General Certificate of Education or the Northern Ireland Certificate of Secondary Education, which are equivalent to those examinations in England and Wales.

The International Baccalaureate, which is offered by several educational institutions in Britain, consists of a two-year curriculum for students at sixth-form level, and leads either to a diploma or to separate subject certificates, the latter being recognised for admission to higher education in Britain and many other countries.

Health and Welfare of School Children

Physical education, including organised games, is part of the curriculum of all schools. Those receiving financial assistance from public funds must have the use of a playing field, and most secondary schools have a gymnasium.

The Department of Health and Social Security is responsible for the medical inspection of school children and for advice and treatment of specific medical and dental problems associated with children of school age.

Local education authorities must provide free school milk, normally one-third of a pint (0·19 litre), on each school day, for all pupils in maintained special schools, pupils up to seven years in other maintained schools, and, on health grounds, to pupils up to eleven. They have discretionary powers to provide free milk for all other junior pupils in maintained schools. The authorities must also provide for all day pupils in maintained schools a mid-day meal at a subsidised charge (which is remitted in cases of need). Under certain conditions the authorities must provide free school transport, and they have discretionary powers to assist financially in the provision of transport for pupils between their home and school and for many other school activities.

School Building   Local education authorities and voluntary bodies are responsible, under the general supervision of the central departments, for providing the schools and other buildings needed for public education in their areas. The central departments determine the maximum size of the authorities' individual programmes in the light of national priorities; they also offer guidance to authorities by means of building bulletins and in other ways.

Since 1945 an extensive school building programme has been carried out resulting in the completion of about 16,300 new schools in Britain, together with extensions, alterations and remodelling of existing state schools; over 9 million new places have been provided.

Grants of up to 85 per cent of the approved cost are normally available from the Department of Education and Science or the Welsh Office for the building of new voluntary aided schools and for alterations and external repairs to existing aided schools. In Northern Ireland capital grants of 85 per cent are available for voluntary schools managed by maintained school committees and voluntary grammar schools which have entered into an agreement under statutory provisions.

The school building programme has provided for new ideas and methods in design and construction. Industrialised building techniques have been widely adopted. New schools are designed to be light, airy and colourful as well as to have enough teaching area and space for auxiliary activities and outdoor games. Space is being used more flexibly, particularly in primary schools to meet the needs of new teaching methods.

POST-SCHOOL EDUCATION   Education for those who have left school is organised very flexibly. It is available to everyone above school-leaving age, is provided at all levels and may be part-time or full-time, vocational or non-vocational.

More than a third of young people receive some form of post-school education compared with a fifth in 1965. Many courses lead to recognised qualifications, varying from degrees and professional qualifications through technician level to qualifications similar to those obtained before leaving school. Further education is a broad term usually taken to refer to all post-school education outside the universities. Higher education (postgraduate, first-degree and similar level work) is provided at universities and on advanced courses at polytechnics and other establishments of further education. Adults of every age make extensive use of widespread and varied facilities for the educational and cultural leisure activities included under the term 'adult education' (see p 149).

Institutions   The principal institutions of post-school education are the 45 universities (see p 146); the 30 polytechnics in England and Wales and the 14 Scottish central institutions, in which advanced (or higher) courses outside the universities are increasingly being concentrated; the Ulster College in Northern Ireland; and well over 600 other colleges which are maintained or assisted from public funds, some of which have a very wide range of courses, while others concentrate on particular subjects. These colleges include the 'liberal arts' colleges and institutions of higher education in England and Wales into which the former colleges of education (for teacher training) have been assimilated. All these institutions offer courses leading to recognised qualifications, while their premises as well as school and other premises are often also used for adult education.

Apart from the universities, most establishments of post-school education are maintained and administered by the local education authorities. The

Scottish central institutions, however, the Scottish colleges of education and the Ulster College do not come under the control of the education authorities, but are managed by independent governing bodies, representative of the authorities and other appropriate interests.

In addition, there are many independent specialist establishments, such as secretarial colleges, correspondence colleges and colleges teaching English as a foreign language; a number of voluntary bodies and private undertakings providing cultural and general education, sometimes with financial or other assistance from local education authorities; and a large number of other education and training schemes run by public or private organisations.

Finance

Most establishments for post-school education are either maintained or assisted from public funds. Where industrial training is provided by a college, the charges are the responsibility of the employer, and broadly reflect the economic cost of provision. Many full-time students are helped by awards from public funds. These awards are mandatory for most students taking university first-degree and other comparable courses. They are assessed to cover tuition fees and a maintenance grant, but parents who can afford to contribute towards the cost are required to do so. In England and Wales these awards are made by local education authorities up to first-degree level, while in Scotland awards to students on advanced level courses are made by the Scottish Education Department. In Northern Ireland awards up to first-degree level are made by the education and library boards. Grants for postgraduate study and research are offered by the education departments and the research councils. In all, about 90 per cent of full-time students on advanced courses receive help from public funds. Some scholarships are available from endowments and from particular industries or companies.

Although largely dependent on public funds, the universities are guaranteed as autonomous institutions by a special financial arrangement. The University Grants Committee is appointed by the Secretary of State for Education and Science to advise on State aid to the universities; its members are drawn from the academic and business worlds. This body acts as a link and buffer between the Government from which it receives a block grant and the universities to which it allocates this grant. So, although the Government is responsible for financing about 90 per cent of universities' central expenditure (colleges within universities may have their own investments, endowments and budgets), it does not control their work or teaching. The Open University (see p 147) is financed directly by the Department of Education and Science, not through the University Grants Committee; and in Northern Ireland, government grants are made direct to the universities by the Department of Education which first seeks the advice of the University Grants Committee.

Students

Well over 900,000 students take full-time and sandwich courses (courses where substantial periods of full-time study alternate with periods of supervised experience on a relevant job) at universities and other major establishments of further education in Britain (1976–77 figures). Of these about 272,000 are at universities while another 250,000 follow advanced courses outside universities, at colleges of further and higher education, polytechnics and Scottish central institutions. More than 400,000 take non-advanced courses, most of them studying for recognised vocational or educational qualifications.

Additionally, there are over 3 million part-time students, over 600,000 of whom are released by their employers for study during working hours. The remainder for the most part take some of the wide variety of adult education classes (see p 149).

Higher Education

The provision for higher education has almost tripled in size since 1960. It caters for about 520,000 full-time and sandwich students and about 230,000 part-time students through a variety of courses and in a variety of institutions. Nearly 14 per cent of 18 year-olds enter courses of higher education. This expansion has been achieved by creating ten new universities; by developing a number of colleges into universities, 30 of them into polytechnics specialising in advanced work; and by widening the range and flexibility of courses.

Student members (excluding teacher training) are evenly divided between science-based and arts-based courses; although this is not a matter for explicit government policy, it has been the subject of much public discussion.

Universities

There are 45 universities in Britain, including the Open University, compared with 17 in 1945. In addition, the University College at Buckingham, which receives no assistance from public funds, began courses in 1976 but has not yet achieved university status.

The English universities are: Aston (Birmingham), Bath, Birmingham, Bradford, Bristol, Brunel (London), Cambridge, City (London), Durham, East Anglia, Essex, Exeter, Hull, Keele, Kent at Canterbury, Lancaster, Leeds, Leicester, Liverpool, London, Loughborough, Manchester, Newcastle upon Tyne, Nottingham, Oxford, Reading, Salford, Sheffield, Southampton, Surrey, Sussex, Warwick, and York. The London Graduate School of Business Studies and the Manchester Business School also have university status. The federated University of Wales includes five university colleges, the Welsh National School of Medicine, and the University of Wales Institute of Science and Technology. The Scottish universities are: Aberdeen, Dundee, Edinburgh, Glasgow, Heriot-Watt (Edinburgh), St. Andrews, Stirling, and Strathclyde (Glasgow). In Northern Ireland there are the Queen's University of Belfast, and the New University of Ulster in Coleraine.

The universities of Oxford and Cambridge date from the twelfth and thirteenth centuries, and the Scottish universities of St. Andrews, Glasgow, Aberdeen and Edinburgh from the fifteenth and sixteenth centuries. All the other universities were founded in the nineteenth or twentieth centuries.

Admission to universities is by examination and selection; there is no religious test and no colour, nationality or sex bar, though in practice there are about twice as many men as women. Prospective candidates for nearly all the universities apply for places through the Universities Central Council on Admissions. The only students to apply directly are applicants to the Open University and British candidates who apply only to the universities of Glasgow, Aberdeen and Strathclyde.

Most students at universities are undergraduates: in 1976–77 there were about 272,000 full-time university students in Britain, including over 50,000 postgraduates. Just under a half lived in colleges and halls of residence, over one-third were in privately rented accommodation, and the remainder lived at home. There were about 32,000 full-time university teachers paid wholly from university funds. The ratio of staff to students was about one to eight or nine, one of the most favourable in the world.

Except at the Open University, first-degree courses are mainly full-time and usually last three or four years, though medical and veterinary courses may require five or six. A full-time course at a university remains the most usual way of obtaining a first degree, in spite of the extension of facilities for obtaining a degree in other ways. About four-fifths of all students on full-time first-degree courses are at universities.

Actual degree titles vary according to the practice of each university; in

England and Wales the commonest titles for a first degree are Bachelor of Arts (BA) or Bachelor of Science (BSc) and for a second degree Master of Arts (MA), Master of Science (MSc), Doctor of Philosophy (PhD); while in Scotland Master is used for a first degree. On the other hand, uniformity of standards between universities is promoted by the practice of employing outside examiners for all university examinations, and the general pattern of teaching (a combination of lectures, small group seminars or tutorials with practical classes where necessary) is fairly similar throughout Britain.

The Open University

The Open University is a non-residential university which provides part-time degree and other courses, using a combination of television and radio broadcasts, correspondence courses and summer schools, together with a network of viewing and listening centres. No formal academic qualifications are required to register for these courses, but the standards of its degrees are the same as those of other universities. The university's first degree, the BA (Open), is a general degree awarded on a system of credits for each course completed; the average amount of study needed for a full course is estimated at 12 to 14 hours a week. The first courses began in 1971, and in 1978 some 60,000 undergraduate and 7,500 associate students were following courses. About 6,000 people a year obtain degrees from the Open University—about 1 in 14 of the total for Britain. The university also has a consultancy service to make its advice and facilities available on a fee-paying but non-profit-making basis to bodies throughout the world interested in 'teaching at a distance' projects.

Teacher Training

In order to teach in a maintained school in England and Wales all new entrants to teaching must generally have taken a course of professional teacher training. Many new entrants have undertaken three-year non-graduate courses leading to the award of the Certificate of Education. With the exception of a few one-year certificate courses for holders of specialist qualifications in subjects where there is a shortage of staff in the schools, however, this qualification is to be phased out as part of the move towards an all-graduate profession. It is to be replaced by a direct-entry Bachelor of Education degree course at ordinary or honours level. The last general entry to the non-graduate certificate courses will be in 1979. From 1980 onwards the most usual route to a teaching qualification will, for non-graduates, be by way of a three- or four-year course leading to the Bachelor of Education degree; for graduates it will be by way of a one-year postgraduate Certificate of Education course.

Teacher training formerly took place in specialist colleges of education but is being integrated with the rest of higher education. By 1981 nearly all training places will be in polytechnics, colleges of higher education and/or further education or universities.

In response to the change in demand for newly trained teachers, caused by restrictions on public expenditure and the continued decline in the size of the school population following the fall in the birthrate, the number of teacher-training places planned for 1981 has been cut to 47,000, to include 10,000 places for in-service training. This substantial reduction from about 100,000 places in 1976–77 has led to the closure of a number of training colleges.

In Scotland all teachers in education authority and grant-aided schools must be registered with the General Teaching Council for Scotland. All teachers of academic subjects in Scottish secondary schools must be graduates. Courses in colleges of education lead to the award of a Teaching Qualification (Primary Education) or a Teaching Qualification (Secondary Education). Graduates and holders of specialist diplomas undergo a one-year course; courses in practical and aesthetic subjects for non-graduates extend to two, three or four years.

Most Scottish colleges of education also offer four-year courses leading to the degree of Bachelor of Education.

In Northern Ireland teacher training takes place in the two university education departments, three colleges of education, the Ulster College and one technical college. The principal courses are three-year (certificate) and four-year (Bachelor of Education) but there are also one-year courses for graduates or holders of other appropriate qualifications.

Increased importance is being given to the continued professional education of practising teachers in Britain, and local authorities, universities and colleges provide a variety of in-service courses.

Other Advanced Courses

In 1976–77 about 372,000 students, over half of them full-time, were taking advanced courses other than in universities in a wide variety of subjects, including architecture, art and design, catering, engineering, natural sciences, social work and business and management studies and teacher training. An increasing proportion of the students were taking courses leading to the awards of the Council for National Academic Awards (CNAA). The Council has power to award degrees and other academic qualifications, comparable in standard with those granted by universities, to students who successfully complete approved courses of study in establishments which do not have the power to award their own degrees. The courses range from science and technology to the arts, social studies, business studies and law, but the proportion of technological, business or other explicitly vocational courses is much higher than in universities and the proportion of arts, language and science courses lower.

In England and Wales higher education provision outside universities and teacher training colleges is being concentrated within 30 major national institutions named 'polytechnics'. These provide all types of courses (full-time, sandwich and part-time) on a wide range of subjects at all levels, though the trend is towards a concentration on advanced work. In Scotland similar provision is made in 14 central institutions and a few further education colleges managed by education authorities, though there is a tendency for the Scottish establishments to specialise more by subjects than do the English polytechnics. In Northern Ireland such higher education provision is concentrated within the Ulster College.

Vocational Courses

The British education systems offer facilities for obtaining all types of vocational education and training, and are notable for providing alternative routes to higher qualifications for those who have found themselves unable to continue full-time education after leaving school.

There is a wide variety of courses for young people in various trades and occupations, leading to appropriate qualifications at the end of a course of up to five years. Other, more academic, courses lead to the National Certificates and Diplomas awarded by joint committees consisting of representatives of education departments, teachers' organisations and appropriate professional bodies. Courses are normally at two levels, ordinary and higher. The Ordinary National Certificate (ONC) courses normally last two years part-time, and students usually follow them between the ages of 16 and 19; the level of the certificate is generally considered to approach that of GCE 'A' level. The Ordinary National Diploma (OND) courses are the full-time or sandwich counterparts of the ONC but involve wider and deeper study. The Higher National Diploma (HND), which requires a further two years' full-time or three years' sandwich study, is recognised, within its more restricted field, as approaching the standard of a pass degree; the Higher National Certificate

(HNC), after two further years' part-time study, is lower in standard because it is more narrowly based, but is nevertheless classified as an advanced course. A Technician Education Council has responsibility for developing a unified system of courses for technicians in England, Wales and Northern Ireland, leading to awards which will eventually replace those of the joint committees; some courses leading to the awards of the Council are already in existence. A similar council has been established in Scotland.

Many further education colleges offer courses in shorthand, typing, book-keeping, and office studies. More advanced level work, however, is generally concentrated in polytechnics or other colleges with a department of business studies, notably those designated as regional centres of management education. Courses for the post-experience postgraduate Diploma in Management Studies are run by about 75 colleges; and some polytechnics run courses leading to the Master's degree of the Council for National Academic Awards (see also p 148). Much business education is related to the specialised examination requirements of various professional bodies, and courses leading to them are provided in many colleges, although numbers of candidates seeking such qualifications do so through correspondence courses. A Business Education Council was established in 1974 with the same functions as the Technician Education Council (see above) in relation to courses of business education. In Scotland, similar courses lead to the Scottish National Certificate, the Scottish Higher National Certificate and the Scottish National Diploma in Business Studies, awarded by the Scottish Business Education Council.

Adult Education

Adult education is generally taken to mean courses of post-school education outside the main areas of higher, professional and technical education. Courses are provided by local education authorities, certain residential colleges, the adult education ('extra-mural') departments of universities and various voluntary and statutory bodies.

A major part of adult education is financed by local education authorities and provided mainly in their establishments, including schools (used for adult evening classes). Most of the courses are part-time, and in some cases 'community schools' where adult education (together with educational, social and cultural opportunities for the wider community) is an integral part of the provision. In addition local authorities maintain or aid most of the short-term residential colleges or centres, of which there are 45 in England and Wales, and which provide courses varying in length between a weekend and a fortnight. Many of the courses are practical, but there are widespread opportunities for academic study.

Long-term residential colleges (seven in England and Wales, one in Scotland) which are grant-aided by the central government departments, provide courses of one or two years, some of which lead to a diploma. The colleges aim to provide a liberal education and do not apply academic entry tests. Most students admitted to them are entitled to full maintenance grants.

The extra-mural departments of the universities and the Workers' Educational Association (WEA), the largest of the recognised voluntary bodies, provide extended part-time courses of more academic studies, though recently there has been a tendency for more short courses organised for special (including vocational) interests. Often the WEA provides the organisation and the teaching is provided by the extra-mural departments, many of which have full-time staff appointed for this purpose and can also call on the services of other departments of the university. Similar work is promoted in some local education authority centres.

There are a large number of other organisations (both national and local) which provide many kinds of education and training. Several non-political bodies, such as the National Federation of Women's Institutes and the National Council of Young Men's Christian Associations, receive government grants; others are commercially or privately financed. Some make their facilities available to the public as a whole, others to a particular group, such as the disabled or the unemployed, or the employees or members of an organisation.

The National Institute of Adult Education provides a national centre of information, research and publication for adult education, as well as a channel of co-operation and consultation for the many interested organisations in England and Wales. It is mainly financed by contributions from local education authorities and assisted by a grant from the Department of Education and Science. The Institute has a Government-funded Adult Literacy Unit to act as a focus for adult literacy work, to commission special projects of relevance to local authorities, and to assist voluntary projects promoting literacy. The Scottish Institute of Adult Education is the Institute's Scottish counterpart.

An Advisory Council for Adult and Continuing Education has been set up to advise on the co-ordination of existing facilities and assist in planning for the future. Northern Ireland has a similar Council for Continuing Education.

Teaching Methods

The general pattern of teaching and learning on full-time courses at universities and colleges remains a mixture of lectures, prescribed or suggested reading, seminars or tutorials, exercises and tests, and, where appropriate, practical work. Nevertheless, each institution has different ways of preparing its course material and different approaches and emphases in teaching it. They make use of the teaching and learning aids provided by radio and television and of other visual aids. Teaching machines and language laboratories are also used, as are computer-assisted and computer-managed learning techniques. All universities have access to computers for educational and research purposes, and most universities and many colleges have closed circuit television.

Radio and television programmes, both specially instructional and general, are perhaps the most penetrating purveyors of adult education, and are often linked to a range of supplementary publications and activities. Most BBC radio study programmes are grouped in hourly sessions on five nights a week and week-end afternoons. Television study programmes are shown on Saturday and Sunday mornings and in the early morning and late evening on weekdays. Both the BBC and Independent Television provide programmes at successive intellectual levels from domestic, social and craft skills to progressive vocational training. The BBC also works with the Open University, producing and broadcasting radio and television programmes as part of the courses. Educational programmes would be one of the main priorities of the 'fourth channel' television service which, under government proposals of July 1978, would be provided and supervised by a new Open Broadcasting Authority (see p 419).

EDUCATIONAL RESEARCH

Research into the theory and practice of education and the organisation of educational services is supported financially by the central government education departments, local education authorities, philanthropic organisations, universities and teachers' associations. Some research is also sponsored at further education institutions and by a few independent organisations. The Schools Council and the Social Science Research Council are important channels for government support.

The major institute undertaking research in education, outside the universities, is the National Foundation for Educational Research in England and Wales, an autonomous body which derives its income mainly from corporate members, including local education authorities, teachers' organisations and universities, and from an annual grant from the Department of Education and Science. There are also the Scottish Council for Research in Education and the Northern Ireland Council for Educational Research.

INTERNATIONAL RELATIONS

There are many opportunities for overseas students to study in Britain and for British students to study abroad, and some British teachers serve overseas for a period. There are also official grant-aided schemes for teacher exchange with other Commonwealth countries (administered by the League for the Exchange of Commonwealth Teachers) and with the United States and various European countries (administered by the Central Bureau for Educational Visits and Exchanges). The United States/United Kingdom Educational Commission promotes the interchange of undergraduates and academic staff to study in the opposite country.

British Council

The promotion of educational work overseas, including advice and assistance in English teaching, is a major concern of the British Council (see also p 388). The Council (founded in 1934) is financed mainly from public funds, and is governed by a board which is broadly representative of many elements of British life and includes members nominated by government ministers. Its purpose is defined in its Royal Charter as the promotion of a wider knowledge of the United Kingdom and the English language abroad and the development of closer cultural relations between Britain and other countries. Through its staff in 78 countries, the Council's activities also include fostering personal contacts between British and overseas people, especially in the educational, professional and scientific fields; running, or helping to maintain, over 170 libraries of British books and periodicals; and presenting British achievements and arts. Its work in Britain is concerned mainly with professional visitors and with the welfare of overseas students.

Britain and the European Community

British membership of the European Community is creating closer educational ties with other member countries. Both at school level and in the colleges and universities there has been an expansion of interest in European studies and languages. Post-to-post exchanges of teachers have been encouraged by government-sponsored schemes which are administered by the Central Bureau for Educational Visits and Exchanges. The Bureau also makes appointments available to European teachers wishing to teach in Britain, negotiates posts on an in-service training basis for British teachers wishing to further their experience in another European country, and operates a scheme for foreign language teaching assistants. Britain has adhered to the Statute of the European Schools (six of which have been established throughout the Community) to provide school education for children of people employed in the European Community institutions. Negotiations are in progress to promote recognition of professional qualifications which will enable qualified people to practise anywhere in the Community.

Two aspects of education being given particular attention within the Community are the relationship between education and working life, and the educational needs of migrant workers' children.

Overseas Students in Britain

Students come to Britain from countries throughout the world to study at universities or other educational institutions or for professional training. In the academic year 1976–77 there were about 125,000 overseas students in

Britain, of whom about 34,500 were at universities, another 47,500 at further education colleges and the remainder learning English or training as teachers, nurses, for the law, banking and accountancy, or in industry. About 45 per cent of all overseas students were from the Commonwealth and about 55 per cent were from developing countries.

A range of public and private study fellowships and scholarships are awarded annually to students and research workers from other countries.

As part of British technical co-operation with developing countries, the Ministry of Overseas Development supports many students with subsistence and fees, encourages the development of special courses of particular value to students from developing countries and of advisory and welfare services to meet their needs. Over 12,000 students and trainees were helped in this way in 1977. Under the Commonwealth Scholarship and Fellowship Plan, the governments of certain Commonwealth countries have made awards available at their own institutions of higher education to men and women from other Commonwealth countries. At the beginning of the academic year 1977-78, 589 scholarships and fellowships (including medical awards) were held in Britain under the plan. The Commonwealth Education Awards Scheme provides opportunities for further training, study and research for teachers and others with appropriate experience. Over 1,000 study fellowships were financed during 1977.

About 450 British Council Scholarships tenable usually for one year in Britain, and 25 British Council Fellowships tenable for two to three years, are offered annually to graduates of overseas universities. Some 30 Marshall Scholarships for two years' study at any university in Britain are offered annually by the British Government to graduates from the United States of America. Over 70 Rhodes Scholarships are awarded annually to graduates from the Commonwealth, the United States and the Federal Republic of Germany for two years of study at the University of Oxford. Other universities and colleges themselves offer many scholarships for which graduate students of any nationality are eligible.

The Association of Commonwealth Universities publishes three handbooks (see Bibliography p 440) which include information about sources of financial aid tenable in Britain. The Association promotes co-operation between Commonwealth universities. Its activities include the provision of publication, information and academic appointments services, and of secretariats for various bodies affecting its member institutions, such as the Commonwealth Scholarship Commission and the Marshall Aid Commemoration Commission.

Fellowships and training awards for study in British institutions are additionally available under the Central Treaty Organisation, the Colombo Plan, and the Special Commonwealth African Assistance Plan. Over 1,500 awards for study or training in Britain are also made under various multi-national programmes such as those of the United Nations and its specialised agencies (UNESCO, FAO, WHO, for example), the Council of Europe, OECD and the European Development Fund of the European Community.

The Atlantic College at St. Donat's, south Wales (one of the three constituent colleges of the United World Colleges) provides two-year residential courses for selected fee-paying pupils of different nationalities prior to their entering university. About 80 per cent of its students benefit from scholarships which are provided mainly by governments and international companies.

The Commonwealth Education Liaison Committee supplements normal direct dealings on education between the countries of the Commonwealth, and regular Commonwealth education conferences are held. The United Kingdom

Council for Overseas Student Affairs is an independent body serving overseas students and organisations, and individuals concerned in student affairs. It provides both a forum for the exchange of ideas, and machinery for consultation with government and other authorities.

British Students Overseas

Many British students follow courses overseas at universities and other institutions of higher education, often in Canada, the United States and France.

In 1977–78 15 British students took up awards in six Commonwealth countries under the Commonwealth Scholarship and Fellowship Plan (see p 152). The United States–United Kingdom Educational Commission (still sometimes called the Fulbright–Hays Commission) offers travel and maintenance grants for postgraduate study in the United States. Notable among other scholarships are the Kennedy scholarship to enable British students to study at an American university, and the Churchill travel scholarships for men and women in all walks of life. British students are also offered scholarships at institutions of higher education in many European and non-European countries outside the Commonwealth.

Teachers Serving Overseas

Between 4,000 and 5,000 British teachers serve overseas in schools, colleges of education, technical colleges, universities, and as teacher trainers and educational advisers in developing countries. Many of them are supported by public funds and most work in Commonwealth countries. Recruitment is carried out by the Ministry of Overseas Development, the British Council and voluntary teacher recruiting agencies, such as Christians Abroad. Some developing countries carry out their own recruitment of British teachers through their offices in London.

Most of the several hundred British people teaching in universities overseas are placed through the Inter-University Council for Higher Education Overseas, the Association of Commonwealth Universities and the British Council. The Government supports a number of schemes of assistance for overseas universities. These are administered by the Inter-University Council and include the Special Commonwealth Awards which are made to leading scholars from British universities who are willing to work for a minimum of two years in important posts in the universities of developing Commonwealth countries.

The Association of Commonwealth Universities publishes lists of sources of financial support for British graduates to study or do research overseas and for overseas graduates to come to Britain (see Bibliography p 440).

In addition, four voluntary organisations, co-ordinated under the British Volunteer Programme, recruit graduate and qualified volunteers for service overseas. Over half the volunteers are teachers. The programme receives financial assistance from the British Government.

Academic Interchange

Several schemes designed to assist interchange between institutions of higher education in Britain and overseas countries through staff visits are administered by the British Council. Study and research visits by British and overseas scholars are supported through programmes of the British Academy, the Royal Society, the Science Research Council, and other British and international bodies.

Schemes under which teachers in Britain exchange posts for a year with teachers overseas include one with the United States and another with Commonwealth countries involving each year over 200 British teachers.

Official exchange schemes also operate between Britain and several European countries, both for teachers and for assistants' posts for language specialists. The largest of these schemes is the modern languages assistants' scheme, administered by the Central Bureau for Educational Visits and Exchanges, which enables students and young teachers to serve overseas, particularly in Europe, and for their counterparts to serve in Britain.

Other Educational Aid

Britain provides assistance, on request, to the developing countries in several other ways, including the loan of educational experts for specialist missions and technical and consultancy services. Areas of particular activity include the introduction of new materials, methods and techniques. This assistance is provided through various educational organisations, the Ministry of Overseas Development and the British Council. In addition, the most extensive language teaching undertaking in the world is provided by the English by Radio and Television service of the British Broadcasting Corporation. English lessons are broadcast weekly by radio with explanations in 30 other languages, and recorded lessons are supplied to some 300 stations in 100 countries. English by television programmes have been used in more than 90 countries.

THE YOUTH SERVICE

The aim of the youth service is to promote the social and informal education of young people by offering them opportunities in their leisure time to mix socially and to develop and enlarge their range of interests. The service is provided by a partnership between public authorities and a large variety of voluntary organisations. Membership of groups is voluntary and there is no attempt to impose uniformity or to create anything in the nature of a national youth movement.

State Involvement

The youth service forms part of the education system. The central government education departments formulate broad policy objectives for the service and encourage their achievement through financial assistance and advice. They assist national voluntary youth organisations through grants towards the cost of administration and building projects. They also make known the Government's attitude by means of circulars to local education authorities and through contacts between departmental officials and representatives of the authorities and the voluntary organisations. The Scottish Education Department is advised by a council representing both statutory and voluntary bodies concerned in youth and community work, while in Northern Ireland the advisory body is the Youth Committee for Northern Ireland. The Youth Service Forum for England and Wales acts as a central forum for the consideration of national policies.

Local education authorities (education and library boards in Northern Ireland) are responsible for local administration of the youth service. Authorities provide and run their own youth clubs and centres (some of which are residential) which may be purpose-built or associated with schools. They also assist local voluntary youth groups by lending premises and equipment and by contributing to their capital and running costs. Many authorities have appointed youth committees on which official and voluntary bodies are represented, and employ youth organisers to co-ordinate youth work in their areas and to arrange in-service training. In Scotland these committees and organisers are normally concerned with services for both young people and adults.

Voluntary Organisations

Although there are many local education authority youth clubs and centres, national voluntary organisations still promote the largest share of youth activities through local groups which raise most of their day-to-day running expenses by their own efforts. These have an estimated combined membership of over 6 million. They vary greatly in character, some concentrating on social and recreational pursuits while others concentrate on educational or religious activities. Most of the national organisations in England are members of the National Council of Voluntary Youth Services, a consultative body which takes action only in the name and with the consent of its member bodies. The Council has 64 national organisations and 46 local co-ordinating bodies as members. In Scotland, Wales and Northern Ireland there are similar representative bodies.

Among the largest of the voluntary youth organisations in membership of the National Council are the Scout and Girl Guides Associations (with about 600,000 and 800,000 members), the National Association of Youth Clubs (about 500,000), the National Association of Boys' Clubs (some 170,000) and the Youth Hostels Association (about 275,000). The three pre-service organisations (the Combined Cadet Force, Army Cadet Force and Air Training Corps) are also members. They are financially assisted by the Ministry of Defence and combine social, educational and physical development with training for possible entry to the armed forces.

Training of Youth Workers

There are some 4,000 full-time youth workers in Britain and these are supported by many thousands of part-time workers, many of them unpaid. Part-time workers usually have no professional qualification in youth work but some have allied qualifications, for instance as teachers, and a large number attend short courses and conferences on youth work. Qualified school teachers are recognised as qualified youth workers.

In England and Wales, there is a basic two-year training for youth and community workers. Provided at further education colleges, the course leads to a professional qualification. In addition a number of teacher training colleges provide a study of youth work as a principal or subsidiary subject within teacher-training courses. In Scotland one- and three-year courses are provided at certain colleges of education and in Northern Ireland courses are provided by the Ulster College.

Other Organisations Concerned with Young People

The Duke of Edinburgh's Award Scheme, which operates through bodies such as local authorities, schools, youth organisations and industrial firms, is designed as a challenge to young people to reach certain standards in leisure-time activities with the voluntary assistance of adults. Over 108,000 young people between the ages of 14 and 25 from Britain and other Commonwealth countries entered the scheme in 1977. There are three awards—Bronze, Silver and Gold—for each of which young people must attempt activities in four out of five sections: service; interests; expeditions; and either physical activity or design for living.

King George's Jubilee Trust is a charitable body which, since its creation in 1935, has distributed £3·3 million in grants to voluntary youth organisations and towards experimental youth projects.

There are, in addition, a number of organisations, which, although primarily concerned with the welfare and out-of-school pursuits of young people, operate in a context broader than that of any individual youth movement. Among the most important are the Sports Councils for England, Wales, Scotland and Northern Ireland, which provide practical and advisory services for many youth organisations; the National Playing Fields Association, which advises local authorities and sports organisations on the acquisition, layout, construction and use of sports grounds; and the Outward Bound Trust, which maintains five schools in areas of outstanding natural beauty and offers full-time residential courses designed to encourage a sense of adventure, responsibility, confidence and achievement.

The National Youth Bureau is a forum for association, discussion and joint action for those concerned with the social education of young people. It provides comprehensive information, training and research services, and has a specialist information unit on social work with young people. In Scotland the Board for Information in Youth and Community Service undertakes similar functions.

Community Service by Young People

Thousands of young people voluntarily take part in community service designed to assist those in need, including the elderly and the disabled. Organisations providing opportunities for community service such as International Voluntary Service, Task Force and Community Service Volunteers receive grants from the Government. Many schools also organise community service activities as part of the curriculum.

The Young Volunteer Force Foundation is an independent body which advises interested organisations in England and Wales on methods of involving young people in providing service to the community. The Foundation is grant-aided by the Government and employs teams of young people who are available on request to assist such bodies as local authorities, voluntary organisations and hospital boards in promoting voluntary service. In Scotland, a similar organisation, 'Enterprise Youth', exists to co-ordinate and promote voluntary community service.

The Queen's Silver Jubilee Trust, launched in 1977, encourages the efforts of young people in Britain and the rest of the Commonwealth in community work to help others of all ages.

8 Planning and the Environment

By comprehensive land-use planning and development control Britain has had considerable success in resolving the conflicting demands of industry, commerce, housing, transport, agriculture and recreation and in reducing environmental pollution. There is no 'national plan' for urban and land development, but there is a statutory system of land-use planning applying over the whole country and to virtually every kind of development, and there are laws dealing specifically with environmental health and the control of pollution. All development requires local 'planning permission', and applications for permission are dealt with in the light of 'development plans' which set out strategies for each area on such matters as housing, transport, industry and open land. The underlying approach is to identify people's needs and possible ways of meeting them, and there is a growing move away from narrow land-use allocation towards broader strategic planning recognising the community's social and economic goals.

The system of land-use planning in Great Britain involves a centralised structure under the Secretaries of State for the Environment, Wales and Scotland, and compulsory planning duties for local planning authorities. The Department of the Environment brings together the major responsibilities in England land-use planning, housing and construction, countryside policy and environmental protection. The Welsh Office and the Scottish Development Department have broadly equivalent responsibilities. Large-scale planning in England and Wales is primarily the responsibility of the county councils and the Greater London Council while district councils and the councils of the London boroughs and the City of London are responsible for most local plans and development control, the main housing functions and many other environmental health matters. In certain areas of planning, the two types of authority exercise concurrent powers. In Scotland, planning functions are undertaken by regional and district councils whose responsibilities are divided on a basis broadly similar to that in England and Wales. In the more rural regions and islands areas, all planning responsibilities are carried out by the regional and islands councils respectively.

In Northern Ireland the Department of the Environment for Northern Ireland is responsible for planning matters through its local offices which work closely with the district councils and the local offices of the Housing Executive (see p 179). District councils have local environmental health responsibilities.

Special provisions, in addition to the general town and country planning measures, control the location of industry and offices (see p 211). General problems of industrial development are dealt with jointly by a number of government departments, but each development scheme, as a rule, requires the local planning authority's consent. Financial incentives from the Government encourage the location of industry in particular areas.

Throughout Britain voluntary organisations take an active interest in planning, conservation and the control of pollution.

**Development
Plans
and
Development
Control**

The development plan system in England and Wales involves 'structure' and 'local' plans. Structure plans are prepared by county planning authorities and require ministerial approval. They set out broad policies for the development and other use of land (including measures for the improvement of the physical environment and traffic management) and indicate 'action areas' where comprehensive development or improvement is expected to start within a specified period. Local plans, which have to conform generally with the structure plan, contain detailed proposals including plans for 'action areas' and are normally prepared by district councils, though sometimes by county councils. Local plans are adopted by the planning authorities without being subject to ministerial approval unless the Secretary of State calls in a plan for his own decision. All plans are under continuous review and may be altered from time to time. Scotland has a similar planning system. In Northern Ireland there is a single-tier system; plans are prepared by the Department of the Environment for Northern Ireland.

Members of the public and interested organisations are given an opportunity to express their views on the planning of their areas during the formative stages of the structure and local plans. The local planning authorities must ensure adequate publicity for matters proposed for inclusion in the plans; representations may be made about them to the authorities. These opportunities for public participation are additional to provisions for objecting to prepared plans. In the case of structure plans the Secretary of State holds an examination in public of matters on which he requires more information in order to reach a decision. In the case of local plans objectors have a right to be heard, and a public local inquiry is normally held for this purpose.

Where specific proposals for development differ substantially from the intentions of a development plan, they must be publicised locally. Other schemes affecting a large number of people are usually advertised by the local planning authority and applications seeking permission for certain types of development must also be advertised. The applicant has a right of appeal to the appropriate Secretary of State if planning permission is refused or granted subject to conditions. Most appeals are transferred for decision to inspectors (in Scotland reporters) appointed by the Secretary of State.

The Secretary of State can direct that a planning application be referred to him for decision. This power is exercised sparingly and usually only in respect of proposals of national or regional importance. The applicant has the right to be heard by a person appointed by the Secretary of State and a public inquiry is normally held for this purpose. In the case of development schemes of national or regional importance or of a technical or scientific nature, and if an ordinary inquiry is inadequate for the purpose, the ministers responsible may decide to set up planning inquiry commissions to carry out investigations and hold inquiries locally. Where highway development is proposed, the government minister concerned can hold such inquiries as he considers appropriate.

Similar provision is made in Northern Ireland for public participation in the planning process and for the hearing of objections. There is a right of appeal to an independent Planning Appeals Commission.

**Regional
Planning**

The Secretary of State for the Environment has responsibilities for regional planning in England, which is carried out with the help of the Regional Economic Planning Councils and Economic Planning Boards. There is a council and a board in each of the eight economic planning regions: the North, Yorkshire and Humberside, East Midlands, East Anglia, the South East, the South West, the West Midlands and the North West. The councils are advisory

ECONOMIC PLANNING REGIONS AND NEW TOWNS

Boundaries of economic planning regions
(these coincide with the standard regions
for statistical purposes)
● New towns
○ Other towns

Glenrothes
Cumbernauld
Glasgow ○ ● Edinburgh
Livingston
East Kilbride
Irvine
Scotland

Northern
○ Newcastle upon Tyne
Washington
● Peterlee
Aycliffe ○

**Yorkshire
and Humberside**

Central Lancashire New Town **North West**
○ Leeds
Bradford
Skelmersdale ● Sheffield
Liverpool ○ Manchester ○
● Warrington
Runcorn

East Midlands

● Telford
Birmingham ● Corby ● Peterborough
○ **East Anglia**
Newtown ● **West Midlands**
Redditch ● Northampton
● Milton Keynes
Wales Stevenage
Welwyn Garden City ● Harlow
Cwmbran ● Hatfield
Cardiff ● Hemel Hempstead ● Basildon
○ Bristol Bracknell ● London
South West **South East** ● Crawley

Londonderry
Ballymena ● Antrim
Northern Ireland ● Belfast
Craigavon

N

bodies and comprise voluntary part-time members with wide experience of their regions; the membership includes local authority representatives, as well as people from industry, commerce and the universities, for instance. The councils help in the preparation of broad economic and land-use strategies which provide a regional framework for national and local planning and investment decisions. The boards consist of senior officials in the regions of the government departments concerned with aspects of regional planning. They co-ordinate the regional work of departments and provide the councils with information and advice.

Scotland also has an Economic Council and an Economic Planning Board; there is a Welsh Council; and Northern Ireland has an Economic Council.

The Community Land Act

The Community Land Act of 1975 established the principle that ultimately all substantial private development should take place on land which has been brought into public ownership and then, except where needed for owner-occupied housing, released on leasehold terms. It gives local planning authorities new powers and duties to buy land needed for development (other than relatively minor development). Under associated tax legislation authorities are empowered to buy land at a price net of the tax payable on its development value. A separate Land Authority for Wales has been set up to assume in Wales the functions connected with acquisitions and disposals of development land which are carried out in England and Scotland by local authorities.

New Towns

The new towns represent one of the most successful achievements of recent British planning. The policy behind their creation was mainly one of encouraging the gradual dispersal of industry and population from congested cities to new areas, planned in advance to become self-contained towns with services and amenities within convenient distance of the whole community. Since 1946 32 new towns have been designated, and nearly a million people have gone to live in them.

Town development (or 'expanding town') schemes, involving the transfer of people and industry from overcrowded areas to existing towns suitable for expansion, offered another way of dealing with the same problems, but are arranged directly between the local authorities of the towns concerned.

A government review of the new towns policy, undertaken against a background of substantial reductions in population forecasts and a need to pay more attention to the regeneration of declining inner city areas (see p 161), has led to a reduction in the long-term target populations of some towns. The momentum of new town development is to be substantially maintained, however, over the next few years.

Of the 32 new towns, most of which had as a nucleus an existing town or village, 21 are in England, 2 in Wales, 5 in Scotland and 4 in Northern Ireland

The planning and growth of each new town is supervised by a government appointed development corporation which is given general powers to acquire by compulsory purchase if necessary, land or property needed for the provision of houses, factories and other buildings and for roads and essential services.

In England four of the new towns have been substantially completed and have become the responsibility of the Commission for the New Towns, a government-appointed agency. In Wales responsibility for one of the two new towns has been taken over by the Development Board for Rural Wales. In Northern Ireland, development of the new towns has been incorporated in a new District Towns Strategy which is the responsibility of the Department the Environment for Northern Ireland.

The capital cost is advanced from public funds and is repayable over 60 years. Parliament has approved a fund to provide for advances to the development corporations, which, for Great Britain, stands at £2,750 million, of which £2,250 million had been advanced by the end of 1977.

The new towns have a total population of over 2 million. Young people form a somewhat higher proportion than in the population of the country as a whole. Several of the more developed towns are becoming regional centres and, as the populations grow large enough to give the necessary support, offices, hotels and department stores, as well as art centres and full entertainment and recreational facilities, are gradually being provided. The new towns programme has included the expansion of large existing towns such as Northampton, Peterborough and Warrington; this has the advantage, among others, that many facilities are already available. Most of the towns expanded under town development schemes (for example, Aylesbury, Basingstoke, Swindon and Thetford) are well established and are providing homes, jobs and amenities for people from large cities.

Inner City Policies

Revitalising the inner areas of many towns and cities presents one of the most important challenges to modern British planning. Past policies have produced many successes (many of the slums have been replaced, much old housing has recently been improved and the clean air legislation has enhanced the general environment and public health) but old problems of poor housing, and in some areas congestion, have still to be overcome. In many areas they have been joined by problems of high unemployment, decay and dereliction and unbalanced population structures with relatively high proportions of the elderly and the disadvantaged. The extent of these problems varies from place to place, and the inter-relationship between them is complex. Government policy is not to seek a universal solution but to work out for each city the package of measures that is most likely to improve conditions.

The Government is giving greater resources and priority to the inner city areas, partly through an expanded urban aid programme which is being increased from a 1977–78 level in England and Wales of under £30 million a year to £125 million a year in 1979–80 (in Scotland from about £6 million a year to £20 million a year by 1980–81). The programme has traditionally complemented the work of major social programmes by providing extra facilities which would otherwise not have been available, such as day nurseries, centres for the elderly and language classes for immigrants, but is being recast so as to cover industrial, environmental and recreational provision as well. The urban programme represents only a small part of the central assistance to urban, and other, local authorities. The main contribution is through the annual 'rate support' grant, transport supplementary grant (in England and Wales only), housing subsidy and other programmes. The Government has also provided £100 million for inner city construction work between 1977 and 1979.

A co-ordinated 'partnership' approach is being adopted in seven English areas whereby central and local government work together to tackle places where the problems are greatest. Each partnership has a three-year action programme based on the needs of the area and its particular priorities. Elsewhere in England 15 areas have been identified where the problems are on a slightly smaller scale but still merit special attention. These areas are preparing their own inner city programmes and will receive greatly increased funds from the urban programme.

In Scotland a major urban renewal exercise in Glasgow to regenerate the city's east end is organised on somewhat similar lines to the partnership areas in England. In Northern Ireland a special effort is being made to tackle Belfast's inner city problems.

The Inner Urban Areas Act 1978 is directed towards the economic revival of inner urban areas, and gives powers to selected inner city local authorities to support the creation of new employment opportunities and to improve the environment of industrial areas.

Historic Buildings and Areas

Lists of buildings of special architectural or historic interest are compiled, as required by the planning Acts, by the Secretary of State for the Environment and the Secretaries of State for Scotland and Wales; nearly 290,000 buildings are already listed. It is an offence to demolish or alter the character of any listed building without special consent from the local planning authority or the appropriate Secretary of State; where consent is given to demolish a building, the Royal Commission on Historical Monuments (for England) and similar bodies for Scotland and Wales have an opportunity to make a photographic record of the building. Emergency 'building preservation notices' can be served by the local planning authority to protect buildings not yet listed.

The respective Secretaries of State (on the recommendation of the appropriate Historic Buildings Council) can make grants and loans for the repair or maintenance of buildings (or groups of buildings) of outstanding interest, and local authorities can make grants and loans for any building of architectural or historic interest even if it is not listed. A Government-sponsored Architectural Heritage Fund provides loans for local historic buildings trusts.

Local planning authorities have designated for special protection over 4,000 'conservation areas' of particular architectural or historic interest. Grants and loans are available for works for the preservation or enhancement of outstanding conservation areas.

The Secretaries of State for the Environment, Scotland and Wales are responsible for the maintenance of royal parks and palaces and for the protection of ancient monuments of which about 800 are in their care. The Ancient Monument Boards recommend which monuments are considered to be of national importance and therefore worthy of preservation.

In Northern Ireland 138 historic monuments are maintained and protected by the State, and there is planning legislation on the listing of buildings of special architectural or historic interest. Grants for repairs and maintenance are made by the Department of the Environment for Northern Ireland, which is also responsible for the designation of 'conservation areas'.

Tree Preservation

The local planning authorities have power to protect trees and woodland in the interest of amenity by means of tree preservation orders. When granting planning permission for development, a local planning authority must, where appropriate, impose conditions to secure the preservation or planting of trees. Landowners are generally required to replace 'preserved' trees, which die or are removed or destroyed in contravention of a preservation order.

Green Belts

In order to restrict the further sprawl of large built-up areas, to prevent adjacent towns merging into one another, and in some cases to preserve the character of a town and the amenities of the countryside, 'green belts' (areas where it is intended that the land should be left open and free from building development and where people can seek recreation) have been established or proposed on the fringes of certain urban areas. Much of London's green belt, for example, is agricultural land or woodland, some of which can be used for recreation. There are also country parks, public open spaces, playing fields and golf courses specifically for recreational use.

The Coast

The maritime local planning authorities are responsible for planning land use at the coast providing, for example, recreational facilities and amenities for holidaymakers and local residents; at the same time they attempt to safeguard and enhance the coast's natural attractions and preserve coastal areas of scientific interest.

A comprehensive study of the coastline of England and Wales, undertaken by the Countryside Commission in 1966–70, recommended that certain stretches of underdeveloped coast of particular scenic beauty should be treated as heritage coast. There is a practical programme aimed at the designation of 42 such coasts which together would cover over 1,300 kilometres (808 miles), some 40 per cent of the underdeveloped coastline. Jointly with local authorities, the Commission has defined 33 of these coasts so far, protecting just over 1,000 kilometres (621 miles).

In 1965 the National Trust (see p 172) launched its Enterprise Neptune campaign to raise funds for the nation to acquire stretches of coastline of great natural beauty and recreational value. More than £3 million has been raised so far and as a result the Trust has under its protection 622 kilometres (387 miles) of coastline in England and Wales. Some 127 kilometres (79 miles) of coast in Scotland are protected by conservation agreements with the National Trust for Scotland. In Northern Ireland 56 kilometres (35 miles) of coast and coastal path have been acquired.

In exceptional cases economic arguments override conservation; the development needs of North Sea oil and gas are making a major impact on remote and unspoiled coastal areas in Scotland, for instance, but special planning guidelines aim to ensure that oil-related activities are sited so as to make the best use of existing labour and infra-structure and to minimise the effect on the coastline. Provision has also been made for funds to be set aside for the restoration of sites once there is no further need for them.

The protection of the coastline against erosion, for which the Department of the Environment, the Welsh Office and the Scottish Office are centrally responsible in Great Britain, presents difficult engineering problems and heavy costs for the maritime local authorities. All sizeable coast protection schemes drawn up by the authorities under the Coast Protection Act 1949 are investigated by government engineering staff. Substantial grants from central funds (up to a maximum of 80 per cent) may be made to the authorities. Protection against sea flooding where there is no question of erosion is the responsibility of the water authorities (see pp 263 and 277). To help to prevent the pollution of the sea and coastline, international conventions restrict the discharge of oil into the sea (see p 169).

Outdoor Advertising

The display of outdoor advertisements is controlled by planning legislation. General consents have been issued for certain classes of advertisement but these can be withdrawn in particular cases where there is a serious threat to amenity or public safety. Consent for advertisements outside these classes must be sought from the local planning authority. Rural areas and urban areas requiring special protection can be designated as areas of special control which may impose more restrictive standards.

Countryside Commissions

Two Countryside Commissions (one for England and Wales, the other for Scotland) encourage the development of facilities for open-air recreation in the countryside. These include the provision by local authorities (sometimes in association with other bodies) and private individuals of country parks within easy reach of towns; the establishment of camping sites and picnic areas; and the increased use of reservoirs, canals and other waterways for bathing, sailing and other activities. Some 150 country parks and 200 picnic sites have been recognised in England and Wales by the Countryside Commission. In Scotland a large number of local authority schemes for the provision of a variety of countryside facilities have been approved for grant aid. The Commissions are also responsible for encouraging and promoting measures to conserve and enhance the natural beauty and amenity of the countryside and may undertake research projects and experimental schemes, working in consultation with local authorities and such bodies as the Nature Conservancy Council (see p 165) and the Sports Councils (see p 421). In England and Wales, the Countryside Commission may give financial assistance to public bodies and individuals carrying out countryside recreation and amenity projects. Attention is increasingly being given to techniques of countryside management to supplement the statutory planning controls.

National Parks and Areas of Outstanding Natural Beauty

The Countryside Commission (for England and Wales) is empowered to designate, for confirmation by the appropriate minister, national parks and 'areas of outstanding natural beauty' and to make proposals for the creation of long-distance footpaths and bridleways. Ten national parks have been established: Northumberland, the Lake District, the Yorkshire Dales, the North York Moors and the Peak District in northern England; Snowdonia, the Pembrokeshire Coast and the Brecon Beacons in Wales; Exmoor and Dartmoor in south-west England. They cover some 13,600 sq km (5,250 square miles), or 9 per cent of the area of England and Wales. Administration is the responsibility of special committees or planning boards which carry out all or most of the planning functions. Some 33 areas of outstanding natural beauty had been designated, covering some 14,500 sq km (5,600 square miles).

The land in these designated areas generally remains privately owned, but agreements or orders to secure additional public access may be made by local authorities. Steps are taken to preserve and enhance the landscape's natural beauty by high standards of development control, and by positive measures for which grants are available, such as tree planting and preservation, and the removal of eyesores. In the national parks, other measures for the benefit of the public include the provision of car parks, camping and caravan areas and information centres. All national parks and some other designated areas have warden services. Most local authority expenditure on national parks is met by central government grants. Some 2,640 km (1,650 miles) of long distance footpaths and bridleways have been approved. Large stretches of these paths are already public rights of way.

In Northern Ireland the Ulster Countryside Committee advises on the establishment of national parks and the designation of areas of outstanding natural beauty. Eight areas of outstanding natural beauty have been designated and six areas are being managed as country parks.

Although there are no national parks in Scotland, there are five national park direction areas, in which all except minor planning applications are subject to scrutiny by the Secretary of State. The areas are: Loch Lomond–Trossachs; Glen Affric–Glen Cannich–Strathfarrar; Ben Nevis–Glen Coe–Black Mount; the Cairngorms; and Loch Torridon–Loch Maree–Little Loch Broom. Ministerial supervision, with the advice of the Countryside

Commission for Scotland, is exercised over planning permission in 'areas of special planning control' which are areas of particular beauty, designated by the Secretary of State. One such area forms part of the Pentland Hills to the south of Edinburgh. Over 98 per cent of the land in Scotland has been designated as countryside within the jurisdiction of the Countryside Commission for Scotland.

Forest Parks

The Forestry Commission (see p 284) has formed, and opened to the public, seven forest parks in some of the finest country in Great Britain: Argyll, Glen Trool, Glen More and the Queen Elizabeth Forest Park in Scotland; the Forest of Dean and the Wye valley woods on the borders of England and Wales; Snowdonia in Wales; and the Border Forest Park on the borders of England and Scotland. They cover some 243,000 hectares (600,000 acres), and camping and other recreational facilities are provided in all of them. The historic New Forest, in Hampshire, although not a forest park, is also open to the public. In addition the Forestry Commission welcomes the public to much of the land under its management. In Northern Ireland, the Department of Agriculture has established six forest parks (Tollymore, Castlewellan, Gortin Glen, Drum Manor, Gosford and Glenariff) and there are also forest scenic drives and many recreational facilities in these and other forests.

Local Footpaths and Open Country

County councils in England and Wales are required to prepare definitive maps showing all public rights of way (footpaths and bridleways), which must be kept free of obstruction. If a path is not shown on the map, a private citizen may claim that it is a public right of way if it has been used and regarded as such without hindrance for at least 20 years. Public footpaths are maintained by local authorities who must also provide signposts and supervise landowners' duties to repair stiles and gates. Local authorities in Great Britain can create paths, close existing paths no longer needed for public use and divert paths to secure either a shorter route or the efficient use of land. Local planning authorities can also convert minor roads into footpaths or bridleways to improve the amenities of their area.

There is no automatic right of public access to open country, although many landowners permit such access more or less freely. Local planning authorities can secure access by means of agreements with landowners; if agreements cannot be obtained, authorities may acquire land or make orders for public access. Similar powers cover Scotland.

Common land, a large proportion of which is open to the public, totals an estimated 600,000 hectares (1·5 million acres) in England and Wales. (There is no common land in Scotland or Northern Ireland.) This land is usually privately owned, but people other than the owner have various rights on or over it, for example, of pasture for farm animals. Commons are protected by law and cannot be built on or enclosed without the consent of the Secretaries of State for the Environment or Wales. The Commons Registration Act 1965 provided for the registration of all commons and village greens. Under the Countryside Act 1968 local authorities can provide facilities for enjoyment on any common land to which the public has access.

Nature Conservation

The official body responsible for nature conservation in Great Britain is the Nature Conservancy Council which has the functions of establishing, maintaining and managing nature reserves, advising ministers, providing general information and advice, and commissioning or supporting research. There are some 162 national nature reserves covering over 126,500 hectares (nearly

313,000 acres). Some 3,600 sites of special scientific interest have been scheduled because of their flora, fauna or geological or physiographical features.

About 8,000 hectares (20,000 acres) of Forestry Commission land are managed as areas in which nature conservation is the main object. Local authorities have declared more than 50 nature reserves, and voluntary organisations, which play an important part in protecting wildlife, have established over 1,000 reserves.

Land Reclamation

Derelict land, often concentrated in places associated with nineteenth century industrial development, presents special problems to planners. With central government grants to help to meet the cost of local authority clearance schemes, however, it is improved in a number of ways. Waste land has been turned to farming or forestry use, as well as into sites for industry, housing, schools, roads and recreational areas. Disused excavations have been filled with water and equipped for water sports. Sometimes where removal of waste heaps is not practicable, they have been made more pleasing to the eye by, for example, covering with vegetation.

The Department of the Environment and the Scottish and Welsh Development Agencies provide central advice and information, and in Northern Ireland grants are paid to landowners who restore or improve the appearance of derelict sites.

Planning controls to prevent the spread of dereliction require that, when permission is granted for mineral working, various measures must be taken to minimise the disturbance caused by the work and to secure whatever restoration is practicable, either progressively or when working ceases. The use of land for disposal of waste materials is also subject to conditions restricting height or requiring treatment on completion.

CONTROL OF POLLUTION

Government measures to control environmental pollution, in which industry and voluntary organisations co-operate, are long established, and are seen as complementary to the planning system and the various measures to conserve amenities and the country's heritage.

Administration

Responsibility for the control of pollution is shared by various central government departments, local and water authorities and statutory agencies. Industry co-operates with these authorities and voluntary organisations help to focus public interest on the process of control. An independent standing Royal Commission on Environmental Pollution advises the Government on national and international matters concerning the pollution of the environment, or the adequacy of research and on the future possibilities of danger to the environment. The Secretary of State for the Environment has a co-ordinating role concerning pollution matters as a whole, exercised through a Central Unit on Environmental Pollution within his department. An independent Standing Commission on Energy and the Environment provides the Government with advice on the inter-action of energy policies and the environment.

Specific responsibilities of the Department of the Environment in England include air pollution control, fresh water pollution control, waste disposal, control of radioactive wastes (jointly with the Ministry of Agriculture, Fisheries and Food), of oil and chemicals on beaches and of noise other than aircraft noise, traffic noise and noise at work. Most of these responsibilities i

Scotland are exercised by the Scottish Development Department, in Wales by the Welsh Office and in Northern Ireland by the Department of the Environment for Northern Ireland.

The Department of Trade is responsible for the control of oil pollution at sea (other than from offshore operations) and its clearance, and for the control of aircraft noise. The Department of Transport is responsible for policies for the control of traffic noise. The Department of Energy is responsible for the control of pollution arising from the exploration and exploitation of oil. The Ministry of Agriculture, Fisheries and Food, the Department of Agriculture and Fisheries for Scotland, the Northern Ireland Departments of Agriculture and the Environment and the Health and Safety Executive are responsible for the control of agricultural chemicals such as pesticides, for the protection of fisheries from pollution and for the prevention of food pollution. The protection of the health of employees at work (see p 327) is the responsibility of the Department of Employment and is controlled by the Factory Inspectorate which forms part of the Health and Safety Executive; in Northern Ireland it is the responsibility of the Department of Manpower Services. Other departments such as the Department of Education and Science, the Department of Health and Social Security and the Scottish Home and Health Department have an interest in health aspects of pollution control.

Local authorities are responsible for matters such as collection and disposal of domestic wastes; control of air pollution from domestic and certain industrial premises and noise abatement measures. Sewerage and sewage treatment and disposal are the responsibilities of water authorities in England and Wales and of local authorities in Scotland. The regional water authorities in England, the Welsh Water Authority in Wales, the river purification boards and islands councils in Scotland and the Department of the Environment for Northern Ireland are responsible for control of water pollution.

The European Community has adopted a Community Environment Programme as a result of which a number of measures for Community action are being developed.

The Control of Pollution Act 1974

The Control of Pollution Act 1974, which applies to Great Britain, constitutes the first comprehensive attempt to tackle pollution problems in different (but related) government areas. It extends a wide range of new powers and duties to local and water authorities, increases the existing powers to deal with controlled wastes, air and water pollution and noise, and contains important provisions on the release of information to the public on environmental conditions. In particular the provisions dealing with waste on land institute a new system for the comprehensive planning of regulation of waste disposal operations so as to ensure that disposal is carried out to satisfactory standards and that the best use is made of waste materials. The Act also increases the penalties for a large number of pollution offences. It is being implemented in stages, and most of it is in operation.

The Land

The main risks of land pollution lie in the indiscriminate dumping of waste materials on land, application of pesticides and chemicals, fall-out of materials from the atmosphere and the deposition of materials from floodwater. The application of sewage sludge on farms, too, involves risks as well as benefits to the land.

The Control of Pollution Act lays a duty on waste disposal authorities (county councils and the Greater London Council in England, for example) to ensure that there are adequate arrangements to dispose of controlled wastes and to draw up and periodically revise a waste disposal plan. It also establishes a licensing system for all waste disposal sites, treatment plants and storage facilities receiving controlled wastes. In addition it provides for a more intensive control system for certain specially hazardous or difficult wastes.

The Pesticides Safety Precautions Scheme is a voluntary scheme set up by the Ministry of Agriculture, Fisheries and Food with the support of the agricultural chemicals industry, under which the Advisory Committee on Pesticides, with its Scientific Sub-Committee and Wildlife Panel, reviews the safety of new pesticides and new uses of existing pesticides. Clearances from the Advisory Committee may be provisional or limited, until sufficient information is available for a full clearance for a particular use to be given. The scheme is being extended to include non-agricultural uses of pesticides. A further voluntary scheme is being introduced to ensure that distributors of pesticides, as well as users, take appropriate precautions.

Under the Litter Act 1958 and the Dangerous Litter Act 1971 it is an offence, subject to a fine of up to £100, to leave litter on land in the open air to which the public have free access. Under the Refuse Disposal (Amenity) Act 1978 the deliberate dumping of rubbish carries a similar maximum fine with the possibility of a £200 fine and three months' imprisonment for subsequent offences.

Recycling and Materials Reclamation

The Government encourages the reclamation and recycling of waste materials wherever this is practicable and economic in order to reduce imports and waste disposal costs and to help to conserve natural resources. Industry already makes considerable use of reclaimed waste material such as metals, paper and textiles. Local authorities collect about 200,000 tonnes of waste paper annually and about 100,000 tonnes of ferrous scrap. Waste disposal authorities are required under the Control of Pollution Act to take full account of opportunities for waste reclamation in drawing up their waste disposal plans. Voluntary organisations also organise collections of waste material.

The Government has set up a Waste Management Advisory Council and launched a National Anti-Waste Programme to co-ordinate policy and promote opportunities for reclamation and recycling through education and advice. Extensive Government-supported research and development in this area is in progress. The Department of the Environment is providing financial and technical help to South Yorkshire and Tyne and Wear County Councils which are constructing full-scale prototype plants for the mechanical sorting of household refuse at Doncaster and Byker. These are expected to come into operation in 1979. In addition Britain participates in discussions on waste reclamation and recycling in the European Community.

Fresh Water

Discharges of polluting matter into rivers, lakes, estuaries and some coastal waters are controlled by law. The Control of Pollution Act contains a number of provisions that will considerably strengthen existing legislation: for example, part of the Act extends powers to control pollution of all inland water, including specific underground waters, and tidal coastal water up to the three-mile (4·8 km) limit. Much of this part of the Act is not yet in force but full implementation is expected by the end of 1979. There has been a steady and significant improvement in water quality. The level of pollution in the tidal Thames, for example, has been reduced to a quarter of the 1950s' level—some 97 kinds of fish have been identified there since 1964.

More than 90 per cent of the British population is provided with main drainage, and public authority sewage treatment works serve over four-fifths of the population—a very high proportion by international standards.

Marine Pollution

Control of marine pollution from ships is based largely on international conventions drawn up under the auspices of the Inter-Governmental Maritime Consultative Organisation, a United Nations agency with headquarters in London, and implemented for British ships by domestic legislation. The Prevention of Oil Pollution Act 1971, which gave effect to the International Convention for the Prevention of the Pollution of the Sea by Oil 1954, as amended in 1962 and 1969, makes it an offence for ships of any nationality to discharge any oil into British territorial waters and for British registered ships to discharge persistent oil anywhere at sea, except in accordance with very stringent regulations. Further amendments to the convention, made in 1971 but not yet in force, relate to the design of tankers and are aimed at reducing the volume of oil that could escape in the event of an accident. The International Convention for the Prevention of Pollution from Ships 1973 (as modified by the 1978 Protocol) will, when in force, replace the 1954 convention by more stringent requirements and will regulate pollution by chemicals, sewage and garbage as well as by oil.

The Department of Trade has developed a nationwide organisation, based on the Coastguard and the Marine Survey Service, to deal with oil spills at sea which threaten to cause coastal pollution or are likely to endanger wildlife. If necessary, action is taken to clear the oil by using low toxicity dispersant and spraying equipment. Central government and local authorities have contingency plans for dealing with oil and chemical pollution of beaches and in inshore waters.

The development of the offshore oil industry has brought an increased risk of oil pollution in the North Sea. Offshore operators are required to ensure that oil does not escape into the sea and are also expected to have contingency plans for dealing with oil spills. Not all traces of oil can be removed from water separated from crude oil before its discharge from production platforms into the sea, and these discharges from offshore installations are normally granted exemption from the 1971 Act subject to strict controls laid down by the Department of Energy. The Department of the Environment, the Welsh Office, the Scottish Development Department and the Northern Ireland Department of the Environment grant exemption subject to similar controls for discharges from land-based sources.

The loading of wastes for dumping at sea by means of vehicles, ships, aircraft, hovercraft, marine platforms and conveyor belts is controlled by the Ministry of Agriculture, Fisheries and Food and the appropriate departments in Scotland and Northern Ireland through the Dumping at Sea Act 1974 which gave statutory backing to the voluntary arrangements which had operated for several years. A licence has to be obtained for the permanent deposit of any substance or article into tidal waters and the sea. Dumping at sea is permitted on the basis of the scientific criteria set out in the annexes to the Oslo Convention (International Convention for the Prevention of Marine Pollution by Dumping from Ships and Aircraft 1972) and the London Convention on the Prevention of Marine Pollution by Dumping Wastes and Other Matter 1972. The 1974 Act does not however control discharges of liquid effluent from pipelines, which are covered by the Control of Pollution Act, nor discharges incidental to or derived from the normal operation of a ship, aircraft, vehicle, hovercraft or marine structure.

Clean Air

Responsibility for clean air rests primarily with local authorities. Under the provisions of the Clean Air Acts 1956 and 1968 they may declare 'smoke control areas' within which the emission of smoke from chimneys constitutes an offence. Over half the premises in the conurbations are now covered by smoke control orders. Emissions from most industrial premises are also subject to the control of local authorities under the Clean Air Acts. The emission of dark smoke from any trade or industrial premises or from the chimney of any building is in general prohibited, and new furnaces must be capable as far as practicable of smokeless operation. The height of the chimney serving a new furnace must generally be approved by the local authority, and approved grit and dust arrestment plant has to be installed. Regulations have been made which prescribe specific limits to the quantities of grit and dust which may be emitted from certain furnaces. Industrial premises that give rise to particularly offensive or dangerous emissions are, in England and Wales, under the control of the Alkali and Clean Air Inspectorate of the Health and Safety Executive. The Inspectorate requires the best practicable means to be used to prevent or abate emissions. Founded in 1863, it was probably the world's first air pollution control agency. Controls are also in force on emissions from motor vehicles, such as the maximum permitted lead content of petrol which was reduced from 0·84 grammes per litre in 1973 to 0·45 grammes per litre at the beginning of 1978.

The Clean Air Council (set up in 1956) and a similar council for Scotland review the progress made in abating air pollution in Great Britain. Notable progress has been made towards the achievement of cleaner air and a better environment, especially in the last twenty years or so. It is estimated that the total amount of smoke in the air has been reduced by about 80 per cent since the early 1950s. The domestic smoke control programme has been particularly important in achieving this result. London no longer experiences the dense smoke-laden 'smogs' of the 1950s and in central London winter sunshine has increased by 70 per cent since 1958. Similar improvement has been achieved in other cities including Glasgow and Sheffield. Control measures have reduced urban ground-level concentrations of sulphur dioxide in Britain by 40 per cent in the last ten years.

Noise

Local authorities enforce noise control and must inspect their areas for noise nuisances and act to secure abatement. The Control of Pollution Act improved and strengthened local authorities' existing powers and enabled them to set up 'noise abatement zones' within which they can require noise levels to be held constant or reduced and within which noise levels may not be increased without their permission. The Act contains special provisions to control noise from construction and demolition sites.

Results of the country's first 'quiet town' experiment, sponsored in Darlington by the Noise Advisory Council are being studied. The aim of the experiment was to reduce unnecessary noise wherever it occurred.

Transport is one of the main offenders in noise pollution, and British measures, like those of other countries, aim to tackle the problem, first by reducing noise at source, by insisting that aircraft and motor vehicles should be made quieter, and secondly by protecting people from its effects. As part of this process, grants have been made towards the sound-proofing of some rooms in houses subject to loud aircraft noise, and sound-insulation grants have been made for rooms in homes likely to be subject to excessive noise levels from traffic on some new trunk roads.

The control of aircraft noise is provided for in a number of statutes relating to civil aviation. Measures taken to abate noise include the insulation of homes against noise—for which the major airport owners have provided grants—and the progressive introduction of quieter aircraft.

All aircraft landing or taking off in Britain must be 'noise certificated' in accordance with noise standards for the manufacture of new aircraft which have been internationally agreed and are kept under review by the International Civil Aviation Organisation. As far as civil subsonic jet aircraft are concerned, the latest of these became applicable in August 1978. When introduced into British legislation it will require noise levels of newly designed aircraft to be significantly lower than those of aircraft meeting the previous standards, which were effective from about 1969, and much lower than those of aircraft presently exempted from the previous standards because they were designed before 1969. Noise standards are also being applied to propeller-driven aircraft, and the International Civil Aviation Organisation is examining the possibility of setting standards for civil helicopter noise and for noise from future civil supersonic transport aircraft (the noise level of the Concorde supersonic aircraft is comparable with that of older subsonic aircraft, although not as quiet as that of the new wide-bodied jets).

There are to be prohibitions on the use of non-noise-certificated subsonic jets acquired by British operators after September 1978, and on the use of all such aircraft on the United Kingdom Register of Civil Aircraft from 1986.

All these measures are expected to reduce substantially the noise nuisance to people living near British airports.

Radioactivity   In the United Kingdom radiation exposure of the population resulting from industrial and other processes represents only a small fraction of that to which the population is exposed from the natural environment. Nevertheless, that fraction is subject to stringent control because of possible effects on health or longer-term genetic effects. Under the Radioactive Substances Act 1960 users of radioactive materials other than those subject to licence under the Nuclear Installations Act (see below) must be registered by the appropriate department, and authorisation is also required for the disposal of radioactive waste, with exemption for very minor uses and disposals. The Health and Safety Executive, through its Nuclear Installations Inspectorate, is the authority concerned with the granting of nuclear site licences for commercial nuclear installations. No such installation may be constructed or operated without a licence granted by the Executive.

The Government is carrying out a review of the existing arrangements for the control of radioactive waste. Various methods are used for disposing of such waste. Most low-level solid waste is buried; intermediate-level solid waste is mostly stored, with some disposed of at sea; and highly radioactive liquid waste is at present stored in tanks while research proceeds on methods of disposal. One such method under investigation is the 'Harvest' process for converting this waste into a solid insoluble glass which would be contained in stainless steel cylinders and might be buried in stable geological formations. The process was developed by the United Kingdom Atomic Energy Authority which, in collaboration with the Institute of Geological Sciences, is participating in a programme of the European Atomic Energy Community to study different types of formation which might be suitable for radioactive waste disposal.

The National Radiological Protection Board established under the Radiological Protection Act 1970 provides an authoritative point of reference on radiological protection and represents British interests internationally.

The Radioactive Waste Management Advisory Committee advises Government ministers on major issues relating to the development and implementation of a policy for the management of civil radioactive wastes, including the waste management implications of nuclear policy, the design of nuclear systems, research and development, and the environmental aspects of the handling and treatment of wastes.

VOLUNTARY ORGANISATIONS

Voluntary organisations are particularly active in ensuring that proposed changes in the use of land take full account of the interests of the public and considerations of amenity. The National Trust for England, Wales and Northern Ireland, founded in 1895, is the largest private landowner in Britain and has 610,000 members. For the benefit of the public it owns 162,000 hectares (400,000 acres) of land and protects from harmful development a further 28,700 hectares (71,000 acres). It owns 232 historic buildings and large stretches of coastline. Properties in Scotland covering some 33,200 hectares (82,000 acres) are protected by the National Trust for Scotland, an independent body founded in 1931, which has over 82,000 members.

The Town and Country Planning Association, founded in 1899, seeks to improve the qualities of land use and planning and operates a planning aid service for local amenity groups; while the Royal Town Planning Institute encourages high standards in town planning. The Civic Trust, established in 1957, encourages the protection and improvement of the environment, high standards in architecture and planning and has been closely associated with the drafting of conservation legislation. It supports and advises over 1,200 local amenity societies. Associate trusts are linked with the Civic Trust in the north-east and north-west of England, Scotland and Wales.

Other voluntary societies concerned with amenity in town and country include: the Council for the Protection of Rural England, the Council for the Protection of Rural Wales, the Association for the Protection of Rural Scotland and the Ulster Society for the Preservation of the Countryside; the National Association for Environmental Education; the Keep Britain Tidy Group; the Commons, Open Spaces and Footpaths Preservation Society and the Scottish Rights of Way Society; the Ramblers' Association; the Society for the Protection of Ancient Buildings and the Ancient Monuments Society; the Georgian Group and the Scottish Georgian Society; the Saltire Society (which encourages the preservation of the architectural heritage in Scotland) and the Ulster Architectural Heritage Society; the Victorian Society; the Pilgrim Trust; the Council for British Archaeology; the Historic Churches Preservation Trust; the Council for National Parks; the Prince of Wales's Committee (which promotes environmental improvements in Wales); the Inland Waterways Association; Friends of the Earth; the Conservation Society; the Noise Abatement Society; and the National Society for Clean Air.

Among a large number of voluntary bodies concerned with nature conservation are the Society for the Promotion of Nature Conservation, the Royal Society for the Protection of Birds, the Scottish Wildlife Trust and the Council for Nature.

The Committee for Environmental Conservation, comprising many of the main voluntary organisations, acts as a liaison body and is concerned with broader questions of amenity than those covered by individual societies. The Centre for Environmental Studies is an independent research body concerned with urban, regional and other planning problems.

9 Housing

A home for all households at a price within their means is a central aim of housing policy. Others include: a better balance between new building and renovation with social as well as financial costs taken into account; reasonable stability in household housing costs; attention to the needs of people with special problems such as the elderly, the disabled and the handicapped; a degree of priority for people who may have problems in finding suitable housing but who are not traditionally thought of as 'in need', such as middle-aged single people; increased scope for mobility; easier means for people to obtain the type of tenure they want; and the safeguarding of tenants' independence.

Although some households still live in unsatisfactory conditions, the proportion of the total is relatively small, and the Government believes that it no longer makes sense to consider housing problems in national totals; attention and resources are therefore being directed more selectively to the areas, often in inner cities, with the most pressing needs. A system of local strategies and investment programmes has been instituted as a means by which local authorities can, in consultation with local bodies concerned, plan comprehensively for development in both public and private sectors.

Public expenditure provision for housing has had to be more strictly limited in recent times, but the expenditure programme is still substantial, standing at over £4,700 million a year.

Housing Characteristics

There are over 20·5 million dwellings, houses being much more common than flats (the ratio is roughly four to one). Nationally the number of dwellings is slightly larger than the number of households, but there continue to be shortages in certain areas and, because of changing social habits, the houses available may not always be of the type in demand.

More than two families in every five live in a post-1945 home, but there remain a large number of old dwellings, some of which have been kept in good repair and modernised, but many others of which (particularly in the centres of cities) are unsatisfactory by modern standards.

Throughout this century pressure on housing accommodation has been increased more by the rapid rise in the number of separate households than by the increase in the population. While the number of people has increased by about two fifths, the number of households has more than doubled. Families are smaller, there has been a substantial reduction in the sharing of homes by three generations, and there has been an increase in the number of one-person households.

Over half of all dwellings are owned by their occupiers, nearly a third are rented from public housing authorities, and most of the remainder are rented from private landlords. There are variations, however, in the distribution of tenure between different parts of the country; in Scotland more than half the dwellings are rented from public authorities. Private rented accommodation is generally more common in the central parts of large towns, while owner-occupation is more frequent in outer suburbs and in country areas.

New house construction is undertaken, on a roughly equal scale, by both public and private sectors, and in addition about five per cent of new building is carried out by voluntary housing associations and societies. Public authorities provide dwellings mainly for renting while private interests build mainly for sale to owner-occupiers. There is very little building of private dwellings to rent.

Administration

Responsibility for formulating housing policy and supervising the housing programme is borne by the Secretary of State for the Environment in England and by the Secretaries of State for Scotland and Wales. (For Northern Ireland see p 179.)

Most of the public housing is provided by 459 local housing authorities, which are responsible for ensuring that the supply of housing in their areas is adequate. The authorities are: in England and Wales (outside London) the district councils; in London, the Greater London Council, the London borough councils and the Common Council of the City of London; and in Scotland, the district and islands councils. Other public housing authorities are the new town authorities, the Scottish Special Housing Association which supplements building by local authorities in Scotland, and the Development Board for Rural Wales.

The central government departments specify certain standards for the construction and equipment of all new dwellings; these are enforced by the local authorities. Subsidies are made available to the authorities to assist them with housing costs, and guidance is given on design and layout.

Local authorities are involved in many other aspects of housing policy, such as the payment of house renovation grants and the implementation of housing renewal programmes. A growing number are establishing housing advisory centres to provide information on most aspects of housing.

Research and Development

Research into building materials and techniques, as well as into the social, economic and design aspects of housing, is undertaken within the Department of the Environment. It is carried out by the Building Research Establishment of the Department's research directorate as well as by the directorates of economics, statistics and housing development. The Research and Development Group of the Scottish Development Department also undertakes research. Sponsored work is carried out by universities, polytechnics, market research firms and the Office of Population Censuses and Surveys, and local authorities may also have housing research programmes.

The Government is advised on the need for, and application of, research and development by the Construction and Housing Research Advisory Council. Advice on ways of increasing productivity in house-building is also provided by the National Building Agency.

Home Ownership

The number of people owning their own houses has more than doubled in the last 20 years, and the 11 million owner-occupied dwellings in Britain account for over half of the total housing stock.

Mortgage Loans

Loans to enable people to buy their own houses are available from various sources, including building societies, insurance companies, industrial and provident societies and local authorities.

Building societies (see also p 349) are by far the largest sources of such funds; their share of the market being over 90 per cent. They do not build houses themselves but lend money upon security by way of a mortgage on the home bought for owner-occupation. They usually advance up to 80 per cent of their valuation of a property but it is possible to borrow up to 100 per cent with the help of an appropriate insurance guarantee. Loans are normally repayable over periods of 20 or 25 years (up to 30 or 35 years in certain circumstances) by equal monthly instalments to cover capital and interest. The average price in Britain of all houses mortgaged to building societies in 1977 was about £13,900. In 1977 the societies advanced some £6,700 million.

Owner-occupiers are entitled to tax relief on their mortgage interest payments arising on up to £25,000 of their mortgages (on one house only) and in 1977–78 this amounted to about £1,055 million. An alternative form of assistance is the option mortgage scheme, designed to help those with smaller incomes. It allows the borrower to receive, instead of tax relief, a subsidy which has the effect of reducing the rate of interest on the loan. Assistance under this scheme in Great Britain amounted in 1977–78 to £150 million. There is an associated guarantee scheme under which mortgage loans of up to 100 per cent of the valuation of a house (not exceeding £14,000) may be made to those participating in the option mortgage scheme. Other ways of helping people with lower incomes to become owner-occupiers include a scheme which allows those buying homes for the first time, subject to certain conditions, to defer part of their mortgage payments that would normally be due in the early years until later in the mortgage term, and equity sharing systems. The Home Purchase and Housing Corporation Guarantee Act 1978 provides for assistance to be given to first-time house buyers who have been saving. The assistance consists of a tax-free cash bonus on savings, payable at the time of house purchase, and a loan of up to £600, interest-free for the first five years and then repayable over the remaining life of the mortgage.

Building
Standards

For building in the private sector the National House Building Council sets standards and enforces them by inspection and certification. Almost all new private houses are covered by the Council's scheme which carries ten-year protection against major structural defects. Two-year protection is also given against faulty workmanship. Most lenders will not grant mortgages on a new house unless it is covered by a Council certificate.

Public Sector
Housing

Public housing authorities own some 6·6 million houses and flats. The number of homes owned by each authority varies widely, several having a stock of well over 100,000.

Local authorities meet the capital costs of new house construction by raising loans on the open market or by borrowing from the Public Works Loan Board. Current expenditure, including maintenance and management costs and loan interest and repayments, is met from rents, supplemented by subsidies from the Government and, where required to balance housing revenue accounts, from the rates. Local authorities are required to charge their tenants reasonable rents (which keep a balance between the interests of tenants and ratepayers) without making a profit. Subsidies for public housing in Great Britain during 1977–78 are expected to total some £1,827 million (including rent rebates payable to poorer tenants to assist in meeting rents of accommodation suited to their needs). Supplementary subsidies assist local authorities with slum clearance.

In selecting tenants for new or vacant dwellings, local authorities normally give preference to families living in overcrowded or unsatisfactory conditions, but they are free to allocate homes according to their own schemes. Authorities normally establish waiting lists and treat applicants (outside priority categories) in order of application; some require applicants to fulfil residence qualifications before they are accepted on waiting lists.

Local authorities have a statutory duty to secure that accommodation (not necessarily an authority house) is available for homeless people who have dependent children or are vulnerable on grounds such as age or disability.

Most building is undertaken by private firms under contract although a number of authorities employ direct labour to build houses. Some authorities work in consortia to make the best use of experience and technical information, and to initiate research and development projects.

Dwellings are constructed to meet the needs of different sizes of household. More than a quarter are of the single-bedroom type suitable for smaller households including the elderly, but the majority are designed for families and have two or three bedrooms, one or two living-rooms and a kitchen, bathroom and lavatory.

Sheltered accommodation (with an alarm system and resident warden) is provided for elderly people who need this degree of support. Increasing importance is also being placed on the housing needs of physically handicapped people, and a small but growing proportion of the new housing stock is suitable for them. Also receiving attention are the needs of other 'disadvantaged' groups such as one-parent families, the mentally handicapped, the ex-mentally ill and women who have suffered from violence within the family.

Public housing is built to a high minimum standard. In England and Wales, for example, some 90 per cent of the new houses built for local authorities in 1976 had central heating and the average floor area of houses to accommodate five people was 88·4 square metres (952 square feet).

Local authorities are being encouraged to take a broad view of their responsibilities for housing management and to consider the wider social and economic consequences of their housing policies. The aim is for them to develop a comprehensive housing service, taking full account of people's needs and preferences, making the best use of all the resources available in both public and private sectors, and adopting a flexible view of the way the housing stock is used. A high standard of skill and organisation is needed to meet this objective, and emphasis is being given to improved training for all grades of housing staff. A Housing Services Advisory Group, composed of central and local government officials, elected councillors and other housing experts, has been set up to advise local authorities on good professional practice in housing management and maintenance. A small Housing Services Advisory Unit has also been created within the Department of the Environment to stimulate an exchange of ideas and information on good management practice and to provide advice on policy within the Department.

Privately Rented Housing   During the last quarter of a century there has been a steady decline in the number of rented dwellings available from private landlords (including tied accommodation)—from over 50 per cent of the housing stock to about 15 per cent (3 million). Major factors have been the increased demand for owner-occupation, the greater availability of public rented housing, and the operation of rent restriction. Privately rented dwellings form a high proportion of the older housing, most landlords being individuals with limited holdings; some rented housing is provided by larger property owners, including property companies.

Most privately rented dwellings are subject to rent restriction. Tenants have a wide degree of security of tenure, and may not be evicted without a court order. Harassment of residential occupiers is a criminal offence. Tenants with incomes up to average levels are eligible for assistance with their rent under a national scheme of rent allowances which is operated by local authorities and financed mainly by government subsidies.

There are three forms of rent restriction: control, regulation and the fixing of a reasonable rent by a rent tribunal. Controlled rents (which apply to dwellings of low rateable value where the tenant has lived continuously since before 1957) are fixed, and may be increased only to an extent which reflects expenditure by the landlord on improvements and repairs. However, if a controlled dwelling reaches a satisfactory standard of amenity, the landlord may transfer it to the alternative system of rent regulation, which applies generally to privately rented accommodation, other than in the luxury class, except for accommodation where the landlord lives on the same premises. In a regulated tenancy a 'fair rent' is fixed by independent rent officers, at the request of the landlord, the tenant, or both; if the rent officer's decision is objected to by the landlord or the tenant, it is referred to a rent assessment committee. Once fixed, the rent is registered and not normally reviewed for at least three years.

The third form of rent restriction applies to tenants with resident landlords and tenants of a few other types of furnished accommodation who may refer their tenancy agreements to a rent tribunal for determination of a reasonable rent. Tribunals may grant tenants security of tenure for up to six months with a possibility of further periods.

Housing Associations

Housing associations extend the choice of housing (which for most people is between owner-occupying or renting from a public authority or a private landlord) by providing an increasing addition to the accommodation available for rent. The associations, which have a tradition dating back to the medieval almshouse trusts, cater for people who would otherwise look to a local authority for a home. In addition to normal family housing, they provide particularly for the special needs of elderly or disabled people.

Since the early 1960s the Government has encouraged the growth of these non-profit-making associations which between them own nearly 300,000 dwellings. The National Federation of Housing Associations has 2,200 associations as its members, and the Scottish Federation of Housing Associations covers 124 associations in Scotland.

Rented housing schemes carried out by housing associations qualify for a government grant but only if the association is registered with the Housing Corporation, a statutory body set up by the Government. The Corporation's register contains details of more than 2,600 associations. Rented dwellings owned by housing associations come within the fair rent and rent allowance arrangements.

Alternative forms of tenure on local authority estates and within the housing association sector are being encouraged in order to give occupiers a greater stake in the ownership or management of their homes. The Housing Corporation is engaged in a pilot programme including co-ownership and community leasehold schemes. The Corporation has also set up a specialist unit, the Co-operative Housing Agency, to advise, assist and finance housing co-operatives (schemes of collective ownership and management).

Improving Older Houses

Modernisation and conversion of substandard housing, with the help of grants from public funds, has increasingly been encouraged as an alternative to clearing and rebuilding and as a way of preserving established communities and of making more economic use of resources. This policy of improvement rather than redevelopment has been reinforced by the Government's decision to give priority to inner city regeneration. Financial assistance is available for the improvement of individual dwellings or of whole areas of older housing.

Renovation grants to improve over 2·35 million homes were approved in Great Britain between 1966 and 1976.

There are four types of renovation grant: improvement grants, for carrying out improvements to a high standard or for conversion into flats; intermediate grants, for the provision of standard amenities and associated repairs; special grants (not available in Scotland) for providing standard amenities in houses of multiple occupation; and repairs grants, available only in 'housing action areas' and 'general improvement areas' (see below). The amount of the award depends on the location of the dwelling: up to 75 per cent (sometimes 90 per cent) of the eligible expense in housing action areas; 60 per cent in general improvement areas; and 50 per cent elsewhere. A government contribution amounting to 75 per cent (90 per cent in housing action and general improvement areas) of each grant is paid to the local authority.

In order to tackle systematically the improvement of whole areas of older housing, local authorities in England and Wales have powers to declare 'general improvement areas' and 'housing action areas'. General improvement areas consist of fundamentally sound houses and a stable population. The aim is to encourage owners to improve their dwellings with the aid of enhanced grants while the local authority improves the environment with financial aid from the Government. In areas of particularly poor housing, where bad physical conditions are combined with social stress, local authorities are empowered to declare housing action areas with the aim of improving living conditions and housing management, for the benefit of the residents, within a five-year period. High rates of grant are available, and the local authority has special powers for compulsory purchase and compulsory improvement in order to secure rehabilitation within the time-scale. Financial aid for environmental improvement is available from the Government, though on a smaller scale than in general improvement areas. By the end of March 1977 there were 1,086 general improvement areas and 212 housing action areas in England and Wales. There are broadly similar arrangements in Scotland where, however, the term 'general improvement area' is not used and where the 'housing action area' powers are available for areas in which at least half the houses fail to meet prescribed physical standards.

Slum Clearance

In urban areas of Britain slum clearance and redevelopment have been major features of housing policy. Since the mid-1950s about 3·3 million people have been rehoused in England and Wales as a result of slum clearance programmes. Clearance of large areas of 'irredeemable' slums is now almost at an end and greater emphasis is placed on renewal and modernisation wherever possible. Local authorities receive special financial assistance from the Government.

Housing authorities are obliged to see that other accommodation exists, or can be provided by them, for people displaced by slum clearance. Owners of land compulsorily acquired during slum clearance programmes receive as compensation either the full market value or, if the land consists of unfit houses, a sum based on the value of the cleared site; additional payments are, however, made to most owner-occupiers of unfit houses to bring their compensation up to market value.

Redevelopment of the slums has presented many problems. Most of the areas were seriously overcrowded; not only were the houses built to a high density but they were themselves over-occupied. While the areas usually lacked social facilities they had the advantage that they were already well provided with the basic utilities, jobs were usually available in the vicinity and town centre facilities were not far away. The aim in carrying out slum clearance was thus to house as many people as possible on the cleared sites. This was most easily achieved if fairly large areas were cleared and high-rise flats built. The results in many areas are now seen as less than satisfactory in spite of the high standard of many of the homes themselves. The main criticisms of multi-storey flats are that they are inhuman in scale and unsuitable for families with young children because of the lack of convenient play space. The need to build to a reasonably high density in inner city areas still exists, but is now being met by carefully grouped low-rise blocks, including individual houses wherever possible.

Northern Ireland Northern Ireland has a major problem of unfit and derelict housing, especially in Belfast. The situation has been made worse by the civil disturbances. With the problem of unfit housing in mind, several recent changes have been made in housing policy emphasis, including a greater concentration on improving the existing stock and a major attack on housing problems in Belfast.

The Housing (Northern Ireland) Order 1976 enables housing action areas to be declared where concerted action can be taken to improve and rehabilitate the housing. A £130-million programme for the rehabilitation of Belfast began in 1977.

The Northern Ireland Department of the Environment is responsible for housing policy in the Province and the Northern Ireland Housing Executive for the provision and management of the public authority housing and for dealing with unfit housing, whether publicly or privately owned.

The development of housing associations is being encouraged so that they can undertake the rehabilitation of older properties, especially in Belfast, and provide new homes for groups such as the disabled and the elderly. A Northern Ireland Committee of the National Federation of Housing Associations encourages the development of housing associations, particularly to help the elderly, the handicapped and those living in older houses which can be improved or rehabilitated.

In the private rented sector legislation is planned to replace the existing rent restriction provisions with a single statute designed to safeguard tenants' rights while providing landlords with sufficient rental income to maintain their property in good condition.

Another trend in housing policy is the attempt to widen housing options available to families, particularly those who wish to own their own homes. The option mortgage scheme is being introduced, and it is intended that the savings bonus and loans scheme for first-time home buyers will also be extended to Northern Ireland.

10 The Churches

Everyone in Britain has the right of religious freedom (in teaching, worship and observance) without interference from the community or the State. Churches and religious societies may own property, conduct schools, and propagate their beliefs in speech and writing. There is no religious or denominational bar to the holding of public office.

Clergy of the established churches of England and Scotland work in services administered by the State, such as the armed forces, national hospitals and prisons, and are paid a salary by the State. Clergy of other denominations are also appointed. Voluntary schools provided by any religious denomination may be wholly or partly maintained from public funds.

There is no precise or uniform information about the number of church adherents since no inquiries are made about religious beliefs in censuses[1] or other official returns, and each church adopts its own criteria in counting its members. Membership figures in this chapter are therefore approximate.

The Church of England

The established Church of England's relationship with the State is one of mutual obligation—privileges accorded to the Church balanced by certain duties which it must fulfil. The Sovereign must always be a member of the Church, and promises to uphold it; Church of England archbishops, bishops and deans are appointed by the Sovereign on the advice of the Prime Minister; all clergy take an oath of allegiance to the Crown. The Church can regulate its own worship. The two archbishops (of Canterbury and York), the bishops of London, Durham and Winchester, and 21 other bishops (according to their seniority as diocesan bishops) sit in the House of Lords. Clergy of the Church (together with those of the Church of Scotland, the Church of Ireland and the Roman Catholic Church) are not allowed to sit in the House of Commons.

The Church has two provinces: Canterbury, comprising 29 dioceses, and York, 14 dioceses. The dioceses are divided into parishes, of which there are some 13,860. The Archbishop of Canterbury is 'Primate of All England', and the Archbishop of York 'Primate of England'. Of the population born and resident in the two provinces (roughly 46 million), about 60 per cent are baptised into the Church and some 20 per cent are confirmed members.

The central governing body, the General Synod, has both spiritual authority and legislative and administrative powers; and bishops, clergy and lay members are involved in decisions. Certain important issues must be referred for the approval of the dioceses before being decided by the Synod. Lay members are associated with church government in the parishes through the ancient office of churchwarden and the modern parochial church councils.

The General Synod is the centre of an administrative system dealing with such matters as education, inter-church relations, social questions, recruitment and training for the ministry, church work at home and overseas and the care of church buildings, particularly those of historic and architectural interest. The Synod is also concerned with church schools; church colleges of education; theological colleges; and establishments for training women in pastoral work.

---

[1] In Northern Ireland, recent full censuses have contained an optional question about people's religious professions.

The Church has its own courts whose jurisdiction today extends only to matters of purely ecclesiastical concern.

Church finance is administered locally by the parishes and the dioceses, with contributions to a central fund for the maintenance of central services, including capital expenditure on training and theological colleges and grants for training candidates for ordination. The State makes no direct financial contribution to church expenses. The Church's endowment income is mainly administered by the Church Commissioners, the body largely responsible for the payment of clergy stipends and pensions.

The Anglican Communion

The Anglican Communion comprises 25 autonomous provinces in Britain and overseas and three regional councils overseas with a total membership of about 67 million. In the British Isles, there are four provinces: the Church of England (established), the Church in Wales, the Episcopal Church in Scotland, and the Church of Ireland.

Every ten years (the last meeting was in 1978), the Lambeth Conference meets for unofficial consultation between all Anglican bishops: presided over by the Archbishop of Canterbury, it has no executive authority, but enjoys great prestige, and its findings on doctrine, discipline, relations with other communions, and attitudes to political and social questions are widely studied. The Anglican Consultative Council—an assembly of laymen and clergy as well as bishops which meets every two or three years—is designed to provide consultations within the Anglican Communion and to serve as an instrument of common action. The council next meets in 1979.

The Church of Scotland

The Church of Scotland has a presbyterian form of government. Its status as the national church derives from the Treaty of Union 1707 and the Church of Scotland Act 1921 which confirmed its complete freedom in all spiritual matters. It appoints its own officers, and its decisions on questions of doctrine and discipline are not subject to parliamentary discussion or modification.

All ministers have equal status, each of some 2,000 churches being governed locally by the Kirk Session, consisting of the minister and the elected elders of the church; above the Kirk Session is the Court of the Presbytery, then the Court of the Synod, and finally the General Assembly, consisting of elected ministers and elders, which meets annually under the presidency of an elected moderator who serves for one year. The Sovereign is represented at the General Assembly by the Lord High Commissioner.

The training for the ministry (to which women may be admitted) has given the Church a high reputation for scholarship and has in turn influenced the standard of education in Scotland. The adult communicant membership of the Church of Scotland is estimated at over 1 million.

The Free Churches

The phrase 'Free Churches' is commonly used to describe the 'nonconformist' churches of England and Wales (which dissent from certain practices of the established church and, generally speaking, have distinctive convictions regarding organisation and worship) and Protestant churches in other parts of Britain (apart from the established Church of Scotland). Certain other churches and religious associations have links with the main Free Churches.

The Methodist Church, the largest of the Free Churches with some 558,000 adult full members, originated in the eighteenth century following the evangelical revival by John Wesley, and is based on a 1932 union of most of the separate Methodist Churches. The Methodist Churches which did not join the union include the Independent Methodists (5,200 members) and the Wesleyan Reform Union (with some 4,200 members).

The United Reformed Church, with some 170,000 members, was formed in 1972 when the Congregational Church in England and Wales (the oldest community of dissenters in Britain) and the Presbyterian Church of England merged—the first transdenominational union of churches in Britain since the Reformation in the sixteenth century.

The Baptists are nearly all grouped in associations of churches, most of which belong to the Baptist Union of Great Britain and Ireland (formed in 1813), with a total membership of about 182,000; in addition there are separate Baptist Unions for Scotland, Wales and Ireland and other Baptist churches.

Among the other Free Churches are the Presbyterian Church in Ireland (with nearly 125,000 regular communicants in Northern Ireland); the Presbyterian (or Calvinistic Methodist) Church of Wales, which arose from the revivalist movement led in 1735 by Howell Harris and now numbers about 91,000; the Union of Welsh Independents; the Free Church of Scotland; the United Free Church of Scotland; the Free Presbyterian Church of Scotland; the Reformed Presbyterian Church of Scotland; the Reformed Presbyterian Church of Ireland; and the Non-Subscribing Presbyterian Church of Ireland.

Other Protestant denominations include: the Unitarian and Free Christian Churches; the Churches of Christ (known also in the United States of America as Disciples of Christ), which have been an organised community in Britain since early in the nineteenth century; the British Province of the Moravian Church, which is an international missionary church; the Free Church of England (or Reformed Episcopal Church), which was formed in 1844 as a direct result of the Oxford Movement; and the Congregational Federation, formed from Congregational churches which did not enter the United Reformed Church. The Religious Society of Friends (Quakers), with about 20,000 members in Britain and over 400 places for worship, came into being in the middle of the seventeenth century under the leadership of George Fox and works for peace and the relief of suffering in many parts of the world.

The Salvation Army, founded in Britain in 1865, has since spread to 82 other countries and has a strength of about 2 million. Within Britain it has some 100,000 active members operating from more than 1,000 centres of worship. Believing in a very practical expression of Christian concern, the Salvation Army has 209 centres to help people in need.

There are also a number of other religious organisations with churches or assemblies in Britain, including the Church of Jesus Christ of Latter-Day Saints (the Mormon Church); and the Christian Scientists with some 300 branch churches and societies in the British Isles.

The Roman Catholic Church

The Roman Catholic hierarchy in England and Wales, which became temporarily extinct during the sixteenth century, was restored in 1850; the Scottish hierarchy became extinct in the early seventeenth century and was restored in 1878. There are now 6 Roman Catholic provinces in Great Britain, each under an archbishop, 26 episcopal dioceses, and some 3,000 parishes. In Northern Ireland, there are 9 dioceses, some of which have territory partly in the Irish Republic. It is estimated that there are some 4·2 million adherents (including children) to the Roman Catholic faith in the whole of Britain.

The Roman Catholic Church attaches great importance to the education of its children and requires its members to try to bring up their children in the Catholic faith. Many schools for Catholic children are staffed by members of the religious orders who also undertake other social work such as nursing, child care, and the conduct of homes for old people.

Jewry

Jews first settled in England at the time of the Norman conquest, but the community in Britain dates from 1656; consisting of some 410,000 people, including both Sephardi (originally from Spain and Portugal) and Ashkenazi (from Germany and Eastern Europe), it has become one of the largest groups of Jews in Europe. The community is divided into two schools of thought—the Orthodox, to which about 80 per cent of practising Jews belong; and the Reform, which originated in 1840 and was followed in 1901 by the Liberal Jewish movement. The Chief Rabbi is the head of the largest group (Ashkenazi) within Orthodox Jewry; the Haham is the head of the Sephardi group. Jewish congregations in Britain number about 450. Jewish denominational schools are attended by about one in five Jewish children.

Other Religious Communities

Immigrants to Britain from Commonwealth and foreign countries have established centres of worship, especially in London, for their own communities. Among the Christian communities represented are Orthodox, Lutheran and Reformed Churches of various European countries and the Armenian Church.

The principal non-Christian communities in Britain, apart from the Jews, are the Muslims, Buddhists, Hindus and Sikhs. For the many Muslims in Britain there are mosques or Islamic centres in London, Birmingham, Manchester, Cardiff, Glasgow and in many other large cities. The community's headquarters are at the London Central Mosque and Islamic Cultural Centre. The Buddhist Society, with headquarters in London and centres in most other large towns and many universities, publishes and makes known the principles of Buddhism and encourages their study and practice. It adheres to no one school of Buddhism. There are other centres for Buddhism, and also many centres of eastern philosophy and religion among immigrant communities.

Co-operation among the Churches

The British Council of Churches, with representatives or observers from all the main Christian churches in the British Isles, facilitates common action and seeks to further Christian unity. It works through five divisions: Christian Aid (which has a separate constitution); Conference for World Mission; Ecumenical Affairs; Community Affairs; and International Affairs.

The Free Church Federal Council (which has a concordat with the British Council of Churches) comprises most of the Free Churches in England and Wales. It promotes unity and joint action among the Free Churches and is a channel for communication with central and local government.

The permanent Anglican-Roman Catholic Commission explores points of possible unity between the two communions.

The Anglican and the main Free Churches in the British Isles also participate in the World Council of Churches (of which the British Council of Churches is an associated national council) which links together some 290 churches in over 80 countries for co-operation and the study of common problems. The Council of Christians and Jews works for better understanding among members of the two religions and deals with problems in the social field.

The New English Bible, a modern English translation completed in 1970, is the result of co-operation among many Christian churches.

The Sharing of Church Buildings Act 1969 enables agreements to be made by two or more churches for the sharing of church buildings.

11 The National Economy

Britain has a mixed economy, nationalised industries accounting for about one-tenth of the national product and about one-seventh of total fixed investment. Manufacturing industry accounts for about 29 per cent of total domestic income and services[1] for 45 per cent. International trade is of great importance and exports of goods and services represent about 34 per cent of gross domestic product. Britain ranks fifth in world trade (after the United States, the Federal Republic of Germany, Japan and France) and accounts for 6 per cent of total world trade. It takes over 7 per cent of the world's exports of primary products, and contributes just over 9 per cent to the main manufacturing countries' exports of manufactured goods. It is among the world's largest exporters of aerospace products, motor vehicles, electrical equipment, finished textiles, and most types of machinery, and is one of the world's largest importers of agricultural products, raw materials and semi-manufactures.

With abundant resources of coal and the discovery and exploitation of North Sea oil and gas, Britain is expected to become self-sufficient in energy by 1980 with substantial benefits to the balance of payments through the reduction of oil imports. The potential balance of payments effect of British production of oil in 1979 has been estimated at £4,500 million (1976 prices). Other economic effects of the offshore oil industry include the growing revenues accruing to the Government through taxation, the new jobs created, and the stimulus provided for the development and sales of highly specialised equipment and services.

A high level of agricultural productivity enables Britain to provide just over half the food it needs from its own soil, although only 2·7 per cent of the employed labour force are engaged in agriculture—a lower proportion than in any other major industrial country.

Britain earns overseas currency by exports of (mainly) manufactured goods and by invisible transactions—earnings on overseas investment, travel, civil aviation, British-owned shipping, and financial, banking, insurance and other services. It accounts for nearly 10 per cent of world invisible receipts (excluding government transactions), more than any country except the United States.

The significant contribution made to export earnings by invisibles is in large measure a reflection of Britain's position as a major financial centre. Its banks, insurance underwriters and brokers and other financial institutions provide worldwide financial services. The City of London contains perhaps the most comprehensive and advanced capital market in the world.

ECONOMIC DEVELOPMENT

Earlier History

As a result of the 'Industrial Revolution' during the eighteenth and nineteenth centuries (when a series of inventions led to a complete change in the character of production), Britain emerged as the first great industrial nation and as a pioneer of new methods in transport, communications and technology. It

---

[1] Services in this context cover transport, communication, distributive trades, insurance, banking, finance and business services, public health and education, and other services excluding public administration, defence and ownership of dwellings.

occupied a leading position as world manufacturer, merchant, carrier, banker and investor, and its fast-growing economy supported a rapidly increasing population. In the period from 1870 to 1890 British industry had a clear though declining lead over that of other countries. Between 1890 and 1914, industrial competition from Europe and North America grew, but its effects on Britain's export industries, particularly cotton textiles and coal, were offset by a number of factors including the rise in world trade and the returns on Britain's large overseas investments.

Following the first world war Britain's older industries met increasing competition, for example, in coal and iron and steel from other European countries and in textiles from some eastern countries where labour was cheaper. The difficulties were increased by the world economic depression which began in 1929 and the associated attempts by many countries to reduce imports. The result in Britain, as in many other countries, was heavy unemployment.

After 1932 levels of production and employment rose. The decade saw a strong expansion in the vehicles, electrical, chemical and aircraft industries, while the construction of 3 million houses brought about a large growth in the building and ancillary industries.

The Second World War and After

During the second world war (1939–45) rapid and far-reaching re-orientation of the economy towards the war effort was secured by central planning. The Government involvement in the economy which this implied has remained, in a modified form, a permanent feature of the British economic system.

In spite of generous aid from the United States and Canada, the war ran down British domestic capital by about £3,000 million, through shipping losses, bomb damage, and arrears of industrial maintenance and replacements. Some £1,000 million worth of overseas investments were sold, nearly half in North America, and new external debts of £3,000 million were accumulated, while exports were greatly reduced.

After the war rationing and other controls were relaxed gradually as civil production expanded and trade recovered. Quantitative restrictions on most imports were gradually removed, exchange controls on transactions between the sterling area and the rest of the world were also for the most part lifted, and convertibility of sterling on current account was introduced for non-residents. The period after 1945 was one of rising production and, until 1970, a low level of unemployment (generally 2·5 per cent or lower); but economic growth, which averaged 2 to 3 per cent up to 1971, was slower than in most other western European countries. There were also certain persistent economic problems, particularly the periodic difficulties with the balance of payments. In spite of the contribution from invisibles, there were substantial deficits on current account in a number of years.

In the 1960s successive governments sought to deal with these problems in a number of ways, sometimes restraining the growth in home demand and implementing policies designed to hold down rises in incomes and prices. Following the devaluation of sterling in 1967, from $2·80 to $2·40=£1, exports recovered, leading to a substantial surplus on visible trade and a record current account surplus in 1971.

Recent Developments

In 1973, the economy achieved an annual growth rate of about 5 per cent in response to government policies introduced from 1971 onwards. However, with, among other things, general inflation and the abrupt increase in the prices of commodities in 1972 and 1973, particularly of oil in late 1973, the world economy entered a phase of recession. At the same time, the very large balance of payments surpluses of the oil-producing countries following the rise in oil prices gave rise to a corresponding deficit for the oil-importing countries collectively, which could not quickly be eliminated. Against this background, economic activity in Britain declined, but initially less steeply than in many other industrialised countries as the Government sought to moderate the depressing impact on employment by increasing public expenditure and reducing indirect taxes. Subsequent policies have been directed towards three integrated aims: to reduce the rate of inflation to the levels of Britain's main trading competitors; to achieve export-led growth based on the strengthening of manufacturing industry; and to maintain overseas confidence in sterling.

Measures Against Inflation

In the last 30 years successive governments have adopted policies (including statutory controls of prices or wages or of both) to slow down the rate of inflation. After the present Government took office early in 1974, counter-inflation policy developed within the framework of the 'social contract' between the Labour Party and the Trades Union Congress (TUC) which involved a wide-ranging understanding on economic and social matters. The Labour Party accepted the need to maintain voluntary collective wage bargaining without statutory control, to control prices, to help the lower paid and pensioners and to aim at full employment; while the TUC acknowledged that, in the absence of a statutory incomes policy, trade unions had loyalties not only to their own members but to other members of the community, and should therefore moderate their pay demands.

A reaffirmation of continuing co-operation on economic policy into the 1980s was endorsed by the TUC-Labour Party Liaison Committee (see p 322) in July 1978.

A voluntary limit on pay increases of £6 a week with no increases for those earning more than £8,500 a year was universally observed in the period 1975–76; this resulted in a sharp fall in real earnings and a reduction in the year-on-year rate of inflation from 26·9 per cent to 12·9 per cent. A second stage, running from 1 August 1976 to 31 July 1977, provided for an average 4·5 per cent limit on pay increases and was also universally observed. The inflation rate rose again in the second half of 1976 as the effects of sterling depreciation and other factors began to work through into the retail price index, which rose to a peak of 17·7 per cent in June 1977. Since then, the rate has fallen, reflecting the effects of earnings limitation through pay policy and of the improved performance of sterling. A third period of restraint between August 1977 and July 1978 was based on guidelines of a 12-month interval between pay settlements and a national earnings increase of no more than 10 per cent (with certain exceptions, notably for self-financing productivity agreements). In the event, the increase was estimated at around 14 per cent. The rate of inflation continued to fall, dropping below 10 per cent in January 1978 and standing at 7·4 per cent in the 12 months to June 1978.

A 5 per cent guideline for earnings increases in 1978-79, excluding self-financing productivity deals, was set by the Government in July 1978. Some other limited exceptions and higher increases for the lowest earners were envisaged.

Price Control

Since 1973 a strict system of price control has been operated by the Price Commission, an independent statutory agency originally set up under the Counter-Inflation Act 1973. Under the Price Commission Act 1977 the Commission has been given new powers to mount specific investigations; it can freeze individual prices for up to a year. The price controls set out in the

Act aim to balance the interests of consumers and the needs of industry to earn a sufficient return on investment.

Money Supply   The Government is committed to exercising firm control over monetary growth as an important support for counter-inflation policy. In doing so, care is taken to ensure that the needs of industry for finance can be met; in particular the Government has acted to limit the size of the public sector borrowing requirement, and the Bank of England has issued directional guidance to the banks requesting them to give priority in their lending to finance for investment and exports, and to exercise strict restraint in lending to persons, property companies and for purely financial transactions. The Government's policy is to keep interest rates as low as possible, consistent with its objectives for monetary growth.

Since 1976 the Government has announced specific objectives for the growth of the monetary aggregates. For the 12 months to mid-April 1979 the Chancellor announced in his April 1978 Budget a target range of 8–12 per cent for the growth of the sterling M3 (which comprises all UK residents, sterling bank deposits, of both public and private sectors, plus notes and coins in circulation with the general public). This target is subject to reassessment after six months, in the light of developments in the economy generally, when it will be rolled forward to cover the succeeding 12-month period. Domestic Credit Expansion (DCE—which measures the total volume of money generated in the domestic economy alone) is to be kept within a ceiling of £6,000 million in the year to mid-April 1979. This ceiling is consistent with the target range for sterling M3 and the Government's ceiling of £8,500 million for the public sector borrowing requirement in the financial year 1978–79.

Other Measures   The Government's industrial strategy, introduced in 1975 (see p 207), aims to improve the prospects of some 40 sectors of manufacturing industry. Measures have also been taken to reduce unemployment (see p 315).

With growing pressure on the exchange rate in the first half of 1976 and substantial withdrawals of official sterling balances by overseas governments in the second quarter, the Government drew a first credit tranche from the International Monetary Fund (IMF) and obtained a stand-by credit of $5,300 million from a group of industrialised countries (drawings on which were repaid in December). The exchange rate came under pressure again in late 1976, minimum lending rate was raised, and a $3,900 million stand-by credit was agreed with the IMF, to be available for drawing in 1977 and 1978. Measures designed to reduce the public sector borrowing requirement were announced in December 1976, and limits were placed on the expansion of domestic credit.

An agreement between Central Bank Governors in Basle on the setting up of a new facility amounting to $3,000 million for the official sterling balances was announced in January 1977 (see p 366). A seven-year $1,500 million loan from a syndicate of banks in the Federal Republic of Germany, North America and Britain was arranged to strengthen the reserves further on a secure medium-term basis. Final repayment is to be made in 1984.

A marked improvement in domestic and external financial confidence occurred in 1977. Although Britain's terms of trade were still about 20 per cent lower than they had been in 1972, the volume of exports had increased much more rapidly than the volume of imports over the period since 1973, so that by the end of 1977 the current account of the balance of payments was in surplus, partly because North Sea oil had begun to make a positive contribution. No drawings on the IMF stand-by were taken up after August 1977. Arrangements were made to repay $2,000 million to the Fund and $1,000 million of commercial loans ahead of schedule; in addition $1,000 million of commercial loans were to be repaid on schedule during 1978.

Developments in 1978

Real personal incomes rose sharply in the last quarter of 1977 and this higher level was maintained into 1978. Tax reductions in the April Budget produced a further increase. Inflation was down to around 7–8 per cent by the summer. There were signs of a revival in economic activity, with industrial production increasing again, following a period of little output growth during 1977, and consumer expenditure on a rising trend.

ECONOMIC MANAGEMENT

The objectives of the Government in managing the economy are to achieve a steady and sustainable rate of growth, a high level of employment and a more equitable distribution of income. This it attempts to do by encouraging investment, output and exports within the constraints imposed by maintaining a satisfactory balance of payments and reducing the rate of inflation. Its policies are carried out by the main government departments with economic responsibilities on a national scale: the Treasury, the Departments of Trade, Industry, Employment, Energy, Prices and Consumer Protection, the Environment, and Transport, and the Ministry of Agriculture, Fisheries and Food.

An important advisory body on general economic policy is the National Economic Development Council, which brings together representatives of government, management and trade unions under the chairmanship of the Prime Minister. It has an independent but publicly financed secretariat and has established a number of economic development committees dealing with different industries and services and different aspects of industry. An industrial strategy (see p 207) was launched at the NEDC in 1975. Other bodies responsible for advice on specific aspects of policy include the Monopolies and Mergers Commission (on action to prevent the abuse of monopoly power, see p 214) and the Office of Manpower Economics (see p 326).

On matters of major public policy such as the broad economic strategy, and problems such as inflation, the Government makes known its purposes, and keeps in touch with developments throughout the economy, by means of informal and continuous links with the chief industrial, financial, labour and other interests. Final responsibility for the broad lines of economic policy rests with the Cabinet. For regional economic planning see Chapter 8.

Public Enterprise

In Britain's mixed economy, direct state intervention in industry and commerce (as well as in social, cultural and other affairs) is often effected through special public corporations set up, usually by statute, to deal with a particular activity. Though not part of a government department, the corporations are under varying degrees of public control. Among the larger nationalised industries are the National Coal Board, British Gas and the electricity industry; the British Steel Corporation; the Post Office; British Rail; the National Freight Corporation; British Airways; British Aerospace; British Shipbuilders; and the National Bus Company. These industries and services, which together employ about 8 per cent of all employees, are described in their relevant sections. The public sector as a whole employs a little over a quarter of the working population.

Recent developments have included the nationalisation of the shipbuilding and aircraft industries and the establishment of the British National Oil Corporation through which the Government exercises its participation rights in the exploitation of Britain's offshore oil resources.

The managing boards and staffs of the nationalised industries are not generally civil servants and although accountable to Parliament for their actions in a variety of ways, it is they and not the ministers of the sponsoring departments who are responsible for management. The Government intends to appoint civil servants to the boards of some industries and to encourage schemes of industrial democracy at all levels. It also sees a role for consumer members on some boards.

The extent to which the responsible minister has power over the working of the boards which have been set up to run the nationalised industries varies from industry to industry, but two features are common to almost all of them. First, the minister appoints (and may dismiss) the chairman and members of each board, and, secondly, he has power to give general directions as to how the industry should be run, but does not interfere in day-to-day management. It is usually also laid down that the board shall give to the minister any information, statistics and financial accounts which he may require. In practice, as the responsible minister is kept fully informed and major policy decisions are reached in consultation with him, there is very seldom occasion for him to issue a general directive. In order to clarify accountability the Government intends, subject to the approval of Parliament, to extend the minister's powers so as to enable him to issue specific as well as general directives on matters affecting the national interest.

The minister also has financial powers and responsibilities. The usual statutory requirement is that the board is required to conduct its business so that receipts at least balance outgoings over a period. However, financial targets have been agreed by the Government for certain industries and targets for the remaining industries are to be set as soon as possible. The main form of target, usually set for 3–5 years, is a real return before interest on average net assets employed. The Government is also discussing with the industries the development of a more direct way of relating the opportunity cost of capital to financial performance. The responsible minister is usually empowered, subject to Treasury approval, to say what shall be done with any surplus revenues which may accrue. As regards finance for capital expenditure, the present system is that finance which cannot be met from internal sources is provided mainly by interest-bearing loans from the Exchequer and by borrowing from abroad. Other sources of finance include grants and Public Dividend Capital on which dividends are paid to the Government.

It is usual for the minister responsible for each nationalised industry to be required by statute to take steps to see that the interests of the industry's customers are protected. This is generally done by the establishment of representative consumers' councils to consider complaints and suggestions, and to advise the board or the minister on the changes they think desirable.

Government policy towards the nationalised industries is subject to the approval of Parliament. Opportunities for parliamentary discussion are afforded by debates, including debates on their annual reports and accounts, and by answers to parliamentary questions, which, in principle, are admissible only if concerned with policy rather than details of administration. A House of Commons Select Committee on the Nationalised Industries examines their reports and accounts. (Its powers of investigation also include several other public corporations such as the Independent Broadcasting Authority, Cable and Wireless Limited and certain activities of the Bank of England.)

State participation and intervention in industry takes several other forms such as the majority shareholdings in certain companies held by the National Enterprise Board (see p 209) and these are described on pp 207–15.

European Community Membership

The main economic adjustments consequent upon Britain's membership of the European Community are set out in Chapter 3 and in other relevant chapters.

TABLE 6: Gross Domestic Product by Industry[a] (*at current prices*)

	1967		1972		1977	
	£m.	per cent	£m.	per cent	£m.	per cent
Agriculture, forestry and fishing	1,105	3·2	1,533	2·8	3,447	2·8
Mining and quarrying	675	1·9	776	1·4	3,627	2·9
Manufacturing	11,194	32·1	16,834	30·6	35,279	28·6
Construction	2,373	6·8	4,205	7·7	8,062	6·5
Gas, electricity and water	1,145	3·3	1,751	3·2	4,296	3·5
Transport	2,087	6·0	3,282	6·0	6,641	5·4
Communications	753	2·2	1,358	2·5	3,603	2·9
Distributive trades	3,910	11·2	5,976	10·9	12,657	10·3
Insurance, banking and finance	2,137	6·1	4,069	7·4	9,171	7·4
Ownership of dwellings	1,672	4·8	3,011	5·5	7,787	6·3
Public administration and defence	2,247	6·4	3,913	7·1	9,159	7·4
Public health and educational services	1,779	5·1	3,304	6·0	8,786	7·1
Other services	4,416	12·6	7,169	13·0	14,546	11·8
Adjustment for financial services	−988	−2·8	−1,892	−3·4	−4,791	−3·9
Residual error	420	1·2	−326	−0·6	1,083	0·9
Gross domestic product at factor cost	34,925	100·0	54,963	100·0	123,353	100·0
Net property income from abroad	378		534		438	
Gross national product at factor cost	35,303		55,497		123,791	

Source: *National Income and Expenditure 1967–77.*

[a] Before provision for depreciation but after deducting stock appreciation.

Differences between totals and the sums of their component parts are due to rounding.

NATIONAL INCOME AND EXPENDITURE

The following sections sketch briefly the structure and disposal of Britain's national income in recent years.

Output

In 1977 Britain's gross national product at factor cost (the measure of the total value of goods and services produced at home and net income from abroad) is estimated to have amounted to £123,791 million. After allowing for price changes, the increase over the ten years since 1967 was nearly 22 per cent.

Over a quarter of total output can be attributed to manufacturing industry, rather less than a decade ago. Expanding industry groups in recent years (in relation to the economy as a whole) have been most of the services, particularly insurance, banking and finance, public administration and health and educational services. Table 6 summarises the contribution of each group.

Use of Resources

Table 7 shows the distribution of total supplies of goods and services in 1967, 1972 and 1977 at 1975 market prices.

The main trends since 1967 are a fall in the proportion of total available output devoted to personal consumption and a significant rise in the proportion devoted to exports.

TABLE 7: Distribution of Total Supplies of Goods and Services
(*at 1975 market prices*)

	1967		1972		1977	
	£m.	per cent	£m.	per cent	£m.	per cent
Consumers' expenditure	54,404	50·0	62,762	49·5	62,732	45·4
General government final consumption[a]	19,100	17·6	20,451	16·1	23,315	16·9
Gross domestic capital formation	19,155	17·6	20,312	16·0	20,789	15·0
Private sector[b]	*9,132*		*12,001*		*12,286*	
Public sector[b]	*9,434*		*8,218*		*7,452*	
Exports of goods and services	16,452	15·1	23,293	18·4	31,357	22·7
Total final expenditure	108,734	100·0	126·713	100·0	138,193	100·0

Source: *National Income and Expenditure 1967–77.*
[a] Current expenditure on goods and services plus non-trading capital consumption.
[b] Excluding value of physical change in stocks and work in progress (£1,051 million in total in 1977).
Sums of component parts differ from totals in some cases owing to the method used to rebase at 1975 prices.

Personal Income and Consumers' Expenditure

Personal incomes before tax at current prices rose rapidly and fairly steadily from £33,850 million in 1967 to £125,140 million in 1977. However, real personal disposable income fell slightly between 1976 and 1977 (although there was a large rise in the final quarter as a result of tax changes and rebates). Consumer expenditure amounted to 68 per cent of total pre-tax income in 1977 compared with 75 per cent in 1967. The difference is accounted for by a higher incidence of both direct taxation and national insurance contributions and by increased personal saving.

Sources of Income

Income from employment in 1977 totalled £85,839 million and accounted for about 69 per cent of total personal income (a slightly lower percentage than in 1967). The three other main sources of personal income were self-employment (9 per cent), income from rent, dividends and interest (10 per cent), and grants from general government (12 per cent).

The combined effect of taxation and transfer payments and benefits in kind is to redistribute income on more egalitarian lines. According to studies by the Central Statistical Office, the effect in 1976 was to raise the share of the poorest fifth of households from 1·2 per cent of total original income to 9·4 per cent of all final income. The share of the richest fifth fell from 44 per cent to 35·2 per cent. Similar conclusions about income redistribution were reached by the standing Royal Commission on the Distribution of Income and Wealth (see p 319), in its fifth report (see Bibliography, p 444). Illustrating trends in income over a period the report also shows a continuing decline in the share of the top 10 per cent of income recipients before tax from 29·4 per cent in 1959 to 26·6 per cent in 1974–75 (25·2 per cent to 23·2 per cent after tax). The increase in the share of the bottom 20 per cent was from 5·3 per cent to 6·2 per cent before tax (6 per cent to 7·5 per cent after tax). The second report, on

Personal income and expenditure 1977 (at current prices)

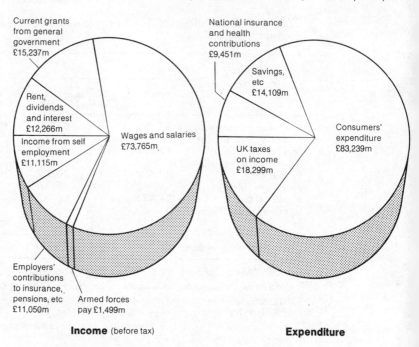

Income (before tax)   **Expenditure**

Note: Figures are preliminary estimates (rounded to nearest million) and exclude items under £125 million

income from companies, shows that rather more than one-third of dividends go indirectly to about 11 million members of occupational pension schemes: 2·25 million taxpayers receiving occupational pensions and 14 million taxpayers who save through life assurance.

Consumers' Expenditure

A rise in the volume of consumers' spending has been accompanied, in Britain as in other advanced industrial countries, by changes in its pattern.

Table 8 shows the amounts and proportions of consumers' expenditure at current prices in 1967 and 1977. Over this period the proportions spent on food, tobacco, and clothing and footwear fell while the proportions spent on alcoholic drink, housing and fuel and light rose. At constant (1975) prices consumers' expenditure fell slightly between 1976 and 1977.

Current Expenditure of General Government

Current expenditure on goods and services by the central Government and local authorities rose by about 20 per cent at 1975 market prices over the period 1967 to 1977 when it amounted to about 20 per cent of the gross domestic product (at current prices). The main cause of this increase was the growth over the period of the social services, especially education. In the same period defence has accounted for a declining share of public expenditure on goods and services—24 per cent in 1977 compared with 33 per cent in 1967 and 48 per cent in 1953.

In addition to their expenditure on goods and services, public authorities transfer large sums to other sectors, mainly the personal sector, by way of national insurance and other social security benefits, grants, and interest and subsidies (see pp 127 and 175). The Government also makes grants to local authorities to finance about 60 per cent of their current expenditure.

TABLE 8: Changes in Pattern of Consumers' Spending
(*at current prices*)

	1967		1977	
	£m.	per cent	£m.	per cent
Food (household expenditure)	5,485	21·5	16,268	19·5
Alcoholic drink	1,739	6·8	6,539	7·8
Tobacco	1,512	5·9	3,632	4·3
Housing (rent, rates, repairs, etc.)	3,088	12·1	12,844	15·4
Fuel and light	1,208	4·7	4,261	5·1
Clothing and footwear	2,219	8·7	6,838	8·2
Cars and motorcycles	777	3·0	2,706	3·2
Other durable goods	1,110	4·4	3,694	4·4
Running costs of motor vehicles	1,228	4·8	4,949	5·9
Other travel expenditure	828	3·2	2,799	3·4
Catering (meals and accommodation)	1,275	5·0	3,739	4·5
Other goods	2,358	9·4	8,074	9·7
Other services	2,528	9·9	8,505	10·2
Other items [a]	136	0·5	−1,318	−1·6
TOTAL	25,491	100·0	83,530	100·0

Source: *National Income and Expenditure 1967–77.*
[a] Consumers' expenditure abroad, less expenditure by foreign tourists in Britain, plus income in kind not included elsewhere.
Differences between totals and the sums of their component parts are due to rounding.

Investment Gross domestic fixed capital formation (total fixed investment) represents about 20 per cent of the gross domestic product at factor cost. The total value of fixed assets in Britain, valued at constant replacement cost, is estimated to have increased by 42 per cent between 1967 and 1977 when their current replacement value, net of depreciation, was some £436,700 million, of which about two-thirds was accounted for by buildings and one-third by plant and machinery, and vehicles.

Within the total of gross domestic fixed capital formation in 1977 (19,738 million compared with £20,240 million in 1972 and a peak of £21,609 million in 1973 at constant 1975 prices) private sector investment accounted for 12·9 per cent of the gross domestic product at factor cost (12·9 per cent in 1972), general government for 3·9 per cent (5 per cent) and public corporations for 3·8 per cent (3·2 per cent). The approximate shares of industry groups in total fixed investment in 1977 were (1972 figures in brackets): manufacturing, 19 per cent (18 per cent), gas, electricity and water, 5 per cent (6 per cent), petroleum and natural gas 8 per cent (1 per cent), transport and communications, 10 per cent (13 per cent), distributive trades, 6 per cent (6 per cent), dwellings, 18 per cent (19 per cent), social and other public services, 12 per cent (16 per cent), and other industries, 22 per cent (21 per cent). There is a marked cyclical pattern in the flow of investment by manufacturing industry; it was at a peak in 1970 and 1974, fell in 1975 and 1976 but increased considerably in 1977. Among the trends in recent years has been an increase in investment in North Sea oil equipment, which reached a peak in 1976.

THE EXTERNAL POSITION

Overseas Trade and Payments

In the years following devaluation in 1967 exports of goods and services increased rapidly in real terms. Helped by a record surplus on current transactions of over £1,000 million in 1971, and by massive capital inflows, the reserves stood at the high level of just over £2,740 million by the end of May 1972, after the repayment of all official short- and medium-term debt.

In 1972 the trade balance began to deteriorate. The marked worsening of Britain's visible trade balance in 1973 and 1974 was much influenced by the increases in world commodity prices, especially oil prices. By 1974 the terms of trade, which were also affected by a fall in the sterling exchange rate, were 27 per cent lower than in 1972. This was partly offset by a growing volume of exports relative to imports. Between 1973 and 1977 the volume of exports increased by about 23 per cent while the volume of imports increased by about 1 per cent. The improved competitive position of British exports, resulting from the floating of the pound in June 1972, contributed to this, while imports were held down in part by the low level of domestic demand. In 1975 the deficit on current account was reduced substantially.

There was a further improvement in 1976, the result of a growing surplus on the invisible account, and a marked improvement in 1977, largely as a result of growing production of North Sea oil. In future years increasing supplies of oil from the North Sea will bring considerable advantage to the balance of payments; it has been estimated that the benefits should rise to between £8,000 million and £9,000 million a year in the mid-1980s (at 1977 prices). For details of overseas trade and payments see Chapter 18.

Exchange Rates

In 1971, a general international realignment of exchange rates was agreed at a meeting held in the Smithsonian Institute in Washington, in which all the main currencies were in effect revalued against the dollar. (The rates of exchange fixed in that agreement are called Smithsonian parities.) As part of this realignment, the sterling rate for the dollar moved up by just over $8\frac{1}{2}$ per cent the new middle rate being $2·60571 compared with the old par value of $2·40. In June 1972 sterling was allowed to float and over the next three years the rate against the dollar fluctuated between $2·30 and $2·60; in 1975 the rate fell to just over $2. Sterling came under pressure in 1976 (see p 187) but recovered somewhat towards the end of the year. Increased confidence in sterling throughout 1977 was shown by rises in the official reserves to record levels and by upwards pressure on the exchange rate. In October 1977 the Government believing that a continuance of the massive inflow of foreign currency would endanger domestic monetary targets, changed the Bank of England's intervention policy and allowed the pound to appreciate on the foreign exchange markets. Since then the sterling/dollar exchange rate has fluctuated within the range of £1 = $1·79 to almost $2. The effective rate for sterling rose by nearly 7 per cent during 1977 rising sharply at the end of the year, but then fell equally sharply to around the levels of mid-1977. At the end of August 1978 it was 62·4 (December 1971 = 100) and the market rate £1 = $1·94.

Five member countries of the European Community (Belgium, Denmark, the Federal Republic of Germany, Luxembourg and the Netherlands) and Norway maintain a scheme, usually called the 'snake', under which rate between any two of their currencies cannot diverge from their cross parities by more than $2\frac{1}{4}$ per cent. Britain, France, Italy and Sweden were formerly members of the scheme.

International Monetary Developments

A second set of amendments to the Articles of Agreement of the International Monetary Fund (IMF) entered into force on 1 April 1978. (The first amendments were made in 1969 when the Special Drawing Right—SDR—was established.) They bring the articles up to date and provide for necessary flexibility. The amendments were drawn up under the guidance of the Interim Committee, which succeeded the Committee of Twenty in 1974.

Members undertake a general obligation to collaborate with the IMF and with other members in order to ensure orderly exchange arrangements and to promote a stable system of exchange rates. Under the new provisions the Fund will be able to determine that, in accordance with specified criteria, international economic conditions permit the introduction of a system based on stable but adjustable par values. Each member will then be able, though not bound, to establish a par value. The amendments provide for a gradual reduction in the role of gold in the international monetary system. The function of gold as the unit of value of the SDR has been eliminated, the official price has been abolished and members will be free to deal in gold in the market and among themselves without reference to any official price, and obligatory payments in gold by members to the Fund and by the Fund to members have been abrogated. The IMF's gold holdings are being reduced; one-sixth is being returned to members, and a further sixth is being auctioned, the major proportion of the proceeds from the auctions being disbursed through a trust fund, set up to provide medium-term balance of payments support to the poorest developing countries. Changes have been made in the role of the SDR in order to enhance its status as an international reserve asset. The amendment also provides for changes in the organisation of the Fund and in its financial operations.

Discussions on reform have been accompanied by measures designed to help recycle oil funds and to assist the developing countries with the problems caused for them by the increases in oil prices and the depression of world trade. After the oil price increases, the IMF set up a borrowing agreement for 1974 (which was continued in 1975), known as the oil facility through which countries could draw on funds lent mainly by the oil-producers. Although the facility was not continued in 1976, the ordinary credit tranches of the IMF were temporarily widened by 45 per cent.

An extended facility for medium-term assistance to members with special balance of payments problems caused by structural economic changes was introduced in 1974. A supplementary financing facility was agreed in principle in 1977, intended to provide financial assistance to members whose payments imbalances are large in relation to their economies and to their quotas in the Fund. By April 1978 a total of more than $10,000 million had been committed for the financing of this facility.

The entry into force of the second set of amendments enabled quotas to be increased under the Sixth General Review of Quotas. Total Fund quotas will be raised from SDR 29,200 million to SDR 39,000 million.

At a meeting in Mexico City in April 1978 the Interim Committee reached a consensus on the general outlines of the co-ordinated strategy for the world economy in the medium term. The strategy is designed to promote non-inflationary growth, leading to higher employment, a reduction in imbalances of international payments and conservation of energy.

12 Industry

Industry (mining and quarrying, manufacturing, construction and gas, electricity and water) and distributive trades together account for more than half of Britain's gross domestic product, manufacturing for some 28 per cent and distributive trades nearly 10 per cent. About 30 per cent of Britain's employed labour force is engaged in manufacturing industry, while over 80 per cent of Britain's visible exports consists of manufactured or semi-manufactured products. This chapter describes the geographical distribution and structure of industry and discusses some general industrial topics—such as trends in production and productivity, investment, the Government's relations with industry, regional development, fair trading and competition policy. It outlines the major sectors of manufacturing industry, construction and distributive and service trades. The chapters following cover other main industries in Britain.

ORGANISATION AND PRODUCTION

Location

The following is a summary of how British industry is distributed through the eight standard regions of England and in Wales, Scotland and Northern Ireland.

South-East Region

London is Britain's capital and main communication centre, and is one of the world's most important financial centres. Lying at the head of ocean navigation on the Thames estuary it is one of the world's largest cities and largest ports, though much deep-sea-going traffic has moved down-river to Tilbury docks. It is the main centre in Britain of printing and the manufacture of clothing, food and drink, furniture, materials for the arts, precision instruments and many other specialised products. Small firms predominate in many of these industries and the average size of manufacturing firms (particularly in the central area) is well below the national average. London is also important, especially in its outer ring, for light engineering, chemicals and consumer goods and has some heavy engineering plants and a number of leading research establishments. There has been in recent years, however, a considerable drop in employment and population in London.

Towards the periphery of Greater London and in the surrounding Outer Metropolitan Area, industry, particularly the electronics and consumer goods industries, has expanded greatly; some of the largest aircraft plants are in these areas, for example at Weybridge and Hatfield, as well as two of the four main motor vehicle manufacturers at Dagenham, Luton and Dunstable. There are other major motor vehicle manufacturing plants at Cowley, Oxford, some 50 miles north-west of London. The computer industry is well represented in Hemel Hempstead and Letchworth, and Chelmsford is an important centre for the electronics industry. Along the lower Thames and Medway estuaries there are large oil refineries as well as some smaller shipyards, engineering works and major concentrations of the paper and pulp and cement industries. There are centres of manufacturing industry at Crawley, Basingstoke, Slough and Reading, in the Medway towns and the Aldershot–Farnborough area. Heathrow and Gatwick airports are also of major importance and are large employers.

A great part of the Channel coast eastwards from Southampton consists of built-up areas, many of which are partly residential areas for people working in London. Holiday resorts fringe the coast. Portsmouth is a naval port with some shipbuilding and general manufactures. Southampton is one of Britain's leading ports for both passengers and freight; its industries include ship repairing, oil refining, cable-making, electronics and synthetic rubber. Dover, Folkestone and Newhaven are ferry ports.

South-West

Though famous for its tourism, leisure industries and agriculture, the south-west of England has a busy manufacturing sector. Bristol, the region's administrative and commercial centre, is a leading port and the largest industrial city, having tobacco, packaging materials, printing, aerospace, chocolate and metal manufacture as well as a wide range of engineering and other industries; there are extensive modern docks at Avonmouth, an industrialised suburb with important basic chemicals and non-ferrous metal plants. Plymouth, with the naval dockyard and electrical and other industries, is an important manufacturing centre. The towns of Gloucester, Poole, Christchurch, Cheltenham and Bath are major producers of machinery, instrumentation and other engineering products. Swindon has vehicle, electrical and electronic engineering. Chemical and engineering products are made at Yeovil, Taunton and Bridgwater. Clothing and other textile products and footwear are made at several centres. In the Camborne, Redruth, Falmouth and St. Austell areas of Cornwall there is china clay and tin mining, and machinery manufacture, ship repairing and other forms of engineering.

East Anglia

Although the smallest of the regions East Anglia has been rapidly growing in terms of both population and employment. A major contribution to this growth has been made by the nine towns receiving overspill of population and industry from London. The area is one of the most productive agricultural regions in the world and this has provided a firm base for the growth of the food processing industry, which is concerned mainly with canning, and more recently freezing local produce. Cambridge is a major centre of research-based industry; Ipswich and Peterborough are noted for diesel engines, agricultural machinery and engineering generally and Norwich for footwear and food manufacture. The east coast ports of Great Yarmouth and Lowestoft are important bases for companies associated with natural gas exploitation in the North Sea.

West Midlands

This is the only landlocked region and it has a greater dependency on manufacturing industry than any other region. However, more than three-quarters of the land is still used for agriculture and includes some areas of great natural beauty, particularly in the south and west. The main concentration of industry is in the West Midlands metropolitan county which includes the districts of Birmingham, Coventry, Dudley, Sandwell, Solihull, Walsall and Wolverhampton. The economy is largely dependent upon the metal-using industries and in particular on motor vehicle manufacture. Other notable industries are mechanical and electrical engineering, machine tools, castings, tubes, locks, jewellery, domestic metalware and rubber manufactures. The metropolitan county also contains the National Exhibition Centre, which is one of the largest and most modern exhibition complexes in the world.

In north Staffordshire, a smaller conurbation centred upon Stoke-on-Trent is the centre of the British pottery and china industry and the region's major coalmining area. Other industries are rubber and electrical products. Coalmining is also important in the Cannock Chase and north Warwickshire areas.

Other important centres include Stafford, with heavy electrical and other engineering; Worcester, mechanical engineering and pottery; Burton-on-Trent, brewing and rubber; Kidderminster, carpets; and Rugby, electrical engineering. Stratford-upon-Avon, the birthplace of William Shakespeare, is an international tourist centre.

The two major new towns, Telford and Redditch, have large metal-based industries.

East Midlands

Although some major industries are heavily concentrated in the East Midlands (over 60 per cent of Britain's hosiery and knitwear, 40 per cent of its footwear and more than 20 per cent of its coal) industry is well diversified. North Nottinghamshire and Derbyshire are traditional coalmining areas where productivity rates are high. In the northern part of the region engineering is also important. In Nottingham a high proportion of employment is in pharmaceuticals, electronics, tobacco and bicycle manufacture. Nottingham lace is famous throughout the world, but textiles and clothing are of more importance. Derby is primarily an engineering town with aero-engines, rail rolling stock, boilers and castings among a wide range of engineering products. The production of rayon is also of considerable importance. Agriculture is significant in Lincolnshire as well as food processing and engineering, much of which produces agricultural and constructional equipment. Lincoln has a substantial engineering industry. Engineering is also a major industry in Leicestershire, much of it supplying other local industries such as textiles and footwear. Electrical engineering is of especial importance in Loughborough. Northamptonshire is famous for high quality footwear. In recent years light engineering, much of it related to the motor and electronics industries, has expanded considerably. Corby has a large and fully integrated steel works.

North-West

The North-West comprises the metropolitan counties of Greater Manchester and Merseyside and the counties of Lancashire and Cheshire. The Department of Industry's administration of this region extends also into parts of Cumbria and Derbyshire. The region is one of the most highly industrialised in Britain. Manchester is Britain's second most important commercial and financial centre and an important port. It is one of the chief centres for electrical and heavy engineering and for the production of a wide range of goods including computers, electronic equipment, petrochemicals, clothing, dye-stuffs and pharmaceuticals. Manchester's traditional role as the centre for the Lancashire textile industry is only a small part of its present-day activities.

The textile towns, while adapting to the decline of traditional textiles and to increasing use of man-made fibres and moving into new textile products, such as carpets, have seen engineering outgrow the textile industry. The largest towns, Bolton, Stockport, Oldham, Blackburn, Preston, Rochdale, Burnley and Bury, are diversified with such industries as paper-making, textile and electrical machinery, light engineering and consumer durables, plastics, foods, chemicals, nuclear process plant, electronics, aircraft and heavy commercial vehicles.

The Manchester Ship Canal, which carries a substantial volume of export traffic, links Manchester and Merseyside. It passes through Warrington, with its metal industries (such as wire-drawing), Widnes, Runcorn with the chemical industry, and Ellesmere Port with its oil refinery installations, before reaching the Mersey estuary. St. Helens, to the north of the canal, is famous for glass manufacture. Liverpool, with its modernised dock system, is one of Britain's leading seaports and, after London, the largest centre for processing and converting imported foodstuffs and raw materials (grain milling, oils, fats and tobacco, sugar refining and rubber products). The centre of economic activity in Merseyside is still its port, but its industrial strength has moved from older industries closely related to the port to the newer industries including motor vehicles, electrical engineering, heavy industrial plant and chemicals.

To the north of this industrial belt lie Blackpool and Lancaster with light industries and chemicals and to the south, the Cheshire plain with agriculture, while a variety of industries such as salt, chemicals, motor vehicles, pharmaceuticals and rail engineering are located among the smaller towns.

The countryside lies close to most towns and the region contains some of Britain's most fertile farmland. There is a large tourist industry on the coast and in historic towns, such as Chester and the four National Parks on or near its boundaries. There are major airports at Liverpool and Manchester, a highly developed rail system and one of the most advanced motorway networks in Britain, providing good access throughout the region, and to the rest of the country and continental Europe through the east coast ports.

Yorkshire and Humberside

Though some parts of Yorkshire and Humberside are heavily industrialised, more than four-fifths of the region is open country.

The region's industrial structure is diverse. About 70 per cent of Britain's worsted and woollen industry is located in West Yorkshire. Bradford is the commercial centre of the wool trade. In addition there are strong sectors of engineering, printing, textile machinery and carpets. The metropolitan district of Leeds is an important commercial centre and also has a variety of industries including men's clothing and various engineering industries. In the south, the steel centre based on Sheffield and Rotherham is noted for the manufacture of high quality steels, tools and cutlery. Yorkshire's coalfields are particularly important and production is to be extended to the Selby area, where major new reserves have been discovered. Doncaster, with tractor and nylon manufacturing, and Barnsley are the largest towns on the coalfield where dependence on steel and coal has been reduced by the introduction of new industries in and around the major towns.

North Yorkshire is mainly agricultural but York, a leading tourist attraction, is also noted for chocolate and confectionery manufacture. It is an important railway centre, and has substantial railway workshops.

Kingston upon Hull is the principal industrial town in Humberside, which is a major centre for maritime trade with ports at Grimsby, Immingham and Goole in addition to Hull. Besides being important fishing ports, Hull and Grimsby contain specialised food processing and cold storage facilities. The Humber ports are strategically situated for direct access to Western Europe. The British Steel Corporation's plant at Scunthorpe is one of Britain's largest steel producers. Close by are chemical, fertiliser, oil refining, and food processing plants. The north bank of the Humber contains a large proportion of Britain's caravan manufacturing industry.

The region has five universities and numerous facilities for further education with long standing links with commerce and industry.

Northern

The greater part of this region (the metropolitan county of Tyne and Wear and the counties of Northumberland, Durham, Cleveland and most of Cumbria) is an area of hills, lakes and moorland. The tourist industry, already strong in the Lake District, is developing in other areas. Industrial activity and the bulk of the population is concentrated in the eastern coastal strip stretching from the coalfields north of the River Tyne southwards to the River Tees, and to a lesser extent, on the western coastal strip of Cumbria.

The region is relatively more dependent than other parts of England on the long-established heavy industries, notably coalmining, iron and steel manufacture, shipbuilding and ship-repairing and chemicals (the complex of chemical plants on both banks of the Tees is probably the most extensive in Europe). Europe's largest steelmaking complex is being developed in the Teesside area. New industries, however, with a broader technological base, have been successfully attracted to the region and the industrial structure is becoming more diversified. Manufacture of electrical plant is a major industry.

Other industries include electric components, plastics, domestic appliances, pharmaceuticals, machine tools, ropes, paint, glass, clothing and scientific instruments as well as mining machinery, rolling mill plant and earth-moving equipment. An aluminium smelter is operating on the Northumberland coast. Atomic energy is important, with two nuclear power stations and other installations in Cumbria, and a further nuclear power station at an advanced stage of construction at Hartlepool. Considerable investment is taking place in the coalmining industry to exploit large coal reserves below the sea bed off the Northumberland and Durham coasts and to boost open-cast coal production. The region is also involved in the North Sea oil programme. The new oil terminal at Teesside has a potential capacity of one million barrels a day of North Sea oil. A major new reservoir at Kielder will, when completed, provide water supplies for industry on Tyneside and Teesside.

Wales

Some two-thirds of the population (which totals 2·8 million) live in industrial south Wales. This area has a diverse range of modern manufacturing industries, including mechanical and electrical engineering, motor vehicle components, plastics, chemicals and textiles. Though coalmining has declined substantially, the south Wales coalfield still produces virtually all Britain's anthracite and much of its steam and other specialised coals. Steel, the other traditional industry of south Wales, is less dominant than formerly but still supplies all of Britain's tinplate and much of its sheet steel. Cardiff, Newport and Swansea are the largest urban centres and, with Barry and Port Talbot, are also the major ports of the region. This latter has one of the largest steelmaking plants in Britain and a deep water harbour for importing iron ore. Milford Haven is one of the finest natural deep water harbours in the world and has developed as Britain's major oil-importing port with four oil refineries and a link with a fifth at Llandarcy.

The other main industrial area is in north-east Wales. Coal mining has now contracted in importance but sheet steel, chemicals, man-made fibres and aircraft construction remain significant sources of employment despite some shedding of labour in recent years. A range of new lighter industry has been introduced in the post-war years, particularly around Wrexham. The remainder of Wales is predominantly rural with agriculture, forestry and tourism the traditional basis of the economy, but here too manufacturing firms have been successfully introduced in many towns, and one or two very large scale undertakings such as an aluminium plant at Holyhead, Anglesey, have been established.

Scotland

About three-quarters of Scotland's population of 5·2 million and most of the industrial activity is concentrated in the central lowlands between the Firth of Clyde and the Firth of Forth. The principal cities in this area are Glasgow, a major commercial centre, and Edinburgh, Scotland's capital, an administrative and cultural centre. There are, in addition, firms which have attracted substantial industrial investment. Clydeside, which includes Glasgow, is a major shipbuilding and marine engineering centre; it produces a great variety of general engineering products, which include modules, pumps and other products for the oil industry. Clydeside is also an important centre for food, drink and tobacco manufactures, carpets and printing and publishing. The steel industry, sited mainly in Central Strathclyde, is being modernised. There are important coalmining works in the Strathclyde, Central, Lothian and Fife regions. The electronics equipment industry is represented in Strathclyde, Fife and Dundee, as well as in Edinburgh, where this and other modern industries are expanding alongside the traditional engineering, printing and publishing and brewing industries. Large-scale plants producing cars in Linwood, near Paisley, and commercial vehicles in West Lothian and the Scotstoun district of Glasgow, are well established, while heavy earth-moving equipment and tracked vehicles are produced in Uddingston and Airdrie. The chemical industry is concentrated in Ayrshire and at Grangemouth, where there is also a major oil refinery. The Firth of Clyde provides central Scotland with valuable deep water facilities.

Outside the central belt there is considerable industrial concentration in and around Dundee and Aberdeen. Numerous towns outside these areas have also attracted light industry in recent years. Dundee's traditional manufacture, jute, has been supplemented by office machinery, clocks and watches, tyres and electronic products.

North-east Scotland is now the centre of the offshore oil industry and a wide variety of oil-related projects have been established. The older industries of whisky distilling, paper manufacture and food and fish processing, however, continue to flourish. In June 1976 between 56,000 and 65,000 people were employed in Scotland as a whole in work directly or indirectly related to oil.

Much of the rest of Scotland is mountainous and therefore sparsely populated. In the Highlands and Islands, the main industries include high quality tweed and knitwear, papermaking and aluminium smelting and there are significant resources of hydro-electric power. Nuclear power is also generated. The development of North Sea oil has led to very substantial oil-related activities including oil platform production yards and a new oil refinery is proposed at Nigg. In the Borders and south-west of Scotland, the wool, cloth and knitwear industries are important, together with food processing and chemicals manufacture. Tourism is important throughout Scotland and there are extensive holiday and recreational facilities.

Northern Ireland Although the area of Northern Ireland is relatively small there is substantial and growing industrialisation, particularly in and around Belfast, the capital city, and Londonderry. Britain's largest single shipyard is in Belfast; other well-established activities include the manufacture of aircraft, textile machinery and a wide range of other engineering products, ropes, twine, tobacco and clothing. Northern Ireland has also long been an important centre for textiles. The textile industry is extensively diversified and Northern Ireland is one of the most important areas in Europe for man-made fibre production, providing over a quarter of Britain's output. There has also been extensive development in vehicle components, oil-well equipment, electronic instruments, telecommunication equipment, carpets and synthetic rubber.

Structure The pattern of ownership and organisation in industry is varied. Personal, corporate, co-operative and public enterprise all assume a number of different forms, and all are important in the economy. Industrial enterprises vary from such large-scale organisations as the General Electric Company (156,000 employees) and Imperial Chemical Industries (125,000), and the public corporations such as the National Coal Board with about 307,000 employees, to the many thousands of small firms. Most manufacturing is in the hands of private enterprise (for the role of public enterprise, see p 188). The Aircraft and Shipbuilding Industries Act 1977 took into public ownership the bulk of the aircraft and shipbuilding industries. Most iron and steel production is already in public ownership. Other state-controlled products include a small range of chemicals from the plants of the British Steel Corporation; locomotives and rolling-stock built in the workshops of British Railways; military equipment and supplies made in establishments of the defence services; and fissile materials and radioactive isotopes. The Government has shareholdings in various companies; it has major holdings in British Petroleum Ltd., and the National Enterprise Board (see p 209) controls British Leyland Ltd. and Rolls-Royce Ltd.

The most recent complete analysis of the size distribution of establishments and enterprises in manufacturing industry, and of the degree of concentration, is contained in the *Report on the Census of Production 1973*. This shows that some 66 per cent (62,500) of the 94,200 or so establishments in manufacturing industry had fewer than 20 employees each and accounted for 6 per cent of total employment; 29,100 establishments had between 20 and 499 employees and accounted for some 38 per cent of the total labour force; 1,963 establishments, each with between 500 and 1,499 employees, were responsible for 21 per cent of employment, while over one-third was in the hands of the 678 establishments each with over 1,499 employees. A high proportion of the biggest establishments were in the heavy industries. An enterprise, as defined in the 1973 census, normally consists of either a single establishment or of two or more establishments under common ownership. In the private sector of British manufacturing industries in 1973 36 per cent of all employment was accounted for by the largest 100 private enterprises.

A further indication of company size is the value of capital employed (net assets). The largest companies, British Petroleum and Shell Transport and Trading have net assets of over £5,100 million and £4,400 million respectively; over 80 companies registered in Britain have each more than £100 million net assets. Of the top 20 industrial groups in Europe in terms of annual sales, four are British.

Merging and regrouping have continued as the effort to reduce overheads have intensified and, in many branches of industry, profitable operation has become dependent on concentration and economies of scale. Larger units of control have been established in almost all the leading industries and in some a small number of big companies and their subsidiaries are responsible for a great proportion of total production. Examples are oil refining, non-ferrous metal smelting, motor vehicles and aircraft, heavy electrical engineering, electronics, machine tools, brewing, textiles, basic chemicals, tobacco and magazine publishing, Shares in these companies are, however, usually distributed among many holders or are held by insurance companies or pension funds representing a broad cross-section of the community, and it is rare for a few holders to have a controlling interest unless they are private companies.

Industrial Association

Voluntary associations are formed by private enterprises for a number of different purposes, including the provision of common services, the exchange of information and representation of their members' point of view; the regulation of trading practices; and negotiation with trade unions on wages and conditions of work. These associations cover, with varying completeness, most of British industry. Trade associations, concerned mainly with representation to the Government, the provision of common services and the regulation of trading practices, are normally composed of firms manufacturing (and/or retailing) a particular product or group of products. Employers' organisations which deal with employment matters usually consist of firms engaged in the same type of operation or manufacturing process. In an industrial sector concerned wholly with an allied group of products, a single association may undertake all the required functions. The national employers' organisations are usually concerned with negotiation of wages and conditions of work (see p 317).

Other voluntary associations include industrial development associations for particular areas or regions, which are sponsored by trade associations, individual firms and local authorities. Four of these bodies (the North of England Development Council, the North West Industrial Development Association, the Yorkshire and Humberside Development Association and the Devon and Cornwall Development Bureau) receive government grants, while the Scottish Council for Development and the Development Corporation for Wales receive grants from the Scottish and Welsh development agencies respectively.

The central body representing British business and industry nationally is the Confederation of British Industry (CBI), recognised by the Government as a channel for consultation between government departments and representatives of both the private and the public sector employers as a whole. The CBI membership consists of nearly 4,500 parent companies and between 11,000 and 12,000 subsidiaries and about 200 employers' organisations and trade and commercial associations and the majority of the nationalised industries. For its members it acts as an advisory and consultative body providing them with information and statistics, ascertaining their collective views and representing them nationally to the Government and the public and also internationally (see p 323). CBI representatives sit on the National Economic Development Council, the Manpower Services Commission, the Health and Safety Commission and other official advisory committees and voluntary bodies concerned with matters affecting industry.

In matters of common concern the CBI often acts jointly with the chambers of commerce. These are open to all kinds of producers and traders and exist to promote the interests of local, regional and national industry and commerce. Most chambers provide export facilities, including the sponsorship of outward trade missions and visits. The Association of British Chambers of Commerce, founded in 1860, is the co-ordinating body to which about 85 local chambers are affiliated, together with 21 British Chambers of Commerce operating in Europe and elsewhere. These chambers have a membership of about 50,000 firms. In Scotland there is an additional central organisation, the Association of Scottish Chambers of Commerce, and in Northern Ireland the Northern Ireland Chamber of Commerce and Industry, to which local chambers are affiliated.

Production

Though industrial production in general has been affected by the world recession in industry, it rose slightly in 1976 and 1977 over the depressed levels of 1975 (see Table 9), as measured by the index of industrial production. Manufacturing production also rose slightly in 1976 and 1977 having increased by 117 per cent in the period 1948–77, the highest increases having been in chemicals and allied industries, in coal and petroleum products, in paper and board, and in engineering—instrument engineering and electrical engineering being the sectors that grew most rapidly.

Productivity   The improvement of productivity, which by international standards has shown a relatively slow rate of growth in Britain, is recognised as being of prime importance for the economy. Productivity, as measured by output per head, increased by 17·7 per cent in manufacturing industries between 1970 and 1977. Both the long-term and the short-term growth of productivity are influenced by such factors as the rate of capital investment, management, advances in products, machinery processes and methods of work, sales promotion and labour. Over the last decade the size of the labour force employed in industry has fallen steadily.

The improvement of productivity rests mainly with unions and management in individual enterprises. It is also a prime objective of the Government's industrial strategy (see p 207). The Department of Industry is responsible for co-ordinating measures to improve industrial productivity. It assists the introduction of advanced machinery and techniques into industry, provides technical advisory services and sponsors the Computer-Aided Design Centre and the National Computing Centre. It is concerned directly with research into such factors as productivity measurement techniques, group technology and production engineering. The Department of Employment advises firms on aspects of productivity connected with manpower utilisation and industrial relations. Many educational establishments also provide advice and assistance.

Within industry, employers' organisations often provide technical assistance and support schemes of vocational education and training, as do many trade unions. The British Council of Productivity Associations is one of many bodies, both public and private, concerned with various aspects of productivity. The council provides information and advisory services to industry through a national network of 45 local associations.

TABLE 9: Index of Industrial Production 1948–76 (1970 = 100)

Industry Group	1948	1970	1974	1975	1976	1977	1948–77 change %
All industries	50·5	100	106·3	100·6	101·3	102·5	+103
Mining/quarrying	129·1	100	79·2	85·9	88·7	103·6	− 20
Total manufacturing	47·8	100	108·9	102·2	103·2	103·8	+117
Food/drink/tobacco	58·4	100	109·9	108·8	110·9	112·3	+ 92
Coal/petroleum products	21·4	100	106·0	92·0	96·5	93·2	+336
Chemical industries	25·5	100	126·9	116·0	127·8	132·2	+418
Metal manufactures	61·8	100	91·7	78·6	85·3	80·6	+ 30
Engineering industries	34·7	100	113·1	108·7	103·6	103·3	+198
Shipbuilding	110·3	100	92·4	97·7	92·0	86·8	− 21
Vehicles (inc. aircraft)	39·0	100	103·0	95·3	91·9	93·3	+139
Other metal goods	64·1	100	103·6	95·0	93·8	98·4	+ 54
Textiles/clothing	73·4	100	103·1	99·7	101·9	101·3	+ 38
Bricks, pottery, etc.	54·4	100	117·1	107·9	111·2	108·9	+100
Timber, furniture, etc.	45·4	100	112·1	110·2	112·6	105·4	+132
Paper/printing/ publishing	42·7	100	108·9	95·6	98·1	114·7	+269
Other manufacturing	30·5	100	114·5	105·5	114·7	120·1	+294
Construction	56·3	100	93·8	86·1	84·5	83·2	+ 48
Gas/electricity/water	31·4	100	118·5	120·3	123·1	128·1	+308

Source: *Economic Trends; Monthly Digest of Statistics*

Investment   Productivity is particularly dependent on the quantity and efficiency of the capital assets which the labour force has at its disposal. Investment in

TABLE 10: Output per head 1968–77 (1970 = 100)

	Employed labour force	All production industries			Manufacturing industries		
		Output	Employ-ment	Output per head	Output	Employ-ment	Output per head
1968	100·4	97·2	101·4	95·9	96·0	99·0	97·0
1969	100·4	99·8	101·5	98·3	99·6	100·3	99·3
1970	100·0	100·0	100·0	100·0	100·0	100·0	100·0
1971	98·3	100·1	96·9	103·3	99·4	96·7	102·8
1972	99·0	102·3	94·7	108·0	102·0	93·6	109·0
1973	101·0	110·0	95·8	114·8	110·5	94·1	117·4
1974	101·3	106·3	95·5	111·3	108·9	94·3	115·5
1975	100·7	100·6	91·5	109·9	102·2	90·1	113·4
1976	100·2	101·4	89·3	113·5	103·2	87·3	118·2
1977	100·5	102·4	89·5	114·4	103·7	88·1	117·7

Source: *Monthly Digest of Statistics*

manufacturing industry tends to reflect the level of demand in the economy as a whole, with some time lag between the start of an increase in output and the implementation of investment plans. There is thus a marked cyclical pattern in the flow of investment by manufacturing industry, and since 1961 there have been three discernible cycles. Details of investment in the period 1968–77 are contained in Table 11.

TABLE 11: Manufacturing Industry's Fixed Capital Expenditure 1968–77 (1970 prices, seasonally adjusted)   £ million

	Total all manufacturing industries	New building work	Vehicles	Plant and machinery
1968	1,851·2 [a] (1,800·2)	335·9	109·2	1,406·1 [a] (1,355·1)
1969	1,977·5 [a] (2,028·5)	390·1	115·9	1,471·5 [a] (1,522·5)
1970	2,129·8	391·2	114·7	1,623·9
1971	1,988·0	353·0	114·8	1,520·2
1972	1,720·8	287·1	123·3	1,310·4
1973	1,730·3	266·7	130·6	1,333·0
1974	1,964·4	295·0	140·2	1,529·2
1975	1,694·9	252·8	105·4	1,336·7
1976	1,632·8	213·8	121·3	1,297·7
1977	1,763·8	228·8	149·6	1,385·4

Source: *Monthly Digest of Statistics*

[a] After allowing for expenditure brought forward into 1968 from 1969 to secure the higher rate of investment grants, estimated at £51 million.

Analysed by industry group, investment in the food, drink and tobacco group in 1977, at current prices, was £757 million, coal and petroleum products totalled £131 million, chemicals £815 million, metal manufacture £653 million; engineering, shipbuilding and metal goods £1,035 million, vehicles £396 million, textiles, leather and clothing £243 million, paper, printing and publishing £252 million and other manufacturing industries £597 million.

Part of the investment in plant and machinery is associated with the introduction of new techniques and equipment. The process of automation is changing the pattern and organisation of many industries and has brought substantial increases in production and efficiency. Much investment, however, still consists of replacements, additions and improvements of a more traditional kind. Industrial technologies of plant maintenance, materials handling, lubrication and corrosion protection, well developed in Britain, make possible large savings in costs.

Management Education

In Britain, as elsewhere, it is recognised that managers require special skills and training. The British Institute of Management (BIM) provides a wide range of information services and has a particular interest in management education and training, and is playing an increasingly representative role for the management and administrative professions. The Institute of Directors also provides information and other services to directors of all types of company. The Industrial Society, whose membership includes trade unions as well as employers and their associations, works to promote better use of human resources; it advises members and conducts conferences and courses.

A large proportion of management education is provided by polytechnics and many of the colleges of further education throughout Britain; 12 regional centres of management education have been established through the association of polytechnics and colleges which have high reputations for management studies. Universities also make an important contribution, especially the full-time postgraduate programmes at the business schools of London and Manchester Universities. Training courses for higher management are offered by several colleges including the Administrative Staff College, Henley-on-Thames, and Ashridge College of Management, Berkhamsted. The Council of Industry for Management Education, jointly sponsored by the CBI, the BIM and the Foundation for Management Education, works to foster the development of business and management education. Many firms provide general management courses for senior executives or systems of informal training. There are also a number of bodies concerned with specialised branches of management, for example, the Institute of Personnel Management, the Institution of Works Managers, the Institute of Administrative Management, the Institute of Supervisory Management, the Institute of Marketing, the Institute of Chartered Secretaries and Administrators and the Institute of Purchasing and Supply.

The large number of professional people working as management consultants indicates the concern for improved management performance in Britain. Such consultancy services are being increasingly used by overseas clients.

Design

Design is an important factor in improving the quality and competitiveness of manufactured goods. Improvement of the design of British goods is the concern of the government-sponsored Design Council and its separate Scottish Committee.

At the council's Design Centres in London and Glasgow there are permanent displays of well-designed modern British goods, together with special exhibitions illustrating new design developments. There is a third, smaller showroom in Cardiff. All the products displayed are chosen from the council's Design Index, a record of some 7,000 current British products, chosen by independent committees for their high standards of design, safety and performance. The council's services include advice on design matters, the organisation of product displays at overseas trade fairs, conferences and seminars on design, help for design education and the publication of a range of material. It provides annual

Design Council Awards for manufacturers of consumer and engineering products and for medical equipment and motor vehicles.

Other bodies concerned with industrial design include the Royal Society of Arts (see p 384), the Society of Industrial Artists and Designers, which is the representative professional body in Great Britain of industrial designers and the Design and Industries Association, a voluntary association of industrial companies, designers, and others interested in the promotion of good design in industry. The Crafts Council of Great Britain, the Crafts Centre of Great Britain and the Scottish Craft Centre are all grant-aided and work to improve craft design and to promote closer relations between craftsmen and industry.

Standards

The British Standards Institution (BSI) is a voluntary non-profit-making body incorporated by Royal Charter, funded in part by sale of standards, by subscription and by government grant. It prepares and promulgates standards which, variously, specify dimensions, performance and safety criteria, testing methods and codes of practice for a large range of products and processes in most fields of production. Voluntary acceptance of such standards by manufacturers, buyers and sellers reduces unnecessary variety and simplifies the specification of requirements. BSI is governed by a council consisting of representatives of the main organisations of employers and workers, professional institutions and the larger government departments.

THE GOVERNMENT AND INDUSTRY

The Government is giving priority to industrial development, in order to reverse the relative decline in this sector that has been continuous for many years. In view of the central importance to the economy of manufacturing industry, government policy is concerned with improving its competitiveness while at the same time developing effective solutions to such major problems as regional imbalance and unemployment. The Government influences industrial activity in a number of ways—through fiscal and monetary policy, through the level of public expenditure, by incentives for industrial investment and by the provision of services, information and advice. For the Government's relations with the public sector of industry, see pp 188–190. Legislative arrangements control aspects of employment, monopolies, mergers and restrictive practices and new industrial and office building and changes in land use.

The Department of Industry is responsible for industrial policy as a whole on both a national and regional level; 1975 saw the transfer of certain regional responsibilities towards industry in Scotland and Wales to the Scottish and Welsh Offices respectively. In Northern Ireland the Department of Commerce deals with industry and industrial development.

There is close association between industry and the Government through such channels as the National Economic Development Council (see p 188) and the Economic Development Committees. These cover particular industrial sectors and bring together representatives of government, management and unions to study, and make recommendations on, the efficiency and prospects of individual industries.

Since 1975 provision has been made for voluntary planning agreements between Government and some leading firms.

Industrial strategy

The Government initiated its industrial strategy in 1975 as a medium-to-long-term programme to strengthen industrial performance. Some 40 tripartite sector working parties have been set up in the National Economic

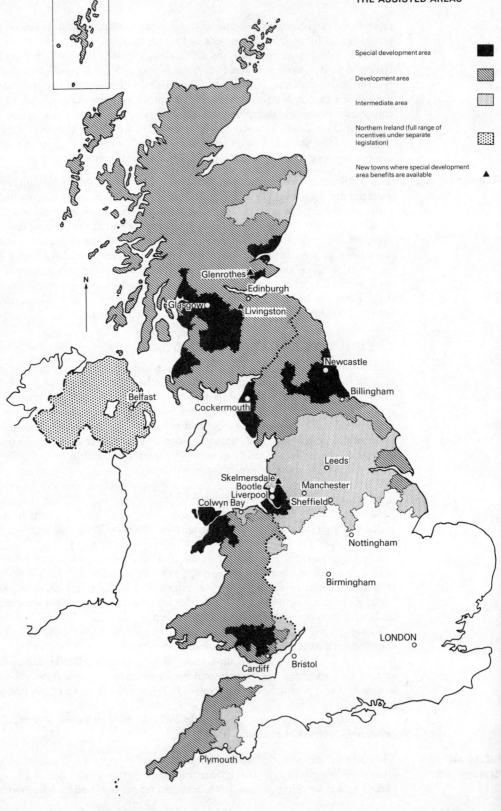

THE ASSISTED AREAS

Special development area

Development area

Intermediate area

Northern Ireland (full range of incentives under separate legislation)

New towns where special development area benefits are available

N

Glenrothes

Edinburgh

Glasgow

Livingston

Newcastle

Billingham

Cockermouth

Belfast

Leeds

Skelmersdale

Bootle

Manchester

Liverpool

Colwyn Bay

Sheffield

Nottingham

Birmingham

Cardiff

Bristol

LONDON

Plymouth

Development Council framework; three sets of reports have been produced, on the basis of which action is being undertaken to help to improve the sectors' shares of home and overseas markets. Comprehensive programmes for action covering such matters as investment, marketing, use of resources, research and development and structure are being developed. There has been special emphasis during 1978 on the need to improve productivity and to communicate the findings of the sector working parties to individual companies.

National Enterprise Board

The National Enterprise Board (NEB), established under the Industry Act 1975, is a public corporation whose principal objectives are to assist the national economy, promote industrial efficiency and international competitiveness and provide productive employment. The NEB's activities include the provision of finance for industrial investment and restructuring. It has a holding company role for shareholdings previously held by the Government, together with its own investments. The NEB is expected to exercise a commercial judgement and to look for an adequate return on its investments. Regional boards promote NEB investment in the Northern and North West regions.

Development Agencies

The Scottish, Welsh and Northern Ireland Development Agencies, established in 1975–76, are designed to stimulate industrial development within their regions by exercising powers similar to those of the NEB with regard to the provision of finance to industry and the establishment and management of industrial undertakings. Where firms are based mainly in Scotland, Wales or Northern Ireland, the development agencies take the initiative for action; where they are more broadly based in Britain, the NEB is responsible. Close consultation takes place between the NEB and the development agencies wherever interests overlap. The Scottish and Welsh agencies also have responsibilities under the regional development programme (see p 211).

Encouragement of Investment

Britain has a generous system of national incentives for industrial development. Under the Finance Act 1972 incentives to encourage capital expenditure in plant and machinery take the form of a system of free depreciation enabling the whole of such expenditure to be written off against profits for tax purposes in the year in which it is incurred; there is in addition a 54 per cent initial allowance on new industrial buildings and structures and an annual writing down allowance of 4 per cent thereafter. Direct investment from overseas is also encouraged, and overseas firms are offered the same facilities and incentives as those applying to British-owned companies. Under the Industry Acts 1972 and 1975 other assistance may be provided throughout Britain where it is judged to be in the national interest. Selective financial assistance is available for certain key sectors of industry to encourage modernisation and increase efficiency.

Regional Development

Economic imbalance between different parts of the country is due partly to the steady decline over the years of older industries, such as coalmining and shipbuilding, causing a high level of unemployment in certain regions and such adverse factors as poor amenities, derelict buildings and land and net outward migration. In addition, the newer and expanding industries have tended to develop mostly in the Midlands and the South-East, and unemployment has remained a persistent problem in Scotland, Wales, Northern Ireland and some parts of England, particularly the North and Merseyside. The ending of regional imbalance has been an objective of successive Governments. Financial and other aid to areas of high unemployment began in the 1930s and has been expanded considerably over the years.

Assisted Areas

The map opposite shows those areas where assistance is offered by the Government to encourage industrial development and the movement of office and other service employment. The assisted areas cover the whole of Scotland and Wales, and in England the Northern, North-West and Yorkshire and Humberside regions; parts of the South-West and East Midlands regions; and Oswestry in the West Midlands. There are three categories of assisted area: special development areas, where the economic situation and consistently high rates of unemployment give rise to the most urgent need for assistance; development areas with similar but rather less severe problems; and the intermediate area, where some assistance is necessary but where the need is relatively less acute than in the other types of area. Northern Ireland is covered by separate legislation. The incentives available are outlined on p 211.

Incentives for Industry

Under the Industry Act 1972 regional development grants are available in the assisted areas to help to meet the costs of buildings and works on premises used wholly or mainly for specified activities in manufacturing, and, in the special development and development areas only, towards the cost of plant and machinery as well. These grants are not limited to projects creating employment, and are thus available to help with improvements and modernisation. In addition they are not treated as reducing the capital expenditure which qualifies for tax allowances.

The Industry Act also provides for selective financial assistance for projects which are likely to provide, maintain or safeguard employment in any part of the assisted areas. Assistance may be provided in a number of forms, the usual ones for employment-creating projects being loans at concessionary rates of interest, interest relief grants, removal grants and service industry grants.

Other forms of assistance available include the provision of modern factories for rent or purchase, free use of government training services, and grants to assist the transfer of key workers to posts in the assisted areas. In the development and special development areas firms are given preferential treatment when tendering for contracts placed by government departments and nationalised industries.

Infrastructure

Special measures to improve the infrastructure in the assisted areas include provisions under the Local Employment Act 1972 for grants towards the improvement of basic services (such as transport, power and water facilities) and towards the acquisition and clearance of derelict land (see p 166).

Administrative Arrangements

Broadly speaking, responsibility for regional industrial development is exercised in England through the Department of Industry and in Scotland and Wales through the Scottish and Welsh Offices respectively. An important exception, however, is the regional development grant scheme, which is operated throughout Great Britain by the Department of Industry.

In England the regional offices of the Department of Industry in the main assisted areas (the North, North-West and Yorkshire and Humberside offices) can handle applications for loans of up to £2 million under the selective financial assistance scheme without reference to the department's headquarters. The Secretary of State for Industry has access to advice from the Industrial Development Advisory Board, a statutory body composed of prominent members of the industrial and financial community, which makes recommendations on industrial opportunities and on applications for selective financial assistance. Non-statutory industrial development boards have also been established for the North, North-West, South-West and Yorkshire and Humberside regions.

In Scotland and Wales, day to day work is carried out by the Scottish Economic Planning Department and by the Industry Department of the Welsh Office. Statutory Scottish and Welsh Industrial Development Advisory Boards advise the respective Secretaries of State for Scotland and Wales. The Scottish and Welsh Development Agencies are responsible for the provision of factories for rent or purchase and are also charged with the reclamation of derelict land and with certain powers to allocate selective financial assistance.

Northern Ireland

Under separate legislation (the Industries Development Acts 1966 and 1971) the Northern Ireland Department of Commerce offers a full range of incentives comparable to those available in the assisted areas of Great Britain.

All firms establishing factories in Northern Ireland, without regard to the number of jobs created, are eligible for capital grants at the rate of 30 per cent of the cost of new buildings, machinery and equipment; for selective employment premiums; for grants towards training and free use of government training services; for grants towards the cost of transferring key workers; and for the derating of industrial buildings by 75 per cent. The capital grants, like regional development grants in Great Britain, are not treated as reducing the capital expenditure which qualifies for tax allowances.

Projects which are especially attractive because of the number of jobs created can obtain special benefits which include industrial development grants of up to 50 per cent of the cost of new buildings, machinery and equipment (as an alternative to capital grants); contributions towards setting-up costs; grants of up to 100 per cent of the cost of transferring plant and machinery; modern factories for rent or purchase; and loans, loan guarantees and interest relief grants.

Grants of up to 50 per cent are available for research and development projects (up to a maximum of £250,000 for any one project).

Assistance is also available to firms in the service sector which have a genuine choice of location within Britain and which create additional net employment. Projects serving primarily local needs are not assisted. The forms of aid available to the manufacturing sector may also be offered to service sector projects.

The Northern Ireland Development Agency may also assist financially with industrial development projects.

Controls on Industrial Location

The Government also influences the location of industry by requiring industrial development certificates before planning permission can be sought for the building of new factories (or for extensions to existing ones) above prescribed limits outside the development areas, special development areas and Northern Ireland. New office development in south-east England is controlled in a similar way by a system of office development permits. However, under a new urban strategy outlined in 1977, the Government is encouraging industrial and office development in deprived inner-city areas, whether or not these are in the assisted areas.

European Regional Development Fund

The European Regional Development Fund was set up in 1975 to assist regions of the European Community suffering from problems of a preponderance of agriculture, industrial change and structural under-employment. In particular payments are made from the fund in respect of approved industrial and infrastructure projects in the assisted areas. Britain's share of the fund in the period 1975–77 was about £150 million.

European Investment Bank

Under a scheme introduced in 1978, loans are available from the European Investment Bank to firms in the development areas, special development areas and Northern Ireland. These loans protect the borrower from any risk of loss due to movements in the sterling exchange rate.

Rural Industries and Small Firms   Encouragement for the development of rural industries in England is provided under the aegis of the Development Commission set up in 1909. Through the agency of the Council for Small Industries in Rural Areas (CoSIRA), the commission provides business advice, credit for manufacturing and service industries in rural areas, and loans for tourism projects in the rural parts of the development and special development areas. In addition the commission provides factory premises in rural areas and lends support for pioneering and experimental schemes bearing on the rural economy, for voluntary bodies aiming to enrich social and cultural life in the countryside, for miscellaneous marketing and co-operative schemes in agricultural and fishing communities, and for surveys and other work in rural areas.

In Scotland and Wales these services are provided by the Scottish and Welsh Development Agencies. Separate bodies, however, cater for particular rural areas. In Scotland the Highlands and Islands Development Board, set up by Act of Parliament in 1965, provides assistance to the Highland region, and surrounding islands, and to parts of the Strathclyde region. It provides grants and loans to industrial and commercial enterprises, builds factories, and has powers to acquire land and set up businesses. The Development Board for Rural Wales has the general function of promoting and undertaking measures for economic and social development in the county of Powys and the districts of Meirionnydd and Ceredigion. It has a particular responsibility for new towns in those areas and can acquire land, carry out building and provide basic services. Within its area the board owns and manages Government estates and factories and also acts as agent for the Welsh Development Agency in the provision of assistance to industry.

The Department of Industry has a separate division which is the focal point for the formation of policy towards small firms. In association with the Scottish and Welsh Offices, the division operates a chain of Small Firms Information Centres throughout Great Britain, which work in co-operation with local business organisations and are linked to a central information bank in London. A number of new measures to assist small firms were taken in 1977–78. These included tax concessions (see p 339), continuation of the scheme to encourage collaboration between small firms and extension of the small firms counselling service. A small firms employment subsidy (see p 315), originally introduced in special development areas, was extended in 1978 to include small manufacturing firms within all the assisted areas and the inner city partnership areas (see p 161).

In Northern Ireland the Local Enterprise Development Unit, established to promote the development of smaller industries, provides grants, loans, premises and management advice to new and expanding companies.

Tourism   Government assistance for tourism is provided under the Development of Tourism Act 1969. The Act established four independent but government-financed statutory bodies—the British Tourist Authority, which is responsible for the overseas promotion of tourism in Britain and has a general responsibility for tourism within Great Britain, and the English, Scottish and Wales Tourist Boards which are responsible for encouraging the development and improvement of facilities and amenities for tourists in their respective countries, and for tourist promotional work and publicity within them. (In Scotland, however, the Highlands and Islands Development Board exercises these responsibilities within its area—see p 212). The Act enables the tourist boards to give financial assistance to selected tourist projects in the development areas. Government policy is to encourage growth in tourism in hitherto unexploited areas (particularly in the development areas) while sustaining the industry in recognised tourist centres. The Northern Ireland Tourist Board, established under separate legislation, has a function broadly similar to that of the other British tourist boards. Financial assistance to tourism projects is available from the Northern Ireland Department of Commerce.

CONSUMER PROTECTION AND COMPETITION POLICY

The encouragement of fair trading, with the particular aim of helping consumers and safeguarding their rights, has become an increasingly important part of government policy in recent years. The Government is also concerned with competition policy and the control of restrictive trade practices. The Department of Prices and Consumer Protection, set up in 1974, is responsible for policy and legislation on consumer affairs and competition policy. The Office of Fair Trading, a government agency, is concerned with the conduct of trade and industry in Britain. Legal redress can, where necessary, be sought by consumers in the county courts in England and Wales and the sheriff courts in Scotland.

Consumer
Protection

The Fair Trading Act 1973 provides machinery (headed by the Director General of Fair Trading) for the continuous review of consumer affairs and for action to meet new problems as they arise, including powers to deal with trading practices which unfairly affect consumers' interests, and to deal with persistent offenders under existing law. Other legislation to safeguard the consumer's economic interests deals principally with quantity, performance and service, price information and credit facilities.

The other major area of legislation is concerned with the prevention of the sale of dangerous or harmful consumer goods. The principal laws here are the Consumer Protection Acts 1961 and 1971, and the Consumer Safety Act 1978 which empower the Government to make regulations to ensure the safety of any class of goods.

Provision of consumer information and advice is an important function of those in local and central Government, and of several independent organisations, concerned with consumer protection. The main outlets are the Citizens Advice Bureaux (see p 134) and the Consumer Advice Centres run by local authorities, both of which receive financial assistance from central government.

The independent, non-statutory National Consumer Council (and associated councils for Scotland, Wales and Northern Ireland), which also receives government finance, ensures that the consumer's view is made known to those in Government and industry whose decisions affect consumers.

Consumer councils for the energy and rail nationalised industries and for the Post Office investigate questions of concern to the consumer, while some trade associations in industry and commerce have established codes of practice designed to protect the consumer. In addition several private organisations work to further consumer interests. The largest is the Consumers' Association, funded by the subscriptions of its membership of 591,000. The association conducts an extensive programme of comparative testing of goods and investigation of services; its views and test reports are published in its monthly magazine *Which?* or its satellite publications. The association also provides an advice service on subscription. Consultancy work on European legislation is undertaken by the association on behalf of the Department of Prices and

Consumer Protection. Local consumer groups, such as the National Federation of Consumer Groups, also promote consumers' interests and provide information and advice.

Competition Policy

Competition policy has led to the development of machinery for scrutinising and regulating monopolies, mergers and restrictive trade practices and of powers to regulate any structural changes or uncompetitive practices which operate against the public interest. The Fair Trading Act 1973 contains all current legislation on monopolies and mergers. The Director General of Fair Trading has certain statutory responsibilities in respect of monopolies, mergers and restrictive practices, in addition to his work on consumer protection.

European Community

The objective of the competition policy of the European Community is to promote free and fair competition in trade between member countries. The Community's rules of competition, which are set out in the Treaty of Rome, apply to industrial and commercial practices likely to affect trade and prevent, restrict or distort competition in the Community. Agreements which fall within the rules must be notified to the European Commission; the Commission has limited powers to exempt agreements which, though restrictive of competition between member countries, benefit the Community in defined ways.

Monopolies and Mergers

The Secretary of State for Prices and Consumer Protection and the Director General of Fair Trading can refer monopoly situations for investigation by the Monopolies and Mergers Commission. The market share by reference to which monopoly is defined is one-quarter; local monopoly situations and arrangements which prevent, restrict or distort competition, and monopolies in public sector industries can also be referred to the commission. If the commission finds that a monopoly situation operates against the public interest, the Secretary of State for Prices and Consumer Protection has powers to make orders and otherwise to remedy or prevent the harm which the commission considers may exist. It is more usual, however, for the Director General to be asked to negotiate undertakings to remedy the adverse effects identified by the commission.

A merger situation (defined as occurring when two enterprises are brought under common ownership or control) may be referred to the commission by the Secretary of State for Prices and Consumer Protection if it results in, or intensifies, a monopoly situation, or if the value of gross assets taken over exceeds £5 million. There are special provisions relating to newspaper and certain other mergers.

Restrictive Trade Practices

The Restrictive Trade Practices Act 1976 requires the entry in a public register of the particulars of a wide range of restrictive agreements which affect the supply of goods or commercial services for the British market. Such agreements must be notified to the Director General of Fair Trading who has a general duty to refer registered agreements to the Restrictive Practices Court.

Unless the restrictions in them are abandoned, the court has powers to prohibit the operation of any which are held by them to be contrary to the public interest. Registration and judicial examination has applied to agreements relating to goods since 1956 and to services since 1976. Not all registered agreements are taken before the court; those containing only insignificant restrictions may be allowed to continue without reference to the court. The Secretary of State for Prices and Consumer Protection may exempt from registration proposed agreements of substantial importance to the national economy or agreements designed to keep prices down. Restrictive agreements relating exclusively to exports are not subject to registration but they must be notified to the Director General of Fair Trading and to the Commission of the European Communities if they fall within the rules of competition of the Treaty of Rome.

MANUFACTURING INDUSTRIES

An outline of the broad sectors of manufacturing industry is given below. Production figures in Table 12 show the relative size of the sectors in the most recent years for which information is available. Over a longer term

TABLE 12: Manufacturing Industry: Net Output 1974–76

Industry Group	£ million			Per-centage of total	per head £		
	1974	1975	1976	1976	1974	1975	1976
Food, drink and tobacco	4,004	4,692	5,900	13·1	5,045	6,089	7,494
Coal and petroleum products	736	833	854	1·9	19,796	22,461	24,270
Chemicals and allied industries	3,225	3,492	4,593	10·2	7,929	8,549	11,334
Metal manufacture	2,565	2,489	3,021	6·7	5,174	5,034	6,339
Mechanical engineering	3,656	4,672	5,135	11·4	3,892	5,052	5,747
Instrument engineering	575	667	795	1·8	3,350	4,000	4,953
Electrical engineering	2,956	3,498	4,284	9·5	3,741	4,564	5,705
Shipbuilding and marine engineering	511	634	728	1·6	2,965	3,698	4,123
Vehicles	2,721	3,115	4,155	9·3	3,476	4,025	5,424
Metal goods not elsewhere specified	1,989	2,312	2,872	6·4	3,566	4,305	5,452
Textiles	1,823	1,879	2,368	5·3	3,153	3,446	4,617
Leather, leather goods and fur	131	147	194	0·4	3,085	3,495	4,697
Clothing and footwear	937	1,144	1,232	2·7	2,155	2,701	2,928
Bricks, pottery, glass, cement, etc.	1,289	1,607	1,916	4·3	4,540	5,891	7,366
Timber, furniture, etc.	1,119	1,191	1,455	3·2	4,125	4,513	5,636
Paper, printing and publishing	2,744	2,912	3,535	7·9	4,641	5,048	6,363
Other manufacturing industries	1,351	1,511	1,834	4·1	3,889	4,539	5,345
All manufacturing industries	32,331	36,796	44,872	100·0	4,201	4,900	6,088

Source: *Census of Production Reports: 1974, 1975, 1976* (1976 provisional results).
Differences between totals and the sums of their constituent parts are due to rounding.

expansion has been particularly marked in those industries using advanced technologies such as electronics (and more recently, micro-electronics), the newer branches of mechanical engineering, instrument engineering, most sectors of the chemical industry and man-made fibres. In other long-established industries (for example, shipbuilding and marine engineering and electrical engineering) extensive reorganisation, re-equipment and modernisation have become essential to meet changing economic conditions.

A major stimulus has been provided by the various needs of the offshore oil and gas industries.

In the following sections, relating to individual branches of industry in 1977, employment statistics are the latest available from the *Department of Employment Gazette* and refer to numbers in Great Britain at March 1978. Sales and output figures are taken from the latest available *Business Monitor* produced by the Business Statistics Office of the Department of Industry and compiled from returns made by firms in industry. Export figures come from *Overseas Trade Statistics of the United Kingdom* published by the Department of Trade. Unless otherwise stated, export and manufacturers' sales figures include parts.

Some sales figures are given in metric terms, where statistics for an industry are normally published in this form. Conversion tables can be found on p 431.

METAL MANUFACTURE

	Employment '000s	Production million tonnes	Exports £ million
Metal manufacture	469·7	57·3	1,718·5
iron and steel products	278·7	53·6	937·5
iron castings	76·4	2·8	60·6
non-ferrous metals	114·6	0·9	720·4

Iron and Steel

Most of the early developments in iron and steel production originated in Britain, today the world's eighth largest steel-producing nation. The Iron and Steel Act 1967 brought together into public ownership 14 major steel companies and created the British Steel Corporation (BSC). BSC currently produces over 85 per cent of Britain's crude steel and is the largest steel undertaking in Europe. It employs some 197,000 people, of which 173,000 are involved in iron and steel manufacturing and 24,000 in other activities, such as constructional engineering and chemicals. The remaining private sector companies are represented by the British Independent Steel Producers' Association whose members employ some 70,000 people and account for over one-third of the value of the industry's turnover. The private sector is particularly strong in the manufacture of alloy and stainless steels and of finished products for the engineering industry. The main steel producing areas are Yorkshire and Humberside (32 per cent of crude steel output in 1977), Wales (29 per cent), the Northern region (14 per cent), Scotland (10 per cent) and the West Midlands (7 per cent).

BSC has invested heavily in modernising its production capacity. Its development strategy includes the replacement of open-hearth steelmaking by basic oxygen steelmaking (for bulk production) and the electric arc process (for more specialised tasks) and the concentration of bulk steelmaking at five main sites (Port Talbot and Llanwern in Wales, Ravenscraig near Glasgow, Lackenby in Cleveland, and Scunthorpe) which have good access to deep water for iron ore imports. During 1977 and 1978 the industry was faced with the serious problem of world over-capacity. In March 1978 the Government published proposals for BSC's capacity to move more into line with demand in order to achieve financial viability. These included the deferral of a number of planned new steel making developments and the closure of a number of old steelworks, in advance of the dates previously agreed. About 80 per cent of production is used by home industry and the remainder for direct export, the major markets for which are the rest of the European Community and the United States. A large part of the steel used by industry in Britain is also subsequently exported as part of other finished products. The BSC is a member of the European Nuclear Steelmaking Club, established to define a strategy for the application of nuclear energy to steelmaking.

Iron Castings

In the production of iron castings, a few large firms are responsible for more than a quarter of total output while fewer, more highly developed units are replacing the numerous small foundries. The main users of iron castings are the motor vehicle industry, the general engineering industry, the manufacturers of pressure pipes and fittings, the building and associated industries and the steel industry. The Government is providing financial assistance for the modernisation of the industry.

Non-ferrous Metals

Britain's non-ferrous metal processing and fabricating industry is one of the largest in Europe. Its major products are aluminium (both virgin and secondary metal); secondary refined copper, lead and primary zinc. Tin mining in Cornwall supplies about 30 per cent of Britain's tin requirements (see p 262) but otherwise British metal smelting and refining industries are based on imported ores and concentrates except for substantial secondary production from scrap metal. Britain is also a major producer of the newer specialised metals including uranium, zirconium and beryllium for the nuclear energy industry, niobium for aircraft production and selenium, silicon, germanium and tantalum for electronic apparatus. Titanium and titanium alloys are also produced and used in aircraft production, power generation and North Sea oil production, where their lightness, resistance to stress, flexibility and resistance to oxidisation are especially valued. Nearly half the industry is situated in the Midlands. Other centres include south Wales, London, Tyneside and Avonmouth, where a zinc smelter of some 100,000 tonnes capacity operates. Three large-scale aluminium smelters provide almost 75 per cent of Britain's requirements for primary aluminium. The large non-ferrous metals fabricating industry uses large quantities of imported refined metals such as copper, lead, zinc and aluminium. A wide range of semi-manufactures is produced in these metals and their alloys, and, particularly in aluminium, firms are engaged in smelting, casting and fabrication by rolling, extrusion and drawing: advanced techniques of powder metallurgy and pressure die-castings are also employed. In recent years considerable progress has been made in the development of 'superplastic' alloys, which are more ductile and elastic than conventional alloys.

Scientific and technological research for the industry is conducted by the Warren Spring Laboratory of the Department of Industry and by the British Non-Ferrous (BNF) Metals Technology Centre.

The main products exported, including alloys and semi-finished products, are copper, nickel, aluminium, lead, tin and zinc, Exports of aluminium and aluminium alloys reached £194 million in 1977, while exports in the same year of copper, brass and other copper alloys totalled over £215 million. Exports of silver, platinum and other metals of the platinum group totalled nearly £203 million in 1977. The major export markets for the whole industry are the United States and the Federal Republic of Germany.

MECHANICAL ENGINEERING

	Employment '000s	Manufacturers' Sales £ million	Exports £ million
Mechanical Engineering	928·1	9,615·8	4,402·5
metal-working machine tools	65·4	514·1	288·2
industrial plant and steelwork	155·6	1,805·3	517·7
industrial engines	29·8	530·9	244·7
pumps, valves and compressors	85·0	966·6	435·4
textile machinery	24·0	243·1	187·5
construction and earth-moving equipment	43·1	833·4	718·8
mechanical handling equipment	61·0	906·6	374·9
agricultural machinery	30·1	232·2	135·7
office machinery	22·4	151·1	137·4
ball, roller and other bearings	*a*	275·3	*a*
other machinery	215·0	2,268·3	1,049·1
general mechanical engineering	196·7	814·5	313·1

a Included in general mechanical engineering.

The mechanical engineering industry comprises a group of industries manufacturing all types of machinery, machine tools, industrial engines, mechanical handling equipment, construction equipment and industrial plant. About half the industry's production is for the home market. The major customers for the heavy equipment sectors are the nationalised fuel industries, the chemical industry and the British Steel Corporation. A wide range of equipment is supplied to the building and construction industry. Demand for other types of equipment comes from all the production industries in Britain.

Machine Tools

Britain was the birthplace of the machine tool industry and many of the more advanced types of metal-working machine tools are produced in Britain. Almost all machine tools produced are purchased by the engineering, vehicles and metal goods industries. Seven large groups account for about 35 per cent of machine tool sales and exports. Dependent as it is on the manufacturing industries and their capital investment plans, demand for the industry's products is highly cyclical.

The most important types of metal cutting machine tools are milling, grinding and turning machines. Manual control for many of these tools is being replaced by automatic control and Britain is an important producer of numerically controlled machine tools, including machining centres. In addition, a range of different sizes and types of metal forming machine tools are manufactured in Britain. The largest export markets for the industry in 1977 were the rest of the European Community, the United States and Poland. The Machine Tool Trades Association represents most of the industry and is responsible for the international machine tool exhibition held in Britain every four years, the next being due in 1980. The Machine Tool Industry Research Association carries out research into design and performance of tools and into production methods.

Manufacturing Plant and Machinery

British industry manufactures almost every type of industrial (including process) plant and steelwork (for nuclear power station construction see Chapter 13). Of particular importance are fabricated products such as pressure vessels, heat exchangers and storage tanks for chemical and oil refining (process) plant, steam-raising boilers (including those of high capacity for power stations), sintering plant, metallurgical furnaces and plant, lime and cement kilns, nuclear reactors, water and sewage treatment plant and fabricated steelwork for bridges, buildings and industrial installations. The industrial plant industry comprises both equipment manufacturers and contractors responsible for the design, engineering, construction and commissioning of complete plants for process industries. British manufacturers have contributed to major advances in process technology: there has been a rapid expansion in the number of plants completed for the chemical, petrochemical, oil refining and gas industries, particularly for North Sea oil and gas operations, and British firms are carrying out major plant projects in many overseas countries. Gas turbine engines for industry, in particular for power generation in the fuel industries, are another thriving section of the industry, where exports have done well in recent years. Three large firms are pre-eminent in the manufacture of industrial engines, including those derived from aero-engines. Industrial pumps, valves and compressors are vital components in many industrial processes, particularly in the chemicals, oil and electric power industries: over half the production of all types of such equipment is exported. The fluid power industry makes oil hydraulic and pneumatic equipment for operating machinery and construction and other equipment. There are many new areas where these powerful and flexible systems may be used.

Machines and accessories for the manufacture and processing of yarns and fabrics from all types of natural and man-made fibres are produced by the textile machinery industry in Britain, which is noted for the range, scale and versatility of its operations. British inventions have remained the foundation of many textile processes in use internationally and progress has been made in developing automation in the industry. In 1977 the industry sold 87 per cent of its output to export markets. Research and development is carried out by the large firms and the four research associations connected with the textile industry. Machinery for food and drink preparation, processing and sterilisation is another important sector.

Refrigerating machinery (excluding domestic equipment) is used for food and drink processing, but the industry also covers plant for ships and vehicles and equipment for conserving drinks, food and ice-cream for the distributive and catering industries.

Construction and Mining Equipment

Almost the whole range of plant required by the construction industry is produced, including excavating, earth-moving and road-making equipment, pile drivers and quarry crushing and screening plant. Overseas sales of construction equipment and of mining machinery and equipment, including coal cutting and coal face loading machinery, are increasing. Mechanical handling equipment is used not only for construction and related activities but throughout industry generally. It extends from individual units and accessories to complete operating systems, the main products being cranes and bridge transporters, lifts, escalators, conveyors, elevators, hoists and powered industrial trucks including forklift trucks. Electronic control and completely automated handling systems are widely available.

Agricultural Machinery

Britain produces a wide range of equipment for general and special use, including many special purpose machines such as hop-picking machines, fruit harvesters and improved root harvesters (for tractors see p 223). Mechanisation is extensively used in the arable farming and dairy farming sectors. Much of the new machinery is designed for use in a variety of conditions to meet the needs of overseas farmers. A large-scale annual exhibition of the industry's products is the Royal Smithfield Show and Agricultural Machinery Exhibition held in London in December. The main trade association for the industry is the Agricultural Engineers Association.

Office Machinery

Sales by this industry have been expanding rapidly. Many products have an increasingly electronic content, particularly in the use of micro-electronics. A large proportion of the industry is owned by multinational companies. The industry includes non-electronic data processing and handling equipment, duplicators, typewriters, accounting machines and cash registers, and electronic calculators. (For electronic computers and data processing equipment see p 222.)

Other Machinery

The other major products of the mechanical engineering industry include printing, bookbinding and paper goods machinery, space heating, ventilating and air-conditioning equipment, packaging and bottling machinery, portable power tools and miscellaneous non-electrical machinery, such as boot and shoe-making machinery, laundry equipment, automatic vending machines, plastic working machinery and other types of specialised equipment.

General Mechanical Engineering

Alongside the firms manufacturing the products of the mechanical engineering industry are enterprises which supply parts and components and undertake general sub-contracting, fabricating and repair work. Particularly important is the production of ball, roller, needle and other bearings, about 25 per cent of which is for the motor vehicle industry, and of other components, such as precision chains, gears and drop-forgings.

INSTRUMENT ENGINEERING

	Employment '000s	Manufacturers' Sales £ million	Exports £ million
Instrument Engineering	148·3	1,304·0	786·2
scientific and industrial instruments	97·5	893·5	428·4
photographic equipment	12·0	147·3	197·4
watches and clocks	11·9	82·1	49·5
surgical instruments and appliances	26·9	181·1	110·9

Instrument engineering is a particularly important sector of the engineering industry. Electronic techniques are widely used, particularly in the industrial instrument sector, which comprises industrial and process measuring and control instruments and equipment, optical instruments and appliances, electrical measuring and testing instruments, nucleonic and ultrasonic testing equipment, analytical instruments and a diverse group of others. About half the market for analytical instruments is in the medical field. The chemicals, power, petroleum and iron and steel industries account for about 80 per cent of process control applications, the largest sector of the industry and one which is expanding. Major advances have been made in automatic testing equipment and analytical instruments for medical diagnosis and pollution control. The industry is served mainly by five trade associations—the Scientific Instrument Manufacturers Association, the Control and Automation Manufacturers Association, the British Industrial Measuring and Control Apparatus Manufacturers Association, the Electronic Engineering Association and the British Photographic Manufacturers Association. The Sira Institute conducts research on behalf of the industry.

Photographic equipment includes photographic and cinematographic cameras, projectors and document copying machines. Other sectors of the instrument industry are concerned with watches, clocks and time recorders and with surgical instruments and appliances and related products.

ELECTRICAL AND ELECTRONIC ENGINEERING

	Employment '000s	Manufacturers' Sales £ million	Exports £ million
Electrical and Electronic Engineering	741·4	7,576·5	3,030·6
electrical machinery	133·7	1,469·8	612·7
insulated wires and cables	43·8	652·0	175·6
electrical domestic appliances	62·1	675·2	177·8
electronic equipment:			
telecommunications	65·9	535·0	122·9
components	128·4	931·4	506·8
consumer goods	50·8	571·8	169·6
computers	45·3	675·1	498·8
capital goods	94·4	1,009·3	440·3

The electrical engineering industry is engaged in the manufacture and installation of a wide variety of equipment, which includes all types of generating, transmission and distribution equipment, motors, telecommunications and broadcasting equipment and domestic electrical appliances. The electronics industry, which makes a vital contribution to the efficiency of many branches of the country's economy, has become one of the most important sectors of British industry.

Leading representative organisations are the British Electrical and Allied Manufacturers Association, the Association of Manufacturers of Domestic Appliances and the Electronic Engineering Association, a member of the Conference of the Electronics Industry which brings together the six principal trade associations for the electronics industry. Scientific and technological research is carried out by the Electrical Research Association.

Electrical Engineering

The main product categories are power equipment (generators, motors, converters, transformers and rectifiers) and switchgear, starting and control gear. Mergers in the industry led to the creation of the General Electric Company, one of the leading electrical engineering groups in Europe for producing equipment used in generating, transmitting and distributing electric power.

The industry produces cables and wires for the distribution of electric power, for telecommunication networks and other purposes; its products include submarine cables and cables insulated by a great variety of materials. Four major groups are responsible for more than half the industry's output and for a large proportion of the world's submarine cable requirements.

A few large firms also dominate the market for other electrical goods, including domestic appliances. Domestic equipment includes heating and cooking equipment, washing machines and dryers, refrigerators, vacuum cleaners, irons and electric kettles. Other major sectors are electrical equipment for motor vehicles and aircraft; electric lamps and light fittings, and batteries and accumulators.

Electronic Equipment

The British electronics industry is one of the largest and most comprehensive in Europe and British scientists and companies have made important contributions to electronics technology. Because of the diversity of the range of products, an exact definition must be arbitrary, but the sectors included are telecommunication equipment, components, consumer goods, computers and communication and other capital equipment, as well as electronic process control and industrial instrumentation (see p 220).

The dependence of the telecommunications industry on electronic techniques is increasing as new switching systems are introduced. The main products are telephone exchange equipment, switching equipment for telegraph and telex, data transmission equipment, facsimile, viewdata and other subscribers' apparatus and long-distance communication equipment. The Post Office is the main customer in the home market, which is largely supplied by four companies and carries out research and development work in co-operation with companies.

The components sector manufactures the whole range of active and passive electronics components, including integrated circuits (in which many circuits are placed on a tiny chip of semiconductor raw material), mainly for the electronics equipment industry. Though the market is dominated by United States manufacturers, some joint ventures with British firms are developing; the NEB (see p 209) is also investing in circuit development.

The major consumer goods produced are radio and television sets, music centres and high-fidelity audio equipment. In the audio field, British manufacturers have a reputation for high-quality goods but are less strong in the mass market.

In the computer sector, an extensive range of computer systems, central processors and peripheral equipment, from large computers for large-scale data processing and scientific work to mini- and micro-computers for use in control and automation systems, are produced. Essential to the sector is the 'software' industry, which produces programs and associated services and complements the hardware industry, enabling the systems manufacturers to provide complete solutions to meet the requirements of users.

An expanding sector of the industry is that which covers the manufacture of radio communication equipment, radar and radio navigational aids for ships and aircraft, alarms and signalling equipment, public broadcasting equipment and other capital goods. An important development in this sector has been the X-ray scanner systems for brain diagnosis and whole body examination manufactured by Electrical and Musical Industries. British equipment is used extensively overseas, for defence, civil aviation, shipping, health, educational and other purposes.

VEHICLES, AIRCRAFT AND SHIPS

	Employment '000s	Manufacturers' Sales £ million	Exports £ million
Vehicles, Aircraft and Ships	943·3	11,495·6	4,798·9
cars and commercial vehicles	484·5	6,681·3	2,697·7
wheeled tractors	35·8	955·6	727·2
motor cycles and pedal cycles	14·0	99·7	68·0
railway vehicles and equipment	43·8	339·8	33·5
aerospace	190·6	2,054·2	942·4[a]
shipbuilding and marine engineering	174·7	1,365·0	330·1

[a] Excluding guided missiles and weapons.

Motor Vehicles

The motor vehicle industry comprises the manufacture of cars and commercial vehicles, caravans and trailers, and parts and components. Output of cars and commercial vehicles is dominated by four large groups (British Leyland, in which there is a majority public shareholding, Ford, Chrysler United Kingdom and Vauxhall) which account for over 99 per cent of car production and some 98 per cent of commercial vehicle output; the remainder is in the hands of smaller, specialist producers of cars, heavy commercial vehicles, buses and coaches. Although there is a balance of trade deficit in cars this is outweighed by a surplus in commercial vehicles and component parts; in 1977 the motor vehicle industry as a whole contributed about £700 million to the British balance of payments.

The principal trade association for the industry is the Society of Motor Manufacturers and Traders which holds a biennial motor industry show at the National Exhibition Centre, Birmingham.

Wheeled Tractors

Britain is the third largest producer of tractors in the world and the world's largest exporter. Agricultural tractors account for the bulk of wheeled tractors produced. Production is dominated by two large firms, with three others responsible for most of the remainder.

Motor Cycles

In recent years the motor cycle industry has contracted and the domestic market is largely supplied by imports.

Railway Vehicles

British Rail's requirements of locomotives and rolling stock are now largely met by their own workshops but there are several major companies in the private sector building these for export as well as components and other equipment such as traction and control gear, signalling, heating and ventilation systems. The private sector also builds the trains for London Transport and other rapid transit networks and is developing a growing export trade.

Aerospace

Britain's aerospace industry is the largest and most comprehensive in Western Europe and second only to that of the United States in the Western world. The products of the industry include civil and military aircraft, helicopters, aero-engines, guided weapons, hovercraft, space vehicles and a comprehensive range of aircraft and airfield equipment and systems.

The public sector, represented by the nationalised corporation British Aerospace (BAe, which was formed in 1977) and the publicly owned companies, Short Brothers and Rolls-Royce, is responsible for the greater part of aircraft, guided weapon and aero-engine manufacture in Britain. BAe, which acquired the assets and manufacturing capacity of the British Aircraft Corporation, Hawker Siddeley Aviation, Hawker Siddeley Dynamics and Scottish Aviation, is the largest of the aircraft and guided weapons manufacturers while Rolls-Royce (see p 202), which is one of the world's three leading aero-engine manufacturers, is responsible for almost the entire output of aero-engines.

The private sector is composed of a number of aircraft companies, including Westland Aircraft and its subsidiary, Westland Helicopters, which specialises in helicopter design and manufacture, together with nearly all of the aviation equipment sector.

Current production of BAe includes such civil aircraft as the HS 748 feeder-liner, the HS 125 business jet, and the BAC One-Eleven airliner. Short Brothers, which is based in Belfast, produces the Skyvan and the 330 commuter airliner. The private sector produces such successful aircraft as the Britten-Norman Islander and Trislander light transports. Military aeroplanes include the unique Harrier vertical/short take-off and landing aircraft (which has achieved substantial sales to the United States), the Hawk advanced trainer aircraft, the Anglo-French Jaguar tactical fighter/operational trainer and the Tornado multi-role combat aircraft, a collaborative venture by Britain, the Federal Republic of Germany and Italy. Westland Helicopters manufacture the successful Sea King and are the British partners in the Anglo-French collaborative programmes on the Puma, Gazelle and Lynx helicopters which are being produced for the armed forces of Britain, France and other countries.

The industry is also a major producer of guided weapons which include
number of export successes, in particular the Rapier ground-to-air missil
Collaborative guided weapon projects between Britain and its NATO partne
are also becoming of increasing importance.

Rolls-Royce aero-engines in production include the Pegasus vectore
thrust engine for the Harrier, the Gem engine for the Lynx helicopter, tl
quiet RB 211-22 engine and its more powerful derivative, the RB 211-52
The new RB 211-535 engine is now being developed. Industrial versions
aero-engines such as the RB 211 and the Olympus (which powers Concord
are being produced for use in oil and gas transmission and as stand-by pow
generators while versions for marine use, in particular of the Olympus ar
the Tyne, are being used to power a new generation of warships for tl
Royal Navy and many overseas navies.

The aviation equipment sector provides a wide range of systems essenti
to the design of engines and aircraft, including engine and flight contro
electrical generation, mechanical and hydraulic power systems, cabin furnis
ings and flight deck information displays, which are sold both in domest
and overseas markets. It also supplies equipment for ground operation inclu
ing that needed for radar and air traffic control, ground power suppliers ar
flight simulators, to airports and airlines throughout the world.

The industry is extensively involved in the manufacture of space system
including satellites for communications and other purposes, and in scientif
research in other European collaborative programmes. It carries out a
extensive programme of research and development on airframes, aer
engines and equipment, including avionics, while considerable research
also undertaken by universities and Government research establishments

Production and exports in the industry, which are fairly evenly divide
between the three sectors of airframes, aero-engines and aviation equipmer
including avionics equipment, have made considerable progress over the pa
few years and now stand at record levels. The principal destinations for expor
are the United States, France and the Federal Republic of Germany.

The main trade association for the industry is the Society of British Aer
space Companies which organises a major international air show at Far
borough, Hampshire, every two years. Major suppliers of avionics equipmer
are also members of the Electronic Engineering Association.

**Shipbuilding
and Marine
Engineering**

Britain has a long-established tradition of shipbuilding. Employment in tl
industry has contracted in recent years as a result of the world econom
recession and an over-capacity in shipping, particularly of oil tankers. The
have been programmes of reorganisation and modernisation in most maj
British shipyards, including construction of several covered-berth sh
'factories'. British yards are among the most modern and efficient in the worl
Nineteen of the principal shipbuilding companies, five companies man
facturing slow-speed diesel marine engines and three training companies ar
their subsidiaries were taken into public ownership in 1977 under a publ
corporation, British Shipbuilders. The public sector accounts for abo
97 per cent of merchant shipbuilding, 99 per cent of warship building, a
slow-speed marine diesel manufacture and some 50 per cent of ship-repairin
The sector also includes a number of companies engaged in general engineerir
work connected with the marine industries. In addition to conventional sh
types, marine structures and modules associated with the offshore oil indust
are constructed. In all, British Shipbuilders employs more than 85,000 peopl

A number of yards in the private sector build smaller vessels, includir patrol boats, fishing and harbour craft, supply vessels, tugs, cargo ships, small tankers and ferries.

About 35 per cent of the output of British yards is exported. Private sector companies in the shipbuilding and ship-repairing industries are represented by the Shiprepairers and Shipbuilders Independent Association. Research into shipbuilding and marine engineering is undertaken by the British Ship Research Association.

METAL PRODUCTS

	Employment '000s	Manufacturers' Sales £ million	Exports £ million
Metal Products	535·5	3,800·2	1,314·7
engineers' small tools and gauges	61·6	376·3	108·5
cutlery	12·9	114·1	61·0
hollow-ware	n.a.	204·0	39·1
hand tools and implements	19·6	140·4	90·3
jewellery, gold and silver ware	22·7	235·2	n.a.

n.a. not available.

A range of metal products other than those described in previous sections are produced by a group of industries made up of a very large number of firms. One of the main groups, in which small firms predominate, manufactures engineers' small tools and gauges, which include jigs and fixtures, press tools and moulds, hard metal-tipped tools and other metal cutting tools. Another group manufactures cutlery and tableware (including safety razors and blades). Although small firms predominate, seven relatively large concerns are responsible for over half of output.

A wide variety of domestic utensils, such as saucepans, buckets and dustbins, made mainly from aluminium and wrought steel, are produced by the hollow-ware industry, together with industrial hollow-ware, such as kegs, drums and barrels. The manufacture of hand tools, including files, saws, hammers, axes and spades, is a long-established industry. About half of its total production is for export. Jewellery, gold and silver ware and the refining of precious metals is an industry in which British craftsmen are world famous: five relatively large firms are responsible for about 60 per cent of total output. Other main groups of metal goods are bolts, nuts and screws, cans and metal boxes, metal furniture, metal windows, metallic closures, metal small-ware such as needles and pins, safes, locks and keys, domestic gas appliances and drop forgings.

CHEMICALS

	Employment '000s	Manufacturers' Sales £ million	Exports £ million
Chemicals	428·6	8,897·9	4,076·2
general chemicals	135·7	4,147·9	1,810·0
pharmaceuticals	72·8	1,367·2	518·8
plastics and synthetics	51·1	1,587·0	635·7
fertilisers	11·2	460·1	60·6
dyestuffs and pigments	22·3	377·2	219·4
paint	26·9	557·1	102·0
toilet preparations, soap and detergents	39·9	1,030·7	268·2

The chemicals industry is one of the most successful industries in Britain as well as being its third largest industrial sector. The industry is also the second largest in Europe and the fourth largest in the Western world and its exports of £4,076 million in 1977 (accounting for 11·7 per cent of total British exports) placed Britain among the top five chemical exporting nations. The industry is undertaking a substantial investment programme. The largest British chemicals group, Imperial Chemical Industries, is the fifth largest chemicals company in the Western world, accounting for about 20 per cent of chemical sales in Britain. A further 30 per cent is in the hands of 24 other large- and medium-sized companies. The industry as a whole is represented by the Chemical Industries Association. Research and development work is financed by the companies themselves. The rest of the European Community and the United States are the major export markets.

General Chemicals

About 22 per cent of the output of the general chemicals industry consists of a limited number of relatively simple inorganic chemicals, such as sulphuric acid and metallic and non-metallic oxides, serving as basic materials for industry. Substantial quantities of inorganic chemicals are used in the manufacture of such products as fertilisers, detergents, paint, glass and metals.

Organic chemicals include the heavy organics produced in bulk and the speciality intermediate products. Over 80 per cent of the output of organic chemicals is made up of petroleum-based chemicals. The most important products (by weight) are ethylene, propylene and benzene. The main outlets for organic chemicals are solvents, plastics and synthetic resins, synthetic rubber, man-made fibres and detergents.

Outside the inorganic and organic sectors is a wide range of general chemicals formulated for specific uses. Radioisotopes are produced by The Radiochemical Centre Ltd.; over half the centre's production is for export.

Pharmaceuticals

The whole range of medicines is produced in Britain, where many of the basic products were discovered and developed. These include antibiotics, sulphonamides, anti-malarial drugs, anti-histamine products, anaesthetics, vaccine sera and naturally occurring drugs. Manufacturers in Britain are among the world's leading producers and exporters of preparations for the treatment of human and animal diseases. This sector is one of the major growth areas of the chemical industry.

Plastics and Synthetics

Many of the basic discoveries in plastics, including polyethylene, were made in Britain. Plastics manufacture is one of the fastest growing sections of industry and 40 per cent of total production is exported. Expansion in recent years has mainly been in thermoplastic materials, of which the most important are polyethylene (used in coverings and packaging—notably for foodstuffs), polyvinyl chloride (known as PVC and used for a wide range of industrial purposes and consumer goods), polystyrene (a material used for toys, light mouldings and many consumer goods) and polypropylene (which can be fabricated as mouldings, films and fibres). A new group of plastics materials reinforced with carbon fibres is also in commercial production in Britain; they have up to three times the strength but are only half the weight of steel. High styrene rubbers for shoe soles and flooring, and nitrile rubbers for use where oil resistance is required, are also in large-scale production, together with neoprene rubber.

Fertilisers and Crop Protection

The development of chemical fertilisers owes much to the pioneer work of British scientists. Production is dominated by three firms, together with a number of firms marketing compound fertilisers from the principal constituents—nitrogen, phosphorus and potassium—and is almost entirely for the domestic market. The use of ammonium nitrate, ammonium phosphate and urea is resulting in more concentrated fertilisers. Notable discoveries by the British crop protection industry include the insecticidal property of BHC (benzene hexachloride), the first selective hormone weed-killer, MCPA, and *Gramoxone*, a non-residual general herbicide. Herbicides are the largest category of sales of pesticides and allied products.

Paint

Britain is a major producer of paints, varnishes and allied products. In recent years many improved techniques have been introduced into the paint and varnish industry, including new ranges of synthetic resins and pigments, non-drip, quick-drying paints and paints needing only one application.

Toilet preparations, Soap and Detergents

These industries include soap and detergents, toilet preparations, cosmetics and perfumes. Many of the firms in the toiletries industry are owned or financed by United States companies but there are a number of long-established British perfume and soap makers. Both sectors are significant exporters.

Other Chemical Products

There is a varied group of chemical products which account for about 10 per cent of the industry's net output. It includes formulated adhesives, printing ink, colours and dyestuffs, photographic chemical materials and floor and furniture polishes.

TEXTILES AND CLOTHING

	Employment '000s	Manufacturers' Sales £ million	Exports £ million
Textiles	468·3	5,517·9	1,610·1
man-made fibres	30·7	595·2	285·4
cotton linen }	85·8	1,137·1	353·7
wool	79·6	1,090·4	392·9
hosiery and knitwear	116·3	1,039·3	219·8
carpets	32·7	548·9	175·9
jute	8·1	80·8	10·3
other textile industries	115·1	1,026·2	172·1
Clothing	290·5	1,867·1	412·0

The historical branches of the industry, based on the natural fibres of cotton and wool, linen and jute, have retained their separate identities but the boundaries between them are becoming blurred with the increasing use of man-made fibres. The growth of man-made fibres has stimulated the development of new processes and new types of yarn and cloth and has strongly influenced the structure of the industry. A small number of large multi-fibre, multi-process groups have emerged, although in many sectors there is still a preponderance of small firms engaged in just one or two operations.

Research for the industry is provided by the Shirley Institute (cotton, silk and man-made fibres), the Lambeg Industrial Research Association, WIRA (the Wool Industries Research Association) and HATRA (the Hosiery and Allied Trades Research Association). The Department of Industry sponsors research and development both for these research associations and also directly within the industry.

Man-made fibres

Much of the early development of man-made fibres took place in Britain and continuing extensive research has produced a wide variety of types with their own special characteristics. The two main types are still those first developed—the cellulosic fibres, such as rayon, and the synthetic fibres, such as nylon and polyester, made wholly by chemical processes. Acrylic fibres, including *Courtelle* (a British discovery), *Acrilan* and *Orlon* are important products, as are the elastomeric or spandex fibres which have inherent properties of stretch and recovery, anti-static synthetic yarns embedded with carbon and various fire-resistant yarns. More recently there has been a greater use of the poly-olefins (polypropylene and polyethylene) in the carpet and carpet backing and packaging fields and still more recently in household textiles and clothing. Output in the man-made fibre industry is concentrated in the hands of a few large firms and has expanded rapidly in recent years.

Cotton

During the nineteenth century cotton was Britain's chief consumer goods industry and cotton piece goods its largest export. Low-cost competition has cut progressively into British markets and made necessary extensive re-organisation, modernisation and the introduction of new techniques. Production includes single and double cotton yarn, spun man-made fibre and mixture yarn, woven cotton cloth and man-made fibre and mixture cloth. The largest markets for cotton fabrics in 1977 were the rest of the European Community, the United States, Zaire, Togo, Finland, and South Africa.

Linen

The linen industry is centred in Northern Ireland, where the lighter types of fabrics for apparel, furnishings and household textiles are produced. The heavyweight canvas for sailcloth, tents, awnings and tarpaulins is mainly produced in Scotland.

Wool

The wool textile industry, of importance to Britain since medieval times, is one of the largest in the world and includes the world's biggest wool textile company, Illingworth, Morris. There are two main branches, woollen and worsted. An increasing amount of man-made fibre is now blended with wool. West Yorkshire is the main producing area but Scotland and the West of England are also famous as specialised producers of high quality yarn and cloth. Large quantities of raw wool are scoured and cleaned in Britain to prepare it for spinning. Government assistance is being given to encourage structural changes in the industry in terms of mergers and rationalisation and to stimulate investment. The largest markets for woollen and worsted fabrics are Japan, the United States and the rest of the European Community.

Hosiery and Knitwear

The hosiery and knitwear industry includes about 500 firms, mainly in the East Midlands and Scotland, of which most are small to medium in size. The industry produces fabrics, outerwear, underwear, tights, socks, stockings and accessories.

Carpets

Some 70 per cent of the output of the carpet and rug industry is made up of tufted carpets, in the production of which the pile, usually with a high man-made fibre content, is inserted into a pre-woven backing. Woven carpets, such as Axminster and Wilton, account for most of the remainder of sales. There is a higher wool content in woven types, although they too are making more use of man-made fibres. The volume of tufted carpets exported is now more than twice as large as that for woven ones, but the high quality and variety of design of the latter make Britain the leading producer of woven carpets.

Jute

Jute products are manufactured in the Dundee area. Jute yarn and the man-made polypropylene yarn are used in the manufacturing of carpets, cordage and ropes and woven into fabrics for a wide range of applications in the packaging, upholstery, building and motor car industries. New uses for jute, for example as a plastics reinforcement, are also being considered.

Other Textile Industries

British textile firms manufacture a wide variety of other goods, including lace, narrow fabrics and household textiles, such as blankets, sheets, towels and tablecloths. Rope, twine, nets and netting are manufactured by the cordage industry, which is one of the largest in Europe. A recent development by British manufacturers is the production of non-woven fabric by the melded process, in which the conventional weaving and knitting stages are omitted.

Clothing

The British clothing industry is one of the largest in Europe; it is highly labour intensive and dominated by small firms, with over 6,000 firms accounting for only 4 per cent of Britain's total employment in manufacturing. The negotiation of the Multi-Fibre Arrangement of the General Agreement on Tariffs and Trade (see p 357) has encouraged investment and exports increased substantially in 1977. The Clothing Export Council, which represents a major part of the industry, co-ordinates its promotional activities.

LEATHER AND FOOTWEAR

	Employment '000s	Manufacturers' Sales £ million	Exports £ million
leather and leather goods	36·9	398·5	128·3
footwear	74·8	609·9	108·0

Leather

Leather tanning and leather goods manufacturing is another long-established industry in Britain. All types of leather (including heavy types for industrial use) and leather goods are produced. Collective research is carried out by the British Leather Manufacturers' Research Association.

Footwear

The British footwear industry is one of the largest in the world. The industry is largely made up of small firms. Production in recent years has been severely affected by the recession and an increase in imports especially in the lower priced categories.

FOOD, DRINK AND TOBACCO

	Employment '000s	Manufacturers' Sales £ million	Exports £ million
Food, Drink and Tobacco	688·7	20,065·2	1,984·0
bread, bakery products, biscuits, flour confectionery	141·5	1,517·8	77.9
chocolate and sugar confectionery	71·6	1,078·3	210·2
bacon curing ⎫ meat products ⎬ fish products ⎭	102·0	1,935·1	338·1
beverages	126·3	3,963·6	666·2
tobacco	30·7	3,108·4	164·7
fruit and vegetable products	60·0	1,103·2	91·0

Bakery Products

About two-thirds of the bread in Britain is manufactured in large mechanised bakeries, most of which use a process developed by the industry's principal research organisation, the Flour Milling and Baking Research Association, and now widely used in other countries. Two groups are predominant. In smaller bakeries production of cakes and other flour confectionery is usually allied to bread production. Biscuits and related products are a major sector of the industry and have gained a world-wide reputation. Another sector is grain milling and the production of various specialised flours and meal.

Confectionery

The cocoa, chocolate and sugar confectionery industry is composed of a small number of very large manufacturers and many medium-sized and small firms. A substantial proportion of total world exports of chocolate and sugar confectionery are supplied by Britain.

Bacon Curing, Meat and Fish Products

The industry comprises the curing of bacon and ham, the canning and preserving of meat and fish, the manufacture of sausages and pies and the preparation of extracts and pastes. In addition to the output of quick-frozen fish, small quantities are also canned.

Fruit, Vegetable and Other Products

Fruit and vegetable products include canned, frozen and dried fruit and vegetables, jam, marmalade, pickles and sauces. Other products of the food processing industry include sugar, sugar preparations and honey, dairy products and eggs, vegetable and animal oils and fats, coffee, cocoa, tea and spices and cereal preparations.

Beverages

Of prime importance among the alcoholic beverages produced in Britain, and in the food and drink industry as a whole, is whisky. Scotch whisky accounts for almost all whisky production in Britain. About four-fifths of annual sales are to overseas buyers; the United States imports a third of the distilled alcoholic beverages exported from Britain. The rest of the European Community and Japan are the other largest markets. Production of gin in Britain has risen steadily since the early 1950s. One company accounts for a large proportion of output. Some of the larger manufacturers also own distilleries abroad.

In the brewing and malting industry there are seven major brewery groups whose products are sold nationally and about 80 smaller enterprises who mainly supply locally, or regionally. Firms have introduced new production methods, including continuous brewing processes, and automated batch production plants are well established. The main raw materials used are malt, hops and some sugar. British malt, which is made almost entirely from home-grown barley, is used by brewers throughout the world. In recent years the popularity of lager has increased considerably.

Three major groups account for much of the cider and perry produced in Britain. The industry is based mainly in Devon, Somerset and Herefordshire. Imported grape and fruit juices are used in the production of most of the made wine. A much smaller, though expanding viticultural industry produces wine from grapes grown in vineyards, mostly in southern England.

The soft drinks industry has expanded markedly in the last decade. There are some very large firms among about 20 producing brands which are marketed on a national scale, while other firms supply regional markets. There is some specialisation among firms in the production of various types, such as carbonated drinks, cola-based drinks, squashes and cordials, tonic waters and 'mixers', fruit juices and health drinks.

Tobacco

The tobacco industry manufactures almost all the cigarettes and tobacco goods sold in Britain. Two big manufacturing groups account for over 90 per cent of total output. Exports, mainly of cigarettes, are shipped to a large number of overseas markets, including Saudi Arabia, the Netherlands and Belgium. Tobacco is imported in large amounts from the United States, Canada and India.

BRICKS, CEMENT, POTTERY AND GLASS

	Employment '000s	Manufacturers' Sales £ million	Exports £ million
brickmaking and refractory goods	39·3	457·3	74·8
cement	13·3	346·6	27·9
pottery	61·1	391·4	150·0
glass	68·3	718·0	167·6

Brickmaking and Refractory Goods

Firms in the industry manufacture such items as bricks, roofing tiles, chimney pots, fireclay ware and heat-resisting products, including furnace and kiln linings. Brickmaking is one of Britain's oldest industries, but most manufacture is now based on highly mechanised systems. One company, the London Brick Company, supplies about 40 per cent of total brick deliveries. Refractory goods include firebricks, silica bricks, magnesite bricks, chrome-magnesite bricks and alumina bricks.

Cement

The cement industry is chiefly concerned with the manufacture of Portland cement for the home market. Invented by Joseph Aspdin and patented in 1824, this material and the methods of its production have been the subject of continuous technical improvement and intensive research. One new variation, glass-reinforced cement composites, consists of ordinary Portland cement and sand combined with an alkali-resistant glass fibre. The capacity of the industry as a whole has been substantially expanded in recent years.

Pottery

The pottery industry, centred largely in Staffordshire, supplies almost all home needs for domestic and industrial pottery. It uses largely indigenous clay from Cornwall and Devon. There has been considerable re-equipment in the industry; kilns fired by gas or electricity have replaced all the coal-fired kilns, and new decorating techniques and automatic and semi-automatic machinery, such as automatic glazing machines, have been introduced. Domestic pottery, including china, earthenware and stoneware, accounts for about half of the industry's output; the other main divisions are glazed tiles, sanitary ware and electrical ware, and such specialised industrial products as acid-proof stoneware, porous ceramics and laboratory porcelain. Production of tableware is concentrated in two major groups. Britain is the world's principal manufacturer of fine bone china, much of which is exported; famous makes include *Wedgwood, Spode, Royal Worcester, Royal Doulton, Minton, Coalport* and *Royal Crown Derby*.

Glass

Britain's glass industry is one of the biggest in the world. The largest section of the industry is devoted to the manufacture of flat glass in its various forms, chiefly 'float' glass, a process developed in Britain and licensed to glassmakers throughout the world. The use of glass for internal decoration and as a finish for internal and external walls has greatly increased in recent years. Large quantities of safety glass are produced for the motor and other industries. Other products include tubular glass, mirrors, lamp and bulb glass, scientific and medical glassware, glass fibres, and all types of glass containers (mostly made automatically). A traditional product is hand-made lead crystal glassware of very high quality. Collective research is undertaken by the British Glass Industry Research Association, and much research work is also carried out by the Department of Ceramics, Glasses and Polymers of Sheffield University.

PAPER, PRINTING AND PUBLISHING

	Employment '000s	Manufacturers' Sales £ million	Exports £ million
Paper and Board			
including converted products	202·4	3,513·7	387·7
paper and board	62·6	1,273·4	205·7
converted products	139·8	2,240·3	182·0
Printing and Publishing	333·9	3,332·8	332·1

Paper and Board Manufacture and Conversion

The British paper and board industry is one of the largest in Europe. The larger British groups hold considerable interests abroad, including pulp and paper producing mills in the United States, Canada, other parts of the Commonwealth and Europe. In recent years paper production has concentrated on printing and writing papers and boards and speciality grades. There has also been a significant trend towards waste-based packaging grades, in order to reduce the industry's reliance on imported woodpulp supplies. Domestically produced woodpulp represents only a small percentage of raw material supplies and the use of recycled waste paper is increasing: together they currently provide nearly 60 per cent of the industry's needs. The Government's recently introduced Paper and Board Industry Scheme has assisted the increased use of both recycled paper and board and of home-produced wood pulp. The main types of paper and board produced are printing and writing papers and board, packaging board, wrapping papers, newsprint, household tissues and industrial and special purpose papers.

The packaging and converting industries manufacture a variety of converted products, including cardboard boxes, cartons, fibreboard packaging and business stationery products.

Printing and Publishing

The printing and publishing industry produces a wide range of products, including national and provincial newspapers, periodicals, books, business stationery and greeting cards. Mergers have led to the formation of large groups in the newspaper, magazine and book publishing sectors, but general printing, engraving, bookbinding and a large part of publishing remain essentially industries of small firms. Production processes include high-speed printing equipment, including electronic engraving, advanced processes of photographic reproduction and computer typesetting. Security printers (of, for example, banknotes and postage stamps) have a high reputation and are important exporters.

The most important overseas markets for printed matter are the United States and Australia.

OTHER MANUFACTURING

	Employment '000s	Manufacturers' Sales £ million	Exports £ million
rubber and rubber manufacturers	110·3	1,422·8	377·8
furniture (wooden), bedding etc.	109·1	1,087·8	151·6
brushes	8·6	65·9	13·6
timber	86·8	890·9	67·1
plastics products, floorcoverings etc.	134·4	1,622·4	n.a.
toys, games, sports equipment	41·0	384·3	167·1

Rubber

Tyres and tubes represent nearly half the output of the industry, but firms make a variety of other goods, the most important being vehicle components and accessories, conveyor belting, cables, hose, latex foam products and rubber footwear, gloves and clothing. Rubber is also used for inflatable liferafts, containers for fuel and other industrial liquids and seals for storage tanks and other products where there are problems of air exclusion and vapour suppression. One of the largest tyre groups in Europe, Dunlop-Pirelli Union, resulted from a merger in 1971 of Britain's leading rubber and tyre company and its Italian equivalent. Tyre manufacturers include several subsidiaries of United States and other overseas companies. The industry's consumption of rubber includes natural, synthetic and recycled rubber.

Furniture, Brushes and Timber

Numerous enterprises manufacture furniture in Britain (including domestic, office, school and other furniture) with a few large firms predominating. In recent years the industry has experienced a sharp increase in demand from overseas. Exports have risen from £98·5 million in 1975 to £211 million in 1977. The industry comprises wooden, metal and plastic furniture, upholstery, bedding and soft furnishings. A Development Council for the industry has existed since 1949. Scientific research and technical and other information services are provided by the Furniture Development Council and the Furniture Industry Research Association.

The brush industry is located throughout Britain and includes highly mechanised establishments as well as small craft units.

Domestic production of timber has been steadily increasing but the timber industries are mainly dependent on imported supplies. A large proportion of timber sales are dependent on the construction industry. Chipboard is the fastest growing sector of the industry; other important sectors are hardwood and plywood.

Plastics Products

In addition to the plastics components and accessories supplied to many different industries, the plastics products industry manufactures a wide range of building materials, such as pipes, sheeting for roofs, sanitary ware, tanks and other products. It also supplies flexible foams, used in the vehicle, furniture and other industries; rigid foams; packaging products, including bottles, containers and bags; domestic and industrial hollow-ware, many kinds of household goods, vinyl and other floorcoverings and leathercloth.

Toys, Games and Sports Equipment

The industry manufactures toys, games, sports equipment and children's carriages. There are about 600 toy and games makers in Britain but some 20 companies dominate the market. The greatest expansion has been in the field of craft and hobby kits. British diecast toys and model construction kits are well known overseas; about half of the output of toys and games is for export. The Federal Republic of Germany and the United States are the major markets for toys while the United States and Canada are the main markets for sports equipment.

CONSTRUCTION

The construction industry, which accounts for about 7 per cent of the total domestic income, includes firms engaged on the design, construction, alteration, repair and maintenance of buildings, highways, airfields, drainage and sewerage systems, docks, harbours and canals, sea defence works, offshore structures, electrical wiring, heating and other installation work, the extractive and materials producing industries, and structural work connected with thermal and hydroelectric power stations and telecommunications. About 1·6 million people are engaged on construction, including the self-employed, and they represent some 7·5 per cent of the total labour force. About 6·5 per cent are employed by public authorities. Some 32 per cent of output consists of maintenance work, and about 45 per cent of all new work is commissioned by public authorities.

Structure

Construction work is carried out both by private contractors and by public authorities which employ their own labour. In 1977 about 87 per cent of the work was done by private firms. Although there were 50,000 firms employing two or more people 92 per cent of them employed fewer than 25 people.

Public authorities as a whole employed about 252,000 operatives but a very large proportion of these were engaged on repair and maintenance work for local authorities.

Some 42 per cent of operatives were occupied on building maintenance, valued at about £2,580 million annually. The total labour force included about 869,000 skilled craftsmen (of whom about 76,000 were trainees), most of whom had been trained under the industry's apprenticeship schemes. The normal apprenticeship period is three years.

Some firms are vertically integrated, owning quarries and workshops, mechanised plant and standard builders' equipment; some undertake responsibility for projects from initial design to finished building. All but the smallest projects are generally carried out under professional direction, either by architects or, in the case of the more complicated civil engineering projects, by consulting engineers. The functions of the latter, acting on behalf of a client, embrace advice on the feasibility of projects, the drawing up of plans and the supervision of the construction work by the contractor.

The Property Services Agency, which is an integral part of the Department of the Environment (see p 45) is responsible for the construction programmes undertaken directly by the Government, including work for the armed forces both in Britain and overseas. The Department of the Environment is responsible for the sponsorship of the construction industry. Among other things, this involves consultation with the industry through the National Consultative Council for the Building and Civil Engineering Industries and less formal contacts. The Department is also responsible for co-ordinating research and development in construction throughout Government and seeks to influence techniques and methods within the industry.

Output

The value of work done in 1977 amounted to £13,491 million, of which £1,640 million represented work carried out by the labour employed directly by public authorities. Private contractors carried out the remaining £11,851 million (£8,879 million on new work and £2,972 million on repair work).

Housing

Some 275,500 houses and flats were started in 1977 and 313,500 were completed, of which 143,300 were for private owners. Of the £3,513 million of new housing carried out by private contractors, £1,786 million, or over half, was for private owners and the remainder for public authorities. Industrialised building methods employing prefabricated components are used in some of the work.

The National Building Agency is an independent advisory body, managed by a board of directors appointed by the Secretaries of State for the Environment and for Scotland and Wales. Its main function is to encourage the adoption of advanced methods of house building, and to provide technical advice and services to government departments, local authorities and other clients.

The Association of Building Centres represents the interests of the 12 building centres throughout Britain most of which provide both a comprehensive permanent exhibition and information services on building materials and products, building services and techniques.

Civil Engineering Projects

Among important construction projects in hand in Britain in 1978 were conventional and nuclear power stations (see p 258), offshore production platforms and onshore terminals for North Sea oil, hospitals, large-scale housing developments, the first stage of the new Jubilee underground line in London, and roads, tunnels and bridges, including the new bridge being built across the river Humber (see p 287).

Overseas Construction

The overseas earnings of all sectors of the construction industry exceeded £2,000 million in 1976–77. This figure is made up of some £320 million from British contractors working abroad, their overseas branches and subsidiaries, a contribution of £250 million from the related professions of consulting engineers, architects and surveyors, and a balance of £1,450 million from the export of building materials, plant and machinery.

In 1976–77 British building and civil engineering firms won new overseas contracts worth £1,700 million in over 100 countries, an increase of £383 million on 1975–76.

A substantial amount of overseas work is being carried out by British engineers, architects and surveyors. British members of the Association of Consulting Engineers were engaged on overseas projects worth £31,000 million at the beginning of 1978.

The Government and the construction industry are represented on the Exports Standing Committee of the National Consultative Council for the Building and Civil Engineering Industries.

Research

Within the Department of the Environment, the Building Research Establishment (BRE) is concerned with all aspects of construction research. In addition, the Building Research Advisory Service of the BRE provides technical advice over a wide range of construction problems. An Agrément Board tests and certifies building products and methods.

The construction industry is served by several of the industrial research associations, while the major construction firms have research departments working on plant, materials and methods. Other bodies concerned with research include the universities and colleges of technology. The larger producers of primary building materials do some research into production methods and new developments.

DISTRIBUTIVE AND SERVICE TRADES

Internal trade can be divided into two broad categories: trade in raw materials, capital goods and intermediate products (for example, packaging materials) and trade in consumer goods, involving the network of distributive trades by which home-produced or imported goods reach the consumer. (For the pattern of consumers' expenditure, see p 192.)

While some of the trade in consumer goods passes through wholesalers to retailers, sales are also made directly to consumers through producers' own selling organisations (including their own retail outlets and mail order businesses), and other sales are made directly by producers to retailers.

Closely connected with the distributive trades are those which offer a service directly to the public, notably catering and hotel trades, laundries and dry cleaners, garage and motor repair trades, hairdressers and shoe repairers.

There have been several major official statistical inquiries into the distributive trades. For wholesale trades, a large-scale inquiry was carried out in respect of 1965, and more recently for 1974, while for service trades there was a large-scale inquiry into the catering trades for 1969 and into motor trades for

1972. The 1971 Census of Distribution covered the retail and certain other service trades. These large-scale periodic inquiries are being replaced by smaller annual sample inquiries in Great Britain that will eventually cover most distributive and service trades. For retailing, the first of these was conducted in 1977 in respect of 1976, and for catering in 1978 in respect of 1977. In Northern Ireland a Census of Distribution has been taken in respect of 1975. About 2·5 million people in Great Britain were employed in wholesale and retail distribution in 1977.

WHOLESALE TRADES

The main areas in which wholesalers are dominant are groceries and provisions, petroleum products and ores and metals. The book value of stocks held by wholesalers and dealers at the end of 1977 was about £5,212 million; fixed capital expenditure by wholesale distributors amounted to about £151 million in 1977 (valued at 1970 prices).

Methods of wholesale distribution vary according to the type of merchandise handled. Fish, for example, is auctioned at the ports to port wholesalers (who may sell to inland wholesalers at the main distribution centres) or, increasingly, is sold by contract to fryers and processors, or direct to retailers. Fruit and vegetables may be sold (or sent on a commission basis) to primary wholesalers who dispose of the produce either to secondary wholesalers or direct to retailers; alternatively the grower may deal direct with retailers or may sell his crop, under contract, to a food-processing company for canning or freezing. The sale of some agricultural products such as milk, hops and potatoes, is regulated by statutory marketing boards.

London's wholesale markets play a leading part in the distribution of foodstuffs. Every year the new Covent Garden market handles over 1 million tons of fruit and vegetables, and about 159,000 tons of carcase meat and 50,000 tons of poultry pass through Smithfield market; Billingsgate is the principal distributing centre for fish.

The co-operative movement in Britain has established its own wholesale organisation to serve the needs of retail societies. The sales of the Co-operative Wholesale Society (CWS), whose membership is restricted to incorporated organisations, amounted to £1,435 million in 1977.

The number of Cash and Carry wholesale warehouses has increased in recent years. By bulk purchasing and limiting their expenditure on premises and credit and delivery facilities they can offer large price discounts to their customers. In 1976 there were about 640 warehouses of this type with total sales of over £1,600 million. Cash and Carry wholesalers accounted for nearly half of all grocery warehousing by turnover in 1976.

RETAIL TRADE

Organisation and Turnover

Retail businesses in Britain may be classified under four main headings: (1) multiple traders with ten or more branches; (2) retail co-operative societies; (3) independent retail businesses, including for this purpose the small multiple stores (that is, chains of stores with nine or fewer branches); and (4) department stores. Other retail outlets include gas and electricity showrooms and mail order businesses (see p 239). Multiple traders have tended to bypass the wholesaler by having their own buying and distribution organisations. In response many wholesalers have joined with independent retailers to form voluntary organisations. This has helped to preserve the existence of retail outlets for the wholesaler and has given to smaller retailers the advantages of bulk-buying and co-ordinated distribution without significant loss of independence. About 30,000 grocers' shops, over a third of all independent grocers, are members of voluntary groups.

The 1971 Census of Distribution covering retail and certain service trades in Great Britain, recorded some 473,000 retail establishments.

TABLE 13: Retail Trades by Type of Business, 1976

Type of trade	Number of outlets	Turnover £ million
Grocers	60,000	7,586
Other food retailers and off-licences	66,000	4,064
Department stores, other general stores and mail order	24,000	7,068
Confectioners, tobacconists and newsagents	44,000	2,515
Footwear, clothing and general textiles	61,000	3,869
Furniture and other household goods	50,000	4,007
Other non-food retailers	57,000	3,656
Other businesses with retail activities	38,000	2,592
Total	400,000	35,358

Source: *Trade and Industry*

Out of this total, grocery and other food retailing groups numbered nearly 198,000 and the clothing and footwear group over 81,000. Provisional results of the retailing inquiry for 1976 (see Table 13) recorded some 400,000 establishments, of which grocery and other food retailing groups accounted for 126,000 and the clothing and footwear group 61,000.

The total value of retail trade in Great Britain (inclusive of electricity and gas showrooms and mail order business), after allowing for price changes, rose by about 6 per cent between 1971 and 1976. Rates of growth (measured in turnover) varied appreciably between different types of trade. The slowest growth was in confectionery, tobacconist, newsagent, clothing and 'other food' sectors. The fastest growth was in department stores, mail order business, combined gas and electricity showroom sales, household goods, groceries and provisions, and 'other non-foods'. However, the growth of sales on a commodity basis has been affected by increased diversification. The results of the retailing inquiry for 1976 indicate a continuation of the trend for a larger volume of trade to be handled by rather fewer shops, particularly in the food sector, along with the continuing expansion of large multiple firms relative to other types of shop. Independent shops accounted for about half of the value of Britain's retail trade, although they made up more than four-fifths of the number of shops.

A very wide range is covered in the size of retailing establishments. Seven shops had a turnover in 1971 exceeding £10 million. At the other extreme there were some 6,500 shops with a turnover of less than £1,000 a year. In addition there were market and street traders, whose volume of business may be very small.

Fixed capital expenditure by retail distributors in 1977 amounted to about £412 million (at 1970 prices).

Multiples and Large Establishments

According to the retailing inquiry for 1976 there were some 169,000 shops owned by multiples (including multiple department stores) in 1976 with a total turnover of over £23,000 million; their share of total turnover was about 65·3 per cent.

Retail Co-operative Societies

Total sales of the retail co-operative societies in 1977 were over £2,600 million, being about 7 per cent of all retail trade. Their share of food shops turnover was some 13 per cent.

The retail co-operative societies are voluntary organisations controlled by their members. Membership is open to anyone paying a small deposit on a minimum share, which entitles the member to an equal voice with other members in the society. Share investment by individual members is limited to £5,000 (less in some societies) and only a low rate of interest is normally paid on the shares. One large society has introduced a scheme of bonus shares carrying a higher rate of interest than the ordinary shares.

Traditionally the trading surplus was paid out to members in the form of a dividend in proportion to their purchases. A large number of societies, accounting for over four-fifths of total co-operative sales, have introduced dividend stamps redeemable for cash, other goods, or credit to a share account, at different redemption rates.

At the end of 1977 there were 231 retail co-operative societies. Amalgamations are rapidly diminishing the number of societies (the total in 1958 was 1,015). The largest single society in Britain is Co-operative Retail Services Limited which in 1977 had 1,300 retail outlets and a turnover of £356 million.

Independent Shops   Independent shops have been giving ground gradually in the face of increased competition from the larger undertakings, but the decline has been partly reduced by the existence of voluntary buying groups (see p 236). The retailing inquiry for 1976 observed that the independent shops' share of trade has continued to fall (to 34·3 per cent); however, they still play an important role, often in terms of convenience, service, and range of goods stocked. The proprietors of some smaller shops have other means of livelihood.

Department Stores   Department stores were defined for the purposes of the 1971 census as having 25 or more persons engaged in selling a wide range of commodities, notably clothing and household goods. There were 818 department stores in Britain, according to the 1971 Census of Distribution, with a turnover of £950 million: 242 were owned by multiples; 343 by independents; and 233, with a turnover of nearly £160 million, by co-operative societies.

Other Methods of Retailing   The development of self-service trading has been a feature of the last two decades. In 1971 there were over 28,000 stores operating wholly or partly on self-service lines, compared with about 9,500 at the end of 1961. This development has been accompanied by a trend to larger shops in terms of both floor space and staff, though the number of staff per square foot of floor space has tended to decrease.

Supermarkets   Supermarkets are defined as self-service shops with a minimum selling area of 2,000 square feet (186 square metres). According to estimates of the Institute of Grocery Distribution there were 6,190 supermarkets in 1977 with sales of £5,097 million. Their share of total retail grocery sales amounted to some 53 per cent.

Superstores   The number of very large stores, generally known as 'hypermarkets' and 'superstores', is increasing. They generally operate a selling area of between 20,000 and 100,000 square feet (1,860 and 9,290 square metres respectively); hypermarkets having a minimum selling area of 50,000 square feet (4,645 square metres). These stores operate on supermarket lines but with a much wider range of goods including food and non-food items. They are generally associated with exclusive car-parking facilities and situated away from established central shopping areas.

Mail Order Sales

Mail order trading, through a mail order business or direct from retailer, wholesaler or manufacturer was one of the most rapidly growing forms of selling in Britain between 1961 and 1966. Its growth rate slowed between 1966 and 1971, but has since increased again. The retailing inquiry for 1976 showed that total mail order sales by retail organisations were £1,875 million, accounting for 5 per cent of total retail sales. The main products sold through mail order in 1976 were clothing, textiles and soft furnishings.

Mobile Shops

Some 31,790 mobile shops and market stalls were reported in the Census of Distribution for 1971, with sales amounting to £147 million. Co-operative societies accounted for 39 per cent of sales through mobile food shops, against 12 per cent in ordinary food shops. Mobile shops were mainly concerned with food sales; about two-fifths were travelling grocers, and greengrocers and butchers each accounted for over one-fifth. Only a small proportion were shops not selling food, and these specialised mainly in paraffin supplies and hardware.

Automatic Vending Machines

There are about 500,000 automatic vending machines in use in Britain, many of them installed in offices and factories. It has been estimated that sales from vending machines in 1971 totalled some £155 million while sales from the 62,500 machines in use in the retail trade totalled some £12 million. The main items sold in them are cigarettes, drinks, confectionery, prepared foodstuffs and other commodities such as postage stamps.

Promotional Offers

Forms of consumer sales promotion include reduced price offers, competitions, gift schemes, and stamp trading. Trading stamps are normally exchanged for goods but, by law, have to be marked with a cash value and, where their aggregate value is £0·25 or more, redeemed for cash on request.

Direct Selling

Sales by the 30 manufacturing and importing companies which are members of the Direct Sales and Service Association Limited and which sell all their products directly to consumers amounted to about £450 million in 1976.

Instalment Credit

The rapid growth of sales of household and durable consumer goods, such as cars, furniture, washing machines, television sets, refrigerators and cookers, has been greatly helped by instalment credit facilities including hire purchase. Total new credit extended by finance houses and retailers in Great Britain in 1977 amounted to £4,392 million, 22 per cent more than in 1976; about 53 per cent was advanced by retailers and the rest by finance companies.

Hire-purchase in Northern Ireland directly financed by the major finance houses operating in Northern Ireland amounted in 1977 to £78·9 million.

Credit Cards

The credit card is widely used in Britain. The cards enable users to have their signatures accepted on bills in participating shops, hotels and restaurants. The issuers, which include banks, then meet the bills and recover the money from the card-holder through a single account presented periodically.

SERVICE TRADES

About 2·3 million people in Great Britain were employed in trades offering a service directly to the public in 1977.

Catering

There were over 130,000 establishments concerned with catering (defined to include public houses, canteens and fish and chip shops, as well as licensed hotels and restaurants) in Britain in 1969. There were 203 catering contractor organisations and over 18,000 industrial and office canteens.

The value of total turnover of all caterers in 1977 was £6,510 million while that of licensed hotels and holiday camps was £1,260 million and that of public houses £3,520 million.

Laundries and Dry Cleaning

In 1971 there were over 8,400 laundry, launderette, dry cleaning and towel, linen and overalls hiring organisations. Turnover in 1971 amounted to some £212 million.

Motor Trades

There were 46,000 businesses in the motor trades in Britain in 1972 with 55,000 establishments and a total turnover of £8,100 million. These trades include motor repairers, distributors, garages and petrol stations. Sales of new vehicles accounted for some 36 per cent of the 1977 total of some £17,200 million and sales of second-hand vehicles for 16 per cent. Sales of accessories, receipts from sales and servicing and sales of petrol and oil accounted for the remaining 48 per cent.

Hairdressing

The 1971 census recorded some 47,200 hairdressing establishments with a total turnover of £166 million. About two-thirds of the number are ladies' hairdressers.

Shoe Repairs

In 1971 there were some 5,500 boot and shoe repair establishments; total takings amounted to £22·4 million.

Presentation of Goods

In Britain the expansion of self-service shops, the spread of branded and standardised products, and developments in partly prepared foods, for example, ready-washed vegetables and ready-made cake mixes, have all been major factors in the changes which have taken place in packaging methods. Packaging products of paper and board remain the most extensively used (turnover of some £900 million in 1976). Other important materials are tinplate, plastics and glass. New uses have been found for tinplate, especially in the canning of soft drinks and beer. The use of plastics continues to develop, particularly poly ethylene film and film products and low-density polyethylene bottles used as an alternative to the traditional glass bottle.

Advertising

Some £1,499 million was spent on all forms of advertising in 1977, as a proportion of the gross national product (1·22 per cent) and of consumer expenditure (1·8 per cent), about the same as in 1956. Of this figure £1,02 million was spent on display advertising and £481 million on classified financial and industrial advertising. Most of the advertising is planned by agencies, which, in some cases, also provide marketing, consumer research and other services; their representative organisation is the Institute of Practitioners in Advertising. The trade association for the whole industry, including agencies advertisers and media owners, is the Advertising Association. It was responsible for the setting up of the Advertising Standards Authority, an independent body whose objective is the promotion and enforcement of the highest standards of advertising, in particular through the British Code of Advertising Practice.

Public Relations

Industry and commerce pay great attention to improving public understanding of their work and objectives. Many have their own public relations advisers and staff, while consultancy firms provide general services and assistance for special public relations activities. The Institute of Public Relations, founded in 1948 is the largest professional public relations organisation in Europe, with some 2,500 members in commerce, industry, public relations consultancies, national associations, and central and local government.

13 Energy and Natural Resources

Much of Britain's energy requirement is supplied from domestic fuel minerals (coal, oil and natural gas), and minerals in general make an important contribution to the economy. The approximate value of minerals produced in 1976 was £3,921 million, of which coal contributed 59 per cent, crude oil 15 per cent and natural gas 6 per cent. The discovery and exploitation of oilfields and gasfields under the British sector of the North Sea are increasing the importance of domestically produced fuel minerals to the economy very considerably. Over the past ten years the production of non-fuel minerals has also increased.

Water resources are normally sufficient for domestic and industrial requirements; supplies are obtained from surface sources such as mountain lakes and from underground sources by such means as wells and boreholes.

Ownership of Mineral Rights

Apart from gold, silver, oil, natural gas (which are owned by the Crown), coal, and some minerals associated with coal, all minerals in Great Britain are privately owned. On the United Kingdom Continental Shelf the right to exploit all minerals except coal is vested in the Crown. The exclusive right to extract coal, or license others to do so, both on land and under the sea, is vested in the National Coal Board. Normally, ownership of minerals runs with the ownership of the land surface but in some areas, particularly where mining has taken place, these rights have become separated. Mining and quarrying, apart from coal, are usually carried out by privately owned companies.

ENERGY

Four main primary sources of energy—petroleum, coal, natural gas and nuclear power—are used in Britain, together with some water power; secondary sources produced from these are electricity, coke and very small quantities of town gas. Inland consumption of energy amounted to 338·4 million tonnes of coal equivalent in 1977, 2·6 per cent higher than in 1976. About three-quarters of all primary energy consumed comes from indigenous sources and the proportion is increasing as growing supplies of oil and gas are obtained from the British sector of the North Sea. These are of major importance as they will enable Britain to become self-sufficient in energy for a number of years from 1980 onwards and will benefit the balance of payments through substantial import savings. The share of natural gas in total consumption has increased substantially, supplies from the North Sea discoveries having expanded rapidly since the first quantities were piped ashore in 1967. Reserves of coal, Britain's richest natural resource, are sufficient to enable production to continue for about 300 years at current rates of extraction. Although coal has accounted for a declining proportion of energy consumption, a major capital investment programme is in progress to end the contraction of the industry. A nuclear power programme has been in progress since 1955 and nuclear power provides a significant share of electricity supplies.

The fuel and power industries, with the exception of most of the petroleum industry and part of that concerned with the extraction of natural gas, are under public ownership. The publicly owned fuel and power industries in Britain employ in total some 600,000 people, 2·3 per cent of the working

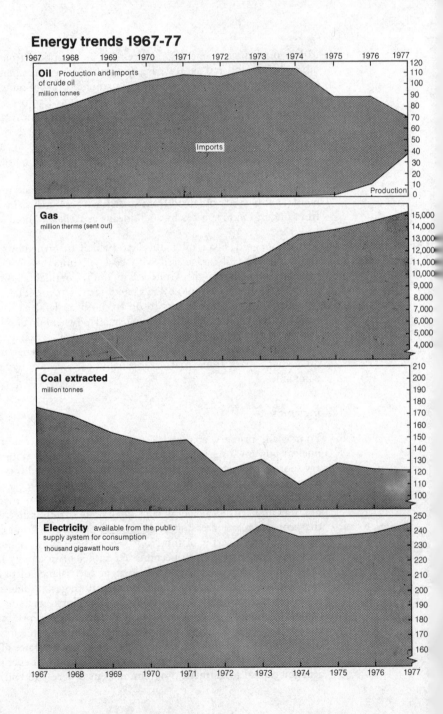

Energy trends 1967-77

Oil Production and imports of crude oil
million tonnes

Imports

Production

Gas
million therms (sent out)

Coal extracted
million tonnes

Electricity available from the public supply system for consumption
thousand gigawatt hours

population, and their annual turnover is about £10,800 million and capital investment about £1,500 million. In Great Britain the Secretary of State for Energy is responsible for these industries, except for electricity in Scotland which is the responsibility of the Secretary of State for Scotland.

The Government wishes to ensure the best use of indigenous resources. It is continuing to develop an integrated approach to energy policy and in February 1978 put forward in a consultative document proposals for developing a long-term energy policy by means of a flexible strategy based on the creation of further capacity in the coal industry, a capability for a quick expansion of nuclear power in the late 1980s and 1990s if this proves economically desirable and publicly acceptable, the avoidance of too rapid a decline in offshore oil and gas production, research and development into alternative sources of energy, and exploitation of the opportunities for energy conservation. The strategy is to be kept under regular review by the Energy Commission, a body set up in 1977 to advise on major issues of energy policy and consisting of representatives of management and employees in the main energy industries and of consumers, industry and other interests.

Britain, which has the richest energy resources of any member State of the European Community, is co-operating fully in the development of the Community's energy policy, a basic objective of which is to reduce dependence on imported energy supplies. Britain is one of the 19 members of the International Energy Agency, an organisation attached to the Organisation for Economic Co-operation and Development, which is engaged on a programme of international co-operation to deal with world energy problems.

ENERGY CONSUMPTION

Trends in primary energy consumption are shown in Table 14 and in the diagram on p 242. In 1977 petroleum accounted for 40·4 per cent of primary consumption, coal 36·3 per cent, natural gas 18·5 per cent, nuclear power 4·2 per cent and hydro-electric power 0·6 per cent. Energy consumption by final users in 1977 amounted to 58,532 million therms[1] on a 'heat supplied' basis. Industrial users consumed about 39 per cent, domestic users 26 per cent, transport 22 per cent, public services 6 per cent and agriculture 1 per cent.

TABLE 14. Inland Energy Consumption (in terms of primary sources)

million tonnes coal equivalent

	1967	1972	1975	1976	1977
Oil	122·6	162·2	136·5	134·2	136·6
Coal	165·8	122·4	120·0	122·0	122·7
Natural gas	2·1	40·9	55·4	58·8	62·8
Nuclear energy	9·0	10·6	10·9	12·9	14·3
Hydro-electric power	2·7	1·9	2·0	1·9	2·0
Total	302·2	338·0	324·8	329·8	338·4

Source: *Department of Energy*

ENERGY CONSERVATION

Although Britain has sufficient supplies of oil and gas for a number of years, worldwide difficulties of energy supply are expected from about the 1990s onwards. Accordingly, energy conservation is an integral part of Britain's energy policy, as in many other countries. The role of the Government is to set a good example in its use of energy, and to guide and stimulate consumers to use energy more efficiently. Britain's continuing energy conservation programme

[1] 1 therm = 105,506 kilojoules.

involves a combination of advisory, financial and mandatory measures aimed at all energy-using sectors. The development of the programme is overseen by a Committee of Ministers on Energy Conservation, while the Secretary of State for Energy is also advised by an independent Advisory Council on Energy Conservation. Studies on energy conservation and alternative sources of energy are undertaken by a number of organisations, notably the Energy Technology Support Unit of the Department of Energy at Harwell (Oxfordshire).

Conservation Measures

In the last four years the Government has introduced a wide range of measures designed to encourage energy saving including an 11-point programme in December 1977. In April 1978 it announced further help for industry and a scheme of grants to private householders for basic insulation. Conservation measures contributed to energy savings estimated at around £2,000 million in the four years to the end of 1977.

Many firms have achieved significant economies through measures such as better use of heating and lighting, improved operational and maintenance techniques, and the installation of draught-proofing and additional insulation.

The Government has encouraged firms to appoint energy managers (of whom there are some 3,000) to draw up and administer energy conservation measures in factories and offices. Several schemes are in operation to assist industry and commerce. Standards of thermal insulation required in new dwellings have been virtually doubled and many householders and organisations have improved thermal insulation in existing properties. In 1977 a ten-year programme was initiated to bring public sector housing up to a basic minimum standard of insulation; over 2 million dwellings will be treated. Other conservation measures have included compulsory limits on heating levels in commercial and industrial buildings; publication of official fuel consumption figures for new cars, so that potential purchasers can assess the petrol usage of different models; and a major government publicity campaign to promote the efficient use of energy.

OFFSHORE OIL AND GAS

Substantial oil and gas reserves have been discovered in the United Kingdom Continental Shelf under the North Sea and their total value is estimated at about £300,000 million. It is one of the world's most attractive offshore areas for oil and gas, the average success rate for exploration drilling comparing very favourably with other offshore areas. Seismic prospecting began in the early 1960s and full-scale exploration activities in 1964. Five rounds of production licensing have been held and a sixth round is planned. The Government's policy is to license small areas of territory at frequent intervals to maintain activity at a constant level. The total area covered by production licences is some 60,000 square kilometres (23,200 square miles) out of a total designated area of about 624,600 square kilometres (241,200 square miles), over which Britain has exercised its rights to explore and exploit the seabed and subsoil.

Work on the development and production of Britain's offshore oil and gas is proceeding rapidly. By the end of July 1978, 781 exploration or appraisal wells and 448 production wells had been drilled or begun; of these 105 and 96 respectively were drilled in 1977.

Large-scale investment is taking place in offshore exploration and development, estimated at £2,000 million in 1977. A further £6,000 million is expected to be invested in the three years 1978 to 1980.

Offshore Supplies

The Department of Energy's Offshore Supplies Office seeks to ensure that British industry can compete effectively for orders for offshore equipment

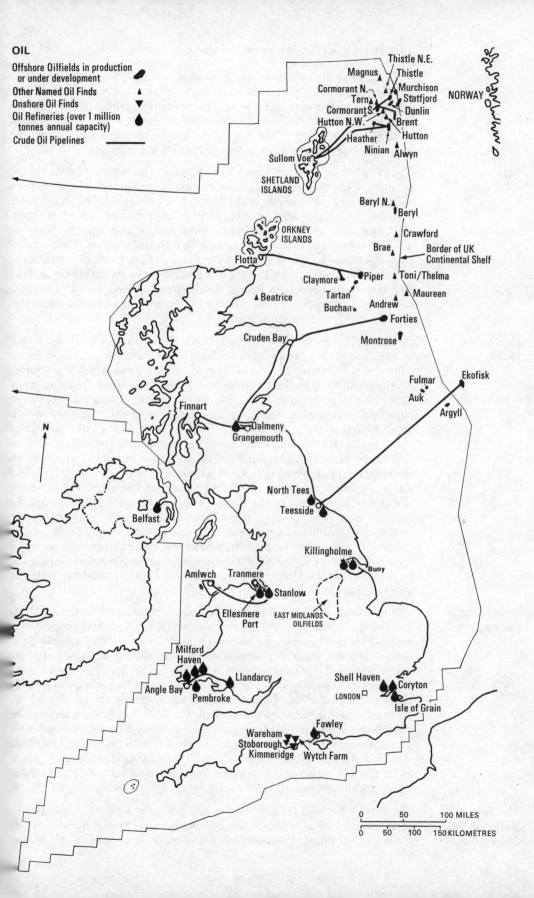

OIL

Offshore Oilfields in production or under development

Other Named Oil Finds

Onshore Oil Finds

Oil Refineries (over 1 million tonnes annual capacity)

Crude Oil Pipelines

NORWAY

Thistle N.E.
Magnus
Thistle
Cormorant N.
Murchison
Tern
Statfjord
Cormorant S.
Dunlin
Hutton N.W.
Brent
Heather
Hutton
Ninian
Sullom Voe
Alwyn

SHETLAND ISLANDS

Beryl N.
Beryl

Crawford

ORKNEY ISLANDS

Brae
Border of UK Continental Shelf

Flotta
Claymore
Piper
Toni/Thelma
Tartan
Maureen
Beatrice
Buchan
Andrew
Cruden Bay
Forties
Montrose

Finnart
Fulmar
Ekofisk
Auk
Dalmeny
Argyll
Grangemouth

North Tees
Teesside

Belfast

Killingholme
Buoy

Amlwch
Tranmere
Stanlow
Ellesmere Port
EAST MIDLANDS OILFIELDS

Milford Haven
Llandarcy
Shell Haven
Coryton
Angle Bay
LONDON
Pembroke
Isle of Grain

Fawley
Wareham
Stoborough
Kimmeridge
Wytch Farm

N

0   50   100 MILES

0   50   100   150 KILOMETRES

by helping firms to identify the needs of offshore operators, assisting operators to identify British suppliers of offshore equipment and services, and promoting new ventures to increase British involvement in the industry. British companies increased their share of the offshore market, worth £1,295 million in 1977, from between 25 and 30 per cent in 1973 to 62 per cent in 1977 and are increasingly involved in supplying other offshore markets.

OIL

The petroleum industry in Britain dates back to 1850, when Dr James Young, a Glasgow chemist, succeeded in obtaining lamp oil and lubricants from natural mineral oil occurring in the Derbyshire coalfields. The Scottish shale deposits, yielding similar products, were worked between 1858 and 1962. With the rapid growth of oil consumption during this century, however, Britain became almost totally dependent on imported supplies. The first discovery of oil in the British sector of the North Sea was made in 1969 and the first oil was brought ashore in 1975. Production has increased rapidly and the first large-scale benefits to Britain, in the form of exports and of imports saved, are being realised. (For estimates of the growing economic benefits of North Sea oil revenues see p 194.)

North Sea Fields

By mid-1978, nine fields in the British sector were producing oil: Brent and Forties, two of the largest offshore oilfields in the world; Argyll; Auk; Beryl; Claymore; Montrose; Piper and Thistle. A further nine fields are under development, while more than 40 further significant finds that have been made may prove to be commercial after further appraisal. Production from most large fields is controlled from production platforms of either steel or concrete which have been built to withstand severe weather including gusts of wind of up to 257 km/h (160 mph) and waves of 30 metres (100 feet).

Offshore oil production from the British sector amounted to nearly 38 million tonnes in 1977, more than three times the level of output in 1976, and was equivalent to nearly half of Britain's primary oil consumption. Production is expected to continue to rise rapidly, reaching between 55 million and 60 million tonnes in 1978, about 100 million tonnes by 1980, and between 100 million and 150 million tonnes a year in the early 1980s, placing Britain among the world's ten leading oil producing countries. Proven reserves of oil in the United Kingdom Continental Shelf amount to 1,405 million tonnes while the total reserves of the United Kingdom Continental Shelf could be as high as 4,500 million tonnes.

Government Policy

The Petroleum and Submarine Pipe-lines Act 1975 provided for the establishment of the British National Oil Corporation (BNOC); tighter controls over exploration, development, installation of pipelines and refining capacity; and control over the rate of depletion to ensure that offshore oil is used at a rate which secures the greatest long-term benefit for Britain. The Government considers that majority State participation in licences for commercial oilfields provides the best means for the nation to share fully in the benefits of offshore oil. Majority participation through the BNOC in existing commercial oilfields has been achieved by negotiations with the licensees; by mid-1978 participation agreements had been concluded with 62 companies. The BNOC or the British Gas Corporation has a majority share in licences awarded under the fifth round of offshore petroleum production licensing and similar arrangements are planned for the sixth round.

The British National Oil Corporation

The British National Oil Corporation was set up as a public corporation in 1976 when it took over the British offshore interests previously held by the National Coal Board. It subsequently acquired a majority of the North Sea interests held by the Burmah Oil Company. The Corporation also holds the Government's participation interest in production licences. It has powers to explore for, produce, transport and refine petroleum; store, distribute and buy and sell petroleum; and provide advisory services and carry out research and training. Other activities, which can be undertaken only with the Government's consent, include overseas exploration and production. The Corporation has a share in the Thistle oilfield and the Viking gasfield, in four oilfields under development and in a number of other oil and gas finds. With its equity and participation interests, the BNOC will have access to substantial amounts of North Sea crude oil in the 1980s. The BNOC's board consists of between eight and 20 members including two civil servants.

Land-based Fields

Onshore production of crude oil in Britain is much less significant than off-shore production, amounting in 1977 to 99,000 tonnes. Twelve onshore fields are in operation, notably Beckingham, Bothamsall and Egmanton in Nottinghamshire, Gainsborough in Lincolnshire and Kimmeridge in Dorset. Britain's largest onshore field, at Wytch Farm (Dorset), should start full production early in 1979.

Consumption

Deliveries of petroleum products for inland consumption (excluding refinery consumption) in 1977 totalled 83·2 million tonnes including 27·8 million tonnes of fuel oil, 19·6 million tonnes of gas and diesel oil (including derv fuel used in road vehicles), 17·3 million tonnes of motor spirit and 6·8 million tonnes of kerosene. Deliveries for electricity generation accounted for 37 per cent of fuel oil deliveries in 1977. The largest industrial users of fuel oil are the steel, chemicals and paper-making industries.

Refineries

In 1978 gross refinery capacity in Britain amounted to 142·7 million tonnes a year. Of the 20 refineries in operation, 17 have a capacity of over 1 million tonnes and are shown on the map on p 245. Four have an annual capacity of over 10 million tonnes: Fawley, near Southampton (18·2 million tonnes); Stanlow, in Cheshire (17·6 million tonnes); one of the four in the area of Milford Haven, Dyfed (15·4 million tonnes); and Isle of Grain (10·5 million tonnes) on the Thames Estuary. Outline planning permission has been given for new refineries at Cliffe (Kent) and Nigg Bay (Highland), and for two projects at Canvey Island (Essex). In future new projects for the construction of refineries of over 1 million tons or the extension of existing refineries by more than 500,000 tons will require an authorisation from the Secretary of State for Energy under the Petroleum and Submarine Pipe-lines Act 1975.

Output of refined products (excluding refineries' own consumption) amounted to 86·3 million tonnes in 1977. In 1977 Britain's imports of crude and process oils were 70·2 million tonnes, valued at £4,094 million, 10·7 per cent less in value than in 1976. Saudi Arabia supplied approximately 25 per cent of crude oil by value, Iran 18 per cent, Kuwait 13 per cent and Iraq 8 per cent. Imports are expected to continue to decline, although heavy crude oil will still be imported for particular uses.

The British sector produces high quality premium oil, much of which has been refined in Britain, although substantial quantities have also gone overseas for refining. Exports have risen considerably and in 1977 were valued at £903 million of crude oil and £1,062 million of petroleum products. Most oil exports are sent to other countries in Western Europe.

Oil Pipelines

Five main crude oil pipelines are in operation in Britain from harbours or offshore moorings capable of berthing very large tankers to refineries (see map, p 245): from Finnart to Grangemouth; from Angle Bay, Milford Haven, to Llandarcy; from Tranmere to Stanlow; from Amlwch (Gwynedd) to Stanlow; and from a single buoy in the Humber estuary to Killingholme. About 700 miles (1,127 kilometres) of submarine pipeline have been built to bring ashore oil from the North Sea. Pipelines connect the Forties field to Cruden Bay (Grampian) and the refinery at Grangemouth, the Piper and Claymore fields to a terminal at Flotta (Orkney), the Ninian and Heather fields to a terminal at Sullom Voe (Shetland), the Brent and several neighbouring fields to Sullom Voe and the Norwegian Ekofisk field to Teesside.

Pipelines also carry refined products and petrochemical feedstocks to major marketing areas; for example, a 300-mile (480-kilometre) pipeline runs from Milford Haven to the Midlands and Manchester.

Research

Research into problems of petroleum technology is carried out mainly by the leading oil companies, which have also endowed research at the universities on a substantial scale. Research centres are situated at Sunbury-on-Thames (British Petroleum), Ellesmere Port in Cheshire, and Woodstock in Kent (Shell), and Abingdon, in Oxfordshire (Esso). Work in progress includes the evolution of new and improved fuels and lubricants, and the development of new uses for petroleum products and of new products based on petroleum, especially chemicals. The main Government research and development effort in offshore technology is undertaken by the Department of Energy with the advice of the Offshore Energy Technology Board (see p 377). In 1978–79 the Department of Energy expects to spend some £15 million in support of offshore technology.

GAS

Public supply of manufactured gas in Britain began in the early nineteenth century in Westminster in central London using gas produced from coal. Gas was originally used almost exclusively for lighting, but between the two world wars it was displaced from this function by electricity. It is now used for domestic cooking and heating and for many industrial and commercial purposes. During the 1960s there was a fairly rapid switch to producing town gas from oil-based feedstocks instead of coal. In 1965 the first commercial natural gas discovery in the British sector of the North Sea was made and production started in 1967. Natural gas has now replaced town gas as the source of gas for the public supply system in Great Britain.

Structure

The Gas Act 1948 brought the industry in Great Britain under public ownership and control in 1949. As a result of the change to natural gas necessitating more centralised control of production and transmission, the British Gas Corporation was set up in 1973 under the Gas Act 1972 to replace the Gas Council and 12 area gas boards. The Corporation's powers in connection with its main duty of developing and maintaining an efficient, co-ordinated and economical system of gas supply and of satisfying reasonable demands for gas are: to search for and extract natural gas and any oil discovered in the course of searching for gas; to manufacture or acquire, transmit and distribute gas; to manufacture, supply, or sell by-products; and to manufacture, install, maintain or remove gas plant and fittings. It has about 100,000 employees.

Natural gas is not available in Northern Ireland and the industry there, which is controlled by nine municipal undertakings and four private sector companies, uses town gas produced from oil feedstocks.

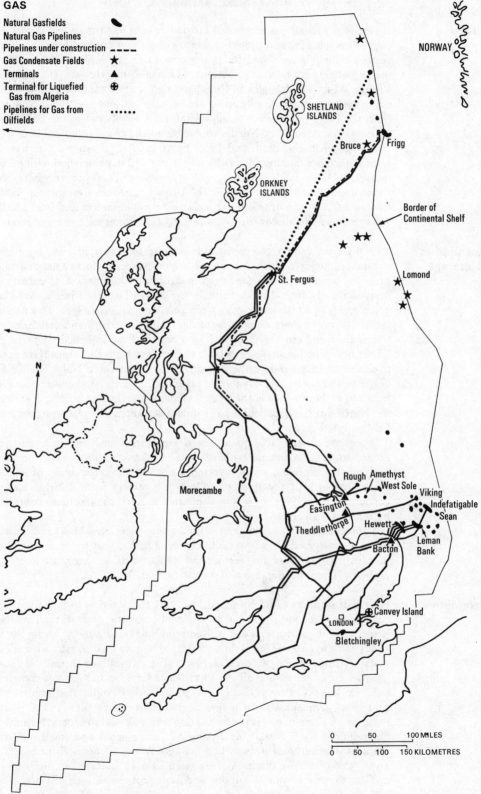

GAS

Natural Gasfields	◗
Natural Gas Pipelines	——
Pipelines under construction	– – –
Gas Condensate Fields	★
Terminals	▲
Terminal for Liquefied Gas from Algeria	⊕
Pipelines for Gas from Oilfields	····

NORWAY

SHETLAND ISLANDS

ORKNEY ISLANDS

Bruce ★   Frigg

Border of Continental Shelf

St. Fergus

★ ★★

★ Lomond
★

N

Rough   Amethyst
West Sole
Morecambe   Viking
Easington   Indefatigable
                            Sean
Theddlethorpe   Hewett
                     Leman
Bacton   Bank

⊕ Canvey Island

□ LONDON

Bletchingley

0   50   100 MILES
0   50   100   150 KILOMETRES

Production

Indigenous natural gas accounted for 96 per cent of primary gas demand in 1977. Between 1972 and 1977 the quantity of gas sent out by the public supply system in Britain increased by 44 per cent to 15,323 million therms. Seven major gasfields are now in production (Leman Bank, Hewett, Indefatigable, Viking, West Sole, Rough and Frigg) and their output totalled 40,166 million cubic metres in 1977. Gas supplies are expected to continue to rise as output from the Frigg field, which straddles the boundary between the British and Norwegian sectors of the North Sea, builds up and as gas produced in association with oil in the Brent and Piper fields is brought ashore. Gas has also been found in a number of smaller structures and in association with oil in a number of other fields; exploration is continuing. Total proven gas reserves remaining in known discoveries in the United Kingdom Continental Shelf at the end of 1977 amounted to 744,000 million cubic metres and total possible reserves in known discoveries amounted to 1·5 million million cubic metres.

Transmission and Storage

The pipeline system commissioned in 1964 for the delivery of liquefied natural gas imported from Algeria has been expanded to form a national high-pressure pipeline system (see map, p 249) for transmission of natural gas derived mainly from British fields in the North Sea. By March 1978 some 3,500 miles (5,633 kilometres) of pipeline were in operation. The national transmission system is supplied by feeder mains from the four North Sea shore terminals and from the Canvey Island terminal for liquefied Algerian gas. Three new pipelines have been built to carry gas from St Fergus (Grampian) to central Scotland and northern England. In the northern North Sea the first of the two 225-mile (362-kilometre) pipelines has been laid between the Frigg field and St Fergus, while the longest offshore pipeline in the British sector of the North Sea has been laid for 281 miles (452 kilometres) between the Brent field and St Fergus.

There are considerable quantities of gas in the North Sea in fields which are too small for economic exploitation. Gas Gathering Pipelines (North Sea) Ltd was therefore set up to investigate the economic feasibility of an integrated network of pipelines to collect gas, mainly from oilfields and gas condensate fields. Its final report, submitted in April 1978, is being considered by the Government.

Various methods of storage of natural gas to meet peak load conditions are being investigated. Storage facilities for liquefied natural gas have been installed at four sites and further facilities, including three salt cavities at Hornsea (Humberside), are under construction.

Consumption

Over half of all gas sold by the British Gas Corporation to its 14·5 million consumers is for industrial and commercial purposes, most of the remainder being for household use. Total consumption increased rapidly during the late 1960s and early 1970s, but is now growing at a more modest rate, with sales in Britain rising by 4·2 per cent in 1977 to 14,579 million therms. A phased programme of converting all gas appliances to use natural gas was completed in Great Britain in 1977. Gas is used particularly in industries requiring the control of temperatures to a fine degree of accuracy such as the pottery industry and certain processes for making iron and steel products. Natural gas not required by the fixed tariff domestic, commercial and small industrial markets is being used in bulk fuel markets and as a chemical feedstock. In 1977, 5,883 million therms of gas were sold to industry in Britain, 519 million therms to public supply and transport power stations and 1,587 million therms to commercial users. The domestic load includes gas for cookers, space heaters, water heaters and refrigerators, but an increasingly large part of domestic demand is for gas for central heating. In 1977, 6,590 million therms were sold to domestic users, 6·4 per cent more than in 1976.

Operations

In 1977–78 the turnover of the British Gas Corporation and its subsidiary companies amounted to £2,568 million, of which sales of gas accounted for £2,218 million. After interest payments there was a profit of £180·3 million. Capital investment amounted to £201 million. The borrowing limit for the Corporation has been fixed by the Gas Act 1972 at £2,500 million, to be raised by order if necessary up to £2,700 million.

Research

The British Gas Corporation conducts research at four research stations into all aspects of gas supply and use. Research is also done on behalf of the Corporation at a number of universities and colleges. The Corporation's total expenditure on research and development and on technical service and testing amounted to £23 million in 1977–78. The Corporation is undertaking various coal gasification projects at its Westfield Development Centre in Fife in collaboration with groups of North American sponsors.

COAL

Coalmining in Britain can be traced back to the thirteenth century. It played a crucial part in the industrial revolution of the early nineteenth century and in its peak year, 1913, the industry produced 287 million tons of coal, exported 94 million tons and employed over a million workers. In 1947 the coal mines passed into public ownership by means of the Coal Industry Nationalisation Act 1946, which set up the National Coal Board (NCB) as a statutory corporation to manage the industry.

The National Coal Board

The NCB has, with minor exceptions, exclusive rights over the extraction of coal in Great Britain, but is empowered to license private operators to work small mines and opencast sites. Under the Coal Industry Act 1977 the NCB has been given powers to work other minerals, where discoveries are made in the course of searching for, or working, coal; and to engage in certain petrochemical activities beneficial to the future of the coal industry; and wider powers to undertake overseas activities, subject to the consent of the Secretary of State for Energy. It has no monopoly in coal distribution and retail sales remain largely in private hands, although it makes bulk sales to large industrial consumers. Two holding companies, wholly owned by the NCB, run most of its non-mining activities. NCB (Ancillaries) Ltd's responsibilities include certain retail fuel distribution operations, computer services and engineering. NCB (Coal Products) Ltd is responsible for solid smokeless fuel manufacture and chemical and by-products plants.

At the end of March 1978 there were 231 NCB collieries in operation grouped into 12 areas, each controlled by a director responsible to the NCB. The main coal-bearing areas are shown on the map on p 253 and the main trends in the coal industry are shown in Table 15.

Consumption

Coal accounted for 90 per cent of primary energy consumption in 1950, but growing competition from oil and gas and the elimination of steam trains on the railways contributed to the fall in demand from the mid-1950s. In 1977–78 internal consumption of coal was 119·7 million tons, of which 65 per cent went to power stations, 14 per cent to coke ovens, 9 per cent to domestic users, 7 per cent to industry and 5 per cent to other inland markets.

Exports of coal in 1977–78 were 1·8 million tons, almost all of which went to Western European countries, while imports amounted to 2·6 million tons.

Production and Productivity

In 1977–78 output of 119 million tons comprised 104·6 million tons from the NCB's deep mines, 13·3 million tons from opencast mines and 1·1 million tons from licensed mines and other sources. Productivity in the NCB's deep mines doubled between 1947 and 1972–73, but thereafter began to decline. However, the upward trend was resumed in 1977–78 following the introduction of a productivity incentive scheme, and output per manshift at the coalface for the year averaged a record 155·7 cwt (7·9 tonnes).

Advances in mining technology are concentrated on the introduction of computerised automatic monitoring and remote control of machines, together with the installation of heavy-duty equipment capable of sustained high performance with minimum maintenance.

TABLE 15: Coal Statistics

	Unit	1967–68	1975–76	1976–77	1977–78
Output	million tons	170·9	123·8	118·9	119·0
of which, opencast	,,	6·7	10·2	11·2	13·3
Consumption	,,	167·5	121·7	124·1	121·5
of which, export	,,	2·0	1·4	1·4	1·8
Average labour force[a]	'000	391·9	247·1	242·0	240·5
Output per man-shift[a]					
at coalface	cwt	119·2	155·4	152·5	155·7
overall	,,	39·0	44·8	43·6	43·1
Collieries in operation[a]	number	376	241	238	231

Source: *National Coal Board*

[a] NCB mines only.

Financial Structure

In 1977–78 the NCB's income was £2,904 million including sales of coal of £2,334 million and grants under the Coal Industry Acts of £75 million. The trading profit was £108·7 million; after interest payments and other items there was a net surplus of £20·4 million. Government assistance to the industry took the form of grants towards the social costs of mine closures, contributions towards the mineworkers' pension scheme, aid towards the cost of stocking coal and coke, and assistance to promote the sale of coal for electricity generation in south Scotland and south Wales. The NCB's borrowing limit is £1,800 million, with provision for further increases up to £2,600 million, subject to parliamentary approval.

Capital Investment

Capital expenditure on collieries amounted to £334 million in 1977–78. In 1974 the Government, the NCB and the coalmining trade unions carried out a tripartite study of the policy towards the coal industry. As a result the Government accepted the Board's Plan for Coal as a general strategy for the following ten years, involving maintenance of deep-mined capacity at the annual level of around 120 million tons and an increase in opencast production to 15 million tons a year. The total cost of the plan is £3,710 million at March 1977 prices including £1,770 million on major projects up to the late 1980s which will generate new deep-mined capacity of 42 million tons a year to replace that lost by exhaustion of old collieries. Since 1974 the NCB has approved over 125 major projects designed to provide about three-quarters of this new capacity at an estimated cost of about £1,000 million including some £500 million for a mining complex at Selby (North Yorkshire) which

COAL

Coalfields

0 20 40 60 80 100 MILES

0 20 40 60 80 100 120 KILOMETRES

N

Glasgow · Edinburgh

Newcastle upon Tyne

Carlisle · Durham

Workington

Selby

Leeds

Doncaster

Liverpool

Manchester · Sheffield

Nottingham

Birmingham

Swansea

Cardiff · Bristol

London ●

Dover

should be producing 10 million tons of coal a year in the late 1980s. Over 30 projects have been completed and new coal mines have been opened at Royston (South Yorkshire) and at Betws (Dyfed).

Although many good seams of coal have now been worked out due to the early development of the industry, total coal reserves in Britain are estimated at 190,000 million tons, of which about 45,000 million tons (sufficient for at least 300 years at present rates of consumption) are recoverable using existing mining technology. The NCB's national exploration programme is proving fresh reserves of economically workable coal at the rate of 500 million tons a year, four times the annual consumption of coal. Major new finds have been located in the North-east Leicestershire coalfield (with recoverable reserves of over 500 million tons), Park (Staffordshire), west of Coventry, under the Firth of Forth off Musselburgh (Lothian), at Margam (West Glamorgan), and in north Oxfordshire.

Research

The NCB has two main research organisations: the Coal Research Establishment, at Stoke Orchard (Gloucestershire), concerned with the combustion and utilisation of coal; and the Mining Research and Development Establishment at Stanhope Bretby (Staffordshire), for research on mining methods and equipment, including underground transport and coal preparation.

In 1977–78 the NCB spent £27 million on research. Following the report in May 1978 of a tripartite group on coal technology, comprising representatives of the Government, the NCB and mining trade unions, the Government is to provide financial support of up to two-thirds of the cost for three new research and development projects designed to convert coal to liquid fuels (including petrol), to produce chemical feedstocks from coal, and, in a project which will be undertaken by the British Gas Corporation, to produce substitute natural gas from coal.

Agreements to exchange technical information have been signed by the NCB with several countries. Britain is responsible through an NCB subsidiary—NCB (IEA Services) Ltd—for managing a programme of international coal research projects on behalf of the International Energy Agency. A programme of five collaborative coal research projects, including a £17 million project to develop pressurised fluidised bed combustion (a method of steam-raising for power generation, which, compared with conventional techniques, uses low-quality coals efficiently and in an environmentally clean way), is being based in Britain.

ELECTRICITY

The first public supply of electricity in Britain was in 1881, at Godalming (Surrey). A measure of public control has always been a feature of the industry and in 1948 all municipal and private undertakings in Great Britain were acquired under the Electricity Act 1947 and vested in the British Electricity Authority and 14 regional boards, except in the north of Scotland where they became the responsibility of the North of Scotland Hydro-Electric Board (NSHEB), which had been set up in 1943. Two subsequent Acts (1954 and 1957) effected a measure of decentralisation and gave the industry its present structure. Electricity supply employs about 183,000 people, including 6,600 in Northern Ireland.

Present Structure

In England and Wales electricity is generated and transmitted by the Central Electricity Generating Board (CEGB), which is responsible for the operation and maintenance of power stations and the main transmission system (national grid), and it is distributed by 12 separate area electricity boards. Co-ordination

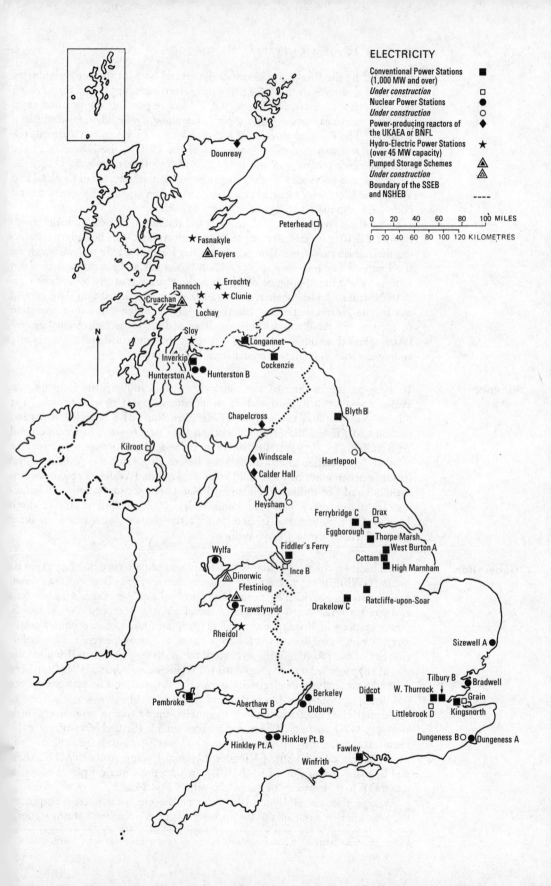

ELECTRICITY

Conventional Power Stations
(1,000 MW and over)   ■
Under construction   □
Nuclear Power Stations   ●
Under construction   ○
Power-producing reactors of   ◆
the UKAEA or BNFL
Hydro-Electric Power Stations   ★
(over 45 MW capacity)
Pumped Storage Schemes   △
Under construction   △
Boundary of the SSEB   ----
and NSHEB

0   20   40   60   80   100 MILES
0 20 40 60 80 100 120 KILOMETRES

Dounreay

Peterhead

★ Fasnakyle
△ Foyers

Rannoch ★ ★ Errochty
Cruachan △ ★ Clunie
Lochay

N

Sloy ★
Inverkip ■
Hunterston A ● ● Hunterston B

Longannet ■
Cockenzie ■

Chapelcross ◆   Blyth B ■

Kilroot □   Windscale ◆   Hartlepool ○
                       Calder Hall ◆

                       Heysham ○

                       Ferrybridge C □   Drax □
                       Eggborough ■   Thorpe Marsh ■
Wylfa ●   Fiddler's Ferry ■   West Burton A ■
△ Dinorwic   Ince B ■   Cottam ■
Ffestiniog   High Marnham ■
● Trawsfynydd   Drakelow C ■   Ratcliffe-upon-Soar ■

Rheidol ★
                                                Sizewell A ●

                              Tilbury B ■   Bradwell ■
Pembroke ■   Berkeley ●   Didcot ■   W. Thurrock ↓ Grain □
Aberthaw B □   Oldbury ●   Littlebrook D   Kingsnorth ■

Hinkley Pt. A ● ● Hinkley Pt. B   Dungeness B ○ Dungeness A ●
                       Fawley ■
                  Winfrith ◆

is effected by the Electricity Council, the central body of the supply industry with a general responsibility for promoting electricity supply and for advising the Secretary of State for Energy; it is also responsible for a number of common services, principally capital financing, research and industrial relations. The Council consists of a chairman and two deputy chairmen, the chairman and two designated members of the CEGB, the chairmen of the area electricity boards and not more than three other members. Under the Government's proposals for the reorganisation of the industry in England and Wales, the Electricity Council and boards would be replaced by a new central body with responsibility for the industry as a whole.

In Scotland two boards, the NSHEB and the South of Scotland Electricity Board (SSEB), generate, distribute and sell electricity. The boundary separating their areas runs from Dumbarton on the Firth of Clyde to Newburgh on the Firth of Tay (see map, p 255). Each board has a chairman and between four and eight members, one of whom is the chairman of the other board.

In Northern Ireland generation, transmission and distribution are carried out by the Northern Ireland Electricity Service which came into operation in 1973 as the result of the amalgamation of four former electricity undertakings. Power stations are located in Belfast, Ballylumford and Coolkeeragh, and a new station is under construction in Kilroot.

Finance

In 1977–78 the income of the electricity supply industry in England and Wales was £4,779 million and its profit after interest payments was £133 million. In Scotland the income of the SSEB and the NSHEB was £408 million and £146 million respectively and their profits were £5·6 million and £1·8 million. In 1976–77 the Northern Ireland Electricity Service's income totalled £133 million and it made a net loss of £19·8 million. Annual capital investment amounts to £671 million in England and Wales, £106 million in Scotland and £66 million in Northern Ireland. The statutory limit to borrowings by the industry in England and Wales is £6,500 million, in Northern Ireland £650 million and in Scotland £1,500 million, with provision for a further increase up to £1,950 million.

Generation

Generation for the public supply in Britain reached a record 262,045 gigawatt hours (GWh)[1] in 1977, 2·8 per cent more than in 1976. Conventional steam power stations provided 84 per cent of the total, nuclear stations 14 per cent and gas turbine, hydro-electric and diesel plant 2 per cent. Public supply power stations in Britain consumed 114 million tonnes of coal equivalent in 1977 of which coal accounted for 70 per cent and oil 16 per cent. The output capacity of the 229 generating stations of the electricity boards in Britain at the end of 1977 totalled 67,276 megawatts (MW) including 1,908 MW in Northern Ireland. An analysis of electricity generation by and output capacity of the public supply system in Great Britain is given in Table 16.

Generation of electricity outside the public supply system is relatively small —21,157 GWh in 1977. The major sources outside the fuel industries are the chemical, engineering, paper, and iron and steel industries and the nuclear power plants of the United Kingdom Atomic Energy Authority (UKAEA) and British Nuclear Fuels Ltd (BNFL). In 1977 these nuclear plants supplied 3,096 GWh of electricity to the public supply system.

Average thermal efficiency (the ratio of the electrical energy output to the heat energy input of the fuel consumed) of conventional steam stations

---

[1] One gigawatt hour = 1,000 megawatt hours = one million kilowatt hours.

in England and Wales rose from 20·75 per cent in 1947 to 31·51 per cent in 1977–78 as new plant was brought into use. The 20 most efficient stations, containing much of the newest plant, had an average thermal efficiency of 33·9 per cent in 1977–78.

TABLE 16: Electricity Generation by the Public Supply System in Great Britain 1977

	Output capacity (end year)	Electricity supplied (net)
	MW	GWh
Electricity Authorities:		
CEGB (including area boards)	56,351	210,741
SSEB	6,930	23,497
NSHEB	2,087	3,103
Method of Generation:		
Steam and oil engines	57,892	202,769
Hydro plant	1,284	3,320
Pumped storage	1,060	−312ᵃ
Nuclear plant	5,132	31,564
Total	65,368	237,341

Source: *Department of Energy*

ᵃ The difference between units supplied (1,296 GWh) and units used in pumping (1,608 GWh).

Advances have been made in the design of steam-generating plant with the introduction of 500 MW and 660 MW single-shaft generating units. Some 46 units of 500 MW have been installed in 13 stations and 11 units of 660 MW have also been installed. Station capacities have increased and there are 11 stations each with a capacity of 2,000 MW including Kingsnorth (Kent), Europe's largest mixed-fuel station burning either coal or oil, while Britain's largest power station is at Longannet (Fife), a 2,400 MW station with four cross-compound units. About 15,000 MW of plant are under construction in 12 power stations including a 3,300 MW oil-fired station at Grain (Kent), which will be the largest in Europe, a 2,000 MW coal-fired extension to the Drax station (North Yorkshire), a 1,320 MW station at Peterhead (Grampian), which will be able to burn natural gas as well as oil, and three nuclear power stations (see p 258).

Large gas turbine units of 55 to 70 MW, based on aero jet engines, have been introduced since 1965 for peak load operation, while others of 17 to 35 MW capacity are being used in new stations to safeguard auxiliary supplies to the large new steam units and also to provide capacity for peak operation. Two 51 MW prototype units at Leicester are powered by industrial gas turbines. Britain's first new power station since 1959 designed to sell waste heat from electricity generation to neighbouring firms is to be built at Hereford. It will be a 15 MW station with diesel generators and thermal efficiency is expected to be around 76 per cent.

Nuclear Power Britain has been implementing a substantial nuclear power programme since the mid-1950s, the primary purpose being to produce an additional energy source for the generation of electricity. In 1956 the world's first large-scale nuclear power station, at Calder Hall (Cumbria), began to supply electricity to the national grid.

Power Stations

There are 11 nuclear power stations in operation controlled by the electricity authorities, while a further five stations are controlled by the United Kingdom Atomic Energy Authority (see p 377) or British Nuclear Fuels Ltd. The UKAEA has three experimental or prototype stations which feed electricity into the national grid: the Advanced Gas-cooled Reactor (AGR) at Windscale, Cumbria (32 MW); the Steam Generating Heavy Water Reactor at Winfrith, Dorset (100 MW); and the Prototype Fast Reactor (PFR) at Dounreay, Highland (250 MW). BNFL operates the two original Magnox stations, both of 198 MW, at Calder Hall and Chapelcross (Dumfries and Galloway).

Nuclear Power Programme

Under the first commercial programme, nine Magnox stations with a total design capacity of 4,800 MW were commissioned between 1962 and 1971. They range in size from Berkeley (Gloucestershire) with a design capacity of 276 MW to the most recent, Wylfa (Gwynedd), which has a design capacity of 1,180 MW. Two 1,320 MW AGR stations at Hinkley Point B (Somerset) and Hunterston B (Strathclyde) began operating in 1976 and the three other stations being built under this second programme (Dungeness B, Kent, 1,200 MW; Hartlepool, Cleveland, 1,320 MW; and Heysham, Lancashire, 1,320 MW) should be commissioned by about 1981. Commercial nuclear power stations, which have lower operating costs than conventional stations, generated 36,420 GWh in 1977, about 14 per cent of public supply electricity production in Britain. As a result of a government review of future policy on thermal reactors, two further AGRs are to be built, at Heysham and Torness (Lothian) and the Government has endorsed the electricity industry's intention to develop the option of proceeding with a pressurised water reactor system in the early 1980s. The Government is considering its policy on fast reactor development including whether or not to proceed with a full-scale demonstration fast reactor, which would use as fuel a mixture of plutonium and uranium dioxides in stainless steel cans and be capable of releasing some 60 times as much energy from uranium feedstock as present nuclear power stations. Any decision to proceed would be subject to a wide-ranging public inquiry.

British Nuclear Fuels Ltd

BNFL provides nuclear fuel services covering the design and development of plant, procurement and processing of uranium, uranium enrichment, fuel element fabrication, transport and reprocessing of spent fuel, and the manufacture of specialised components and preparation of radioactive materials. All of BNFL's shares are held by the UKAEA. BNFL is organised into three divisions covering uranium enrichment, based at Capenhurst (Cheshire) where a £50 million plant using the gas centrifuge process was opened in September 1977; fuel manufacture at Springfields (Lancashire); and reprocessing at Windscale (Cumbria) where uranium, plutonium and radioactive wastes are separated from irradiated fuel. It is engaged on a ten-year investment programme, costing about £1,500 million. This includes the refurbishing of facilities for storing and reprocessing spent fuel from Magnox power stations, the manufacture of centrifuge enrichment plant, a new thermal oxide reprocessing plant (THORP) at Windscale which will deal with spent fuel from Britain's AGRs and will also reprocess spent fuel for a number of overseas electricity authorities, and a demonstration plant for vitrifying radioactive waste (see p 171).

Hydro-electric Power

Hydro-electric generation is confined almost entirely to Scotland and Wales. Most of the water-power so utilised is drawn from high-level reservoirs with their own natural catchment areas. In 1977–78, 2,880 GWh were sent out by the NSHEB from 54 main and 25 small conventional hydro-electric station with a total installed capacity of 1,052 MW; the largest station, Sloy, has a capacity of 130 MW. The NSHEB also operates pumped-storage schemes at Cruachan, Strathclyde (400 MW), and Foyers, Highland (300 MW). (In pumped-storage schemes electricity generated in off-peak periods is used to pump water to high-level reservoirs from which it descends to drive turbines, rapidly providing a large supply of electricity at peak periods or to meet sudden increases in demand.) Work is in progress on the construction of a pumped-storage station at Dinorwic (Gwynedd), which will be the largest of its type in the world when completed in 1983 and will have an average generated output of 1,681 MW.

Transmission and Distribution

The British system is the largest fully interconnected power network under unified control in the western world. By 31st March 1978 the main transmission lines of the CEGB totalled 13,958 circuit kilometres, of which 11,555 circuit kilometres were at 400,000 volts and the remainder at 275,000 volts. Primary distribution in England and Wales is at 132,000 volts, secondary distribution at 33,000 volts, tertiary at 11,000 volts or below and general low voltage distribution at 240 volts single phase. In Scotland there were 8,406 circuit kilometres of main transmission lines at the end of March 1978, of which 340 kilometres operated at 400,000 volts, 3,025 circuit kilometres at 275,000 volts and the remainder at 132,000 volts. Primary distribution in Scotland is at 33,000 volts. The national grid in England and Wales is divided into seven grid control areas and the operations are co-ordinated by a National Control in London. The grid in Scotland is operated from the control centres at Pitlochry (NSHEB) and at Kirkintilloch (SSEB).

Twin cross-Channel cables between Lydd and Boulogne are capable of transmitting up to 160 MW; by this means advantage is taken of the differences between France and Britain in the timing of peak loads. The CEGB and Electricité de France are negotiating on proposals for a 2,000 MW cable link between the two countries.

Consumption

Sales of electricity in 1977 amounted to 225,655 GWh. Industry took 39 per cent of the total, domestic users 38 per cent and commercial and other users 23 per cent. About one-fifth of domestic sales is for space heating, one-quarter for water heating and one-tenth for cooking. Electricity is used in industry almost entirely for motive power, melting, heating and lighting.

The electricity industry supplies 22·6 million consumers of whom 20 million are in England and Wales; of the remainder 1·6 million are supplied by the SSEB, 520,000 by the NSHEB and 512,000 by the Northern Ireland Electricity Service.

Research

The Electricity Council, in consultation with the Secretary of State for Energy, is responsible for drawing up a general programme of research comprising direct research carried out by the Council and electricity boards supported by co-operative research with selected industrial research associations and by research contracts placed with universities and other organisations. Collaboration on research between the supply industry and the plant manufacturers is co-ordinated by the Power Engineering Research Steering Committee. The research establishments run by the CEGB comprise the Central Electricity Research Laboratories at Leatherhead (Surrey), the Berkeley Nuclear Laboratories in Gloucestershire and the Marchwood Engineering Laboratories on Southampton Water. Research on distribution technology and electricity utilisation is undertaken at the Electricity Council Research Centre at Capenhurst (Cheshire) and by the area boards.

Both Scottish electricity boards carry out research and experimental work on their own and in co-operation with other electricity authorities.

RENEWABLE SOURCES OF ENERGY

Research is proceeding on alternative sources of energy (sea-wave, wind and tidal power for electricity generation, and solar and geothermal energy for low-grade heat for domestic and industrial uses). Little contribution to Britain's energy supply is expected before the year 2000, although the contribution could begin to become more significant in the first quarter of the twenty-first century. In principle, the most promising long-term alternative sources are wave power (because of Britain's long coastline and favourable geographical position) and solar heat.

Research on wave power is concerned with examining the feasibility of the large-scale extraction of power from waves. Four main devices are being evaluated, while work is under way on problems common to all the devices, such as that of bringing power ashore. The programme aims to produce a full-scale prototype for testing at sea by the mid-1980s, and work on two devices has progressed to trials on models at 1:10 scale. In 1977 a four-year government-funded programme of research and development on solar energy was inaugurated to identify its potential contribution and to stimulate the development of cost-effective solar technologies, particularly on water and space heating in houses (the areas of greatest potential return).

Research on geothermal energy involves collection of data in the areas considered to have the most suitable conditions and identification of the markets for the relatively low-grade heat produced. The Department of Energy and an industrial consortium are working on a project to establish the technical and economic potential for generating electricity from wind power. Work includes a detailed design study for a large aerogenerator and an examination of suitable sites in Scotland with favourable wind conditions. Studies have been made of a project for harnessing the tides in the Severn Estuary, one of the world's most suitable sites for tidal power, and the Government has set up an independent Severn Barrage Committee to assist in reaching a decision on whether to proceed with such a project.

NON-FUEL MINERALS

Although much of Britain's requirements of industrial raw materials is met by imports, non-fuel minerals produced in Britain make an important contribution to the economy. Output of non-fuel minerals in 1976 totalled 330 million tonnes, valued at £750 million. The total number of employees in the industry was 42,500 in 1976. The geographical locations of some of the more important minerals produced in Britain are shown on the maps on p 261.

Exploration

The exploration for and exploitation of indigenous mineral resources to meet the requirements of British industry are being encouraged by the Government to minimise dependence on imports. Under the Mineral Exploration and Investment Grants Act 1972 there is provision for financial assistance of up to 35 per cent of the cost of searching for mineral deposits in Great Britain and on the United Kingdom Continental Shelf, and evaluating them for commercial purposes. Minerals included in the scheme are the ores of non-ferrous metals, fluorspar, barium minerals and potash. By the end of March 1978 45 companies had sought assistance totalling £2·6 million in respect of 15 exploration projects, mainly for non-ferrous metals. Work on 107 projects had been completed.

SOME MINERALS PRODUCED IN BRITAIN

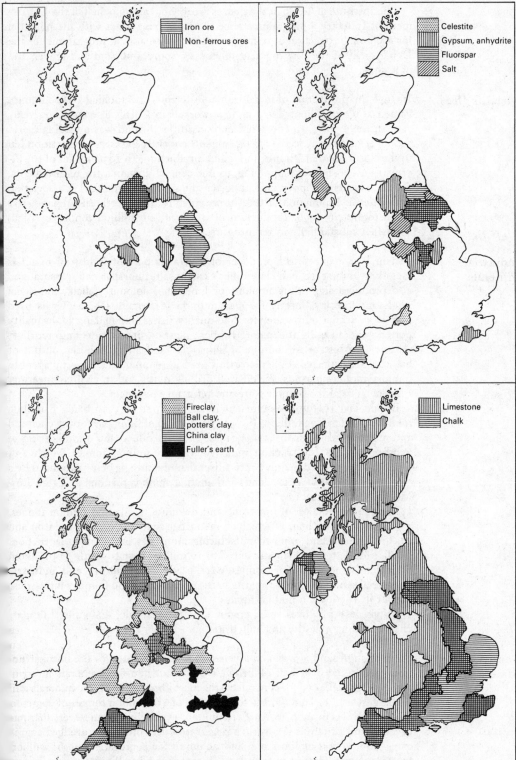

Iron ore
Non-ferrous ores

Celestite
Gypsum, anhydrite
Fluorspar
Salt

Fireclay
Ball clay, potters' clay
China clay
Fuller's earth

Limestone
Chalk

The maps above are based on county or regional boundaries and not those for geological outcrops.

The Institute of Geological Sciences is carrying out on behalf of the Department of Industry a programme aimed at identifying areas with the potential for economic extraction of minerals. It also has an annual programme for the Department of the Environment to assess resources of sand and gravel, and limestone.

Metallic Ores

In 1976 the production of metal from non-ferrous ores totalled 16,600 tonnes, valued at £29 million. Tin was first worked in Cornwall over 2,000 years ago. In the eighteenth and nineteenth centuries Britain was a leading world producer of copper, lead and tin, but subsequently overseas competition led to the closure of many mines and falling production. In 1976 output of tin-in-ore was 4,000 tonnes, supplying 30 per cent of Britain's tin requirements. Small amounts of copper, zinc, tungsten and silver are produced in association with the tin. Production of lead-in-ore, mainly from northern England, was 7,100 tonnes in 1976. Production of iron ore (4·6 million tonnes in 1976) has fallen substantially in recent years.

Industrial Minerals

Britain is a major world producer of several important industrial minerals including china clay, ball clay, fuller's earth, salt, fluorspar and gypsum, and also produces significant amounts of limestone, dolomite, chalk, industrial sands and fireclay, mostly for consumption in Britain. China clay is used mainly as a filler and coater for fine-quality paper, for making high-quality pottery and also in the paint, rubber, plastics, insecticide and fertiliser industries. Most of the output of china clay and about half the output of ball clay are exported. Fuller's earth is used in refining, as a bonding agent in foundry moulding sands, for oil-well drilling muds and in civil engineering. Fireclay is used for ceramic ware and refractory products.

Britain is virtually self-sufficient in salt, output in 1976 being 8 million tonnes valued at £33 million. In 1976 production of fluorspar for the chemical and metallurgical industries was 217,000 tonnes valued at £9 million and of gypsum for the construction industry was 3·3 million tonnes worth £11 million. Potash, used mainly for fertiliser manufacture, is being produced by a new mine at Boulby (Cleveland) and another mine is planned at Egton Low Moor (North Yorkshire).

In 1976 production of limestone and dolomite totalled 89 million tonnes, valued at £177 million, of which about 14 per cent was used in the iron and steel, chemicals and other manufacturing industries excluding construction. Chalk production in 1976 amounted to 16 million tonnes worth £15 million, of which some 2 million tonnes were used in agriculture and industry. Industrial sands are used primarily in the glassmaking and foundry industries; output in 1976 was 6 million tonnes.

Britain also produces small amounts of barytes, talc, diatomite, calcspar, chert and flint, celestite and anhydrite.

Construction Materials

Production of sand, gravel and crushed rock as aggregates for use in construction constituted over half of Britain's output of non-fuel minerals in 1976. Sand and gravel, used for concrete, is the most important of these minerals and the largest user of land. Of the total output of 118 million tonnes of common sand and gravel in 1976, worth £210 million, 15·9 million tonnes were marine-dredged and Britain is the world's largest producer of marine-dredged aggregates. Production of limestone and dolomite for aggregates was 61 million tonnes in 1976. Output of sandstone in 1976 was 14 million tonnes valued at £42 million and of igneous rock 37 million tonnes valued at £115 million. Small amounts of limestone, sandstone, igneous rock and slate are used as building stone and architectural facing material.

Production of limestone, chalk and clay as raw materials for cement manufacture was 10 million, 13 million and 3 million tonnes respectively in 1976. Some 17 million tonnes of clay and shale were produced for the manufacture of bricks, pipes and tiles.

WATER

Britain's water resources are, with progressive development, normally sufficient for domestic and industrial requirements. Supplies are obtained partly from surface sources such as mountain lakes, streams impounded in upland gathering grounds and river intakes (one-third comes from rivers), and partly from underground sources by means of wells, adits and boreholes. In 1975–76 the driest period of weather since records began to be kept in 1727 led the Government to pass the Drought Act 1976, which enabled water authorities in England and Wales to limit or prohibit the use of water and, if necessary, to restrict domestic water supplies. Subsequent very heavy rainfall replenished surface and underground sources by the spring of 1977, but the Act has been retained as providing important reserve powers. Water consumption in Britain continues to increase and in 1976 amounted to about 17·2 million cubic metres a day (mcmd), comprising 16·6 mcmd of potable (drinkable) water and 0·6 mcmd of non-potable water. Average daily consumption per head amounts to around 309 litres.

In general, householders pay for their domestic water supply, sewerage and sewage disposal services through charges based on the rateable value of their property, whereas industrial users are charged for their water supply according to actual metered consumption.

England and Wales

Water services in England and Wales are being consolidated and developed within a reorganised national industry. Responsibility for promoting a national policy for water in England and Wales rests with the Secretaries of State for the Environment and for Wales and the Minister of Agriculture, Fisheries and Food who, under the Water Act 1973, are charged with responsibility for securing the conservation, augmentation, distribution and proper use of water resources and the provision of water supplies; the provision of sewerage and sewage disposal services; the restoration and maintenance of the wholesomeness of rivers and other inland waters; the use of inland waters for navigation and recreation; the provision of land drainage; and the protection and development of fisheries.

National Water Council

The National Water Council advises and assists ministers and water authorities. It consists of a chairman appointed by the Secretaries of State, the chairmen of the water authorities, and ten other members with special relevant knowledge, of whom eight are appointed by the Secretaries of State and two by the Minister of Agriculture, Fisheries and Food.

Water Authorities

Nine regional water authorities in England and the Welsh Water Authority in Wales are responsible for the management of water services; the development of water resources; water distribution and supply; the prevention of pollution (see p 168); sewerage and sewage treatment; river management, land drainage; sea defences; recreation; and freshwater fisheries. The board of each water authority consists of a chairman and several members appointed by the Secretary of State for the Environment (or, in the case of the Welsh Authority, by the Secretary of State for Wales), a few members appointed by the Minister of Agriculture, Fisheries and Food and a small majority, usually of only one, of members appointed by the county and district councils within the area of the authority. District councils usually also act as agents of water authorities for the design, construction, operation and maintenance of public sewers in their areas.

Statutory Water Companies

The Water Act 1973 provides for 29 existing statutory water companies to continue to supply water. In 1976 they accounted for 19 per cent of total supplies. Special arrangements govern the relationship of statutory water companies to the water authorities.

Central Water Planning Unit

The Central Water Planning Unit, part of the Department of the Environment, provides a common service to the Government, the National Water Council and the water authorities. Its principal functions are to keep under review national and strategic aspects of water services planning and operation.

Water Data Unit

The principal functions of the Water Data Unit, also part of the Department of the Environment, are to advise on information required for water management purposes, to ensure common standards and methods of data collection and to publish such data on a national basis.

Supplies

Some 13,429 million cubic metres of water were abstracted in England and Wales in 1976. Public water supplies, reaching over 99 per cent of the population, accounted for 5,451 million cubic metres. The Central Electricity Generating Board took 4,743 million cubic metres, primarily for cooling in connection with electricity generation, other industry 3,121 million cubic metres and the remainder was used in agriculture. Water authorities' revenue totalled £1,141 million in 1977–78. Capital expenditure in 1977–78 on water supply, sewerage and sewage disposal is estimated at £470 million.

The provision of piped supplies for rural areas has been assisted by grants under the Rural Water Supplies and Sewerage Acts 1944 to 1971. By March 1978 schemes costing some £129 million had been completed or were in progress with the aid of grants under these Acts totalling £36 million.

New Proposals

The Government has announced its intention of strengthening the industry at the centre by introducing legislation to establish a National Water Authority (NWA) which will replace the National Water Council, and incorporate the Water Research Centre, the Central Water Planning Unit and part of the Water Data Unit. One of the NWA's main tasks will be to prepare a national water strategy which will form the framework for the plans, investment programmes and operations of the industry.

Scotland

In Scotland responsibility for public water supply, sewerage and sewage disposal rests with the nine regional and three islands councils. Additionally the Central Scotland Water Development Board, established under the Water (Scotland) Act 1967, is primarily responsible for developing large water sources and supplying water in bulk to its six constituent member authorities, the regional councils in Central Scotland.

Scotland has a relative abundance of unpolluted water from upland sources. Over 98 per cent of the population has a public water supply. About 820 million cubic metres of water were abstracted in Scotland in 1976 for public water supplies. Capital expenditure in 1977–78 on water supply, sewerage and sewage disposal is estimated at £52 million. The Secretary of State for Scotland is responsible for the promotion of the conservation of water resources and of the provision by water authorities of adequate water supplies, and also has a duty to promote the cleanliness of rivers and other inland waters and the tidal waters of Scotland. The Scottish River Purification Advisory Committee advises the Secretary of State on matters relating to the cleanliness of rivers in Scotland.

Northern Ireland

Northern Ireland has abundant potential supplies of water for both domestic and industrial consumption. Over 90 per cent of the population has a piped supply. The Government is responsible for water supply and sewerage services, and these are provided by the Northern Ireland Department of the Environment. Capital expenditure during 1977 amounted to around £23 million.

The largest source for water supply is Lough Neagh and in order to conserve the potential and to co-ordinate the various interests and demands on this water resource system a comprehensive water management programme has been prepared.

Research

The central research organisation for the water industry in Britain is the Water Research Centre at Henley-on-Thames (Oxfordshire). The Centre's laboratory at Stevenage (Hertfordshire) is concerned with water pollution including sewage and industrial waste water treatment, sludge treatment and disposal, flow measurement, estuarine pollution and the development of analytical methods and quality monitoring systems. Its laboratory at Medmenham (Buckinghamshire) deals with water resources, water treatment, health aspects of water quality, distribution and operational research.

The Hydraulics Research Station of the Department of the Environment at Wallingford (Oxfordshire) predicts the performance of hydraulic civil engineering works and their effects on the environment. Its work covers background research and specific investigations into the flow of water over weirs and spillways, the performance of flood prevention and sea defence works, silting in rivers and estuaries, and harbour and offshore structure design.

The Institute of Hydrology of the Natural Environment Research Council at Wallingford studies the whole hydrological cycle, and the Meteorological Office (see p 383) is concerned with rainfall.

14 Agriculture, Fisheries and Forestry

AGRICULTURE

Although Britain is a densely populated, industrialised country relying on imports for nearly half its food supply, agriculture remains one of its most important industries. It occupies 661,000 people or 2·7 per cent of the total civilian working population, provides about 2·5 per cent of the gross domestic product, and uses 19 million of the 24 million hectares (47 million of the 60 million acres) of land. Exports in the agricultural sector (including machinery and fertilisers) in 1977 amounted to nearly £3,400 million.

THE LAND AND ITS USES

The soils of the country are varied (see p 4). Land used for farming is conventionally divided into land suitable for cultivation (crops and grass) and rough grazing. In hill country the area of cultivated land is often small, but is usually supplemented by grazing on a comparatively large area of hill land.

There are 12 million hectares (30 million acres) under crops and grass. Cultivated land, rough grazing, woodland and other land on agricultural holdings together represent 78 per cent of the land area. The rest is mountain and forest, or put to urban and kindred uses. The area available for farming is gradually decreasing to meet the needs of housing and industry; so far, the loss has been offset by the increase in productivity on the land being farmed.

Size and Ownership of Farms

There are about 261,000 farming units in Britain. Some 50 per cent are very small units, mostly farmed part-time, and accounting for less than 10 per cent of the industry's total output. Of the 127,000 full-time farm businesses some 29,000 are classified (by standard man-days) as large farm businesses (capable of employing four or more men full-time); these, accounting for less than 10 per cent of the number of holdings, produce about half of the industry's total output. There are about 45,000 medium-sized (two–three men) and some 53,000 small full-time farm businesses.

Amalgamation of small farms into larger, more viable units has been encouraged by successive governments. The average size of full-time holdings is about 113 hectares (279 acres) of crops and grass and rough grazings.

Some 32,000 of the total of significant farming units are in Northern Ireland; their average size is 25 hectares (62 acres). Over half of these units provide a full-time occupation for the owner. Other holdings, of which there are about 21,000, are either extremely small or let in conacre (seasonal lettings for crops or grazing).

In Great Britain more than half of the farms, and in Northern Ireland almost all farms, are owner-occupied.

Types of Farming

The increasing use of intensive methods of production both in crops and in animal husbandry has led to greater specialisation. Three-fifths of the full-time farms in Britain are devoted mainly to dairying or beef cattle and sheep; one in six is a cropping farm and the remainder specialise in pigs, poultry or horticulture, or are mixed farms. The farms devoted primarily to arable crops are found mainly in the eastern parts of England and Scotland. Large-scale potato and vegetable production is characteristic of the Fens (south Lincolnshire and Cambridgeshire), the alluvial areas around the rivers Thames and Humber and the peaty lands in south Lancashire. Early potatoes are an important crop in Dyfed and south-west England. Elsewhere, horticultural crops are widely dispersed amongst agricultural crops.

Dairying occurs widely, but there are concentrations in south-west Scotland, the western parts of England and south-west Wales, where the wetter climate encourages the growth of good grass. Sheep and cattle are reared in the hill and moorland areas of Scotland, Wales and northern and south-western England. Beef fattening takes place partly in better grassland areas and partly in yards on arable farms.

In Northern Ireland dairying is the main occupation on 41 per cent of the full-time farms, while a further 37 per cent concentrate on beef and sheep production. The remainder are either specialised cropping and horticultural holdings, intensive pig and poultry units, or mixed farms with no predominant single enterprise.

Mechanisation

Britain has one of the heaviest tractor densities in the world, with 519,000 tractors in 1977 or one to every 13 hectares (33 acres) of arable land. Power-take-off implements now characterise arable farming; and some 58,000 combine harvesters were in use in 1977. A wide variety of machines for harvesting and preservation of grass are employed. Milking machines are installed on all except the smallest farms.

Over 90 per cent of the farms in Great Britain have an electricity supply and accompanying equipment. Through machinery syndicates farmers have the use of expensive equipment whose capital cost is shared among members.

Research, development and testing of farm machinery are carried out by the National Institute of Agricultural Engineering.

AGRICULTURAL PRODUCTION

The increase in production which has occurred over the past decades is a result of the effort of individual farmers, of farmers' organisations, of research workers and advisers and of government action. The role of the Government is described on pp 273–7. Some production is carried out on a co-operative basis (see p 273).

The steady expansion in production and in yield per hectare of arable land which has taken place since 1936 despite falling manpower is summarised in Table 17 which also shows the effect of the drought during 1975–76. Total cattle stocks reached a record of 15·2 million in 1974 but fell to 13·9 million in 1977. Over the past decade there has been a substantial growth in the number of beef cattle and poultry and a less marked increase in the number of dairy cattle, sheep and pigs. Arable production has shown a greater diversification since the second world war. Total cereals production reached about 17 million tonnes in 1977. Potato production is susceptible to weather conditions but, on average, adequate supplies are maintained from a steadily declining area. Increases in output of meat and milk have been associated with higher consumption of feedingstuffs, mostly from home resources. In 1977 some 5·5 million tonnes of concentrated feeds were imported; the level of imports depends, however, on the size of the home crop of cereals.

The index of agricultural net product (1975 = 100), which stood at 103 in 1967, is estimated to have risen to 112 in 1977. The lower levels in 1975 (the base year) and 1976 (89) were the result of unfavourable weather.

TABLE 17: Manpower, Land Use, Produce and Livestock

Item and Unit	Averages 1936–38	Averages 1967–69	1976	1977	1977 imperial unit equivalents
Manpower in Agriculture ('000)	[a]	808	669	661	
Land Use ('000 hectares)					
Total crops and fallow	3,605	4,981	4,821	4,863	12,016[c]
Grass (excluding rough grazings)	9,280	7,346	7,235	7,127	17,611[c]
Rough grazings	6,668	7,115	6,513	6,400	15,814[c]
Other land on agricultural holdings	[b]	[b]	419	451	1,115[c]
TOTAL	19,552	19,515	18,987	18,841	46,556[c]
Main crops					
Wheat: area ('000 hectares)	751	915	1,231	1,076	2,659[c]
harvest ('000 tonnes)	1,677	3,579	4,740	5,274	5,191[d]
yield *(tonnes per hectare)*	2·23	3·91	3·85	4·90	1·95[e]
Barley: area ('000 hectares)	376	2,418	2,182	2,400	5,932[c]
harvest ('000 tonnes)	777	8,717	7,648	10,531	10,365[d]
yield *(tonnes per hectare)*	2·08	3·61	3·51	4·39	1·75[e]
Oats: area ('000 hectares)	972	391	235	195	481[c]
harvest ('000 tonnes)	1,971	1,305	764	790	778[d]
yield *(tonnes per hectare)*	2·03	3·33	3·25	4·06	1·62[e]
Potatoes: area ('000 hectares)	293	272	222	232	575[c]
harvest ('000 tonnes)	4,951	6,763	4,789	6,621	6,517[d]
yield *(tonnes per hectare)*	16·82	24·9	21·6	28·5	11·3[e]
Sugar area ('000 hectares)	136	186	206	201	497[c]
beet: harvest[f] ('000 tonnes)	422	882	632	638	628[d]
yield *(tonnes per hectare)*[g]	3·11	5·7	3·1	3·2	1·3[e]
Livestock ('000 head)					
Cattle and calves	8,675	12,289	14,069	13,854	
Sheep and lambs	25,786	27,831	28,265	28,104	
Pigs	4,466	7,425	7,947	7,736	
Poultry	76,236	126,532	142,222	133,886	
Livestock Products					
Milk (million litres)	7,069	11,908	13,819	14,594	3,210[h]
Eggs (million dozen)	558	1,226	1,153	1,159	
Beef and veal ('000 tonnes)	587	946	1,069	1,032	1,016[d]
Mutton and lamb ('000 tonnes)	198	244	248	229	225[d]
Pigmeat ('000 tonnes)	442	844	843	903	889[d]
Poultry meat ('000 tonnes)	90	509	663	679	668[d]

Source: *Agricultural Departments*

[a] Not available.
[b] Figures not collected before 1969, and incomplete before 1974.
[c] '000 acres.   [d] '000 tons.   [e] Tons per acre.
[f] Sugar production 1936–38: raw equivalent basis; 1967–76: refined basis.
[g] Sugar-in-beet per crop hectare.
[h] Million gallons.
Differences between totals and the sums of their constituent parts are due to rounding.

Crops

Cereals

Wheat is grown mainly in the eastern half of England. About 5·3 million tonnes were harvested in 1977, with average yields estimated at 4·90 tonnes per hectare (1·95 tons per acre). About one-half of the wheat crop is normally used for flour milling, the remainder going mainly for animal feed.

Since 1960 the area under barley has increased by about 75 per cent. In recent years, between 15 and 23 per cent of the crop has been used for malting and distilling; most of the remainder is used as feed for livestock.

The universal use of combine harvesters has necessitated the installation of drying and storage facilities on many farms. Such equipment is also often used on a co-operative basis.

Fodder Crops The total area of fodder crops has fallen since 1960 because in many cases farmers can provide winter feed more economically by increased grass production and improved methods of conservation. The principal fodder crops are turnips, swedes and kale in England, and turnips and swedes in Scotland. Their principal use is to supplement conserved grass (mainly hay and silage) for winter feeding.

Sugar Beet Beet is grown under contract to the British Sugar Corporation Ltd. (the sole British processor) which also provides technical advice and assistance. The corporation contracts annually for the area from which it will buy beet; the contracted area has risen over the past few years to about 209,000 hectares (517,000 acres) in 1978. At normal yields this should produce about one million tonnes of sugar—about 42 per cent of total British consumption. (The balance is largely supplied, under the Lomé Convention (see p 358), by developing countries which export raw cane sugar.)

Potatoes First supplies of early potatoes normally come at the end of May, and the lifting of maincrop varieties usually starts in September. Seed potato production for Britain and for export is chiefly centred in Scotland and Northern Ireland.

The total area planted with potatoes in 1977 was 232,000 hectares (575,000 acres) and the average yield per hectare was 28·5 tonnes. Although potato production is becoming increasingly mechanised, much hand labour is still needed.

Hops Hops, which are grown for the brewing industry, occupy only about 6,000 hectares (14,000 acres) but have a very high yield per hectare and value by weight.

Grassland The British climate suits grassland farming. Grassland is important in the economy of most farms. Grassland production has been enhanced over recent years by the development and application of new techniques, notably the increased use of fertilisers, new methods of grazing control, improved herbage conservation for winter feed and irrigation. Rough grazings are used for extensively grazed flocks and herds, producing young animals for fattening elsewhere.

Livestock A great number of specialised breeds of livestock have been developed over the centuries in Britain. Substantial sales of animals and semen are made to overseas buyers seeking to replenish and improve their herds and flocks. In recent years farmers have introduced a number of breeds from the continent of Europe.

Artificial insemination plays an important part in cattle breeding, about 60 per cent of the dairy herd in England, Scotland and Wales being bred in this way.

Dairy Farming In England, Scotland and Wales more milk goes for liquid consumption than for manufacture, but in Northern Ireland the greater part of the milk is used for manufactured products. Average consumption of liquid milk per head in 1977 was 2·71 litres (about 4·7 pints) a week.

Average yields per dairy cow have increased during the last decade by about 23 per cent and were some 4,450 litres (979 gallons) in 1977. Freedom from tuberculosis has reduced herd wastage, and a campaign to eradicate brucellosis is well advanced. Milk production has been stimulated by advances in grass-land management, new methods of grass conservation and controlled concentrate feed programmes.

The average size of dairy herds has also been increasing over the years and in 1977 was some 44 cows a herd, the largest in the European Community.

Beef Cattle

Although there are several breeds of beef cattle, about two-thirds of home-fed beef production derives from the dairy herds, some females being mated to beef sires. Large numbers of store cattle are moved for fattening from hill and upland areas to lowland pastures, on which cattle imported from the Irish Republic are also fattened.

Sheep

Britain has a long tradition of sheep production, and more than 40 breeds and innumerable crosses are to be found in the country. Research has provided vaccine and sera protection against nearly all the epidemic diseases.

Draft ewes and lambs are brought every autumn from the hill areas, where winters are usually severe, to swell the lowland flocks, usually in two stages: first, to farms at intermediate altitudes, where they are mated with rams of a larger and more rapidly maturing breed; then, the cross-bred progeny pass on to the milder lowland conditions, where they become crossed again with Down rams for fat lamb production. The hill breeds bring in hardiness, and the lowland sires fecundity and early maturity. Store and fat lamb production provides the main source of income for sheep farmers but wool is also of considerable importance, especially to farmers in hill areas.

Pigs

Pig production is carried on in most parts of Britain but is particularly important in the eastern and southern counties of England and in Northern Ireland. There is an increasing concentration into specialist units and larger herds. Artificial insemination is available nationally.

About 30 per cent of the pigmeat is used for bacon and 70 per cent for pork and manufacturing into sausages and other processed forms.

Poultry

The British poultry industry has expanded rapidly in recent years, aided by the application of improved husbandry and management techniques in intensive production units and by genetic improvements in stock. Some 80 per cent of the laying birds on farms are in flocks of 5,000 or more, while about 75 per cent of the broilers are in flocks of 50,000 or more. The average yield of eggs per bird is about 240 a year. Nearly all eggs and poultry meat consumed in Britain are home-produced.

Horticultural Industry

The horticultural industry produces a wide variety of fruit, vegetables and flower crops which are worth about 10 per cent of the total value of agricultural output; in 1977 their value was estimated at £704 million.

At the June 1977 census the land on which these crops were grown amounted to nearly 300,000 hectares (740,000 acres), about 2·5 per cent of the land used for crops and grass. Fruit accounted for about 65,000 hectares (161,000 acres), vegetables, excluding potatoes, for about 221,000 hectares (547,000 acres) and flowers, bulbs and nursery stock for about 13,000 hectares (32,000 acres). Crops under glass, plastic and in sheds, including mushrooms, occupied about 2,000 hectares (5,000 acres).

Horticultural crops are largely grown on specialised holdings, but some, particularly vegetables for processing, are produced on arable farms. Most horticultural enterprises are increasing output per unit area with the help of improved planting material, new techniques of cultivation and environmental control, and the widespread use of machinery.

Vegetable Crops

Field vegetables, with approximately 74 per cent of the horticultural output and about 221,000 hectares (547,000 acres) in area (excluding potatoes), are the most important horticultural sector. They are widely spread over the country, with the most intensive concentrations in the Thames Valley and Hereford and Worcester and extensive production in the eastern counties. Some 38 per cent are destined for processing.

Fruit

Of the land used for fruit growing in 1977, 16,000 hectares (39,000 acres) were devoted to soft fruit and the remainder was under orchards. The area of apple orchards (excluding cider apples) is some 31,000 hectares (76,000 acres). Dessert apples are the most important fruit crop. England and Northern Ireland are among the few countries which grow varieties of apples especially suitable for cooking. There are about 4,000 hectares (11,000 acres) in the western Midlands and the south-west of England devoted to cider apple production.

Although pears thrive best in the warmer continental climate, some high-quality varieties are produced in the east and south-east of England, where the conditions are most suitable. Cherries and plums are grown in Kent, and plums also in the Vale of Evesham and parts of East Anglia. Around Perth in Scotland is the largest concentration of raspberry plantations in the world.

Strawberries are the most widely grown soft fruit, accounting for some 6,000 hectares (16,000 acres), with early production in the south and west of England. Blackcurrants are also widely grown in Britain, mainly for the preparation of juice for the manufacture of soft drinks and flavours for confectionery. Other fruits include gooseberries, red and white currants, loganberries and blackberries.

Glasshouse Crops

Much of the glasshouse sector of the horticultural industry has been re-equipped since the mid-1960s with the aid of grants. Widespread use is now being made of units with automatic control of heating and ventilation, and semi-automatic control of watering coupled with carbon-dioxide enrichment of the atmosphere. Tomatoes form the most important glasshouse crop, and, together with lettuce and cucumbers, represent some 95 per cent of the total value of glasshouse vegetable output. The area under sweet peppers and celery has increased significantly. Mushrooms, whose farmgate value is estimated at over £35 million for 1977, are grown in specially constructed sheds in most parts of Britain, with concentrations in the eastern and northern counties of England.

Other Crops

Bulbs occupied some 5,000 hectares (12,000 acres) and hardy nursery stock some 7,000 hectares (17,000 acres) in June 1977; flowers in the open took about 1,000 hectares (2,500 acres).

FOOD SUPPLIES

Britain now produces just over half of its total food requirements or about two-thirds of those supplies that can be produced in temperate climates.

Home Production

Home production of the principal foods is shown as a percentage by weight of total supplies in Table 18.

TABLE 18: British Production as a Percentage of Total Supplies

Food product	1957	1965–67 average	1977 (provi-sional)
Carcase meat and offal	63	69	76
Bacon and ham	42	35	45
Shell eggs	99	98	100
Milk for human consumption (as liquid)	100	100	100
Cheese	48	43	63
Butter	11	10	30
Oils and fats (crude oil equivalent)	16	37	33
Sugar (as refined)	19	30	35
Wheat and flour (as wheat equivalent)	21	45	58
Potatoes for human consumption	na	95	88

na Not available.

Source: *Ministry of Agriculture, Fisheries and Food*

MARKETING AND CO-OPERATION

Agricultural products are marketed in many ways: mainly through private trade channels, through producers' co-operatives or through marketing schemes. Marketing schemes are established under the Agricultural Marketing Act 1958 or under similar Northern Ireland legislation; they are essentially producers' organisations with certain statutory powers to regulate the marketing of particular products. There are ten schemes, each of which must be approved by Parliament, and also in Great Britain by a majority of producers of the regulated product. Each scheme is administered by a board, the majority of whose members are elected from among registered producers; a small minority of independent members are appointed by agricultural ministers (see pp 273–4). Various safeguards exist to protect the public interest generally, including the interests of individual producers and consumers.

Marketing boards fall into two categories: first, those which are sole buyers of the regulated product from all producers not specially exempted, or those which control all contracts between producers and first buyers; and, secondly, boards which maintain only a broad control over marketing conditions, leaving producers free otherwise to deal individually with buyers. The boards for hops, milk and wool, and the Northern Ireland pigs and seed potato boards fall into the first category, and the Potato Marketing Board into the second.

For certain other commodities there are broadly based organisations representing producer, distributor and independent interests.

The Home-Grown Cereals Authority was set up to improve the marketing of home-grown cereals. It provides a market intelligence service, and promotes research and development. It also acts as agent for the Intervention Board for Agricultural Produce (see p 274) in respect of the support buying, storage and disposal of cereals and oilseed rape.

The Meat and Livestock Commission's wide range of functions covers the promotion and improvement of many activities concerning livestock and livestock products in Great Britain, extending from breeding to retail distribution; the Commission also acts as agents for the agricultural departments and the Intervention Board in administering price support schemes. In Northern Ireland, the Livestock Marketing Commission promotes better organisation, development and marketing in the livestock and livestock products' industry.

The Eggs Authority has the general duty of improving the marketing of eggs. It provides market intelligence, carries out promotional work and undertakes research and development projects.

Under the Common Agricultural Policy of the European Community (see p 274) a wide range of horticultural produce is subject to common quality standards which, with certain minor exceptions, apply at all stages of distribution. The Community standards apply to all produce entering Britain and to British produce sold on the domestic market. Community regulations prescribe grades consisting of a range of up to four classes, and specify requirements concerning colour, size, packaging, presentation and labelling. All fruit and vegetables subject to the standards, and exported from or imported into the Community, must meet the requirements of at least Class II.

Co-operation

Agricultural co-operatives are concerned with supply of farmers' requirements, with marketing, production, and services. There are, in addition, pest control societies and machinery syndicates.

The Central Council for Agricultural and Horticultural Co-operation promotes and develops co-operation in agriculture and horticulture, and administers a scheme of grants. The Agricultural and Horticultural Co-operation Scheme 1971 provides grants (including capital grants) for co-operative production and marketing of agricultural and horticultural produce.

FARM EXPENDITURE AND EARNINGS

Estimates of farm expenses and sales and the aggregate net income of agricultural producers are prepared annually by the agricultural departments. The aggregate net income of farmers in 1977 is estimated at £1,348 million (excluding stock appreciation). Of the total farm output, estimated at £6,473 million in 1977, nearly two-thirds is in the form of livestock and livestock products.

Feedingstuffs amount to approximately one-third of agriculture's total cost, and wages and machinery (including depreciation) to about one-fifth each. In recent years agricultural workers' earnings have risen considerably in real terms, but this has been offset by the manpower economies made possible by increasing mechanisation and larger farms. Labour productivity rose by nearly 4 per cent a year between 1967 and 1977.

Capital Requirements

It is estimated that £258 million was added to the value of buildings and works and £614 million was invested in new plant, machinery and vehicles in 1977. Most of the capital for investment is generated from within the farm business; however, outside capital is also important, with bank advances providing the main source of short- and medium-term credit. Agricultural merchants are also an important source of short-term credit. Mortgage loans form the chief source of long-term credit and are provided by specialised financial institutions (see pp 275-6) and private sources.

Net Incomes

In 1976-77 the average net income for farms of different types in England and Wales was generally within the range of £50 to £140 per hectare (£20 to £57 per acre) with the exception of pig and poultry farms and horticultural holdings, which are more intensive in their use of land. Net income per hectare on dairy and arable farms has nearly always been higher than on stock-rearing farms, which are generally larger in area than the other types and are situated on poorer land.

THE ROLE OF THE GOVERNMENT

In England the Ministry of Agriculture, Fisheries and Food (see p 42) operates through functional divisions. Its relations with individual farmers are conducted mainly through its local offices, grouped in regions, with Chief Regional Officers.

Responsibility for agricultural and fisheries functions in Wales was transferred from the Minister of Agriculture, Fisheries and Food to the Secretary of State for Wales on 1 April 1978 and is discharged through the Agriculture Department of the Welsh Office.

The Advisory Council for Agriculture and Horticulture in England and Wales provides the agricultural ministers (Minister of Agriculture, Fisheries and Food and Secretary of State for Wales) and their departments with independent advice on any agricultural or horticultural subjects remitted to it.

In Scotland most of the agricultural functions of the Secretary of State are discharged through the Department of Agriculture and Fisheries. The Secretary of State for Scotland also appoints the members of the Crofters Commission (see p 276) and the Red Deer Commission, which deals with the conservation and control of red deer.

The Northern Ireland Department of Agriculture is responsible for implementing agricultural policy. It is organised on similar lines to the Ministry of Agriculture, Fisheries and Food, for which it acts as agent in the administration in Northern Ireland of British agricultural schemes.

Within the machinery of the Economic Development Committees (see p 207) there is a committee for agriculture, comprising representatives of farmers, workers and landowners, as well as official and independent members.

Since February 1973 Britain has applied the European Community system of agricultural support under the Common Agricultural Policy (CAP) (see below). Market arrangements under the CAP are administered by the Intervention Board for Agricultural Produce which is responsible to the agricultural ministers.

Annual Review

Each year, in accordance with the requirements of the 1947 Agriculture Act, the agricultural ministers review the economic condition and prospects of the agricultural industry in consultation with representatives of producers. The conclusions drawn from the review contribute, together with views expressed on behalf of agricultural workers, landowners, consumers and the food industry to the formulation of government agricultural policy.

Common Agricultural Policy

The prices of most agricultural commodities produced in Britain are supported through the Common Agricultural Policy of the European Community (CAP). (For products supported by Britain's national price guarantees, see p 275.) Under the CAP, producers' returns for most of the main commodities are supported by a combination of charges on imports from outside the Community and internal support prices which, for some of the more important products, are maintained by intervention buying when necessary. In addition export refunds enable Community exporters to sell on world markets when world prices are below Community price levels. There is also provision for certain direct payments to producers, including beef premiums. The Community's support price levels have been operating fully in Britain since the beginning of 1978, following a five-year transitional period. These prices, and levels of aid, are converted into the currencies of the member states by means of fixed representative or 'green' rates (for Britain the 'green pound') in order to avoid fluctuations as market exchange rates change. Monetary compensatory amounts, based on the percentage difference between the representative and market rates of each currency, are applied to prevent distortions in trade. They operate as import subsidies and export levies for countries whose currencies' market rates are below the representative rates, and as import levies and export subsidies in the opposite case.

The level of support prices under the CAP is reviewed by the Community each year, and the results of the British Annual Review (see p 274) help to shape the Government's approach to the negotiations on CAP support.

Some of the grants paid to farmers under the schemes mentioned below also come within the scope of the CAP.

Price Guarantees In the light of the British Annual Review, agricultural ministers determine guaranteed prices for the coming year for potatoes, fat sheep, and wool. Guaranteed prices for other commodities have been terminated in accordance with the Treaty of Accession (see p 72).

Sheep producers receive guarantee payments if the average market prices fall below the guaranteed levels. For wool the Government operates the guarantee through the British Wool Marketing Board (see p 272), to which a fixed price is guaranteed for every kilogram of fleece wool it buys from producers.

For potatoes ministers fix each year a target area designed to achieve self-sufficiency. In Great Britain the Potato Marketing Board ensures, as far as possible, that this area is planted, and may with government agreement undertake support buying of any surplus, re-selling as much as possible for stockfeed. In Northern Ireland the Department of Agriculture undertakes any support measures. Most of the cost is met by the Government.

Other Grants and Subsidies In addition to market support under the CAP and the British guaranteed prices, producers also receive support through certain capital and production grants. These include grants to help producers with the costs of capital investment under the Farm Capital Grant Scheme and the Horticulture Capital Grant Scheme. Grant aid is also available to producers undertaking development plans under the Farm and Horticulture Development Scheme.

There is also a Payments to Outgoers Scheme designed to assist in the improvement of farm structure and a Milk Non-Marketing and Conversion Scheme under which grants are available to farmers who cease production of milk for sale, with advantageous rates if they also convert to beef or sheep production. Special financial assistance, involving headage payments on breeding cows and ewes, and higher rates of capital grant, is also available under Community arrangements for farmers in less favoured (hill) areas. Community assistance may also be made available for improvements to facilities for the marketing and processing of agricultural products.

Cost of Support Estimated 1977–78 expenditure in Britain on price guarantees, grants and subsidies is about £204 million, of which about £27 million is expected to be reimbursed from the European Agricultural Guidance and Guarantee Fund (FEOGA). Expenditure in Britain under CAP market regulation in 1977–78 is estimated at about £204 million, of which some £146 million is likely to be reimbursed from FEOGA.

Agricultural Credit In England and Wales finance for the purchase or improvement of agricultural land and buildings is available on the security of a first mortgage from the Agricultural Mortgage Corporation Ltd., a company which enjoys a measure of government financial backing but raises its funds on the London capital market. The Scottish Agricultural Securities Corporation Ltd. fulfils a similar role in Scotland.

In Northern Ireland loans are available to farmers from the Agricultural Loans Fund, administered by the Department of Agriculture and financed out of public funds.

In any part of Britain, where a farmer, grower or co-operative requires a bank loan for business purposes but cannot provide sufficient collateral, the Agricultural Credit Corporation Ltd. may be able to provide the bank with a guarantee. The Minister of Agriculture, Fisheries and Food has power to make grants to the Corporation where the guarantees have to be fulfilled; and in some circumstances the minister can also meet the guarantee charges normally paid to the Corporation by the borrower.

Agricultural Advisory Service

In England and Wales scientific, technological and management advice and services are available through the Agricultural Development and Advisory Service (ADAS) which operates mainly from the regional and divisional offices of the Ministry of Agriculture, Fisheries and Food and of the Welsh Office. The Service also helps to identify problems requiring investigation and research, to suggest priorities for such work, and, where appropriate, to contribute to possible solutions. ADAS provides free, impartial advice to landowners, farmers and growers, but charges are made for certain services.

In Scotland the agricultural advisory service is provided by the three regional independent colleges of agriculture which are financed almost entirely by public funds.

Advisory work in Northern Ireland is under the direction of the Chief Agricultural Officer of the Department of Agriculture, and Advisory Centres are located in the main provincial towns. The resources of the agricultural colleges, the research centres and the specialist divisions of the Department are available to the advisory service.

Smallholdings and Crofts

Local authorities provide about 8,500 smallholdings in England and about 1,000 in Wales. In England about 800 lettable holdings are provided by the Ministry of Agriculture, Fisheries and Food. The minister and local authorities may make loans of up to 75 per cent of required working capital to their smallholding tenants.

Land settlement in Scotland has always been carried out by the central Government, which owns and maintains about 169,000 hectares (418,000 acres) of land settlement estates, comprising some 2,850 crofts and holdings.

Crofting

Within the crofting areas of Scotland (situated in Strathclyde, Highland, Western Isles, Orkney Islands and Shetland Islands) much of the land is held by crofters, that is, tenants whose holdings are generally either rented at a cost of not more than £100 a year or have an area not exceeding 30 hectares (75 acres).

The Crofters Commission is responsible for the administration and regulation of crofting. It also acts as the Secretary of State for Scotland's agent in administering grants to crofters for cropping and land improvement.

Tenancy Legislation

A code of landlord-tenant relationships has been written into legislation in order to protect the respective interests of landlords and tenants and to eliminate uncertainty as to their rights and obligations.

Legislation in Great Britain provides for any tenancy of agricultural land, with the exception of certain short-term lettings, to continue in force from year to year until terminated by a valid notice to quit. With certain exceptions the tenant can contest it by serving a counter-notice; the notice to quit then becomes inoperative unless the landlord obtains consent to its operation from an independent body (in England and Wales the Agricultural Land Tribunal and in Scotland the Scottish Land Court).

There is a code of compensation to which the tenant is entitled on termination of the tenancy. Rent is a matter for negotiation between landlord and tenant and may be varied by agreement or, failing agreement, by arbitration.

There are provisions for succession of a close relative on the death of a tenant farmer.

Safety at Work

The Agricultural Branch of the Health and Safety Executive (see p 327) is responsible for the enforcement of regulations relating to the health and safety of workers in agriculture. These regulations cover such matters as the guarding of field and stationary machinery, farm safety, the fitting of safety cabs to tractors, and the use of agricultural chemicals. The executive's Agriculture Industry Advisory Committee assists it in resolving problems of health and safety in agriculture, including horticulture and forestry.

Arterial Drainage and Sea Defence

Ten regional water authorities are responsible for land drainage (including flood protection) in England and Wales. In Scotland local authorities deal with the coast protection and flood prevention, while arterial drainage of agricultural land is the owners' responsibility.

Most of the funds needed by the water authorities are obtained from local authorities, but the Government pays grants toward the cost of improvement schemes, varying from 10 per cent to 80 per cent according to the financial position of the authority, with an additional premium for sea defence works.

Within the water authority areas, in low-lying areas where there are special local problems of land drainage, there are 282 internal drainage districts administered by internal drainage boards which carry out work for the special benefit and protection of their districts. The boards finance their work from drainage rates levied on owners and occupiers. They also receive a government grant at a flat rate of 50 per cent for improvement schemes.

Local authorities in England and Wales also have general land drainage powers and may receive government grants of between 20 per cent and 50 per cent of the cost of improvement work. In Scotland 60 per cent grants (70 per cent if for the benefit of less favoured (hill) areas) are available to owners or occupiers of agricultural land who carry out arterial drainage work.

In Northern Ireland the Department of Agriculture is the drainage authority for watercourses designated by the Drainage Council as main or minor watercourses, and also has responsibility for urban drainage.

CONTROL OF DISEASES AND PESTS

Animals

The day-to-day work of treating animal disease is the responsibility of the practising veterinary surgeon. Control of animal disease in Great Britain in accordance with the Government's policy is the responsibility of the Agricultural Development and Advisory Service (ADAS). The ADAS Veterinary Service also deals with the welfare of farm livestock.

The work of the Veterinary Service is backed by extensive laboratory facilities. In addition, in England and Wales 24 investigation centres perform work requiring specialist knowledge and give advice on disease problems to private practitioners. In Scotland a similar service is provided by the investigation centres of the three Scottish agricultural colleges.

Great Britain has been free from many serious animal diseases for a number of years. Strict veterinary controls are exercised on the import of all animals, meat and meat products, live poultry and other captive birds and poultry meat so as to prevent the introduction of animal or poultry diseases into Great Britain. Sheep scab, eradicated in 1952, reappeared in 1973, and rigorous measures are being taken to eradicate it again. Enzootic bovine leucosis was found for the first time in 1978; a survey is being carried out to furnish a basis for long-term policy; meanwhile, legislation provides for the slaughter of affected animals and the payment of compensation to owners. The campaign to eradicate swine fever was successfully completed in 1966 and, although three cases of the disease occurred in 1971, the infection was quickly eliminated. An epidemic of a previously unknown swine vesicular disease began in December 1972 and has been combated by a stringent slaughter policy; the last outbreak occurred in June 1977. Foot-and-mouth disease was eradicated after the 1967–68 outbreak. In 1960 the whole of Britain became a bovine tuberculosis attested area. The incidence of the disease is now very low; cattle (except for certain categories) are tested at regular intervals and reactors to the test are slaughtered; compensation is paid to the owners. Voluntary schemes for the eradication of brucellosis have been in operation since 1967; compulsory eradication on an area basis began in 1972. By March 1978, 80 per cent of all herds in Great Britain were declared free of the disease. Newcastle disease (fowl pest) has declined to a low level due to the operation of a vaccination policy.

Non-farm animals are subject to import licence and six months' quarantine as a precaution against the introduction of rabies, and there are severe penalties for those breaking the law. There have been only two cases of rabies in animals outside quarantine in Great Britain since 1922 and both were in imported animals.

In Northern Ireland the veterinary services are organised similarly to those in Great Britain but are administered separately by the Department of Agriculture for Northern Ireland. Animal health control policies and the geographical situation have kept the country free from rabies and nearly all the major epizootic diseases, including swine vesicular disease. A Brucellosis Eradication Scheme has been successfully carried out and in December 1971 Northern Ireland was declared brucellosis-free. The full-time veterinary service is supplemented by the central veterinary laboratory.

Plants

The plant health services, operated by the agricultural departments, are responsible for statutory controls designed to limit the spread of plant pests and diseases present in Britain and prevent the introduction of new ones from abroad. They also issue the health certificates required by other countries to accompany plant material imported from Britain. Certification schemes are operated to encourage the development of healthy, vigorous and true-to-type planting stocks. The Plant Pathology Laboratory at Harpenden, Hertfordshire, and the Agricultural Scientific Services Station, East Craigs, Edinburgh, provide scientific and technical advice on which statutory controls and certification schemes are based.

Pests and Storage

The Pest Infestation Control Laboratory at Slough, Berkshire, undertakes research and provides advice on harmful mammals and birds and on insects, mites and moulds associated with grain and other stored food products. The Laboratory is responsible for regional pest officers who advise farmers, local authorities and others on control techniques. In Scotland the Agricultural Scientific Services of the Department of Agriculture and Fisheries have a similar function and maintain close liaison with the Laboratory.

Agricultural Chemicals

Safeguards against the dangers which could arise from uncontrolled use of pesticides have been devised and are operating successfully. Products must be cleared for safety under the Pesticides Safety Precautions Scheme (see p 168), and may be submitted through the Agricultural Chemicals Approval Scheme for efficacy approval.

Veterinary Medicinal Products

The Medicines Act 1968 provides through a system of licensing for the control of the manufacture, sale and supply of veterinary medicinal products (including those used in animal feedingstuffs). The licensing authority (the agricultural ministers) is advised by the Medicines Commission, the Veterinary Products Committee, whose functions are to advise on the safety, quality and efficacy of veterinary medicinal products, and by other expert committees. (For other provisions of the Act, see p 120.)

RESEARCH, EDUCATION AND TRAINING

Research

An outline of the organisation of agricultural research and development in Britain, including that carried out by the Agricultural Research Council and the universities, is given on p 372. The Ministry of Agriculture, Fisheries and Food carries out research and development at its own laboratories and on the 22 experimental husbandry farms and horticulture stations operated by ADAS, and commissions work from the Agricultural Research Council, the Natural Environment Research Council and outside research organisations. In Scotland the three colleges which provide the advisory services (see p 276) also undertake development and experimental work. In England and Wales, research in agricultural economics is undertaken by 12 university departments of agricultural economics. At the University of Reading, the Centre for Agricultural Strategy provides an assessment of British agriculture with a view to developing long-term strategies.

The Ministry of Agriculture, Fisheries and Food has four economic divisions and two statistics divisions. In Scotland, agricultural economists are on the staff of three agricultural colleges and the Department of Agriculture and Fisheries for Scotland.

In Northern Ireland, the Department of Agriculture has nine research divisions.

Education and Training

Fifteen British universities provide degree and postgraduate courses in agriculture or agricultural sciences. The National College of Agricultural Engineering at Silsoe, Bedfordshire, offers degree and postgraduate courses. Sandwich courses leading to a Higher National Diploma are available at eight agricultural colleges in England and Wales and there are nearly 50 local authority and other agricultural colleges providing full-time courses on different aspects of agriculture, horticulture, forestry and farm management. A centre for European agricultural studies is based at London University's Wye College at Ashford.

In Scotland the three agricultural colleges which have the advisory and development functions are also teaching establishments. They mainly provide sandwich courses leading to Higher and Ordinary National Diplomas, post-diploma courses and certain short courses. In Northern Ireland degree courses in agriculture and food science are provided at Queen's University, Belfast. Courses below this level are provided at three residential colleges run by the Department of Agriculture.

Local education authorities throughout Britain provide full-time and part-time courses for farmers, farm workers and horticulturists, as well as an advisory service for domestic producers.

In Great Britain the Agricultural Training Board provides a training advisory service, organises training courses and pays training grants. In Northern Ireland training courses are organised by the Department of Agriculture.

FISHERIES

The industry catches demersal fish (caught on or near the bottom of the sea), pelagic fish (caught nearer the surface) and shellfish. The major element of the catch (about 54 per cent by weight) is demersal fish; the catches of pelagic fish comprise over 37 per cent and the shellfish about 9 per cent of the total catch. The principal demersal fish (in terms of value) are cod, haddock and plaice. The most important pelagic species are herring and mackerel. Shellfish include crustacea (such as lobsters and crabs) and molluscs (such as mussels and oysters).

Fishery Limits

From the beginning of 1977, Britain's fishery limits have been extended to 200 miles (or, where the distance between two countries' coasts is less than 400 miles, up to the median line, that is, half-way between the two countries' base lines). This followed the European Community member states' agreement to adopt such limits jointly, after similar extensions, with resulting restrictions on Community vessels, had been announced by many maritime nations.

Community countries and non-Community countries having temporary agreements with the Community have the right to fish up to 12 miles off the British coast. Access to waters within 12 miles is restricted; no foreign vessels are permitted within 6 miles and only certain authorised countries (Norway and Community countries) may fish in specified regions within 6 to 12 miles.

Common Fisheries Policy

Internal Regime

With the extension of fishery limits to 200 miles, it is necessary to revise the Community fisheries' internal régime to allow for controlled Community fishing in the greatly extended area. Britain has a particularly strong interest in such control, since about 60 per cent of the total catch within the new limit is taken in British waters, while the loss of fishing opportunities in distant waters (such as Iceland) has reduced the British industry's total catch more than that of other Community states. As a result, the British fishing industry is looking for a substantial share of the quotas proposed for the fish stocks around Britain's coasts.

There is also a need for effective and enforceable conservation measures within the waters of member states. The Government is continuing to work towards a common fisheries policy which meets these needs. In the absence of an agreed Community policy, the Government has introduced a number of conservation measures, some of which implemented Community decisions often taken as a result of a British initiative. Other essential elements of a comprehensive revised internal regime are rules which set common standards of enforcement and give member states the responsibility for operating them in their own waters, and a common structural policy (see p 281).

External Regime

The Community has negotiated exchanges of fishing rights within member states' limits for reciprocal rights within the waters of several non-member countries; for 1978, reciprocal quotas have been negotiated with Norway and the Faroe Islands, which are the countries of greatest interest to British fishermen, and also with Sweden. Quotas have also been granted to the Community by Canada and the United States. Framework agreements, intended to establish the general lines of fishery relations between the Community and each of the other countries, have been reached with the Faroes, Sweden and the United States, and the text of an agreement with Norway has been worked out. British fishermen have been excluded from the traditionally important grounds off Iceland, and reciprocal fishing with the Soviet Union and the rights of certain other East European states to fish in member states' waters have been terminated.

Marketing and Structural Policy

From February 1973 those provisions of the common fisheries policy which are based on the establishment of a common organisation of the market and a common structural policy have applied in Britain. The common organisation of the market aims at assisting in the adaptation of supplies to marketing requirements, while ensuring, as far as possible, a reasonable return to producers, by means of the establishment of a common grading and price system, and common rules on competition. Provision is also made for the protection of the Community market against disruption by imports from non-member countries. The responsibility for market organisation is placed largely in the hands of the industry itself through producers' organisations. In 1977, following transitional arrangements similar to those applying to industrial products (see p 72), tariffs on intra-Community fish trade were abolished, and the common external tariff became applicable. The common structural policy aims at promoting the harmonious and balanced development of the fishing industry and the rational exploitation of resources. It includes common measures for the financing of the improvement of the structure of the fishing industry and the provision of an equitable standard of living for those engaged in it.

Fishing Ports

The principal fishing ports in England and Wales are Hull, Grimsby, Fleetwood, North Shields, Lowestoft, Plymouth, Brixham, Newlyn and Milford Haven. In Scotland the chief ports are Aberdeen, Peterhead, Fraserburgh, Lerwick, Ullapool, Mallaig, Ayr and Stornoway. In Northern Ireland the main fishing ports are Kilkeel, Portavogie and Ardglass.

Employment

In the British fishing industry in 1977 there were about 16,350 fishermen in regular employment and some 5,500 occasionally employed; about 48 per cent of the former and 28 per cent of the latter were based on Scottish ports. In Northern Ireland there are about 540 regular fishermen and about 285 part-time. It is estimated that for every fisherman there are between three and five jobs in associated trades.

Fishing is an important source of employment and income in certain areas of Britain, in many of which unemployment is well above the national average. Maintenance of fishing opportunities, through conservation of stocks and through the preservation or restoration of British fishermen's access to their traditional distant grounds, is thus vital to Britain.

Methods of Sea Fishing

The chief methods of catching fish are by trawling and seining on the sea bed and, in midwater, by trawling and purse-seining. Bottom trawling is carried out in the distant and near waters for all species of demersal fish. Seining is also used for catching demersal fish all the year round, mainly in the North Sea, the Minches, the Firth of Clyde and the Irish Sea. Lines and set nets are also used to catch demersal fish. Midwater trawls and purse-seines are used to catch pelagic fish, especially herring, mackerel and sprats.

The inshore fisheries comprise a great diversity of types of vessel and methods of capture. They yield all sorts of fish, and shellfish are important; there are extensive fisheries for crabs, lobsters, shrimps, mussels, escallops, cockles and oysters, and off Scotland and north-east England and in the Irish Sea there are valuable catches of *Nephrops* (Norway lobsters or Dublin Bay prawns).

The Fishing Fleet

At the end of 1977, the deep-sea fleet comprised some 329 vessels; of these, distant-water trawlers, which operate mainly from Hull and Grimsby, numbered 97. They are 140 feet (42·7 metres) and over in length and are of two types, the older, traditional side trawlers, which can only preserve their catches on ice, and modern stern freezer/factory trawlers (38 in number). Traditionally all have fished in the north-east Arctic and still do within the constraints of quota agreements which have reduced activity. Some side trawlers have been diverted to North Sea grounds hitherto fished by middle-water trawlers. Stern trawlers also fish the north-east Arctic but have recently been successful in local mackerel fishing. Middle-water trawlers between 110 and 140 feet in length (33·5–42·7 metres) have also had to diversify their activity into northern North Sea grounds consequent upon reduced quota allocations off the Faroes. The inshore group consists of some 2,024 vessels of over 40 feet (12·2 metres) and about 4,600 smaller vessels.

Supplies

In 1977 landings of all types of fish (excluding salmon and trout) by British fishing vessels totalled 916,000 tonnes (496,000 tonnes of demersal fish, 342,000 tonnes of pelagic and 78,000 tonnes of shellfish), valued at £252 million. Cod accounted for 34 per cent of the total value of demersal and pelagic fish landed by British vessels; haddock (21 per cent) and plaice (7 per cent) were the other most important sources of earnings to the industry.

Increasing attention is being paid to the culture of fish and shellfish, and the farming of some species of sea fish is being developed.

Imports of all fresh, frozen and cured fish and shellfish totalled 202,000 tonnes valued at £210 million. Imports of canned and preserved fish and shellfish amounted to 82,000 tonnes valued at nearly £114 million. Imports of fish meal amounted to 214,000 tonnes, worth £60 million, and those of fish oils to 185,000 tonnes worth nearly £51 million. Exports and re-exports of fish and fish products amounted to 156,000 tonnes and were valued at nearly £92 million.

Total fish consumption was running at a level of approximately 17·6 lb (8 kg) a head in 1977. Home production provided about 88 per cent of supplies.

Sea Fish Processing

The growth of quick-frozen fish production radically altered the structure of the processing industry. With the increase in quick-freezing, export outlets for white fish account for about 75 per cent of the total exports of fish and fish preparations. Experiments are being carried out in the catching and processing, for human consumption and fish meal, of previously under-exploited species of fish (for example, blue whiting and mackerel) of which large stocks are known to exist in the sea adjacent to the British Isles.

A valuable by-product of the industry is the manufacture of fish meal for animal feed. Home production of fish meal in 1977 was about 78,000 tonnes. Fish oil production was about 21,000 tonnes.

Freshwater Fisheries

The most valuable freshwater fish are salmon and sea-trout. Sea fishing for salmon is prohibited in a wide area around the British Isles outside the 12-mile zone. Within the zone drift netting and certain other methods are prohibited off the coast of Scotland but are permitted under licence off England, Wales and Northern Ireland. In Scotland salmon fishing is a private right. In England and Wales, water authority licences are required for coastal and estuary netting. The landed value of the salmon catch in 1977 was approximately £1,550,000 in England and Wales, about £3·8 million in Scotland, and some £352,000 in Northern Ireland. Eels worth about £968,000 were caught in Northern Ireland in 1977.

Distribution System

The principal method of distribution is through wholesalers, located at the ports, who buy fish at the auctions and sell to inland wholesalers as well as directly to retail outlets. Fish lorries, including insulated and refrigerated vehicles, transport the catch daily from the ports to inland centres, although rail transport is still used from some ports. The principal inland wholesale distributing centre for fish is Billingsgate Market in London. The increasing popularity of quick-frozen consumer packs has encouraged trawler-owning companies to enter the marketing and distribution system.

Promotion and Regulation of the Industry

The government departments mainly responsible for the administration of legislation concerning the fishing industry and for fisheries research are the Ministry of Agriculture, Fisheries and Food, the Department of Agriculture and Fisheries for Scotland, the Welsh Office Agriculture Department (see p 274) and the Department of Agriculture for Northern Ireland. The safety and welfare of crews of fishing vessels and other matters common to shipping generally are provided for under the Merchant Shipping Acts administered by the Department of Trade.

The Herring Industry Board

The Herring Industry Board was set up to reorganise, develop and regulate the herring industry. Its members are appointed jointly by the Minister of Agriculture, Fisheries and Food, and the Secretaries of State for Scotland, Wales and Northern Ireland. The Board, whose activities are financed partly by levies and licence fees and partly by government grants and loans, is advised by the Herring Industry Advisory Council, which represents all sections of the industry and consumers.

The functions of the Board include the promotion of sales of herring and the application of the benefit of technical progress to the industry. In England, Scotland and Wales, the Board administers the government grant and loan schemes which provide for assistance towards the purchase of new fishing vessels and the improvement of existing vessels. Up to 31 December 1977 about £7·5 million in loans and £8·6 million in grants had been approved by the Board.

The White Fish Authority

The function of the White Fish Authority is to reorganise, develop and regulate the white fish industry, and that of its Committee for Scotland and Northern Ireland is to advise the authority about the exercise and performance of its functions in Scotland and Northern Ireland. Membership is by ministerial appointment. The White Fish Industry Advisory Council, which represents the various interests of the fishing industry, advises the Authority about the exercise and performance of its functions.

In England, Scotland and Wales the Authority administers government grant and loan schemes for the purchase of new fishing vessels and engines and the improvement of existing vessels. It also administers loans to processors, co-operatives, etc., for the acquisition, reconditioning or improvement of facilities. Up to 31 March 1978 about £53 million in loans and £64 million in grants had been approved. Its other activities are financed by levies on first-hand sales of most white fish, and a government grant towards research and development. In 1973 the Herring Industry Board and White Fish Authority formed a unified administration for the development of fisheries administration under the European Community's marketing and structural policy (see p 281).

Northern Ireland

The Department of Agriculture for Northern Ireland operates grant and loan schemes for the purchasing of new fishing vessels and engines and the improvement of existing vessels, and for processors, co-operatives and fish farmers. Up to 31 March 1978, about £3 million in grants and £4·2 million in loans had been approved.

FORESTRY

The estimated total area of woodland in Britain is 2·056 million hectares (5·084 million acres), or about 8·5 per cent of the total land area; 44 per cent of the area is in England, 12 per cent in Scotland, 12 per cent in Wales and the remainder in Northern Ireland.

The area of productive forest in Great Britain managed by the Forestry Commission, at 0·841 million hectares (2·078 million acres), constitutes 50 per cent of this category. The annual rate of productive forest expansion is currently 23,100 hectares (57,080 acres) by the Commission mainly in Scotland, and some 7,700 hectares (19,000 acres) by private woodland owners. The Commission's programme includes considerable planting in upland areas, and consists mainly of conifers because of the difficult site conditions encountered.

Total employment in state and private forests in Great Britain was estimated at 21,150 in 1977.

Except for the period of the two world wars, when felling was abnormally heavy, home woodlands have until recent years made only a limited contribution to the nation's consumption of wood and wood products, as less than half of the Commission's woodlands are yet in production. Britain imports more than 90 per cent of its needs, the total import cost of wood and wood products including pulp and paper being £2,000 million in 1977.

The Forestry Commission and Forestry Policy

The Forestry Commission is the national forestry authority charged with promoting the interests of forestry, the development of afforestation and the production and supply of timber in Great Britain. The Commissioners comply with directions given by the forestry ministers, who are the Minister of Agriculture, Fisheries and Food and the Secretaries of State for Scotland and Wales. Northern Ireland has its own separate organisation (see p 285). In pursuing its main objective, that is, timber production, Great Britain's forestry policy also takes into account amenity, environmental and employment criteria.

The Commission's total estate covers some 1·250 million hectares (3·090 million acres) of which 0·841 million hectares (2·078 million acres) are under trees in 249 forests. All these forests are covered by management plans which are concerned not only with planting and timber production but also with facilities for public recreation, wildlife conservation and the landscaping of plantations.

As more of its coniferous woods reach the production stage, the Commission has assumed an increasingly important role as a timber seller and has encouraged the setting up of some 20 major new timber-using industries since the mid-1960s.

Production of timber from the Commission's woodlands amounted to 1·8 million cubic metres in 1977–78. The timber is used in coal mines (for roof props), in the pulp industry, in sawmills, and in factories producing chipboard, fibreboard and wood wool.

Finance

The expenditure of the Forestry Commissioners is paid out of the Forestry Fund, into which are paid amounts voted annually by Parliament, together with the Commission's receipts from sales of produce, rentals and other sources. In the period ended 31 March 1978, expenditure amounted to about £61 million, and receipts were approximately £36 million.

Private Forestry

Privately owned woods comprise 57 per cent of the total forest area in Great Britain. About half of the private woodland area is in ownerships of under 80 hectares (198 acres) in extent.

The effective management of private woodlands is encouraged by the provision of grants administered by the Forestry Commission in return for which owners accept a continuing obligation to manage their woodlands in accordance with sound forestry practice. Woodland owners are represented, in their relations with the Forestry Commission, by the Forestry Committee of Great Britain, which co-ordinates the work of the Timber Growers' Organisation (for owners in England and Wales) and the Scottish Woodland Owners' Association.

Advisory Bodies

The Home Grown Timber Advisory Committee advises the Forestry Commission on certain statutory functions, including promoting the interests of forestry and the production and supply of timber. It includes representatives of associations of woodland owners, timber merchants, processors, and other major timber users and the trade unions.

The Forestry Commissioners also maintain National Committees for England, Scotland and Wales, which act in an advisory capacity, particularly on the social, recreational and amenity aspects of the Commissioners' activities and relationships with other land users. The Commissioners also maintain a regional advisory committee for each conservancy and a consultative panel for the New Forest.

Forestry Education and Research

Forestry education is the responsibility of the central government education departments (see p 138). Degree courses in forestry and associated studies are provided at four universities and there are supervisory, craft and managerial level courses.

The Forestry Training Council, set up by the Forestry Commission, assists the development of systematic training and the co-ordination of training in the state and private sectors.

The Furniture and Timber Industry Training Board is concerned with training for private-sector employees in the home timber trade.

Forestry research is carried out by the Forestry Commission, universities and other institutions (see p 379).

Forestry in Northern Ireland

The Department of Agriculture is the forest authority for Northern Ireland. The Department may acquire land for afforestation and give financial and technical assistance for private planting. It has introduced measures to control felling, fires near plantations and damage by certain animals. Financial provision is made annually by Parliament.

The state forest area has grown steadily since the end of the second world war. By 1978, 67,700 hectares (167,300 acres) of plantable land had been acquired of which 50,100 hectares (123,800 acres) were planted. There were about 12,000 hectares (30,000) acres of privately owned forest.

Some 1,700 people worked in state and private forests in 1978, of these, about 800 were employed under the Urban and Rural Improvement Campaign for developing recreational facilities, mostly in state forests.

15 Transport and Communications

The application of technological developments to Britain's transport and communications network is helping to make travel quicker and more convenient. Major improvements in the movement of passengers and freight within Britain or between Britain and other countries have resulted from the construction of a network of motorways, the extension of fast inter-city rail services (such as those operated by high speed trains), the modernisation of many ports, the increased use of containers and other modern methods in shipping, the use by airlines of larger or speedier aircraft (such as the Concorde supersonic aircraft) and the expansion of facilities at many of Britain's airports.

Transport and communications contribute 8 per cent of Britain's gross national product and are responsible for a rather higher proportion of the nation's gross domestic fixed capital formation. These activities employed some 1·4 million people in Great Britain in March 1978 and accounted for 6 per cent of the employed labour force. Of these, 396,000 employees were engaged in road passenger transport and road haulage contracting, 207,000 in railways, 405,000 in postal services and telecommunications, 147,000 in sea transport, port and inland water transport, 82,000 in air transport and 153,000 in other transport services and storage.

INLAND TRANSPORT

The passenger and freight traffic of Great Britain is carried mainly by road. However, rail, coastal shipping and, to a lesser extent, pipelines and inland waterways are important in carrying certain types of freight, particularly bulk goods. In 1976 about 67 per cent of freight, in terms of tonne-kilometres, travelled by road, 16 per cent by rail, 14 per cent by coastal shipping, and 3 per cent by pipeline and inland waterway. Much of the inland transport system of Great Britain is publicly owned, although road haulage and coastal shipping are almost entirely in the hands of private enterprise.

In mid 1978 there were 17·7 million vehicles licensed for use on the roads of Great Britain. Of these 14 million were motor cars, 1·7 million road goods vehicles, 1·2 million motor cycles, scooters and mopeds and 112,000 public road passenger vehicles (including taxis). Private ownership of cars has been growing rapidly for many years and the car is now the most popular form of travel within Great Britain.

Government Policy

The Government's transport policy is directed towards helping economic growth and higher national prosperity, and ensuring a reasonable level of personal mobility, while improving safety, particularly on the roads, minimising damage to the environment and taking account of energy considerations. In a major policy statement in June 1977, the Government announced that higher priority would be given to maintaining public transport, with particular help for rural areas, and that local government would be given more responsibility for planning and integrating local transport. It also announced a more selective approach to roadbuilding, with emphasis on specific schemes instead of a strategic network.

Roads

There are three main categories of road in Great Britain: trunk roads (including most motorways) on which much of the long-distance traffic travels; classified roads; and unclassified roads. Road mileage in Britain totalled 222,752 miles (352,484 kilometres) in mid-1977 (see Table 19). Motorways and other major roads are shown on the map at the end of the book.

TABLE 19: Road Mileage

	Public roads[a]	Trunk roads[a] (including motorways)	Trunk motorways[b] in use[c]	under construction
England	158,643	6,470	1,261	101
Scotland	30,383	2,022	115	15
Wales	19,249	1,042	59	8
Northern Ireland	14,477	397	67	2
Britain	222,752	9,931	1,502	126

Sources: *Department of Transport, Northern Ireland Department of the Environment, Scottish Development Department and Welsh Office.*

[a] As at April 1977.

[b] As at April 1978.

[c] In addition, there were 59 miles (95 kilometres) of local authority motorway in use in England and 9 miles (14 kilometres) in Scotland.

The Government's programme of trunk road construction and improvement in England concentrates on improving the main routes between the major centres of population and industry, ports and airports, although there are also some local schemes on the less important trunk roads. The general aim is to enable journey times, accidents and vehicle operating costs to be reduced, while many towns and villages also benefit by the removal of heavy through traffic. Priority in the programme is being given to the orbital route around London and to other schemes of industrial importance. In Wales the Government's priorities are to complete the motorway across south Wales, reconstruct the coast road in north Wales and improve roads which are important for industrial redevelopment. The main objectives of the programme in Scotland are to complete the remaining links in the motorway/dual carriageway network in central Scotland and to continue improving roads which are important for North Sea oil-related activities. Priority for new roads in urban areas of Great Britain is being given to those designed to meet the needs of industry and commerce, serve new industrial or housing estates, provide links to the national trunk road network or to complement traffic management schemes.

Motor vehicle traffic in Great Britain rose in 1977 by 1·8 per cent to a record 259,382 million vehicle-kilometres, of which cars and taxis accounted for 80 per cent.

Bridges and Tunnels

The suspension bridges across the Firth of Forth and the Severn Estuary, completed in the mid-1960s, both incorporated major advances in suspension bridge design. Their main spans are among the longest suspension bridge spans, but the bridge being built across the river Humber and due to be opened in 1979 will have a span of 1,410 metres (4,626 feet), longer than any existing bridge span in the world.

A few road tunnels have been built to cross major estuaries, notably the Mersey, the Thames, the Tyne and the Clyde. A second crossing of the Thames at Dartford (Kent) is being built and is due to be completed in April 1979.

Administration

In England the Secretary of State for Transport, in Scotland the Secretary of State for Scotland, and in Wales the Secretary of State for Wales are responsible for the administration of trunk motorways and other trunk roads, and the costs of their construction, improvement and maintenance are paid for by central Government. Work on major trunk road and motorway schemes in England is controlled by regional road construction units which include staff from the Department of Transport and county councils. The highway authority for non-trunk roads in England and Wales is, in general, the county council in whose area the roads lie, and in Scotland the regional or islands council.

In Northern Ireland the Northern Ireland Department of the Environment is responsible for public roads and bears the cost of maintenance and construction.

Road Safety

The road accident record in Great Britain is considerably better than that of many other countries, even though it has one of the highest densities of road traffic in the world; in 1977, 6,614 people were killed on the roads, about 81,700 seriously injured and 259,800 slightly injured.

Modern roads, designed for present-day traffic and segregating pedestrians from vehicles, have been shown to produce a marked decrease in casualties. There are two classes of national speed limit: a limit of 70 mph (113 km/h) on motorways and other dual carriageway roads; and a limit of 60 mph (97 km/h) on single carriageway roads. In built-up areas there is a general limit of 30 mph (48 km/h). To meet local needs the urban limit can be raised and the other limits lowered on specific stretches of road. Other measures directed primarily towards road safety include pedestrian crossings and the system of road markings and traffic signs. A computer-controlled signalling system has been installed on most busy motorways to warn motorists of advisory speed limits in certain conditions and of lane closures.

The design of vehicles, their use on the roads, and the maintenance of their mechanical condition are controlled by regulations which are amended when necessary in the interests of safety or for control of pollution and noise. On 1 August 1978 a 'type approval' scheme came into operation whereby the use of cars manufactured after 1 October 1977 is not permitted unless they are of a type that has been certified as meeting the required standards. In Great Britain private cars and light vans which are three or more years old must be tested annually at private garages authorised as test stations. (In Northern Ireland private cars seven or more years old are tested at official vehicle inspection centres.) Heavy goods vehicles are tested annually at government test stations. Public service vehicles must be specially approved before being licensed to carry passengers, and are tested at regular intervals. Any vehicle may be stopped on the road at any time by the police and examined.

Minimum ages for driving are: 16 for driving invalid carriages and mopeds; 17 for cars and other passenger vehicles with nine or fewer seats (including that of the driver), motorcycles and goods vehicles not over 3·5 tonnes maximum permissible weight; 18 for goods vehicles over 3·5 but not over 7·5 tonnes; and 21 for passenger vehicles with over nine seats and goods vehicles over 7·5 tonnes. All drivers of motor vehicles, unless they have either held a full British licence or passed the driving test in the last ten years, are required to pass a test before being granted a full licence to drive. Until they pass the test they must hold a 'provisional' licence, display 'L' (learner) plates on their vehicle and be accompanied while driving (with certain exceptions) by a qualified driver. In Northern Ireland a driver having passed the test is required to display an 'R' (restricted) plate for a one-year period during which he must not exceed 45 mph (72 km/h). There are schemes for special licensing and testing of drivers of heavy goods vehicles and public service vehicles.

The Road Traffic Acts embody most of the law relating to road users. A person convicted of any of the most serious offences is liable to be disqualified from driving for a specified period. The standard of conduct for all road users and a summary of the requirements of the law are set out in the *Highway Code*. A failure to observe the code does not render a person liable to criminal proceedings but may be taken into account in such proceedings. The Road Safety Act 1967 strengthened existing measures to discourage drinking and driving, and set a maximum permissible blood alcohol level of 80 milligrams of alcohol per 100 millilitres of blood. The Government intends to introduce further measures to tighten the law on drinking and driving. Legislation will also be drawn up requiring the wearing of seat belts where they are fitted in the front seats of cars or vans. Riders of motor cycles, who are very vulnerable in accidents, are required to wear safety helmets and are encouraged to wear clothes that can be easily seen by other road users.

Campaigns to persuade people to take greater care on the roads are conducted nationally by government departments and the Royal Society for the Prevention of Accidents and locally by local authorities. In recent years major publicity campaigns have been undertaken to increase the wearing of seat belts, to reduce casualties to child pedestrians and to riders of motor cycles, and to reduce the incidence of drinking and driving.

Traffic in Towns Traffic in the centres of cities and towns in Britain is increasingly being managed so as to minimise congestion and its environmental effects, and to improve road safety. Local authorities have powers to introduce a range of measures which, when combined, form comprehensive traffic management schemes covering a particular area. Such schemes may include one-way systems, streets reserved for pedestrians, bus priority measures, parking controls and limited road construction.

Parking control is an important element of comprehensive traffic management. In most town centres parking is restricted and waiting limits apply. Major city centres often have controlled parking zones, where payment is required for on-street parking.

Several cities have new shopping precincts, some of them enclosed, which are specially designed for pedestrians and from which motor vehicles are excluded. In the centres of many towns, areas containing several streets have been wholly or partly converted to pedestrian use, and this has resulted in a more attractive environment.

Urban traffic control systems, which link traffic signals and some traffic signs to a central computer, represent an important addition to local authorities' ability to control traffic. They are confined to large towns and cities, but they are being adapted and extended for use in smaller towns. The Department of Transport is sponsoring two of the new systems at Torbay and Hull; these are due to become operational in 1979.

Research The Transport and Road Research Laboratory (TRRL), jointly sponsored by the Department of the Environment and the Department of Transport, provides technical and scientific advice and information to help in formulating, developing and implementing the Government's transport policy. It employs nearly 1,000 people of whom about half are scientists and engineers.

ROAD HAULAGE Goods vehicle traffic reached a record 42,700 million vehicle-kilometres in 1977. Considerable growth is taking place in international road haulage traffic and British hauliers are increasingly running goods vehicles to the rest of Europe and as far afield as North and West Africa and the Middle East. Much internal road haulage traffic is carried over short distances with about three-fifths of the tonnage being carried on hauls of 25 miles (40 kilometres) or less. A growing number of larger, more efficient and better designed road haulage vehicles are being operated.

Structure of the Industry Road haulage is predominantly an industry of small businesses. Many of the 124,400 holders of an operator's licence in September 1977 had only one vehicle and the average size of a vehicle fleet is only about four. Most of the industry is privately owned, but the biggest operator in Great Britain is the publicly owned National Freight Corporation (NFC). Turnover of the NFC's freight transport subsidiaries amounted to £373 million in 1977 and at the end of 1977 it had 40,100 employees and owned or leased 20,300 vehicles, 14,400 trailers and 12,200 containers and demountable bodies. Public haulage (private road hauliers and the NFC carrying other firms' goods) accounts for 63 per cent of freight carried in Great Britain in terms of tonne-kilometres. In Northern Ireland the biggest operator is Northern Ireland Carriers Ltd, owned jointly by the Northern Ireland Transport Holding Company and the NFC.

Licensing and Other Controls Those operating goods vehicles of over $3\frac{1}{2}$ tonnes gross weight (with certain special exemptions) require an operator's licence, obtained on showing good repute and ability to maintain vehicles properly and control loading and hours worked by drivers. Licences are divided into restricted licences for firms carrying their own goods and standard licences, sub-divided into 'national only' and 'international', for hauliers operating for hire or reward. Proof of professional competence is required to obtain a standard licence. Over 1 million goods vehicles not exceeding $3\frac{1}{2}$ tonnes gross laden weight are exempt from operators' licensing. A wide-ranging review of the operators' licensing system is in progress.

Regulations control the emission of smoke and noise by lorries and the carriage of dangerous goods by road. There are limits on the hours worked by drivers of goods vehicles. International road haulage is governed mainly by bilateral agreements, which are in force with 23 other European countries and allow British road hauliers to carry goods to or through these countries. Permits are required in some cases and with special exceptions these are limited to a quota negotiated annually. Within the European Community there is also a quota which authorises holders of a limited number of permits to carry out hire and reward operations between any two member countries; a similar arrangement exists between the 19 states (including Britain) which are members of the European Conference of Ministers of Transport.

PASSENGER TRANSPORT Bus and railway services in Britain are provided mainly by publicly owned operators, coach and air services partly by publicly owned bodies, and taxis and hire cars almost entirely by privately owned businesses. Buses and coaches account for about 12 per cent of passenger mileage within Great Britain, rail for 7 per cent and air 0·5 per cent.

Metropolitan Passenger Transport

In the metropolitan counties of Greater Manchester, Merseyside, West Midlands, Tyne and Wear, South Yorkshire and West Yorkshire, the metropolitan county council, acting as the passenger transport authority (PTA) is responsible for local transport policy as a whole, and appoints a professional passenger transport executive (PTE) to be responsible for day-to-day management and operations. In Scotland the Strathclyde Regional Council is the PTA for Greater Glasgow although the passenger transport area does not cover all of the region. The PTEs operate bus services in their areas and are responsible for reaching agreements with other passenger transport operators in their areas, including the British Railways Board, concerning the provision of such services as are considered necessary by the PTAs. In London the bus and Underground rail services are operated by the London Transport Executive which is responsible to the Greater London Council.

Buses and Coaches

In the public sector in Great Britain 23,000 vehicles are operated by the National Bus Company and the Scottish Transport Group, 11,000 by the seven PTEs, 6,800 by the London Transport Executive and 6,000 by other local authority undertakings. There are some 6,000 privately owned undertakings (of which the majority have fewer than five vehicles) comprising about 28,000 vehicles; only a small proportion of these operators are concerned with scheduled bus services.

Improvements to bus services are being undertaken in many areas of Britain to try to halt the substantial decline in their use due primarily to the growth in ownership of private cars. These include express and/or limited-stop bus services, 'park and ride' bus services between suburban car parks and town centres, and 'postbus' services (Post Office minibuses carrying mail and passengers) in rural areas. Bus operators have taken action to contain costs and to improve productivity by introducing larger buses, increasing the proportion of bus services operated by one man and reducing or rationalising services. Many uneconomic bus services have been withdrawn, particularly in rural areas, leaving some villages without access to public transport. To assess ways of meeting the transport needs of rural communities, experimental transport schemes, co-ordinated by a government steering committee, have been introduced in four areas (north Devon, Dinefwr in Dyfed, North Yorkshire and south Strathclyde). The Government is also providing substantial financial support, estimated at £150 million in 1977–78, to ensure the maintenance of essential local bus services.

Publicly Owned Operators

The National Bus Company operates in England and Wales through locally based subsidiaries, such as the Western National Omnibus Company, Ribble Motor Services Ltd and Crosville Motor Services Ltd, and has a network of long-distance coach services. At the end of 1977 it owned some 18,800 vehicles and employed 65,100 people. In 1977 passenger journeys on the Company's buses amounted to 1,800 million, gross revenue was £392 million and the Company had a net surplus of £9·6 million.

The Scottish Transport Group (with about 4,000 vehicles) operates all the main bus services in Scotland outside the major cities. It also runs shipping services to the main islands off the west coast of Scotland; modernised vehicle ferries have been introduced on many of these services.

In Northern Ireland almost all road passenger services are provided by subsidiaries of the Northern Ireland Transport Holding Company. Citybus Ltd operates services in the city of Belfast and Ulsterbus Ltd operates most of the services in the rest of Northern Ireland. These companies have 320 and 930 vehicles respectively.

Licensing   There are 11 traffic areas in Great Britain each under the jurisdiction of an independent body of three traffic commissioners. The commissioners are responsible for ensuring the fitness of vehicles used to carry passengers for hire or reward, and for licensing public road passenger services in order to secure proper co-ordination and to avoid unnecessary competition; to this end they may settle routes, timetables and fares. Under the Transport Act 1978 the licensing system has been modified to allow regular car-sharing schemes and to reduce restrictions on community buses run by volunteers.

Taxis   There are about 36,000 taxicabs in Great Britain, mainly in urban areas, especially London where some 12,500 taxicabs that ply for hire in the streets are privately operated by companies or owner-drivers and are licensed annually by the Metropolitan Police. There are about 16,500 licensed cab drivers in London. Numerous car-hire firms are also in operation. Elsewhere taxis are licensed by local authorities.

Urban Railways   There are underground railway services in three British cities: London, Glasgow and Liverpool. London Transport has 4,323 railway cars and serves 278 stations, while its trains operate over 255 miles (410 kilometres) of railway, of which nearly 100 miles (161 kilometres) are underground.

Urban rail projects are proceeding in several areas. London Transport is engaged on a 20-year modernisation programme for the Underground. The Piccadilly line was extended to Heathrow Airport in December 1977, enabling passengers to travel directly between Heathrow and central London by the Underground. The first stage of the new Jubilee line, which is projected to link north-west and central London, should be opened in 1979. Two major rail projects are in progress in Glasgow, one of which involves the complete modernisation of the underground railway which should be reopened in 1979. A light rapid transit system under construction on Tyneside involves the electrification of two suburban railway lines, linked by new tunnels under Newcastle upon Tyne and Gateshead, and a new bridge over the Tyne. The first section should be open in 1979 and the whole system, 34 miles (55 kilometres) long with over 40 stations, should be in operation by the mid-1980s. The project is the largest provincial urban transport scheme to have been undertaken in Britain in the twentieth century.

RAILWAYS   Railways were pioneered in Britain, and the Stockton and Darlington Railway, opened in 1825, was the first passenger public railway in the world to be worked by steam power. Under the Transport Act 1947 the four large railway companies in Great Britain were brought under public ownership and in 1963 the British Railways Board was set up to manage railway affairs and subsidiary activities. The Government has confirmed support for the present rail network through the Railways Act 1974, under which the Secretary of State for Transport has directed the British Railways Board to provide a public service generally comparable with that provided in December 1974.

Operations   In 1977 the railway network operated by British Rail amounted to 11,168 route-miles (17,973 kilometres) of which 2,341 miles (3,767 kilometres) were electrified. A total of 702 million passenger journeys was made, representing 18,200 million passenger-miles (29,290 million kilometres). Some 170 million tonnes of freight were carried by rail and freight business amounted to 12,534 million net tonne-miles (20,172 million tonne-kilometres). Receipts amounted to £593·4 million from passengers and £348·2 million from freight.

In 1977 the Board had an operating surplus of £68·4 million, £54·7 million more than in 1976. It received £364 million from the Government and the

MAIN RAILWAY PASSENGER ROUTES

Inter-City services ▬▬▬▬
Other services (for Scotland and Wales) ▬▬▬▬

```
0    20   40   60   80   100 MILES
0  20 40 60 80 100 120 KILOMETRES
```

N

Inverness
Aberdeen
Dundee
Perth
Glasgow
Edinburgh
Berwick
Dumfries
Carlisle
Newcastle upon Tyne
Sunderland
Hartlepool
Darlington
Londonderry
Larne
Belfast
Barrow
Blackpool
Preston
Leeds
York
Hull
Bradford
Manchester
Grimsby
Liverpool
Doncaster
Retford
Holyhead
Sheffield
Newark
Crewe
Stoke
Nottingham
Derby
Grantham
King's Lynn
Stafford
Shrewsbury
Leicester
Peterborough
Norwich
Wolverhampton
Coventry
Birmingham
Rugby
Cambridge
Ipswich
Worcester
Northampton
Colchester
Harwich
Hereford
Cheltenham
Fishguard
Gloucester
Oxford
Swansea
Newport
Bristol
Swindon
Reading
LONDON
Margate
Cardiff
Bath
Ashford
Dover
Folkestone
Taunton
Southampton
Portsmouth
Hastings
Exeter
Bournemouth
Eastbourne
Worthing
Brighton
Newton Abbot
Weymouth
Newhaven
Penzance
Plymouth
```
```

PTEs for providing uneconomic, but socially necessary, passenger trains, £40 million less than the limit set in advance.

At the end of 1977 the Board employed 240,100 people, of whom 178,200 were engaged on the railways (12,600 less than at the end of 1973). British Rail operated 3,290 diesel and 320 electric locomotives, 76 high speed train (HST) power cars and 302 HST passenger carriages, 3,313 diesel and 7,343 electric passenger multiple-unit vehicles, 6,086 other passenger coaches and a fleet of 166,900 freight vehicles.

In Northern Ireland the Northern Ireland Railways Company Ltd, a subsidiary of the Northern Ireland Transport Holding Company, operates the railway service on 200 miles (322 kilometres) of track.

Other Activities   British Rail has a group of other companies, of which British Rail Engineering Ltd (BREL) has the largest number of employees, about 35,000 at 13 engineering factories. BREL mainly constructs locomotives, coaches, wagons and containers for British Rail, and undertakes heavy maintenance and overhauls. It also carries out work for export and won export orders worth £42 million in 1977. Transmark, which provides consultancy services overseas on railway and associated operations, undertook consultancy work on 47 projects in 31 countries in 1977. British Transport Hotels Ltd runs 29 hotels and controls Travellers-Fare, which is responsible for catering facilities at stations and on trains, and provides meals and snacks on more trains than any other railway company in Europe. British Rail's Shipping and International Service Division, with 43 vessels, is the largest partner in the international Sealink consortium, and operates passenger and ferry services between Great Britain and Ireland and on the short-sea routes to the continent of Europe, as well as on some domestic routes. British Rail Hovercraft Ltd provides hovercraft services in conjunction with Société Nationale des Chemins de Fer Français under the Seaspeed banner (see p 301). The Railway Technical Centre at Derby is the largest in the world; its most important achievement has been the development of the advanced passenger train (APT), capable of speeds up to 155 mph (250 km/h). Development work has involved fundamental research into the guidance and stability of railway vehicles which would enable these high speeds to be attained on existing track.

Development   In recent years the main developments have been the improvement of inter-city passenger services with the emphasis on speed, reliability, comfort and better train connections; and an increase in freight trainload traffic, allowing higher speeds and greater mechanisation in the carrying of coal, other bulk commodities and containers. The standards of track and signalling are being raised to allow faster running speeds and improved operating efficiency.

Passenger Services   The passenger network (see p 293) comprises a fast inter-city network linking the main centres of Great Britain; local stopping services; and commuter services in and around the large conurbations, especially London and the South East. British Rail introduced the world's fastest diesel rail service known as Inter-City 125, in October 1976 on the route from London to Bristol and south Wales. The service is operated by 27 high speed trains, which travel at maximum sustained speeds of 125 mph (201 km/h). The first six of further HSTs inaugurated a similar service between London and Edinburgh in May 1978 and the construction of HSTs to operate between London and south-west England and on the route linking Edinburgh, Newcastle upon Tyne, Birmingham, and south-west England or south Wales has been approved by the Government. Three prototype electric APTs are being built

Postal Services

Carrying 35,000 mail sacks a day, the Post Office's unique underground railway runs for six and a half miles under London.

Postbuses, carrying passengers and mail, provide a vital transport link in remote rural areas.

Expresspost, a speedy special delivery service, operates in London and other major cities.

Communications Research

Testing a computer that will control the working of System X exchanges, part of the advanced telephone network planned by the Post Office for the 1980s.

An almost echo-free chamber used in the research for achieving clearer speech over the telephone.

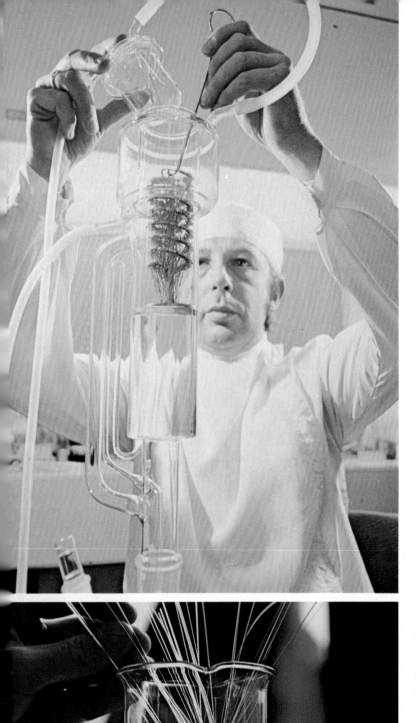

Working on a transistor 'header' used for boosting telephone conversations through underwater cables.

Glass-fibre rods, stretched into strands as fine as a human hair, are used for carrying telephone calls over the new optical fibre links.

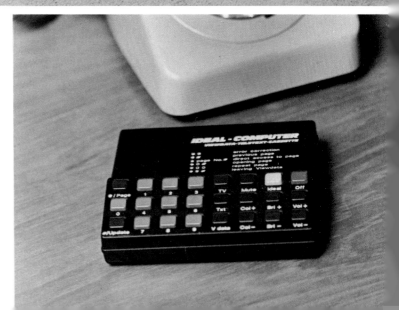

'Prestel' brings together two familiar pieces of domestic equipment—the television set and the telephone. It will be the world's first public viewdata service when established in 1979.

The keypad used in selecting information for display on the screen.

and the first set will enter service between London and Glasgow in 1979, covering the 400-mile (644-kilometre) journey in just over four hours.

Electrification is continuing and work started in 1977 on an £80 million scheme to electrify the line between London and Bedford. Proposals for commuter services include the development of new electric multiple-unit trains to replace old stock, while several urban railway projects are in progress (see p 292). The Government is reviewing with the British Railways Board the case for further main-line electrification.

Freight

The most important freight commodities handled in 1977 were coal and coke (94 million tonnes) and iron and steel (26 million tonnes). Other commodities, such as petroleum products, cars, refuse, roadstone and construction materials, are becoming more important and British Rail is concentrating on traffic particularly suitable for carriage by rail, especially long-distance and bulk trainload traffic. Trainload traffic accounts for about 80 per cent of freight tonnage, compared with 31 per cent in 1968.

Increased efficiency is being obtained as new types of wagon are introduced with larger capacities and capable of higher speeds. A network of 'Speedlink' high-speed freight services using these new wagons is being established between the major industrial centres. Over 30 Speedlink trains run each day and the number is being increased to around 50 by the end of 1978. Freight traffic is being concentrated at fewer and better equipped and sited marshalling yards and terminals. A computer-based total operations processing system, which monitors continuously all consignments and freight train and wagon movements in Great Britain, has reduced costs by allowing the more intensive use of rolling stock and the withdrawal of many obsolete freight vehicles. The 'merry-go-round' system, whereby trains are loaded and discharged automatically while in motion, is being used increasingly where there are heavy flows of mineral traffic, such as the carriage of coal to power stations and iron ore to steelworks.

The Government provides grants of 50 per cent towards the cost of construction or modernisation of privately owned rail freight facilities where this leads to significant environmental benefits by the removal of heavy goods vehicle traffic from the roads. By mid-1978, 43 schemes had been approved for grants totalling £10 million.

Private Railways There are several small privately owned passenger-carrying railways in Great Britain, mostly operated on a voluntary basis and providing limited services for tourists and railway enthusiasts; the principal aim of many of these railways is the preservation of steam traction. Some are narrow gauge railways, while others run on former British Rail track.

INLAND WATERWAYS Inland waterways are popular for recreation (see p 423), continue to carry freight and are important for land drainage and water supply. Of the 2,000 miles (3,219 kilometres) of canal and river navigations controlled by the publicly owned British Waterways Board, some 340 miles (547 kilometres) are maintained as commercial waterways for use by freight-carrying vessels. Freight traffic of about 4 million tonnes a year is carried on the Board's commercial waterways. In addition, some freight is carried on about 600 miles (966 kilometres) of inland waterways owned by other bodies. The Board also operates docks, warehouses and inland freight terminals, and has two freight carrying fleets, although most of the traffic on its waterways is conveyed by independent carriers. Limited improvements are being undertaken for freight traffic. The Board is operating on some of its commercial waterways a specially designed 'push-tow' barge system.

In 1977 the Board's turnover amounted to £10·7 million and it received government grants of nearly £12·4 million, most of which were used to maintain its waterways to statutory standards. As part of the Government's proposals to reorganise the structure of the water industry (see p 264), the British Waterways Board would be merged within a centralised structure to form the nucleus of a national navigation authority.

PORTS

There are some 250 port authorities or public wharf operators in Britain, and about 800 other undertakings engaged in various harbour operations, such as stevedoring, towage, warehousing and lighterage. Port authorities are of four main types: nationalised bodies, public trusts, local authorities and statutory companies.

Ports run by nationalised undertakings represent over a quarter of total capacity, the majority, including Southampton, Hull, Immingham, Newport, Cardiff and Swansea, being owned by the British Transport Docks Board. In 1977 shipping arrivals and departures at the Board's docks totalled 129·8 million net registered tons (including fishing vessels) and total cargo handled was 77·2 million tonnes. The Board's revenue totalled £110·5 million and it achieved a net surplus of £7·3 million. The British Railways Board controls certain ports, including Fishguard, Folkestone, Holyhead, Parkeston Quay (Harwich) and Stranraer, which are largely used for its shipping services, while the British Waterways Board owns Sharpness (Gloucester) and Weston Point in Runcorn. Major ports controlled by public trusts include London, Milford Haven, Tees and Hartlepool, Medway, Forth and Clyde. Local authorities own about one-third of Britain's ports, including Bristol and Sunderland. Port undertakings owned by statutory companies include Manchester and Liverpool. Many private ports deal with the traffic of individual industrial firms in commodities such as china clay and petroleum.

Port authorities, in the main, operate with statutory powers and responsibilities set out in private Acts of Parliament. Most are members of the British Ports Association which aims to further the common interests of port authorities in their relations with the Government, shipowners and traders.

National Ports Council

The National Ports Council, set up under the Harbours Act 1964, is financed principally by a levy on port authorities. It advises the Government on major port developments and has various responsibilities in relation to research, training, statistics and charges.

Port Traffic

Over 336 million tonnes of cargo a year pass through the ports of Great Britain. Coastal traffic accounts for over 100 million tonnes consisting largely of petroleum and coal. Of some 158 million tonnes of imports from overseas, about 81 million tonnes consist of petroleum and petroleum products. Manufactured goods form about 30 per cent of exports.

A large proportion of the general cargo traffic through British ports is handled by unitised transport methods in containers and roll-on goods vehicles, which carried 35 million tonnes of goods in 1977. Felixstowe, Dover, London, Southampton and Hull all handled large amounts.

Principal Ports

London is Britain's largest port for non-fuel traffic. In 1977, 43 million tonnes of goods were handled, including 22 million tonnes of petroleum. Southampton is the main trading port on the south coast. Medway is important for petroleum and petroleum products, while some of the other ports in the South East and East Anglia are growing rapidly with modern facilities especially for roll-on/roll-off and container traffic. Dover is Britain's leading port for passengers and roll-on/roll-off passenger and goods vehicles.

Liverpool is a very important export outlet, especially to countries outside Europe and the Mediterranean. The inland port of Manchester, reached from the Mersey via the 58-kilometre (36-mile) Manchester Ship Canal, exports particularly chemicals and petroleum products.

The port of Tees and Hartlepool handles petroleum products, chemicals, iron and steel, and iron ore. Some of the ports on the north-east coast of England, such as Blyth and the Tyne, have an important outward trade in coal. Grimsby and Hull are Britain's two main fishing ports. Immingham handles imports of iron ore and crude oil and exports of ferrous and petroleum products.

Milford Haven, handling 37 million tonnes a year, is Britain's major oil port. Much of the traffic through the south Wales ports is connected with the local steel industry—imports of iron ore and exports of iron and steel, and tinplate.

In Scotland the principal port facilities serving the central industrial area are Greenock (handling particularly petroleum and petroleum products, containers and raw sugar) and Glasgow (iron ore and grain) on the Clyde, and Grangemouth (containers and timber) and Leith (grain and whisky) on the Forth. The Clyde and Forth estuaries have major crude oil terminals.

Belfast is the principal port of Northern Ireland and with Larne handles the main traffic across the Irish Sea.

Tanker Terminals

Most of the oil tankers coming to Britain to discharge crude oil are berthed at special tanker terminals owned and operated by the oil companies to serve their refineries. Milford Haven can accommodate fully laden vessels of up to 275,000 deadweight tons on all tides at five private oil company terminals and Finnart on the Clyde will accept vessels of 325,000 deadweight tons. At Tetney Haven, off the mouth of the Humber, tankers discharge oil at an offshore buoy and it is carried by pipeline to the shore; the first oil was discharged at a similar buoy at Amlwch (Gwynedd) in 1977.

The first purpose-built terminal for oil from the British sector of the North Sea was completed at Hound Point on the Forth in 1975 and other terminals have been built on the Tees and at Flotta (Orkney). The oil port being built at Sullom Voe in Shetland is expected to become the largest in Britain and should handle its first oil later in 1978. Of the four jetties being built, three are designed to take tankers of up to 300,000 deadweight tons.

Development

Modernisation of Britain's ports is in progress, primarily to accommodate technological changes, notably the growth in size of tankers and bulk carriers and the increase in the proportion of goods carried in container ships and roll-on vessels, and the changing nature and direction of Britain's trade. However, port investment in real terms has been declining in the 1970s and most current developments are concerned with specific energy or industrial needs or to accommodate specialised container or roll-on services rather than with general purpose port facilities.

Recent major schemes have included a £16 million container terminal at Tilbury (London) covering 64 acres (26 hectares), which is due to open later in 1978, making Tilbury the world's largest terminal for refrigerated containers; the £37 million Royal Portbury Dock at Bristol, containing six berths and the largest entrance lock in Britain; and one of the world's biggest hoverports, a £12 million terminal at Dover to handle cross-Channel hovercraft, which became fully operational in July 1978. A terminal for handling iron ore and coal is being built at Hunterston on the Clyde and will be able to accommodate ships of up to 350,000 deadweight tons. It is the biggest terminal of its type in Europe and should be operational towards the end of 1978.

The exploration for, and production of, offshore oil and gas has led to other port developments, mainly in Scotland. Supply bases for offshore vessels have been built at a number of ports including Leith, Dundee, Montrose, Aberdeen, Peterhead, and Lerwick in Shetland.

Labour

At the end of 1977 about 65,000 people were employed in Britain's ports industry; of these, 29,000 dockers responsible for the physical and mechanical handling of cargo were registered with the National Dock Labour Board (NDLB), which administers the Dock Workers Employment Scheme. The system of casual labour common among dock workers in the past has been virtually eliminated. The Dock Work Regulation Act 1976 enables statutory control of dock work to be modified to meet changing conditions in the industry. The NDLB has been reconstituted as a statutory corporation with wider representation.

SHIPPING

Of the world's active sea-going tonnage of 100 gross tons[1] and over at 1 January 1978, 8 per cent was registered in Britain, making the British merchant fleet at 31·2 million gross tons the fourth largest in active employment after those of Liberia, Japan and Greece. The oil tanker fleet (14·6 million gross tons) was the world's third largest and the ore and bulk carrier fleet (8 million gross tons) the fifth largest. The British fleet is one of the most modern in the world with some 42 per cent of the tonnage less than five years old. In the last ten years some £4,500 million has been spent on new ships and other capital investment by Britain's 300 shipping companies.

Role of the Government

The Department of Trade is the government department responsible for most matters connected with merchant shipping, including general policy towards the industry and Britain's relations with other governments and international organisations on shipping matters. Under the Merchant Shipping Acts it administers many regulations for marine safety and welfare, and for preventing and cleaning up pollution from ships (see p 169). For instance, it certifies the load-line (or Plimsoll line) that shows that a ship is not overloaded; ensures that standards of safety are observed in ship construction; ensures the provision of adequate life-saving, fire-fighting and radio equipment; and deals with the discipline, professional standards, health and accommodation of seamen. These duties are carried out from marine survey offices and mercantile marine offices located at various ports. The Acts also contain certain reserve powers for protecting shipping and trading interests from measures adopted or proposed by overseas governments. In the offices of the Registrar General of Shipping and Seamen, at Cardiff, a record of all British ships is kept.

---

[1] One gross ton = 100 cubic feet (2·83 cubic metres). One deadweight ton = 1 long ton (2,240 lb or 1,016 kilogrammes). Gross tonnage indicates the total capacity of the enclosed space on a ship. Deadweight tonnage denotes the maximum load which a vessel can carry before submerging the load-line.

THE MERCHANT FLEET

In July 1977, 29·4 million gross tons of trading vessels of 100 gross tons and over were both owned and registered in Britain.[1] These ships are usually employed as follows: 15·3 million gross tons as tankers; 9·2 million gross tons as tramps and 5 million gross tons as passenger and cargo liners. Rapid technological change in the merchant fleet is reflected in the current composition. Vessels are becoming obsolete over a shorter period and as they do so are being replaced by larger ships, incorporating labour-saving devices.

The tendency to greater size has been most marked in tankers, bulk carriers and container vessels. Tanker size has increased from a maximum of 30,000 deadweight tons in the early 1950s to about 500,000 deadweight tons for the largest ocean-going tankers. The largest modern container ships of up to 60,000 gross tons have a capacity of 2,800 containers of 20-foot (6-metre) equivalent units.

Lloyd's Register of Shipping surveys and classifies ships with particular regard to their safety and operational efficiency.

OWNERSHIP

Nearly the whole of the British merchant fleet is privately owned, apart from some ships which are owned and/or operated by nationalised industries as part of their normal commercial operations, one example being British Rail (see p 294). Over half of the tanker fleet belongs to the oil companies, although there are a few independent tanker operators. British liner tonnage is dominated by a relatively small number of large groups, the largest liner company being the Peninsular and Oriental Steam Navigation Company. Some shipowners have delegated the management of their fleets to specialist ship management companies. Several companies are participating in consortia, particularly where heavy investment in ships and facilities is required, as with container and bulk cargo vessels. Chartering of ships of all nationalities takes place on the Baltic Exchange, the largest market of its type in the world. The representative body for shipowners (excluding owners of fishing vessels) is the General Council of British Shipping.

TRAFFIC

Almost all Britain's overseas trade by weight, over four-fifths by value, is carried by sea. Ships registered in Britain carry 35 per cent by weight, 44 per cent by value, of seaborne trade between Britain and other countries. Tanker cargoes, mostly imports of crude oil, account for nearly half this trade by weight but only about 13 per cent by value, and foodstuffs and manufactured goods account for over three-quarters by value.

Traffic in container or roll-on/roll-off vessels is accounting for a growing proportion of general cargo trade. Many of the deep-sea liner services from Britain are operated by container ships. Roll-on services, accommodating passengers and their cars and, in some cases, commercial vehicles are increasing in number, particularly between Britain and the continent of Europe. Several roll-on services for freight only operate to the Irish Republic, the continent of Europe, and to more distant countries, especially in the Middle East, North Africa and West Africa.

The proportion of passengers travelling to or from Britain by sea is about one-third, compared with about one-half in the early 1960s. Almost all passengers travel to or from the continent of Europe or the Irish Republic, services on other routes having virtually ceased as a result of the growth of air services. Remaining long-distance passenger ships are used for cruising and about 100,000 passengers a year embark on pleasure cruises from British ports.

---

[1] The remaining tonnage included fishing vessels, tugs, river and estuary craft, Ministry of Defence vessels (mostly tankers) not usually engaged in the commercial carriage of cargo, and shipping registered in Britain but owned in other Commonwealth countries.

Conferences

British shipping companies operating liner services have associated with each other and with the companies of other countries operating on the same routes in a series of 'conferences' designed to secure standardisation and stability of rates, and to maintain frequency and regularity of services. The essential principle of a conference is the establishment of a common tariff of freight rates to be applied by each member line. Each conference regularly reviews existing rates and the share of the trade carried by member lines. Rates are reviewed in consultation with shippers' organisations. There are about 100 conferences dealing with trade to and from Britain.

EMPLOYMENT OF SEAFARERS

Various qualifications are required for employment on board ship in certain grades. Responsibility for holding examinations and issuing certificates of competency rests with the Department of Trade, except in the case of radio officers where this is the function of the Home Office.

There are some 50 establishments providing full-time vocational training for seafarers. Most deck and catering junior ratings are trained at the National Sea Training College at Gravesend (Kent), the world's largest ratings' establishment, which can accommodate some 2,000 ratings a year. The Merchant Navy Training Board promotes the instruction and studies of apprentices, cadets and ratings who are preparing for their examinations for the various certificates of competency.

Conditions of Employment

Wages and conditions of employment of most seafarers are negotiated by the National Maritime Board, composed of equal numbers of representatives of the General Council of British Shipping and seafarers' trade unions. The Merchant Navy Established Service Scheme, introduced in 1947, removed a great deal of the uncertainty formerly associated with seafaring. Under the latest scheme seafarers are employed either as 'registered seafarers' or they may enter into a company service contract, for a minimum of one year, for employment on the ships of a particular company. Registered seafarers receive special benefits between voyages in addition to the normal state benefits. The benefits paid to company service contract seafarers must be at least equivalent to those paid to registered seafarers. The industry is studying ways of improving seafaring conditions of work and leisure.

SAFETY AT SEA

The Department of Trade's responsibilities for safety include administration of the Marine Survey Service, the Coastguard Service, and certain administrative functions concerning lighthouses and pilotage. The Department makes regulations to ensure safety of navigation at sea and conducts inquiries into shipping casualties and accidents. Britain's merchant fleet is one of the safest in the world; it has a consistently lower record of ship losses than the world average.

Sea Rescue

The Coastguard Service co-ordinates search and rescue action for vessels in distress off the coasts of Britain, and gives direct assistance where appropriate. There are some 600 regular coastguards and about 9,000 voluntary auxiliary coastguards. Constant watch is maintained all the year round at certain main stations and at times of casualty risk at a number of others. During 1977 life-saving action was taken on 4,030 occasions and 7,433 people were rescued.

The Coastguard Service calls upon shipping, the lifeboats of the Royal National Life-boat Institution (RNLI), and Service aircraft to assist as necessary. It can also call upon the services of a long-range civilian helicopter based at Aberdeen. The RNLI is supported entirely by voluntary contributions, and depends for its operation on voluntary workers. Lifeboats were launched 2,737 times in 1977 and rescued 1,131 people.

Lighthouses   The general lighthouse authority for England and Wales, the Channel Islands and Gibraltar is the Corporation of Trinity House, which is administered by a board of Elder Brethren elected from the Royal Navy and the Merchant Navy. Lighthouses in Scotland and Ireland are the responsibility respectively of the Northern Lighthouse Board and the Commissioners of Irish Lights. These authorities control about 350 lighthouses, many minor lights and buoys, and a number of lightships, some of which are being replaced by unattended sea marks or by light towers.

Pilotage   In Britain there are 46 pilotage authorities for the 86 pilotage districts and over 1,500 licensed pilots. Trinity House is the chief pilotage authority, licensing some 700 pilots in 41 districts in England and Wales. In some cases the harbour authority or local council is the pilotage authority.

Traffic Control   There are a number of traffic separation schemes around the shores of Britain. Observance of traffic separation schemes adopted by the Inter-Governmental Maritime Consultative Organisation (a United Nations agency with headquarters in London) has been required of British shipping since 1972 and in 1977 it became mandatory for vessels of countries contracting to revised international collision regulations. The most important scheme affecting British waters is in the Dover Strait, one of the world's busiest seaways. It consists of traffic lanes for shipping passing through the strait and inshore traffic zones for use by local shipping. The number of collisions has fallen considerably since the introduction of the scheme. Britain and France operate radar surveillance services which keep watch on ships not conforming to the traffic separation scheme and broadcast navigational information to ships in the Dover Strait. 'Mancheplan', a joint contingency plan for handling maritime disasters in the English Channel and the Dover Strait, was brought fully into force by the British and French Governments in May 1978. The Anglo-French Safety of Navigation Group, comprising representatives of British and French government departments, is responsible for improving safety in the English Channel.

HOVERCRAFT   The hovercraft, a vehicle which rides on a cushion of air over both land and water surfaces, was invented in Britain and has been in regular public passenger service since the mid-1960s. Services are concentrated on cross-Channel routes and on routes across the Solent between Southampton and the Isle of Wight. Two operators provide cross-Channel services: Seaspeed with routes between Dover and Boulogne, and Dover and Calais; and Hoverlloyd Ltd, which has a purpose-built hoverport at Pegwell Bay for its car and passenger ferries between Ramsgate and Calais. A hovercraft crossing takes about one-third of the time taken by ships and hovercraft have gained about one-third of the short-sea traffic in this area. Several hovercraft have had or are to have their capacity increased to meet the growing demand. In the summer of 1978 Seaspeed placed in service the world's largest hovercraft, a British Hovercraft Corporation SR.N4 which has been structurally enlarged to accommodate 416 passengers and 60 cars.

CIVIL AVIATION

Britain has a growing civil aviation industry which is continuing to develop to meet the increasing demand for air travel, particularly international travel. Airline services are operated by British Airways and by a number of independent airlines. The most modern types of aircraft are operated including wide-bodied aircraft and the Concorde supersonic aircraft with which British Airways inaugurated in 1976, jointly with Air France, the world's first supersonic passenger services. To cater for the growing number of air passengers, many airports are being substantially modernised and new terminals installed.

Role of the Government

The Secretary of State for Trade is responsible for international matters (including negotiation of air service agreements with other countries, the licensing and control of public transport operations into Britain by overseas operators and British participation in the activities of international aviation bodies), airports policy, amenity matters such as aircraft noise, aviation security policy and investigation of accidents.

Civil Aviation Authority

The Civil Aviation Authority (CAA) is an independent statutory body, responsible for the economic, technical and operational regulation of the industry; the provision by the National Air Traffic Services, jointly with the Secretary of State for Defence, of air navigation services and the aerodrome navigation services at certain British airports; and the operation of eight aerodromes in Scotland. The Secretary of State for Trade appoints the members of the CAA, and issues a written guidance on the general policies to be followed, which requires approval of both Houses of Parliament.

The CAA has been given the objective of recovering as soon as possible the whole of its costs and a reasonable return on capital from the users of its services. Meanwhile the Government is paying the CAA a grant to meet the deficit on its revenue account; it amounted to £16·6 million in 1977–78.

Air Traffic

Since 1962 more passengers have entered or left Britain by air than by sea. In 1977 a total of some 34·6 million passengers travelled by air (international terminal passengers), compared with 18·3 million by sea. Total capacity offered on all services by British airlines amounted to 10,279 million capacity-tonne-kilometres in 1977, 5·7 per cent more than in 1976. British Airways accounts for some 92 per cent of scheduled services flown by British airlines, whereas the charter market is dominated by independent companies.

The value of overseas trade by air rose by 28 per cent in 1977 to £10,973 million, and the proportions of Britain's overseas trade carried by air amounted to 17 per cent of the value of exports and 14 per cent of imports. Air freight is important for the carriage of goods with a high value-to-weight ratio, especially where speed of movement is essential. Precious stones (particularly diamonds), live animals, medicinal and pharmaceutical products, clothing, leather and skins, and scientific instruments are major categories where a relatively high proportion of exports is sent by air.

British Airways

British Airways is one of the world's leading airlines, and in terms of international passengers carried and of international passenger-kilometres flown it is the largest in the world. During 1977–78 British Airways' turnover was £1,355 million (including £1,156 million from airline operations), and it made a net profit of £33 million. Overseas earnings amounted to £775 million. In March 1978 British Airways employed about 57,300 staff. Its assets of £819 million included £662 million of aircraft and spares and £99 million of land and buildings. In 1977 a reorganisation of the airline, involving the replacement of three airline divisions by a number of functional departments, was implemented to create a unified airline, with a simpler organisation, and to increase efficiency and profitability.

Airline Operations

British Airways' route network covering some 579,800 kilometres (360,200 miles) of unduplicated route is among the largest in the world. The airline serves 149 destinations in 78 countries. In 1977–78 some 13·4 million passengers were carried on scheduled services, which are operated to the rest of Europe, the Middle East, the Far East, Australasia, East and South Africa, North America and Guyana in South America. Within Britain it runs over 1,000 services a week to 26 towns and cities throughout the country. The airline's Concorde services are operated from London (Heathrow) to New York, Washington and Bahrain. Initial experience has exceeded expectations with high passenger load factors on the routes to the United States. In 1975 British Airways inaugurated Europe's first air 'shuttle' service (a regular scheduled no-reservation service with back-up aircraft to carry extra passengers) between Heathrow and Glasgow, and similar services have been introduced from Heathrow to Edinburgh and Belfast. Joint shuttle services with national airlines to a number of other European countries are being investigated.

Other Activities

British Airways Associated Companies Ltd is responsible for the group's investments connected with a number of hotel companies and air companies in different parts of the world. British Airways Helicopters Ltd operates a scheduled service between Penzance (Cornwall) and the Isles of Scilly, undertakes charter work, provides links between oil rigs in the North Sea and the mainland and operates air-sea rescue services from Aberdeen. Engine overhaul work for British Airways and other airlines is carried out by British Airways Engine Overhaul Ltd. International Aeradio Ltd plans, installs, operates and maintains airport technical services and general communications and manufactures specialised equipment for use in these services.

Aircraft

British Airways operated 208 aircraft and helicopters in 1978. Aircraft included 25 BAC One-Elevens, 9 Boeing 707–436s, 11 Boeing 707–336s, 25 Boeing 747s, 5 Concordes, 2 HS 748s, 5 Merchantmen (converted Vanguard passenger aircraft), 15 Trident Ones, 16 Trident Twos, 25 Trident Threes, 9 TriStar 1s, 15 Super VC10s, and 19 Viscounts. Major orders include 19 Boeing 737s, 19 Boeing 757s and 6 TriStar 500s. Helicopters operated comprise 23 Sikorsky 61Ns, 2 Sikorsky 58Ts, 1 Bell Jet Ranger and 1 Bell 212.

Independent Airlines

The independent airlines carry nearly 4 million passengers a year on scheduled services and over 9 million on charter flights. The main independent scheduled airline is British Caledonian Airways, which operates a fleet of 27 aircraft and carries over 1 million scheduled service passengers a year. Its scheduled services are primarily to the continent of Europe, West and Central Africa, South America and Houston in the United States. Other independent operators of scheduled passenger services include British Island Airways, British Midland Airways and Dan-Air Services. A pioneering development in transatlantic air travel was the inauguration in September 1977 by Laker Airways of its daily 'Skytrain' service, a service with cheap fares and no advance bookings operating between London (Gatwick) and New York. Britannia Airways, Dan-Air Services, Laker Airways and Monarch Airlines are the leading independent airlines running charter passenger services.

Over 290 aircraft operated by some 130 public transport companies are engaged in air-taxi operations. Helicopters are also used to transport businessmen, but are being employed increasingly in operations connected with the development of Britain's offshore oil and gas resources. Light aircraft and helicopters are also involved in other activities, such as charter operations, search and rescue services, crop-spraying, aerial survey and photography, and flying instruction.

Licensing

Under the CAA's air transport licensing system, British operators apply for licences for scheduled and charter services, or for revocation or variation of existing licences including alterations to fares. With certain exceptions the CAA is required to license only one British airline to provide scheduled services on a long-haul international route. British Airways is the preferred airline for all long-haul routes other than those to the areas in the 'sphere of interest' of British Caledonian Airways, as defined in the policy guidance of 1976. The CAA also licenses air travel organisers. The Air Transport Users Committee advises the CAA on the interests of passengers and other airline users, and investigates individual complaints against airlines.

Safety

The CAA is responsible for the regulation of the safety of civil aircraft registered in Britain. Its Operations Division deals with the preparation and application of safety requirements concerning airline operations, flight crew licensing and training, aerodromes, and fire and rescue services. The Airworthiness Division is responsible for functions such as the airworthiness certification of aircraft, the licensing of aircraft maintenance engineers, the approval of work schedules to which transport aircraft are maintained, and the publication of the British Civil Airworthiness Requirements, a code with which all aircraft built in Britain or flown by British airlines must comply. It has similar duties in relation to hovercraft. The CAA is advised in these duties by the Airworthiness Requirements Board. Recent safety measures have included a mandatory system of reporting of incidents and structural or mechanical defects, and the requirement for fitting ground proximity warning systems in public transport aircraft registered in Britain.

Air Operators'
Certificates

Every operator of aircraft above a certain weight used for public transport must possess an Air Operator's Certificate which is granted by the CAA when it is satisfied that the operator is competent to secure the safe operation of its aircraft. The CAA's flight operations inspectors (who are experienced airline pilots) check that satisfactory operating standards are maintained.

Flight Crew
Qualifications
and
Training

Each member of the flight crew of a British registered aircraft must hold the appropriate official licence issued by the CAA. Applicants for professional pilots' licences are required to attend approved courses of training before attempting qualifying examinations and flight tests.

Air Traffic
Control and
Navigation
Services

Responsibility for civil and military air traffic control over Britain and the surrounding seas rests with the National Air Traffic Services. The planning and provision of the facilities necessary for control of aircraft at the higher flight levels are carried out in conjunction with Eurocontrol, a European international agency of which Britain is a member.

A system of airways, introduced in 1950 and covering the main traffic routes with control zones around the major airports, has been gradually extended. The primary navigation aids have been the very high frequency omnidirectional ranges (VORs) and distance measuring equipment. Re-equipment with the more accurate Doppler VOR system began in 1974 and should be completed before 1980. During the last few years virtually the whole of the airspace over Britain above 5,000 feet (1,500 metres) has been brought under surveillance by modern primary and secondary radar equipment. There are two main air traffic control centres, located at West Drayton (Greater London) and Prestwick, and a subsidiary centre at Manchester. Extensive use is made of automatic data processing and other advanced electronic techniques.

The development of all-weather landing systems, on the basis of an improved version of the standard instrument landing system, was pioneered in Britain and most of Britain's major airports use this improved version.

Airports

Of the 128 licensed civil aerodromes in Britain, just over one-quarter each handles more than 100,000 passengers a year. In 1977 Britain's civil airports handled a total of 47·1 million passengers (45·9 million terminal passengers and 1·2 million in transit), 2·6 per cent more than in 1976, and 705,000 tonnes of freight. The two major airports in the London area (Heathrow and Gatwick) handled most passengers, 23·8 million and 6·7 million respectively. Other leading airports were Manchester 2·9 million passengers, Glasgow 1·8 million, Luton, Birmingham and Belfast. While the number of air passengers has, in general, risen in recent years, there has not been a corresponding increase in air transport movements owing to the growing use of wide-bodied aircraft.

Ownership and Control

The British Airports Authority (BAA), an independent statutory body operating on a commercial basis, owns and manages seven airports—Heathrow, Gatwick and Stansted in the south-east, and Glasgow, Edinburgh, Prestwick and Aberdeen in Scotland—which handle 75 per cent of air passengers and 85 per cent of air cargo traffic in Britain. In 1977–78 the BAA's income was £125·1 million and it recorded a pre-tax profit of £24·3 million.

Eight small aerodromes in the Highlands and Islands of Scotland are controlled by the Civil Aviation Authority and Belfast's airport (Aldergrove) is managed by Northern Ireland Airports Ltd, a subsidiary of the Northern Ireland Transport Holding Company. Most of the other public airports are controlled by local authorities. All airports and aerodromes in Britain (apart from those controlled by the Government or by the CAA) must be licensed annually by the CAA. Stringent requirements, such as the provision of adequate fire-fighting, medical and rescue services, suitable runways, and of air traffic control services and visual aids, must be satisfied before a licence is granted. Strict security measures are in force at airports. Policing of airports is generally the responsibility of the local police forces.

Development

A major £73 million modernisation programme is almost complete at Heathrow, the world's busiest centre for international travel, to develop the capacity of the three terminals to their ultimate limit of about 30 million passengers a year. Plans for a fourth terminal, raising Heathrow's annual capacity to 38 million passengers, are being considered at a local planning inquiry. Gatwick airport, 28 miles (45 kilometres) south of London, is the second major airport for the London area and was the first in the world to bring together road, rail and air transport connections in one unit. A £100 million redevelopment programme has been virtually completed, increasing Gatwick's annual capacity to some 16 million passengers. The Government has announced measures to ensure greater use of Gatwick so as to relieve congestion at Heathrow.

Work is in progress to develop facilities at several of Britain's other airports. A five-year development scheme, costing some £15 million, started in 1977 for the expansion of terminal facilities at Aldergrove. Conditions at Edinburgh airport have been improved considerably as a result of a £15 million redevelopment scheme which involved the construction of a 2,560-metre (8,400-ft) runway and of a new terminal building. Offshore oil and gas activities have stimulated a major expansion programme at Aberdeen airport, where a new terminal was opened in 1977 and which has become the world's busiest heliport, and developments at other airports including Inverness and Sumburgh (Shetland).

Government Policy on Airport Development

In 1978 the Government set out its policy for the development of airports in Great Britain up to 1990, to accommodate the substantial increase expected in the number of air passengers. The emphasis is on developing existing airports rather than on constructing new ones. The Government envisages a build-up of traffic to use the large modern facilities at Gatwick and a limited expansion of other airports in the London area. Manchester has been designated as the principal 'gateway' international airport in England and Wales outside the south-east. Developments in the rest of England and Wales will be concentrated at the selected regional airports of Birmingham, Cardiff-Wales, East Midlands, Leeds/Bradford and Newcastle upon Tyne.

THE POST OFFICE

The Post Office, founded in 1657, provides postal, telecommunications, data processing and Giro services. It was set up as a public authority under the Post Office Act 1969, having previously been a government department. The chairman and other members of the board are appointed by the Secretary of State for Industry. With some 401,000 employees, it is the largest commercial employer in Europe.

In 1977–78 the Post Office's income, excluding internal transactions, was £4,183 million and a profit of £367·7 million was recorded, with profits of £325·5 million on telecommunications and £40·4 million on posts. Capital expenditure on fixed assets amounted to £870 million in 1977–78. Some £56 million a year is spent on research and development, mostly at the Post Office's research centre at Martlesham Heath (Suffolk).

POSTAL SERVICES

The Post Office pioneered postal services and was the first service to issue adhesive postage stamps as proof of advance payment for mail. It provides deliveries each working day to 22 million addresses. In 1977–78 the Post Office handled some 160 million parcels and 9,325 million items of other correspondence (including 8,840 million inland letters).

Postal operations are being mechanised and by 1984 there will be a national network of 83 mechanised high-speed sorting offices. Large parcel centres, each serving a group of counties, are gradually taking over the work of the 1,200 offices which handle parcels manually. Mechanised sorting is aided by the use of postcodes, of which there are 1·5 million; Britain's postcode system is one of the most sophisticated in the world.

Post Offices

Britain has 22,900 post offices, of which nearly 1,600 are operated directly by the Post Office and the remainder on an agency basis by sub-postmasters. At a post office counter, besides making use of its postal and telegraph facilities, a person may draw a pension or a family allowance, buy a dog licence, a television receiving licence, renew a motor vehicle licence, obtain a British visitor's passport, buy national insurance stamps, and use the facilities of the National Savings Bank (see p 346) and of the National Girobank (see p 344). In much of its counter service the Post Office acts as agent for government departments and local authorities.

Other Services The Post Office provides a range of 40 specialist services, mainly for commerce. 'Datapost', a door-to-door overnight delivery service originally for computer data, has been expanded to include documents, medical samples and spare parts, and handles 2·7 million packets a year. There are International Datapost links with 12 countries. An 'Expresspost' messenger service, for rapid delivery of mail within or between cities, was started in London in 1976 and has been extended to 15 centres. About one-third of the Post Office's philatelic business, which mainly involves the sale of stamps to collectors or dealers, is conducted by the Philatelic Bureau in Edinburgh. The British Postal Consultancy Service offers advice and assistance on all aspects of postal business to overseas postal administrations, and over 20 countries have used its services.

TELE-COMMUNICA-TIONS Britain has the world's third largest telecommunications system, after the United States and Japan, with more than 23 million telephones, 15 million exchange connections, 72,000 telex connections and 50,000 data transmission terminals (more than in any country except the United States). The Post Office's telecommunications business employs 225,000 people, has assets of nearly £6,500 million, and runs eight factories and a fleet of nearly 49,000 telecommunications vehicles.

Telephone Services In 1977–78 some 17,454 million telephone calls were made in Britain comprising 14,600 million local calls, 2,703 million trunk calls and 151 million international calls. Virtually all local and trunk calls can be dialled direct. To back up its nationwide system of cables, the Post Office has built a network of radio towers for transmitting telephone calls, television programmes and computer data over microwave channels.

Special Telephone Services Several specialised services are available by telephone, including the '999' emergency dialling service enabling subscribers to be connected rapidly and free of charge to the police, ambulance or fire brigade. Of the 534 million calls a year made to recorded information services, 383 million are to the speaking clock. Other recorded information services include weather forecasts, motoring information, recipes, cricket scores, Financial Times Share Index and Business News Summary, and 'Dial a Disc'.

Exchanges Over 870 electronic exchanges are in use in Britain and orders for a further 300 have been placed. They are more reliable than conventional electro-mechanical exchanges as they have very few moving parts and so require less maintenance. Most electronic exchanges are of the TXE2 type, with a capacity of up to 7,000 lines. Larger TXE4 exchanges, with a capacity of up to 40,000 lines, have been brought into service since February 1976.

Overseas Services Britain leads the world in the provision of international direct dialling; about 85 per cent of Britain's telephone subscribers can dial direct to 76 countries. About 88 per cent of all international calls are dialled direct. The demand for international calls is doubling every four or five years and the Post Office has substantially increased the amount of equipment in its international exchanges and raised the number of cable and satellite circuits linking Britain with other countries from nearly 3,000 in 1970 to 26,000 in mid-1978. Over 60 per cent of the intercontinental telephone traffic to or from Britain is carried by satellite. Three aerials at the Goonhilly earth station in Cornwall provide commercial telecommunications services via high-capacity geostationary satellites positioned over the Atlantic and Indian Oceans. Britain has the second largest interest, after the United States, in the world space communications satellite network and a second earth station is being built at Madley (Hereford and Worcester) to cope with the growth in international traffic.

Submarine Cables

Some 243 submarine cables, covering a total of 905 nautical miles (1,677 kilometres), are part of Britain's internal cable network. There are 28 cables, covering a total of 4,445 nautical miles (8,237 kilometres), from Britain to the continent of Europe, the Irish Republic, the Channel Islands and the Faroe Islands, and four cables between Britain and North America.

Maritime Communications

The Post Office provides day-to-day communications links and radio services for shipping of all nations through one long-range and 11 medium-range radio stations around the coastline of Britain. At all medium-range stations a continuous watch is maintained on the international distress frequencies, as part of a safety of life at sea service provided on behalf of the Department of Trade. A number of remotely controlled short-range coast radio stations are being installed to provide radiotelephone links with ships at sea at a range of up to 50 miles (80 kilometres).

Oil and gas production platforms in the North Sea are linked to Britain's telecommunications network by transhorizon radio. Two new radio stations have been built in south Shetland and one near Fraserburgh (Grampian).

Datel Services

Post Office Datel services provide for transmission of information for computers and other automatic processors. A wide variety of data transmission facilities, at speeds from 50 bits a second to 48,000 bits a second, are provided using Post Office circuits. The services consist of a suitable telegraph or telephone line and, when necessary, a modem (which converts digital signals into voice frequencies for transmission). The Post Office will introduce in 1978 a service at 4,800 bits a second over the public telephone network. An internationally compatible Datel service at 2,400 bits a second was introduced in 1977.

Telex

The British telex service is fully automatic. Demand for inland and international telex services is growing and the number of connections has nearly doubled since 1971. Customers can dial direct to over 110 countries and 98 per cent of all international calls are dialled direct.

Telegrams

International telegrams are transmitted through the Post Office's computer-controlled Telegram Retransmission Centre in London, the largest of its kind in the world, which has greatly improved efficiency by reducing the average handling time of international telegrams. It has direct access to terminals in over 90 countries.

Developments

The Post Office is developing several new telecommunications services. A public test service of 'Prestel', the new Post Office viewdata service, in which people can telephone for information stored in a computer and have it displayed on a television set in words and simple diagrams, started in June 1978. Prestel will be the world's first public viewdata service when it is established in the first quarter of 1979 and will have an initial capacity of over 100,000 pages of information. Plans are being drawn up for Prestel centres in London, Birmingham, Cardiff, Edinburgh, Leeds, Manchester and Norwich. The Post Office has exported the system to telecommunications authorities in a number of countries.

A radiopaging service, which provides direct dialling access to very high frequency pocket 'bleepers' over the public telephone network, is operating in three areas (Greater London, Birmingham and the Thames Valley) and a service in other major centres is planned to start between late 1978 and mid-1979.

The Post Office Experimental Packet Switched Service, which came into full operation in 1977, is Europe's first public service for sending computer data by this technique, in which it is assembled in blocks, or packets, each with a built-in address to route the data independently through the network to its destination. A service to the United States started in July 1978 and a European service, known as Euronet, is due to start in 1979.

A series of new switching and associated systems for telephone exchanges, known as System X, using microelectronics technology, integrated digital transmission and switching, stored program (software) control and common channel signalling, has been developed. The first production exchanges are expected to be ordered before the end of 1978 and they should enter service three years later.

DATA PROCESSING

The Post Office has a corporate Data Processing Service for internal services, and a comprehensive bureau service, known as National Data Processing, for industry and commerce. It operates some of the most comprehensive data processing systems in Europe and has implemented more than 400 projects.

16 Employment

As a major industrial country, Britain has a labour force characterised by a high level of technical and commercial skill which has often shown its capacity to adapt to changing economic conditions and technical progress. To ensure as far as possible that Britain's working population, like the country's other economic resources, is fully utilised, the Government intervenes in the labour market in a number of ways: by providing public employment and training services; by policies to promote regional development and labour mobility; by measures to alleviate unemployment; through legislation to regulate terms and conditions of employment and improve industrial relations; by providing for security of employment and incomes; and through legislation relating to health and safety at work.

THE WORKING POPULATION

The total working population of Britain at the middle of June 1977 was 26·3 million, about 48 per cent of the total population. If the unemployed, the self-employed, and the Armed Forces are omitted from the working population, there remained 22·7 million employees (13·4 million men and 9·3 million women) in employment. The percentage of women (particularly those working part-time) in the labour force continues to rise, although at a reduced rate compared with previous years. The great majority of the working population work for a wage or salary, but nearly 2 million are employers or self-employed. The working population increased slowly until 1966, then declined between 1966 and 1971, since when it has been rising again (see Table 20). One reason for the fall after 1966 was the increased number in full-time education. During the next few years the male labour force is expected to increase slowly, while the number of females is expected to continue to increase. In June 1977 men accounted for 59 per cent of all employees and women for 41 per cent (about two-fifths of whom worked part-time).

TABLE 20: Manpower in Britain 1970–77 *Thousands*[a]

Year	Employees in employment[b]	Employers and self-employed	Unemployed[c]	Armed Forces[d]	Total working population[d]
1970	22,471	1,902	555	372	25,300
1971	22,122	1,909	724	368	25,123
1972	22,120	1,899	899	371	25,194
1973	22,662	1,947	575	361	25,545
1974	22,790	1,925	542	345	25,602
1975	22,707	1,886	866	336	25,795
1976	22,539	1,886	1,332	336	26,093
1977	22,661	1,886	1,450	327	26,367

Source: *Department of Employment Gazette*
[a] Discrepancies between totals and their constituent parts are due to rounding.
[b] Part-time workers are counted as units.
[c] Excluding adult students.
[d] The working population figures and the Forces figures include ex-Service personnel on leave after completing their service.

Though successful development policies in the less-prosperous regions may raise the working population above the levels forecast, any increasing demand for labour must in general be met by better deployment of manpower, improved productivity and more training. In general, non-employed married women form the only substantial reserve.

The distribution of employees by industry in 1970 and 1977 is shown in Table 21.

Northern Ireland

The total working population of Northern Ireland, including employers and self-employed, was about 623,000 in June 1977 (394,000 males and 229,000 females). The number of employees in employment was about 489,000. The largest non-service industries are agriculture, engineering, textiles and clothing. Most of the agricultural workers in Northern Ireland are family workers. Farmers and small-holders working their own holdings account for about 6 per cent of the working population.

MANPOWER POLICY

In Great Britain the Department of Employment is generally responsible for employment policy, industrial relations and pay policy, and for the payment of unemployment benefit, but the Manpower Services Commission (MSC) advises the Government on manpower policy issues and, with the agreement of

TABLE 21: Analysis of Civil Employment in Britain 1970 and 1977

Industry or Service	1970 Thousands	1970 Per cent	1977[a] Thousands	1977[a] Per cent
Agriculture, forestry and fishing	468	1·9	391	1·6
Mining and quarrying	410	1·7	349	1·4
Manufacturing industries	*8,339*	*34·2*	*7,343*	*29·9*
Chemicals and allied industries	491	2·0	466	1·9
Metals, engineering and vehicles	4,315	17·7	3,795	15·5
Textiles	678	2·8	516	2·1
Clothing and footwear	455	1·9	390	1·6
Food, drink and tobacco	792	3·2	723	2·9
Other manufactures	1,609	6·6	1,453	5·9
Construction	1,335	5·5	1,265	5·2
Gas, electricity and water	391	1·6	350	1·4
Transport and communications	1,573	6·5	1,449	5·9
Distributive trades	2,676	11·0	2,734	11·1
Professional, financial, scientific and miscellaneous services[a]	5,801	23·8	7,144	29·1
National and local government service	1,479	6·1	1,633	6·7
Total : employees	22,471	92·2	22,661	92·3
Employers and self-employed persons (all industries and services)	1,902	7·8	1,886	7·7
Total in Civil Employment	24,373	100·0	24,547	100·0

Sources: *Department of Employment* and *Northern Ireland Department of Manpower Services*

[a] Excludes private domestic service.
Discrepancies between totals and their constituent parts are due to rounding.

the Government, has set itself the long-term aim of developing a comprehensive manpower policy with a dual function: to enable the country's manpower resources to be developed and contribute fully to economic well-being; and to ensure that there is available to each worker the opportunities and services he or she needs in order to lead a satisfying working life. Responsibility for the activities of the MSC in Scotland and Wales rests with the Secretaries of State for Scotland and Wales respectively, while, in Northern Ireland, corresponding responsibilities are undertaken by the Department of Manpower Services.

The MSC, which is separate from the Government but accountable to the Secretaries of State for Employment, Scotland and Wales, has a chairman and nine other members appointed after consultation with employers and employees, and local government and educational interests; responsibility for the management and development of the commission's services thus belongs directly to representatives of those who use them. Scottish and Welsh committees of the MSC consider special Scottish and Welsh dimensions of manpower issues.

The MSC carries out its functions within a general policy framework agreed with the Secretaries of State, and was responsible for expenditure of about £432 million in 1977–78. Most of its activities are financed from public funds. The MSC is advised by a network of district manpower committees on which employers, employees and other local interests are represented, to secure the full benefit of local knowledge and the co-operation of employers and employees. The main statutory duty of the MSC is to make such arrangements as it considers appropriate for assisting people to select, train for, obtain and retain employment, and for assisting employers to obtain suitable employees. The services in Northern Ireland are run on similar lines by the Department of Manpower Services but there are some variations related to the much smaller area of administration.

EMPLOYMENT SERVICES

The main public employment services (other than the careers service) are provided in Great Britain by the MSC's employment service division, the principal aim of which is to provide a comprehensive service for employers needing staff and for people, whether or not already in employment, seeking jobs. It operates through a network of nearly 1,000 local employment offices and 'jobcentres', which handle the full range of occupations and deal with full-time, part-time and temporary vacancies. Employment offices are being replaced by jobcentres which provide self-service facilities in addition to other services.

Though use of the service by both employers and job-seekers is voluntary, in the year to March 1978 over 5·8 million people registered for employment, 2·4 million vacancies were notified and 1·6 million were placed in employment.

Special Services

Special employment services include services to the disabled, occupational guidance, services to assist the geographical mobility of workers, Professional and Executive Recruitment and the Careers Service.

Services to the Disabled

The public employment service has long provided a resettlement service to disabled people. This is provided by over 500 specialised disablement resettlement officers (DROs) who also give advice on the various courses of rehabilitation or training available, and to employers on aspects of employing disabled people and the grants available for adaptation of equipment. The DROs administer the quota scheme which, under the Disabled Persons (Employment) Act 1944, requires employers to include a percentage of registered disabled people among their workforce. Employment rehabilitation is provided at 26 centres (including one linked with a medical rehabilitation unit); in 1977 some 15,000 people attended the wide range of courses available. The MSC also gives financial assistance to voluntary and local authority bodies concerned with specific disabilities such as blindness, cerebral palsy and psychiatric disorders; in 1977 more than 650 people passed through these courses.

There are vocational training facilities for the disabled at 'skillcentres', educational institutions and employers' establishments. For the more seriously disabled there are special residential training colleges run by voluntary organisations with the help of the MSC's training services division. Grants are available to disabled people qualified to undertake study or training for professional or comparable employment.

Sheltered employment is provided for the severely disabled in Great Britain by Remploy Ltd, a non-profit making company, and in Northern Ireland by Ulster Sheltered Employment Ltd, a company constituted similarly to Remploy, and by local authorities and voluntary organisations. The MSC also works in close co-operation with the National Advisory Council on Employment of Disabled People.

In 1977 the MSC and the Northern Ireland Department of Manpower Services helped with the cost of providing places for over 13,000 severely disabled people, of which approximately 2,000 were blind or partially sighted and some 200 were trainees.

Occupational Guidance

Occupational Guidance is a free advisory service available to anyone seeking advice on changing or choosing a job. It operates through a national network of 49 occupational guidance units, helping about 55,000 people a year. The service is based on interviews with specially trained staff who can call on the services of occupational psychologists if necessary.

Geographical Mobility Schemes

In order to ease unemployment, particularly in the assisted areas (see p 209), the MSC administers various grants and allowances under the Employment Transfer Scheme to enable the unemployed, and those under threat of redundancy, to take up jobs in other areas; the Job Search Scheme to provide the cost of fares and subsistence in order to attend interviews and to move to other areas temporarily to look for work; and the Key Workers Scheme, which helps people who move temporarily or permanently to occupy key posts in establishments set up by their employers in assisted areas.

Professional and Executive Recruitment

Professional and Executive Recruitment (PER) provides a specialist employment service at managerial, professional, scientific and technical levels. It is organised separately from the rest of the MSC and operates through a network of 36 offices staffed by experienced consultants. PER has a computer-assisted matching and selection system but also offers an interviewing service and an advertising service. The service is free to candidates while employers are charged a fee on all successful placings based on the starting salary. A broadly similar service, free to both employers and candidates, is operated in Northern Ireland.

Careers Service

Local education authorities have a statutory obligation under the Employment and Training Act 1973 to provide a careers service, a vocational guidance service for people attending all educational institutions (except universities) and an employment service for those leaving them. Authorities also provide an employment service for people, especially young people, in their early years at work. There is close co-operation with the MSC's employment service division which also caters for those who have left school and choose to use its facilities in preference to those of the careers service.

In Northern Ireland the careers service is an integral part of the Department of Manpower Services.

The Careers and Occupational Information Centre (COIC) publishes a wide range of material to help people looking for jobs to make an informed choice, and distributes careers literature to some 15,000 schools, careers offices and other centres.

Immigrant Workers

In general, people coming to Britain for employment (including Commonwealth citizens who do not have the right of abode, see p 12, but excluding nationals of European Community countries and Gibraltar) need a work permit issued by the Department of Employment. This must be applied for by the prospective employer for a specific person and is issued for a specific job and for a fixed initial period not exceeding 12 months in the first instance. People admitted as holders of work permits may change their jobs only with the approval of the Department of Employment. Normally further leave to remain will be given on application to the Home Office if they remain in approved employment. Under current immigration rules the Home Office will consider an application to remove the conditions attached to their stay after four years in approved employment, and if granted, a worker may change employment without restriction. Among other conditions, work permits are issued only for work requiring a professional qualification, skill or experience, where the Department of Employment is satisfied that the worker is necessary and there is no suitable resident worker to fill the post offered, and where the wages and conditions are not less favourable than those generally available in the area for similar work.

Permits for nursing auxiliaries and resident domestic workers in hospitals, schools and similar establishments and private households are subject to overall numerical limits decided annually. Permits for resident domestic employment are issued only for unmarried people and for married couples if they are to work in a joint post. They are not issued to those with children under 16 years of age. Permits for nursing auxiliaries are issued only for unmarried people without dependants.

Commonwealth citizens and foreign nationals (other than nationals of European Community countries and Gibraltar) are generally eligible for permits on the same terms. In addition, Commonwealth citizens may be admitted for fixed periods of training 'on the job' arranged in advance if they hold trainee permits issued by the Department of Employment. Foreign nationals may also enter Britain as holders of student employee permits for short-term employment to enable them to improve their English and widen their business experience.

European Community regulations establish the rights of workers to move freely between member States (of which Britain is one, see p 71) for the purposes of employment. European Community workers entering another member State are entitled to be treated in the same way as nationals of that State as regards facilities of the national employment services, pay and working conditions, trade union rights, vocational training and retraining facilities, access to housing and property, and social security and industrial injury benefits. Workers who wish to remain in the United Kingdom for longer than an initial period of six months must apply to the Home Office for a residence permit. If they are in permanent employment the residence permit is normally valid for five years. If the employment is temporary (that is, for less than a year) the permit is valid for the expected duration of the employment.

Race Relations Race relations employment advisers, based in the Department of Employment's regional offices, provide advice and information to employers, trade unions and other organisations with the aim of improving employment opportunities for workers from the ethnic minorities.

UNEMPLOYMENT In common with many other industrial countries, unemployment in Britain has risen in the 1970s to the highest level for 40 years, though the seasonally adjusted level fell slightly towards the end of 1977, a trend which continued during the first half of 1978. Over recent years it has been increased by the growth of the labour force, due mainly to larger numbers of young people and married women seeking work.

Unemployment has been relatively low in the south-east of England, and consistently higher in those parts of the country which have the greatest dependence on shipbuilding, coalmining, and certain branches of the heavy engineering and metal manufacturing industries, notably parts of Scotland and Wales, and north-east England and Merseyside. The general unemployment rate in Great Britain in July 1978 was 5·6 per cent: the areas with the highest rates were Wales and Scotland and the north of England.

The unemployment rate in Northern Ireland has remained higher than in other parts of the United Kingdom. In July 1978 it was 11·2 per cent of all employees.

Government Action The Government's programme for alleviating unemployment (which rose particularly rapidly during 1975 and 1976) has to be viewed within the context of a succession of measures designed to assist industrial investment and help industry generally (see p '209). These measures have been introduced progressively since August 1975 to check the rise in unemployment and at the same time to safeguard and expand Britain's industrial potential so as to provide the base for more jobs in the medium term.

The measures include: a temporary employment subsidy for firms who agree to defer redundancies which would otherwise have taken place; a small firms employment subsidy for extra jobs provided by small manufacturing firms in certain areas; a youth opportunities programme to provide a range of training and work experience opportunities for young people; a special temporary employment programme to provide worthwhile temporary jobs for adults who have been unemployed for a long time; a 'job release' scheme to encourage older workers, close to pensionable age, to leave work early and release jobs for younger unemployed people; and a 'job introduction' scheme for disabled people.

From April 1975 until March 1978 expenditure on the special employment and training measures amounted to £560 million. The estimated expenditure for these measures in 1978–79 is £530 million. It is estimated that by March 1979 some 400,000 people will be being assisted under these schemes.

TRAINING SERVICES The main responsibility for carrying out industrial and commercial training lies with individual employers, but in recent years the MSC, with government support, has evolved a comprehensive strategy to help to improve the supply of trained manpower needed by the economy, to provide opportunities for individuals to acquire new skills, and to improve the efficiency and effectiveness of training generally. The MSC's training services division is responsible for putting these programmes into effect.

Training in Industry

There are 23 industrial training boards and one industrial training committee, covering firms employing nearly 60 per cent of all employees, which are responsible for promoting training in their respective industries. They receive Exchequer funds to meet their advisory service and other costs and to enable them to pay grants to employers to encourage training activities of national importance (supplemented, during the current economic recession, by special grants to support craft and technician training). The boards' five-year strategies and short-term operating plans and budgets are agreed with the MSC. From 1979 grant support will be subject to strengthened criteria designed to increase the responsibility of employers for removing skill imbalances and securing a more flexible workforce.

The MSC also promotes training for some 11 million people employed in industries not covered by industrial training boards, maintaining liaison with major training organisations in this sector.

Training Opportunities Scheme

The Training Opportunities Scheme (TOPS) is intended to supplement the training given in industry and commerce by providing individuals over the age of 19 with the opportunity to acquire new skills. Training is carried out at 68 'skillcentres' and at many colleges and employers' establishments. Skillcentre courses concentrate mainly on engineering, construction and automotive trades and those at colleges on clerical and commercial skills, but in all about 600 different courses are available in a wide range of occupations. Trainees are paid allowances which vary with domestic responsibilities and may receive, among other things, an earnings-related supplement, travelling expenses and a lodging allowance. Some 78,500 adults were trained under TOPS in 1977–78.

Other Training Services

The MSC also provides a number of other direct training services to employers.

The Training Within Industry (TWI) scheme is intended to develop the skills of supervisors in developing leadership, instructing and communicating, improving methods and improving safety practices. Special courses are available for supervisors employed in offices, retail distribution and hospitals. Courses in international trade procedures are available for staff employed in export/import offices and (at advanced level) for customs entry clerks. Courses in instructional techniques are available to skillcentre staff and industrial and commercial firms at the MSC's two instructor training colleges (one in England and one in Scotland) and at three instructor training units attached to skillcentres. In-plant courses are also available.

Employers are able to sponsor their own employees for refresher and upgrading training at skillcentres, on courses designed specifically to meet the needs of the employer and of the employees concerned. There is also a complementary mobile instructor service for employers, which provides specific training for employees in their own workshops.

Training services at skillcentres and courses at instructor training colleges are also available to trainees from overseas. These facilities are increasingly being used by overseas governments and organisations, and in every case programmes are structured to meet agreed training objectives.

Terms and Conditions of Employment

EMPLOYMENT LAW

Britain has been a pioneer in the introduction of protective legislation for the safety, health and welfare of employees. The determination by statute of minimum wages, holidays and holiday pay was until recently confined in principle to those trades and industries where the organisation of employers or workers, or both, was inadequate to negotiate collective agreements and to ensure their observance. However, recent legislation, in particular the Employment Protection Act 1975, provides considerable safeguards for the employee in his terms of employment as well as working conditions. This Act also provides machinery, under certain conditions, for enforcing the observance of the relevant terms and conditions of employment. The Contracts of Employment Act 1972 requires an employer to give an employee written information on his terms and conditions of employment, the disciplinary rules applicable to him and the procedure available to him where he has a grievance about his employment or is dissatisfied with any disciplinary decision relating to him; it also lays down the right of both employers and employees to minimum periods of notice when employment is to be terminated. Under the Redundancy Payments Acts 1965 and 1969 employees with a minimum period of service of 104 weeks are entitled to lump-sum redundancy payments if their jobs cease to exist (for example, because of technological improvements or because of a fall in demand) and their employers cannot offer suitable alternative work, the cost being partly met from a fund subscribed to by industry. The Trade Union and Labour Relations Acts 1974 and 1976 give protection against unfair dismissal by providing machinery under which an employee may complain against an employer of unfair dismissal, and obtain reinstatement, re-engagement or compensation; and give legal support to the right to trade union organisation by making it unfair to dismiss a person because of his membership or participation in the activities of an independent trade union. The Employment Protection Act 1975 improves the remedies for unfair dismissal and extends the rights of employees regarding dismissal and penalisation short of dismissal because of trade union membership or activities, and payment when work is not available for reasons other than as a result of a trade dispute. It also introduces maternity rights for women employees which include protection from dismissal because of pregnancy, maternity pay, and the right to return to work after confinement.

Discrimination

The Race Relations Act 1976 (see p 136) makes unlawful, discrimination on grounds of colour, race, nationality or ethnic or national origin, in employment, training and related matters. Employers may not discriminate when recruiting workers or in their treatment of employees in regard to their terms and conditions of employment, promotion, transfer, training and access to other benefits, and dismissal.

The employment provisions of the Sex Discrimination Act (see p 134) make sex discrimination unlawful in employment, training and related matters. An employer may not discriminate between men and women either in recruitment or in treatment of existing employees in such matters as promotion, training, transfer, benefits and facilities and dismissal. It is also unlawful for a married person to be treated less favourably than a single person of the same sex.

Wage Rates and Earnings

PAY, HOURS OF WORK AND HOLIDAYS

Pay for manual occupations, and increasingly for non-manual occupations, is normally set by collective bargaining (see p 324). In a small number of industries, legally enforceable minimum rates are set by wages councils.

Basic rates of pay vary widely, though in private industry local rates normally exceed the rates specified in national agreements. Higher rates are usually paid for overtime and shift work, and weekly earnings may be further increased by incentive bonus schemes. Piecework, or payment-by-results, is still common, though of declining importance as production methods in a number of industries increasingly dictate employees' output.

Earnings, wage rates, retail prices, wages and salaries 1973-78

average 1970 = 100   log scale

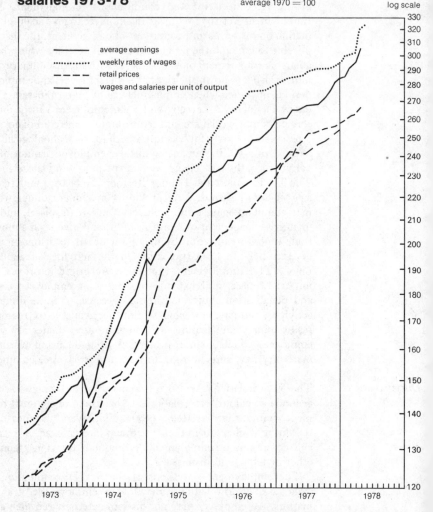

```
———————  average earnings
·············  weekly rates of wages
— — —  retail prices
— —  wages and salaries per unit of output
```

According to the latest annual survey conducted by the Department of Employment into earnings and hours of work, the average weekly earnings of full-time male adult manual workers in April 1977 were, including overtime, £71·50; while for full-time female adult manual workers they were £43·70. The corresponding figures for non-manual workers were £88·90 and £53·80. Women's earnings are thus markedly lower than those of men, partly because on average they work shorter hours, with less overtime paid at premium rates, and partly because they tend to be concentrated in the less well-paid jobs. The Equal Pay Act 1970 requires that a woman doing the same or broadly similar work to a man qualifies for equal pay and conditions of employment.

Between April 1970 and April 1977 the average weekly earnings of manual workers before tax and national insurance deductions increased by 167 per cent for men and by 220 per cent for women. Part of the increase has been offset by a rise in retail prices of about 140 per cent and by larger national insurance contributions and income tax. For trends between 1973 and 1978 in earnings, wage rates, retail prices, wages and salaries, see the diagram on p 318.

Salaries and Fees

Remuneration in commercial, technical and professional careers is normally by annual salary paid monthly, often on a scale carrying annual increments, and such careers generally afford opportunities for promotion to posts with higher remuneration. Starting salaries may be in the range of £2,500 to £3,000 (lower for trainees from 16–18 years of age and higher for some graduates entering industry).

Most of the senior posts in business, the professions and the Civil Service command salaries in the range of £10,000 to £15,000 a year gross before tax. The posts with salaries in the range of £15,000 to £30,000 a year include those of Cabinet Ministers, top-ranking judicial appointments, the highest positions in government departments and the largest municipal authorities, editors of daily newspapers, some persons outstanding in their professions and in the higher managerial posts in industry, commerce and banking. Salaries of chairmen of major companies exceptionally exceed £50,000 a year gross, though highly successful people (such as star entertainers) often receive more through fees or fixed contracts. The range of net incomes in the country as a whole is, however, reduced by a system of progressive taxation and by provisions for social security.

Royal Commission on the Distribution of Income and Wealth

The Royal Commission on the Distribution of Income and Wealth was set up in 1974 to examine and report on various aspects of the distribution of personal incomes, both earned and unearned, and wealth as are referred to it by the Government. The commission has produced six reports both on the general state of, and trends in, income distribution, and on specific subjects such as higher incomes and lower incomes. The Government attaches great importance to the results of the commission's inquiries, as a means of establishing a sound basis for policy guidance on such matters as pay, industrial relations and social security.

Hours of Work

The normal working week in Britain is in the range 39–40 hours for manual work and 37–38 for non-manual work; a five-day week is usually worked. Actual hours worked in manual occupations differ from their standard hours; in October 1977 they were 44·2 for men compared with 37·4 for women. Men and women in non-manual occupations generally work less overtime than manual workers.

National legislation limits and defines permissible hours of work for women and young people in a number of industries or trades—the maximum, with limited exceptions, being 48 hours a week and 10 hours a day (9 hours a day for 6-day-week workers) in premises covered by the Factories Act for adult women over 18 and young people between 16 and 18. The employment of women and young people at night is prohibited in industrial undertakings, except for young men over 16 working in some continuous-process industries (subject to certain conditions). The Department of Employment can make exemptions from these restrictions on grounds of public interest. In general the hours of work of adult men, or of people not working in factories, are not restricted by statute.

Holidays with Pay and Public Holidays

Holiday entitlements are normally determined by collective agreements. These generally provide for at least three weeks paid holiday a year. However about one-third of manual workers covered by agreements have entitlements of four weeks. Non-manual workers generally have longer holidays than manual workers. Additional holidays, dependent upon length of service, are also quite common.

In addition to annual holidays, most agreements provide for bank holidays or public holidays. In England and Wales, in addition to Christmas Day and Good Friday, regular bank holidays take place on New Year's Day, Easter Monday, the last Monday in May, the last Monday in August and 26 December, and there is also a holiday in respect of May Day. In Scotland public holidays are declared locally; regular bank holidays are New Year's Day, 2 January, Good Friday, the first Monday in May, the last Monday in May, the first Monday in August, Christmas Day and 26 December. The English and Welsh bank holidays apply also to Northern Ireland, where in addition St Patrick's Day (17 March) and 12 July are public holidays; in certain areas the Tuesday after Easter is also a customary holiday for industry and trade.

Provision for an alternative day to be observed is made when any bank or public holiday falls on a Saturday or Sunday.

'Fringe' Benefits

A variety of additional benefits exist in varying degree. It has been estimated that at the end of 1975 11·5 million employees were covered by occupational pension schemes. Many employees are also covered by occupational sick pay schemes, additional or complementary to the State schemes (see p 129). A smaller number are covered by schemes for redundancy payments above the statutory minimum. Such benefits are more usual among clerical and professional employees receiving a standard salary than among manual workers, who have a chance to increase their pay—for example, by working overtime. Senior members of firms may use a company car and some firms provide profit-sharing and share-saving schemes.

Social Security

Social security benefits, which include unemployment, sickness and industrial injury benefits, are described in the Social Welfare chapter.

INDUSTRIAL RELATIONS

The structure of industrial relations in Britain has been established mainly on a voluntary basis. The system is based chiefly on the organisation of employees and employers into trade unions and employers' associations, and on freely conducted negotiations between them at all levels. The State is ready to provide assistance where the organisation of employees, employers, or both, is inadequate to conduct negotiations, or where the usual methods of resolving disagreements have failed.

For the most part, this voluntary system (supported by certain basic legal provisions) results in good industrial relations, and the closer involvement of the trade union movement in economic management in recent years has resulted in a considerable reduction in the number and extent of industrial disputes.

Industrial Disputes

According to figures published by the International Labour Office covering the mining, manufacturing, construction and transport industries, over the ten years 1967–76 Britain lost fewer days per 1,000 employees through industrial disputes than several other major industrial countries; moreover there was a considerable decline in strike activity in 1975 and 1976. Figures for the number of strikes and the number of working days lost through strikes in 1977 were broadly in line with Britain's record on average over the last ten years. The results of research carried out by the Department of Employment and published in 1976 and 1978 show that in the period 1971–75 an average per year of 98 per cent of manufacturing plants in Britain were free of strikes.

Northern Ireland's industrial relations record is better than that of the rest of Britain, with proportionately fewer disputes and working days lost through strikes.

TRADE UNIONS　　In nearly all industries and occupations some workers (and in some industries nearly all workers) are organised into trade unions. These have grown up gradually and independently over many years and, consequently, their form and organisation vary considerably, as do their traditions. In the last decade or so, trade unionism has again increased particularly among clerical, supervisory, technical and administrative workers. Trade unions may be organised either by occupation (for example, they may recruit clerks or fitters wherever employed) or by industry. Some are based on a combination of both principles. At the end of 1976 the total membership of British trade unions was 12·4 million. There were 462 unions, but nearly 80 per cent of all trade unionists were in the 25 largest unions, each with a membership of 100,000 or over, while only 0·6 per cent were in the 250 smallest unions with under 1,000 members each.

The Certification Officer appointed under the Employment Protection Act 1975 is required to maintain a list of trade unions. To be eligible for entry on the list a trade union must show that it consists wholly or mainly of workers and that its principal purposes include the regulation of relations between workers and employers, or between workers and employers' associations.

Under the Employment Protection Act 1975 and other legislation, certain rights and privileges are reserved for independent trade unions. A trade union on the list may apply to the Certification Officer for a certificate that it is independent, such a certificate being conclusive evidence of independence.

The central organisation of most large unions consists of a national executive council, usually elected by and responsible to the annual conference of delegates from local branches. Between conferences, councils are the highest authority of unions, and carry out policy decisions made by conference delegates. Most unions also have regional and district organisations. At the level of the individual member there are local branches, covering one or more factories. Members may attend branch meetings, make suggestions about terms and conditions of employment, discuss the work of the union, and take part in the election of the union's officers. The branch takes action on certain matters considered to be entirely, or mainly, of local interest and forwards its views on wider issues for action by the union's national or regional bodies. The organising of members in individual places of work, and the negotiation of local pay agreements with managements at the factory or plant, may be done by full-time district officials of the union, or, increasingly, by 'shop stewards', who are chosen by their fellow members in the place of work to represent them. Trade unions vary in the degree to which shop stewards are integrated into their organisation. Where two or more unions have members in the same workplace, shop stewards' committees may be formed to discuss matters of common concern.

Unions often provide dispute benefit ('strike pay') for members involved in official industrial action. They also provide legal advice for members who suffer injury or contract diseases at work, and may pay members' legal costs where a case for compensation goes to court. Some unions pay benefits in case of illness, accident, death and retirement (additional to those payable under the national insurance scheme) financed out of membership contributions. Many trade unions are affiliated to the Labour Party.

Trades Union Congress

In Britain the national centre of the trade union movement is the TUC, which was founded in 1868. The TUC's objects are to promote the interests of its affiliated organisations and to improve the economic and social conditions of working people. Its affiliated membership comprises 115 trade unions which together represent 11·5 million workpeople, or 93 per cent of all trade unionists in Britain. The TUC deals with all general questions which concern trade unions both nationally and internationally and gives assistance on questions relating to particular trades or industries.

The annual Congress convenes in September to discuss matters of concern to trade unionists and to employees generally. It elects a General Council which represents it between successive Congresses and is responsible for carrying out Congress decisions, watching economic and social developments, providing educational and advisory services to unions, and presenting to the Government the trade union viewpoint on economic, social and industrial issues. The council is also empowered to mediate in inter-union disputes in certain circumstances, and uses its authority to deal with unauthorised and unconstitutional stoppages of work, as well as official disputes.

The TUC as well as many individual unions conduct extensive educational services for members, mainly concerned with industrial subjects, trade unionism and the principles and practice of industrial relations.

The TUC plays an active part in international trade union activity, through its affiliations to the International Confederation of Free Trade Unions and the European Trade Union Confederation. It also nominates the British workers' delegation to the annual International Labour Conference.

There are eight TUC regional councils in England, based on the Government's eight planning regions (see p 158) with a further similar body for Wales known as the Wales Trades Union Council. These bodies, whose function is to make representations to the Government's various regional bodies, co-ordinate the activities of trade unions in the regions and keep them in touch with the policy of the TUC at national level.

Scotland and Northern Ireland

Scottish trade unions also have their own national central body, the Scottish Trades Union Congress (STUC), which in many respects is similar in constitution and functions to the TUC. Trade unions whose membership includes Scottish workers may affiliate to the STUC and a number of trade unions are in fact affiliated to both bodies. Trade unions in Northern Ireland are represented by the Northern Ireland Committee of the Irish Congress of Trade Unions (ICTU), though the majority of trade unionists in Northern Ireland belong to unions based in Great Britain. Almost 90 per cent of Northern Ireland trade unionists are members of organisations affiliated to the ICTU while the majority belong to unions which are also affiliated to the TUC.

TUC–Labour Party Liaison Committee

The TUC–Labour Party Liaison Committee was set up in 1972 after the General Council of the TUC, the national executive committee of the Labour Party and the parliamentary committee of the Labour Party had agreed to establish a liaison committee to discuss policies on industrial relations and management of the economy. In 1973 the committee reached an agreement on the 'social contract' (see p 186) which was reaffirmed in July 1976.

EMPLOYERS'
ORGANISATIONS

Many employers in Britain are members of employers' organisations, a large number of which are wholly or partly concerned with labour matters. The primary aims of such organisations are to help to establish suitable terms and conditions of employment, including a sound wage structure and proper standards of safety, health and welfare; to promote good relations with employees and the efficient use of manpower; and to provide means of settling any disputes which may arise. They may also represent members' points of view as manufacturers or traders to the Government on commercial matters.

Employers' organisations are usually organised on an industry basis rather than a product basis. A few are purely local in character or deal with a section of an industry; others are national in scope and are concerned with the whole of an industry. In some of the main industries there are local or regional organisations combined into national federations, while in others, within which different firms are engaged in making different principal products, there is a complex structure with national and regional federations for parts of an industry as well as for the industry as a whole. Altogether there are some 150 national employers' organisations, which negotiate the national collective agreements for their industry with the trade unions concerned. Many of these national organisations belong to the CBI.

The final authority of local or small national organisations may be a meeting where all member firms are directly represented; but in larger organisations some form of indirect representation is necessary, either through local organisations or through regions or sections into which these are grouped.

The representatives thus chosen, together with a number of office holders, form a general council or central committee, which meets perhaps once a quarter, mainly to make major policy decisions, to elect committees and to ratify their work. A paid staff under a director or secretary carries out the day-to-day work of the organisation. There is usually a small working group, consisting of senior officials and committee chairmen, which meets to deal with urgent questions and co-ordinate the work of committees. Employers' associations (as defined in the Trade Union and Labour Relations Act 1974) may apply to the Certification Officer for inclusion in the list of employers' associations maintained by the officer.

Confederation
of British
Industry

The central body of employers is the CBI which deals with all matters affecting the interests of employers and represents them nationally to the Government and the public and also internationally, for instance, in the International Labour Organisation and in the various institutions of the European Community. It is also the British member of the Union of Industries of the European Communities (UNICE) and the Business and Industry Advisory Committee to the Organisation for Economic Co-operation and Development, and a member of the British national committee of the International Chamber of Commerce (ICC). The majority of national employers' organisations and nationalised industries and a large number of individual companies, both large and small, belong to the CBI, whose representatives or nominees sit on various official bodies and take part in the discussion of matters of importance to the national economy through their membership of the NEDC (see p 188).

Legal
framework

The Trade Union and Labour Relations Act 1974 defines the status of trade unions and employers' associations and sets out certain legal requirements which they must observe. The Act confers immunities on trade unions in respect of actions taken in support of a trade dispute, allows peaceful picketing, and also provides that collective agreements shall not be legally enforceable unless they are written agreements and specifically provide for this.

The Employment Protection Act 1975 extends the rights of employees in a number of respects and strengthens voluntary collective bargaining. The Act placed the Advisory, Conciliation and Arbitration Service (ACAS) on a statutory basis, provided for the appointment of a Certification Officer and for the setting up of the Central Arbitration Committee; and established an Employment Appeal Tribunal to hear appeals concerning decisions of the Certification Officer and of industrial tribunals. (Industrial tribunals deal, in general, with complaints from employees on infringements of individual rights under a number of Acts concerning, for example, redundancy payments, contracts of employment, equal pay, unfair dismissals and sex discrimination.)

Northern Ireland

Northern Ireland has a similar but separate system of industrial relations under which certain responsibilities devolve upon the Labour Relations Agency. Industrial relations legislation enacted in 1976 has brought the province largely into line with similar legislation enacted in Great Britain since 1974.

COLLECTIVE BARGAINING AND JOINT CONSULTATION

In most industries terms and conditions of employment and procedures for the conduct of industrial relations are settled by negotiation and agreement between employers and trade unions. Whereas in the past the emphasis has been on formal industry-wide agreements supplemented as necessary by informal local agreements in firms or factories, a gradual change of attitude and structure has led to increasing emphasis being placed on agreements at firm and factory level (plant bargaining), though there have been some important exceptions to this trend, for example in the motor industry. In some industries, firms and factories, negotiations are conducted by meetings held when necessary, while in others, joint negotiating councils or committees have been established on a permanent basis. The scope of the various joint bodies (from the national joint industrial councils for whole industries to the works councils and committees in individual workplaces) varies widely, and has frequently been extended to cover such additional matters as production plans, absenteeism, training, education and welfare (see below). Normally these arrangements for collective bargaining suffice to settle all questions which are raised, but provision is sometimes made for matters not so settled to be referred for settlement to independent conciliation or arbitration. The Employment Protection Act 1975 makes provision for information needed for collective bargaining purposes to be disclosed by employers to trade unions, subject to certain safeguards.

Standing arrangements exist for consultation at national level between the Government, the TUC, the CBI, and the nationalised industries through the National Economic Development Council on matters in which employers and workers have a common interest. The operation of collective bargaining has from time to time been restricted in an attempt to control inflation (see p 186

Advisory, Conciliation and Arbitration Service

The Advisory, Conciliation and Arbitration Service (ACAS) is charged with the general duty of promoting the improvement of industrial relations, and in particular of encouraging the extension of collective bargaining, and the development and (where necessary) reform of collective bargaining machinery.

ACAS was placed on a statutory basis under the Employment Protection Act in 1976, and is controlled by a council consisting of a chairman and nine other members experienced in industrial relations, of which three are nominated by the CBI, three by the TUC, and three are independent.

The service may offer conciliation in industrial disputes in both the public and private sectors of industry where this is thought to be helpful, and has discretion in meeting requests for conciliation subject only to the need to pay regard to agreed procedures in the industry or area of employment concerned.

At the joint request of the parties in dispute, and having regard to the need to safeguard negotiating procedures, ACAS may appoint single arbitrators or boards of arbitration to determine differences on the basis of agreed terms of reference. Alternatively ACAS may refer cases for arbitration to the Central Arbitration Committee (see below). Some 300 joint requests for arbitration were made to ACAS during 1977.

Although ACAS has prime responsibility for intervention in disputes, the Secretary of State retains powers to appoint a court of inquiry or committee of investigation into a dispute, whether existing or foreseen.

The service gives advice on all aspects of industrial relations and personnel management. It conducts surveys to diagnose the causes of industrial relations problems and suggests remedial action to management and trade unions or employee representatives. It also carries particular responsibility for attempting conciliation on complaints of infringement of individual employee rights (such as individual complaints of unfair dismissal, complaints under the Equal Pay Act 1970 and complaints on employment matters under the Sex Discrimination Act 1975).

The service is concerned with the long-term improvement of collective bargaining and, with the consent of the parties involved, conducts detailed inquiries in particular firms or industries. It also considers claims by independent trade unions that they should be recognised by an employer.

Central Arbitration Committee

The Central Arbitration Committee (CAC) is a permanent body for the settlement of disputes by voluntary arbitration. Disputes may be referred to the CAC by ACAS at the joint request of the employers and trade unions concerned.

The committee is also called upon to arbitrate on claims made under various Acts, including the Equal Pay Act 1970 and the Employment Protection Act 1975, and acts as the independent tribunal to which the Secretary of State for Employment refers questions relating to the payment of wages and conditions of employment observed by Government contractors.

Industrial Democracy

The need for better communication between management and workers has led to movement towards greater industrial democracy, that is, towards enabling workers to have a more decisive voice in the way in which their firms are run. There are worker directors in certain nationalised industries and public corporations; moreover, some private sector companies have long had a system of works councils, while others are conducting experiments in greater worker participation in one form or another.

In May 1978 the Government published a White Paper giving its views on the majority recommendations of the report of the Committee of Inquiry on industrial democracy (the Bullock report, see Bibliography, p 449) that, among other things, employees should have a right to representation on the boards of management of companies with 2,000 or more employees, following an application for such representation from a recognised trade union and confirmation by a ballot of all employees. The White Paper proposes that employees in companies employing 500 or more people in Britain should have a statutory right to have all major proposals of the company affecting them discussed with their representatives before decisions are taken; but that the development of industrial democracy should otherwise proceed on a step-by-step basis.

Public Authorities

While industrial relations in government service and in the nationalised industries are, in general, organised on the same principles as in private industry, there are some special features.

Central and Local Government

Non-industrial employees in central Government service, where salaries and conditions of service are dealt with by the Civil Service Department, are permitted and encouraged to join the appropriate Civil Service unions and there is a highly developed system of negotiation and joint consultation by means of the National and Departmental Whitley Councils. Unresolved disputes may, subject to certain limitations, be reported to the Secretary of State for reference to the Civil Service Arbitration Tribunal, an independent body appointed by the Secretary of State. Government industrial employees are similarly encouraged to belong to trade unions and machinery exists for joint consultation. There are four Trades Joint Councils on which representatives of the Government and the trade unions sit to consider pay and conditions of employment affecting individual grades and certain other limited matters. A Joint Co-ordinating Committee, on which the Government and Trades Joint Councils are represented, deals with national pay negotiations, conditions of service and other matters of general application. In the main employing departments there are departmental joint councils for the discussion of domestic matters. Disputes on wages or conditions of employment that cannot be resolved by the existing machinery can be referred to the Central Arbitration Committee.

In local government service there are separate National Joint Councils for the main grades of employees (such as manual, clerical and technical employees) which deal with wages and conditions of service as well as other matters. There are corresponding regional and district councils.

Nationalised Industries

The major nationalised industries have a statutory duty to establish satisfactory arrangements for collective bargaining and for joint consultation with their employees. Unlike firms in the private sector, the corporations are not usually members of employers' associations (although the majority are 'public sector members' of the CBI). In some industries they are sole or main employers, but even where part of the industry is in private hands, as for example in road transport, the corporations are separately and directly represented on wage negotiating bodies.

Wages and conditions of service in the nationalised industries are generally settled by negotiation between representatives of management and trade unions at the national level; in most cases there are also regional and local bodies similarly representative, to deal with local issues but not normally to negotiate separate local agreements. Most of the industries use the facilities for arbitration offered to industry generally by the ACAS, but coalmining and rail transport have their own special arrangements. Consultation at all levels including the workplace, has been arranged in all the nationalised industries.

Office of Manpower Economics

The Office of Manpower Economics, established in 1971 as an independent non-statutory body, acts as secretariat for the three review bodies set up to advise on the remuneration of certain groups in the public sector for which negotiating machinery is not appropriate, such as chairmen and members of boards of nationalised industries, the higher judiciary and senior civil servants; the armed forces; and doctors and dentists. It also services special inquiries on particular pay structures and related problems.

STATUTORY NEGOTIATING MACHINERY In a number of industries and trades where the organisation of employers or employees or both is not strong enough to provide a basis for successful voluntary arrangements, there are statutory wage-regulating bodies, known as wages councils. These are composed of equal numbers of representatives of employers and employees in the respective sectors of industry, with three independent members. Wages councils publish proposals for minimum remuneration, holidays, holiday remuneration and other terms and conditions of employment. After considering any representations the councils make orders giving statutory force to such proposals. The Department of Employment's Wages Inspectorate enforces the provisions of these wages orders. About 2·8 million workers are covered by such arrangements.

Agricultural wages boards (there are boards for England and Wales and for Scotland) perform similar functions in relation to employment in agriculture.

The Secretary of State for Employment has power to convert a wages council into a statutory joint industrial council (SJIC), a body which functions in the same way as a wages council, except that it has no independent members. Such conversion is intended to assist in the development of collective bargaining, an SJIC being seen as a halfway stage between the statutory system and full voluntary collective bargaining.

HEALTH AND SAFETY AT WORK

Employers have a duty at common and criminal law to take reasonable care of their employees and provide a safe system of working, while employees have a duty of care towards each other and also to take care for their own safety. In addition, minimum required standards of safety in certain kinds of workplaces or work are laid down under a number of statutes; some of these also deal with health and welfare. The Health and Safety at Work etc. Act 1974 reorganised the system under which safety and health at work was safeguarded and extended it to cover everyone at work and to further the protection of the general public from industrial hazards.

Health and Safety Commission The Health and Safety Commission, appointed by the Secretary of State for Employment after consultation with the TUC, CBI and local authorities, has responsibility for supervising the application and enforcement of health and safety legislation. Its operational arm is the Health and Safety Executive, consisting largely of the government inspectorates covering factories, mines and quarries, agriculture, explosives, nuclear installations and alkali works; the Employment Medical Advisory Service; and the Health and Safety Laboratories, which include the Safety in Mines Research Establishment.

The basic obligations laid down in the Act are supported by ministerial powers to make regulations dealing with a wide range of health and safety matters. Regulations will be supplemented where appropriate by codes of practice approved by the commission, and by guidance notes and other codes. In particular the Act gives inspectors the power to issue improvement and prohibition notices, which enable them to require practical improvements to be made within a specified time or to require preventive measures immediately without first having to obtain a court order. There are provisions for appeals to industrial tribunals against such notices.

Safety Regulations

About 207,000 industrial premises (factories, warehouses, shipyards, docks and construction sites) are regulated under the Factories Act 1961, which is enforced mainly by the Factory Inspectorate, part of the Health and Safety Executive. Likewise about 770,000 premises are subject to the Offices, Shops and Railway Premises Act 1963, whose enforcement is shared by the Factory Inspectorate and the Mines and Quarries Inspectorate (also part of the new Executive), the Railway Inspectorate (see below) and local authorities.

The Acts and regulations made under them are designed to secure the health, safety and welfare of employees, and deal with such matters as the fencing of machinery; precautions against the exposure of people to toxic gases and dusts; precautions against fire, dangerous substances and special risks; the safe condition of premises; and cleanliness, lighting, temperature and ventilation. They also contain provisions concerning the employment of women. Anyone intending to employ other people in industrial or commercial premises to which either the Factories Act or the Offices, Shops and Railway Premises Act applies has to notify the enforcing authority of his intention and there is a statutory duty to report every accident which is either fatal or causes more than three days' incapacity. The Factories Act includes provisions for the compulsory notification and investigation of certain types of dangerous occurrence.

Comparable provision with appropriate variations covers mines and quarries, agriculture and transport (including aviation and shipping, the responsibility of the Department of Trade). As with the Factories Act these other provisions are, with some exceptions, enforced through inspectorates—the Mines and Quarries Inspectorate, the Agricultural Inspectorate, and the Railway Inspectorate of the Department of Transport. Safety requirements in all other places of work including hotels, places of entertainment and educational establishments but excluding domestic work in the home, are covered by the Health and Safety at Work etc. Act or (in respect of their offices and shops) by the Offices, Shops and Railway Premises Act, while fire authorities are responsible for general fire precautions and means of escape.

The Health and Safety Executive, through its Nuclear Installations Inspectorate, is the authority concerned with the granting of nuclear site licences for commercial nuclear installations. No such installation may be constructed or operated in Britain without a licence granted by the executive under sections of the Nuclear Installations Act 1965 which are relevant statutory provisions under the Health and Safety at Work etc. Act. Conditions attached to such licences in the interests of safety are imposed and enforced by the inspectorate.

The Health and Safety Commission also has responsibility under the Mineral Workings (Offshore Installations) Act 1971 and the Petroleum and Submarine Pipelines Act 1975 for the health and safety of all persons (including divers) engaged in the offshore oil and gas industry.

Other Measures

Transport operators and ministries concerned with road and air travel give high priority to safety measures affecting crews and passengers. Every effort is made to counter the higher risks resulting from rising traffic densities by improving the design of vehicles and transport equipment, by control of standards of maintenance, by traffic regulations and by training crews in safety awareness.

To minimise the hazards which may arise from the use of pesticides, a voluntary scheme has been established under which pesticides are vetted by the Ministry of Agriculture, Fisheries and Food's Advisory Committee on Pesticides and Other Toxic Chemicals (see p 168) before being marketed. The committee gives clearance for specific uses, subject to its recommendations on such matters as safety precautions and labelling being agreed to.

There are also the Health and Safety Laboratories, which are concerned with research into health and safety problems in industry (see p 382).

Employment of
Women and
Children

Legislation forbids any employment of children under 14 years of age, and employment in any industrial undertaking of children who have not reached the statutory minimum school-leaving age (now 16); of women and young people underground in mines and in certain other dangerous occupations (for example, certain processes connected with lead manufacture); and of women in factories and workshops within four weeks after childbirth. It also limits and defines the permissible hours of employment for women and young people.

Promotion of
Safety Measures

The Health and Safety Commission encourages the development of voluntary central organisation within each industry at national level for the consideration of safety matters and the formulation of policy and accident prevention. Its inspectorates, besides inquiring into notified accidents and safety aspects of machine design and specification, circulate expert advice to both sides of industry and to the general public, and maintain a health and safety centre in London, at which various types of guards for machinery are displayed, as well as a wide range of protective clothing and equipment. Regulations coming into force in October 1978 provide that recognised trade unions may appoint safety representatives to represent the employees in a workplace; also, two or more such representatives may make a written request to the employer to establish a safety committee, which must then be set up within three months of the request being made.

Organisations in industry participate also in joint standing and advisory committees appointed by the Secretary of State for Employment, but these arrangements are being superseded. The Health and Safety Commission has appointed four major advisory committees in addition to the Committee on Major Hazards set up in 1975; these include one on asbestos, one on toxic substances, one on dangerous substances and one on medical matters. Proposals have also been made for the appointment of 18 industry-based committees, four of which have already been set up. The Royal Society for the Prevention of Accidents (RoSPA) and the British Safety Council are national bodies concerned with accident prevention and sponsor a number of local accident prevention groups.

Training and
Research in
Safety

Training is important in accident prevention and the Manpower Services Commission provides a course in job safety for supervisors in its Training Within Industry scheme (see p 316). The industrial training boards include specific provisions for safety training in their training recommendations.

RoSPA provides a variety of safety courses for special needs, mainly at its Industrial Safety Training Centre in Birmingham, and also helps the accident prevention movement by providing publicity and organising conferences; its regional industrial safety officers work to promote safety activity among top-level managers. The British Safety Council also offers safety training courses. Other courses are organised by local accident prevention groups and organisations such as the Federation of Civil Engineering Contractors.

A substantial amount of research is being done by industry, universities and other academic bodies, and government research organisations into problems of guarding machines, ergonomics, safe handling, electrical hazards, nuclear safety, protective personal equipment, construction methods, fires and explosions, psychological factors and causes of accidents, both generally and in particular sectors of industry. Industrial research associations include among their more purely economic research projects the improvement of working conditions and the reduction of hazards.

The National Coal Board conducts courses of safety training for workmen and officials. Its research programme includes a number of projects with a direct bearing on safety. In addition, the Health and Safety Executive has a statutory responsibility for research concerning the safety and health of coal miners, largely exercised through its Safety in Mines Research Establishment.

The University of Aston in Birmingham helps to meet the need for academically trained safety officers and engineers whose careers will be concerned with the technical aspects of insurance and forensic work.

Employment Medical Advisory Service

The Employment Medical Advisory Service (EMAS), set up under the Employment Medical Advisory Service Act 1972 and now part of the Health and Safety Executive, provides a nation-wide service of advice on the medical aspects of employment problems to employers, employees, trade unions, doctors and others. It carries out medical examinations of workers in hazardous occupations and surveys of employment hazards, advises the staff of the Manpower Services Commission on medical aspects of job placement, rehabilitation and industrial training and co-operates with school medical officers and careers officers in helping to solve the employment problems of handicapped school leavers. The service, headed by the Health and Safety Executive's Director of Medical Services, has over 100 employment medical advisers based in the country's main industrial centres. The TUC, the CBI and other interested organisations are associated with the work of the service through advisory committees.

Scientific Support for Occupational Health

The Occupational Medicine and Hygiene Laboratories (which are part of the Health and Safety Laboratories, see p 327) at Cricklewood, north London, provide laboratory services and undertake research in the field of occupational health. Among other things these laboratories assist EMAS in the analysis of blood and urine samples; while the Factory Inspectorate also looks to the laboratories as a main source of laboratory assistance.

Research facilities are provided by government agencies such as the Medical Research Council; by university faculties of industrial health and social medicine; and by the research departments of various industries and large industrial concerns. Field investigations are carried out by the Factory Inspectorate, which has specialised technical branches, and by the EMAS.

Employers' Health Services

Many employers voluntarily maintain medical services for their employees over and above the statutory requirements. The big employers, including the State and the boards of nationalised industries, have taken the lead but a number of smaller factories also provide medical services and in a few cases have joined together in group medical services.

Other Amenities

An increasing number of firms pay part or all of the cost of recreational facilities. Some have their own rehabilitation centres or support convalescent homes. The provision of low-priced meals at the place of employment has become usual in large undertakings and quite common in smaller ones. Many offices and shops which are unable to provide canteen facilities for their staff have adopted luncheon voucher schemes.

Human Relations in Industry

Both official and voluntary organisations are concerned with promoting better human relationships in industry. The Government has sought to extend by research the available knowledge of the factors influencing human relations in industry and human efficiency. Such research is sponsored or conducted by the Social Science Research Council (see p 375) and the Medical Research Council (see p 373). In addition, the Department of Employment's Work Research Unit provides information on how particular jobs can be redesigned to create greater satisfaction, helps industry and others in initiating and evaluating changes in the content of work, and administers a research programme. Voluntary organisations include bodies which deal with management problems and provide a service to subscribing firms; professional associations, linking individuals with a common interest in particular functions of management; and bodies providing specialist services, usually on a fee-paying basis.

Safety, Health and Welfare in Northern Ireland

The safety, health and welfare of employees in Northern Ireland have been the subject of legislation which is embodied in the Factories Act (Northern Ireland) 1965 and the Office and Shop Premises Act (Northern Ireland) 1966. A number of firms voluntarily employ safety officers, and industrial safety groups, supported by representatives of industry, insurance companies and public authorities, make a valuable contribution to accident prevention.

Legislation for Northern Ireland in line with the Health and Safety at Work etc. Act 1974 (see p 327) has been passed and will come into effect during 1979.

17 Finance

THE PUBLIC SECTOR

PUBLIC EXPENDITURE

Public expenditure comprises the current and capital expenditure of central government and local authorities (collectively known as general government), excluding expenditure charged to the operating account of trading bodies; central government finance in the form of grants, loans or public dividend capital provided towards the cost of capital investment by the nationalised industries; the capital expenditure of other public corporations; the contingency reserve; and those debt interest payments which constitute a charge on taxation. Public expenditure, excluding debt interest, in 1977–78 amounted to about £54,300 million (at 1977 Survey prices) of which 70 per cent was undertaken by the central Government; and 28 per cent by local authorities, the remaining 2 per cent representing the capital expenditure of public corporations other than the nationalised industries.

The wide range of functions and purposes of this expenditure and its distribution is shown in Table 22.

The social services programmes accounted for nearly 53 per cent of the total programmes, and defence expenditure for about 12 per cent.

Out of the total public expenditure of £56,220 million in 1977–78 some £32,372 million or 58 per cent was spent by the public sector directly on goods and services (wages and salaries, other current expenditure on goods and services, gross domestic fixed capital formation and stocks). Transfer payments to individuals, companies and other institutions in the private sector (for example, social security payments, capital grants, subsidies, and debt interest) made up the balance. Unlike public authorities' direct purchases of goods and services, transfer payments do not represent a direct demand on the nation's resources. The gross sums transferred create a proportionately lower indirect demand for goods and services because of taxes paid and savings made by the recipients.

Between 1972–73 and 1977–78 total public expenditure programmes grew in real terms by about 5·3 per cent. The growth previously envisaged in the expenditure programme after 1976–77 was reduced to make possible a shift of resources into industrial investment and exports. The low level of economic activity led to further downward adjustments to the medium-term expenditure plans during 1976. The improvement in Britain's financial situation in 1977, however, enabled the Government to plan for resumed expansion of many expenditure programmes including an addition of £1,000 million to the plans for 1978–79. The Government has also stated its aim of having a greater degree of stability in public spending than has been achieved in recent years.

Planning and Control of Public Expenditure

Major importance is attached to adequate planning and control of public expenditure. There are three principal and interdependent ways in which this is done. First, the annual public expenditure survey, which leads to the publication of a report describing the Government's medium-term expenditure plans on a constant price basis; secondly, the Supply Estimates by means of which Parliament votes the cash required to run certain central government services in the coming financial year; and thirdly, the system of cash limits under which, for the financial year immediately ahead, the volume of expenditure at constant prices shown in the survey plans is translated into cash provision which will not normally be exceeded. These arrangements are described in more detail below.

TABLE 22: Public Expenditure 1977–78

	£ million at 1977 Survey prices
Defence and external relations (UK)	
Defence	6,255
Overseas aid and other overseas services	1,351
Commerce and industry	
Agriculture, fisheries and forestry	899
Trade, industry and employment	1,796 [a]
Government lending to Nationalised industries	420
Environmental services	
Roads and transport	2,590
Housing	4,475
Other environmental services	2,532
Law, order and protective services	1,906
Social services	
Education and libraries, science and arts	8,010
Health and personal social services	7,390
Social security	13,226
Other services	
Other public services	844
Common services	883
Northern Ireland [b]	1,742
Total programmes	54,320
Debt interest	1,900
TOTAL	56,220

Source: *The Government's Expenditure Plans 1978–79 to 1981–82*

[a] Net of £559 million for proceeds of sale of shares in the British Petroleum Company.
[b] Including the other services shown above except Defence and external relations.

Public Expenditure Surveys

Each year a survey is made of the whole range of projected public expenditure covering the period five years ahead. It is carried out by officials in the Treasury and other government departments, under the direction of the Public Expenditure Survey Committee.

The primary purpose of the survey is to present to ministers an up-to-date assessment of the cost of their existing policies and proposed changes as a basis for decisions about the total and the composition of public expenditure in the five-year period covered. This gives the Government the opportunity to plan ahead any necessary changes without causing wasteful disruption in existing services, and to have regard to the overall economic outlook when taking decisions.

A report on the survey is prepared in the first half of the year. This is followed by ministerial consideration of the report and then by the publication of the Government's public expenditure plans (see Bibliography, p 450). This provides the basis for an annual public expenditure debate in the House of Commons. The plans contain a contingency reserve to provide for additions to the programmes set out. This has been developed into a more operational instrument, as one of the means of securing that actual expenditure is kept within the plans. The object is, as far as possible, to limit claims on the reserve by meeting the cost of new measures, or increased estimates for existing measures, within existing departmental totals. Recourse to the reserve to meet additional expenditure is subject to the approval of Treasury ministers, who may refer the larger or more difficult claims for consideration by the Cabinet as a whole.

Estimates

Each department submits its estimates of cash requirements to the Treasury in the December before the financial year beginning on the following 1 April. Estimates cover central Government's own expenditure. (Not all this expenditure is classified as public expenditure—for example, payments to local authorities. Only when the money is spent by the local authorities is public expenditure recorded.) After they have been approved by the Treasury, the Supply Estimates are presented to Parliament shortly before the Budget (see p 335) and are approved by Parliament for one year ahead, by means of an annual Appropriation Act, in July (expenditure to this date from 1 April is covered by a Vote on Account approved by Parliament before the beginning of the financial year). There are 29 allotted days (known as supply days) in each session on which the choice of subject for debate rests with the Opposition and on which estimates can be debated. Broad issues of policy are normally discussed.

Certain expenditures are not approved annually, but are covered by Acts of Parliament allowing payments to continue from one year to another and are paid direct from the Consolidated Fund. These include the financial provision for members of the royal family, and salaries and pensions of judges. The Consolidated Fund, into which tax revenue and other receipts are paid, finances most of the Government's expenditure; its balance is held in the Exchequer account at the Bank of England. The National Loans Fund covers most of the Government's domestic lending and borrowing, and is operated as an official account at the Bank of England. The two funds deal only with sterling receipts and payments; official dealings in foreign exchange are carried out by the Exchange Equalisation Account (see p 343).

Cash Limits

Cash limits, first introduced on an extensive scale in 1976–77, have been applied to public spending wherever they can make a useful contribution to financial discipline. They also contribute to the Government's policy for reducing inflation and help in forecasting the Government's maximum financing requirements. About half of public expenditure is covered by cash limits. Certain services such as social security payments are excluded because, once policy and rates of payment have been determined, cash spending in the short term depends on factors outside the Government's direct control. Cash limits are also placed on the financial assistance given to local authorities by central Government and on local authority capital expenditure. The estimates of the financing requirements of the nationalised industries are also treated as a form of cash limit.

Spending departments and authorities are required to provide within their cash limits for any increase in costs due to pay and price changes. The cash limits for 1978–79 were published in April 1978 (see Bibliography, p 450).

Monitoring

Expenditure by government departments is monitored by the Treasury and compared with profiles of expected expenditure prepared at the beginning of the financial year in accordance with the approved Public Expenditure Survey, Supply Estimate and cash limit provisions.

The Comptroller and Auditor General

The Comptroller and Auditor General is appointed by the Crown and his independence of the Executive is secured by specific statutory provisions. Since 1866 he has had two functions: as Comptroller he ensures that all revenues and other public money payable to the Consolidated Fund and the National Loans Fund are duly paid over and that all issues from these funds are authorised by statute; and as Auditor General he audits departmental and other accounts and, as required by statute, submits his reports on Appropriation Accounts and other accounts to Parliament. For many years and with the encouragement of the Public Accounts Committee (see below) his statutory audit functions have been extended to include general financial administration, cost-effectiveness and cases of apparent waste or extravagance.

Expenditure Committee

The House of Commons Select Committee on Expenditure considers papers on public expenditure and estimates presented to the House. As part of its activities it examines ministers and senior officials, and questions whether the policies underlying the planning figures may be carried out more economically; and examines critically the form and content of the Public Expenditure Plans and Estimates. The Committee's reports provide information for the House for its debate on public expenditure. The Committee operates by means of sub-committees which cover, for example, general government financial control and the efficient execution of government policies; and individual public expenditure programmes such as defence and external affairs, education and social services. The sub-committees are able to call for oral and written evidence from departmental ministers and officials; they also take evidence from witnesses outside central government. The committee is appointed for the life of a Parliament.

The Public Accounts Committee

The accounts of each department and the reports of the Comptroller and Auditor General upon them are considered by a House of Commons select committee called the Public Accounts Committee. This was established in 1861 to ensure that expenditure was properly incurred in accordance with the purposes for which it was voted and with the relevant Acts of Parliament. The committee's terms of reference are simply that it must examine and report upon the accounts laid before Parliament and these terms are widely interpreted. Successive committees have investigated whether full value has been obtained for the sums spent by departments and have reported in detail on cases in which administration appeared faulty or negligent. The committee has become a powerful instrument for the exposure of waste or inefficiency. It embodies its findings in regular reports to Parliament and its recommendations are given serious consideration by departments. The Government's formal reply to these reports is presented to Parliament by the Treasury in the form of a Treasury Minute, and the reports and the Minute are made the subject of an annual debate in the House of Commons.

THE BUDGET

The Budget (an old word which meant a bag containing papers or accounts) is a set of proposals, usually put forward in March or April, for financing government expenditure. Supplementary budgetary measures may also be introduced at other times of the year. The proposals are described by the Chancellor of the Exchequer in the Budget speech, against the background of a statement of the Government's past and prospective revenue and expenditure, and his assessment of the position and prospects of the economy.

The Budget speech is followed by the moving of a set of Ways and Means resolutions, in which the proposals are embodied. These resolutions, when passed by the House, become the foundation of the Finance Act, which expresses the proposals in statutory form.

A major function of the Budget is to act as an instrument of economic management, and the Budget statement is normally the main occasion for a review of general economic policy. The scale of public expenditure and taxation has an important influence on the general level of output and distribution of resources. The Budget judgment is therefore concerned with the balance between the total of goods and services which are likely to be available to the nation and the total claims which are likely to be made on them. Through taxation the Government can exert a considerable influence on the demand for goods and services; its measures can also have a broader influence on the pattern of demand and the long-term performance of the economy.

The Budget deals with the means of financing expenditure and particularly with changes in taxation and not primarily with expenditure itself. On occasions, changes affecting expenditure, such as increases in pensions and family allowances, have been announced in the Budget statement as have financial and monetary measures such as changes in exchange control policies. Such measures, however, are not generally reflected in the resolutions or the Finance Act but are applied by the appropriate procedure, that is, separate legislation, statutory instruments or administrative action.

The scope of the Budget and that of the Finance Act which follows it are different although they are closely interrelated. The Budget is essentially concerned with the measures that give effect to the Chancellor's decision to increase or reduce to an appropriate extent the predicted level of demand on economic resources by use of the instruments at his disposal, and especially by increasing or reducing the yield of central government taxes. The tax changes proposed on the basis of the Budget judgment are enacted in the form approved by Parliament in the Finance Act, which also provides the annual opportunity for non-Budgetary changes in the tax system and for certain other financial matters, such as provisions relating to Government borrowing.

The bulk of the taxation proposals in the Budget are concerned with changes in the rates or coverage of existing taxes, the introduction of new taxes or the abolition of existing ones, and changes in the administrative machinery relating to taxation. In two cases (income tax and corporation tax), however, annual Ways and Means resolutions followed by a Finance Act clause are necessary to maintain the taxes in existence at all, since they are annual taxes. Thus a Budget at or about the beginning of each financial year is a necessity.

New taxes and changes in certain existing taxes, like other changes in statute law, do not come into effect until the appropriate Bill—in this case the Finance Bill—has received Royal Assent (in the case of the spring Budget, normally about the end of July) or at some other date laid down in the Bill. Some changes, however, come into effect earlier, usually from Budget Day or from the start of the tax year, under the Provisional Collection of Taxes Act. This enables the Government to collect certain taxes provisionally, income tax for example, either at the rates previously in operation or at new rates following the passing of the appropriate Ways and Means resolutions.

Public Sector Accounts   The economic background to the spring Budget and the transactions of the central government and the public sector as a whole are presented in the

Financial Statement and Budget Report (see Bibliography, p 450) which is laid before the House of Commons by the Chancellor of the Exchequer when he presents the Budget. The report is in three parts: the economic context of the Budget; the accounts of the public sector for the past financial year and the one immediately ahead; and the accounts of the central government for the same two years. The accounts are designed to assist in assessing the impact of changes in revenue and public expenditure on the economy.

The accounts of the public sector show the transactions of the central government, local authorities, nationalised industries and other public corporations combined into a consolidated account covering the whole of the public sector. The transactions within the public sector cancel out on consolidation and the net balance on the consolidated account represents therefore the borrowing which is required by the public sector from the private and overseas sectors.

The accounts of the central government show transactions both on the conventional cash basis of Exchequer accounting and in accordance with the framework of the national income accounts.

To raise the money it requires over and above tax revenue the Government offers a great variety of claims on itself designed to attract different types of lender. Broadly there is marketable debt, and non-marketable debt. Marketable debt is made up of short-term floating debt consisting of Treasury bills, and funded or longer-term debt made up of government securities which are of varying maturities and publicly quoted on the Stock Exchange. Non-marketable debt comprises the various forms of national savings designed to attract the smaller saver; certificates of tax deposits; and ways and means advances, which basically is very short-term internal government borrowing. The bulk of public corporations' borrowing is met by central government through the National Loans Fund, although public corporations' temporary borrowing needs are met largely from the market under Treasury guarantee. That part of local authority borrowing met by central government is dealt with through the Public Works Loan Board which has recourse to the National Loans Fund. The local authorities also borrow directly from the market, both short-term and long-term, through a range of different investments. Some public corporations also borrow, under special statutory power and with Treasury consent, in foreign currencies.

After allowing for the changes introduced by the Budget of April 1978 the central government's borrowing requirement for 1978–79 was expected to be £7,957 million, compared with an estimated outturn of £4,494 million in 1977–78 and that for the public sector as a whole £8,537 million compared with an estimated £5,713 million in 1977–78.

Table 23 shows total revenue from taxation and other sources in 1977–78 and the forecasts for 1978–79 together with the effects of the Budget changes.

SOURCES OF REVENUE

The three principal sources of tax revenue are first, taxes on income, which include income tax and corporation tax; second, taxes on capital, which include capital transfer tax and capital gains tax; and third, taxes on expenditure (including taxes on the ownership or use of certain assets)—these include protective and excise duties, value added tax (VAT), the National Insurance Surcharge, local rates (see p 67), stamp duties and licence duties (for example, on motor vehicles). Taxes on individual (but not corporate) incomes are progressive in that larger incomes bear a proportionately higher rate of tax. The Board of Inland Revenue assesses and collects the taxes on income and capital and the stamp duties; the Board of Customs and Excise collects the most important taxes on expenditure (the customs and excise duties and VAT) while a variety of authorities is responsible for the collection of the remainder.

Taxes on Income   Income tax is imposed for the year of assessment beginning on 6 April. The rates of tax introduced in the Finance Act 1978 are as follows: a new lower tax
Income Tax   rate band of 25 per cent applies to the first £750 of taxable income (that is,

TABLE 23: Taxation and Miscellaneous Receipts 1977–78 and 1978–79

£ million

	1977–78			1978–79 Forecasts	
	Budget forecast	Forecast changes[a]	Estimated Outturn	Before Budget changes	After Finance Act
Taxation					
Inland Revenue:					
Income tax	18,065	17,069	17,420	21,227	19,310
Surtax	30		30	15	15
Corporation tax	2,560	2,587	3,346	4,188	4,170
Petroleum revenue tax	5		—	170	170
Capital gains tax	330		340	390	375
Development land tax	5		7	10	10
Estate duty	70		87	50	50
Capital transfer tax	320	310	312	320	320
Stamp duties	320		375	440	440
Total Inland Revenue	21,705	20,726	21,917	26,810	24,860
Customs and Excise:					
Value added tax	4,250		4,226	4,795	4,775
Oil	2,550	2,400	2,465	2,500	2,500
Tobacco	2,150		2,056	2,440	2,450
Spirits, beer, wine, cider and perry	2,050		2,062	2,400	2,400
Betting and gaming	315		320	350	350
Car tax	250		286	325	325
Other revenue duties	10		10	10	10
Protective duties, etc.	690		676	765	765
Agricultural levies	135		183	175	175
Total Customs and Excise[b]	12,400	12,250	12,284	13,760	13,750
Motor vehicle duties	1,068		1,072	1,120	1,120
National insurance surcharge	1,159		1,163	1,475	1,928
Total Taxation	36,332	32,976	36,436	43,165	41,658
Miscellaneous Receipts:					
Broadcast receiving licences	250		294	317	317
Interest and dividends	225		240	264	264
Other[c]	935		1,803	960	960
Total	37,742	34,386	38,773	44,706	43,199

Source: *Financial Statement and Budget Report 1978–79 and Treasury*
[a] Changes in the Finance Act 1977 and the Finance (Income Tax Reliefs) Act 1977.
[b] Includes customs duties and agricultural levies accountable to the European Communities as 'own resources'.
[c] Includes the 10 per cent of 'own resources' refunded by the European Communities to meet the costs of collection.

total income less deductions and personal allowances) with up to a further £750 if there are wife's earnings, after which a basic rate of 33 per cent is charged on the balance of taxable income of up to £8,000, 40 per cent on the £8,001–£9,000 band of taxable income and thereafter the rate for successive bands rises generally in steps of 5 per cent until a maximum rate of 83 per cent is reached at a level of over £24,000 of taxable income. These rates are charged on both earned and investment incomes. Investment incomes are also liable to a surcharge on the amount by which they exceed £1,700 (£2,500 for the elderly); the surcharge is 10 per cent on the first £550 of investment income (£500 for the elderly) above the relevant threshold and 15 per cent on the remainder. The tax imposed on an individual is graduated by means of personal allowances and reliefs. In general, married couples receive higher allowances than a single person. Husband and wife may choose to have the wife's earnings charged separately for tax on condition that the former receives the single instead of the married personal allowance. But even then the married couple are taxed jointly on their investment income.

For 1978–79 a single person earning £5,000 a year pays £1,264·95 in income tax, while a married man with the same earned income pays £1,083·45; if he has two children under the age of 11 and his earnings plus child benefits total £5,000 his tax falls to £929·27. The amount of tax payable by a single person varies from, for example, £274·95 on an earned income of £2,000 a year to £9,091·25 on an earned income of £20,000.

Most wage and salary earners pay their income tax under a PAYE ('Pay as You Earn') system whereby tax is deducted (and accounted for to the Inland Revenue) by the employer, thus enabling them to keep as up to date as possible with their tax payments.

In general, income tax is charged on all income which originates in the United Kingdom and on all income arising abroad of persons resident in the United Kingdom. Interest on certain United Kingdom government·securities belonging to persons not ordinarily resident in the United Kingdom is exempt. The United Kingdom has entered into agreements with many countries providing for relief from double taxation; where such agreements are not in force unilateral relief is allowed.

Corporation Tax   Companies pay corporation tax at a single rate on all their profits, whether distributed or not. Only a proportion of any capital gains is included in total profits, with the result that chargeable gains as a whole are subject to a lower effective rate of tax. Income tax is not deducted from dividends but a company which distributes profits to its shareholders is required to make to the Inland Revenue an advance payment of corporation tax. In general, this payment is set against a company's corporation tax bill and the recipient of the distribution in respect of which the advance payment was made is entitled to a tax credit, which satisfies the liability to income tax at the basic rate.

The rate of corporation tax is fixed retrospectively in the Budget for the past financial year; for the financial year 1977 (1 April 1977–31 March 1978) it is 52 per cent with a reduced rate of 42 per cent for small companies (as defined in the Finance Acts 1972, 1974, 1976, 1977, and 1978). The tax is assessed on the profits of accounting periods, the rate of tax being the rate for the financial year in which the accounting period falls. Where an accounting period straddles 31 March the profits are apportioned on a time basis. Relief is given by an interim scheme for the rise in the value of stocks and work in progress due solely to inflation between the beginning and the end of each accounting period. The form of a permanent scheme will be considered when the outcome of the current debate on inflation accounting becomes clear and its methods have been reviewed in practice. Meanwhile legislation is planned for introduction in 1979 which would limit the build up of deferred tax liabilities.

Petroleum Revenue Tax

Under the Oil Taxation Act 1975 a petroleum revenue tax of 45 per cent (deducted in computing profits for corporation tax) is charged on profits from the winning, as opposed to refining or other form of processing, of hydro-carbons under licence in Britain and on its continental shelf. The Government proposes to increase petroleum revenue tax to 60 per cent on 1 January 1979. Each licensee of an oilfield is to be charged on the profits for that field, computed for half-yearly periods.

Taxes on Capital

Capital Transfer Tax

A comprehensive tax, capital transfer tax, applies to transfer of personal wealth in three main areas: lifetime gifts; transfers on death; and transfers relating to settled property (that is, any property held in trust). The tax is chargeable in respect of a person's lifetime transfers as they occur and on a cumulative basis. The final stage of cumulation is the inclusion of the property 'passing' on an assumed transfer of the whole of the deceased's estate immediately before the death. The rates of tax applicable are progressively higher on successive slices of the cumulative total of chargeable transfers, with a lower scale of tax for lifetime transfers than for transfers on death. Under both scales the first £25,000 of transfers is exempt; the rates on the remainder rise from 5 per cent on the slice between £25,000 and £30,000 to 75 per cent on the excess over £2·01 million for lifetime transfers and from 10 per cent on the slice between £25,000 and £30,000 to 75 per cent on the excess over £2·01 million for transfers on death.

Capital Gains Tax

Capital gains accruing on the disposal of assets are liable to capital gains tax or, in the case of companies, to corporation tax. The rate of tax is normally 30 per cent, but in the case of individuals may be less, depending on their circumstances. For small businesses the tax on gifts and certain deemed disposals of business assets may be deferred until the assets are sold. Certain assets may be exempt from tax, including the principal private residence, chattels worth less than £2,000 (and any chattels, except those used for the purpose of a trade, with a predictable life of less than 50 years), private motor cars and National Savings Certificates. An individual is exempt from capital gains tax where the total net gains do not exceed £1,000 in any year; where the gains do not exceed £5,000, the excess over £1,000 is charged at a reduced rate of 15 per cent; where the gains exceed £5,000, liability is limited to tax of £600 plus half of the excess over £5,000. This marginal relief runs out at £9,500. In addition, the gains on gilt-edged securities are exempt from the tax if the securities were held for more than 12 months.

Development Land Tax

The Development Land Tax Act 1976 introduced a development land tax (DLT) on development value in place of the charge on development gains and on first letting introduced in the Finance Act 1974. The rate of DLT is 80 per cent but the first £10,000 of development value realised in any financial year is completely exempt and for a transitional period up to 31 March 1980 the next £150,000 in any financial year will be liable at a rate of 66·6 per cent. Exemptions from DLT include the sale or development of owner-occupied residences.

Taxes on Expenditure

The largest group of taxes on expenditure are those administered by the Board of Customs and Excise namely, VAT, car tax and the excise duties on tobacco, hydrocarbon oil and alcoholic drinks and betting and gaming, and the protective duties, chargeable as Community customs duty in accordance with the EEC Common Customs Tariff (no such duties are chargeable on goods which qualify as Community goods). These taxes are usually referred to as indirect taxes since they are normally paid by the importer, manufacturer, or wholesaler, who adjusts the prices charged to customers accordingly.

All the excise duty goods (other than hydrocarbon oil) are subject to the standard rate of VAT. The Chancellor of the Exchequer has power to vary between Budgets the amounts of the VAT rates by up to 25 per cent, and the rate of any of the other main groups of excise duties (that is, tobacco, alcoholic drinks, oil and the minor excise duties) by up to 10 per cent. This power, known as the 'regulator', requires annual renewal. The April 1978 Budget imposed a supplementary duty on cigarettes with a higher tar yield.

Value Added Tax

Value added tax (VAT) is collected at each stage in the production and distribution process. The final tax is borne by the consumer. A taxable person (generally, a trader carrying on a business with a turnover of more than £10,000 a year) is charged by suppliers of goods and services with VAT ('input' tax). The trader then charges the customer with VAT on goods and services supplied ('output' tax). The trader pays to Customs and Excise the difference between output and input tax. Although VAT falls on imported goods, most exports are zero-rated and VAT entering directly into export costs can be reclaimed.

VAT is a broadly based tax falling on final consumers' expenditure except where there are strong social or economic reasons for giving relief. There are two basic methods by which supplies of goods and services may get relief from VAT: zero-rating, when a trader does not have to charge tax to a customer, but can reclaim any input tax paid to suppliers, and exemption, when a trader does not have to charge a customer any output tax but is not entitled to deduct or reclaim any input tax relating to the goods or services which he sells. The most important supplies to which zero-rating applies are most types of food (except in the course of catering); books, newspapers and periodicals; fuel (except for petrol and other fuels for road use); construction of buildings; exports (goods and many services); public transport fares; young children's clothing and footwear; and drugs and medicines supplied on prescription. Exemption applies to land (including rents), insurance, postal services, betting, gaming other than by means of a gaming machine and lotteries, finance, education, health and burial and cremation.

VAT is chargeable at a standard rate of 8 per cent except for certain goods which are charged at a higher rate of 12·5 per cent. These include petrol, most domestic electric appliances (excluding cookers, space heaters and fitted water heaters), radios, televisions, hi-fi equipment, boats, aircraft, caravans, cameras, binoculars, furs and jewellery.

Car Tax

New cars and motor caravans, whether British made or imported, are chargeable with car tax at 10 per cent on the wholesale value. VAT falls on the price including car tax.

Betting and Gaming Duties

The principal betting duties are: the pool betting duty (which applies to football pools and betting by coupon at fixed odds) charged at a rate of 40 per cent of the stake money; and the general betting duty, which is charged at the rate of 7·5 per cent of stake money except for on-course betting which is charged at 4 per cent. Gaming is taxed at different rates mainly by licence fees.

Vehicle Excise Duty

The annual tax on motor vehicles is collected by the Department of Transport; the proceeds are paid into the Consolidated Fund. The licence duty on a private motor car is £50 a year; motor cycles and three-wheel vehicles, etc., pay £5, £10 or £20 a year according to engine capacity. Goods vehicles are taxed by unladen weight, and taxis and buses by seating capacity.

National Insurance Surcharge

The national insurance surcharge is a new tax which took effect from the start of the 1977–78 financial year. It takes the form of a levy paid by employers, along with their national insurance contributions, in respect of their employees and is equal to 3·5 per cent of employees' earnings up to £120 per week (earnings of less than £17·50 per week are exempt). Generally it is assumed that the incidence of this tax will be passed forward into prices, so that it ranks as a tax on expenditure.

The National Debt

On 31 March 1978 the total National Debt was estimated at £79,083 million, of which £4,629 million was repayable in currencies other than sterling, mainly to the United States Government. Of the £74,454 million of internal debt, £12,703 million was short-term debt, mainly in the form of 91-day Treasury bills, while the long-term loans included a variety of stocks, bonds, loans and certificates carrying fixed rates of interest and with fixed or indeterminate dates of repayment.

PUBLIC FINANCE IN NORTHERN IRELAND

The general system of public finance in Northern Ireland is, in its main features, similar to that operating in the United Kingdom as a whole. The major sources of revenue are the main national taxes imposed by the United Kingdom Parliament over the whole country. The Northern Ireland share of the yield of United Kingdom taxes is paid out of the Consolidated Fund of the United Kingdom into that of Northern Ireland. Revenue also accrues from local resources such as the regional rate and from certain non-tax revenue. There is also an annual grant-in-aid voted by Parliament (£682 million in 1977–78 which together with the attributed share of United Kingdom taxes, rates and miscellaneous sums, amounted to a total of £1,601 million). Loans from the United Kingdom National Loans Fund are available (up to a limit of £1,000 million) to finance capital expenditure programmes in Northern Ireland.

Various funds have been established in Northern Ireland, in addition to statutory Reserve and Sinking Funds, for specific purposes. In general, these funds follow the United Kingdom pattern, the principal funds being those relating to national insurance and government loans. The latter constitutes a pool of money available mainly for local and public authority borrowings; on 31 March 1978 a sum of approximately £290 million was outstanding against such borrowers.

FINANCIAL INSTITUTIONS

THE BANKING SYSTEM

The British banking system comprises a central bank; deposit banks which perform the usual main banking services; the British offices of domestic and overseas banks whose main business is in other countries; merchant bank and other specialised institutions.

The Central Bank

The Bank of England was established in 1694 by Act of Parliament and Royal Charter as a corporate body; the entire capital stock was acquired by the

Government under the Bank of England Act 1946. As the central bank, the Bank acts as banker to the Government, to overseas central banks and to deposit banks and is the lender of last resort to the banking system; it is the note-issuing authority and the registrar for some 200 government, nationalised industry, local authority, public board and Commonwealth government stocks. As agent for the Government the Bank administers exchange control. On behalf of the Treasury it manages the Exchange Equalisation Account (EEA), which holds Britain's official reserves of gold, foreign exchange and Special Drawing Rights (SDRs) on the International Monetary Fund. Using the resources of the EEA, the Bank may intervene in the foreign exchange market both to prevent undue fluctuations in the exchange value of sterling and to conserve the means of making payments abroad.

As banker to the Government, the Bank examines and seeks to anticipate banking and financial problems and undertakes the appropriate operations in the money, capital and the foreign exchange markets; consequently it has a major responsibility for advising the Government on the formulation of monetary policy and for its subsequent execution. It is also the main channel of communication between the deposit banks and other financial institutions of the City of London on the one hand and the Government on the other.

The Bank's implementation of monetary policy is carried out primarily through control over interest rates and through direct controls over the banking system. It administers directly the official discount rate, known as Minimum Lending Rate (MLR), which is the rate at which the Bank will normally provide funds to the discount market as a lender of last resort. MLR in turn can be expected to have an influence on other short-term interest rates. In addition, the authorities can influence interest rates through their daily operations in the money market and the terms on which they offer gilt-edged stock.

The Bank's direct controls over the banking system include the setting of a 12·5 per cent minimum ratio of specified reserve assets to total eligible liabilities (broadly, sterling deposits drawn from outside the banking system with an original maturity of two years or less plus the banks' net foreign currency liability). Second, the Bank can call for special deposits as a percentage of total eligible liabilities, which generally bear interest at the Treasury bill rate but which do not count as reserve assets and which therefore contract the banks ability to lend. In addition, a supplementary special deposits scheme can be operated; this requires a bank to place non-interest bearing supplementary special deposits with the Bank of England for every percentage growth in the interest-bearing element of its eligible liabilities beyond a certain specified rate over a defined period. The Bank of England has also issued qualitative guidance on the direction of bank lending; this provides for priority to be given to the finance required by manufacturing industry, for the expansion of exports and for import saving.

The Bank of England has the sole right in England and Wales of issuing bank notes. The note issue is fiduciary, that is to say, it is no longer backed by gold but by government and other securities. The Scottish and Northern Ireland banks have limited rights to issue notes; these issues, apart from an amount specified by legislation for each bank, must be fully covered by holdings of Bank of England notes. The provision of coin for circulation is the responsibility of the Royal Mint, a government department.

The Deposit Banks

The primary business of the deposit banks is the receipt, transfer and the encashment of deposits. The principal deposit banks are the six London clearing banks, three Scottish clearing banks and two Northern Ireland banks. Mergers have resulted in the formation of six banking groups, four based in London and two in Scotland. The two Northern Ireland banks are owned by London clearing banks, but two groups of banks based in the Irish Republic also operate in Northern Ireland.

In April 1978 sterling sight and time deposits with these banks from non-bank customers amounted to £27,438 million and accounted for over 72 per cent of the total of such deposits with all banks in Britain, that is including the accepting houses, overseas banks and other British banks. Sight accounts are repayable on demand and no interest is generally paid on them, but on time deposits interest is paid (at a rate below individual banks' base rates). The deposit banks provide full banking services throughout Britain, and operate through some 14,000 branches. Several of them have interests in British overseas and Commonwealth banks, and in other banks which have been formed specially to compete in international markets. They have also acquired substantial interests in hire-purchase finance houses, and some have set up their own unit trusts and merchant banks.

The deposit banks' reserve assets consist of balances at the Bank of England, money at call (mainly loans to discount houses), their holdings of Treasury and some other bills and short-dated British Government securities. The banks also hold a proportion of their assets as portfolio (mainly longer-dated British Government securities) or trade investments.

The banks' profits are largely earned through their advances to customers partly in the form of overdrafts and partly in the form of loans (with or without collateral security). In April 1978 sterling advances by the London clearing banks amounted to about 63 per cent of their total deposits.

The bank giro, a credit transfer scheme, and the direct debiting by which a creditor with the prior approval of the debtor may claim money due to him direct from the latter's banking account, have helped to improve the money transmission services. Many banks have automatic cash dispensing machines in operation and an increasing number of banks are introducing more auto-mated banking facilities. Credit cards are in widespread use for the settlement of accounts in retail shops; and cheque cards enable the card holder to cash a cheque up to any prearranged credit limit at any office of the major British and Irish banks, and at offices of many banks overseas.

Membership of the London Bankers' Clearing House consists of the Bank of England and the London clearing banks together with the Co-operative Bank and the Central Trustee Savings Bank which became members in 1975. In 1977 cheques and drafts passing through the London clearing system averaged in value nearly £216,000 million monthly.

National Girobank

The Post Office National Girobank (known as National Giro until 1978), which was introduced in 1968 to provide a low-cost current account banking and money transfer service, is operated through most post offices in Britain. All accounts and transactions are maintained by means of a computer complex at the National Girobank Centre near Liverpool. In March 1978, Girobank had 590,000 accounts with deposits of over £230 million. The number of yearly transactions has risen from 80 million in March 1969 to 242 million by March 1978. In addition to its services to individuals, Girobank's services to commerce, industry and the public utilities include a facility whereby organisations with dispersed branches, depots and representatives can rapidly channel receipts into their central accounting system. Over 140 local authorities as well as voluntary housing associations use Girobank's rent collection services. Girobank's international services also provide money transfer facilities in Europe linking over 18 million account holders in the European Community and other countries in Western Europe. Following the granting of powers to Girobank in 1976 to provide a wider range of banking services, personal loans, a guarantee card, limited overdrawing for personal customers and overdrafts for corporate customers were introduced. Other new services introduced in April 1978 include deposit accounts, budget accounts and bridging loans.

Overseas Banks

Altogether some 360 overseas banks are represented in London, through branches, subsidiaries, representative offices and consortia. There are about 290 banks directly represented in London, while over 70 different foreign banks and financial institutions are represented through 37 consortium banks operating in London. Of those directly represented, 65 are from the United States, 23 from Japan and 109 from Europe, of which 51 are from the European Community. They provide a comprehensive banking service in many parts of the world and engage in the financing of trade not only between Britain and other countries but also between third countries.

The Merchant Banks

The merchant banks have an influence on Britain's financial affairs which is much greater than their size in relation to other financial institutions might suggest. Traditionally merchant banks have been primarily concerned with acceptance credits[1] and with the sponsoring of capital issues on behalf of their customers. Today they have a widely diversified and complex range of activities with an important role in international finance and the short-term capital markets, the provision of expert advice and financial services to British industrial companies especially where mergers, takeovers and other forms of corporate reorganisation are involved, and in the management of investment holdings, including trusts, pensions and other funds.

The Discount Market

The Discount Market is an institution which is unique to the City of London. Its function in the monetary system is to provide a financial mechanism designed to promote an orderly flow of short-term funds. The market consists of 11 discount houses, five money traders and two discount brokers, all of which borrow money 'at call' or short notice and lend for somewhat longer periods. The discount houses have recourse to the Bank of England as lender of last resort. The Bank lends to them generally overnight or for seven days at minimum lending rate, although it may charge a higher rate. Most of the market's borrowed funds come from the banks, which are thus provided with a flexible means of earning a yield on surplus funds which they have at any given time, although an increasing proportion is also coming from industry.

The assets of the discount houses mainly consist of Treasury and commercial bills, government and local authority securities and negotiable certificates of deposit denominated in both sterling and US dollars. The discount houses accept as a formal responsibility that they should cover the Government's need to borrow on Treasury bills which are offered on tender each week.

National Savings

The Department for National Savings is responsible for the administration of Government savings schemes: National Savings Bank accounts, National

---

[1] Acceptance credits are usually short-term (90 days) arrangements to finance exports from, and imports to, Britain and other markets. The expression is derived from the method of financing trade by which commercial bills are 'accepted' or guaranteed by a merchant bank against documents, after which they may be discounted for cash by a discount house.

Savings Certificates, British Savings Bonds, Premium Savings Bonds and Save As You Earn contracts. Government policy is directed towards encouraging investment, primarily of personal savings, in these schemes. At the end of May 1978 National Savings totalled £10,335·5 million. Facilities are provided by National Savings for the purchase of Government stocks ('gilts'); a selection of about 55 stocks is held on the National Savings Stock Register. National Savings Gift Tokens are also available at most post offices.

National Savings Bank

The National Savings Bank provides a countrywide system for depositing and withdrawing small savings at post offices. There are about 21 million active accounts. Ordinary Accounts bear interest at 5 per cent and the first £70 of annual interest is tax-free. Up to £50 can be withdrawn on demand at any savings bank post office, but a few days' notice is required for larger amounts. The money is lodged with the National Debt Commissioners and is invested in Government securities. Deposits bearing a higher rate of interest may be made in Investment Accounts. All deposits carry a government guarantee. At the end of May 1978 the sum of the two accounts totalled £3,336 million.

National Savings Certificates

National Savings Certificates, in units of £1 (minimum purchase £5), are encashable at par at any time. Interest, which is free of income tax and capital gains tax, is paid only on encashment. The maximum permitted holding of the current Fourteenth Issue is £3,000. Index-linked National Savings Certificates Retirement Issue are available only to men aged 65 and over and women aged 60 and over at £10 for each one unit certificate. Interest does not accrue periodically but instead, subject to the certificate being held for one year, the repayment value is related to the movement of the general index of retail prices. If held for five years a bonus of 4 per cent of the purchase price will be added to the repayment value. The maximum permitted holding is £700.

British Savings Bonds

British Savings Bonds, 9·5 per cent, are sold in units of £5. If the bonds are held to maturity (five years from the date of purchase) they are repaid with a tax-free bonus of 4 per cent. The maximum permitted holding is £10,000.

Premium Savings Bonds

Premium Savings Bonds are in units of £1 (minimum purchase is £5) and individual holdings are limited to £3,000. After a qualifying period of three months the bonds give investors a chance to win tax-free prizes. There is a weekly draw for prizes of £75,000 and £50,000 and a monthly draw for well over 110,000 prizes ranging from £25 to £100,000. At the end of May 1978, £1,300 million was invested in this form of savings.

Save As You Earn

The Third Issue of the Save As You Earn (SAYE) scheme is index-linked. The scheme enables savings to be made in fixed regular monthly amounts over five years, with a minimum of £4 and a maximum of £20, by means of deductions from pay or by other regular payments. At the end of five years, the repayment value will be the total contributions plus any increase due to index-linking of monthly contributions. Completed savings which are not withdrawn will qualify for fresh index-linking and a bonus equal to two monthly contributions at the end of seven years. Savers who wish to stop payments will be able to withdraw the total sum saved (but there cannot be partial withdrawals). Tax-free compound interest will then be paid at the rate of 6 per cent a year on amounts withdrawn after the first year.

Ulster Savings

Northern Ireland issues separately Ulster Savings Certificates and Ulster Development Bonds on similar terms to the corresponding National Savings Certificates and British Savings Bonds.

Trustee Savings Banks

The Trustee Savings Banks (TSBs), most of which were founded in the nineteenth century, operate under their own trustees but are subject, under the Trustee Savings Banks Acts 1969 and 1976, to the supervision of the Trustee Savings Banks Central Board and the Registrar of Friendly Societies. Following a planned programme of amalgamations, there were 19 individual banks in June 1978 (compared with 67 in 1975) operating in a network of about 1,650 branches with 14 million accounts and total deposits in excess of £4,000 million. The 1976 Act empowered TSBs to provide a full banking service including credit services and removed the requirement, as from November 1979, that deposits be invested with the National Debt Commissioners. The TSB credit services, including personal loans, temporary overdrafts and bridging loans, were introduced during 1977. The TSBs also operate their own unit trust, and Central TSB, which is responsible for the clearing operation of the TSBs, is a functional member of the Committee of London Clearing Banks.

OTHER FINANCIAL INSTITUTIONS

Many special financial facilities, which are supplementary to the credit facilities of the banks, are provided through institutions outside the banking system. These include finance corporations, hire-purchase finance companies, the Stock Exchange, investment trust companies, unit trusts, building societies and the insurance market. The firms engaged in such activities are in the main highly specialised, for example, finance houses, stockbrokers, insurers and insurance underwriters and brokers.

Finance Houses

Although there are a large number of firms engaged in the financing of hire purchase and other instalment credit transactions, 90 per cent of all finance house business is accounted for by the 37 firms which constitute the Finance Houses Association. At the end of March 1978 the value of instalment credit debt outstanding to finance houses, including those recognised as banks, amounted to £2,300 million. About 65 per cent of new credit extended by finance houses related to cars and commercial vehicles, including motorcycles and caravans, the remainder relating to industrial and building equipment and other goods.

The leading finance houses comply with the authorities' policies on lending similar to those applied to banks, and all finance houses are required to observe term controls affecting the minimum deposits and maximum repayment period for specific goods financed by certain forms of lending. Finance houses with total eligible liabilities exceeding £5 million are subject to the same system of credit control as that applied to banks (see p 343).

Finance Corporations

Finance for Industry Ltd (FFI) was formed in 1973 as the holding company for two previously separate but related corporations, the Finance Corporation for Industry (FCI) and the Industrial and Commercial Finance Corporation (ICFC). The purpose of the merger was to provide, in one specialist financial institution, the capacity to support investment programmes over the whole range of industry. The FCI provides medium-term funds at fixed and variable interest rates for large companies in excess of £2 million. At the end of March 1978 it had approved £267 million in 39 companies plus £58 million which had been committed but not drawn. The ICFC provides medium- and long-term funds at fixed interest rates for the small and medium sectors of industry. The ICFC has investments of over £239 million in 2,375 companies and its normal lending limits range from £5,000 to £2 million for periods between seven and 20 years.

Equity Capital for Industry Ltd (ECI) was formed in 1976 as a new specialist long-term institution with the primary purpose of providing equity or equity-type capital for industry in Britain which cannot appropriately be provided through the normal market mechanism. Its authorised capital is £50 million and the shares are largely held by insurance companies and life offices, investment trust companies, unit trusts and FFI. There is an unauthorised unit trust associated with ECI whose units are held by pension funds so as to enable them to participate in the provision of capital.

The Commonwealth Development Finance Company (CDFC) is no longer confined to the Commonwealth in its activities. It supports business enterprise overseas by providing finance in the form of share capital and loans on mutually acceptable terms. Its authorised share capital is £30 million, of which about 14½ million 'A' ordinary shares of £1 (£0·10 paid) are held by industrial, shipping, mining and banking interests in Britain, and 11¾ million 'B' ordinary shares of £1 (£0·50 paid) are held by the Bank of England and certain central banks in the Commonwealth. At 31 March 1978 the CDFC held investments of about £30 million spread over a wide range of industries in 40 countries.

The Agricultural Mortgage Corporation was established in 1928 for the purpose of making loans to farmers. Its authorised share capital is £1·5 million and at 31 March 1978 loans and investments amounted to £355·4 million.

The Commonwealth Development Corporation (CDC) was set up in 1948 and undertakes projects for the promotion and expansion of a wide range of enterprises within and outside of the Commonwealth. At the end of 1977 the CDC had a total capital commitment of £270 million.

Investment Trust Companies and Unit Trusts

Investment trust companies and unit trusts enable investors to spread their risks and obtain the benefit of skilled management.

The usual type of investment trust company is constituted as a public company registered under the Companies Acts with limited liability; its business is to invest its capital in a range of stocks and shares. Like other companies, it may issue several types of stocks or shares and may retain part of its profits to build up reserves. Investment trust companies grew to importance in the latter half of the nineteenth century and have been prominent in directing capital towards overseas investment. At the end of 1977, such companies held assets worth £6,500 million, of which 31 per cent were in overseas securities.

Unit trusts are constituted by trust deed between a management company and a trustee company which holds the assets. Normally, the managers sell units to the public and must invest the proceeds in a fairly wide range of stock exchange securities. The costs of running the trust are defrayed partly by an initial charge which forms part of the price of a unit and partly by a half-yearly service charge which is usually taken out of the income of the trust. The level of both charges is controlled by the Department of Trade, from which authorisation is required before units can be offered to the public; this is only granted if the trust deed meets the Department's requirements.

The first British unit trust was formed in 1931 and by 1939 there were 98 trusts, with assets estimated at £80 million. At the end of 1977 there were almost 2 million unit holdings. The value of the funds invested in authorised trusts depends on the value of the underlying securities; from only £60 million at the end of 1958 they had risen to £3,461 million at the end of

1977. There is a wide variety of trusts, both in the range of investments covered and in the ways of catering for the differing needs of investors.

Building Societies

Building societies are non-profit-making mutual institutions which borrow mainly short-term from individual savers, who are generally able to withdraw their money on demand, and provide long-term loans at variable rates of interest on the security of private dwellings purchased for owner occupation. They also lend to a limited extent to house builders and on the security of business or commercial property. Most societies pay and charge interest on the basis of a structure of rates recommended periodically by the Building Societies Association, the movement's representative body.[1]

Building societies have existed in Britain for some 200 years and have been subject to specific legislation governing their operations (now consolidated in the Building Societies Act 1962) since 1836. The present legislation is administered by the Chief Registrar of Friendly Societies, to whom the societies must provide regular statements of their financial position and who has discretionary powers to restrict or suspend a society's operations if he considers that the way in which its business is being conducted may put investors' money at risk.

Building societies account for about 90 per cent of all lending for house purchase in Britain and in recent years they have overtaken the banks as the principal repository for the personal sector's total liquid assets. This growth has been accompanied by a concentration of most of the business in the hands of a few large societies. At the end of 1977 there were 339 registered building societies with total assets of about £34,290 million; over half this amount was accounted for by the five largest societies and almost 90 per cent of it by the 30 largest. The amount lent on mortgages in 1977 was a record £6,720 million, a 10 per cent increase on 1976.

The Stock Exchange

The stock exchanges of the United Kingdom and Irish Republic amalgamated in 1973 to become 'The Stock Exchange' with its main trading floor and central administration in London. There are also trading floors in Glasgow, Liverpool, Manchester, Birmingham and Dublin.

The number and variety of securities officially listed on the Stock Exchange are greater than in any other market in the world and its turnover of company securities is roughly equivalent to that of all the European bourses combined. Some 8,200 securities are quoted on the Stock Exchange; at the end of December 1977 these had a total market value of £294,554 million. About 6,600 securities of companies were quoted, including a number of leading overseas companies. Company issues represented more than four-fifths of the securities at market valuation, the remainder being United Kingdom, Irish Republic and other overseas government and corporation stocks.

The Stock Exchange does not fix dealing prices; the terms on which bargains are made between members reflect the interaction of supply and demand for the securities concerned.

In 1978 a new market in traded share options opened on the Stock Exchange. The market, initially in the shares of ten prominent British companies, enables investors not only to buy options to purchase shares in future at pre-fixed prices but also to trade in the options themselves.

---

[1] The income tax on interest is paid by the society on behalf of individual investors, at a rate equal to their average tax rate. This means that while those not liable to tax cannot reclaim the tax paid on their behalf, investors who pay at the basic rate receive a better return than would otherwise be the case.

The Council for the Securities Industry was set up in 1978 as a supervisory body for the securities industry. Its main function is to sustain proper conduct and high standards in the industry.

The Foreign Exchange Market

The market consists of about 270 authorised banks and several firms of foreign exchange brokers which act as intermediaries between the banks. It provides those engaged in international trade with foreign currencies for their transactions. The foreign exchange banks are in close contact with financial centres abroad and are able to quote buying and selling rates for both spot and future delivery. An important function of the market is to engage in arbitrage transactions which serve to eliminate differentials in exchange rates between different centres. The forward market enables traders, who at a given date in the future are due to receive or make a specific foreign currency payment, to contract in advance to sell or buy the foreign currency involved for sterling at a precise fixed exchange rate.

The London Gold Market

All authorised banks may deal in gold but, in practice, dealings are largely concentrated in the hands of the five members of the London gold market. The five members meet twice daily to establish a London fixing price for gold. This price provides a reference point for world-wide dealings in gold. Although much interest centres upon the fixings, active dealing takes place throughout the day. Forward prices may also be quoted on request.

The Insurance Market

Although a certain amount of insurance is provided by friendly societies, banks and trade unions, most insurance services in Britain are in the hands of mutual or joint stock insurance companies or Lloyd's underwriters.

Insurance Companies

There are about 800 insurance companies authorised to carry on one or more classes ·of insurance business in Britain of which about 150 are overseas companies. A number of other overseas insurance companies are represented by agents in Britain although they do not write business here.

Some 310 companies belong to the British Insurance Association and these account for about 95 per cent of the world-wide business of the British insurance companies market.

Lloyd's

Lloyd's is an incorporated society of private insurers in London. The name 'Lloyd's' is derived from Edward Lloyd's coffee house, established in the late seventeenth century, where merchants with maritime and other interests gathered to transact business. Although Lloyd's activities were originally confined to the conduct of marine insurance business, a very considerable world-wide market for the transaction of other classes of insurance business in non-marine, aviation and motor markets has been built up.

Lloyd's is regulated by a series of special Acts of Parliament starting in 1871. The affairs of the Society of Lloyd's in its corporate capacity are administered by the Committee of Lloyd's. The society does not accept insurance itself.

Lloyd's is not a company but a market for insurance, where business is transacted by individual underwriters for their own account and risk and in competition with each other. Insurance may only be placed through Lloyd's brokers, who negotiate with Lloyd's underwriters on behalf of the insured. Only elected underwriting members of Lloyd's, who must transact insurance with unlimited liability and who have met the most stringent financial regulations laid down by the Committee of Lloyd's, are permitted to transact business at Lloyd's; these financial safeguards give security to the Lloyd's policy. Since 1969 non-Commonwealth underwriters have been admitted to membership of Lloyd's if they satisfy the requirements.

There are some 14,130 underwriting members of Lloyd's grouped into about 370 syndicates and represented at Lloyd's by underwriting agents who accept risks on behalf of the members of their syndicates.

Alongside its marine insurance business Lloyd's has built up a world-wide organisation for the collection and diffusion of shipping intelligence.

Insurance Brokers

The insurance market is completed by the insurance brokers, acting on behalf of the insured; brokers are an essential part of the Lloyd's market and a valuable part of the company market. Many brokers specialise in re-insurance business, acting as intermediaries in the exchange of contracts between companies, both British and overseas, and often acting as London representatives of the latter. The Insurance Brokers (Registration) Act 1977 provides for the registration of insurance brokers by a Registration Council.

International Insurance Services

Over 60 per cent of the general (that is, non-life) business of members of the British Insurance Association is carried on overseas, partly by re-insurance on the London market and partly through branches and agencies established in over 100 countries. The basic principle of this international business is that resources capable of meeting any potential loss are instantly available for use in any part of the world.

Behind this large and international volume of business stand the very substantial assets of the companies, in addition to substantial reserves of uncalled capital, and the deposits, underwriting trust funds and other resources of Lloyd's underwriters.

In accordance with the Treaty of Rome, insurance and re-insurance in the European Community are regulated by directives addressed to the governments of member states. The purpose of the directives is to harmonise the legislation of the various member countries, thus providing a 'common market', which would avoid distortion of competition. Directives abolishing restrictions on freedom of establishment and freedom to provide services in respect of reinsurance, and on compulsory motor insurance were in force when Britain joined the Community and have since been accepted. A directive relating to freedom of establishment in non-life insurance came into force in 1976 while one relating to insurance intermediaries came into force in July 1978. Draft directives relating to other classes of insurance are under consideration or in preparation.

Commodity Markets

Britain remains the principal international centre for transactions in a large number of commodities, although most of the sales negotiated in London relate to consignments which never pass through the ports of Britain. The need for close links with sources of finance and with shipping and insurance services often determined the location of these physical markets in the City of London. There are also futures markets in cocoa, coffee, grains (wheat and barley), rubber, soya bean meal, sugar, wool and non-ferrous metals (copper, lead, silver, tin and zinc).

The Crown Agents

The Crown Agents for Oversea Governments and Administrations provide financial, professional and commercial services for some 100 governments, mostly of independent countries, and over 200 overseas public authorities and international bodies. The individual Crown Agents are appointed by the Minister for Overseas Development, but the office is not a government department. It is a public service which is responsible to its principals for business operation. In April 1976 the Government announced its intention to incorporate the Crown Agents.

18 Trade and Payments

Although small in area and accounting for only about 1·4 per cent of the world's population, Britain is the fifth largest trading nation in the world—and, as a member of the European Community, part of the world's largest trading area which accounts for about one-third of all trade.

For hundreds of years, and especially since the mid-nineteenth century, when the rapid growth of Britain's industry, commerce and shipping was accompanied by its development as an international trading centre, overseas trade has been of vital importance to the country's economy. Britain's exports of goods represent more than one-quarter of the gross domestic product. It is a major supplier of machinery, vehicles, aircraft, metal manufactures, electrical apparatus, chemicals and textiles. Britain relies upon imports for almost half of its total consumption of foodstuffs, and for most of the raw materials needed for its industries. It is among the world's largest importers of foodstuffs, timber and paper, metals and ores, and other raw materials, petroleum and many other products. Invisible trade is also of great significance to the economy, Britain having the largest share of world invisible trade after the United States.

A sound commercial banking system and a wide range of financial institutions ensure that commercial needs are met for both short- and long-term finance for international trade. The facilities provided by merchant banks and accepting houses, for example, have long been used to finance shipments of goods not only to and from Britain, but also between overseas countries.

This chapter describes the pattern of British overseas trade including its commodity and area distribution, outlines British commercial policies and government services to overseas trade, summarises the balance of payments and gives an account of government aid to developing countries.

OVERSEAS TRADE

PATTERN OF TRADE

Changes in the value, volume, composition and geographical distribution of imports and exports are outlined in the following paragraphs.

Value and Volume

In 1977 Britain's exports of goods were valued at about £32,200 million f.o.b. and its imports of goods at about £33,900 million f.o.b. on a balance of payments basis (as distinct from an overseas trade statistics basis, which for imports includes the costs of insurance and freight, and for both imports and exports includes returned goods). Between 1976 and 1977 the value of exports rose by 27 per cent while that of imports increased by 17 per cent. Over the same period the volume index of exports increased by 8 per cent and of imports by 1·4 per cent; but the unit value index of exports rose by 18 per cent and of imports by 16 per cent. The small increase in the volume of imports reflects a low level of demand in Britain and increasing production of North Sea oil.

The value and volume of imports and exports, together with the terms of trade index, from 1970 to 1977, are shown in Table 24.

TABLE 24: Imports and Exports: 1970–77[a]

	1970	1974	1975	1976	1977
Value (£ million):					
Imports c.i.f.[b][g]	9,163	23,492	24,423	31,569	36,996
Imports f.o.b.[c][f]	8,146	21,734	22,667	28,932	33,788
Exports of British produce and manufactures, and re-exports f.o.b.[c][g]	8,170	16,820	20,111	26,024	33,308
Exports f.o.b.[c][d][f]	8,121	16,539	19,462	25,422	32,176
Volume Index Nos.[f] (1975 = 100)					
Imports	80·2	107·9	100	105·5	107·0
Exports	79·5	103·9	100	109·9	118·9
Unit Value Index Nos.[f] (1975 = 100)					
Imports	40·6	88·5	100	121·9	141·4
Exports	50·5	81·8	100	120·6	142·4
Terms of Trade[e][f] (1975 = 100)	124·4	92·4	100	98·9	100·7

Source: *Trade and Industry*

[a] Figures for recent years are subject to slight revision from year to year.
[b] 'Cost, insurance and freight', that is, including shipping, insurance and other expenses incurred in the delivery of goods as far as their place of importation in Britain. Most of these expenses represent earnings by British firms.
[c] 'Free on board', that is, all costs accruing up to the time of placing the goods on board the exporting vessel having been paid by the seller.
[d] Including an allowance for under-recording of exports.
[e] Export unit value index as a percentage of the import unit value index.
[f] On a balance of payments basis.
[g] On an overseas trade statistics basis.

Commodity Composition
Imports

Although Britain is still one of the largest importers of food in the world the value of its imported food supplies has been growing less rapidly than the value of total imports and the ratio of imported foodstuffs to total imports, on an overseas trade statistics basis, has fallen from 36 per cent in 1954 to 16 per cent in 1977. There has been a similar downward trend in the proportion accounted for by basic materials—from 30 per cent in 1954 to about 10 per cent in 1977.

Imports of petroleum and petroleum products amounted to about 14 per cent of the total value of imports during 1977, when their value was £4,769 million on a balance of payments basis. This was 7·3 per cent lower than in 1976, increased prices being offset by a fall in volume, itself the result of increasing production of North Sea oil.

In recent years there has been a significant rise, in Britain as in other industrial countries, in the proportion of imports of finished manufactures. Such imports rose from about 6 per cent of the total imports in 1957 to 32 per cent in 1977, when they were valued at £11,803 million. Imports of semi-manufactures have also been increasing and since 1962 have formed a larger part of the total import bill than basic materials, partly the result of a shift of the early stages of the manufacturing processes to the supplying countries. Imports of semi-manufactured goods (including chemicals) totalled £9,878 million in 1977 and accounted for 27 per cent of total imports.

Exports

About 82 per cent of Britain's exports consist of manufactured goods both finished and semi-manufactured. By far the most important group of goods is machinery and transport equipment, which in 1977 increased by 22 per cent, to account for 38 per cent of total exports. Exports of machinery alone accounted for 25 per cent of total exports in 1977. The share of chemicals has grown fairly steadily, to reach nearly 12 per cent in 1976 and 1977. The share

of textiles has fallen from 18 per cent in 1948 to 7 per cent in 1960 and 3·6
per cent in 1977.

TABLE 25: Commodity Composition of Trade 1977[a]

Exports (f.o.b.)[b]	£ million	Per cent
Food, beverages and tobacco	2,217	6·7
Basic materials	895	2·7
Fuels	2,078	6·2
Manufactures:	27,172	81·6
Machinery and transport equipment	*12,680*	*38·1*
Machinery	8,337	25·1
Road motor vehicles	2,871	8·6
Other transport equipment	1,473	4·4
Chemicals	*3,821*	*11·5*
Metals and metal manufactures	*2,879*	*8·6*
Textiles	*1,193*	*3·6*
Other manufactures	*6,599*	*19·8*
Miscellaneous	945	2·8
TOTAL	33,308	100·0
Imports (c.i.f.)[c]		
Food, beverages and tobacco	5,945	16·0
Fuels	5,252	14·2
Industrial materials:	13,491	36·5
Basic materials	*3,612*	*9·8*
Chemicals	*2,365*	*6·4*
Other semi-manufactures	*7,513*	*20·3*
Finished manufactures:	11,803	31·9
Machinery and transport equipment	*8,780*	*23·7*
Machinery	5,298	14·3
Road motor vehicles	2,133	5·8
Other transport equipment	1,349	3·6
Other manufactures	*3,023*	*8·2*
Miscellaneous	505	1·4
TOTAL	36,996	100·0

Source: *Trade and Industry*
[a] On an overseas trade statistics basis.
[b] See footnote [c] under Table 24.
[c] See footnote [b] under Table 24.

**Geographical
Distribution of
Trade**

Although Britain's trade has, in general, grown fastest in recent years with the
rest of the European Community, there was a marked change in the pattern
of British exports following the oil price rise at the end of 1973. As a result of
this rise, which generated large reserves for the oil-exporting countries,
British exports to these countries rose in value by 52 per cent between 1973 and
1974, accounting for nearly one-tenth of the total growth in exports over this
period. On the other hand, the slowdown in activity in most of the developed
economies during 1974 adversely affected British exports to these economies.
This pattern was repeated in 1975, when the value of exports to the oil
exporting countries grew by 86 per cent, compared with a growth of 16 per
cent to other member countries of the European Community and of only 4 per
cent to North America (implying a substantial fall in volume). In 1976 and 1977
there was a return to growth in world trade and exports to the developed
industrial countries continued the recovery which began in the latter part of
1975 as economic conditions in the European Community and the United

States improved. Details of Britain's principal export markets and sources of supply in 1976 and 1977 are given in Tables 26 and 27.

TABLE 26: Principal British Markets 1976–77

Exports to (f.o.b.) ^{a}	1976 (£ million)	1977 (£ million)	Percentage change 1976–77
United States ^{b}	2,465	3,127	+27
Federal Republic of Germany	1,843	2,518	+37
Netherlands	1,517	2,173	+43
France	1,732	2,162	+25
Belgium–Luxembourg	1,406	1,841	+31
Irish Republic	1,264	1,650	+31
Switzerland	1,004	1,437	+43
Sweden	1,052	1,201	+14
Nigeria	775	1,079	+39
Italy	830	983	+18
Denmark	657	800	+22
Norway	474	767	+62
Australia	692	761	+10
Canada	630	713	+13
Iran	513	655	+28
Developed countries	18,612	23,689	+27
EEC	*9,249*	*12,128*	+31
Rest of Western Europe	*4,298*	*5,594*	+30
North America	*3,116*	*3,863*	+24
Other ^{c}	*1,949*	*2,104*	+ 8
Developing countries	6,630	8,613	+30
Oil-exporting countries ^{d}	*3,221*	*4,368*	+36
Other	*3,409*	*4,245*	+25
Centrally planned economies ^{e}	726	910	+25

Source: *Trade and Industry*

^{a} On an overseas trade statistics basis.
^{b} Including dependencies.
^{c} Australia, New Zealand, South Africa, Japan.
^{d} Algeria, Bahrain, Brunei, Ecuador, Gabon, Indonesia, Iran, Iraq, Kuwait, Libya, Nigeria, Oman, Qatar, Saudi Arabia, Trinidad and Tobago, United Arab Emirates, Venezuela.
^{e} Soviet Union, Poland, German Democratic Republic, Hungary, Czechoslovakia, Albania, Bulgaria, Romania, Chinese People's Republic, North Korea, Vietnam, Mongolia.

Invisible Transactions

As far back as estimates have been made (for nearly two centuries) Britain has usually earned a surplus from its invisible transactions. These fall into three main groups: services (receipts and payments arising from services, as distinct from goods, supplied to and received from overseas residents); interest, profits and dividends (income arising from outward and inward investment); and transfers between Britain and other countries (see below). Table 28 shows the breakdown of the figures from 1970 to 1977. Services of the private sector (and public corporations) include sea transport and civil aviation, travel, financial services (including insurance) and 'other services' which include commissions on imports, royalties, services between related companies, construction work overseas, agency expenses and many other services.

The balance on invisibles in 1977 was £1,998 million. Gross earnings of £16,135 million from invisible exports were about half the total of £32,182 million from visible exports. The surplus in 1977 was substantially below that of £2,452 million in 1976, largely as a result of the increasing profits of foreign companies operating in Britain, particularly oil companies. Earnings from tourism were particularly high in 1977 and earnings from construction work overseas and insurance also increased strongly.

The deficits on government services have related predominantly to military services overseas which have remained fairly steady in recent years, though currency changes have caused the sterling value to rise. Substantial government transfer payments relate to economic grants to developing countries and subscriptions to international organisations including, since 1973, Britain's contribution to the common budget for the financing of European Community expenditure.

TABLE 27: British Principal Sources of Supply 1976–77

Imports from (c.i.f.)[a]	1976 (£ million)	1977 (£ million)	Percentage change 1976–77
United States[b]	3,100	3,729	+20
Federal Republic of Germany	2,770	3,602	+30
France	2,112	2,689	+27
Netherlands	2,456	2,530	+ 3
Belgium–Luxembourg	1,303	1,686	+29
Italy	1,110	1,543	+39
Switzerland	967	1,333	+38
Irish Republic	1,052	1,295	+23
Sweden	1,194	1,270	+ 6
Canada	1,165	1,230	+ 6
Saudi Arabia	986	1,133	+15
Japan	797	1,065	+34
South Africa	615	885	+44
Norway	625	853	+36
Denmark	708	816	+15
Developed countries	22,569	27,420	+21
EEC	*11,510*	*14,161*	+23
Rest of Western Europe	*4,645*	*5,582*	+20
North America	*4,280*	*4,997*	+17
Other[c]	*2,134*	*2,680*	+26
Developing countries	7,860	8,167	+ 4
Oil-exporting countries[d]	*4,296*	*3,804*	−11
Other	*3,564*	*4,362*	+22
Centrally planned economies[e]	1,109	1,357	+22

Sources: *Trade and Industry*

[a] On an overseas trade statistics basis.
[b] Including dependencies.
[c] See footnote [c] under Table 26.
[d] See footnote [d] under Table 26.
[e] See footnote [e] under Table 26.

COMMERCIAL POLICY

Britain has long been an advocate of the removal of artificial barriers to trade, and to this end has taken a leading part in the activities of such organisations as the General Agreement on Tariffs and Trade (GATT), the International Monetary Fund (IMF), the Organisation for Economic Co-operation and Development (OECD) and the United Nations Conference on Trade and Development (UNCTAD). As a member of the European Community Britain participates in the development of the Community's commercial policy. The Community's Common Customs Tariff (CCT) is, on average, at a similar level to the tariffs of other major industrial countries.

General Agreement on Tariffs and Trade

Protective tariffs have been considerably modified in recent years as a result of negotiations held under the auspices of GATT which also seek to reduce tariffs and other barriers to trade, and to eliminate discrimination in international commerce.

As a result of the 'Kennedy Round' (1964–67), a series of GATT tariff negotiations, average reductions of over 30 per cent were made by the major trading countries, including Britain, in their tariffs on industrial goods. A new series of negotiations was formally launched in Tokyo in 1973; substantive negotiations took place in early 1978 and a framework of understanding was agreed in July with a view to a conclusion to the negotiations early in 1979. The negotiations cover a wide range of both tariff and non-tariff barriers to trade in both individual and agricultural products. (The European Community operates as a single unit both in these negotiations and GATT generally.)

TABLE 28: Britain's Invisible Overseas Transactions 1970–77

£ million

	1970	1974	1975	1976	1977
Total invisibles					
Credits	5,030	10,046	11,024	14,354	16,135
Debits	4,257	8,402	9,643	11,902	14,137
Invisible balance	+773	+1,644	+1,381	+2,452	+1,998
Constituent items					
Services:					
General government [a]	−309	−538	−620	−757	−788
Private sector (and public corporations):					
SEA TRANSPORT	−76	−122	+56	+25	+21
CIVIL AVIATION	+50	+96	+116	+241	+244
TRAVEL	+50	+154	+245	+627	+1,077
FINANCIAL SERVICES	+439	+777	+1,014	+1,287	+1,372
OTHER SERVICES	+257	+436	+340	+559	+875
Interest, profits and dividends:					
General government	−269	−352	−514	−648	−685
Private sector (and public corporations)	+825	+1,634	+1,277	+1,963	+1,123
Transfers:					
General government	−177	−320	−379	−792	−1,127
Private sector	−17	−121	−154	−53	−114

Source: *United Kingdom Balance of Payments 1967–77*
[a] Central government and local authorities.

Anti-Dumping

The GATT Anti-Dumping Code, to which Britain is a party, together with the Customs Duties (Dumping and Subsidies) Act 1969 and a European Economic Community regulation, control the anti-dumping action that may be taken to protect British industry against unfair competition and the criteria by which allegations of dumping are judged.

Community preference

All tariffs on trade in industrial products between Britain and the other European Community countries have been eliminated. Britain applies the common customs tariff to all countries neither belonging to, nor having any special arrangement with, the Community, subject to special arrangements for some industrial materials. Virtually all industrial tariff barriers between the

European Community and the remaining member countries of the European Free Trade Association (EFTA), to which Britain belonged between 1960 and 1972, have been dismantled.

Commonwealth and Developing Countries

Preferential tariff treatment for British imports from other independent Commonwealth countries dating from the Ottawa Conference of 1932 has been phased out since accession to the European Community. In the case of 22 developing Commonwealth countries in Africa, the Caribbean and the Pacific (ACP), Commonwealth preference has been replaced by the trade provisions of the Convention of Lomé, which came into effect on 1 July 1975. This established new trade, aid and co-operation links between the European Community and a total of 46 developing ACP countries. In 1976 and 1977 seven newly independent countries acceded to the Convention, bringing the total number of members to 53 (24 Commonwealth and 29 non-Commonwealth).[1] The Convention safeguards the interests of Commonwealth and other countries dependent on the export of particular agricultural products including sugar for which access to Community markets has been guaranteed for an indefinite period at prices related to those in the Community and in quantities which the producing countries have undertaken to supply.

All British dependent territories (with the exception of Gibraltar, Hong Kong and Bermuda), together with the Overseas Countries and Territories (OCT) of other Community members, were formally linked with the Community as a whole in 1976 under arrangements similar to those embodied in the Convention of Lomé.

Other special arrangements have been agreed relating to continued access into the Community for New Zealand dairy products.

The Community has stated its continuing objective of expanding and reinforcing existing trade relations with the Commonwealth countries of Asia taking into account the scope of the generalised system of preferences (see below) from which they derive considerable benefit. A commercial co-operation agreement between the Community and India came into effect in 1974, one with Sri Lanka in 1975, and one with Bangladesh in 1976. An agreement with Pakistan was signed in 1976.

To secure greater stability in world commodity trade, discussions are under way in UNCTAD on a number of primary products and on the creation of a Common Fund to support international commodity agreements. Britain has consistently supported the negotiation of such agreements on a product-by-product basis where feasible and economic and is committed to the establishment of a Common Fund.

Generalised System of Preferences

The establishment of a generalised system of preferences for manufactures and semi-manufactures exported by developing countries was agreed in principle at the second UNCTAD Conference in New Delhi in 1968. Britain's scheme started early in 1972, but, as a member of the European Community, Britain adopted in 1974 the scheme of the enlarged Community. Since enlargement the Community's scheme has been considerably improved in the interests of the poorer developing countries.

---

[1] The Commonwealth ACP countries are: The Bahamas, Barbados, Botswana, Fiji, The Gambia, Ghana, Grenada, Guyana, Jamaica, Kenya, Lesotho, Malawi, Mauritius, Nigeria, Papua New Guinea, Seychelles, Sierra Leone, Swaziland, Tanzania, Trinidad and Tobago, Tonga, Uganda, Western Samoa and Zambia.

The non-Commonwealth ACP countries are: Benin, Burundi, Cameroon, Cape Verde, Central African Republic, Chad, Comoros, Congo, Djibouti, Ethiopia, Gabon, Equatorial Guinea, Guinea, Guinea-Bissau, Ivory Coast, Liberia, Madagascar, Mali, Mauritania, Niger, Rwanda, Sao Tomé and Principe, Senegal, Somalia, Sudan, Surinam, Togo, Upper Volta, Zaïre.

CONTROLS ON TRADE AND PAYMENTS

There are now very few restrictions imposed by Britain on the movement of goods and services.

Import and Export Control

Under the Import, Export and Customs Powers (Defence) Act 1939 the Department of Trade is empowered to prohibit or regulate the import or export of goods. Most goods may be freely imported under the provisions of the Open General Import Licence. Controlled goods require an individual import licence. Several other departments have separate powers to control imports and exports for specific purposes.

Import Controls

In accordance with its international obligations under the GATT, and to the IMF and the European Community, Britain has progressively removed quantitative restrictions from almost all its imports from the market economies; those controls that remain (for example the GATT Multi-Fibre Arrangement, approved by the European Community in December 1977) predominantly affect textile goods. There are comparatively few quantitative restrictions on imports from centrally planned economies, and progress towards liberalisation continues to be made wherever possible. In accordance with its obligations to the European Community, Britain has also removed all quantitative restrictions on imports of goods of Community origin, with the exception of potatoes and certain internationally recognised restrictions. In 1975 the importation of gold coins, gold medals and similar articles, minted or made after 1837, was stopped (except by authorised banks and then only for sale abroad); in 1977 the cut-off date was changed to 1937; the remaining controls include those recognised internationally on a few goods such as arms, ammunition and radioactive materials. Some further restrictions or prohibitions are applied by other Departments under separate legislation for the protection of health or public safety, in the interest of conservation, and for other non-economic reasons (for example, on animals, drugs and explosives).

There is a general import restriction on goods from Rhodesia as part of the Government's sanctions policy against the illegal régime.

Export Controls

Except for the control necessary to ensure that exports to destinations outside the scheduled territories are paid for in the proper manner most British exports are not subject to any government control or direction. (The scheduled territories comprise the United Kingdom, the Channel Islands, the Isle of Man, the Irish Republic and Gibraltar.) The few controls that are in operation are imposed to supervise exports of military and strategic significance; on diamonds, to assist exchange control operations (see below) in preventing the export of capital in that form; on cattle, sheep and pigs, horses, asses and mules, for humanitarian purposes; on cocoa and cocoa products and on endangered species of animals and plants, in accordance with international agreements; on antiques over 100 years old and documentary and photographic material over 70 years old, to restrict the export of items of national importance; on salmon and trout, to inhibit out-of-season fishing; on controlled (dangerous) drugs; on currency notes, gold coin and gold bullion; on British spirits (beverages) in casks of less than nine gallons; and on EEC Common Agricultural Policy (CAP) products. All exports to Rhodesia are subject to control.

Exchange Control

Britain applies exchange control principally in order to conserve its reserves of gold and foreign exchange. The powers under the Exchange Control Act 1947 are conferred mainly on the Treasury which has delegated the administration of most parts of the Act to the Bank of England and to HM Customs and Excise.

The Bank has in turn authorised most commercial banks in Britain to execute a wide range of transactions.

The general effect of exchange control rules is to control transactions between residents of the scheduled territories and non-residents. Payments in sterling may in general be made freely between residents, but the acquisition of other currencies by them is subject to control.

The aim of exchange control policy is not to discourage investment abroad but to regulate the manner in which investment outside the scheduled territories is financed. Official exchange is usually available only for projects which promise early and continuing benefits to the balance of payments. Where the use of official exchange is not permitted investors can finance their approved projects in other ways, for example, by borrowing foreign currency or purchasing investment currency (which, because it is drawn from a limited pool of currency, normally changes hands at a premium).

Payments for goods exported from the scheduled territories must be received in foreign currency or in sterling from non-resident sources—normally within six months of export unless they are covered by an approved export credit arrangement. Control is also exercised over imports to ensure that currency authorised for their payment is used for that purpose. British merchants conducting trade between countries outside the scheduled territories are normally allowed to pay non-residents for goods only with foreign currency borrowed for that purpose, the borrowing to be repaid from the sale proceeds of the goods when they are sold to non-residents. Sterling credit provided by British banks for foreign trade is therefore restricted to the financing of trade between the scheduled territories and the rest of the world.

There are certain restrictions on dealings in gold bullion and on the use of gold for manufacturing and industrial purposes. Purchases of gold coins minted after 1937 by United Kingdom residents other than authorised dealers in gold are allowed only if the coins are in Britain and are being sold by a resident who is not selling on behalf of a non-resident.

Residents are entitled to purchase up to £500 in foreign currency for their travel expenditure on each journey outside the scheduled territories, other than to Rhodesia, irrespective of the purpose of the journey. Further travel funds may be obtained for business, professional or other reasons. Non-residents are normally allowed by the Bank of England to hold an external account in a British bank and are entitled to change their sterling on external account for other currencies and to make and receive payments in any currency to and from non-residents in any other part of the world. Special restrictions apply to transactions with residents of Rhodesia.

People living outside the scheduled territories who visit Britain temporarily are regarded as non-resident and not subject to most of the exchange control provisions. On the other hand, people coming to Britain from outside the scheduled territories and intending to take up permanent residence in Britain are normally regarded as resident, though they may be eligible for certain exemptions from their obligations under the Exchange Control Act 1947.

Visitors to Britain may import notes in any currency, travellers' cheques and letters of credit without limit. On departure, visitors may take with them sterling or scheduled territory notes up to a value of £100, foreign currency notes up to a value of £500 and, as a concession, any foreign currency notes which they brought in with them.

GOVERNMENT SERVICES

The Government assists exporters by its efforts to create conditions favourable to the export trade and by providing information and advice about opportunities for trade in other countries and credit insurance facilities. Export promotion is also assisted by the Scottish Council (Development and Industry), the Development Corporation for Wales and in Northern Ireland by the Department of Commerce.

British Overseas Trade Board

The British Overseas Trade Board (BOTB) directs Britain's official export promotion services, which include the provision of export intelligence, assistance to British exporters in appointing agents and locating potential importers, help to exporters at trade fairs and other promotional events overseas, and support for firms participating in missions overseas and for inward commercial visits to Britain. It includes representatives of commerce and industry, the Trades Union Congress, the Department of Trade and the Foreign and Commonwealth Office and operates under the general authority of the Secretary of State for Trade who is the President.

Information and Advice to Exporters

Exporters wanting assistance and advice can consult the offices of the BOTB throughout Britain and, through these offices, the commercial posts of the British Diplomatic Service overseas.

Overseas officers work closely with the BOTB in the provision of services for exporters. They regularly report on local economic and commercial conditions and generally assist the exporter to overcome any difficulties he encounters in trade with the country in question, particularly those arising out of governmental regulations.

Export Credit Insurance

The Export Credits Guarantee Department (ECGD) provides credit insurance for more than a third of the country's export trade and insures exports of both goods and services.

The main risks covered include insolvency or protracted default of the buyer, governmental action which stops the British exporter receiving payment, new import restrictions, war, or civil disturbance in the buyer's country. Cover may commence from the date of contract or (at lower premiums) from the date of shipment.

This insurance may be supplemented by unconditional guarantees of repayment given direct to banks financing the exporter. Alternatively, for contracts over £1 million ECGD will guarantee loans direct to overseas buyers enabling them to pay on cash terms, or 'lines of credit' similarly covering an agreed buying programme of an overseas country. The banks provide finance against these guarantees.

In order to facilitate a switch from sterling to foreign currency financing of exports, ECGD has, since 1977, underwritten larger projects only where these are financed in foreign currency.

Since 1975 ECGD has offered a measure of cover against high and unpredictable cost escalation to exporters with capital goods contracts worth over £2 million which involve a manufacturing period of over two years. ECGD is also prepared to support the issue of performance bonds in the commercial market in respect of cash or near-cash contracts worth over £1 million.

Investment insurance is also provided for new British investment against expropriation, war damage and restrictions on remittances.

Trade Fairs

Britain stages many exhibitions and trade fairs and British products are shown at most of the large international trade fairs throughout the world.

Participation in trade fairs and store promotions overseas are forms of export promotion for which the Government provides information and financial assistance to exporters. In 1973 a British Export Marketing Centre was opened in Tokyo to provide exhibitions and other marketing facilities for individual British firms or organisations.

BALANCE OF PAYMENTS

Britain's balance of payments has usually been characterised by a deficit on visible trade partially offset by a surplus on invisible earnings. Estimates of the balance of payments and its main constituent items from 1970 to 1977 are given in summary in Table 29, and in greater detail since 1975 in Tables 30 and 31. The balance of payments statistics contain two indicators of particular importance. The first is the balance on current account, covering both visible (exports and imports of goods) and invisible (trade in services, investment income and transfers) transactions. This, together with capital transfers, provides a measure of how far Britain is paying its way abroad and thus adding to or using up overseas assets. The second indicator.is the balance for official financing. This is the net result of all external transactions, that is, the current account, capital transfers, investment and other capital transactions (including official long-term capital transactions, investment flows, trade credit, and

TABLE 29: United Kingdom Balance of Payments 1970–77

£ million

	Current balance	Balance for official financing	SDR al- location Gold sub- scription to IMF[a]	Official financing		
				Total	Official borrowing[b]	Official reserves[c]
1970	+731	+1,287	+133	−1,420	−1,295	−125
1971	+1,090	+3,146	+125	−3,271	−1,735	−1,536
1972	+135	−1,265	+124	+1,141	+449	+692
1973	−999	−771	—	+771	+999	−228
1974	−3,591	−1,646	—	+1,646	+1,751	−105
1975	−1,855	−1,465	—	+1,465	+810	+655
1976	−1,137	−3,629	—	+3,629	+2,776[d]	+853
1977	+289	+7,361	—	−7,361	+2,327	−9,588

Source: *United Kingdom Balance of Payments 1967–77*
[a] Gold subscription to IMF in 1970 was −£38 million.
[b] Drawings (+)/ repayments (−).
[c] Drawings on (+)/ additions to (−).
[d] Includes a credit of £1,113 million from the IMF.

changes in Britain's net external banking and money market liabilities in sterling and in overseas currencies) and other flows including unidentified transactions reflected in the balancing item. The balance for official financing shows the impact of all external transactions on the reserves and official debt position, that is, how much is available to add to the reserves and repay any official borrowing in the case of a net surplus, or how much must be financed by drawing on the reserves or by borrowing if there is a net deficit. Table 30 gives details of the current account since 1975. The increase in oil prices (see p 186) was the main cause of a substantial rise in the visible deficit in 1974 to £5,235 million, offset to some extent by a surplus on invisibles of £1,644 million. In 1975, the low level of domestic activity and substantial de-stocking reduced the volume of imports, more than offsetting the decline in the volume of exports resulting from the setback in world trade. The visible trade deficit consequently declined to £3,236 million while that on non-oil goods was almost eliminated. After a slight worsening in the terms of trade in 1976, the visible deficit stood at £3,589 million and the total current deficit at £1,137 million. In 1977 the visible deficit fell to £1,709 million, largely due to increased production of North Sea oil. The current account showed an overall surplus of £289 million.

There was a net inflow in 1977 on identified investment and other capital transactions of some £4,410 million and a balancing item of £2,662 million. The outflow on investment and other capital transactions in 1976 was largely the result of a rundown of overseas residents' sterling balances and the extension of sterling lending overseas. The inflow in 1977 was caused by a large build-up of non-official overseas holdings of sterling deposits and government stocks and a marked slowdown in sterling lending overseas.

The direct benefit of the North Sea oil and gas programme to the balance for official financing has increased substantially from about £500 million in 1975 to over £2,300 million in 1977.

TABLE 30: Current Account 1975–77

£ million

	1975	1976	1977
Visible trade:			
Exports (f.o.b.)	19,463	25,424	32,182
Imports (f.o.b.)	22,699	29,013	33,891
Visible balance	−3,236	−3,589	−1,709
Invisibles:			
Credits	11,024	14,354	16,135
Debits	9,643	11,902	14,137
Invisible balance	+1,381	+2,452	+1,998
Current balance	−1,855	−1,137	+289

Source: *United Kingdom Balance of Payments 1967–77*

Britain participates in the Special Drawing Rights (SDRs) scheme which came into effect in 1970 in order to supplement world reserves. SDRs are reserve assets created and distributed by decision of the members of the IMF. Any member of the IMF may join the scheme, and its share is based on its IMF quota. Participants in the scheme accept an obligation to provide convertible currency, when designated by the IMF to do so, to another participant in exchange for SDRs up to a total amount equal to twice the net amount of their own allocation of SDRs. Only those countries with a sufficiently strong balance of payments are so designated by the IMF. SDRs may also be used in certain direct payments between participants in the scheme and for payments of various kinds to the IMF. The role of SDRs as a central standard of value in international transactions (see p 195) is being enhanced.

EXTERNAL ASSETS AND LIABILITIES

The significance of any inventory of Britain's aggregate external assets and liabilities[1] is limited because a variety of claims and obligations are included that are very dissimilar in kind, in degree of liquidity and in method of valuation. The inventory for the end of 1977 shows that Britain had a net debtor position estimated at some £1,700 million, due to heavy official financing of balance of payments deficits in recent years. In the past a net creditor position

[1] Figures for the end of 1977 and for earlier years are published in the *United Kingdom Balance of Payments 1967–77* produced by the Central Statistical Office (see Bibliography, p 450).

has been usual and this is likely to be quickly restored as North Sea oil allows for repayment of external debt.

TABLE 31: Analysis of Capital Flows and Official Financing 1975–77

£ million

	1975	1976	1977
Current balance	−1,855	−1,137	+289
Investment and other capital transactions:			
Official long-term capital	−288	−158	−291
Overseas investment in UK public sector [a]	+43	+203	+2,182
Overseas investment in UK private sector	+1,697	+2,061	+3,019
UK private investment overseas	−1,281	−2,156	−2,282
Overseas currency borrowing or lending (net) by UK banks [a, b, c]:			
Borrowing to finance UK investment overseas	+320	+165	+520
Other borrowing or lending (net)	−85	−271	−136
Exchange reserves in sterling [d]:			
British government stocks	+7	+14	+5
Banking and money market liabilities	−624	−1,421	−24
Other external banking and money market liabilities in sterling	+550	+255	+1,471
Import credit [e]	+224	+165	+179
Export credit [e]	−570	−1,145	−408
Other short-term transactions	+285	−608	+175
Total investment and other capital transactions	+278	−2,896	+4,410
Balancing item	+112	+404	+2,662
Balance for official financing	−1,465	−3,629	+7,361
Net transactions with:			
IMF	—	+1,018	+1,113
Other monetary authorities	—	−34	—
Foreign currency borrowing:			
By the British Government [f]	+423	—	+871
By the public sector under the exchange cover scheme	+387	+1,792	+243
Drawings on (+)/additions to (−) official reserves [g]	+655	+853	−9,588
Total official financing	+1,465	+3,629	−7,361

Source: *United Kingdom Balance of Payments 1967–77*

[a] Excluding foreign currency borrowing by the public sector under the exchange cover scheme.
[b] Including certain other financial institutions.
[c] Excluding changes in levels resulting from changes in sterling valuation.
[d] Sterling reserves of overseas countries and international organisations, other than the IMF, reported by banks etc. in Britain.
[e] Excluding trade credit between related firms; after deducting advance and progress payments to suppliers.
[f] Borrowing on the $2,500 million Euro-dollar facility.
[g] Valued in sterling at market-related rates of exchange.

External Assets Britain's assets arising from private investment overseas are estimated to have been £26,550 million at the end of 1977. Direct investment[1] excluding oil, banking and insurance accounted for £15,550 million of the total figure for end 1977, portfolio investment for £7,300 million and oil for £3,700 million.

[1] Direct investment refers mainly to the establishment of subsidiary companies and banks, while portfolio investment refers to investment in company securities.

United Kingdom banking and commercial claims at the end of 1977 totalled £7,983 million. Within this total banking claims were £4,216 million; suppliers' export credit to unrelated firms was £3,264 million. Official external assets, including re-financed export credit, amounted at the end of 1977 to £4,701 million, which included outstanding inter-government loans by Britain of £1,243 million. These assets, together with official reserves of £10,975 million, £7,983 million in banking and commercial claims and private investment overseas of £26,550 million, resulted in aggregate identified external assets at the end of 1977 of some £50,200 million.

Outward Private Investment

Approval is readily obtained for financing direct investment projects by borrowing abroad on appropriate terms, and there is also scope for the investment of retained profits of subsidiary companies overseas. In recent years a considerable proportion of net direct investment outflow has been financed in this way. Foreign currency finance out of the official reserves is available for direct investment only when projects promise early and substantial benefits to Britain's balance of payments, such as may be provided by the returns to direct investment overseas, which take the form of interest, profits and dividends. Examination of these returns in conjunction with the methods of financing direct investment overseas (such as the use of unremitted profits and foreign currency borrowing) indicated that, overall, British direct investment overseas has a beneficial effect on the official reserves and the balance of payments.

Direct investment outflow, excluding oil, was £1,899 million in 1977 compared with £2,108 million in 1976. (The latest available area analysis indicates that of the 1976 figure £451 million was placed in developing countries, £490 million in other member countries of the European Community and £567 million in North America.) With the inclusion of oil, portfolio and other investment, aggregate private investment outflows totalled £2,282 million in 1977, compared with £2,156 million in 1976.

External Liabilities

Identified external liabilities at the end of 1977 are estimated to have been some £51,900 million. Net drawing on the IMF accounted for £2,129 million of this sum and foreign currency borrowing by the Government for a further £2,085 million. Foreign currency borrowing by the rest of the public sector under the exchange cover scheme[1] totalled £5,656 million. Inter-governmental loans to Britain and other official liabilities, mainly a consequence of the second world war and its aftermath, totalled £2,017 million at the end of 1977 of which £1,577 million was owed to the United States and £374 million to Canada. The Government has also drawn a loan of £65 million from the Federal Republic of Germany under the 1969 Anglo-German Offset Agreement. Other public sector liabilities of £6,257 million comprised overseas holdings of British government and public corporations' sterling securities, holdings of Treasury bills and notes, local authorities' securities and mortgages and borrowings by British public corporations and local authorities other than under the exchange cover scheme. British banking and commercial liabilities, including liabilities in sterling and in foreign currencies, totalled £12,483

---

[1] A scheme first introduced in 1969 whereby local authorities and public corporations raise foreign currency from overseas residents either directly or through British banks and surrender it to the Exchange Equalisation Account in exchange for sterling for uss to finance expenditure in Britain. The Treasury sells the borrower foreign currency to service and repay the loan at the exchange rate that applied when the loan was taken out.

million.[1] Liabilities in the form of overseas investment in Britain's private sector excluding oil, banking and insurance totalled £8,500 million at the end of 1977.

The 'sterling balances', or foreign holdings in Britain of sterling in the form of British government securities, bank deposits, deposits with local authorities and hire purchase companies, and Treasury bills totalled £7,790 million at the end of 1977. Of this, £2,107 million was held by residents of oil-exporting countries, £1,483 million by residents of other member countries of the European Community and £4,200 million by other holders. About 36 per cent of the balances were official holdings (mostly those of central monetary institutions) and 64 per cent were private holdings used by overseas residents to finance their international transactions. The total of these liabilities (excluding the counterpart of borrowing) remained broadly constant between the end of 1945 and 1970, then rose sharply in the early 1970s to a peak in 1975, but fell in 1976, mainly as a result of reductions in the amounts held by central monetary institutions. It rose again to a new peak in 1977 as confidence in sterling increased.

As trade and payments arrangements have become more diversified in recent years the relative importance of sterling as a reserve currency has declined. Nevertheless, following the increase in oil prices the official sterling balances grew rapidly as a number of oil-producing countries deposited part of their financial surpluses in Britain. During 1976, however, they fell sharply as official holdings were reduced because of fears about Britain's relatively high inflation rate and trade deficit which undermined the sterling exchange rate, and this depressed the exchange rate further. The facility for the sterling balances, set up for two years early in 1977, with provision for a possible extension for a third year (see p 187), aims to ensure that sterling and the exchange markets cease to be affected by pressures associated with any run down of the official sterling holdings and to achieve greater international monetary stability. It also enables the Government to achieve an orderly reduction in the role of sterling as a reserve currency. The Government offered official holders the option to convert part of their holdings into negotiable medium-term foreign currency bonds issued on market-related terms; some £395 million of the official balances were converted in this way.

Inward Private Investment

Overseas liabilities arising from investment in the private sector of the British economy rose from £7,385 million in 1970 to £21,240 million at the end of 1977.

Overseas investors in Britain are free to repatriate the proceeds of the sale of their investments, including any capital gains that may have accrued. Earnings and dividends are transferable irrespective of their size. In 1977 the inflow of direct, portfolio and other private investment, including oil, amounted to £3,019 million.

The value of overseas investment in the private sector at the end of 1977 comprised: the book value of direct investment in Britain by companies incorporated abroad (excluding oil, banking and insurance)—£8,650 million (this figure has been extrapolated from the book value at the end of 1974, taking account of subsequent annual transactions); portfolio holdings of British securities—£4,720 million; the book value of the net assets in Britain of

---

[1] This sector covers the London banks' operations in the Euro-currency markets in which very large non-sterling currency liabilities are broadly matched by non-sterling assets. Only net liabilities of £6,591 million (the difference between assets of £82,999 million and liabilities of £89,590 million) are included in the external liabilities figure.

overseas oil companies—£5,300 million; and borrowing by British companies overseas—£2,570 million.

Of the £711 million inflow of direct investment excluding oil, banking and insurance into Britain in 1976 (the latest year for which detailed figures are available) £466 million originated in North America and £159 million in other member countries of the European Community. Foreign investment inflow brings a number of benefits to British industry, including technological development which in turn will strengthen the economy and its balance of payments position.

BRITISH GOVERNMENT AID TO DEVELOPING COUNTRIES

Britain's aid programme to the developing countries, which is the responsibility of the Ministry of Overseas Development, consists of grants and loans for economic and social development, technical co-operation, budget support and contributions to multilateral aid giving agencies. To complement the official programme private investment is encouraged by the provision of government insurance to private investors by the ECGD. In addition an important contribution is made to economic development by private voluntary organisations engaged in relief, development and educational work.

Since 1945 total official aid disbursements have amounted to about £5,877 million. The average gross annual disbursement over the four years 1974–77 was about £471 million. In 1977 official aid flows totalled some £589 million, of which £576 million represented official development assistance (see Table 32) and £13 million other official flows. Of the overall total, bilateral aid accounted for £374·5 million including technical co-operation funds of £126·6 million; assistance provided through multilateral agencies was £201·7 million. Repayments of capital and payments of interest during the year on loans made previously came to £52·5 million and £37·8 million respectively.

In recognition of the special importance of the role of official development assistance, the strategy for the Second UN Development Decade, adopted in 1970, included a recommendation that each developed country should progressively increase its official development assistance to the developing countries and exert its best efforts to contribute a minimum net amount of 0·7 per cent of its gross national product (GNP) to them by the middle of the decade. Britain has accepted in principle the 0·7 per cent GNP target and is seeking in the years ahead to move towards it. The speed at which it can do so, however, must be subject to the pace of Britain's own economic recovery and to other calls on its resources. In 1977, net disbursements of official development assistance amounted to £523·7 million, 0·38 per cent of GNP (the net official flow figure was £536·7 million, 0·39 per cent of GNP). Britain has also accepted the UN target of 1 per cent of GNP for total net financial flows (that is, including private and official flows) to developing countries.

In 1975, in a major policy statement, contained in a report entitled *The Changing Emphasis in British Aid Policies—More Help for the Poorest* (see p 450), the British Government outlined its intention to adapt its aid policies to meet the needs of the poorest countries and the poorest communities within these countries, with particular emphasis being placed on rural development.

Bilateral Financial Aid

Bilateral financial aid in 1977 totalled £247·9 million; over 73 per cent was in grants and the rest in loans. Budgetary aid, £10·44 million in 1977, is provided in the form of grants. Development aid is in grants or loans, depending on the economic and constitutional circumstances of the recipient countries. The greater part of it is provided in grants following the decision in June 1975 to provide future aid to the poorest developing countries (which include India,

Bangladesh, Sri Lanka and many African countries) in grant form only. The terms of new development loans from Britain have been progressively softened since 1958 and a policy of making interest-free loans to lighten the repayment burdens of the poorer developing countries was introduced in 1965. In 1977 the total value of bilateral loan commitments entered into by the British Government, excluding investments by the Commonwealth Development Corporation (see p 369), was £6 million and of this over 92 per cent was on interest-free terms. Where loans bear interest it is at fixed concessionary rates ranging from 3 per cent to 6 per cent, and both kinds of loan carry from three to seven years' grace periods during which repayments of capital are not made. Of all loans committed in 1977 the average maturity was 25 years. Britain has more than fulfilled the 1972 recommendations of the Development Assistance Committee of the Organisation for Economic Co-operation and Development (OECD) on easing the terms of financial aid. In July 1978 Britain announced its intention to cancel debts worth £900 million owed on past development loans by 17 of the poorest countries.

Loans and grants are tied to the purchase of goods, equipment and services from Britain, although there may be a limited element for local costs and a foreign content not exceeding 20 per cent in contracts financed from tied aid in appropriate cases. Since October 1975, new loan commitments can be untied, if the recipient agrees, to the extent that goods can be purchased from the poorest developing countries as well as from Britain.

TABLE 32: Official Development Assistance (ODA) to Developing Countries 1974–1977

£ million

	1974	1975	1976	1977
Bilateral	261·3	298·4	381·1	374·5
Commonwealth countries (including dependent territories)	211·2	233·3	304·3	251·0
Grants	*40·2*	*57·7*	*163·9*	*151·2*
Technical co-operation (*grants*)	*57.5*	*70·0*	*94·9*	*60·1*
Loans	*113·5*	*105·5*	*45·5*	*39·7*
Other countries	50·1	65·2	76·8	123·5
Grants	*7.5*	*11·2*	*21·7*	*30·1*
Technical co-operation (*grants*)	*18·9*	*26·2*	*32·5*	*66·5*
Loans	*23·7*	*27·7*	*22·6*	*27·0*
Contributions to multilateral agencies	91·0	133·5	140·8	201·7
Total	352·3	431·9	521·9	576·2
Total net of amortisation (as used for calculation of the 0·7 per cent target)	308·6	388·3	462·1	523·7
Interest receipts	40·1	38·5	38·4	37·8

Source: *British Aid Statistics*

Differences between totals and the sum of their constituent parts are due to rounding.

Commonwealth Countries

Historically, Britain's aid programme began as part of the discharge of its responsibilities towards dependent territories, and the main emphasis remains on the Commonwealth which includes among its members some of the world's poorest countries. In 1977 £251 million (67 per cent) of the bilateral programme was disbursed to Commonwealth countries. Of this, £31·2 million went to Britain's remaining dependencies, which are a first charge on the aid programme, and £5·3 million to the Associated States in the Caribbean.

An important role in development assistance is played by the Commonwealth Development Corporation (CDC), set up by the British Government in 1948, to assist the economic development of the then dependent territories. Subsequent legislation extended its area of operations to independent Commonwealth countries and, with the approval of the Minister of Overseas Development, to other countries. By the end of 1977 some £260·6 million had been invested out of a total commitment of £333·9 million. Of the latter, £82·9 million was in East Asia and the Pacific Islands, £56·6 million in the Caribbean and virtually all of the remainder in Africa. Commitments approved in 1977 totalled over £45 million.

Technical Co-operation

Expenditure on bilateral technical co-operation (the provision of skilled personnel, advice and training) has increased in recent years and was £126·6 million, 33 per cent of bilateral aid, in 1977. The largest component of expenditure (£59 million in 1977) was on sending or maintaining experts overseas, including volunteers; the next largest was for students and trainees in Britain (£20 million).

During 1977, of the 8,625 British persons other than volunteers who were working in developing countries and financed by the British Government, some 3,846 were engaged in the field of education, 1,590 in public works and communications, 1,303 in public administration, 1,096 in agriculture and allied fields, 249 in health services, and 241 in industrial posts.

In addition, under the British Volunteer Programme in 1977 there were 1,641 volunteers, mainly graduates or otherwise qualified, working in developing countries, the majority of them teaching. Recruitment, training and placing overseas is undertaken by four voluntary bodies; 80 per cent of the British costs were met by the British Government.

Britain receives large numbers of students and trainees from developing countries. Over 14,615 were financed in Britain in 1977 under regional programmes of technical co-operation, by awards under the Commonwealth Education Co-operation Scholarships and Education Fellowship Schemes, and under the various schemes of the British Council.

Multilateral Contributions

Britain is the second largest subscriber (after the United States) to the World Bank group of institutions—the International Bank for Reconstruction and Development, the International Development Association (IDA) and the International Finance Corporation. The British commitment to the IDA's Fourth Replenishment, covering 1975–77, was over £206 million, while that to the Fifth Replenishment, which became effective in July 1977, is £474 million. Britain has contributed, or has agreed to contribute, to the Asian Development Bank, the Inter-American Development Bank, the Caribbean Development Bank and the African Development Fund. Since its inception in 1950 Britain has contributed £158 million to the United Nations Development Programme and has provided more experts and training places under multilateral schemes than any other country. Other contributions include those to the United Nations Relief and Works Agency for Palestine Refugees (UNRWA), the United Nations High Commissioner for Refugees (UNHCR), the World Food Programme, the United Nations Fund for Population Activities (UNFPA) and the United Nations Children's Fund (UNICEF). As part of its contribution to the International Year of the Child (1979) the Ministry of Overseas Development is giving £30,000 to £40,000 to the international child-to-child programme which is designed to teach and encourage school children to concern themselves with the health of their younger brothers and sisters.

An increasing proportion of British development assistance is being channelled through the European Community's aid programme. Community financial aid takes the form principally of assistance from the European Development Fund (EDF) to those countries which have a special relationship with the Community under the Convention of Lomé (see p 358). The EDF for 1975–80 amounts to some £2,000 million, including expenditure on a new export-earnings stabilisation scheme. Assistance to a number of Mediterranean countries linked to the Community by trade agreements is being extended. Britain also contributes fully to the Community's food aid programme.

Britain has played a leading part in urging the Community to adopt a new aid and development policy based on the criterion of need and applicable on a world-wide basis, thereby encompassing those developing countries (many of which are among the world's poorest) not covered by the Lomé Convention or having any other special relationship with the Community. The basis of a programme has been agreed with a budget allocation of 70 million units of account in 1978.

19 Promotion of the Sciences

Britain has for centuries provided an atmosphere of learning congenial to its scientists, whose record of achievements in relation to size of population is in many respects unsurpassed. A feature of the present century has been the increased allocation of national resources by the Government to assist in research and development, partly because of the benefits of science to society and partly because of the increasing cost of the equipment and facilities needed. This has led to the development of means for determining priorities in allocating resources and for accounting for their uses. The resulting organisational structure, as described in this chapter, is, however, less centralised than it appears and allows flexibility in maintaining much of the freedom which scientists in Britain have traditionally enjoyed.

The Government keeps under review facilities for training scientists and ensures that adequate research is devoted to matters of national interest, which include defence (see Chapter 5), industrial innovation, health, environmental protection, use and conservation of natural resources, the provision of good food, shelter and energy and of efficient transport and communications. Though the Government finances just over half the research and development in Britain it carries out only one-quarter in its own establishments. Funds are also provided by private and public corporations, and by private endowments and trusts. Research is carried on in a wide range of institutions—private firms, research associations, contract research institutions, government research laboratories, universities, polytechnics, schools and hospitals.

The Pattern of Expenditure
Total expenditure in Britain on scientific research and development in 1975–76 (the latest year for which complete estimates are available) was £2,111 million, or 1·93 per cent of gross national product. Net Government expenditure on research and development rose from £776 million in 1972–73 to £1,382 million in 1975–76, of which £25 million was for the social sciences. Private industry spent £743 million in 1972–73 which increased to £1,185 million in 1975–76. The Government funded £403 million of this, £782 million being privately funded.

THE GOVERNMENT AND SCIENTIFIC RESEARCH
Central responsibility for basic civil science rests with the Secretary of State for Education and Science, who is advised by the Advisory Board for the Research Councils (see p 372). Responsibility for technology rests mainly with the Secretary of State for Industry. Other government departments are responsible for research and development related to their executive responsibilities. In 1972 the Government extended the customer-contractor approach to all its applied research and development, whereby each department as customer, with advice from its Chief Scientist, defines requirements and the work is undertaken by contractors (government laboratories, research councils, research associations, industry and the universities).

Advisory Council for Applied Research and Development
The Lord Privy Seal is responsible for ensuring that there is adequate co-operation and co-ordination between departments in science and technology. An Advisory Council for Applied Research and Development has been established under the Lord Privy Seal's chairmanship to provide a central

forum of external advice to ministers and to publish reports as necessary on the deployment of applied research and development in both public and private sectors and on the role of Britain in international collaboration in such activities.

Parliamentary Committees

The Select Committee on Science and Technology, one of the specialist select committees of the House of Commons (see p 33), has published reports on such subjects as alternative sources of energy, energy conservation, university-industry relations, advanced ground transport and nuclear reactors which have raised the level of public debate and influenced ministers. The Parliamentary and Scientific Committee provides for a regular exchange of information between Members of Parliament and scientists. Membership is open to Members of Parliament of any party in both Houses, and also to nominated representatives of such non-profit-making scientific and technological organisations as may be affiliated under its constitution.

The Department of Education and Science

The Department of Education and Science (see also p 44) discharges its responsibilities for basic and applied civil science mainly through the five research councils: the Agricultural Research Council, the Medical Research Council, the Natural Environment Research Council, the Science Research Council and the Social Science Research Council; it also provides financial grants to the British Museum (Natural History) and to the Royal Society (see p 383). The Department spent about £249 million in 1977 on the research councils which in addition received commissions of about £52·5 million from other departments under the customer-contractor principle. The Department is also responsible for some aspects of international scientific relations (see p 387) and helps to co-ordinate government policy regarding scientific and technical information.

The Advisory Board for the Research Councils

The Advisory Board for the Research Councils advises the Secretary of State on responsibilities for civil science with special reference to the research council system, the support of postgraduate students and the proper balance between national and international scientific activities, and on the allocation of the science budget between research councils and other bodies; and promotes close liaison between the councils and users of their research. Its membership includes the chairman or secretary of each of the five research councils, the chairman of the University Grants Committee, the Chief Scientists from departments with a major interest in the work of the research councils, and independent members drawn from the universities, industry and the Royal Society of London.

Computer Board

The Computer Board advises on requirements for central computer installations at universities, research councils and similar establishments.

Agricultural Research Council

The Agricultural Research Council (ARC), established in 1931 under Royal Charter (since amended), consists of a chairman and 18–21 other members. It is supported in part by grant-in-aid provided by Parliament through the Secretary of State for Education and Science; over half its expenditure is for work commissioned by the Ministry of Agriculture, Fisheries and Food.

The ARC is responsible for 15 independent state-aided agricultural research institutes and also has eight institutes under its direct control and seven units under distinguished scientists associated with universities. Also there are eight independent institutes in Scotland financed by the Department of Agriculture and Fisheries for Scotland with advice from the ARC on their scientific programmes, staffing and equipment.

The ARC makes special research grants to support promising new lines of work in university departments. It makes a limited number of postgraduate training awards.

Medical Research Council

The Medical Research Council (MRC) was established under Royal Charter in 1920, as successor to a Medical Research Committee first appointed in 1913. The Council, which consists of a chairman and 14–18 other members, was granted a new Charter in 1966 (since further amended). It is supported mainly by a grant-in-aid provided by Parliament through the Secretary of State for Education and Science and also receives funds from the health departments and Department of Employment for the support of commissioned research.

The Council is assisted by four advisory boards: the Neurobiology and Mental Health Board; the Cell Biology and Disorders Board; the Physiological Systems and Disorders Board; and the Tropical Medicine Research Board. In addition, the MRC is advised by committees concerned with particular aspects of its work and with research grants. The MRC's arrangements for the support of research fall under four main headings: investigations by members of its scientific staff, mostly working in its own establishments; short-term ('project') grants to workers in universities and elsewhere; long-term grants in support of specific research programmes in university departments ('programme grants'); and research training awards (fellowships and studentships) tenable both at home and overseas.

The MRC's main research establishments are the National Institute for Medical Research at Mill Hill, London, and the Clinical Research Centre at Northwick Park, London, which forms an integral part of Northwick Park Hospital. In addition the Council has over 60 research units, mostly located in university departments, medical schools and hospitals in Britain.

The MRC also undertakes work overseas and, with additional support from the Ministry of Overseas Development, maintains laboratories in The Gambia and in Jamaica.

Other Medical Research

Besides financing the MRC, the Government also supports medical research through block grants to universities distributed through the Department of Education and Science and the University Grants Committee, and through the research and development programme of the Department of Health and Social Security (see p 381). Certain government-financed research for defence purposes has civil applications related to medical science.

Important contributions to the support of research in particular subjects are made by industry, especially the pharmaceutical industry, and by the many private charities or voluntary organisations which raise money for particular branches of research.

The Natural Environment Research Council

The Natural Environment Research Council (NERC) was established by Royal Charter in 1965 with responsibility to encourage, plan and execute research in sciences, physical and biological, relating to man's natural environment and its resources. These researches are broadly grouped and defined as: the Solid Earth—its physical properties and mineral resources; Seas and Oceans—their behaviour and living and mineral resources; Inland Waters— their behaviour and living resources; Terrestrial Environments—wild-life communities and their resources; Atmosphere—its structure and interactions; and a number of interdisciplinary studies including pollution and the physical and biological properties of the Antarctic environment.

The Council carries out research and training through its own institutes, grant-aided institutes, and by grants, fellowships and other postgraduate awards to universities and other institutes of higher education.

The Council's research institutes are: the British Antarctic Survey, the Institute of Geological Sciences, the Institute of Hydrology, the Institute of Marine Biochemistry, the Institute for Marine Environmental Research, the Institute of Oceanographic Sciences, the Institute of Terrestrial Ecology, the Sea Mammal Research Unit and the Unit of Invertebrate Virology. The Council also maintains central service units which include the Research Vessel Base and the Experimental Cartography Unit.

Research institutes aided by council grants are: the Freshwater Biological Association, the Marine Biological Association of the United Kingdom, the Scottish Marine Biological Association, the Unit of Marine Invertebrate Biology, the Unit of Comparative Plant Ecology and other units attached to universities.

The statutory council consists of a chairman and up to 18 members. The Council is financed by a grant-in-aid from Parliament, received through the Department of Education and Science, and by commissioned research from government departments.

Science Research Council

The Science Research Council (SRC), comprising a chairman and 14–18 other members, was established under Royal Charter in 1965 and is supported by parliamentary grants-in-aid through the Secretary of State for Education and Science. The SRC supports basic research in astronomy, the biological sciences, chemistry, engineering, mathematics and physics in furthering its primary purpose of sustaining standards of education and research in the universities. Most of the SRC's resources are devoted to helping university and polytechnic staff to carry out basic research at the forefront of their subjects in their institution, in one of the Council's research establishments, or elsewhere; to encouraging active collaboration in research between the higher education institutions and industry; to identifying and supporting areas of special importance, such as polymer engineering, manufacturing technology, marine technology and energy; and to enabling suitable graduates to receive further training in methods of research or a specialised branch of science or engineering of importance to British industry. The SRC provides grants for research projects and awards studentships for training in methods of research or advanced courses of study, and fellowships to promising scientists or engineers to enable them to carry out independent research programmes that they themselves have put forward.

The SRC maintains five research establishments: the Appleton Laboratory at Slough (Berkshire), the Daresbury Laboratory at Warrington (Cheshire), the Royal Greenwich Observatory at Herstmonceux (East Sussex), the Royal Observatory, Edinburgh, and the Rutherford Laboratory at Chilton (Oxfordshire). Their main purpose is to support the research of universities and polytechnics. The five establishments are each centres of specialised research but are also used for the development and operation of research equipment beyond the resources of a university (for example, the high-power laser facility at the Rutherford Laboratory). They provide support for scientists whose research needs access to facilities run by international research organisations, such as the powerful particle accelerators at the European Organisation for Nuclear Research (CERN) and the high-flux neutron source at the Institut Laue Langevin (ILL).

The SRC provides national contributions to CERN, the civil science programme of the North Atlantic Treaty Organisation, the Anglo Australian Telescope, the European Incoherent Scatter Project and part of the European Space Agency contribution. It also contributes to, and shares with its French and German partners, the control of the ILL reactor at Grenoble.

The provision of facilities for university research in nuclear physics is the function of the SRC. The SRC establishments concerned are the Rutherford Laboratory, which supports university teams engaged in experiments in particle physics at CERN, and the Daresbury Laboratory, where a 30 million volt tandem accelerator for research into nuclear structure is under construction.

At the Rutherford Laboratory, the SRC has built a central laser facility for plasma physics and compression study, and is constructing a new spallation source based on a proton synchrotron (particle accelerator). At the Daresbury Laboratory the Council is building a source of high intensity electromagnetic radiation which will be used in a wide range of research projects in the physical and biological sciences.

Astronomy

Astronomy uses both ground-based techniques, such as optical and radio telescopes, and space-based methods (see p 389). Optical astronomy is carred out in university departments and in the Royal Greenwich Observatory and the Royal Observatory, Edinburgh, under the SRC. Instruments include the Isaac Newton Telescope, of diameter 2·5 metres (8 feet), for which the Royal Greenwich Observatory is responsible; the Anglo Australian Telescope, of diameter 3·9 metres (13 feet), at Siding Spring, Australia, in a joint project with the Australian Government; a 1·2-metre (4-ft) Schmidt Telescope on the same site; and optical telescopes operated by the South African Astronomical Observatory, to which the SRC contributes. A 3·8-metre (12-ft) infra-red telescope is being completed on Mauna Kea, Hawaii, by the SRC.

Cambridge and Manchester Universities are the main centres for research in radio astronomy with substantial support from the SRC. The fully steerable 76·2-metre (250-ft) telescope at Jodrell Bank (University of Manchester) has been modernised and a radio-linked interferometer system is under construction. The Cambridge University group at Lord's Bridge has developed and made substantial use of the aperture synthesis technique; two arrays of telescopes with 1·6-kilometre (1-mile) and 0·8-kilometre (0·5-mile baseline have been complemented by a 5-kilometre (3·1-mile) array.

The Social Science Research Council

The Social Science Research Council (SSRC) was established under Royal Charter in 1965 to encourage, support and carry out research in, and to disseminate knowledge about, the social sciences. The SSRC consists of a chairman and 13–19 other members, and is supported by grant-in-aid provided by Parliament through the Secretary of State for Education and Science. It initiates research into such topics as health policy, energy policy, population studies, pollution policy, pre-school education, transmitted deprivation, and the social impact of North Sea oil. It provides grants for research projects at universities and other institutions, and makes training awards to postgraduate students. It has also four research units: the Industrial Relations Unit, the Cambridge Population Unit, the Ethnic Relations Unit, and the Socio-legal Studies Centre. The SSRC's fields of interest include economics; political science; psychology; social anthropology; social and economic statistics; sociology and social administration; social science and government; education; management and industrial relations; human geography; linguistics; planning and various aspects of a wide range of other disciplines.

**Other
Social
Research**

Several government departments have funds allocated for social research related to their responsibilities, including the Home Office, which has a large research unit carrying out a wide variety of sociological studies. The Social Survey conducts sample survey inquiries at the request of government departments and from time to time also carries out studies in collaboration with universities and other independent research organisations. Trends based on departmental data are indicated by the Central Statistical Office in its publication *Social Trends*.

**The Universities
and Institutions
of University
Status**

Of total estimated university expenditure on scientific research in the academic year 1976–77 (over £232 million), the largest government contribution (over £138 million) was through the University Grants Committee (UGC).

Scientific research in the universities (and other institutions of higher education) is also supported through the research councils. This support takes two forms. First, about half the postgraduate students in science and technology in the universities and other institutions receive maintenance awards from the research councils, through postgraduate studentships. These awards are in some cases for periods of up to three years of training in research work and in others for shorter periods for advanced studies. The cost of these awards is about £33 million a year. Second, grants and contracts are given to the universities and other institutions by the research councils for specified projects, particularly in new or developing areas of research. These total about £50 million a year. The ARC, MRC and SSRC maintain a number of research units within universities. In addition, the research councils provide central facilities in their own establishments for use by university research workers.

The other main channels of support for scientific research in the universities are various government departments, the Royal Society, industry and the independent foundations. The contributions from sources other than the UGC amount to about a third of the total university expenditure on research.

Universities in industrial centres have tended to acquire outstanding reputations in studies relating to their local industries, and on a national scale close relationships are fostered between the universities, industries and the Government in numerous joint projects.

*Statistics of
Qualified
Manpower*

There were in 1976 some 585,000 persons with qualifications in engineering, technology and science in Great Britain, of whom 307,000 were qualified in science and 278,000 in engineering and technology. Of those economically active in 1975 (465,000), about half (237,000) held engineering qualifications.

**The Department
of Energy**

The Department of Energy (see p 44) is responsible for the United Kingdom Atomic Energy Authority (UKAEA); research in support of the exploitation of North Sea oil and gas; research into alternative sources of energy and conservation of energy; co-ordination of energy research within government departments; general approval of the research programmes of the coal, gas and electricity supply industries; and co-ordination of British contributions to energy research and development programmes sponsored by international organisations.

An Advisory Council on Research and Development for Fuel and Power advises the Secretary of State on the general programme of research and development of the nationalised energy industries and on other matters related to energy research and development. An Energy Technology Support Unit at Harwell assists the Department in assessing technological possibilities in energy policy, advises on long-term research and development programmes, and assists in their management.

An Offshore Energy Technology Board advises the Secretary of State for Energy on research and development in offshore oil and gas technology and is responsible for programmes designed to ensure the safety and efficiency of offshore operations and improve the competitive efficiency of the offshore equipment industry in Britain.

Nuclear Energy The Secretary of State for Energy is responsible for promoting and controlling the development of nuclear energy and ensuring that the proper degrees of importance are attached to its various applications. The UKAEA is the main body carrying out relevant research and development. Its programme includes work in support of the Government's nuclear power programme, and it builds and operates experimental and prototype reactors (see p 258). The authority also works outside the nuclear field. Research and development work is undertaken at the Atomic Energy Research Establishment at Harwell and at the Culham Laboratory, both in Oxfordshire; at the Atomic Energy Establishment at Winfrith (Dorset) and at establishments of the Authority's northern division, which is directed from the Risley Nuclear Power Development Establishment, near Warrington, Cheshire: the Risley Nuclear Power Development Laboratories, the Dounreay Nuclear Power Development Establishment, Highland, the Springfields Nuclear Power Development Laboratories, Lancashire, and Windscale Nuclear Power Development Laboratories, Cumbria. The Safety and Reliability Directorate at Culcheth (Cheshire) is the focal point of the UKAEA's work in relation to the safety of nuclear reactors and related plants and processes.

Co-operation in nuclear energy between Britain and other countries takes place within a framework of intergovernmental agreements and membership of bodies such as the International Atomic Energy Agency (which operates under the aegis of the United Nations) and the Nuclear Energy Agency of the Organisation for Economic Co-operation and Development, and through direct research links between the UKAEA and counterpart organisations in other countries.

Euratom Britain takes part in the co-operative research programmes of the European Atomic Energy Community (Euratom, see p 72) including that concerned with establishing the feasibility of achieving controlled thermonuclear fusion. The Joint European Torus project, partly financed by Euratom, is to be sited at the UKAEA's laboratory at Culham (Oxfordshire) where a Euratom design team has been working since 1973. This project is intended to carry forward research into a completely new source of energy through the fusion of the nuclei of light elements, using cheap, readily available and hitherto untapped resources.

The Department of the Environment and the Department of Transport The Departments' research programme is the responsibility of the Directorate General of Research which provides a common service to both Departments. It is formulated on the basis of the customer-contractor relationship, the main contractors being the Departments' research establishments. Guidance on research priorities is given by six research requirement committees, which bring together the main customer-contractor and research policy interests. The Departments receive external advice on the broad shape and priorities of their research programme from the Construction and Housing Research Advisory Council and the Planning and Transport Research Advisory Council. There are also a number of procedures to ensure that outside interests, such as those in local government and industry, are fully consulted about the programme's contents.

About half the Departments' programme is carried out at the Building Research Establishment (see p 235), the Transport and Road Research Laboratory (see p 289) and the Hydraulics Research Station. The other half is the subject of contracts placed with, or grants given to, a wide range of organisations, either by the research establishments, or by the Departments.

The Departments give grants-in-aid to a number of research organisations which include: the Centre for Environmental Studies; the Local Government Operational Research Unit of the Royal Institute of Public Administration; and the Retail Planning Institute. The Construction Industry Research and Information Association, the Building Services Research and Information Association, the Timber Research and Development Association and the Water Research Centre receive grants to support their co-operative research and related activities. The Royal Society receives a grant to meet costs it incurs as British representative on the International Institute of Applied Systems Analysis.

The Nature Conservancy Council

The Nature Conservancy Council (see p 165), funded by the Secretary of State for the Environment, may give grants to anyone (including voluntary bodies) to carry out research projects relevant to its functions. The Council carries out certain research and also commissions research mainly from the Institute of Terrestrial Ecology, a component body of the NERC (see 373).

The Department of Industry

The Department of Industry is responsible for the sponsorship of manufacturing industries and for technical services to industry, and for six Government laboratories. Of these, the National Physical Laboratory has responsibilities for the national system of measurement, for technical aspects of standards (including the British Calibration Service) and for research in computing, numerical analysis, chemical standards and materials applications. The National Engineering Laboratory carries out research in mechanical engineering aimed at helping industry improve designs and production processes by the application of improved technology. The Warren Spring Laboratory undertakes research in control engineering, materials handling, metals extraction, mineral processing, waste materials processing and environmental technology. The National Maritime Institute has special facilities and expertise relating to the characteristics and performance of ships and offshore structures, marine traffic and navigation safety, wind and water forces on structures and in conducting marine trials and measurements at sea. The Computer Aided Design Centre is concerned with increasing and optimising the use of computer aided design by industry. The Laboratory of the Government Chemist offers analytical services and scientific advice to all government departments. All these laboratories undertake contract research for British industry and overseas firms.

The Department sponsors research by extra-mural contracts with industry, universities and research associations. In accordance with the Government's customer-contractor principle, the Department administers a number of requirements boards to determine the objectives and balance of the relevant research and development programmes, to further the practical application of technology and to advise on science and technology matters in their fields. They cover ship and marine technology; mechanical engineering and machine tools; engineering materials; computers, systems and electronics; chemicals and minerals; metrology and standards; garment and allied industries; and electrical technology. They are responsible to the Secretary of State for Industry and include representatives from other departments, industry and bodies in the public sector. The Chief Scientist and Engineer's Board covers other relevant branches of technology.

Industrial Research

Within the total expenditure of £1,178 million on research and development carried out within or financed by private industry in 1975–76, expenditure in individual industries, including funds from government sources, was as follows (in £ million): aerospace 291, electronics (including computers) 251; other electrical engineering 64; petroleum products 18; other chemical products 221; mechanical engineering 63; motor vehicles 87; scientific instruments 21; food, drink and tobacco 48; textiles 25. Firms in science-based industries commit large private funds to research and development in the course of business.

A number of institutes for sponsored research have been established to extend the facilities for private research for industrial firms by studying problems which are not within the scope of the average industrial laboratory.

Research Associations

A scheme by which the Government helped firms with similar interests to form organisations known as research associations, to carry out industrial research co-operatively, was started in 1917. Encouragement by government grants, related to the contributions made by the industries concerned, has lately been phased out in favour of extra-mural contract support, such as that offered by the Department of Industry's Requirements Boards (see p 378). About 30 of these research associations operate in areas of interest to the Department of Industry. In addition there are four (buildings services; construction industry; timber; and water) linked with the Department of the Environment and five (Flour Milling and Baking; Campden Food Preservation; British Food Manufacturing Industries; British Industrial Biological Research; and Processors' and Growers') linked with the Ministry of Agriculture, Fisheries and Food. Among the largest of the industrial research associations are those dealing with production engineering, ships, welding, electrical manufacturing, cotton and man-made fibres, non-ferrous metals and motor manufacturing. (See also Chapter 12.) The Textile Research Council serves as a focal point for the collective interests of the various textile research associations.

Public Corporations

Some of the public corporations which run the nationalised industries have their own research organisations, in particular those concerned with energy (see Chapter 13), steel and transport. These organisations also give support to other organisations concerned with research on matters of interest to them.

Agricultural, Food, Fisheries and Forestry Research

Agricultural research is carried out by the Agricultural Research Council, the government agricultural departments and by private industry. Fisheries research is conducted by the government fisheries departments, the White Fish Authority, and the Natural Environment Research Council. Expenditure on research and development by the Ministry of Agriculture, Fisheries and Food is estimated to be £45·1 million in 1978–79.

Advice is given to the government agricultural departments and to the ARC on priorities for all state-aided research and development in agriculture and food in England, Wales and Scotland, by the Joint Consultative Organisation (JCO). The JCO comprises members of the farming and food industries, scientists, economists and members of the departments' professional, technical and administrative services and consists of five advisory boards concerned with animals; arable crops and forage; horticulture; food science and technology; and engineering and buildings.

Government Agricultural and Food Departments

The Ministry of Agriculture, Fisheries and Food does both applied and basic research. At its Central Veterinary Laboratory at Weybridge, research and laboratory investigations are carried out into the causes, pathology, epidemiology and control of diseases of farm livestock, including poultry; the diagnosis of animal and poultry diseases (other than foot-and-mouth disease); and the making and supplying of certain biological products. The laboratory is, by appointment of the World Health Organisation, the third international laboratory for biological standards. In discharging its responsibilities in regard to plant health services, the Plant Pathology Laboratory at Harpenden, Hertfordshire, provides the scientific basis for essential legislation against plant pests and diseases, and acts as a liaison centre for the collection and dissemination of information on pests and diseases of crops and plants and on the uses and toxic hazards of pesticides used in agriculture and horticulture. It carries out research and development on plant health problems, and also on the detection of pesticide residues in treated crops and crop products, and on the formulation of pesticides. The Pest Infestation Control Laboratory at Slough, Berkshire (with stations at Tolworth and Worplesdon, Surrey), engages in research work on insects, mites and fungi affecting food storage and on harmful mammals and birds. It provides the scientific basis for advisory work on their detection and control and acts as an instruction and liaison centre for home and some overseas work. It is also concerned with the safe use of pesticides in food storage and in animal husbandry, and with the effect on wildlife of pesticides of all kinds.

With the guidance of the Chief Scientific Adviser (Food), the Food Science Division provides advice on scientific and technical aspects of food. Particular attention is paid to the safety, quality and nutritive value of food, including consideration of food additives and contaminants. Close liaison is maintained with the Department of Health and Social Security, which has responsibilities for public health, and with other government departments. The division has Food Science Laboratories in Norwich and London concerned with storage of certain foods, interaction of food additives and food components, heavy metal contamination and studies arising from food legislation and safety. There is an increasing demand for advice in connection with international work, including the European Community food legislation, and also regarding the new government policies for the support of research at the four food research associations and elsewhere.

In Scotland research work at East Craigs, Edinburgh, by the Agricultural Scientific Services of the Department of Agriculture and Fisheries is mainly concerned with the problem of cultivar taxonomy, seed testing, healthy seed potato production, plant pathology, and the ecology of birds, mammals and insects harmful to agriculture and stored products. In Northern Ireland the Department of Agriculture is responsible for promotion of research in food produced by agriculture and in veterinary sciences with the aim of improving efficiency of production, marketability of foods and the health of plants and animals. The Department is also responsible for work on forest science, ecology of freshwater and marine fish as well as on the biology of freshwater resources.

Government Fisheries Departments

The Ministry of Agriculture, Fisheries and Food's research work is carried out by the Directorate of Fisheries Research at Lowestoft and by the Torry Research Station in Aberdeen. The former includes a Marine Fisheries

Laboratory and Fisheries Radiobiological Laboratory at Lowestoft, a Shellfish and Marine Pollution Laboratory at Burnham-on-Crouch (Essex), a Salmon and Freshwater Fisheries Laboratory in London, a Shellfish Cultivation Station at Conwy (Gwynedd) and a Fish Disease Centre at Weymouth. Torry Research Station and an outstation at Hull are concerned with the investigation of all aspects of fish technology. There are seven research vessels engaged on sea-going, inshore and estuarine work. The Department of Agriculture and Fisheries for Scotland maintains a marine research laboratory and six sea-going research ships at Aberdeen, and a freshwater fisheries research laboratory at Pitlochry.

A Fisheries Research and Development Board, representative of government departments and the industry, advises fisheries ministers on research programmes, objectives and priorities. A Controller of Fisheries Research and Development, responsible jointly to the Minister of Agriculture, Fisheries and Food and the Secretary of State for Scotland, co-ordinates the programmes of the research laboratories.

Forestry

Forestry research is carried out by the Forestry Commission at the Forest Research Station, Alice Holt Lodge, Surrey, and the Northern Research Station, Roslin, near Edinburgh. By means of grants, aid is also given for forestry research work undertaken by various universities and other institutions, including the Commonwealth Forestry Institute, Oxford. Expenditure by the Commission on research work in Great Britain amounted to £2·7 million in 1977–78. Research into the quality and uses of home-grown timber is carried out by Princes Risborough Laboratory in Buckinghamshire, and also by grant-aided associations. An extensive research programme on Dutch elm disease has been carried out by the Commission since the outbreak of the disease in 1969.

Other Government-sponsored Research

The Procurement Executive, Ministry of Defence, engages in research for defence purposes at its research and development establishments and through contracts placed with industry and universities (see p 111). It also undertakes certain research for civil purposes, including meteorology (see p 383), civil aviation (see p 111), medical research and space research.

The Department of Health and Social Security spent over £25 million on research and development in 1977–78 of which over £8·5 million was on bio-medical research through the Medical Research Council. The Department is advised by a Chief Scientist supported by a group of independent advisers covering a wide range of scientific disciplines.

The Department of Employment has a Research and Planning Division to conduct and advise on its programme of research on socio-economic problems. Assistance is given to the Department in social research by the Office of Population Censuses and Surveys and close contact is maintained with the Social Science Research Council.

The Department of Prices and Consumer Protection (see p 49) has responsibility for standards and weights and measures, for government support for the British Standards Institution (see p 207) and for the Metrication Board set up to facilitate the transition to the metric system of weights and measures in Britain.

Some other branches of research for which government departments are responsible are given below.

Aeronautical Research

Britain's aerospace industry carries out from its own resources a substantial programme of research and development. Supplementary government assistance is given by the Ministry of Defence and the Department of Industry. Their work is, wherever possible, integrated into a single programme managed by the Procurement Executive of the Ministry of Defence and carried out in government establishments such as the Royal Aircraft Establishment, the National Gas Turbine Establishment and the Royal Signals and Radar Establishment as well as in industry, in research associations and in universities. The work is subject to the oversight of the Aeronautical Research Council and the Joint Research Committee, which bring together the research interests with the aircraft manufacturing and operating industries and with eminent academics.

Similar methods are used by the Civil Aviation Authority for research needed to support their statutory responsibilities in aircraft operation; in this case, advice is obtained on research and development work from the Civil Aviation Research and Development Programme Board.

Botany

The Royal Botanic Gardens, Kew (founded in 1759), together with its 200-hectare (500-acre) estate at Wakehurst Place, Ardingly (Sussex) is administered by the Ministry of Agriculture, Fisheries and Food and has the largest collection of living plants in the world. The Herbarium (also the largest in the world with nearly 5 million specimens) is concerned primarily with research into the classification and accurate determination of plants, as well as producing several major descriptions of flora in various parts of the world. The Jodrell Laboratory undertakes the study of plant anatomy and plant physiology, biochemistry, cytology and genetics. There is also a seed bank and seed testing unit. There is a Conservation Unit concerned with various aspects of plant conservation, and in particular the threatened plants of the world. The Museums Division is concerned with public exhibitions and the care of reference collections of economic plant products. The Library, founded in 1852, consists of more than 120,000 botanical books, about 140,000 reprints and separately issued items and a collection of over 170,000 drawings and paintings of plants.

The Royal Botanic Garden, Edinburgh (founded in 1670), has, since 1969, been administered by the Department of Agriculture and Fisheries for Scotland. Together with the associated Logan Botanic Garden at Ardwell, near Stranraer, and the Younger Botanic Garden at Benmore, near Dunoon, it maintains large collections of living plants (both temperate and tropical) used for taxonomic research (into classification of plants), including tropical plants. The herbarium and library (the finest outside London) are used for taxonomy, cytology, anatomy, mycology and other subjects.

Communications

The Post Office, responsible to the Department of Industry, undertakes research and development on many aspects of the science and engineering of communications (see pp 308–9).

Environmental Pollution

Research into the effects of pollutants on man and the environment and on methods of controlling them is spread throughout research establishments of all kinds, sponsored by research councils and central government departments with control responsibilities (see p 166). The Royal Commission on Environmental Pollution advises on the adequacy of such research.

Health and Safety

The Health and Safety Executive, through its Health and Safety Laboratories, carries out research into matters affecting the health and safety of people at work. Fields of study include explosion risks, fires, protective equipment, methods for monitoring and measuring airborne contaminants, the safety of engineering systems and fluid mechanics. The Executive also places research contracts with outside organisations.

Meteorology

The Ministry of Defence finances the Meteorological Office, which is responsible for research in meteorology and some aspects of geophysics, mainly for civil purposes. The headquarters of the Office and most of its research sections are at Bracknell (Berkshire). The Ministry also makes grants for fundamental meteorological research carried out under the auspices of the Royal Society or in university departments.

Radiological Protection

A National Radiological Protection Board (see p 171) carries out research, makes public and occupational health assessments and provides services in connection with radiological protection. The Board is financed by Parliament through the Secretary of State for Social Services by grants from the UKAEA and the MRC, and by income from services.

THE LEARNED SOCIETIES

Although today most research is conducted under other auspices, the learned societies, of which there are more than 300, have retained their traditional function of facilitating the spread of knowledge. The most eminent of those concerned with science in its broadest aspects (as distinct from those societies with specialised interests and activities) are the Royal Society, Royal Society of Arts, Royal Institution and British Association.

Royal Society

The Royal Society, or, more fully, the Royal Society of London for Improving Natural Knowledge, founded in 1660, occupies a unique place in the country's scientific affairs and is equivalent to national academies of sciences in other countries. It is the oldest such academy in the world to have enjoyed continuous existence. Election to it is regarded by scientists as a high honour. The Queen is Patron. There are today three main categories of Fellowship: Royal Fellows, Foreign Members, of whom there are about 80, and the main body of Fellows numbering about 860. Election to the Fellowship, which is for life, is restricted to 40 persons a year. The Royal Society is governed by a council of 21 members.

Its activities include the holding of scientific meetings; publication of research work, mainly in the *Philosophical Transactions* and the *Proceedings*; the presentation of medals; the giving of endowed lectures; and the award of research appointments and grants. Among its research appointments are the Foulerton, Wolfson, Henry Dale and Napier Research Professorships and 14 other research professorships supported by a parliamentary grant-in-aid. Research fellowships in human nutrition supported by the J. Sainsbury Centenary Grant were inaugurated in 1974. The highest medal awarded is the Copley Medal, for which scientists from all countries are eligible; there are also three Royal Medals, and the Rumford, Davy, Darwin, Buchanan, Sylvester, Hughes, Leverhulme and Mullard Medals, and the Esso Award for the conservation of energy. There are seven lectureships: the Croonian (biology); the Bakerian (physical sciences); the Ferrier (nervous system); the Wilkins (history of science); the Leeuwenhoek (microbiology); the Bernal (social functions of science); and the Clifford Paterson (for electrical science and technology). There are also the Rutherford Memorial, the Blackett Memorial and the Isaac Newton Lectures which are given overseas. The Council has set up committees, some of them jointly with other bodies, to promote improvements in education in science and to emphasise the importance of applied sciences, especially engineering.

Although an independent private corporation, the Society has always had a special relationship with the Government, which makes grants for certain of

its activities. The President of the Society is consulted on scientific appointments to research councils and Fellows serve on most governmental advisory
councils and committees concerned with research.

The international relations of the Royal Society are extensive. It represents
Britain in the international unions comprising the International Council of
Scientific Unions and appoints national committees for each of them. The
Society represents Britain on the Council of the International Institute for
Applied Systems Analysis, and is a member of the European Science Foundation and certain other organisations. It also plays a leading part in international scientific programmes and promotes exchange visits of scientists
with many academies throughout the world. Its international fellowship
scheme to foster relations with scientists of Western Europe receives financial
support from the British Government and from partner organisations in
Europe.

Royal Society of Arts

The Royal Society of Arts (properly, the Royal Society for the Encouragement
of Arts, Manufactures and Commerce) is concerned with scientific, artistic
technical, industrial and commercial subjects. Since its foundation in 1754
one of the Society's principal objects has been to promote the progress and
useful application of all departments of science. Today it fulfils this purpose
chiefly by disseminating new scientific knowledge. The Society regularly holds
lectures, and publishes a monthly *Journal*, thus enabling the exposition and
assessment by leading authorities of developments which have a public as well
as a specialist interest.

Royal Institution

The Royal Institution was founded in 1799 as a public body for facilitating
the introduction of useful mechanical inventions and improvements, and for
teaching the application of science to everyday life. Later it undertook the
'promotion of chemical science by experiments and lectures for improving
arts and manufactures', and 'the diffusion and extension of useful knowledge'.
Its character, however, was largely determined by the work of Sir Humphry
Davy and Michael Faraday, who established a tradition of research. Today
the Royal Institution has extensive research laboratories, and lectures are
given on recent developments in science and other branches of knowledge.

British Association

The British Association for the Advancement of Science was founded in 1831
to promote general interest in science and its applications. One of its chief
activities is the annual meeting, attended by many young students as well as
by eminent scientists. In addition the Association plans special lectures
exhibitions and discussions (some designed for young audiences), the publication of pamphlets, the organisation of conferences, the appointment of study
groups and liaison with the Press and with sound and television broadcasting
services. The Association has area committees and three lectureships for
young scientists (the Kelvin, the Darwin and the Lister lectureships, dealing
respectively with the physical, biological and sociological sciences) to encourage scientists to make their activities known to wider audiences. The
British Association has made an important contribution to the development of
science by taking or recommending action to remove obstacles to the discovery and application of scientific knowledge.

Professional Institutions

There are numerous technical institutions and professional associations, many
of which are playing a distinguished part in promoting their own discipline
or are interested in the education and professional well-being of their members.

The Council of Engineering Institutions, the federal body for the chartered engineering institutions, promotes the co-ordination of the engineering profession. The Council of Science and Technology Institutes is a federal body with five member institutes representing biologists, chemists, mathematicians, metallurgists and physicists.

Fellowship of Engineering

A Fellowship of Engineering, envisaged as complementary to the Royal Society and forming an independent and authoritative forum of eminent engineering opinion, was formed in 1976. The founder members were Fellows of the Royal Society, together with a number of other distinguished engineers who were selected by the chairman of the Council of Engineering Institutions and the Presidents of the individual engineering institutions. Further Fellows, up to a total of 1,000, but not more than 60 in one year, are being elected by the Fellowship.

Major Awards

MacRobert Awards of £25,000 and a gold medal have been presented since 1969 by the Council of Engineering Institutions on behalf of MacRoberts Trusts, for successful technological innovations contributing to the national prestige and prosperity of Britain. A fund was endowed in 1972 by the late Lord Rank to be used to reward outstanding contributions to human nutrition and crop husbandry, and to opto-electronics and nearly related phenomena. The first Rank prizes were announced in 1976. In giving awards for technological innovation, the Queen's Award to Industry scheme concentrates on the potential application in industry of outstanding achievements in advanced technology in the form of processes or products.

Science and Society

There are at least two bodies concerned with the relationship between science and society: the British Society for Social Responsibility in Science; and the Council for Science and Society, formed by specialists in the natural and social sciences, the law, and medicine to support and stimulate research into the social effects of scientific and technological development.

Zoological Gardens

Zoological research is among the many activities of The Zoological Society of London. The society also runs the world-famous London Zoo, opened in 1828, which occupies 14 hectares (36 acres) of Regent's Park, London. In 1931, the Society opened Whipsnade Park Zoo in Bedfordshire, where hundreds of animals roam a 200-hectare (500-acre) park. Other well-known zoos are those at Edinburgh, Bristol, Chester, Dudley, Chessington and Jersey (a small collection of some of the rarest animals in the world). There are also a number of 'safari parks' containing reservations of wild animals through which the public can pass in closed motor cars.

Scientific Museums

The British Museum (Natural History) is the principal centre in the Commonwealth for the general study of natural history, particularly for research into classification (taxonomy); it has extensive collections of extant and fossil animals and plants and of minerals, rocks and meteorites. The Science Museum illustrates the development of pure and applied science in all countries, but chiefly in Britain, which has always held a leading place in engineering, agriculture, navigation, mining, aeronautics, and in the development of industrial machinery and processes. The geology of Britain is probably known in more exact detail than that of any other country in the world, and the Institute of Geological Sciences has an outstanding collection of exhibits in its Geological Museum. These three museums are in South Kensington, London. Other important collections are those of the Museum of Science and Industry, in Birmingham, and the Museum of the History of Science, at Oxford.

DISSEMINATION AND APPLICATION OF RESULTS OF RESEARCH

The dissemination of the results of research to other research workers and to ultimate users has become a major problem as the volume of information has grown. The leading learned societies have for long been important agencies for communicating scientific information. The traditional method of scientific publication, in which results are written up into papers and published in journals or are presented at scientific meetings, is still the main means of communication among scientists, but access to information through computer networks is becoming of increasing importance.

Information Services

A description of general library services which also cater for scientific needs is given on p 402.

Two constituents of the British Library are concerned with science and technology—the Lending Division, and the Science Reference Library. The Lending Division collects for loan purposes all literature which is likely to be of interest to the practising scientist and technologist, covering all branches of science and technology (including agriculture and medicine) and the social sciences. The Science Reference Library is divided between the Holborn Division, formerly the Patent Office Library, and the Bayswater Branch which has substantial collections, especially in the life sciences and scientific literature written in Slavonic and oriental languages.

The rehousing in a new London headquarters of the world's largest library devoted to the social sciences, the British Library of Political and Economic Science, part of the London School of Economics, is planned for completion by the end of the present decade.

Aslib, representing special libraries and information units in industry, government departments, universities, colleges and other institutions, carries out research into the collection, utilisation and dissemination of information, provides consultancy and advisory services and training courses and offers members an inquiry and reference service covering all subjects.

The Department of Industry and the UKAEA devote considerable sums to advisory and information services. The former has nine regional offices which make contacts with local industries to promote greater use of existing scientific and technical knowledge. Its Technology Reports Centre is a national clearing house for unpublished technical reports made available by various bodies in Britain and overseas. The industrial research associations circulate research reports and provide information services to members. Besides information services provided by its various groups, which include the Ceramics Centre and the Non-destructive Testing Centre at Harwell, the UKAEA has an information centre in London and a network of regional advisers on the use of radioisotopes.

In agriculture, the Commonwealth Agricultural Institutes and Bureaux (see p 388) provide abstracts and an information service in various branches of agricultural science. The ARC publishes an *Index of Agricultural Research in Progress*, and gives an account of current developments in its annual reports. The advisory services of the agricultural departments bring research results directly to the farmer.

Medical research results are communicated mainly through journals and periodicals but the MRC issues special reports and includes special articles in its annual reports.

National Research Development Corporation

The National Research Development Corporation (NRDC) is an independent public corporation supported as necessary by government loans through the Department of Industry. The NRDC's functions are to promote the manufacture by industry, under NRDC licence, of new products and processes invented in government laboratories, universities and elsewhere, advancing money where necessary to bring them to a commercially viable stage, and to speed up technological advance by investing money with British industrial firms, on a joint venture basis, for the development of their own inventions and projects. Its borrowing power for government advances is £50 million. Outstanding advances total £7·9 million and the Corporation is currently funding its annual investment in research and development from its income from licences and levies. Projects so far sponsored include the *Cephalosporin C* antibiotic, hovercraft, computers, advanced types of electric motor, diving and other oceanological equipment, packaging equipment, insecticides, micro-electronics and plastics.

INTERNATIONAL SCIENTIFIC RELATIONS

Britain is represented on the Scientific and Technical Research Committee of the European Economic Community, the object of which is to co-ordinate national policies on these matters and to implement joint projects of interest to the Community. Other intergovernmental organisations involved in scientific co-operation with which Britain is concerned include: European Co-operation in Science and Technology; specialised agencies of the United Nations such as the United Nations Educational, Scientific and Cultural Organisation; the International Atomic Energy Agency; the Nuclear Energy Agency and the International Energy Agency of the Organisation for Economic Co-operation and Development; the European Organisation for Nuclear Research; the European Space Agency; the European Molecular Biology Conference; the European Molecular Biology Laboratory; the International Agency for Research on Cancer; and the North Atlantic Treaty Organisation Science Committee. Among non-governmental organisations Britain is represented in the international unions comprising the International Council of Scientific Unions (see p 382). The five research councils, the Royal Society and the British Academy became founding members of the European Science Foundation set up in 1974. In nuclear energy Britain also co-operates within the framework of international agreements; through direct links between the UKAEA and its counterparts; and through joint companies in, for example, nuclear fuel and radioisotope manufacture.

There are scientific counsellors in the British Embassies in Washington, Paris, Bonn, Moscow and Tokyo who among other things promote contacts in science and technology between Britain and the countries to which they are accredited. These counsellors serve all central government departments concerned in overseas scientific affairs, as well as the research councils and the Royal Society, which is the main representative of Britain in areas of non-governmental collaboration. Administrative support for the counsellors is provided in Britain by the Department of Industry's Overseas Technical Information Unit.

The Ministry of Overseas Development

The Ministry of Overseas Development promotes scientific activities in the interests of developing countries. These include research covering a wide range of disciplines, specialist advice from Britain, advisory visits, conferences for exchange of information, training scientists from overseas in universities and research institutions in Britain, recruiting scientific staff from Britain, and providing support for existing research services and research projects overseas. Equipment is sometimes provided for research purposes and to encourage scientific training. There are two organisations forming part of the Ministry, which are wholly engaged on scientific work to assist developing countries. They are the Tropical Products Institute, which specialises in the post-harvest aspects of agricultural, fish and animal products, and the Centre for

Overseas Pest Research, which is concerned with the development and application of pest control techniques relevant to tropical agriculture. In addition, the Ministry meets the cost of a number of scientific units which do substantial research work of benefit to developing countries. The Ministry also supports the International Agricultural Research Centres under the aegis of the Consultative Group for International Agricultural Research. The Ministry provides over £17 million a year for scientific activities including research for the benefit of developing countries.

Commonwealth Science Council

The Commonwealth Science Council (CSC) consists of administrators and scientists nominated by the Governments of Commonwealth member countries and has been brought into close association with the Commonwealth Secretariat. The Council concentrates on the organisation of collaborative projects in science and technology to be undertaken by member countries.

Commonwealth Agricultural Bureaux

The Commonwealth Agricultural Bureaux, financed by contributions from the governments of 25 Commonwealth countries, comprise four institutes and ten bureaux, all of which except one institute are in Britain and each of which is concerned with a particular branch of agricultural science. They act as clearing houses for the interchange of information of value to research and other workers in agricultural science throughout the Commonwealth and increasingly throughout the world.

The British Council

The principal aims of the British Council (see p 151) in science (including agriculture, medicine and technology) are to foster co-operation between British scientists and scientists of other countries, to promote among overseas specialists a better understanding and knowledge of Britain and its scientific achievements, and, in the developing countries, to identify and manage development projects in the technological, scientific and educational sectors.

There are 70 staff overseas with science qualifications who work to advance technological, educational and scientific development, and collaboration with Britain. One of their priorities is to make British know-how available, increasingly through consultancy schemes; others are to establish research and development facilities, to provide trained manpower, and to assist with the establishment of technical teaching institutes.

Interchange of scientists, technologists and educationalists is considered to be of prime importance. British specialists in a very wide range of subjects are sent overseas to advise on research and development and on teaching, and to give courses of lectures, while scientists, technologists and technical teachers are recruited or seconded to posts in overseas universities, technical teaching institutes, teacher training colleges, education authorities, schools or curriculum reform centres.

The Council invites senior overseas people to Britain and arranges programmes of visits or attachments. It makes its own awards for postgraduate study in Britain and supervises programmes for senior specialists and students who come to Britain through the United Nations agencies or bilateral technical assistance schemes. The Council administers the Academic Interchange with Europe Scheme, the European Academic Links Scheme, the Younger Research Workers' Interchange Scheme, the Commonwealth University Interchange Scheme and scientific exchange with Eastern Europe. Professional courses organised by the Council in various parts of Britain for overseas specialists include science and medicine. At the Council's headquarters in London, extensive professional, advisory and information facilities within specialist departments and libraries covering education, medicine, science, technology and science education are available to overseas people.

SPACE ACTIVITIES

Government responsibility for space activities is undertaken by the Secretary of State for Education and Science (through the SRC), the Secretary of State for Defence and the Secretary of State for Industry, according to the nature of the project. Expenditure on space activities in 1977 was about £60 million.

The United Kingdom is a member of the European Space Agency (ESA) together with Belgium, Denmark, France, the Federal Republic of Germany, the Irish Republic, Italy, the Netherlands, Spain, Sweden and Switzerland; Austria, Norway and Canada have observer status. Britain actively participates in the ESA's science and applications programmes in its four applications development satellites (for general communications, meteorology, and air and maritime communications) and in Spacelab, a manned laboratory to be carried aboard the United States Space Shuttle Orbiter.

Scientific research, notably in astronomy and geophysics, using satellites, rockets and balloons, is supported by the SRC (see p 374). The programmes of the ESA and bilateral arrangements with other countries provide flight opportunities for British experiments. Britain is co-operating with the United States in a programme which includes American launching of the British *Ariel* series of scientific satellites, the incorporation of British experiments in American satellites, and the analyses of lunar surface samples. The SRC's Appleton Laboratory provides support and services for the universities' space-based experiments and also operates the United States National Aeronautics and Space Administration Spaceflight Tracking and Data Network station at Winkfield. Optical tracking of satellites is undertaken by many individual observers in Britain; the prediction and co-ordination centre is at the Appleton Laboratory, which is also the home of one of the three World Data Centres for space research.

The Royal Society represents Britain in non-governmental international scientific groups such as the Committee on Space Research of the International Council of Scientific Unions.

The Department of Industry is responsible for leading the British delegation to the ESA and for industrial sponsorship of Britain's space industry. It participates in a joint departmental industry technology programme designed to improve Britain's industrial capability in space applications systems; the programme is supervised on behalf of the Department by the Procurement Executive of the Ministry of Defence. The Space Department of the Royal Aircraft Establishment at Farnborough also undertakes long-term research and development to assist industry.

The Department of Industry, through the Post Office, is responsible for the use of satellites for civil communications purposes and undertakes research work in connection with communications systems using satellites, including those of Intelsat.

20 The Arts

The wealth of artistic and cultural activity in Britain, ranges from the highest standards of professional performance to the enthusiastic support and participation of amateurs. London is one of the leading world centres for music, drama, opera and dance; and festivals held in Bath, Cheltenham, Edinburgh and other centres are also well known. Many British playwrights, composers, sculptors, painters, writers, actors, singers, choreographers and dancers enjoy international reputations. At an amateur level, activities take many forms, of which a common characteristic is the use of local talent and resources. Amateur choral, orchestral, operatic, dramatic and other societies for the arts abound; and increasing numbers of people take an interest in crafts such as pottery, weaving and woodwork.

Promotion and patronage of the arts are the concern of both official and unofficial bodies. The Government and local authorities take an active part, and an increasing amount of help also comes from private sources, including trusts and commercial concerns. Policies towards support for the arts are broadly similar, however, and there are two main aims. One is to maintain and improve the traditional arts and cultural heritage, and to make them more accessible to greater numbers of people. The other is to provide financial aid to working artists and craftsmen, and to encourage more ordinary men and women to take part in creative leisure pursuits.

Ministerial responsibility for general arts policy is borne by a Minister of State at the Department of Education and Science; the Secretaries of State for Wales, Scotland and Northern Ireland are also concerned with cultural matters. In addition, the Government is responsible for the upkeep of ancient monuments and historic buildings, and grants are made towards the maintenance of privately owned historic buildings (see p 162).

The main educational functions concerning the arts are carried out through the central Government education departments. They are concerned, in partnership with local education authorities and voluntary bodies, with arts education in schools, further education colleges, polytechnics, evening institutes and community centres, and with the public library service.

Arts Councils — Most government support for the arts takes the form of grants to independent agencies. The most important of these is the Arts Council of Great Britain, established by Royal Charter in 1946, whose main objects are to develop and improve the knowledge, understanding and practice of the arts, to increase their accessibility to the public, and to advise and co-operate with government departments, local authorities and other organisations.

Government allocations to the Arts Council in 1978–79 amount to £49 million. The Council gives financial help and advice to over 1,200 organisations, from the major opera, dance and drama companies, orchestras and festivals, to the smallest touring theatres and experimental groups. It encourages such diverse interests as contemporary dance, photography and art films, and helps professional creative writers, choreographers, composers, artists and photographers by means of bursary and award schemes. It promotes art exhibitions and tours of opera, dance and drama companies. Funds are provided for specialist training courses in the arts and the Council

The Police

The Metropolitan Police Force is 150 years old in 1979.

Left: Traffic Control Room and (*below*) Information Room at New Scotland Yard.

Thames Barrier

A tidal flood barrier for the 1980s is being built across the River Thames at Woolwich. It will be a series of moveable gates resting side-by-side on the river bed which can be raised to form a continuous steel wall within 15 minutes.

One of the support structures.

A concrete sill to house one of the gates.

Ironbridge Gorge Museum

The museum, an area with many examples of early industrial structures, won the first European Museum of the Year Award in 1978.

Above right: The Coalport China Works Museum.

Above left: Davis and Samson engines at Bliss Hill Open Air Museum.

View showing the first iron bridge ever built. The bridge was cast in 1779 and bicentenary celebrations are taking place during 1979.

Sport

Aston Villa,
Birmingham, one of
the football clubs to
be given a grant,
through the Sports
Council, for
providing greater
sports opportunities
for young supporters.

Skateboarding on a
specially prepared
rink.

also assists projects for the construction of new buildings or improvements to existing theatres, concert halls and other arts buildings under its 'Housing the Arts' scheme.

Members of the Council are appointed by the minister responsible for the arts. Advised by panels responsible for different aspects of the arts, the Council itself allocates subsidies to the main professional arts promoting organisations. Organisations in Scotland and Wales receive their subsidies from the Scottish and Welsh Arts Councils which are committees of the Arts Council of Great Britain having a large measure of autonomy.

A growing proportion of the Council's funds is channelled to regional arts associations, which are independent bodies set up to develop the arts in the regions. A recent assessment by the Council indicated that about 30 per cent of its revenue funds were applied to activities in London (compared with over half ten years ago), and 70 per cent to Scotland, Wales and the English regions. In Scotland about a fifth of the Council's grant to the Scottish Arts Council is applied to activities in Edinburgh.

In Northern Ireland there is an independent Arts Council with aims and functions similar to those of the Arts Council of Great Britain. It receives an annual grant from the Northern Ireland Department of Education.

British Council   The British Council promotes knowledge of British culture and literature in English overseas (see p 151), and maintains libraries in most of the countries in which it is represented. The Council may give administrative and financial help to overseas tours by British theatre companies, orchestras, choirs and opera and dance companies, as well as by individual actors, musicians and artists. It promotes fine arts and other exhibitions overseas, and organises British participation in international exhibitions. The Council distributes overseas a wide range of specialised films, many of them on the arts, and encourages professional interchange in all cultural fields between Britain and other countries.

Broadcasting   A major contribution to the arts (particularly music and drama) is made by the
Organisations   British Broadcasting Corporation (BBC) and, to a lesser extent, by the independent television and radio programme companies and the Independent Broadcasting Authority (IBA). The BBC has orchestras employing about a third of the country's full-time professional musicians, and each week it broadcasts some 90 hours of serious music (both live and recorded) on its Radio 3 channel. It regularly commissions new music, particularly by British composers, and sponsors concerts, competitions and festivals. Independent television companies make grants for the promotion of the arts in their regions, particularly to regional arts associations, and transmit general magazine programmes on the arts. Both the BBC and IBA broadcast a wide range of new drama together with adaptations of novels and stage plays. They also screen a variety of feature films including British and overseas productions.

Local Support   Local authorities support the arts in many ways. In addition to their responsibilities for education (including specialised art education) and the public library service, many provide and maintain local museums and art galleries. In Great Britain the authorities have power to incur expenditure on entertainment in all its forms (including cultural activities). Many authorities make contributions to regional arts associations and towards the expenses of professional symphony orchestras and local theatre companies. Grants are often made towards the capital cost of new arts buildings, especially theatres; the Greater

London Council, for example, made a substantial contribution towards the cost of the new National Theatre.

Private Contributions

Valuable support for the arts comes from many voluntary sources including charitable trusts and foundations, and supporters' organisations of the major national institutions. Industrial and commercial concerns provide a certain amount of patronage, and an Association for Business Sponsorship of the Arts has been formed to advise interested companies. Sponsorship may take the form of grants to regional arts associations, local arts festivals and orchestras; and donations towards individual cultural events. Tax advantages and exemptions are available to encourage such support.

Regional Arts

The Government encourages regional co-operation in arts patronage through 15 regional arts associations in England and Wales whose aim it is to ensure that the whole range of the arts is more widely available to people throughout their areas. They can offer financial assistance to local and other regional arts organisations and advise on and promote all sorts of local arts activities. They are financed by a combination of local authority, Arts Council and private funds; local authorities and a wide range of other interests are represented on the associations. Other examples of co-operative patronage are the orchestra boards which support symphony and chamber orchestras and the societies formed to present some of the many arts festivals in Britain.

Festivals

Considerable interest and enthusiasm is shown for more than 200 professional arts festivals which take place each year. Most are subsidised by a combination of local authority, regional arts association and private funds, while the major ones receive Arts Council assistance. Some arts festivals concentrate particularly on music. These include: the Three Choirs Festival which has taken place annually for about 250 years in Gloucester, Worcester or Hereford, the Cheltenham Festival which is largely devoted to contemporary British music, and the Aldeburgh and English Bach festivals. Others cater for a number of art forms; among the better known are the Edinburgh International Festival, the Royal National Eisteddfod of Wales, and those held in the City of London, Bath, Brighton, Malvern, Harrogate, Chichester, Windsor and York. A festival is held in Belfast under the auspices of the Queen's University.

Arts Centres

There are more than 150 arts centres and the number is increasing steadily. They provide opportunities for enjoyment of and participation in the arts. The centres are supported mainly by regional arts associations and local authorities with some help from the Arts Council and other organisations. They may be small centres for amateur activities or they may offer a professional programme. A growing number of theatres and art galleries also provide a focal point for the community by offering facilities for other arts.

DRAMA

Britain is one of the world's major theatre centres. In London during the summer season, theatres are packed with overseas visitors, while in the provinces there is growing support for the work of regional theatres. From what was once called the 'fringe' theatre, and was based on London, a network of informal touring companies has developed, which visit many of the new arts centres and community festivals.

Support for much of this development in British drama comes jointly from the Government, through the Arts Councils of Great Britain and Northern Ireland, from local authorities and regional arts associations, and from some private sponsorship. In particular the Arts Council assists developments in new drama by encouraging co-operation between theatres and playwrights by means of bursaries, commissions and guaranteed royalties. Schemes are also in operation to train stage designers, directors, technicians, actors and those wishing to take up theatre administration.

Professional Theatre

Over 250 theatres in professional use in Britain can accommodate more than 200 people. Some are owned or rented by non-profit-distributing companies, the majority of which are receiving Arts Council subsidies, while the remainder are operated commercially or are owned by local authorities.

London is the centre of theatrical activity with some 40 principal theatres in or near the centre and eight in the suburbs. Most of the theatres are let to producing managements on a commercial basis but four are occupied by major subsidised companies, including the National Theatre which stages classical and modern plays from various countries in its three auditoria on the south bank of the River Thames, and the Royal Shakespeare Company which presents Shakespearean plays at Stratford-upon-Avon and a mixed repertoire in London.

Outside London there are a number of theatres which accommodate pre- and post-West End tours of the major London productions and performances by companies specially formed for touring. (Both the National Theatre and Royal Shakespeare companies have toured in Britain and overseas.) A decline in the number of these theatres has been stemmed in response to the demand by audiences outside London for the larger opera, dance and drama companies. Some theatres have been purchased by local authorities. Many non-repertory theatres outside London present all kinds of drama and many also put on variety shows and other entertainments. There has, however, been a growth in the activities of almost 50 resident theatre companies which receive financial support from the Arts Council and the local authorities. These companies employ leading producers, designers and actors, and standards are high. Some companies have their own theatres, others rent from local authorities.

There is no censorship of plays, but the Theatres Act 1968 makes it an offence to present or direct an obscene performance of a play in public or in private (including theatre clubs), an obscene performance being defined as one which tends to 'deprave and corrupt persons who are likely . . . to attend it'. Provision is made for a defence against an obscenity charge on the grounds that the performance is for the public good in the interests of, for example, drama, opera or literature.

Amateur Theatre

There are several thousand amateur dramatic societies in Britain; they are encouraged by local education authorities, by other public bodies, and by four special organisations—the British Theatre Association, the National Drama Conference, the Scottish Community Drama Association and the Association of Ulster Drama Festivals. Most universities have active amateur drama clubs and societies; an International Festival of University Theatre is held annually.

Dramatic Training

Training for the theatre is provided mainly in drama schools. Among the most important are the Royal Academy of Dramatic Art, the Central School of Speech and Drama, the London Academy of Music and Dramatic Art, and the Guildhall School of Music and Drama, all of which are in London; and the Old Vic School in Bristol. There is the Royal Scottish Academy of Music and Drama in Glasgow; and in Cardiff, the Welsh College of Music and Drama. Several universities offer major courses in drama.

Theatre for Young People

Theatre for young people has increasing importance. In 1970 the Young Vic was opened as a theatre for young people, the National Youth Theatre has a base in London, and the Scottish Youth Theatre was established in 1970. There are some ten specialist companies, including the Unicorn Theatre for Young People, Theatre Centre and the Polka Company, some of which are supported by the Arts Council. Outside London about 35 repertory companies provide programmes and engage in other types of theatre activity for young people. In Northern Ireland a company called Interplay Theatre, which is sponsored and administered by the Arts Council of Northern Ireland, works mainly in schools.

Most of the many amateur youth theatres in Britain are supported by local authorities. Many schools and youth clubs put on plays and provide some education in drama. The London education service provides special drama centres for young people.

MUSIC, OPERA AND DANCE

Music plays an important role in British cultural life. Pop music, folk music, jazz, light music and brass bands all have substantial followings while the widespread interest in classical music is reflected in the large audiences at choral and orchestral concerts and at performances of opera, dance and chamber music.

The Arts Councils provide subsidies for orchestras, opera and dance companies, music societies and festivals. They also provide bursaries and commissions for composers, musicians, designers and choreographers. The Master of the Queen's Music holds an office within the Royal Household, and whose responsibility includes organising and writing music for state occasions.

Music

Seasons of orchestral concerts are promoted every year in many of the large towns and cities. In central London the principal concert halls are the Royal Festival Hall, adjacent to which are the Queen Elizabeth Hall and the Purcell Room which accommodate smaller-scale performances; the Royal Albert Hall, where the annual summer season of Promenade Concerts is given; the Wigmore Hall, a recital centre; and St John's, Smith Square.

Orchestras

The leading symphony orchestras are the London Philharmonic, the London Symphony, the Philharmonia, the Royal Philharmonic, the Royal Liverpool Philharmonic, the Hallé (Manchester), the City of Birmingham Symphony, the Bournemouth Symphony, the Ulster and the Scottish National. The BBC runs a number of orchestras, including four symphony orchestras, providing broadcast concerts which are often open to the public. There are also specialised string and chamber orchestras such as the English Chamber Orchestra, the Academy of St Martin-in-the-Fields, the London Mozart Players, the Bournemouth Sinfonietta, the Northern Sinfonia (Newcastle upon Tyne), the Scottish Philharmonic, the Scottish Baroque Ensemble and the Scottish Chamber Orchestra. Most orchestras (other than those of the BBC) receive financial aid from the Arts Councils, local authorities and industrial sources.

Choral Societies

Among the principal choral societies are the Bach Choir, the Swansea Philharmonic Choir, the Edinburgh Royal Choral Union and the Belfast Philharmonic Society. Almost all the leading orchestras have their own choirs, but they also combine with others in major choral works. The majority of choral societies are affiliated to the National Federation of Music Societies.

Amateur Interest

Interest in amateur music-making is encouraged by the work of County Music Committees (some of which are voluntary and some sub-committees of local education authorities), which are aided by the Carnegie United Kingdom

Trust and united in the Standing Conference for Amateur Music. The National Federation of Music Societies, the organisation for chamber music societies, amateur choirs and amateur orchestras, receives an annual grant from the Arts Council to assist affiliated societies with the cost of engaging professional soloists. Over 1,100 music societies are members of the Federation, which advises them on concert planning and promotion. The Welsh Amateur Music Federation, funded by the Welsh Arts Council, assists amateur music-making activities in Wales.

Opera and Dance

Regular seasons of opera and ballet are given at the Royal Opera House, Covent Garden, London, which receives financial assistance from the Arts Council and from private and business sponsorship. The Royal Opera House has a permanent orchestra which plays for the Royal Opera and the Royal Ballet. Both organisations have a high international reputation and make overseas tours. Seasons of opera and operetta in English are given by the English National Opera which plays in the London Coliseum, and makes provincial tours supplemented by the English National Opera based at Leeds. Sadler's Wells Theatre provides for the London performances of visiting opera and dance companies and for the Sadler's Wells Royal Ballet. The Scottish Opera has regular winter seasons at its permanent home, the Theatre Royal in Glasgow, and tours Scotland and northern England.

Opera Groups

At Glyndebourne, in Sussex, an opera season, for which international casts are specially assembled, is held every summer, followed by an autumn tour by Glyndebourne Touring Opera with different casts. Other opera companies include Kent Opera, the English Music Theatre Company which specialises in the performance of works by British composers, the New Opera Company which is associated with the English National Opera, and the Welsh National Opera Company. Opera in Northern Ireland is promoted by the Northern Ireland Opera Trust and the Studio Opera Group.

Dance Companies

Dance companies also include London Festival Ballet, Ballet Rambert (Britain's oldest ballet company, which re-formed in 1966 as a leading modern dance company), Scottish Ballet, London Contemporary Dance Theatre (which provides regular seasons of contemporary dance in London besides touring extensively) and Northern Ballet Theatre (which concentrates its activities in the north of England, although it makes periodic tours elsewhere). Many small modern groups also give performances.

Training in Music, Opera and Dance

Professional training in music is given at colleges of music, of which the Royal Academy of Music, the Royal College of Music and Trinity College of Music in London, and the Royal Scottish Academy of Music and Drama in Glasgow are grant-aided. Other leading colleges include the Guidhall School of Music and Drama in London, the Royal Northern College of Music in Manchester and the Birmingham School of Music. The National Opera Studio provides advanced training courses. The leading dance schools are the Royal Ballet School, the Rambert School of Ballet and the London School of Contemporary Dance which, with many private schools, have helped in raising British dance to its present high standard.

A Youth and Music organisation, affiliated to the international *Jeunesses Musicales*, encourages attendances by young people at opera, dance and concert performances. The Royal Ballet's work includes a small group, Ballet for All, which offers an introduction to ballet to the public and to schools. Educational Dance Drama Theatre and Dance for Everyone receive financial support for their work with young people.

Many children learn to play musical instruments at school, and some take the examinations of the Associated Board of the Royal Schools of Music. The National Youth Orchestra of Great Britain, the National Youth Orchestra of Wales and other youth orchestras are noted for their high standards. Almost a third of the players in the European Community Youth Orchestra come from Britain.

FILMS

British films, actors and the creative and technical services which support them have achieved successes at international film festivals and other events. Cinema and television films are exported to most countries of the world.

There are about 1,500 cinema screens in Great Britain, and estimated attendance in 1977 amounted to 107 million. Cinema attendance figures have been declining since the mid-1950s as television has become generally accessible. In 1953 the average weekly cinema audience was some 25 million; by 1977 it was just over 2 million.

An Interim Action Committee is studying the future of the film industry. Among the ideas being considered are the establishment of a British Film Authority and additional help for the industry.

The Government does not invest directly in films but the National Film Finance Corporation lends money for feature film production from capital advanced by the Government and private interests. The Corporation also administers the National Film Development Fund which provides loans for script-writing and other pre-production costs.

A levy on cinema admissions, known as the Eady Levy, provides a fund, administered by the British Film Fund Agency, to benefit the makers of eligible films. Subject to the approval of the Secretary of State for Trade, grants from the levy can be made to the Children's Film Foundation, to the British Film Institue Production Board, the National Film School, and the National Film Finance Corporation. The rest of the fund is distributed to makers of eligible films in proportion to a film's takings.

A specified proportion of British or European Community films must be shown in British cinemas each year. For main feature films the quota is 30 per cent and for supporting programmes 25 per cent.

Cinema Licensing and Film Censorship

Local authorities are the only public authorities with powers to license cinemas and censor films. They have a legal duty to prohibit the admission of children under the age of 16 to unsuitable films, and may also exercise censorship over films for adults. In considering the suitability of films the authorities normally rely on the judgment of an independent body, the British Board of Film Censors, to which most films for public showing (other than newsreels) are submitted.

The British Board of Film Censors was set up in 1912, on the initiative of the cinema industry, to ensure that a proper standard was maintained in the films offered to the public. The board, which does not use any written code of censorship, may require cuts to be made before granting a certificate to a film; very rarely, it refuses a certificate. Films passed by the board are placed into one of four categories: 'U' (for general exhibition); 'A' (for general exhibition but parents are advised that the film contains material which they may not wish children under the age of 14 years to see); 'AA' (for persons of not less than 14 years of age); and 'X' (for persons of not less than 18 years of age).

Documentary Films

The documentary tradition in short film production in Britain goes back to 1929, when a group of directors began making factual films of a distinctive and imaginative kind on behalf of the Government, and later for commercial organisations. The war years saw a big expansion in this field and, since then, British documentary technicians have continued to produce, for both cinema and television, high quality factual films which have won numerous international awards. The British Industrial and Scientific Film Association promotes the use of films in industry, science and commerce. The Federation of Specialised Film Associations is the trade association of documentary, short, industrial, advertising and cartoon film makers. The National Panel for Film Festivals, under the aegis of the British Council, is responsible for the selection of British entries for international short and documentary film festivals.

The Government sponsors a wide range of films for use in Britain and overseas, including documentary films, television programmes and newsreels. They are produced through the Central Office of Information (COI), which commissions their production by private companies.

A large number of films are sponsored by industrial concerns and other organisations, such as the British Tourist Authority and the British Productivity Council. The best are available through the COI's Central Film Library and other agencies. The Films of Scotland Committee promotes the production of films covering the industries and cultural traditions of Scotland.

Children's Films

Cinemas which give children's shows require a special licence from local authorities which may impose conditions. There are about 470 children's cinema clubs which provide special programmes on Saturday mornings. An important contribution to these programmes is made by the Children's Film Foundation, which, with the aid of grants from the British Film Fund Agency, produces and distributes entertainment films specially designed for children.

British Film Institute

The development of the film and television as an art is promoted by the British Film Institute, founded in 1933, which is financed mainly by an Exchequer grant, and by the Scottish Council for Educational Technology which also receives a government grant. The Institute offers financial and technical assistance to both new and experienced film makers who cannot find support elsewhere. The Institute administers the National Film Theatre in London and the National Film Archive and maintains a film library from which films may be hired, a library of scripts and books on the film and television, a British National Film Catalogue recording all non-fiction and short films available in Britain, and an information service. It makes grants to the Federation of Film Societies, the British Universities Film Council and the Society for Education in Film and Television.

The Institute's Educational Advisory Service offers guidance to teachers in formal education at all levels on film and television courses, and its Editorial Department produces a range of publications including a critical journal *Sight and Sound* and the *Monthly Film Bulletin*.

The National Film Archive contains about 25,000 films, including newsreels and other miscellaneous items, and 3,725 television programmes, besides art designs, posters and over 1 million photographic stills, selected to illustrate the history and the art of the film and as social and historical records.

The National Film Theatre has two cinemas showing films of outstanding historical, artistic or technical interest. It is unique as a cinema offering regular programmes unrestricted by commercial considerations or by the age or nationality of the films shown. Each year it organises a London Film Festival. The British Film Institute has promoted the development of some 50 regional film theatres on the lines of the National Film Theatre and may make grants towards their costs. In Scotland the Scottish Film Council, as a committee of the Scottish Council for Educational Technology, is responsible for regional film theatres and administers the Scottish Central Film Library. Grants in Northern Ireland are made by the Arts Council of Northern Ireland.

Training in Film Production

An independent National Film School offers three-year courses for writers, directors, producers and cameramen. The school, which is financed by grants from the Department of Education and Science and the British Film Fund Agency, has about 75 students. Training in film production is also given at the London International Film School which has some 150 students, and at some polytechnics and other institutions of further education.

VISUAL ARTS

A number of modern British painters and sculptors have a high international reputation, and have received many international prizes and commissions for major works in foreign cities. The growth of interest in the visual arts at home has been stimulated by improved methods of display by museums and galleries, and by the activities of many institutions, societies, private galleries and the growing number of local arts centres.

State support for painting and sculpture mainly takes the form of maintenance and purchase grants for the national museums and galleries, purchase grants for municipal museums and galleries, and grants towards the cost of local education authority art education. The Government also encourages high standards of industrial design and craftsmanship through grants to the Design Council.

In addition to direct state assistance, the Arts Council runs the Hayward Gallery in London, where major loan exhibitions are shown, and the Serpentine Gallery, which mainly presents the work of young artists. The council also maintains its own collection of contemporary British art, and organises or offers grants or guarantees towards a variety of touring and other exhibitions. It also supports art societies and independent galleries, and provides commissions and awards for artists. The Scottish and Welsh Arts Councils maintain galleries in Edinburgh, Glasgow, and Cardiff respectively, and the Northern Ireland Arts Council owns a gallery in Belfast.

The Art Market

London is a major centre for the international art market and regular sales of works of art take place in the main auction houses. Certain items are covered by export control: these are works of art and other antiques over 100 years old and worth more than £4,000; documentary and photographic material over 70 years old; and British archaeological material over 100 years old. A licence is required before such items can be exported but this is granted automatically in the case of objects imported into Britain within the last 50 years. In other cases the application for a licence is considered by the Department of Trade, and if the department's expert advisers recommend the withholding of a licence, the matter is referred to the Reviewing Committee on the Export of Works of Art. If the committee regards a work to be of national importance it can advise the Government to withhold the export licence for a specified time to enable a public museum or art gallery to purchase the object at a fair price.

Museums and Art Galleries

Over 950 museums and art galleries are open to the public including the major national collections and a wide variety of municipally and independently owned institutions.

An increasing number of people visit major national art galleries and museums (about 23·3 million in 1977 compared with 16·2 million in 1971).

National
Collections

Of the national museums and art galleries, those in London contain between them one of the most comprehensive collections of objects of artistic, archaeological, scientific, historical and general interest ever to exist within one city. They are the British Museum, the Victoria and Albert Museum, the National Gallery, the Tate Gallery, the National Portrait Gallery, the Imperial War Museum, the National Army Museum, the Royal Air Force Museum, the National Maritime Museum, the Museum of London, the Wallace Collection, the British Museum (Natural History), the Geological Museum and the Science Museum.

There are three national museums and art galleries in Edinburgh: the National Museum of Antiquities of Scotland, the Royal Scottish Museum (including the Scottish United Services Museum), and the National Galleries of Scotland (comprising the National Gallery of Scotland, the Scottish National Portrait Gallery, and the Scottish National Gallery of Modern Art). The National Museum of Wales, in Cardiff, has a branch at St. Fagan's Castle where the Welsh Folk Museum is housed and has recently opened an Industrial and Maritime Museum in Cardiff's dockland. In Northern Ireland there are two national museums: the Ulster Museum in Belfast and the Ulster Folk and Transport Museum, County Down.

Some national museums have also opened branches outside the capital cities, an example being the National Railway Museum at York which is administered by the Science Museum.

Most of the national collections are administered by trustee bodies, but the Victoria and Albert and Science Museums are the responsibility of the Department of Education and Science; the Royal Scottish Museum has a similar relationship with the Scottish Education Department.

Other Collections

Other important collections in London include the Armouries (housed in the Tower of London), the Public Record Office and the Sir John Soane's Museum. In Buckingham Palace the Queen's Gallery has exhibitions of pictures from the extensive royal collections.

Most cities and towns have a museum devoted to art, archaeology and natural history, usually owned by the local authority but sometimes by a local learned society or by individuals or trustees. Both Oxford and Cambridge are rich in museums, many of them associated with the universities (for example, the Ashmolean Museum in Oxford, founded in 1683, the oldest in the country, and the Fitzwilliam Museum in Cambridge). There are important museums and art galleries in Aberdeen, Belfast, Birmingham, Bristol, Cardiff, Dundee, Glasgow, Leeds, Leicester, Liverpool, Manchester, Norwich, Reading, Sheffield, Southampton and York. Many private art collections housed in historic family mansions, including those owned by the National Trust, are open to the public. An increasing number of open air museums depict the regional life of an area or preserve early industrial remains (for example, the Weald and Downland Museum in Sussex, the North of England Open Air Museum in Durham, and the Ironbridge Gorge Museum in Salop which won the first European Museum of the Year Award in 1978).

Finance

All national collections are financed chiefly from government funds. Besides meeting administrative and maintenance costs, the Government provides annual purchase grants (£6·5 million in 1978–79). It also provides special purchase grants. Pre-eminent works of art accepted by the Government in place of capital transfer tax are allocated to public collections.

Local museums and art galleries, which are maintained from rates or endowments, receive help in building up their collections through the annual government grant administered by the Victoria and Albert, Science and Royal Scottish Museums. Financial and practical assistance is also given to museums and galleries by trusts and voluntary bodies, including the Calouste Gulbenkian Foundation, the National Art Collections Fund, the Contemporary Art Society and the Association for Business Sponsorship of the Arts.

Policy and Co-ordination

The Government is advised on policy matters by the Standing Commission on Museums and Galleries, which also promotes co-operation between national and provincial institutions. Eight area museum councils, grant-aided by the Government, provide technical services and advice on conservation, display, documentation, publicity and other matters.

The Museums Association, to which museums and art galleries and their staffs throughout the country belong and which also has many overseas members, is an independent organisation. It serves as a central body for the collection of information and discussion of matters relating to museum administration, and as a training and examining body for professional qualifications.

Exhibitions

Temporary exhibitions provided by the Arts Councils, the national museums and galleries, the Art Exhibitions Bureau and the area museum councils are a regular feature of many museums. In London the Hayward Gallery, the Tate Gallery, the British Museum, the Victoria and Albert Museum and the Royal Academy are the main centres for loan exhibitions; these are also held at the Whitechapel Art Gallery, the Camden Arts Centre and the Institute of Contemporary Arts. Commercial exhibitions are held in the galleries of the London dealers. The Serpentine Gallery in London's Kensington Gardens houses Arts Council exhibitions of contemporary artists, and another small gallery in London is run by the Crafts Advisory Committee.

There are a number of national art exhibiting societies, some of which, notably the Royal Academy at Burlington House, have their own galleries in London. The Royal Scottish Academy holds annual exhibitions in Edinburgh. An increasing number of amateur art societies throughout Britain hold local exhibitions and encourage local interest in the fine arts. There are also children's exhibitions, including the National Exhibition of Children's Art.

Training in Arts and Design

Art and design education is provided in maintained colleges of art, further education colleges and polytechnics, which are administered by local education authorities. Other institutions offering art and design courses include universities, the Royal Academy Schools and some private art schools. At postgraduate level there is the Royal College of Art which awards its own degrees. Art is also taught at an advanced level at the four Scottish Central (Art) Institutions administered by the Scottish Education Department.

The leading academic institutions for the study of the history of art are the Courtauld Institute of the University of London, the Department of Classical Art and Archaeology in University College, London, and the Warburg Institute, also a part of London University.

Art has a place in all school curricula, and the Society for Education through Art encourages, among other activities, the purchase by schools of original works of art by organising an annual Pictures for Schools exhibition. Pictures may also be borrowed from many public libraries.

Crafts

Government grants for the crafts, amounting to some £840,000 in 1978–79, are administered in England and Wales by the Crafts Advisory Committee. Set up in 1971 to advise the minister responsible for the arts on the needs of artist-craftsmen, the committee also promotes exhibitions of work and gives financial assistance to enable craftsmen to be trained and to establish or expand their businesses. Its activities include crafts associated with conservation and renovation. Scotland receives a separate government grant which is similarly administered by the Joint Crafts Committee.

Architecture Official responsibility towards the nation's architecture is concerned mainly with encouraging the best in new building and conserving the best that has been inherited from the past (for conservation, see p 162).

Several government departments, notably the Department of the Environment, provide advice on building and architecture. In collaboration with the Royal Institute of British Architects, the Secretary of State for the Environment makes annual awards for good housing design in both the public and private sectors. Royal Fine Art Commissions for England and Wales and for Scotland advise the departments, planning authorities and other public bodies on questions of public amenity or artistic importance.

The Royal Institute of British Architects is the leading professional institution with a membership of 20,750 in Britain and 5,850 overseas. It exercises control over standards in architectural education, and maintains one of the largest architectural libraries in the world. The Royal Incorporation of Architects in Scotland is allied to it.

Other bodies with an interest in architecture include the Civic Trust (see p 172) which seeks to promote high standards in civic building and planning, and the National Trust (see p 172) which acquires land and buildings in order to protect them for the benefit of the public from harmful development. The number of people visiting National Trust properties rose from just over a million in 1960 to more than 5 million in 1977.

LITERATURE AND LIBRARIES The study of literature is included in the curricula of all schools, colleges and universities. There are free public libraries throughout the country, private libraries and a large number of private literary societies. Book reviews are featured in the press and on television and radio and there are numerous periodicals concerned with literature. Recognition of outstanding literary merit is provided by a number of awards, including the Booker, W. H. Smith & Son, and Whitbread prizes. Awards to encourage young writers are made, for instance, by the Somerset Maugham Trust Fund and the E. C. Gregory Trust Fund.

Government help is given through the Arts Councils which support literature in a number of ways, including grants awarded to writers, translators, publishers, little presses and magazines. The title, Poet Laureate, is conferred on a poet who receives a stipend as an officer of the Royal Household.

Literary and Philological Societies Societies for the promotion of literature include the English Association and the Royal Society of Literature. The British Academy for the Promotion of Historical, Philosophical and Philological Studies (known as the British Academy) is the leading society of humanistic studies and receives a government grant.

Other specialist societies include the Early English Text Society, the Bibliographical Society, the Harleian Society, the Saltire Society, and several societies devoted to particular authors of which the largest is the Dickens Fellowship. A number of societies sponsor poetry readings and recitals, among which the Poetry Society and the Apollo Society are the best known. There are also a number of clubs and societies, such as the New Fiction Society and the Poetry Book Society, which distribute selected new books to their members.

Books

In 1977 British publishers issued 36,000 separate titles: more than 27,000 new ones, and over 8,000 reprints and new editions. An increasing proportion of books—including specialised non-fiction—is sold in paperback form. Book clubs make available hardback books at a lower price.

Leading organisations representing the interests of those concerned with book production and distribution are the Publishers' Association and the Booksellers' Association. The British Council also publicises British books and periodicals through its libraries in over 60 countries, its programme of book exhibitions (263 exhibitions were mounted in 1977–78) and its bibliographical publications including the monthly *British Book News*. The Book Development Council promotes British books overseas. (For sales and exports of books in 1977 see p 232). The National Book League has a membership including authors, publishers, booksellers, librarians and readers. It encourages an interest in books and arranges exhibitions in Britain and overseas.

Libraries

The British Library, created in 1973 from a merger of the British Museum Library with other libraries and institutions, is organised in three divisions. The Reference Division includes the Department of Printed Books holding nearly 10 million titles, the Department of Manuscripts, the Department of Oriental Manuscripts and Printed Books, and the Science Reference Library. The Lending Division at Boston Spa, West Yorkshire, has nearly 2·9 million volumes including some 47,000 current periodicals available on loan to other libraries in Britain and overseas. It also has access to many millions of books in other libraries and is the national centre for inter-library lending within Britain and between Britain and foreign countries. The Bibliographic Services Division processes the acquisitions of the British Library for inclusion in its catalogues and provides other bibliographic services; it publishes the *British National Bibliography* which lists in a classified order (with indexes) all new books and new editions, excluding reprints, published in Britain. The British Library automatically receives a copy of each new book, pamphlet or newspaper published in Britain. In addition the National Library of Scotland, the National Library of Wales, the Bodleian Library of Oxford University and the Cambridge University Library are entitled to claim copies. The Government has announced plans to start work on a new building for the British Library in London during 1979–80. When completed the building will cater for about 3,500 readers, will carry a stock of 25 million books and have a staff of some 2,500. The building will cover 3·80 hectares (9·5 acres). The first stage will take about ten years to complete and will cost an estimated £77 million.

London's Victoria and Albert Museum and Natural History Museum, correctly known as the British Museum (Natural History), also have large libraries and many government departments have old-established libraries of considerable size and importance. The Public Record Office contains the records of the superior courts of law and of most government departments, as well as such famous historical documents as Domesday Book. In Scotland, the Scottish Record Office serves the same purposes. The National Register of Archives (maintained by the Historical Manuscripts Commission) contains particulars of local and private records.

Besides the few great private collections, such as those of the Signet Library, Edinburgh, and the London Library, there are the rich resources of the learned societies and institutions (for scientific societies and institutions, see p 383). Examples are the libraries of the Royal Institute of International Affairs, the Royal Commonwealth Society, the Royal Geographical Society, the Royal

Society of Edinburgh, the British Theatre Association, the Royal Academy of Music, the National Library for the Blind and the National Book League.

Many libraries have collections of records and musical scores for loan to the public. The City of Westminster houses the Central Music Library which lends to other libraries and to individuals. Another well-known collection is the Henry Watson Music Library at the Manchester Central Library.

Libraries in Education

The ancient university libraries of Oxford and Cambridge are not matched by any of the more recent foundations, although the combined library resources of the colleges and institutions of the University of London total some 5·5 million volumes, the John Rylands University Library in Manchester contains some 2 million volumes, and the university libraries of Edinburgh and Glasgow have over 1 million volumes each, while Birmingham, Leeds, Liverpool and St Andrews each has over 750,000 volumes. Many universities have built up large and important research collections in special subjects; for example, the Barnes Medical Library at Birmingham, and the British Library of Political and Economic Science at the London School of Economics. Other universities and the polytechnics are also building collections.

The importance of good libraries is recognised at all levels of the education system. School libraries, most of which are maintained by local education authorities, often receive important support services from the public library service, including loans of books.

Public Libraries

Britain is served by a network of public libraries, administered by local public library authorities. These libraries have a total stock of some 114 million books (not including the libraries in publicly maintained schools).

Qualified and specialist staff are available for consultation in all but the smallest service points. About one-third of the total population are members of public libraries. The Secretary of State for Education and Science is responsible for the supervision of the public library service in England and is advised by the Library Advisory Council for England. The Secretary of State for Wales has similar responsibility in Wales and is advised by the Library Advisory Council for Wales. Public library authorities in England and Wales have a duty to provide an efficient and (with some limitations) free lending and reference library service of books and periodicals. They maintain nearly 5,000 public library service points; some areas may be served by mobile libraries, of which almost 600 are in service, and domiciliary services exist for people who are unable to visit a library. In Scotland local authorities have a duty to provide library facilities, and similar duties are imposed on education and library boards in Northern Ireland.

In addition to lending books, most library authorities now lend gramophone records of various kinds and a number also lend from collections of works of art, either originals or reproductions. Nearly all libraries provide children's departments, while reference sections and art, music, commercial and technical departments meet the growing and more specific demands in these fields. Most libraries possess a significant collection of books and documents on the history of their localities.

The public library is often a centre for local cultural activities. Film shows, lectures, adult education classes, book-week exhibitions, drama groups, gramophone recitals and children's story hours are among the many activities provided by or based upon the local library.

A voluntary system of library co-operation in England and Wales has grown up since the first quarter of this century. The eight regional library bureaux in

England and Wales (consisting mainly of public libraries in each area) aim to be largely self-sufficient in the interlending of current British books, achieved in some regions by a system of co-operative subject specialisation. The British Library is responsible for national and international inter-library lending.

A number of local schemes for the exchange of specialist titles and information involve industrial, commercial and sometimes university libraries, and are normally centred on a major public or technical college library.

The National Library of Scotland and the National Library of Wales carry out functions similar to those of the regional bureaux and the lending division of the British Library. In Northern Ireland access to the stocks of all co-operating libraries is available on application to the libraries under the control of the five education and library boards and to the Queen's University and New University of Ulster libraries.

Library
Associations

The principal professional organisation is the Library Association. It maintains a Register of Chartered Librarians, publishes books, pamphlets and official journals, and holds regular conferences. There are also associations of libraries, for example, the Association of Special Libraries and Information Bureaux and the Standing Conference of National and University Libraries.

21 The Press

More daily newspapers, national and regional, are sold per person in Britain than in most other countries. Despite a slight long-term decline in national newspaper sales, some papers have circulations comparable with the largest in the world. National papers have a total circulation of about 14 million on weekdays and 19 million on Sundays, and a total readership nearly three times greater.

The press caters for a variety of political views, interests and levels of education. It is subject neither to state control nor to censorship.

Although pronounced views may be expressed in some newspapers and their political leanings may be obvious, they are almost always financially independent of any political party and are not obliged to follow any specific party line. In order to preserve their character and traditions, a few newspapers and periodicals are governed by arrangements which vest ownership of the undertaking in trustees, or operate it in accordance with a deed of trust, or provide that the transfer of shares be controlled by trustees. Others have management arrangements to ensure editors' authority and independence.

Unlike most of its European counterparts the British press receives no subsidies and relatively few tax and postal concessions. Newspaper and magazine sales and advertising receipts are zero-rated for value-added tax purposes. Registered newspapers receive a concession on postal rates, and there are concessions on 'per-word' rates for international press telegrams and phototelegrams. In common with all postal customers, newspaper and magazine publishers can obtain reduced charges for regular bulk postings.

About 130 daily (Monday to Saturday) and Sunday newspapers and over 1,000 weekly newspapers are published. These figures include certain specialised papers with circulations limited not by region but by interest; for instance, business newspapers, sporting newspapers, newspapers in foreign languages for people of other countries resident in Britain and religious newspapers. Newsprint forms roughly a third of average national newspaper costs. Three-quarters of Britain's requirements are imported.

A Royal Commission on the Press reported in 1976 on the economic problems of the national newspaper industry, recommending investment in new equipment and rationalisation of the use of manpower. The Royal Commission's final report in 1977 covered the press as a whole and made recommendations on a wide range of matters, including editorial standards, concentration of ownership, industrial relations, the economics of the press, the training of journalists and the role of the Press Council. The Royal Commission's reports are listed in the Bibliography (see p 453).

Ownership

Newspaper ownership, as it affects the national, London-evening and regional daily newspapers, is concentrated mainly in the hands of a comparatively small number of large press publishing groups (see, for example, the details of the groups controlling the national press which are given in Table 33).

Although most enterprises are organised as limited liability companies, individual and partner proprietorship survives. The large national newspaper and periodical publishers are major corporations with diversified interests over the whole field of publishing and communications; some have shares in independent television and radio contracting companies; and others are involved in industrial and commercial activities which have no connection with publishing or the mass media.

The law provides safeguards against the risks inherent in undue concentration of the means of communication. For instance, if it appears that newspaper shareholdings in television programme companies have led or are leading to results which are contrary to the public interest, the Independent Broadcasting Authority may, with the consent of the Home Secretary, notify the companies that their programmes may cease to be transmitted. There is a similar stipulation for independent local radio; if a local newspaper has a monopoly in the area, it is not allowed to have a controlling interest in the local radio station. In addition, it is unlawful to transfer a newspaper or newspaper assets to a proprietor whose newspapers have an average daily circulation amounting, with that of the newspaper to be taken over, to 500,000 or more copies unless the Secretary of State for Prices and Consumer Protection gives written consent. Except in certain limited cases, which include transfers of very small newspapers, consent may be given only after the Secretary of State has referred the matter to the Monopolies and Mergers Commission and received its report.

The 'National' Press

Nine morning daily papers and seven Sunday papers (see Table 33) circulate throughout the country, and are known as national newspapers. All are produced in London (where Fleet Street is the traditional centre for the press), but five of the dailies and four of the Sundays also print northern editions in Manchester (accounting for about a quarter of the total production of the national press). Prices of the national newspapers vary from 7p to 15p for the dailies and 12p to 22p for the Sundays.

The leading Scottish papers, *The Scotsman* and the *Glasgow Herald,* have a considerable circulation outside Scotland. Each of London's two evening papers has a distinctive style and draws its readership from a wide area, but both have ownership affiliations with a national daily (see Table 33).

National newspapers are often divided into 'quality' and 'popular' papers on the basis of differences in format (broadsheet or tabloid, though this is not a rigid distinction), style and content. Four dailies and three Sundays are usually described as quality newspapers. The three Sunday qualities produce colour supplements which are distributed as part of the paper.

The slight long-term decline in newspaper circulations conceals the different experiences of individual papers and the fact that, while the circulation of the popular press as a whole has declined over the years, that of the quality press has generally remained steady.

English Regional Newspapers

The regional newspapers of England (outside London, 78 morning or evening dailies and Sundays and some 700 newspapers appearing once or twice a week) provide mainly regional and local news. The daily newspapers also give coverage to national affairs, and a number co-operate to provide their own foreign news service.

Generally speaking, regional evening newspapers are non-political, while the morning newspapers adopt a more positive political stance and tend to be independent or conservative in outlook.

The total circulation of the regional morning and evening papers is estimated at over 6 million. Of the morning papers the *Yorkshire Post* (Leeds) and the *Northern Echo* (Darlington) have circulations of over 100,000 and two provincial Sunday papers—the *Sunday Sun* (Newcastle upon Tyne) and the *Sunday Mercury* (Birmingham)—have circulations of over 160,000 and 200,000 respectively. Individual circulation figures of regional evening papers start at about 15,000; most are in the 30,000–100,000 range, although the *Manchester Evening News* and the *Birmingham Evening Mail* have circulations

TABLE 33: National and London-Evening Newspapers

Title and foundation date	Controlled by	Circulation[a] average Jan.–June 1978
NATIONAL MORNINGS		
'Populars'		
Daily Express (1900)	Trafalgar House Ltd[b]	2,400,907
Daily Mail (1896)	Associated Newspapers Group Ltd	1,932,808
Daily Mirror (1903)	Reed International Ltd	3,778,038
Morning Star (1966)	The People's Press Printing Society Ltd	35,463
The Sun (1969)	News International Ltd	3,930,554
'Qualities'		
The Daily Telegraph (1855)	The Daily Telegraph Ltd	1,344,968
Financial Times (1888)	Pearson Longman Ltd	180,793
The Guardian (1821)	The Guardian and Manchester Evening News Ltd	273,201
The Times (1785)	The Thomson Organisation Ltd	293,989
NATIONAL SUNDAYS		
'Populars'		
News of the World (1843)	News International Ltd	4,934,532
The Sunday People (1881)	Reed International Ltd	3,853,561
Sunday Express (1918)	Trafalgar House Ltd	3,242,777
Sunday Mirror (1963)	Reed International Ltd	3,832,394
'Qualities'		
The Observer (1791)	The Atlantic Richfield Co. and The Observer Trust	688,458
Sunday Telegraph (1961)	The Daily Telegraph Ltd	844,589
The Sunday Times (1822)	The Thomson Organisation Ltd	1,409,296
LONDON EVENINGS		
Evening News (1881) Monday–Friday Saturday	Associated Newspapers Group Ltd	547,786 489,350
Evening Standard (1827) Monday–Friday	Trafalgar House Ltd	398,316

[a] Circulation figures are those of the Audit Bureau of Circulations (founded in 1931 and consisting of publishers, advertisers and advertising bureaux) and are certified average daily or weekly net sales for the period. The circulation figure of the *Morning Star* is otherwise independently audited.
[b] Trafalgar House Ltd has announced plans for a new national morning daily newspaper.

of over 340,000. Weekly papers are mainly of local appeal; they are also a valuable medium for local advertising. Most have circulations in the 5,000–40,000 range.

There are also many free distribution advertising newspapers (mostly weekly), some published by orthodox newspaper publishers.

London Suburban Papers

The London local weeklies (120) include papers for every district in Greater London. They circulate in as many as six to eight local editions of individual papers, affiliated in some cases to larger groups.

A number of evening newspapers, using the latest production technology, are published in the outer metropolitan area on the fringe of the circulation areas of the two London evening newspapers.

Wales

Wales has one daily morning newspaper, the *Western Mail*, published in Cardiff; its circulation of just under 100,000 is mainly in south Wales. In north Wales the *Liverpool Daily Post* gives wide coverage to events in the area. Evening papers published in Wales are the *South Wales Echo*, Cardiff; the *South Wales Argus*, Newport; the *South Wales Evening Post*, Swansea; and the *Evening Leader,* Wrexham. Their circulation range is between 22,000 and 120,000. North Wales is also served by the *Liverpool Echo*, the *Shropshire Star* covers parts of mid and north Wales, and there is coverage to a smaller extent by the *Manchester Evening News*.

The weekly press (nearly 60) includes English language papers, some of which carry articles in Welsh, bilingual papers, and Welsh language papers.

Scotland

Scotland has six morning, six evening and three Sunday newspapers. The morning papers, with circulations of between 89,000 and 712,000, are *The Scotsman* published in Edinburgh; the *Glasgow Herald*; the *Daily Record* (sister paper to the *Daily Mirror*); the Dundee *Courier and Advertiser*; the Aberdeen *Press and Journal*; and the *Scottish Daily Express* (published only in Manchester although production in Inverness is also planned). The evening papers have circulations in the range of 16,000 to 212,000 and are the *Evening News* of Edinburgh, Glasgow's *Evening Times*, Dundee's *Evening Telegraph and Post*, Aberdeen's *Evening Express,* the *Paisley Daily Express* and the *Greenock Telegraph*. The Sunday papers are the *Sunday Mail*, the *Sunday Post* and the *Scottish Sunday Express*.

Weekly and local newspapers number about 130, of which the *Hamilton Advertiser* and the *Falkirk Herald* have the largest circulations.

Northern Ireland

Northern Ireland has two morning newspapers, one evening paper and one Sunday paper, all published in Belfast with circulations ranging from 50,000 to 170,000. They are *The News-Letter* (Unionist) and the *Irish News* (Nationalist), the evening *Belfast Telegraph* and the *Sunday News*.

There are over 40 weekly newspapers.

The Periodical Press

The 4,300 periodical publications are classified as 'general', 'specialised', 'trade', 'technical' and 'professional'. There are also about 635 'house magazines' produced by industrial undertakings, business houses or public services for the benefit of their employees and/or clients. The 'alternative' press probably includes a further 500 titles, most of which are devoted to radical politics, community matters, religion, the occult, science or ecology.

General and specialised periodicals include magazines of general interest; women's magazines; publications for children; religious periodicals for all denominations; fiction magazines; magazines dealing with sport, gardening hobbies and humour; journals specialising in various subjects such as politics, finance and economics, science, agriculture, medicine and the arts; and the publications of learned societies, trade unions, regiments, universities and other organisations.

The weekly periodicals with the highest sales are: *Radio Times* and *TV Times* which have circulations of over 3 million and *Woman's Weekly, Woman's Own, Woman, Weekly News* (which sells mainly in Scotland) and *My Weekly* with circulations in the 800,000 to 1·6 million range. The leading journals of opinion are *The Economist*, a politically independent publication covering topics from a wider angle than its title implies; the *New Statesman*, which is a review of politics, literature and the arts with an independent socialist political tendency; the *Spectator*, which covers much the same subjects from an independent conservative standpoint; *Tribune*, which represents the views of the left-wing of the Labour Party; *New Society*, covering the sociological aspects of current affairs; and *New Scientist*, which reports on science and technology in terms which the non-specialist can understand. *Punch*, traditionally the leading humorous periodical, and *Private Eye*, a satirical fortnightly, also devote attention to public affairs.

Literary and political journals and those specialising in international and Commonwealth affairs, published monthly or quarterly, appeal generally speaking to the more serious type of reader.

The publication of trade, technical, business, scientific and professional journals (covering hundreds of subjects, many of them in considerable depth) has become one of the more important aspects of the British publishing industry. In addition to circulating in Britain, these journals have a considerable circulation overseas and are an important medium for selling British goods. Their publication ranges in frequency from weekly to quarterly.

Periodicals published in England circulate throughout Britain. In Wales there are also several monthly and quarterly journals published in both Welsh and English; in Scotland there are three monthly illustrated periodicals, a weekly paper devoted to farming interests, a number of literary journals (of which the most famous is probably *Blackwood's*), and numerous popular magazines; and Northern Ireland has weekly, monthly and quarterly publications covering farming, the linen industry, building, motoring, politics and social work.

New Technology New techniques are continually being introduced into all the stages of newspaper production, but the national newspapers are generally concentrating investment in the composing and plate-making processes. The introduction of new technology in these departments involves computerised photocomposition in place of Linotype machine composition, and substitutes electronic and chemical methods of plate-making for manual. These methods allow savings to be made with newspapers' labour costs and have been adopted particularly by the provincial press where composing represents a very high proportion of total costs.

News Agencies There are three principal British news agencies registered in Britain: Reuters Ltd; The Press Association Ltd; and The Exchange Telegraph Company Ltd.

Reuters Ltd, a world news organisation, is owned by four associations: the Newspaper Publishers Association; The Press Association; the Australian Associated Press; and the New Zealand Press Association. They are parties to a trust deed which safeguards the independence and integrity of the news service. Founded in Aachen in 1850 and transferred to London in 1851,

Reuters now has about 1,150 correspondents in 183 countries and territories, and links with 120 national or private news agencies, which give it access to coverage by many hundreds of local reporters. Some 700,000 words of general news, sports, and economic reports are received in London every day and are retransmitted to 154 countries and territories over a global network of leased teleprinter lines, satellite links and cable and radio circuits. These news services are specially tailored to the needs of recipients in Britain and overseas, and are distributed to information media, either direct or through national news agencies. Reuters Economic Services, one of the world's largest financial and business news services, supplies information to business houses throughout the world by means of computer-based video display units, teleprinters and bulletins.

The Press Association Ltd, the British national news agency founded in 1868, is co-operatively owned by the principal newspapers of the United Kingdom outside London, and of the Irish Republic. It provides newspapers, the broadcasting organisations, Reuters (of which it is a major joint owner) and other international agencies with a complete service of home news, including general and parliamentary news, legal reports, and all branches of financial, commercial and sports news; and includes in its services to regional papers the world news of Reuters and the Associated Press. News is teleprinted 24 hours a day from head office in London over a network of lines leased from the Post Office—certain items being available in teletypesetting form. Through its photographic department The Press Association serves London and regional newspapers with a daily picture service from home and overseas; these are wired to the regional press. Its Special Reporting Service supplies reports of local or special interest to daily and weekly papers and periodicals. Press Association Features provides exclusive rights to syndicated articles and visual features.

The Exchange Telegraph Company Ltd (Extel), an independent news agency founded in 1872, is a wholly owned subsidiary of The Exchange Telegraphy Company (Holdings) Ltd, a public company. It supplies financial and sporting news to newspapers and broadcasting organisations. In conjunction with The Press Association Ltd, racing services are also supplied by teleprinter and telephone to subscribers in London and the provinces from offices in all important cities and towns.

The British press and broadcasting organisations are also served by Associated Press Ltd, and by United Press International, which are British subsidiaries of United States news agencies.

A number of other British, Commonwealth and foreign agencies and news services have offices in London, and there are minor agencies in other cities, mostly specialising in various aspects of newspaper and periodical requirements. Syndication of features is not as common in Britain as in some countries, but a few agencies specialise in this type of work.

Training for Journalism

The National Council for the Training of Journalists (NCTJ), which represents the principal press organisations, sets and conducts examinations, and organises short training courses for journalists.

The two methods of entry into newspaper journalism are selection for a one-year NCTJ pre-entry course or direct recruitment by a regional or local newspaper. Both categories of entrant take part in an apprenticeship scheme consisting of 'on-the-job' training, and block release courses for those who have not attended a pre-entry course. A number of centres provide courses for reporters. Other training facilities include one-year postgraduate courses in journalism at the University College of South Wales in Cardiff, and at the City University (London), and courses provided by the Newspaper Society Training Service for regional newspapers in such subjects as circulation, advertising, industrial relations and management.

The NCTJ co-operates closely with the Printing and Publishing Industry Training Board which is responsible for training in printing, publishing and professional photography.

Under the Commonwealth Press Union Harry Brittain Memorial Fellowship Scheme, several young Commonwealth journalists each year spend three months working and studying in Britain. The Thomson Foundation holds training courses for journalists from all parts of the world at its studies centre in Cardiff, and provides consultants and tutors for courses in journalism held overseas.

Press Institutions

The most important organisations to which employers in the industry belong are the Newspaper Publishers Association, whose members publish national newspapers in London and Manchester; the Newspaper Society, which represents the regional, local and London suburban press; the Scottish Daily Newspaper Society, which represents the interests of daily and Sunday newspapers in Scotland; the Scottish Newspaper Proprietors Association, which represents the owners of weekly newspapers in Scotland; Associated Northern Ireland Newspapers, whose members are the proprietors of weekly newspapers in Northern Ireland; and the Periodical Publishers Association, whose membership embraces the independent publishers of trade and technical publications and general magazines.

On the journalists' side there are the Institute of Journalists (IOJ), with some 2,300 members, and the National Union of Journalists (NUJ), with 29,600 members. All practising journalists (including those engaged in radio, television, public relations, freelance journalism and book publishing editorial work) are eligible for membership of either. Four main printing unions are concerned with the press.

The Guild of British Newspaper Editors with about 450 members aims to maintain the professional status and independence of editors, defend the freedom of the press, and improve the education and training of journalists. The British Association of Industrial Editors is the professional organisation to which most editors of house journals belong.

The Press Council

The Press Council has a membership consisting of equal numbers of press and non-press members, with an independent chairman. Its aims are: to preserve the established freedom of the press; to maintain the character of the press in accordance with the highest professional and commercial standards; to keep under review any developments likely to restrict the supply of information of public interest and importance; to deal with complaints about the conduct of the press or the conduct of persons and organisations towards the press (the Council's complaints committee comprises equal numbers of press and non-press members); to report on developments in the press which may tend towards greater concentration or monopoly; to make representation on appropriate occasions to the Government, to organs of the United Nations and to press organisations abroad; to publish its adjudications and periodic reports recording its work; and to review from time to time developments in the press and the factors affecting them. The Council publishes annual reports, which include statistics of the newspaper and periodical press and a series of articles examining the structure of the leading press groups.

The Press and the Law

The press has generally the same freedom as the individual to comment on matters of public interest.

Apart from enactments relating directly to such matters as the registration of newspapers for postal purposes, there are no specific press laws but certain statutes include sections which apply to the press. These relate to such matters as the extent of newspaper ownership in television and radio companies; the transfer of newspaper assets; the drawing up between employers and unions of 'closed shop' membership agreements[1]; restrictions on the reporting of preliminary hearings of indictable offences (in England, Wales and Northern Ireland); the right of press representatives to be admitted to meetings of local authorities; restrictions on the publication of (a) certain details of divorce, domestic and rape proceedings in courts of law, (b) legal proceedings involving children, (c) advertisement and investment circulars, which are governed by Acts dealing with the publication of false or misleading descriptions of goods and services and with fraud, and (d) advertisements of remedies for certain diseases, which are covered by public health legislation; agreements between the Post Office and newspaper proprietors on telegraphic communications, which must comply with telegraphs legislation; restrictions on certain types of prize competition; and copyrights, which come under copyright laws.

Of particular relevance to the press are the laws on libel and contempt of court. A newspaper may not publish comments on the conduct of judicial proceedings which are likely to prejudice their reputation for fairness before or during the actual proceedings nor may it publish before or during a trial anything which might tend to influence the result. The obtaining and publication of information from state and official sources of a confidential or security nature is affected by the Official Secrets Acts. Newspapers are also liable to proceedings for seditious libel and incitement to disaffection.

Legal proceedings against the press are comparatively infrequent; the majority are libel actions brought by private individuals. In such cases, the editor, proprietor, publisher, printer and distributor of the newspaper, as well as the author of the article, may all be held responsible.

---

[1] In order to safeguard the interests of journalists, contributors and others involved in writing newspaper articles, the Trade Union and Labour Relations (Amendment) Act 1976 provides for the drawing up of a charter containing practical guidance on matters affecting the freedom of the press. Following talks within the industry the Secretary of State for Employment is holding consultations about provisions for a charter. The Royal Commission on the Press recommended a number of safeguards it considered essential, together with voluntary methods for securing them.

22 Television and Radio

All British broadcasting is based on the tradition that it is a public service accountable to the people through Parliament. Television and radio are the responsibility of two broadcasting authorities, the British Broadcasting Corporation (BBC) and the Independent Broadcasting Authority (IBA), which work to broad requirements and objectives placed on them by Parliament, but are quite independent in the day-to-day conduct of business.

The BBC operates two national television channels, four national radio services and 20 local radio stations. It also broadcasts to countries overseas through its External Services division. The IBA supervises the operation of a single television channel (Independent Television, ITV) and 19 local radio stations. The Home Secretary regulates broadcasting generally under the Wireless Telegraphy Acts 1949 and 1967 which prohibit the sending or receiving of wireless communications except under licence. He is answerable to Parliament on broad policy questions, and may issue directions on a number of technical and other matters.

Television viewing is by far the most popular leisure pastime in Britain, and some 96 per cent of the population have television in their homes. It is estimated that about 10 per cent of households have two or more sets. Average viewing time per person is over 17 hours a week. Practically every home also has a radio set, and car radios and portable sets have made radio, national and local, one of the country's major day-time diversions.

Households with television sets must buy a licence each year—£9 for black and white sets, £21 for colour. Of about 18 million licences current in April 1978 approximately 11 million were for colour and 7 million for black and white television. The revenue from licences meets most of the cost of the BBC's domestic services. Independent television and independent local radio are self-supporting, with revenue drawn from the sale of advertising time.

In July 1978 the Government published proposals for the future constitution, structure and organisation of broadcasting, resulting from its consideration of the Annan Committee's report on the future of domestic broadcasting (see Bibliography, p 453). (For some of the main proposals, see p 419.)

The British Broadcasting Corporation

The constitution and finances of the BBC are governed by the Royal Charter and by a Licence and Agreement. The Corporation consists of 12 governors (including a chairman, a vice-chairman and separate national governors for Scotland, Wales and Northern Ireland), each appointed by the Queen on the advice of the Government. The governors are responsible for the whole broadcasting operation, including television and radio programmes and installations and equipment. Committees advise them on such matters as the social effects of television, religious broadcasting, music, agriculture, schools broadcasting, further education, programmes for immigrants, science and engineering and charitable appeals. There is also a programme complaints commission. The governors appoint the chief executive officer (the Director General) with whom they discuss major matters of policy and finance. He is chairman of the BBC's board of management, which also includes the managing directors for television, radio and external broadcasting, and the directors of personnel, finance, public affairs and engineering.

The National Broadcasting Councils for Scotland and Wales control the policy and content of television and radio programmes intended primarily for reception in their respective countries. Local radio councils, representative of the local community, are appointed by the BBC to advise on the development and operation of local radio stations.

The domestic services of the BBC are financed principally by the income from the sale of television licences less certain deductions for collection and other expenses. This is supplemented by profits from trading activities, including television programme exports, the sale of records and publications connected with BBC programmes, the hire and sale of educational films, film library sales and exhibitions based on programmes and other BBC activities. Nearly three-quarters of the BBC's expenditure on domestic services relates to television. The BBC meets the cost of local radio stations but some local education authorities help to make educational programmes.

The BBC's External Services are financed by a grant determined each year by the Government.

The Independent Broadcasting Authority

The IBA's constitution and finances are governed by the Independent Broadcasting Authority legislation and a Licence. It consists of a chairman, a deputy chairman and nine other members (three of whom have responsibility for Scotland, Wales and Northern Ireland) appointed by the Home Secretary. The IBA does not itself produce radio or television programmes; these are provided by commercial programme companies. Its main functions are to appoint the companies, to supervise programme arrangements, to control advertising and to build, own and operate transmitting stations.

The IBA is advised by a General Advisory Council, by Scottish, Northern Ireland and Welsh committees, and by committees on educational broadcasting, religious broadcasting, charitable appeals and advertising. A specialist panel advises on medical and allied advertisements. A Complaints Review Board reviews reports of complaints received and investigated by the IBA's staff. Local advisory committees provide advice on local radio services.

The chief executive officer of the IBA, the Director General, is supported by a headquarters and regional office staff covering all technical and administrative services.

The IBA's finance comes from annual rental payments made by the television and radio programme companies. The television programme companies also pay to the IBA, for transfer to the Government, a levy related to their profits.

The Programme Companies

Fifteen television programme companies hold contracts to provide television programmes in the 14 independent television regions (two companies share the contract for London, one providing programmes during the week and the other at the weekend). The companies operate on a commercial basis, deriving their revenue from the sale of advertising time. The financial resources, advertising revenue and programme production of the companies vary considerably, depending largely on the size of population in the areas in which they operate.

Although newspapers can acquire an interest in programme companies, there are safeguards to prevent their shareholdings leading to results contrary to the public interest.

In consultation with the IBA, each company plans the content of the programmes to be broadcast in its area. These consist partly of material produced by the company itself, partly of that produced by the other programme companies, and partly of that purchased from elsewhere. The five largest companies (Thames, ATV, Granada, Yorkshire and London Weekend) produce a larger proportion of their own programmes and provide more programmes for broadcast elsewhere on the national network than do the smaller ones. A common news service is provided by Independent Television News Ltd., a non-profit-making company in which all the programme companies are shareholders. The negotiations concerning the supply, exchange and purchase of programmes and their co-ordinated transmission through the independent television network take place largely on the Network Planning Committee which consists of representatives of all the programme companies and of the IBA.

Local radio is broadcast by independent stations on the same principles. The companies providing programmes are under contract to the IBA, operate under its control and are financed by advertising revenue. News coverage is supplied as a common service by Independent Radio News. In certain circumstances local newspapers have a right to a share in the control of local radio companies.

When a company, on the basis of negotiations with the other companies, has decided on a programme schedule for its area, it is required to submit this to the IBA for approval. The IBA has wide-ranging powers to regulate the content and quality of programmes; for example, it ensures that a 'proper balance' of views is expressed and, for television, has drawn up a code on violence which includes special precautions to be taken when children are likely to be viewing.

Television

Three television channels are in operation: BBC-1 and ITV broadcasting on both 405 lines very high frequency (vhf) and 625 lines ultra high frequency (uhf), and BBC-2 which broadcasts on 625 lines uhf only. Some 99 per cent of the population live within range of vhf, and almost 98 per cent within range of uhf transmissions, which are still being extended. The vhf transmissions are expected to cease within a few years. A high proportion of programmes on the three uhf services is transmitted in colour, though they can also be received in black and white. Most television sets are designed to receive four channels, and the Government has made proposals for a new type of service to be provided on the fourth channel (see p 419).

Apart from a break during the war years the BBC has been providing regular television broadcasts since 1936. All BBC-2 programmes and the majority of those on BBC-1 are broadcast on the national network. Of the BBC's 1976–77 television output over 44 per cent was produced in London and 36 per cent elsewhere in Britain, 11 per cent comprised feature films and series, and 9 per cent Open University programmes. Current affairs, features, documentary, news, schools, further education, Open University and religious programmes comprised some 46 per cent of the total.

Through co-ordinated planning of programmes on its two services the BBC is able to cater simultaneously for people of differing interests. While both services cover the whole range of television output, BBC-1 presents a higher proportion of programmes of general interest, such as light entertainment, sport, current affairs, children's programmes and outside broadcasts, while BBC-2 places greater emphasis on minority interests, providing a larger element of documentaries, travel programmes, serious drama, music, programmes on pastimes and international films.

The first regular independent television broadcasts began in London in 1955. ITV services are provided on a regional basis by the programme companies.

On average every ITV region transmitted nearly 103 hours of television each week in 1977, nearly two-fifths of which comprised informative programmes—including news, documentaries, current affairs, education and religion. Nearly three-quarters of the programmes seen on ITV are produced by the programme companies themselves. There are about three short advertising intervals an hour, during and between programmes.

British Television Overseas

British television programmes have won many international awards, and the country is one of the world's foremost exporters of television productions. It is estimated that Britain exports roughly £25 million-worth of television programmes a year, and there are few countries in the world where British programmes have not been shown.

Cable Services

Over 14 per cent of households with television rely on cable systems for the reception of programmes. The systems are usually used to improve reception quality, to avoid 'screening' by buildings or the local topography, or because external aerials are not allowed in some residential buildings. There are cable networks in almost every urban area; some cover a whole town, some homes scattered throughout an area, and others particular housing estates. Of some 2·6 million subscribers to cable networks in 1978 nearly 1·6 million subscribed to commercial systems, 909,000 to systems operated by local authorities and other non-commercial bodies, and nearly 85,000 to housing associations' systems. Commercial relay operators are represented by The Cable Television Association of Great Britain. All operators of cable systems are licensed by the Home Secretary and the Post Office.

In the past few years several experiments have been authorised for local stations to distribute locally-originated material by cable systems to subscribers. Three stations are still in operation. At Greenwich in London funds are provided by the local commercial cable television company, while at Swindon they are provided by a number of non-commercial bodies and from the promotion of a weekly lottery. At Milton Keynes the new town development corporation is using public funds to provide locally-originated programmes over the Post Office cable system. All the experiments enable people not only to see programmes about local activities but also to participate in making programmes.

Radio

BBC Radio's four national channels each have a distinct character. Radio 1 provides a programme of pop music, while Radio 2 provides light music as well as being the principal channel for the coverage of sport. Radio 3 provides mainly classical music (much of which is in stereo) and in the evening offers, in addition, adult education programmes and works of artistic and intellectual interest. Radio 4 is the main speech programme, providing the principal news and information service as well as a wide range of drama, music, talks, entertainment and schools broadcasts. Many radio programmes are transmitted in stereo.

Local radio is provided by 20 BBC stations in England and by 19 independent stations distributed throughout Britain. Local broadcasts provide a comprehensive service of local news and information, music and other entertainment, education, consumer advice and coverage of local events, and offer residents a chance to air their views, often by using the phone-in technique.

Five experiments in locally-initiated sound programmes over cable distribution systems are being licensed. By August 1978 two experimental stations, at Newton Aycliffe and Thamesmead, were in operation.

External Services

The BBC broadcasts to most countries overseas (in 39 languages, including English) for a total of some 705 hours a week. The main objectives are to give unbiased news, to reflect British opinion and to project British life and culture. News bulletins, current affairs programmes, political commentaries and topical magazine programmes form the main part of the output. A full sports service, all kinds of music, drama, and a wide range of general entertainment are also included.

The languages in which the External Services broadcast and the length of time each language is on the air are prescribed by the Government. Apart from this the BBC has full responsibility and it is completely independent in determining the content of news and other programmes.

The foreign language services are divided into areas: the African, Arabic, Eastern, Far Eastern, Latin American, French (to Europe and Africa), Central European, South European, German and East European Services. Broadcasts range from 45 hours a week in Arabic to 35 minutes in Maltese. A review of the service is in progress.

The BBC's English by Radio and Television Service is the most extensive language teaching undertaking in the world. English lessons are broadcast weekly by radio with explanations in 26 other languages, and recorded lessons are supplied to some 280 stations in 90 countries. English by Television programmes are shown in more than 60 countries.

The BBC World Service broadcasts for 24 hours a day in English and is supplemented at peak listening times by additional series of programmes designed to be of special interest to Africa.

BBC news bulletins and other programmes are rebroadcast by the domestic radio services of many countries. Rebroadcasting involves direct relays from BBC transmissions and the use of recorded programmes supplied through the BBC tape and disc transcription service. There are some 3,000 rebroadcasts weekly of World Service programmes in about 50 countries. The Transcription Service offers programmes to some 110 countries.

Another part of the External Services is the Monitoring Service which listens to and reports on foreign broadcasts, supplying a daily flow of significant news and comment from overseas to the BBC, the press, and the Government.

The BBC External Services are complemented by the radio services of the Central Office of Information (COI) which produce a range of material for transmission by radio stations overseas. In addition, COI television services provide material such as documentary and magazine programmes for distribution to overseas television stations.

Transmitters and Studios

The BBC's domestic television and radio services operate from over 1,000 transmitters, and its external services from some 47 transmitters in Britain and 32 overseas. Most of the circuits used to link studios and transmitters are rented from the Post Office. For its domestic radio, the BBC uses 101 studios in London and the regions, and for its external services 52 in London. In addition, there are semi-automatic studios which can be operated by programme officials without engineering staff. Each BBC local radio station has at least two studios. BBC television productions come from main studios at the Television Centre in west London and other studios in various parts of London, and six fully-equipped regional studio centres and eight television studios in other towns. Outside broadcasting is covered by a number of mobile units.

The IBA uses a total of more than 400 television and sound radio transmitting stations throughout Britain, programme links being rented from the

Post Office. Independent television programmes are produced at 18 studio centres throughout the country. These studios reflect the IBA's policy of encouraging regional television, and the programmes are designed for either local broadcasting or for national transmission. All companies have facilities for colour transmission.

Advertising

The BBC does not give publicity to any individual firm or organised interest by mentioning its name or branded products, except when it is necessary in order to provide effective and informative programmes. Under the terms of its licence and agreement it must not broadcast sponsored programmes.

Advertisements are broadcast on independent television but there is no sponsoring of programmes by advertisers. Advertisements must be clearly distinguishable and separate from programmes, and the amount of time given to advertising must not be so great as to detract from the value of the programmes as a medium of information, education and entertainment. In any one hour of broadcasting the amount of advertising time on independent television is normally limited to seven minutes. Averaged over the day's programmes it must not exceed six minutes per hour. The independent local radio stations are normally limited to up to nine minutes of advertising each hour. The IBA has drawn up a code governing standards and practice in advertising on television and radio and giving guidance about the types and methods of advertisement that may not be used. Some types of advertising are prohibited, notably those with a political or religious object or on behalf of cigarettes or betting. Advertisements may not be inserted in certain types of programme, such as broadcasts to schools.

Government publicity material designed to support non-political campaigns may be broadcast on independent radio and television. It is prepared through the COI and is broadcast and paid for on a normal commercial basis. The Government has no general access to radio or television. Short public service features on safety, health and welfare schemes are also produced for free transmission by the BBC and ITV.

Political Broadcasting

Broadcasts on political issues include a daily factual and impartial account of proceedings in Parliament, transmitted on BBC's Radio 4 when Parliament is in session, and there is frequent coverage of political subjects in news bulletins and current affairs programmes on both radio and television. Ministerial and party political broadcasts are transmitted periodically under rules agreed between the major political parties, the BBC and the IBA. Certain parliamentary proceedings are broadcast on radio.

Technical Developments

Research into technical problems is carried out by the scientific and engineering staffs of the BBC, the IBA, the Home Office, the Post Office, the Government and the radio industry. Advances by the BBC have included the electronic conversion of monochrome and colour television pictures between the European and the American systems, and the development of a sound-and-vision system known as 'sound-in-syncs' which enables the television sound and picture to be carried over a single 625-line vision circuit, and thus eliminates the operational complexity and expense of a separate circuit for the sound. IBA engineers were the first in the world to introduce a fully digital field rate standards converter (DICE) to improve the interchange of programmes between areas using the 525-lines system (for example, North America) and those using the 625-lines system (for example, Europe).

Both the BBC and IBA have produced 'teletext' systems, known respectively as CEEFAX and ORACLE, which allow the broadcasting of written and simple graphical information to television receivers fitted with special adaptors. Both systems enable viewers to select a display of 'pages' of written information on the television screen 'Prestel', a service providing a wide range of information via the telephone which can be displayed on the screen of a television receiver is being developed by the Post Office (see p 308).

International Relations

The BBC and the IBA (together with the Independent Television Companies Association) are active members of the European Broadcasting Union (EBU), which was established to advance international broadcasting projects. The EBU manages Eurovision, is responsible for the technical and administrative arrangements for co-ordinating the exchange of programmes over that network and for intercontinental satellite links, and maintains a technical monitoring station where frequency measurements and other observations on broadcasting stations are carried out.

The BBC belongs to the Commonwealth Broadcasting Association whose members extend to each other such facilities as the use of studios, recording channels, and programme contributions. The BBC also provides technical aid, particularly in training the staff of other broadcasting organisations throughout the world; members of the BBC's staff are seconded for service overseas.

The BBC is a partner in Visnews, which supplies a service of world newsfilm to some 134 television organisations in 94 countries and is the most widely used newsfilm agency in the world. The BBC is also a member of the International Television Federation (Intertel), which produces high-quality information programmes which are exchanged overseas. United Press International, Paramount Pictures and Independent Television News jointly provide an international newsfilm service to more than 100 overseas television organisations via the Eurovision network and by satellite.

The Government spends a considerable amount each year on broadcasting training for overseas students and largely finances the British Council (see p 151), which includes in its activities training in educational television and radio for members of broadcasting organisations overseas. Training in television work is also provided for overseas trainees at the Thomson Television College in Glasgow, run by the Thomson Foundation, a charitable trust.

The BBC and the IBA participate in the work of the International Telecommunication Union (ITU), the United Nations specialised agency responsible for the regulation and control of all international telecommunication services (including radio and television), for the allocation and registration of all radio frequencies and, through its international consultative committees, for the promotion and co-ordination of the international study of technical problems in broadcasting. The BBC is also represented on the United Kingdom Committee of the International Special Committee on Radio Interference.

Government Proposals

Government proposals for the future of domestic television and radio were announced in July 1978. A few of the main points are mentioned below.

The BBC and the IBA would continue to be responsible for the broadcasting service they already provide, and the IBA's supervisory responsibilities would be extended to embrace cable services, including pilot schemes of pay-television and other forms of local broadcasting. Both the BBC and the IBA would be authorised to establish a number of new local radio stations.

An Open Broadcasting Authority would be established to provide a fourth-channel television service in which priority would be given to education, interests not catered for on the three existing channels, and programmes produced outside the existing broadcasting organisations. A Welsh language service would be given priority on the fourth channel in Wales. The proposed Authority would not make programmes itself. Some finance would come from the Government, especially in the early years, but advertising would also be a source of revenue.

Changes are proposed in the BBC's internal structure so as to distance the governors from detailed involvement in management and to enable them to concentrate more on their supervisory and regulatory functions. Proposals are made for changes in the governing instruments of the BBC and the IBA so that they may better meet the special needs of Scotland, Wales and Northern Ireland.

Broadcasting authorities would from time to time conduct public hearings to sound out people's views, and an independent Broadcasting Complaints Commission would be set up to adjudicate complaints of misrepresentation, unfairness or invasion of privacy.

23 Sport and Recreation

There is widespread interest in sport in Britain. Large crowds attend such occasions as the association football 'Cup Final' at Wembley Stadium, the international rugby matches at Twickenham, Murrayfield and Cardiff Arms Park, the Wimbledon lawn tennis championships, the classic horse races, Grand Prix motor racing and the cricket Test Matches; millions also watch them on television. Enthusiasm for active participation in sport and recreation has grown considerably in recent decades and there is a large variety of opportunities and facilities available. Physical recreation tends to be informal and non-competitive and may include, for example, climbing, rambling, riding, boating, angling and other water-based activities.

ORGANISATION AND PROMOTION

An important feature of British sport and recreation is its amateur element (the people who devote time and energy to the organising, teaching and training of individual activities). Although the Government is not directly concerned with the organisation of sport and recreation, a Minister of State in the Department of the Environment has responsibility for the co-ordination of policies and the promotion of research in the field of active recreation. The Secretaries of State for Wales, Scotland and Northern Ireland exercise similar responsibilities in their countries.

The Government's policy is to stimulate the provision of facilities and encourage their full use. It provides financial and other assistance through a number of official bodies. Some of these, such as the Sports Councils (see below) and the Countryside Commissions, have specific responsibilities relating to sport and recreation, and assist other public and private bodies in the provision of facilities. Others, for example, the Forestry Commission, the British Waterways Board, the Nature Conservancy Council and the regional water authorities, provide recreational amenities in addition to their main functions.

Sports Councils

The main responsibility for the general development of sport in Great Britain rests with three independent bodies—the Sports Council (for England and for general matters affecting Britain as a whole), the Sports Council for Wales and the Scottish Sports Council. Members of the councils are appointed by the Government. The Councils have the task, subject only to general ministerial directives, of allocating funds made available by the Government (in 1978–79 amounting to some £18 million). They award grants for sports development, coaching and administration to the governing bodies of sport and to other national organisations; and administer national sports centres. Grants and loans are made to voluntary organisations and local authorities to assist in the provision of sports facilities. The Councils also assist British representatives at international sports meetings and encourage links with international and overseas organisations. The Sports Council consults with the Central Council of Physical Recreation, comprising members of the national governing and representative bodies of sport and physical recreation in England. The Sports Council is linked with nine regional councils for sport and recreation in England on which are represented local authorities and sport and countryside interests in each region. The Scottish Sports Council consults with the Scottish Standing Conference of Sport which comprises representatives of the national governing bodies of sport in Scotland; and the Sports Council for Wales maintains, through a standing committee, a close liaison with the governing bodies of sport in Wales.

In Northern Ireland the Department of Education provides financial assistance to local authorities and voluntary sports bodies for the provision of facilities. The Sports Council for Northern Ireland acts in an advisory capacity and can assist voluntary clubs with the cost of equipment, coaching and administration.

A bibliographic service about sport is provided by the National Documentation Centre, set up by the Sports Council and based at the University of Birmingham. The Council also has an information centre providing data on a wide range of sports topics; similar services are provided by the Sports Council for Wales and the Scottish Sports Council.

Organisations

There are a number of voluntary organisations whose activities are concerned with recreation. Some, such as the Ramblers' Association, safeguard the interests of particular leisure pursuits; others, such as the National Trust (see p 172), provide for recreation in addition to their main responsibilities. Most, however, exist to provide recreational opportunities for young people. A description of the youth service and an outline of the work of individual organisations is contained in Chapter 7.

The British Olympic Association

The British Olympic Association, founded in 1905, organises the participation of British teams in the Olympic Games. The Association's committee consists of representatives of the 26 sports in the programme of the Olympic Games (summer and winter). It determines the size of the British team (which competes under the name of 'Great Britain'); raises funds; makes all the arrangements for the team's travel and comfort at the games; organises the provision and transport of clothing and equipment; and provides a headquarters staff for the management of the team.

The National Playing Fields Association

The National Playing Fields Association aims to stimulate the provision of playing fields, playgrounds and recreational facilities. It maintains a technical advisory service, and specialises in the play and recreational needs of children and young people including young handicapped people. It is a national charity established by Royal Charter, and depends mainly on voluntary contributions. It is helped by its seven regional play advisers and by affiliated associations in Scotland and Northern Ireland and in English and Welsh counties.

The British Sports Association for the Disabled

The British Sports Association for the Disabled, founded in 1961, encourages sporting activities for the physically handicapped. The Association, which receives an annual Sports Council grant, provides advice on physical recreation for the disabled, arranges sports meetings and encourages the provision of facilities (including sports clubs) for disabled people. Regional and branch committees of the Association organise local, regional and national games. Annual national and international paraplegic games are arranged by the British Paraplegic Sports Society. At Stoke Mandeville Hospital, the first sports stadium in the world designed for disabled people was opened in 1969. In Scotland and Wales there are associations which co-ordinate sporting activities and facilities for disabled people.

Private Sponsorship

Increasing numbers of sports receive financial sponsorship from commercial concerns. Sponsorship may take the form of financing specific events, or it may be granted to individual sports organisations, for example, to provide better accommodation for spectators or to encourage more people to participate in the sport.

A Sports Aid Foundation has responsibility for raising and distributing funds from industry, commerce and private sponsors in order to assist the training of talented individual sportsmen and sportswomen. The Foundation makes grants on the recommendation of the governing bodies of sport. The Sports Council also runs a sponsorship advisory service which links potential sponsors with suitable sports.

PROVISION OF FACILITIES Local authorities are the main providers of land and large-scale facilities for community recreation and their total expenditure on sport and outdoor recreation in England and Wales amounted to some £490 million in 1976–77. In Scotland, total expenditure on sports and recreation facilities by local authorities in 1976–77 was about £69·2 million. The facilities provided include parks, playing fields, sports halls, tennis courts, golf courses, lakes, swimming baths and sports centres catering for a wide range of indoor and outdoor activities.

All publicly maintained schools are required to provide for the physical education (for example, gymnastics, games, athletics, dancing and swimming) of their pupils. All (except those solely for infants) must have a playing field, or the use of one, and most secondary schools have a gymnasium. Some have other amenities such as swimming pools, sports halls and halls designed for dance and movement. In some areas, physical education facilities in schools are available to the whole community outside school hours. Sport and recreation facilities are likewise provided at universities (some of which have departments of physical education), and there are 'centres of sporting excellence' at universities and other colleges which enable selected young athletes to develop their talents and provide for their educational needs.

Opportunities for outdoor recreation in national parks, nature reserves, forest parks and country parks are provided by public bodies (see p 163). Water-based activities on canals, rivers, lakes and reservoirs are increasingly popular. The British Waterways Board, for example, maintains about 1,760 kilometres (1,100 miles) of cruising waterways for navigation, about 960 kilometres (600 miles) of other waterways and some 90 reservoirs. An Inland Waterways Amenity Advisory Council advises the Board on the use of its waterways for pleasure purposes, and a Water Space Amenity Commission provides advice on the recreational use of water in England generally.

In addition to the recreational facilities provided by public authorities, many facilities are made available by local voluntary clubs. Some of these cater for indoor recreation, but more common are those providing sports grounds, particularly for games such as cricket, association and rugby football, hockey, tennis and golf. Clubs linked to industrial business firms often cater for a wide range of activities, and in many cases make their facilities available to members of the public. Commercial facilities, provided as profit-making businesses, include tenpin bowling centres, ice and roller skating rinks, squash courts, golf driving ranges and riding stables.

Sports Centres National sports centres, some of which were initially financed by funds from voluntary sources, are maintained by the sports councils and provide facilities and a wide range of courses for instructors and performers in many recreational activities. As well as making residential courses available for enthusiasts from all over Britain, the centres are used extensively by local clubs and the community generally.

There are seven national centres in England and Wales. Combined facilities for ranges of sports are provided at three centres: the Crystal Palace National Sports Centre in London and the Bisham Abbey and Lilleshall National Sports Centres in Buckinghamshire and Salop respectively. The centre at Crystal Palace has a main stadium seating 17,000 spectators, a sports hall seating 2,000 spectators, a swimming hall with pools meeting Olympic requirements and seating 2,000, two teaching pools, ten squash courts, an indoor cricket school, practice rooms for most indoor sports and a hostel for 132 residents. These facilities are available for international competitions as well as for training purposes, and are supported by a grant from the Greater London Council in addition to the Sports Council grant. The other four are specialist centres: the Plas-y-Brenin National Centre for Mountain Activities in north Wales, the National Sailing Centre in the Isle of Wight, the Holme Pierrepont National Water Sports Centre in Nottinghamshire, and Harrison's Rocks, a small rock-climbing centre in Sussex. In addition there is a National Sports Centre for Wales in Cardiff which is supported by local authorities, and by a grant from the Sports Council for Wales.

The Scottish Sports Council operates three national sports training centres: Glenmore Lodge near Aviemore for outdoor activities, Inverclyde at Largs for general sports activities, and a national water sports training centre in Cumbrae Isle on the Firth of Clyde.

As well as the national sports centres, other centres (such as the Meadowbank Sports Centre administered by Edinburgh District Council) cater for a wide range of recreational activities and often attract more than purely local interest. Over 300 indoor sports centres serve local rather than national needs; more are planned, some as 'dual' projects on school sites. There are also several national centres catering for specialised interests and generally administered by the sponsoring organisations. These include the National Equestrian Centre, run by the British Equestrian Federation, and the Stoke Mandeville Sports Stadium for the Paralysed and Other Disabled, run by the British Paraplegic Sports Society (see p 422).

In Northern Ireland eight indoor sports centres are provided by district councils and several more are being built. The Sports Council for Northern Ireland has a Mountain Centre at Tollymore, County Down.

POPULAR SPORTS　Some of the major sports in Britain are described below. Sportsmen may be professionals (paid players) or amateurs. Some sports, such as rugby union football, hockey and rowing, are entirely amateur but in others the distinction between amateur and professional status is less strictly defined.

Association Football　Probably the most popular spectator sport is association football, dating as an organised game from the nineteenth century, and controlled by separate football associations in England, Wales, Scotland and Northern Ireland. In England over 400 clubs are affiliated to the English Football Association (FA) and some 37,000 clubs to regional or district associations.

The principal clubs in England and Wales belong to the Football League (92 clubs) and in Scotland to the Scottish Football League (38 clubs); the clubs play in four divisions in England and Wales and three in Scotland. During the season attendances at Football League matches total about 25 million.

The annual competitions for the FA Challenge Cup, the Football League Cup, the Scottish FA Cup and the Scottish League Cup are organised on a knock-out basis, and the finals (four of the most important matches of the year) are played at Wembley Stadium, London, and at Hampden Park, Glasgow.

National teams representing England, Wales, Scotland and Northern Ireland compete against each other annually and take part in European competitions, the World Cup competition and other international matches.

The Sports Council is giving grants to some Football League clubs to enable them to provide greater sports opportunities for young supporters.

Athletics

In England amateur athletics (including track, road and cross-country running, relay racing, jumping, vaulting, hurdling, steeplechasing, throwing and race walking) are governed, for men, by the Amateur Athletic Association and, for women, by the Women's Amateur Athletic Association. Scotland, Wales and Northern Ireland have their own associations and, as in England, there are separate women's associations. The various organisations encourage the development of the sport, establish uniform rules and regulations and promote regional and national championships. Hundreds of clubs are affiliated to the various national associations.

International athletics and the selection of British teams are the concern of the British Amateur Athletic Board which is composed of representatives of the national associations. British teams compete in the Olympic Games and in other international matches, and separate teams representing England, Wales, Scotland and Northern Ireland compete in the Commonwealth Games. The board also administers coaching schemes.

The Highland Games

The Highland Games, traditional gatherings of local people in the Highlands of Scotland, at which sports (including tossing the caber, putting the weight and throwing the hammer) and dancing and piping competitions take place, are unique spectacles which attract large numbers of spectators from all over the world. Among better-known Highland Games are the annual Braemar Gathering (traditionally attended by the Royal Family), the Argyllshire and Cowal Gatherings and the meeting at Aboyne.

Boxing

Boxing as a British sport is one of the oldest, probably originating in Saxon times. Its modern form, also adopted in many overseas countries, dates from 1865 when the Marquess of Queensberry drew up a set of rules eliminating much of the brutality that had characterised prize fighting and making skill the basis of the sport. Boxing is both amateur and professional.

The Amateur Boxing Association controls all amateur boxing in England including schoolboy, club and association boxing, and boxing in the armed services. There are separate associations in Scotland, Wales and Northern Ireland. The associations organise various amateur boxing competitions, and teams from England, Wales, Scotland and Northern Ireland take part in international competitions.

Professional boxing is controlled by the British Boxing Board of Control, founded in 1929. The Board has strict medical regulations which provide for an examination of boxers before and after each contest, and for an extensive annual medical examination. In addition the Board appoints inspectors, medical officers and representatives to ensure that the regulations are observed and to guard against over-matching and exploitation.

Amateur and professional boxing championships are decided at various weights—11 in amateur and 10 in professional boxing.

Cricket

Cricket is among the most popular of summer sports and is sometimes called the English national game. It is known to have been played as early as the 1550s. Among the many clubs founded in the eighteenth century was the

Marylebone Cricket Club (MCC) which was founded in London and which reframed the laws of the game. Cricket in Britain is now governed by the Cricket Council which consists of representatives of the MCC, the Test and County Cricket Board (representing first class cricket) and the National Cricket Association (representing club and junior cricket).

The game is played in schools, colleges and universities, and in most towns and villages there are amateur teams which play weekly games from late April to the end of September. In the Midlands and the north of England there is a network of League cricket contested by teams of Saturday afternoon players reinforced by professionals, some of whom come from overseas.

Some of the best supported games are the annual series of five-day sponsored Test Matches played between England and a touring team from Australia, New Zealand, India, Pakistan or the West Indies. A team representing England tours one or more of these countries in November–March. There is also a sponsored First Class County Championship of three-day games played by 17 county teams who also take part in three one-day sponsored competitions—two of these are knock-out competitions and the other is a Sunday League.

Cricket is also played by women and girls, the governing body being the Women's Cricket Association, founded in 1926.

Field Sports

The British Field Sports Society looks after the interests of all field sports (including hunting, game shooting and fishing) which have a long history and play a considerable part in the life of the countryside. The Society is a member of the British Shooting Sports Council which is the representative body of recreational shooting.

Fox hunting on horseback with a pack of hounds is the most important British hunting sport but there is also stag hunting, and hunting the hare. The fox hunting season lasts from early November to April and is preceded by the hunting of young foxes when young hounds are trained. There are over 320 packs of hounds of all kinds in Britain and hunts are financed mainly by members' subscriptions and by the proceeds of such events as steeplechase point-to-points.

Game shooting as an organised country sport probably originated in the early part of the nineteenth century. Game consists of grouse, black-grouse, partridge, pheasant and ptarmigan, these species being protected by law during a close season when they are allowed to breed in security on numerous estates supervised by privately employed game-keepers. It is necessary to have a licence to kill game, and a certificate must be obtained from the local police by anyone who possesses, purchases or acquires a shot gun. The Game Conservancy, formed by landowners, farmers and others interested in game conservation, collects information and studies factors controlling game population.

Other shooting sports are wild-fowling which takes place on marshes and fenlands, and deer stalking.

The most popular country sport is fishing, there being about 4 million anglers in Britain. Many fish for salmon and trout particularly in the rivers and lochs of Scotland, but in England and Wales the most widely practised form of fishing is for coarse fish such as pike, perch, carp, roach, dace, tench, chub and bream. Angling clubs affiliate to the National Federation of Anglers and many clubs organise angling competitions. National championships are organised by the federation which also enters a team in the World Angling Championship. Freshwater fishing usually has to be paid for; most coarse fishing is let to angling clubs by private owners while trout and salmon fishermen either rent a stretch of river, join a club, or pay for the right to fish by the day, week or month. Coastal and deep sea fishing are free to all (apart from salmon and sea trout fishing which is by licence only). In Northern Ireland the Ulster Provincial Council of the Irish Federation of Sea Anglers and the Ulster Angling Federation look after the interests of the sport.

Golf

Golf originated in Scotland where it has for centuries borne the title of the Royal and Ancient Game, the headquarters of the Royal and Ancient Golf Club being situated at St. Andrews on the east coast. The sport is played throughout Britain and there are golf courses in the vicinity of most towns, some of which are owned by local authorities. The main event of the golfing year is the Open Golf Championship; other important events include the Walker Cup match for amateurs and the Ryder Cup match for professionals, both of which are played between Britain and the United States.

Lawn Tennis

The modern game of lawn tennis was first played in England in 1872 and the first championships at Wimbledon in 1877. The controlling body, the Lawn Tennis Association, was founded in 1888. The main event of the season is the annual Wimbledon fortnight for players from all over the world; these draw large crowds, the grounds at the All-England Club accommodating over 30,000 spectators. There are also county championships and national competitions for boys' and girls' schools. International events include the Davis Cup and Kings Cup for men and the Federation Cup for women. Women from Britain and the United States compete for the Wightman Cup.

Motor Sports

Among the most popular spectator sports is motor racing. The governing body, the Royal Automobile Club Motor Sports Association Ltd., issues competition licences to motor clubs registered with it covering all events from hill climbs to full international race meetings. In addition it organises the British Grand Prix which counts towards the Formula One World Motor Racing Championship, and the RAC Rally which counts towards the World Rally Championship.

Motor cycle racing is governed by the Auto Cycle Union and the most important events of the year are the Isle of Man Tourist Trophy races, the British Grand Prix, and the Formula 750 World Championship. Motor cycle speedway racing is governed by the Speedway Control Board.

Racing

Horse racing takes two forms—flat racing (from late March to early November) and steeplechasing and hurdle racing (from August to June). The Derby, run at Epsom, is the outstanding event in the flat racing calendar. Other classic races are: the Two Thousand Guineas and the One Thousand Guineas, both run at Newmarket; the Oaks, run at Epsom; and the St. Leger, run at Doncaster. The most important steeplechase and hurdle race meeting is the National Hunt Festival Meeting at Cheltenham. The Grand National, run at Aintree near Liverpool, is the best known single steeplechase.

The Jockey Club administers all horse racing in Britain. Its rules are the basis of turf procedure and it also licenses racecourses.

Racing takes place on most weekdays throughout the year and about 11,600 horses are in training.

The racing of greyhounds after a mechanical hare (now considered to be among Britain's most popular spectator sports) takes place at 105 tracks licensed by local authorities. Meetings are usually held two or three times a week at each track, up to a maximum of 130 days a year. Rules for the sport are drawn up by the National Greyhound Racing Club, but its overall administration and organisation is the responsibility of the British Greyhound Racing Federation.

Riding

The authority responsible for equestrian activities (other than racing) is the British Equestrian Federation which co-ordinates the work of the British Horse Society and the British Show Jumping Association at international level and runs the National Equestrian Centre at Stoneleigh, Warwickshire.

The British Horse Society promotes the interests of horse and pony breeding and of riding. It provides lectures, publications, a film library, courses and examinations and, together with riding schools approved by it, helps to promote horsemastership. With over 25,430 members the Society is also the parent body of the Pony Club and the Riding Club movement. These hold their own rallies, meetings and competitions, culminating in annual national championships at the National Equestrian Centre.

Horse trials are held during the spring and summer under the auspices of the Society. The three-day events held each year (in April at Badminton, Avon, in May at Tidworth, Hampshire, and in September at Burghley House, Lincolnshire) include dressage, cross-country riding and show jumping.

Show jumping is promoted by the British Show Jumping Association which draws up competition rules and prescribes the general standards and height of obstacles. The Association keeps a register of horses and ponies taking part in shows and seeks to improve the standard of jumping and to provide for British representation in international competitions. It has over 14,000 members and 1,000 shows are affiliated to it. The two major show jumping events each year are the Royal International Horse Show and the Horse of the Year Show.

Rugby Football

Rugby football is played according to two different sets of rules: Rugby Union (a 15-a-side game) is played by amateurs while Rugby League (a 13-a-side game) is played by professionals as well as amateurs.

Rugby Union is played throughout Britain under the auspices of the Rugby Football Union (in England), the Welsh Rugby Union, the Scottish Rugby Union and the Irish Rugby Football Union. International matches between England, Scotland, Wales, Ireland and France are played each year and there are tours by international teams.

Rugby League is played mostly in the north of England. The governing body of the professional game is the Rugby Football League which sends touring teams to Australia and New Zealand. Annual matches are also played against France. The Rugby League Challenge Cup Final is the major match of the season and is played at Wembley Stadium in London. The amateur game is governed by the British Amateur Rugby League Association.

Sailing

Sailing has always been popular on Britain's inland and coastal waters. The Royal Yachting Association has over 1,400 clubs and about 54,000 members. There are about 500 teaching establishments recognised by the Association including the National Sailing Centre at Cowes in the Isle of Wight where instructors are coached and tested. One of the world's principal regattas takes place each year at Cowes and major events are held at other British sailing centres.

Swimming

Swimming is enjoyed by millions of people in Britain, many of whom learn to swim at public baths, schools or swimming clubs. Instruction and coaching is provided by qualified teachers who hold certificates awarded by the Amateur

Swimming Association, to which over 1,700 clubs are affiliated. The Association also draws up and enforces regulations for amateur swimming, diving and water polo championships and competitions in England. Separate associations control sport in Scotland, Wales and Northern Ireland.

Underwater swimming (sub-aqua) is governed nationally by the British Sub-Aqua Club which promotes underwater exploration, science and sport. Formed in 1953, the club has become the largest in the world with some 25,000 members and more than 1,000 branches in Britain and overseas.

Other Sports   The governing bodies of some other sports played in Britain are given below. Most of these are organised on the basis of clubs and regional organisations linked to a national body. The governing bodies' functions are broadly similar and usually include drawing up the rules of the sport, organising regional and national competitions and maintaining relations with sporting bodies overseas.

Many of the sports listed below have separate national bodies for Scotland, Wales and Northern Ireland.

Sport	Governing Body
Aerosports:	
Private Flying	Aircraft Owners and Pilots Association
Gliding	British Gliding Association
Hang Gliding	British Hang Gliding Association
Parachuting	British Parachuting Association
Archery	Grand National Archery Society
Badminton	Badminton Association of England
Basket Ball	English Basket Ball Association
Billiards and Snooker	Billiards and Snooker Control Council
Bowls	English Bowling Association
Canoeing	British Canoe Union
Croquet	Croquet Association
Curling	Royal Caledonian Curling Club
Cycling:	
Cycle Racing	British Cycling Federation
Touring	Cyclists' Touring Club
Fencing	Amateur Fencing Association
Gymnastics	British Amateur Gymnastics Association
Hockey	Hockey Association (men)
	All England Women's Hockey Association
Jogging	National Jogging Association
Judo	British Judo Association
Karate	British Karate Control Commission
Lacrosse	All England Women's Lacrosse Association
Mountaineering	British Mountaineering Council
Netball	All England Netball Association
Orienteering	British Orienteering Federation
Polo	Hurlingham Polo Association
Race Walking	Race Walking Association
Rowing	Amateur Rowing Association
Shooting (Target)	British Shooting Sports Council
	National Rifle Association
	National Small-Bore Rifle Association
	Clay Pigeon Shooting Association
Skateboarding	Skateboard Association

Sport	Governing Body
Skating	National Skating Association of Great Britain
Skiing	National Ski Federation of Great Britain
Squash Rackets	Squash Rackets Association
Surfing	British Surfing Association
Table Tennis	English Table Tennis Association
Tenpin Bowling	British Tenpin Bowling Association
Volleyball	English Volleyball Association
Water Skiing	British Water Ski Federation
Weightlifting	British Amateur Weightlifters' Association
Wrestling	British Amateur Wrestling Association

GAMBLING

Various forms of betting and commercial gaming are permitted under strict regulations and estimated money staked in Great Britain in 1977 was about £8,000 million; of this some £7,700 million was returned in winnings. It is estimated that some 94 per cent of adults gamble at some time or another, 39 per cent regularly.

Gaming includes that at casinos, on gaming machines and on licensed bingo which is thought to be played by about 5·5 million people on a fairly regular basis. Betting takes place mainly on horse and greyhound racing, and on football matches (usually through football pools). Racing bets may be made at racecourses and greyhound tracks, or through some 13,250 licensed off-course betting offices which take nearly 90 per cent of the money staked. A form of pool betting (totalisator betting) is organised on, and off, course by the Horserace Totalisator Board (HTB). Bookmakers and the HTB have to contribute a 'betting levy' to the Horserace Betting Levy Board which promotes the advancement of veterinary science and the improvement of horseracing and breeds of horses.

In addition legislation allows local authorities and certain bodies to hold lotteries.

A Royal Commission on Gambling reported in 1978 (see Bibliography, p 452). One of its principal recommendations was that there should be a national lottery with the proceeds going to sport, the arts and other deserving causes.

Appendix

Currency

The unit of currency is the pound sterling divided into 100 new pence (p). There are six denominations: 50p; 10p; 5p; 2p; 1p; and ½p.

Bank of England notes are issued for sums of £1, £5, £10 and £20.

Metric Equivalents for British Weights and Measures

Adoption of Metric System

The Metrication Board was set up in 1969 to promote the planning and publicising of the changeover to the international system of units for weights and measures throughout the country.

Length

	1 inch	=	2·54 centimetres
12 inches =	1 foot	=	30·48 centimetres
3 feet =	1 yard	=	0·914 metre
1,760 yards =	1 mile	=	1·609 kilometres

Area

	1 square inch	=	6·451 square centimetres
144 square inches =	1 square foot	=	929·03 square centimetres
9 square feet =	1 square yard	=	0·836 square metre
4,840 square yards =	1 acre	=	0·405 hectare
640 acres =	1 square mile	=	2·59 square kilometres

Capacity

	1 pint	=	0·568 litre
2 pints =	1 quart	=	1·136 litres
4 quarts =	1 gallon	=	4·546 litres
8 gallons =	1 bushel =		36·37 litres
8 bushels =	1 quarter =		2·909 hectolitres

Weight (Avoirdupois)

	1 ounce (oz.)	=	28·35 grammes
16 oz.	= 1 pound (lb.)	=	0·454 kilogramme
14 lb.	= 1 stone (st.)	=	6·35 kilogrammes
112 lb.	= 1 hundredweight (cwt.) =		50·8 kilogrammes
20 cwt. (2,240 lb.)	= 1 long ton	=	1·016 tonnes
2,000 lb.	= 1 short ton	=	0·907 tonne

Double Conversion Tables for Measures and Weights

(Note: the central figures represent either of the two columns beside them, as the case may be, for example, 1 centimetre = 0·394 inch, and 1 inch = 2·540 centimetres.)

Centi-metres		Inches	Metres		Yards	Kilo-metres		Miles	Hec-tares		Acres
2·540	1	0·394	0·914	1	1·094	1·609	1	0·621	0·405	1	2·471
5·080	2	0·787	1·829	2	2·187	3·219	2	1·243	0·809	2	4·942
7·620	3	1·181	2·743	3	3·281	4·828	3	1·864	1·214	3	7·413
10·160	4	1·575	3·658	4	4·374	6·437	4	2·485	1·619	4	9·884
12·700	5	1·969	4·572	5	5·468	8·047	5	3·107	2·023	5	12·355
15·240	6	2·362	5·486	6	6·562	9·656	6	3·728	2·428	6	14·826
17·780	7	2·756	6·401	7	7·655	11·266	7	4·350	2·833	7	17·298
20·320	8	3·150	7·315	8	8·749	12·875	8	4·971	3·237	8	19·769
22·860	9	3·543	8·230	9	9·843	14·484	9	5·592	3·642	9	22·240
25·400	10	3·937	9·144	10	10·936	16·094	10	6·214	4·047	10	24·711

Kilo-grammes		Av. Pounds	Litres		Pints	Litres		Gallons	Metric Quintals per Hectare		Hun-dred-weight per Acre
0·454	1	2·205	0·568	1	1·760	4·546	1	0·220	1·255	1	0·797
0·907	2	4·409	1·136	2	3·520	9·092	2	0·440	2·511	2	1·593
1·361	3	6·614	1·705	3	5·279	13·638	3	0·660	3·766	3	2·390
1·814	4	8·818	2·273	4	7·039	18·184	4	0·880	5·021	4	3·186
2·268	5	11·023	2·841	5	8·799	22·730	5	1·100	6·277	5	3·983
2·722	6	13·228	3·409	6	10·559	27·276	6	1·320	7·532	6	4·780
3·175	7	15·432	3·978	7	12·319	31·822	7	1·540	8·787	7	5·576
3·629	8	17·637	4·546	8	14·078	35·368	8	1·760	10·043	8	6·373
4·082	9	19·842	5·114	9	15·838	40·914	9	1·980	11·298	9	7·169
4·536	10	22·046	5·682	10	17·598	45·460	10	2·200	12·553	10	7·966

Thermometrical Table

0° Centigrade = 32° Fahrenheit.

100° Centigrade = 212° Fahrenheit.

To convert °Fahrenheit into °Centigrade: subtract 32, then multiply by $\frac{5}{9}$; °Centigrade into °Fahrenheit: multiply by $\frac{9}{5}$, then add 32.

Bibliography

This bibliography is in no sense comprehensive: it is only intended to be a guide to further reading on the subjects covered in this handbook.

Readers are asked to note that in Britain the Central Office of Information reference documents marked with an asterisk may be obtained, on payment of a charge, from the Central Office of Information, Reference Division Distribution Unit, Hercules Road, London SE1 7DU; and overseas they may be obtained from British Information Offices.

Certain reference pamphlets produced by the Central Office of Information can be purchased from Her Majesty's Stationery Office and its agents overseas. These pamphlets are listed here with their respective prices (postage extra).

Acts of Parliament referred to in the text can be obtained at various prices from H.M. Stationery Office and its agents overseas.

International Standard Book Numbers (ISBN) should be quoted when ordering publications. So that readers will be supplied with the latest edition no ISBNs are given for annual and periodical publications.

1 The Land and the People

Physical Background

	ISBN		£
Chandler, T. J. and Gregory, S., *Editors.* The Climate of the British Isles			
Longman	0 582 48558 4	1977	7·95
Cheatle, J. R. W. A Guide to the British Landscape			
Collins	0 00 219240 3	1976	3·95
Fitter, R. S. R., Heinzal, H. and Parslow, J. The Birds of Britain and Europe			
Collins	0 00 212034 8	1972	1·95
Martin, W. Keble. A Concise British Flora in Colour. 2nd edn.			
Sphere Books	0 7221 5850 5	1972	3·50
Mitchell, J. B., *Editor.* Great Britain: Geographical Essays			
Cambridge University Press	0 521 09986 2	1975	4·50
Stamp, L. Dudley and Beaver, S. H. The British Isles: A Geographic and Economic Survey, 6th rev. edn.			
Longman	0 582 48144 9	1971	9·95
Trueman, A. E. Geology and Scenery in England and Wales. Rev. edn.			
Penguin	0 14 020185 8	1972	2·50
British Regional Geology Handbooks. *HMSO*		1947 to 1976	0·40 to 2·25
Meteorological Office Annual Report. *HMSO*		Annual	

Demographic Background

Halsey, A. H., Change in British Society			
Oxford University Press	0 19 289119 7	1978	1·95
Kelsall, R. K. Population. 3rd edn.			
Longman	0 582 48182 1	1975	1·75

	ISBN		£
Census 1971, various reports. *HMSO*			various
Demographic Review. *HMSO*	0 11 690680 4	1978	2·75
Population and the Social Services. Report by the Central Policy Review Staff			
HMSO	0 11 700571 1	1977	2·25
Population Trends. *HMSO*		Quarterly	
Report of the Population Panel. Cmnd 5258 *HMSO*	0 10 152580 X	1973	0·90
Ulster Year Book. *Belfast, HMSO*		Annual	
1981 Census of Population. Cmnd 7146 *HMSO*	0 10 171460 2	1978	0·40

Annual Statistics:
Family Expenditure Survey. *HMSO*
General Household Survey. *HMSO*
Office of Population, Censuses and Surveys Annual Series
of Statistics: A series of volumes covering medical and
population statistics. *HMSO*
Registrar General, Northern Ireland
Belfast, HMSO
Registrar General, Scotland:
Part I. Mortality Statistics. *HMSO*
Part II. Population and Vital Statistics. *HMSO*
Social Trends. *HMSO*

2   Government

General Survey

	ISBN		£
Blondel, J. Voters, Parties and Leaders: the Social Fabric of British Politics			
Penguin	0 14 020638 8	1969	0·80
Bromhead, P. Britain's Developing Constitution			
Allen & Unwin	0 04 320100 8	1974	2·50
Butler, David and Sloman, Anne. British Political Facts, 1900–1975			
Macmillan	0 333 17838 6	1975	15·00
de Smith, S. A. Constitutional and Administrative Law			
Penguin	0 14 080223 1	1977	3·95
Hartley, T. C. and Griffith, J. A. G. Government and Law			
Weidenfeld & Nicolson	0 297 76792 5	1975	4·50
Hood Phillips, O. Constitutional and Administrative Law			
Sweet & Maxwell	0 421 15480 2	1973	6·40
Keir, *Sir* D. Lindsay. The Constitutional History of Modern Britain since 1485. 9th edn.			
A & C Black	0 7136 0939 7	1969	5·00
Yardley, D. C. M. Introduction to British Constitutional Law. 4th edn.			
Butterworth	0 406 69004 9	1974	2·80
Our Changing Democracy: Devolution to Scotland and Wales. Cmnd 6348 *HMSO*	0 10 163480 3	1975	0·95
Devolution to Scotland and Wales: Supplementary Statement. Cmnd 6585 *HMSO*	0 10 165850 8	1976	0·28
Royal Commission on the Constitution [Kilbrandon Report]:			
Vol. I. Report. Cmnd 5460 *HMSO*	0 10 154600 9	1973	3·35
Vol. II. Memorandum of Dissent. Cmnd 5460–1 *HMSO*	0 10 154601 7	1973	1·30

The Monarchy

	ISBN		£
Burke's Guide to the Royal Family			
Burke's Peerage	0 85011 015 7	1973	10·00
Hardie, F. The Political Influence of the British Monarchy 1868–1952			
Batsford	0 7134 1113 9	1970	3·95
Howard, Philip. The British Monarchy			
Hamish Hamilton	0 241 89564 2	1977	7·50

	ISBN		£
Liversidge, Douglas. Crown & People			
Franklin Watts	0 85166 267 6	1972	1·50
Longford, Elizabeth. The Royal House of Windsor			
Sphere Books	0 7221 5599 9	1976	2·50
The Monarchy in Britain. (COI Reference Pamphlet			
R5526/77) No. 118. *HMSO*	0 11 700915 6	1977	0·90

Parliament

	ISBN		£
Bond, Maurice. Guide to the Records of			
Parliament. *HMSO*	0 11 700351 4	1971	3·25
Dod's Parliamentary Companion		Annual	
Dod's Parliamentary Companion Ltd.			
Gregory, Roy and Hutchesson, Peter. The Parliamentary			
Ombudsman			
Allen & Unwin	0 04 328009 9	1975	18·00
Hollis, Christopher. Parliament and its Sovereignty			
Hollis and Carter	0 370 01358 1	1973	2·50
King, Anthony. British Members of Parliament:			
a Self-Portrait			
Macmillan	0 333 17170 5	1974	5·95
——— and Sloman, Anne. Westminster and Beyond			
Macmillan	0 333 14492 9	1973	4·95
May, Erskine. Parliamentary Practice. 19th edn.			
Butterworth	0 406 29102 0	1976	25·00
Punnett, R. M. Front-Bench Opposition			
Heinemann	0 435 83735 4	1973	2·75
Rose, Richard. Politics in England Today			
Faber	0 571 10534 3	1974	1·95
———The Problem of Party Government			
Penguin	0 14 021954 4	1976	1·60
The Times: Guide to the House of Commons, October 1974			
The Times	0 7230 0124 3	1974	7·00
Walkland, S. A. and Ryle, M. The Commons in the 70's			
Fontana	0 00 634497 6	1977	1·50
The British Parliament. (COI Reference Pamphlet			
R5448/75) No. 33. *HMSO*	0 11 700779 X	1975	1·50
Organisation of Political Parties in Britain			
Reference Paper R4769/77 *COI*		1977	*
Parliamentary Elections in Britain.			
(COI Reference Pamphlet R5513/78)			
No. 159. *HMSO*	0 11 700977 6	1978	0·65

The Prime Minister, The Cabinet, Government Departments, the Civil Service

	ISBN		£
Blake, Robert. The Office of Prime Minister			
Oxford University Press	0 19 725724 0	1975	3·00
Hanson, A. H. and Walles, M. Governing Britain			
Fontana	0 00 632374 X	1976	1·25
Headey, Bruce. British Cabinet Ministers			
Allen & Unwin	0 04 320098 2	1975	6·50
Mackintosh, John P. The British Cabinet. 3rd edn.			
Stevens	0 420 44680 X	1978	6·00
———The Government and Politics of Britain. 4th edn.			
Hutchinson University Library	0 09 131341 4	1977	2·95
Stacey, Frank. British Government 1966–75:			
Years of Reform			
Oxford University Press	0 19 876036 1	1975	2·75
Central Government of Britain. (COI Reference Pamphlet			
R5564/77) No. 40. *HMSO*	0 11 700805 2	1977	0·75
The Civil Service. Report of the Committee 1966–68			
[Fulton Report]. Cmnd 3638 *HMSO*	0 10 136380 X	1968	0·87½
Reform of the Official Secrets Act 1911. Cmnd 7285 *HMSO*	0 10 172850 6	1978	0·70
The United Kingdom's Overseas Representation.			
Cmnd 7308 *HMSO*	0 10 173080 2	1978	1·35

	ISBN		£

Annual Reports:
Civil Service Department. *HMSO*
Her Majesty's Civil Service Commissioners. *CSC*
Parliamentary Commissioner for Administration. *HMSO*

Local Government

	ISBN		£
Arnold-Baker, Charles. The Local Government Act 1972 *Butterworth*	0 406 11280 0	1973	8·00
Cross, C. A. Principles of Local Government Law *Sweet & Maxwell*	0 421 19240 2	1974	4·00
Hart, *Sir* William O. Introduction to the Law of Local Government and Administration. 9th edn. *Butterworth*	0 406 59403 1	1973	6·80
Hepworth, N. P. The Finance of Local Government. 3rd edn. *Allen & Unwin*	0 04 352062 6	1976	7·95
Municipal Year Book and Public Services Directory *Municipal Journal*		Annual	
Redcliffe-Maud, *Lord* and Wood, Bruce. English Local Government Reformed *Oxford University Press*	0 19 888091 X	1974	1·50
Richards, Peter G. The Reformed Local Government System *Allen & Unwin*	0 04 352057 X	1975	2·25
Schofield, A. N. Local Government Elections *Shaw and Sons*	0 7219 0342 8	1976	12·00
Local Government Finance (the Government's response to the report of the Layfield Committee) Cmnd 6813 *HMSO*	0 10 168130 5	1977	0·70
Local Government in Britain. (COI Reference Pamphlet R5505/75) No. 1. *HMSO*	0 11 700679 3	1975	0·90
Local Government in England and Wales: a Guide to the System. *HMSO*	0 11 750847 0	1974	4·00

The Fire Service

Fire Services in Britain. Reference Paper R5580/76. *COI*		1976	*

Annual Reports:
H.M. Chief Inspector of Fire Services (England and Wales). *HMSO*
H.M. Inspector of Fire Services for Scotland. *HMSO*

3   Membership of the European Community

	ISBN		£
Paxton, John. A Dictionary of the European Economic Community *Macmillan*	0 333 21381 5	1977	7·50
Britain in the European Community. (COI Reference Pamphlet R5999/75) No. 137. *HMSO*	0 11 700786 2	1975	1·00
Britain in the European Community: The Developing Countries (COI Reference Pamphlet R 6030/77) No. 154. *HMSO*	0 11 700938 5	1977	0·75
Britain in the European Community: Social Policy. (COI Reference Pamphlet R5996/75) No. 136. *HMSO*	0 11 700782 X	1975	0·50
Developments in the European Communities. *HMSO*		Biannual	
Political Co-operation by the Member States of the European Communities. Cmnd 5432 *HMSO*	0 10 154320 4	1973	0·10½
Report on Renegotiation. Cmnd 6003 *HMSO*	0 10 160030 5	1975	0·38
Treaty establishing the European Coal and Steel Community Cmnd 5189 *HMSO*	0 10 151890 0	1973	1·00

	ISBN		£
Treaty of Accession to EEC and Euratom:			
Part I. Cmnd 5179–I *HMSO*	0 10 151790 4	1973	1·65
Part II. Cmnd 5179–II *HMSO*	0 10 151791 2	1973	1·90
(including texts of the Rome and Euratom treaties)			

4 Justice and the Law

The Law

Collins, Lawrence. European Community Law in the United Kingdom			
Butterworth	0 406 26920 3	1975	7·80
Latham, C. T. and Richman, J., *Editors* Stone's Justices' Manual			
Butterworth		Annual	
Halsbury, Lord. Laws of England, 4th edn.			
Editor-in-Chief Lord Hailsham. 56 vols.			
Butterworth		various	
Jackson, R.M. The Machinery of Justice in England. 7th edn.			
Cambridge University Press	0 521 29231	1977	8·95
James, Philip S. Introduction to English Law			
Butterworth	0 406 60497 5	1976	3·60
Kiralfy, A. K. R. The English Legal System			
Sweet & Maxwell	0 421 23890	1978	4·00
Owens, Joan Llewelyn. The Law Courts			
Dent	0 460 06665 X	1976	3·30
Pollock, Seton. Legal Aid: the First 25 years			
Oyez	0 85120 263 2	1975	4·50
Street, Harry. Freedom, the Individual and the Law. 4th edn.			
Penguin	0 14 020646 9	1977	1·20
Walker, D. M. The Scottish Legal System. 4th edn.			
William Green	0 414 00591 0	1976	7·00
Wraith, R. E. and Hutchesson, P. G. Administrative Tribunals			
Allen & Unwin	0 04 347002 5	1973	5·75
Criminal Justice in Britain. (COI Reference Pamphlet R5984/75) No. 129. *HMSO*	0 11 700763 3	1975	0·65
The Legal System of Scotland. *HMSO*	0 11 491332 3	1977	1·15
The Legal Systems of Britain. (COI Reference Pamphlet R6000/76) No. 141. *HMSO*	0 11 700792 7	1976	1·10

Annual Reports:
Civil Judicial Statistics (England and Wales). *HMSO*
Civil Judicial Statistics (Scotland). *HMSO*
Council on Tribunals. *HMSO*
Criminal Statistics, England and Wales. *HMSO*
Criminal Statistics, Scotland. *HMSO*
The Law Commission. *HMSO*
The Law Society of Scotland on the Legal Aid Scheme. *HMSO*
Legal Aid—The Law Society and the Lord Chancellor's Advisory Committee. *HMSO*
Scottish Law Commission. *HMSO*

The Police Service

Critchley, T. A. A History of Police in England and Wales			
Constable	0 09 461490 3	1978	5·50
Leigh, L. H. Police Powers in England and Wales			
Butterworth	0 406 84540 9	1975	5·60
Mark, Sir Robert. Policing a Perplexed Society			
Allen & Unwin	0 04 363006 5	1977	2·50
Wegg-Prosser, Charles. The Police and the Law			
Oyez	0 85120 166 0	1973	1·25

Annual Reports:
Commissioner of Police of the Metropolis. *HMSO*
H.M. Chief Inspector of Constabulary. *HMSO*
H.M. Chief Inspector of Constabulary for Scotland. *HMSO*

Penal Systems

	ISBN		£
Bochel, Dorothy. Probation and After-Care: its Development in England and Wales			
Scottish Academic Press	0 7011 2179 3	1976	7·50
Jones, Howard and Cornes, Paul (assisted by **Stockford, Richard**). Open Prisons			
Routledge & Kegan Paul	0 7100 8602 4	1977	7·95
Prisons and the Prisoner: the work of the Prison Service in England and Wales. *HMSO*	0 11 340759 9	1977	5·25
The Sentence of the Court. A Handbook for Courts on the Treatment of Offenders. *HMSO*	0 11 340146 9	1978	2·00
Sentences of Imprisonment: A Review of the Maximum Penalties (Report of the Advisory Council on the Penal System). *HMSO*	0 11 340145 0	1978	3·75
Young Adult Offenders (Report of the Advisory Council on the Penal System). *HMSO*	0 11 340559 6	1974	1·65

Annual Reports:
Criminal Injuries Compensation Board. *HMSO*
Parole Board. *HMSO*
Parole Board for Scotland. *HMSO*
Prisons in Scotland. *HMSO*
The Work of the Prison Department. *HMSO*

5   Defence

NATO Facts and Figures		
NATO Information Service, Brussels	1976	
Jane's All the World's Aircraft, edited by John W. R. Taylor		
Macdonald and Jane's	Annual	
Jane's Fighting Ships, edited by J. E. Moore		
Macdonald and Jane's	Annual	
Jane's Weapon Systems, edited by R. T. Pretty		
Macdonald and Jane's	Annual	
RUSI and Brassey's Defence Yearbook		
Brassey's Publishers Ltd	Annual	
The Military Balance		
International Institute for Strategic Studies	Annual	
Supply Estimates, Defence. *HMSO*	Annual	
Statement on the Defence Estimates. *HMSO*	Annual	

6   Social Welfare

General

	ISBN		£
Brown, Muriel. Introduction to Social Administration in Britain			
Hutchinson	0 09 131351 1	1977	3·25
Brown, R. S. G. The Management of Welfare: a Study of British Social Service Administration			
Fontana	0 00 633321 4	1975	1·50
Family Welfare Association. Charities Digest			
FWA		Annual	
Guide to the Social Services. *FWA*		Annual	
Hall, Phoebe; Land, Hilary; Parker, Roy and Webb, Adrian. Change, Choice and Conflict in Social Policy			
Heinemann	0 435 82671 9	1975	2·90
Mays, John; Forder, Anthony and Keidan, Olive. Penelope Hall's Social Services of Modern England and Wales. 9th edn.			
Routledge & Kegan Paul	0 7100 8252 5	1975	2·95
National Council of Social Service, Voluntary Social Services: Directory of organisations and handbook of information. *NCSS*	0 7199 0945 7	1978	2·75

	ISBN		£
Watkin, Brian. Documents on Health and Social Services: 1834 to the present day *Methuen*	0 416 18080 9	1975	5·50
Wolfenden Committee. The Future of Voluntary Organisations *Croom Helm*	0 85664 660 1	1978	2·95

Health and Personal Social Services

	ISBN		£
Abel-Smith, Brian. Value for Money in Health Services *Heinemann*	0 435 82006 0	1976	2·25
Barnard, Keith and Lee, Kenneth, *Editors.* Conflicts in the National Health Service *Croom Helm*	0 85664 420 X	1977	6·95
Bloomfield, Ron and Follis, Peggy. The Health Team in Action *British Broadcasting Corporation*	0 563 10825 8	1974	1·30
Darnbrough, Ann and Kinrade, Derek (Compilers). Directory for the Disabled: a handbook of information and opportunities for the disabled and handicapped *Woodhead-Faulkner*	0 85941 066 8	1977	4·25
Freeman, M. D. A. The Children Act 1975. Text with concise commentary *Sweet & Maxwell*	0 421 21790 1	1976	1·70
Hall, Phoebe. Reforming the Welfare: the Politics of Change in the Personal Social Services *Heinemann*	0 435 82400 7	1976	5·50
Howe, G. Melvyn. Man, Environment and Disease in Britain: A Medical Geography through the Ages *Penguin*	0 14 021808 4	1976	1·25
Levitt, Ruth. The Reorganised National Health Service *Croom Helm*	0 85664 657 1	1977	3·50
Owen, Dr. David. In Sickness and in Health: the Politics of Medicine. *Quartet Books*	0 7043 3123 3	1976	1·95
Pringle, M. L. Kellmer and Naidoo, Sandhya. Early Child Care in Britain *Gordon and Breach*	0 677 05200 6	1975	6·30
Sainsbury, Eric. The Personal Social Services *Pitman*	0 273 01097 2	1977	4·95
The School Health Service 1908–74. *HMSO*	0 11 270409 3	1976	1·00
Prevention and Health. Cmnd 7040 *HMSO*	0 10 170470 4	1977	1·60
Priorities for Health and Personal Social Services in England. *HMSO*	0 11 320654 2	1976	1·60
Priorities in the Health and Personal Social Services. The Way Forward. *HMSO*	0 11 320676 3	1977	1·00
Sharing Resources for Health in England: Report of the Resource Allocation Party. *HMSO*	0 11 320227 X	1976	1·70
Care of Disabled People in Britain. (COI Reference Pamphlet R4972/75) No. 131. *HMSO*	0 11 700772 2	1975	1·20
Care of the Elderly in Britain. (COI Reference Pamphlet R5858/77) No. 121. *HMSO*	0 11 700809 5	1977	0·90
Health Services in Britain. (COI Reference Pamphlet R5154/77) No. 20. *HMSO*	0 11 700927 X	1977	1·75
Social Services in Britain. (COI Reference Pamphlet R5595/77) No. 3. *HMSO*	0 11 700930 X	1977	1·50

Annual Reports:
Central Health Services Council. *HMSO*
Department of Health and Social Security. On the State of the Public Health. *HMSO*
Health Education Council. *The Council*
Scottish Education Department. Social Work in Scotland. *HMSO*
Scottish Home and Health Department. Health Services in Scotland. *HMSO*
Scottish Health Services Planning Council. *HMSO*
Supplementary Benefits Commission. *HMSO*

Social Security

	ISBN		£
Calvert, Harry. Social Security Law			
Sweet & Maxwell	0 421 22120 8	1978	6·85
Better Pensions Fully Protected Against Inflation:			
Proposals for a New Pensions Scheme. Cmnd 5713 *HMSO*	0 10 157130 5	1974	0·26
Social Security Provision for Chronically Sick and			
Disabled People. *HMSO*	0 10 227675 7	1974	0·34
Social Security in Britain. (COI Reference Pamphlet			
R5455/77) No. 90. *HMSO*	0 11 700807 9	1977	0·90
Supplementary Benefits Handbook. 5th edn. *HMSO*	0 11 760435 6	1977	0·65

Community Relations

	ISBN		£
Ethnic Minorities in Society. A Reference Guide			
British Council of Churches and the Runnymede Trust	0 902397 39 7	1976	0·40
Smith, David J.			
Racial Disadvantage in Britain: the PEP Report			
Penguin	0 14 021979 X	1977	1·25
Immigration into Britain. Reference Paper R5976/77. *COI*		1977	*
Race Relations in Britain. (COI Reference Pamphlet			
R5934/77) No. 108. *HMSO*	0 11 700929 6	1977	1·00

Annual Reports:
Commission for Racial Equality. *The Commission*
Control of Immigration: Statistics. *HMSO*

7 Education

	ISBN		£
Association of Commonwealth Universities.			
Commonwealth Universities Yearbook			
The Association		Annual	
——Awards for Commonwealth University Staff			
(and two supplements)			
The Association		Biennial	
——(For the Committee of Vice-Chancellors and Principals			
of the Universities of the United Kingdom.) The Compendium			
of Entrance Requirements for First-Degree Courses			
in the United Kingdom			
The Association		Annual	
——Financial Aid for First-Degree Study at			
Commonwealth Universities			
The Association		Biennial	
——Scholarships Guide for Commonwealth			
Postgraduate Students (and two supplements)			
The Association		Biennial	
Boyle, Edward and Crosland, Anthony. The Politics of			
Education			
Penguin	0 14 080607 5	1971	1·25
British Council and the Association of Commonwealth			
Universities. Higher Education in the United Kingdom:			
A Handbook for Students from Overseas			
Longman		Biennial	
Cantor, Leonard M. and Roberts, I. F. Further Education			
in England and Wales. 2nd edn.			
Routledge & Kegan Paul	0 7100 7359 3	1972	3·75
Council for National Academic Awards.			
Directory of First-Degree Courses			
CNAA		Annual	free
——Directory of Postgraduate Courses			
CNAA		Annual	free
Dent, H. C. Education in England and Wales			
Hodder & Stoughton	0 340 21488 0	1977	2·25
National Association of Teachers in Further and			
Higher Education. Handbook of Institutions Providing			
Both Teacher Training and other Full-time Advanced Courses			
NATFHE/Lund Humphries		Annual	

	ISBN		£
Education Committees Year Book			
Councils & Education Press		Annual	
Evans, K. The Development and Structure of the English Educational System			
Hodder and Stoughton	0 340 17606 7	1975	5·60
Findlay, Ian R. Education in Scotland			
David & Charles	0 7153 5744 1	1973	3·50
Furneaux, Barbara. The Special Child: The Education of Mentally Handicapped Children			
Penguin	0 14 080092 1	1969	0·75
Lawson, John and Silver, Harold. A Social History of Education in England			
Methuen	0 416 08680 2	1973	3·95
National Institute of Adult Education. Yearbook of Adult Education			
National Institute of Adult Education		Annual	
O'Connor, Maureen. Your Child's Primary School			
Pan	0 330 25153 8	1977	0·75
———Your Child's Comprehensive School			
Pan	0 330 25152 X	1977	0·75
Peers, R. Adult Education. A Comparative Study			
Routledge & Kegan Paul	0 7100 3372 9	1973	9·50
Perry, Walter. Open University. A personal account by the first Vice-Chancellor			
Open University Press	0 335 00042 8	1976	7·50
Van der Eyken, William, *Editor.* Education, the Child and Society: A Documentary History 1900–1973			
Penguin	0 14 080341 6	1973	1·20
Ward, Colin, *Editor.* British School Buildings. Designs and Appraisals 1964–74			
Architectural Press	0 85139 085 4	1976	15·00
Wardle, D. English Popular Education 1780–1975			
Cambridge University Press	0 521 29073 2	1976	1·95
Bristow, Adrian. Inside the Colleges of Further Education. 2nd edn. *HMSO*	0 11 270331 3	1976	1·20
Burgess, Tyrrell. Inside Comprehensive Schools. *HMSO*	0 11 270149 3	1970	0·30
Adult Education: A Plan for Development [Russell Report]. *HMSO*	0 11 270336 4	1973	1·90
Children and their Primary Schools. Report of the Central Advisory Council for Education (England) [Plowden Report]			
Vol. I. Report. *HMSO*		1967	1·75
Vol. II. Research and Surveys. *HMSO*		1967	1·62½
Education in Schools: a Consultative Document. Cmnd 6869 *HMSO*	0 10 168690 0	1977	1·10
Educational Disadvantage and the Educational Needs of Immigrants. Cmnd 5720 *HMSO*	0 10 157200 X	1974	0·15
Health Education in Schools. *HMSO*	0 11 270456 5	1977	2·50
A Language for Life. Report of the committee on reading and the use of English [Bullock Report]. *HMSO*	0 11 270326 7	1975	7·00
A New Partnership for our Schools: Report of the Committee of Enquiry into Management and Government of Schools. *HMSO*	0 11 270457 3	1977	3·25
Progress in Education: a report on recent initiatives. *HMSO*	0 11 270483 2	1978	0·90
The Reorganisation of Secondary Education in Northern Ireland			
Belfast, HMSO	0 337 04080 X	1977	0·25
Schools in Britain. (COI Reference Pamphlet R6024/78) No. 156. *HMSO*	0 11 700968 7	1978	1·25
Special Educational Heeds (Report of the Warnock Committee). Cmnd 7212 *HMSO*	0 10 172120 X	1978	5·65
Teacher Education and Training [James Report]. *HMSO*	0 11 270236 8	1972	0·85
University-Industry Relations. Cmnd 6928 *HMSO*	0 10 169280 3	1977	0·50

Annual Reports and Statistics:
British Council. *BC* Council for National Academic Awards. *CNAA*
Education Statistics for the United Kingdom. *HMSO*
Department of Education and Science. *HMSO*
Department of Education for Northern Ireland:
Education in Northern Ireland. *Belfast, HMSO*
Education Statistics. *Belfast, HMSO*

	ISBN		£
Scottish Education Department:			
Education in Scotland. *HMSO*			
Scottish Educational Statistics. *HMSO*			
Statistics of Education (6 volumes) England and Wales:			
Vol. 1. Schools. *HMSO*			
Vol. 2. School Leavers, GCE and CSE. *HMSO*			
Vol. 3. Further Education. *HMSO*			
Vol. 4. Teachers. *HMSO*			
Vol. 5. Finance and Awards. *HMSO*			
Vol. 6. Universities. *HMSO*			
Statistics of Education in Wales. *HMSO*			
Universities Central Council on Admissions			
(and Statistical Supplement). *UCCA*			
University Grants Committee. Annual Survey. *HMSO*			

The Youth Service

	ISBN		£
Eggleston, J. Adolescence and Community. The Youth Service in Britain			
Edward Arnold	0 7131 5887 5	1976	3·50
Thomas, Michael and Perry, Jane. National Voluntary Youth Organisations. PEP Broadsheet No. 550			
Political and Economic Planning	0 85374 132 8	1975	2·40
The Youth Service and Similar Provision for Young People. *HMSO*	0 11 700128 7	1972	3·00

8 Planning and the Environment

	ISBN		£
Civic Trust. Environmental Directory			
Civic Trust	0 900849 89 4	1978	1·20
Burke, Gerald. Townscapes			
Penguin	0 14 021821 1	1976	2·25
Cullingworth, J. B. Town and Country Planning in Britain. 6th edn.			
Allen & Unwin	0 04 352060 X	1976	7·95
Garner, J. F. and Crow, R. K. Clean Air—Law and Practice. 4th edn.			
Shaw and Sons	0 7219 0680 X	1976	6·00
Hall, Peter. Urban and Regional Planning			
Penguin	0 14 021725 8	1975	2·00
Heap, *Sir* Desmond. Outline of Planning Law			
Sweet & Maxwell	0 421 22800 8	1978	6·75
Ryan, Peter, *Editor*. The National Trust and the National Trust for Scotland			
Dent	0 460 04223 8	1974	6·50
Schaffer, Frank. The New Town Story			
Paladin	0 586 08067 8	1972	0·75
Taylor, Ray; Cox, Margaret and Dickens, Ian, *Editors*. Britain's Planning Heritage			
Croom Helm	0 85664 192 8	1975	5·75
An Outline of Planning in the United Kingdom. *HMSO*	0 11 750902 7	1976	2·00
Policy for the Inner Cities. Cmnd 6845 *HMSO*	0 10 168450 9	1977	0·60
Historic Buildings and Conservation Areas: Policy and Procedure. *HMSO*	0 11 751172 2	1977	0·75
Nuclear Power and the Environment. The Government's response to the Sixth Report of the Royal Commission on Environmental Pollution. Cmnd 6820 *HMSO*	0 10 168200 X	1977	0·60
Planning in the United Kingdom			
Department of the Environment	0 903197 61 8	1976	10·00
Pollution Control in Great Britain: How it Works. *HMSO*	0 11 751123 4	1976	1·40
River Pollution Survey of England and Wales. *HMSO*	0 11 751020 3	1978	16·00
Royal Commission on Environmental Pollution:			
First Report. Cmnd 4585 *HMSO*	0 10 145850 9	1971	0·45
Second Report. Cmnd 4894 *HMSO*	0 10 148940 4	1972	0·45
Third Report: Pollution in some British Estuaries and Coastal Waters. Cmnd 5054 *HMSO*	0 10 150540 X	1972	0·85
Fourth Report: Pollution Control: Progress and Problems. Cmnd 5780 *HMSO*	0 10 157800 8	1974	1·10

	ISBN		£
Fifth Report: Air Pollution Control: An Integrated Approach. Cmnd 6371 *HMSO*	0 10 163710 1	1976	1·75
Sixth Report: Nuclear Power and the Environment. Cmnd 6618 *HMSO*	0 10 166180 0	1976	2·65
The Countryside: Problems and Policies. *HMSO*	0 11 751104 8	1976	0·55

Annual Reports:
Commission for the New Towns. *HMSO*
Countryside Commission (E & W). *HMSO*
Countryside Commission for Scotland. *HMSO*
Nature Conservancy Council
The Council
New Town Development Corporations:
England. *HMSO*
Wales. *HMSO*
Scotland. *HMSO*

9 Housing

	ISBN		£
Hoath, David. Council Housing *Sweet & Maxwell*	0 421 23860 7	1978	2·00
Tiplady, David. Housing Welfare Law *Oyez*	0 85120 262 4	1975	3·25
Digest of Housing Statistics for Northern Ireland *Belfast, HMSO*		Quarterly	
Housing Corporation Report. *HMSO*		Annual	
Housing Design Bulletins. *HMSO*		various	
Housing and Construction Statistics, Great Britain. *HMSO*		Quarterly	
Housing Policy: A Consultative Document. Cmnd 6851 *HMSO*	0 10 168510 6	1977	2·50
Housing Return for Scotland *Edinburgh, HMSO*		Quarterly	
Housing Summary Tables Census 1971, Great Britain. *HMSO*	0 11 690411 9	1974	0·95
Local Housing Statistics. England and Wales. *HMSO*		Quarterly	
Report on Research and Development: Department of the Environment. *HMSO*		Annual	
Scottish Housing: A Consultative Document. Cmnd 6852 *HMSO*	0 10 168520 3	1977	1·75

10 The Churches

		£
Sources of Statistics on Religion *Central Statistical Office*	1976	free
Most of the religious denominations in Britain publish handbooks and reports.		

11 The National Economy

	ISBN		£
Morris, Derek, *Editor.* The Economic System in the United Kingdom. *Oxford University Press*	0 19 877078 2	1977	4·95
Murphy, Brian. A History of the British Economy 1086–1970: Part I. 1086–1740 *Longman*	0 582 35033 6	1973	2·25
Part 2. 1740–1970 *Longman*	0 582 35034 4	1973	2·75
Prest, A. R. and Coppock, D. J. The UK Economy: A Manual of Applied Economics *Weidenfeld & Nicolson*	0 297 77231 7	1976	3·65
The Challenge of North Sea Oil. Cmnd 7143 *HMSO*	0 10 171430	1978	0·45
Economic Trends. *HMSO*		Monthly	
National Institute Economic Review *National Institute of Economic and Social Research*		Quarterly	
The Nationalised Industries. Cmnd 7131 *HMSO*	0 10 171310 X	1978	0·75
Royal Commission on the Distribution of Income and Wealth: Report No. 1. Initial Report on the Standing Reference. Cmnd 6171 *HMSO*	0 10 161710 0	1975	3·10

	ISBN		£
Royal Commission on the Distribution of Income and Wealth: Report No. 2. Income from Companies and its Distribution. Cmnd 6172 *HMSO*	0 10 161720 8	1975	2·45
——Report No. 3. Higher Incomes from Employment. Cmnd 6383 *HMSO*	0 10 163830 2	1976	3·15
——Report No. 4. Second Report on the Standing Reference. Cmnd 6626 *HMSO*	0 10 166260 2	1976	1·85
——Report No. 5. Third Report on the Standing Reference. Cmnd 6999 *HMSO*	0 10 169990 5	1977	4·65
——Report No. 6. Lower Incomes. Cmnd 7175 *HMSO*	0 10 171750 4	1978	6·75
Winning the Battle Against Inflation. Cmnd 7293 *HMSO*	0 10 172930 8	1978	0·25

Statistics:

Regional Statistics. *HMSO*		
Annual Abstract of Statistics. *HMSO*		Annual
Digest of Welsh Statistics. *HMSO*		Annual
Monthly Digest of Statistics. *HMSO*		Monthly
National Income and Expenditure. *HMSO*		Annual
Northern Ireland Digest of Statistics. *HMSO*		Half-yearly
Scottish Abstract of Statistics. *HMSO*		Annual

12   Industry

General Structure and Organisation

	ISBN		£
Allen, G. C. The Structure of Industry in Britain. 3rd edn. *Longman*	0 582 44572 8	1970	2·50
British Standards Institution. Year Book *BSI*			
Ganz, G. Government and Industry. *Professional Books*	0 903486 34 2	1977	5·80
Guenault, P. H. and Jackson, J. M. The Control of Monopoly in the United Kingdom. 2nd edn. *Longman*	0 582 44053 X	1974	4·50
Korah, Valentine, Competition Law of Britain and the Common Market *Elek*	0 236 31031 3	1975	12·50
Rees, M. The Public Sector of the Mixed Economy *Batsford*	0 7134 1372 7	1973	2·25
An Approach to Industrial Strategy. Cmnd 6315 *HMSO*	0 10 163150 2	1975	0·22
Economic and Industrial Strategy for Northern Ireland. Report by Review Team. *Belfast, HMSO*	0 337 23211 3	1976	2·60
The Nationalised Industries. Cmnd 7131 *HMSO*	0 10 171310 X	1978	0·75
Regional Development in Britain. (COI Reference Pamphlet R5804/76) No. 80. *HMSO*	0 11 700800 1	1976	1·20
Report of the Committee of Inquiry on Small Firms [Bolton Report]. Cmnd 4811 *HMSO*	0 10 148110 1	1971	2·55

Annual Reports:

Design Council.   *Design Council*
Industries Development Assistance. *Belfast, HMSO*
Industry Act 1972. Annual Report by the Secretary of State for Industry. *HMSO*
Office of Fair Trading. *HMSO*
Scottish Development Department. *HMSO*

Manufacturing Industries

	ISBN		£
Allen, G. C. British Industries and their organisation *Longman*	0 582 48002 7	1970	3·95
British Steel Corporation. Report *BSC*		Annual	
Hayes, Samuel P. Studies in the British Economy: The Engineering Industries *Heinemann*	0 435 845527	1972	0·95
Society of Motor Manufacturers and Traders. The Motor Industry of Great Britain *SMMT*		Annual	

	ISBN		£
British Industry Today: Chemicals. (COI Reference Pamphlet R6025/78) No. 151. *HMSO*	0 11 700933 4	1978	1·75
British Industry Today: Electronics. (COI Reference Pamphlet R6013/76) No. 145. *HMSO*	0 11 700802 8	1976	1·40
British Industry Today: Textiles and Clothing. (COI Reference Pamphlet R6017/77) No. 150. *HMSO*	0 11 700932	1977	1·25
British Steel Corporation; the Road to Viability. Cmnd 7149 *HMSO*	0 10 171490 4	1978	0·35

Construction

	ISBN		£
Construction Industry, UK *House Information Services*	0 903716 08 9	1976	8·00
National Economic Development Office. Before you build: what a client needs to know about the construction industry. *HMSO*	0 11 700539 8	1974	1·00
Annual Report: Building Research Establishment. *HMSO*			

Distributive and Service Trades

	ISBN		£
The Distributive Trades in the Common Market. National Economic Development Office. *HMSO*	0 11 700540 1	1973	1·00
Report on the Census of Distribution and other Services 1971:			
Part I. Retail Outlets (Establishment Tables) *HMSO*	0 11 511104 2	1975	1·60
Parts 2–11. Area Tables *HMSO*		1975	various
Part 12. Area Summary Figures *HMSO*	0 11 511115 8	1976	2·00

13   Energy and Natural Resources

Energy

	ISBN		£
Coal for the Future: Progress with 'Plan for Coal' and Prospects to the year 2000 *Department of Energy*		1977	free
The Development of Alternative Sources of Energy. Cmnd 7236 *HMSO*	0 10 172360 1	1978	0·40
Energy Conservation. Cmnd 6575 *HMSO*	0 10 165750 1	1976	0·30
Energy Papers. Department of Energy. *HMSO*		1975 to 1978	various
Energy Policy: A Consultative Document. Cmnd 7101 *HMSO*	0 10 171010 0	1978	2·15
Nuclear Energy in Britain. (COI Reference Pamphlet R5151/75) No. 28. *HMSO*	0 11 700794 3	1975	1·00
Reorganisation of the Electricity Supply Industry in England and Wales. Cmnd 7134 *HMSO*	0 10 171340 1	1978	1·60
Structure of the Electricity Supply Industry in England and Wales [Plowden Report]. Cmnd 6388 *HMSO*	0 10 163880 9	1976	0·95
United Kingdom Offshore Oil and Gas Policy. Cmnd 5696 *HMSO*	0 10 156960 2	1974	0·25
The Windscale Inquiry: Report by the Hon. Mr Justice Parker. Vol 1. Report and Annexes 3–5. *HMSO*	0 11 751314 8	1978	3·75

Annual Reports and Statistics:
British Gas Corporation. *HMSO*
British National Oil Corporation
BNOC
Central Electricity Generating Board. *HMSO*
Central Electricity Generating Board. Statistical Yearbook. *CEGB*
Development of the Oil and Gas Resources of the
United Kingdom. *HMSO*

	ISBN		£

Digest of United Kingdom Energy Statistics. *HMSO*
Electricity Council. *EC*
Electricity Council. Statement of Accounts and
Statistics. *HMSO*
Electricity, Department of Energy. *HMSO*
National Coal Board. Annual Report and Accounts. *HMSO*
National Coal Board. Statistical Tables. *NCB*
Northern Ireland Electricity Service. *NIES*
North of Scotland Hydro-Electric Board. *NSHEB*
South of Scotland Electricity Board. *SSEB*
Statistical Review of the World Oil Industry
British Petroleum Co.

Non-fuel Minerals

Mineral Resources Consultative Committee: Reports on individual minerals. *HMSO*		1971 to 1978	various

Annual Reports and Statistics:
Mineral Exploration and Investment Grants Act 1972.
Annual Report by the Department of Industry. *HMSO*
United Kingdom Mineral Statistics. Institute of
Geological Sciences. *HMSO*

Water

Analysis of trends in public water supply *Central Water Planning Unit*	0 904839 15 X	1976	free
A Background to Water Reorganisation in England and Wales. *HMSO*	0 11 750570 6	1973	0·53
The Water Industry in England and Wales: the Next Steps. Cmnd 6876 *HMSO*	0 10 168760 5	1977	0·60
Water Resources in England and Wales:			
Vol. 1. Report. *HMSO*	0 11 780012 0	1973	3·50
Vol. 2. Appendices. *HMSO*	0 11 780013 9	1973	4·20

Annuals:
Ground Water Year Book. *HMSO*
National Water Council. *NWC*
Reports of the Regional Water Authorities and the Welsh
Water Authority. *Water Authorities*
Surface Water Year Book. *HMSO*
Water Data. *Department of the Environment Water Data Unit*

14   Agriculture, Fisheries and Forestry

Agriculture

The Agricultural Research Service *Agricultural Research Council*		1975	free
Agricultural Statistics, England and Wales. *HMSO*		Annual	
Agricultural Statistics, Scotland. *HMSO*		Annual	
Agriculture in Britain. (COI Reference Pamphlet R5961/77) No. 43. *HMSO*	0 11 700918 0	1977	1·40
Agriculture into the 1980s: A set of six reports. EDC for Agriculture. *NEDO*	various	1977	various
The Common Agricultural Policy *Commission of the European Communities*		1977	free
Food From Our Own Resources. Cmnd 6020 *HMSO*	0 10 160200 6	1975	0·45
Farm Productivity, EDC for Agriculture. *HMSO*	0 11 700542 8	1973	0·50
Output and Utilisation of Farm Produce in the United Kingdom. *Ministry of Agriculture, Fisheries and Food*		Annual	
UK Farming and the Common Market. . . . Series on specific producers. EDC for Agriculture. *NEDO*		Various	free

Annual Reports:
Agricultural Development and Advisory Service. *HMSO*

	ISBN			£

Agricultural Marketing Schemes. *HMSO*
Animal Health. *HMSO*
Annual Review of Agriculture. *HMSO*
Department of Agriculture for Scotland:
Agriculture in Scotland. *HMSO*
Farm Incomes in England and Wales. *HMSO*
Department of Agriculture, Northern Ireland. *Belfast, HMSO*
National Food Survey Committee: Household Food
Consumption and Expenditure. *HMSO*

Fisheries

Fishing Industry Index International
Haymarket Press   Irregular

Annual Reports:
Fisheries of Scotland. *HMSO*
Herring Industry Board. *HMSO*
White Fish Authority (and Accounts). *HMSO*

Annual Statistical Tables:
Scottish Sea Fisheries. *HMSO*
Sea Fisheries. *HMSO*

Forestry

British Forestry
Forestry Commission   1974   1·00
Forestry in Scotland
Forestry Commission   1970   free
Census of Woodlands, 1965–67. A Report on Britain's
Forest Resources. *HMSO*   0 11 710123 0   1970   0·60
Forestry Policy Consultative Document. *HMSO*   0 11 710125 7   1972   0·18
Forestry Commission Guides. *HMSO*   various

Annual Reports:
Forestry Commission. *HMSO*
Forest Research. *HMSO*

15   Transport and Communications

Inland Transport

Thomson, M. J. Great Cities and their Traffic
Victor Gollancz   0 575 02146 2   1977   8·95
British Industry Today: Freight Transport. (COI Reference
Pamphlet R5900/78) No. 101. *HMSO*   0 11 700975 X   1978   1·25
Town Traffic in Britain. (COI Reference Pamphlet
R5860/77) No. 130. *HMSO*   0 11 700967 9   1977   0·75
Transport Policy. Cmnd 6836 *HMSO*   0 10 168360 X   1977   1·35

Annual Reports and Statistics:
National Freight Corporation. *NFC*
Transport and Road Research Laboratory. *HMSO*
Transport Statistics. *HMSO*

Roads

Drinking and Driving [Blennerhassett Report]. *HMSO*   0 11 550396 X   1976   1·05
The Highway Code. *HMSO*   0 11 550433 8   1978   0·25
Report of the Advisory Committee on Trunk Road
Assessment (Leitch Report). *HMSO*   0 11 550458 3   1978   7·25

Annual Reports and Statistics:
Basic Road Statistics.
British Road Federation
Policy for Roads: England. *HMSO*
Road Accidents Great Britain. *HMSO*

Passenger Transport

	ISBN		£
Barker, T. C. and Robbins, M. A History of London Transport. Vol. 2. The Twentieth Century to 1970 *Allen & Unwin*	0 04 385063 4	1974	7·50
Simmons, Jack, *Editor*. Rail 150: the Stockton and Darlington Railway and what followed *Methuen Paperbacks*	0 413 32310 2	1975	2·50
The Role of British Rail in Public Transport. Cmnd 7038 *HMSO*	0 10 170380 5	1977	0·75

Annual Reports:
British Railways Board. *HMSO/BRB*
London Transport Executive. *LTE*
National Bus Company. *HMSO/NBC*
Northern Ireland Transport Holding Company. *NITHC*
Railway Accidents. *HMSO*
Scottish Transport Group. *STG*

Inland Waterways

	ISBN		£
Hadfield, Charles. British Canals *David & Charles*	0 7153 6823 0	1974	2·95
British Waterways Board. The Last Ten Years: Progress and Achievement 1963–72. *BWB*		1973	0·45

Annual Report:
British Waterways Board. *HMSO*

Ports

	ISBN		£
British Industry Today: Ports. (COI Reference Pamphlet R5970/74) No. 119. *HMSO*	0 11 700668 8	1974	0·45

Annual Reports and Statistics:
Annual Digest of Port Statistics. 2 vols.
National Ports Council
British Transport Docks Board. *BTDB*
National Ports Council. *NPC*

Shipping

	ISBN		£
International Shipping and Shipbuilding Directory *Shipping World/Benn*		Annual	
United Kingdom Marine Search and Rescue Organisation 1975. *HMSO*	0 11 511641 9	1975	1·50

Annual Reports and Statistics:
British Shipping Statistics
General Council of British Shipping
Casualties to Vessels and Accidents to Men. *HMSO*
General Council of British Shipping. *GCBS*

Civil Aviation

	ISBN		£
'Flight' Directory of British Aviation *IPC*			
Airports Policy. Cmnd 7084 *HMSO*	0 10 170840 8	1978	0·85
Future Civil Aviation Policy. Cmnd 6400 *HMSO*	0 10 164000 5	1976	0·30

Annual Reports:
British Airports Authority. *BAA*
British Airways Board. *BAB*
Civil Aviation Authority. *CAA*
CAA Annual Statistics. *CAA*

The Post Office

	ISBN		£
The Post Office. Cmnd 7292 *HMSO*	0 10 172920 0	1978	0·80
Report of the Post Office Review Committee. Cmnd 6850 *HMSO*	0 10 168500 9	1977	2·35

Annual Reports and Accounts:
Cable and Wireless Ltd. *HMSO*
Post Office. *HMSO*

16   Employment

	ISBN		£
Clegg, H. A. The System of Industrial Relations in Great Britain. 3rd edn. *Blackwell*	0 631 17160 6	1976	5·50
Huggett, Frank E. Factory Life and Work *Harrap*	0 245 50886 4	1973	2·20
Perry, P. J. C. The Evolution of British Manpower Policy. Available from the British Association for Commercial and Industrial Education *P. J. C. Perry*	0 905675 00 2	1976	14·00
Slade, Elizabeth. Tolley's Employment Handbook *Tolley*	0 510 49352 1	1978	6·50
Department of Employment Gazette. *HMSO*		Monthly	
Manpower and Employment in Britain: Industrial Relations. (COI Reference Pamphlet R6019/76) No. 148. *HMSO*	0 11 700921 0	1976	0·90
Manpower and Employment in Britain: Industrial Training. (COI Reference Pamphlet R5777/77) No. 153. *HMSO*	0 11 7009369	1977	0·90
Manpower and Employment in Britain: The Role of Government. (COI Reference Pamphlet R5943/77) No. 152. *HMSO*	0 11 700935 0	1977	0·75
Manpower and Employment in Britain: Trade Unions. (COI Reference Pamphlet R5682/77) No. 128. *HMSO*	0 11 700926 1	1977	0·75
Report of the Committee of Enquiry on Industrial Democracy [Bullock Report]. Cmnd 6706 *HMSO*	0 10 167060 5	1977	3·00
Industrial Democracy. Cmnd 7231. *HMSO*	0 10 172310 5	1978	0·50

Annual Reports and Statistics:
Advisory, Conciliation and Arbitration Service. *HMSO*
Central Arbitration Committee. *CAC*
Certification Office for Trade Unions and Employers' Associations. *HMSO*
British Labour Statistics. Year Book. *HMSO*
Manpower Services Commission. *MSC*
Time Rates of Wages and Hours of Work. *HMSO*

17   Finance

	ISBN		£
Clayton, G. British Insurance *Elek*	0 236 17618 8	1971	9·50
Davies, Glyn. National Giro: Modern Money Transfer *Allen & Unwin*	0 04 332054 6	1973	5·00
Kay, J. A. and King, M. A. The British Tax System *Oxford University Press*	0 19 877105 3	1978	2·95
McRae, H. and Cairncross, F. Capital City, London as a Financial Centre *Eyre Methuen*	0 417 01620 4	1974	0·85
Morgan, E. V. and Thomas, W. A. The Stock Exchange: Its History and Functions *Elek*	0 236 30952 8	1970	9·50
Prest, A. R. Public Finance in theory and practice. 5th edn. *Weidenfeld & Nicolson*	0 297 76858 1	1975	4·00
Pringle, Robin. Banking in Britain *Methuen*	0 416 81220 1	1975	1·90
Rees, Graham L. Britain's Commodity Markets *Elek*	0 236 31076 3	1972	7·50
Revell, Jack. The British Financial System *Macmillan*	0 333 14925 4	1973	3·95

	ISBN		£
Sayers, R. S. Modern Banking. 7th edn.			
Oxford University Press	0 19 828154 4	1967	1·40
Banking and Credit Unions Bills. Cmnd 7303 *HMSO*	0 10 173030 6	1978	1·75
The British System of Taxation. (COI Reference Pamphlet R5271/76) No. 112. *HMSO*	0 11 700917 2	1976	0·90
Capital Transfer Tax. Cmnd 4929 *HMSO*	0 10 157050 3	1974	0·11
Cash Limits 1978–79. Cmnd 7161 *HMSO*	0 10 171610 9	1978	0·35
The Development of National Giro. Cmnd 6344 *HMSO*	0 10 163440 4	1975	0·20
Financial Statement and Budget Report. *HMSO*		Annual	
Financial Statistics. *HMSO*		Monthly	
Future of the Crown Agents. Cmnd 6445 *HMSO*	0 10 164450 7	1976	0·30
Insurance Business, Department of Trade. *HMSO*		Annual	
Public Expenditure. *HMSO*		Annual	

Annual Reports:
Commissioners of Customs and Excise. *HMSO*
Commissioners of Inland Revenue. *HMSO*
Deputy Master and Comptroller of the Royal Mint. *HMSO*

18   Trade and Payments

	ISBN		£
Anthony, Vivian S. British Overseas Trade. 3rd. edn.			
Heinemann	0 435 84566 7	1976	1·10
Davies, Brinley. The United Kingdom and the World Monetary System			
Heinemann	0 435 84350 8	1975	0·95
Tew, Brian. The Evolution of the International Monetary System 1945–77			
Hutchinson	0 09 129211 5	1977	3·25
Britain and the Developing Countries: Overseas Aid. A Brief Survey. (COI Reference Pamphlet R5762/78) No. 77.			
HMSO	0 11 700980 6	1978	1·00
British Aid Statistics. *HMSO*		Annual	
Overseas Development: The Changing Emphasis in British Aid Policies—More Help for the Poorest. Cmnd 6270			
HMSO	0 10 162700 9	1975	1·35
Overseas Trade Statistics of the United Kingdom. *HMSO*		Monthly	
United Kingdom Balance of Payments. *HMSO*		Annual	

Annual Reports:
Commonwealth Development Corporation. *HMSO*
The British Council *British Council/HMSO*

19   Promotion of the Sciences

	ISBN		£
Cardwell, D. S. L. The Organisation of Science in England. (Rev. edn. 1972)			
Heinemann	0 435 54154 4	1972	1·25
Government Organisation of Science and Technology in Britain.			
British Council	0 900229 22 5	1976	1·50
Industrial Research in Britain. 8th edn.			
Francis Hodgson	0 85280 171 8	1976	47·00
A Survey of Learned Societies			
The Royal Society	0 85403 086 7	1976	2·00
Thomson, Sir A. Landsborough. Half a Century of Medical Research:			
Vol. I. Origins and Policy of the Medical Research Council (U.K.). *HMSO*	0 11 450025 8	1973	4·60
Vol. II. The Programme of the Medical Research Council (U.K.). *HMSO*	0 11 450029 0	1975	10·00
Yearbook of the Royal Society of London			
The Royal Society		Annual	
Zuckerman, Lord. Beyond the Ivory Towers. The Frontiers of Public and Private Science			
Weidenfeld & Nicolson	0 297 00236 8	1970	3·75

	ISBN		£
Britain and International Scientific Co-operation. (COI Reference Pamphlet R5814/78) No. 81. *HMSO*	0 11 700970 9	1978	1·75
Cabinet Office. Government Research and Development. A Guide to Sources of Information. *HMSO*		Annual	
Changes in the Population of Persons with Qualifications in Engineering, Technology and Science 1959–1976. *HMSO*	0 11 512071 8	1977	3·25
Framework for Government Research and Development. Cmnd 5046 *HMSO*	0 10 150460 8	1972	0·13
Notes on Science and Technology in Britain. NST Series. *COI*		1962 to 1977	*
Report of the Working Group on Scientific Interchange. Cmnd 4843 *HMSO*	0 10 148430 5	1972	0·42
Scientific Research in British Universities and Colleges, 1974–75:			
Vol. I. Physical Sciences. *HMSO*	0 11 880231 3	1975	14·80
Vol. II. Biological Sciences. *HMSO*	0 11 880232 1	1975	11·25
Vol. III. Social Sciences. *HMSO*	0 11 880233 X	1975	10·65
Second Report of the Advisory Board for the Research Councils, 1974–75. *HMSO*	0 10 164300 4	1976	0·50
The Select Committee on Science and Technology Session 1974–75: Scientific Research in British Universities. *HMSO*	0 10 277876 0	1976	7·90
Studies in Official Statistics No. 27. Research and Development Expenditure and Employment. *HMSO*	0 11 630139 2	1976	2·00
University-Industry Relations. Cmnd 6928 *HMSO*	0 10 169280 3	1977	0·50

Annual Reports:
Agricultural Research Council. *HMSO*
Comptroller General of Patents, Designs and Trade Marks. *HMSO*
Departmental Research:
   Agriculture and Fisheries. *HMSO*
   Employment. *HMSO*
   Energy. *HMSO*
   Environment. *HMSO*
   Health and Social Security. *HMSO*
   Industry. *HMSO*
   Overseas Development. *HMSO*
   Requirement Boards. *HMSO*
Medical Research Council. *HMSO*
Metrication Board. *HMSO*
National Research Development Corporation. *NRDC*
Natural Environment Research Council. *HMSO*
Science Research Council. *HMSO*
Social Science Research Council. *HMSO*
United Kingdom Atomic Energy Authority. *HMSO*

20   The Arts

The Arts

	ISBN		£
Minihan, Janet. The Nationalisation of Culture. The development of state subsidies to the arts in Great Britain *Hamish Hamilton*	0 241 89537 5	1977	8·50
Redcliffe-Maud, Lord. Support for the Arts in England and Wales *Calouste Gulbenkian Foundation*	0 903319 06 3	1976	1·50
White, E. W. The Arts Council of Great Britain *Davis-Poynter*	0 7067 0108 9	1975	6·00

Annual Reports:
Arts Council of Great Britain
Arts Council
British Council. *HMSO*
Export of Works of Art, Report of the Reviewing Committee. *HMSO*

Drama

	ISBN		£
Kerensky, Oleg. The New British Drama			
Hamish Hamilton	0 241 89628 2	1977	5·95
Lambert, J. W. Drama in Britain 1964–73			
Longman	0 582 02111 1	1974	0·50
Taylor, John Russell. The Penguin Dictionary of the Theatre			
Penguin	0 14 051033 8	1970	1·00
The Oxford Companion to the Theatre			
Editor, Phyllis Hartnoll. 3rd edn.			
Oxford University Press	0 19 211531 6	1967	10·00
The Theatre Today in England and Wales. Report of the			
Arts Council. *HMSO*	0 11 980916 8	1970	0·50

Music

	ISBN		£
Scholes, Percy. The Oxford Companion to Music, 10th edn.			
Oxford University Press	0 19 311306 6	1970	9·00
Young, Percy M. A History of British Music			
Benn	0 510 37311 9	1967	8·00

Films

	ISBN		£
Betts, Ernest. The Film Business: A History of			
British Cinema, 1896–1972			
Allen & Unwin	0 04 791028 3	1973	5·50
Future of the British Film Industry. Report of the			
Prime Minister's Working Party. Cmnd 6372 *HMSO*	0 10 163720 9	1976	0·50
Proposals for the setting up of a British Film Authority,			
Report of the Interim Action Committee on the Film Industry.			
Cmnd 7071 *HMSO*	0 10 170710	1978	0·35
Screen Violence and Film Censorship (Home			
Office Research Unit Report). *HMSO*	0 11 340680 0	1977	2·75

Annual Reports:
British Film Fund Agency. *HMSO*
Cinematograph Films Council. *HMSO*
National Film Finance Corporation (and Statement of
Accounts). *HMSO*

Visual Arts

	ISBN		£
Guide to Stately Homes, Museums, Castles and Gardens.			
Automobile Association	0 09 132171 9	1978	1·95
Historic Houses, Castles and Gardens in Great Britain and			
Northern Ireland			
ABC Travel Guides		Annual	
Jencks, Charles. Modern Movements in Architecture			
Penguin	0 14 021534 4	1973	2·95
Maxwell, Robert. New British Architecture			
Thames and Hudson	0 500 34054 4	1973	7·50
Sunderland, John. Painting in Britain 1525–1975			
Phaidon Press	0 7148 1716 3	1976	12·95
Museums and Galleries in Great Britain and Ireland			
ABC Travel Guides		Annual	

Literature

	ISBN		£
Atkinson, F. The Public Library			
Routledge & Kegan Paul			
Harvey, Sir Paul, *Editor.* The Oxford Companion to			
English Literature. 4th edn.			
Oxford University Press	0 19 866106 1	1967	6·75
Saunders, W. L., *Editor.* British Librarianship Today			
Library Association	0 85365 498 0	1976	8·25

Annual Report:
The British Library
The British Library

21 The Press

	ISBN		£

Lee, Allan J. The Origins of the Popular Press in England,
1855–1914. *Croom Helm*   0 85664 392 0   1976   9·50
Smith, Robert Callender, Press Laws
Sweet and Maxwell   0 421 23450 4   1978   2·75
The British Press. (COI Reference Pamphlet R5572/76)
No. 97. *HMSO*   0 11 700796 X   1976   0·90
Contempt of Court: a Discussion Paper. Cmnd 7145
HMSO   0 10 171450 5   1978   0·45
Royal Commission on the Press:
   Final Report. Cmnd 6810 *HMSO*   0 10 168100 3   1977   4·25
   Final Report: Appendices. Cmnd 6810–1 *HMSO* 0 10 168101 X   1977   2·60
   Interim Report: the National Newspaper Industry.
   Cmnd 6433 *HMSO*   0 10 164330 6   1976   1·50
   Industrial Relations in the National Newspaper Industry.
   Cmnd 6680 *HMSO*   0 10 166800 7   1976   5·00
   Industrial Relations in the Provincial Newspaper and
   Periodical Industries. Cmnd 6810–2 *HMSO*   0 10 168102 X   1977   2·60
   Analysis of Newspaper Content. Cmnd 6810–4 *HMSO*   0 10 168104 6   1977   5·25
   Attitudes to the Press. Cmnd 6810–3 *HMSO*   0 10 168103 8   1977   5·50
   Concentration of Ownership in the Provincial Press.
   Cmnd 6810–5 *HMSO*   0 10 168105 4   1977   2·10
   Periodicals and the Alternative Press. Cmnd 6810–6 *HMSO*   0 10 168106 2   1977   1·35
   New Technology and the Press. *HMSO*   0 11 730073 X   1975   0·85
   Review of Sociological Writing on the Press. *HMSO*   0 11 730074 8   1976   1·05
   Studies on the Press. *HMSO*   0 11 730075 6   1977   5·50
   The Women's Periodical Press in Britain 1946–76. *HMSO*   0 11 730076 4   1977   1·50

Annuals:
Benn's Press Directory
Benn
Press Council Annual Report
The Council
Willing's Press Guide
Thomas Skinner Directories
Writers' and Artists' Year Book
A. & C. Black

22 Broadcasting

Briggs, Asa. The History of Broadcasting in the
United Kingdom:
Vol. I. The Birth of Broadcasting
Oxford University Press   0 19 212926 0   1961   3·50
Vol. II. The Golden Age of Wireless
Oxford University Press   0 19 212930 9   1965   4·75
Vol. III. The War of Words
Oxford University Press   0 19 212956 2   1970   8·00
Burns, Tom. The BBC: Public Institution and Private World
Macmillan   0 333 19720 8   1977   8·95
Goldie, Grace Wyndham. Facing the Nation:
Television and Politics 1936–1976
Bodley Head   0 370 01383 2   1977   7·50
Broadcasting. Cmnd 7294 *HMSO*   0 10 172940 5   1978   1·25
Report of the (Annan) Committee on the Future of
Broadcasting. Cmnd 6753 *HMSO*   0 10 167530 5   1977   7·25

Annual Reports:
British Broadcasting Corporation. BBC Handbook
BBC
Guide to Independent Television and Independent Local Radio.
IBA
Independent Broadcasting Authority. *IBA*

23 Sport and Recreation

	ISBN		£
Arlott, J., *Editor.* The Oxford Companion to Sports and Games *Oxford University Press*	0 19 211538 3	1975	8·50
Coppock, J. R. and Duffield, B. S. Recreation in the Countryside: A Spatial Analysis *Macmillan*	0 333 15170 4	1975	3·95
Indoor Sports Centres (Sports Council Study). *HMSO*	0 11 750393 2	1972	1·20
Royal Commission on Gambling. Final Report. Cmnd 7200 *HMSO*	0 10 172000 9	1978	7·50
Sport and Recreation. Cmnd 6200 *HMSO*	0 10 162000 4	1975	0·45
Sport and Recreation in Britain. (COI Reference Pamphlet R4296/76) No. 107. *HMSO*	0 11 700799 4	1976	1·00

Annual reports are published by the Sports Council, the Scottish Sports Council, the Sports Council for Wales and the Sports Council for Northern Ireland. In addition, most of the organisations concerned with sport publish year-books covering results and records of the previous season and future prospects. Many weekly or monthly periodicals on sport are also published.

Index

Bold type in a sequence of figures indicates main references.

As the main purpose of this book is to inform readers overseas about Britain, organisations and societies are generally indexed under their subject matter rather than under *Association of*, *British*, *National*, *Royal*, etc. (*that is, Accidents, Royal Society for the Prevention of; Archives, National Register of*). In cases where the first word is not separable, however (*for example, Royal Air Force, Royal Society*), entries will be found appropriately.

Items are indexed under England, Northern Ireland, Scotland or Wales only where they are matters peculiar to these countries; otherwise they are indexed under the relevant subject headings.

M